DEVIANCE ACROSS CULTURES

DEVIANCE ACROSS CULTURES

CONSTRUCTIONS OF DIFFERENCE

SECOND EDITION

Robert Heiner

PLYMOUTH STATE UNIVERSITY

New York   Oxford
OXFORD UNIVERSITY PRESS

Oxford University Press is a department of the University of Oxford. It furthers the University's objective of excellence in research, scholarship, and education by publishing worldwide.

Oxford   New York
Auckland   Cape Town   Dar es Salaam   Hong Kong   Karachi
Kuala Lumpur   Madrid   Melbourne Mexico City   Nairobi
New Delhi   Shanghai   Taipei   Toronto

With offices in
Argentina   Austria   Brazil   Chile   Czech Republic   France   Greece
Guatemala   Hungary   Italy   Japan   Poland   Portugal   Singapore
South Korea   Switzerland   Thailand   Turkey   Ukraine   Vietnam

Copyright © 2014, 2008 by Oxford University Press

For titles covered by Section 112 of the US Higher Education Opportunity Act, please visit www.oup.com/us/he for the latest information about pricing and alternate formats.

Published by Oxford University Press
198 Madison Avenue, New York, New York 10016
http://www.oup.com

Oxford is a registered trademark of Oxford University Press

Library of Congress Cataloging-in-Publication Data
Heiner, Robert, 1956
    Deviance across cultures : constructions of difference / Robert Heiner, Plymouth State University.—Second edition.
      pages cm
    ISBN 978-0-19-997352-1
    1. Deviant behavior—Cross-cultural studies. I. Title.
    GN493.5.H45   2014
    302.5'42—dc23
                                                      2013010933

Printing number: 9 8 7 6 5 4 3 2 1

Printed in the United States of America
on acid-free paper

This book is dedicated to the works and memory of
Gresham M'Cready Sykes (1922–2010)

CONTENTS

PREFACE

One of the more resounding principles in the sociology of deviance is that the defining quality of deviance resides in the audience and not in the person or the behavior. That is, there is nothing inherent in the behavior or the person that makes it or him or her deviant. Rather, a behavior or person is deviant because an audience defines it or him or her as such. This proposition is the essence of labeling theory and of social constructionism, and it suggests that a sociological understanding of deviance requires us to study the audience. Further, an understanding of the audience requires us to examine its cultural milieu because, quite simply, audiences react differently depending upon the cultural and historical contexts in which they reside. Thus, for example, behaviors which led to the label of "witch" in medieval Europe would be seen as normal, rebellious, idiosyncratic, or the product of mental illness in other times and cultures.

The subtitle of this edition, "Constructions of Difference," reflects its emphasis on social constructionism as a means of understanding deviance. Different societies at different times construct different categories by which people differentiate among themselves. As social constructions, these categories have little or no inherent meaning, but they often have very real social and economic meaning. "Race," for example, has little or no scientific meaning. All of us are descended from the same first human ancestors and fall onto a continuum of skin colors, with few of us sharing the exact shade of coloring. There is no scientific reason for choosing skin color as a relevant basis for differentiating among people and no scientific basis for slicing up that continuum of skin color into different races. While "race" has no inherent meaning, as a category of difference it has impacted the lives of millions of people, justifying centuries of slavery and then continued inequality. When we think about deviance, most of us probably do not consider race; but race is a prime example of how societies create categories of "otherness," and the sociology of deviance is largely about this process.

While this volume emphasizes a social constructionist perspective, it does not do so to the exclusion of all other perspectives. Enormously valuable contributions have been made to the sociology of deviance outside of social constructionism. These contributions are presented particularly, but not exclusively, in the first section of readings on theories of deviance. Sociological theories are often classified among three broad theoretical perspectives: functionalism, conflict theory, and symbolic interactionism. Social constructionism is more closely affiliated with the latter perspective, but from my viewpoint it is not incompatible with either functionalism or conflict theory, and, quite often, it complements them.

Since deviance is socially constructed, it is culturally relative, and the study of deviance is most appropriate for a cross-cultural analysis such as this book is designed to facilitate. We tend to judge other cultures and their standards by the standards of our own. This tendency is called "ethnocentrism" and it is, to an extent, natural and unavoidable; but it stands in the way of objective understanding, and it is one of the great bugaboos of social scientific inquiry. One very common manifestation of ethnocentrism is the tendency to view customs in other cultures as being strange, exotic, or bizarre, and a book such as this runs the risk of catering to this tendency. I was ever-conscious of this dilemma when selecting articles for this volume and did my best not to make this a look-how-weird-they-are book. It is my hope that the combination of articles contained herein and the introductions that precede each article will make it clear to the reader that his or her own country is just as "weird" as "they" are and that the same processes that generate and influence deviance in other cultures do so in their own. Further, I expect that our ethnocentric tendencies will be counterbalanced by the fact that deviance in other cultures will be seen as more distant and therefore less threatening than deviance in our own culture, thus improving our ability to understand the phenomenon of deviance more objectively.

This new edition of *Deviance Across Cultures* is substantially different from the first edition. Specifically, new to this edition are:

- Introductions to each section of readings.
- Discussion questions following each article.
- Eight articles have been deleted; twenty-one have been added.
- The "Prostitution" section of readings has been folded into the "Sex and Sexuality" section.
- The "Corporate Deviance" section has been replaced with the Corporate, State, and Occupational Deviance" section with all new readings.
- A new section of readings on "Studying Deviance" (i.e., Methods).

Together, with the additional articles, the section introductions, the individual article introductions, and the discussion questions, this book is intended to be used either as a principal textbook or as a supplementary text.

This book was made possible by a host of friends, scholars, and professionals who assisted and inspired me. I want to thank the various reviewers of this and an earlier version of this project who provided me with encouragement and very useful criticism. They include:

- Phillip Davis – Georgia State University
- Kim Fendley – Shenandoah University
- Risa Garelick – Northern Arizona University
- Dr. Gary O'Bireck – Anna Maria College
- Nicholas Parsons – Connecticut State University
- Elizabeth Scheel – St. Cloud State University
- Johnny Spraggins – University of Texas at San Antonio

Very special thanks go to my editor at Oxford University Press, Sherith Pankratz. We have worked together on many projects for many years now, and it has never been anything but a pleasure working with her. Thank you to Caitlin Greene, Katy Albis, Joyce Bruce, and Philip Haskell. They have always been ready with their able assistance whenever I have faltered. Thanks also to Katherine Donahue, Kathryn Melanson, Nikki Nunes, Alice Staples, and Cynthia Vascak for their support and encouragement. Lastly, I want to thank my wife, Sheryl, and daughter, Laurel, for their love and for putting up with me when I was skipping out early in the morning on weekends and school breaks to go work on this book.

ACKNOWLEDGMENTS

Bancroft, Angus, from *Drugs, intoxication and society*. Cambridge, UK: Polity Press, 2009, pp. 47–59. Reprinted with permission of the publisher.

Bartholomew, Robert E., "Penis panics: The psychology of penis-shrinking mass hysterias." *Skeptic*, vol. 7, no. 4, 1999, pp. 45–49 (edited). Reprint permission conveyed through Copyright Clearance Center.

Bayley, David H., Republished with permission of the University of California Press from *Forces of order: Policing modern Japan* (revised edition). Berkeley: University of California Press, 1991, pp. 168–182 (edited); permission conveyed through Copyright Clearance Center, Inc.

Bellis, Mark A., Karen Hughes, and Helen Lowey, Reprinted from *Addictive Behaviors*, vol. 27, no. 6, Mark A. Bellis, Karen Hughes, and Helen Lowey, "Healthy nightclubs and recreational substance use: From a harm minimisation to a healthy settings approach," pp. 1025–1035, Copyright 2002, with permission from Elsevier.

Bonger, Willem, from *Criminality and economic conditions*, Translated by Henry P. Horton, Boston: Little, Brown and Co., 1916 (originally published 1905), pp. 669–672. Public domain.

DeYoung, Mary, "The devil goes to day care: McMartin and the making of a moral panic." *Journal of American Culture*, vol. 20, no. 1, Spring 1997, pp. 19–25. Permission conveyed through Copyright Clearance Center.

Durkheim, Emile, Reprinted with permission of Free Press, a Division of Simon and Schuster Inc., from *The rules of sociological method by Emile Durkheim*, translated by Sarah A. Soloway and John H. Mueller. Edited by George E. G. Catlin, Copyright © 1938 by George E. G. Catlin. Copyright renewed © 1966 by Sarah A. Solovay, John Muller, George E. G. Catlin. All rights reserved.

Erikson, Kai T., *Wayward puritans: A study in the sociology of deviance*, Classic edition, 1st edition, © 2005, pp. 8–19. Reprinted by permission of Pearson Education, Inc., Upper Saddle River, NJ.

Gibbs, Jack P., "Conceptions of deviant behavior: The old and the new." *Pacific Sociological Review*, vol. 9, Spring 1966, pp. 9–11. Reprinted with permission from the University of California Press as conveyed through Copyright Clearance Center.

Heiner, Robert, "Crime scares," from *Social problems: An introduction to critical constructionism*, 4th edition, 2013, pp. 145–153. New York: Oxford University Press, Reprinted with permission.

Heiner, Robert, "Cross-cultural and historical methodology," from *The Routledge handbook of deviant behavior*. Edited by Clifton D. Bryant, London: Routledge, 2011, pp. 82–88. Reprinted with permission.

Heiner, Robert, "The medicalization of deviance," adapted from *Social problems: An introduction to critical constructionism*, 4th edition, 2013, pp. 172–174. New York: Oxford University Press. Reprinted with permission.

Heiner, Robert, "Nones on the run," from "Evangelical heathens: The deviant status of freethinkers in Southland." *Deviant behavior*, vol. 13, no. 1, 1992, pp. 1–20 (edited). Reprinted with permission from Taylor and Francis (http://www.tandfonline.com).

Heiner, Robert, "Prostitution and the status of women in South Korea." *International Journal of Contemporary Sociology*, vol. 29, no. 1, April 1992, pp. 115–123.

Hills, Stuart, From *Corporate violence: Injury and death for profit*. Totowa, NJ: Rowman and Littlefield Publishers, 1987, pp. 190–203. Reprinted with permission.

Hirschi, Travis, *Causes of delinquency*. Piscataway, NJ: Transaction, 2002, pp. 16–30. Reprinted with permission.

Ihara, Hiroshi, Reprinted from *International Journal of Risk and Safety in Medicine*, vol. 24, Hiroshi Ihara, "A cold of the soul: A Japanese case of disease mongering in psychiatry," pp. 115–120, Copyright 2012, with permission from IOS Press.

Kappeler, Victor E. and Gary W. Potter, Reprinted by permission of Waveland, Inc. from Victor E. Kappeler and Gary W. Potter, *The mythology of crime and criminal justice*, 4th edition. (Long Grove, IL: Waveland Press Inc., 2005). All rights reserved.

Kendall, Kathryn, "Women in Lesotho and the (Western) construction of homophobia," from *Female desires: Same-sex relations and transgender practices*. Edited by Evelyn Blackwood and Saskia Wieringa, New York: Columbia University Press, 1999, pp. 157–178 (edited). Reprinted with permission from the author.

Knief, Amanda, "Liberté, egalité—de femenistes!: Revealing the burqa as a pro-choice Issue." *The Humanist*, vol. 70, no. 5, Sept./Oct. 2010, pp. 13–17. Reprinted by permission of the author.

Lancaster, Roger N., Republished with permission of the University of California Press from *Life is hard: Machismo, danger, and the intimacy of power in Nicaragua*. Berkeley: University of California, 1992, pp. 237–245 (edited); permission conveyed through Copyright Clearance Center, Inc.

Li, Ling, "Performing bribery in China: Guanxi-practice, corruption with a human face." *Journal of Contemporary China*, vol. 20, no. 68, January 2011, pp. 7–14, 19–20. Reprinted by permission of the publisher (Taylor and Francis Ltd, http://tandf.co.uk/journals).

Merton, Robert K., "Social structure and anomie." *American Sociological Review*, vol. 3, 1938, pp. 672–682. Public domain.

Nanda, Serena, Reprinted by permission of Waveland Press, Inc. from Serena Nanda, *Gender diversity: Crosscultural variations*. Long Grove, IL: Waveland Press, Inc., 2000, pp. 11–26. All rights reserved.

Nepstad, Sharon Erickson, "Religion, violence, and peacemaking." *Journal for the Scientific Study of Religion*, vol. 43, no. 3 (August 2004), pp. 297. Reprinted by permission of the publisher (John Wiley and Sons) as conveyed through Copyright Clearance Center.

Palmer, Susan J., "Caught up in the cult wars: Confessions of a Canadian researcher," from *Misunderstanding cults: Searching for objectivity in a controversial field*. Edited by Benjamin Zablocki and Thomas Robbins, © University of Toronto Press, 2001, pp. 99–121 (edited). Reprinted with permission from the publisher.

Pisani, Elizabeth, From *The wisdom of whores: Bureaucrats, brothels, and the business of AIDS*, Copyright © 2008 by Elizabeth Pisani. Used by Permission of W. W. Norton & Company, Inc. and Penguin Group (Canada), a Division of Pearson Canada, Inc., pp.48–59, 83.

Reiman, Jeffrey, *The rich get richer and the poor get prison*, 8th edition, © 2007. Adapted by permission of Pearson Education, Inc., Upper Saddle River, NJ. Reprinted by permission.

Reinarman, Craig, "The social construction of drug scares." Reprinted by permission of the author.

Rosenhan, David. L., "On being sane in insane places." *Science*, vol. 179, 1973. Copyright © 1973 AAAS. Reprinted with permission from AAAS.

Rubenstein, Richard, Excerpts from pp. 22–7, 33–5 (2,740 words) from *The cunning of history: The Holocaust and the American future* by Richard L. Rubenstein. Copyright © 1975 by Richard L. Rubenstein. Introduction copyright © 1978 by William Styron. Reprinted by permission of HarperCollins Publishers.

Schubert, Sarah, Susan Hansen and Mark Rapley, "There *is* no pathological test: More on ADHD as rhetoric." *Journal of Critical Psychology, Counseling and Psychotherapy*, vol. 9, no. 4, pp. 151–160. Reprinted with permission of PCCS Books.

Silva, Ana Paula da, and Thaddeus Gregory Blanchette, "Sexual tourism and social panics: Research and intervention in Rio de Janeiro." *Souls: A Critical Journal of Black Politics, Culture, and Society*, Columbia University Institute for Research in African American Studies, vol. 11, no. 2, June 2009. Reprinted by permission of the publisher (Taylor and Francis Ltd, http://www.tandf.co.uk/journals).

60 Minutes, "Rx Drugs," © CBS Worldwide Inc., All Rights Reserved, Originally broadcast on 60 MINUTES on December 27, 1992, over the CBS Television Network.

Sykes, Gresham M. and David Matza, "Techniques of neutralization: A theory of delinquency." *American Sociological Review*, vol. 22, 1957, pp. 664–670. Public domain.

Tannenbaum, Frank, From *Crime and community*. New York: Columbia University Press, 1938 (reprinted 1951) pp. 17–22. Public domain.

Thompson, Kenneth. From *Moral panics*, Kenneth Thompson, Copyright © Routledge 1998. Reproduced by permission of Taylor and Francis Books UK, pp. 31–41. Quotations from Cohen reprinted with permission. Stanley Cohen, Folk devils and moral panics, Copyright 2011, Routledge. Reproduced by permission of Taylor and Francis Books UK.

Victor, Jeffery S., *Satanic panic: The creation of a contemporary legend.* pp. 195–200. Reprinted by permission of Open Court Publishing Company, a division of Carus Publishing Company, Peru, IL from *Satanic panic: The creation of a contemporary legend* by Jeffery S. Victor, Copyright © 1993 by Open Court.

Warner, Richard, From *Recovery from schizophrenia*, 3rd edition, Richard Warner, Copyright © 1998 Brunner-Routledge. Reproduced by permission of Taylor and Francis Books UK.

Watters, Ethan, "The Americanization of mental illness" *The New York Times*, January 10, 2010 © The New York Times. All rights reserved. Used by permission and protected by the Copyright Laws of the United States.

Weinberg, Martin S., "The nudist management of respectability," originally from *Deviance and respectability*. Edited by Jack D. Douglas. Basic Books, © 1970. Updated by the author in 2012. Reprinted by permission of the author and the publisher.

DEVIANCE ACROSS CULTURES

EXPLAINING DEVIANCE

Introduction

This section on theories of crime and deviance begins with the classic work of Emile Durkheim. Durkheim was a nineteenth-century French intellectual who was largely responsible for introducing the field of sociology into university curricula, and he was a pioneering figure in the development of the sociological perspective known as functionalism. Early functionalists likened society unto a living organism and, like other living organisms, society has its component parts that contribute to the functioning of the whole. Just as with the human organism, the pancreas can only be understood in terms of how it contributes to the functioning of the whole body; any given social phenomenon must be understood in terms of how it contributes to the functioning of the whole of society.

Durkheim examines the phenomenon of crime and applies a similar logic. He starts with the observation that all societies have had and will always have crime. He reasons that a society without crime, or as he put it "a society of saints," is not possible unless all members of a society think and act exactly alike. Otherwise, the slightest deviation from the norm would be treated as a serious deviation. Thus, within a society of saints, while there may be no murders, robberies, or burglaries, etc., masturbation would be treated as a very serious crime. Durkheim further posits that since crime occurs in all societies, it cannot be taken as a sign of an unhealthy society and it must, therefore, exist for a reason. The excerpt included in this section concludes with the following line: "If crime is not pathological at all, the object of punishment cannot be to cure it, and its true function must be sought elsewhere." This passage leads us directly to the next article in this section of readings.

Kai Erikson's article, "On the Sociology of Deviance," is another, more recent classic written in the functionalist tradition. Erikson argues that all societies need to have moral boundaries that separate members of the community from non-members, or, as sociologists say, members of the in-group from members out the out-group. Much like Durkheim, Erikson argues that this is necessary to enhance group identity and social cohesion, giving members a reason to take pride in their membership and to follow the group's norms. People, he says, "need to sense what lies beyond the margins of the group before they can appreciate the special quality of the experience which takes place within it." Societies need deviants in order to locate and maintain their moral boundaries. Deviance and deviants, and, more specifically, reactions to them serve to publicize the moral boundaries of the community and let its members know which behaviors are tolerated and which are not.

Erikson argues that given this crucial function served by deviance, societies develop ways of ensuring a steady supply of deviants; and here we arrive at Durkheim's assertion that the true function of punishment lies somewhere other than curing crime. Do we really believe that if we take a deviant (i.e., criminal) and lock him up for years in an extremely deviant environment (i.e., prison) he will come out less deviant? Erikson helps us make sense of this most ironic response to deviance in arguing that the true purpose of incarceration is not to protect society from the threat of deviance, but rather to ensure a steady supply of deviants to "patrol" our moral boundaries. Thus, according to Erikson, the high rates of ex-convicts who are returned to prison after re-offending are not an indication of the failure of our criminal justice system, but rather a sign of its success.

The next article in this section, "Social Structure and Anomie" by Robert Merton, is by far one of the most famous, most often cited works written in the sociology of crime and deviance. In this piece, Merton starts with a theoretical foundation already built by Durkheim in another one of his classics, *Suicide* (1897/1951), but he diverges considerably from Durkheim and develops a theory specific to American society. Merton notes that all societies set goals for which their members should strive. One society, for example, might emphasize family honor as a goal; another might emphasize military service; and the United States, he argues, is distinctive in the emphasis it places on the goal of financial success. All well-socialized Americans are supposed to strive for financial success and their ability to achieve this goal becomes a measure of their success in life. This is where Merton diverges from Durkheim, who argued that our goals in life are moderated by our social class. For Merton, they are not; everybody wants to be financially successful.

All societies also specify the legitimate means by which we are to attain the goals specified for us. In the United States, people learn that if they are ambitious, work hard, and follow the rules, then they will achieve financial success. The goal of financial success for all presupposes that the condition of equal opportunity exists, that all who are ambitious, work hard, and follow the rules will attain financial success. This, however, is not the case. It is much easier for people born rich to stay rich than it is for people born poor to get rich. Thus, while all well-socialized Americans are striving for financial success, tens of millions are being set up for failure—especially those on the lower rungs of the class hierarchy—because society's institutions simply are not equipped to provide wealth for all. The theory is also called "strain theory" because all Americans are under this strain to achieve and the strain and frustration is especially acute for the poor.

Merton also works with Durkheim's concept of *anomie*. In *Suicide*, Durkheim argues that the norms are what anchor us in society and the norms that regulate our goals are the most important norms of all. When these norms lose their salience or become irrelevant, other norms start to lose their salience as well and people (or individuals) lose their anchor and are set adrift in a sea of meaninglessness or, to use Merton's term, "normlessness."

Now I will summarize Merton's theory and relate it to deviance. The well-socialized American learns that his or her main goal in life should be to achieve financial success and that their ability to achieve this goal is a measure of their value as a person. They are also being told that there is equal opportunity to achieve financial success when, in fact, there is not. In essence, they are being lied to and the result is anomie. Those most important norms that regulate our goals lose their meaning and other norms start to lose their meaning also. People under this strain may adapt by breaking the rules in order to achieve financial success or by dropping out of the "game" altogether. Merton discusses other modes of adaptation as well.

Undoubtedly, the resilience of Merton's theory rests in part in his critique of the American economic culture. His theory is one of the best in the history of the sociology of crime and deviance to explain the connection between crime and poverty in a specifically American context and it also helps us to understand white-collar crime as well as some acts of non-economic deviance, such as drug addiction and what might have been called the "tramp phenomenon" in 1938 when Merton wrote the article. It is a theory that draws heavily on the functionalist tradition, but, in its critique of American capitalism, it also has strong appeal to those who are inclined toward conflict theory (discussed later). The two theoretical perspectives are often seen as antithetical; but Merton's theory is one among a few that shows that the two can complement one another.

The next article, "Techniques of Neutralization" by Gresham Sykes and David Matza, was written during a spate of theories emerging from sociology that dealt with lower class male gang delinquency in the 1950s. One of the more influential of these was developed by Albert Cohen in his book *Delinquent Boys,* published in 1955 (Cohen, 1955/1971). Much like Merton, Cohen argued that deviance often occurs when people's goal aspirations are frustrated. For Merton, the goal is wealth; for Cohen, it is status or self-esteem. Kids born into poverty, he argued, are deprived of ascribed status and they are deprived of legitimate opportunities to achieve status. Consequently, many kids react to this situation by rejecting or inverting society's dominant values and by joining gangs where they can earn status from other gang members by committing acts that are offensive to the middle class (Cohen, 1971).

Sykes and Matza begin by challenging Cohen's notion that the behavior of delinquent kids represents an "inversion of the values held by respectable, law-abiding society." They argue that lower class delinquent males have the same values as most kids. Kids' idols—heroes, famous movie stars and athletes—represent their values and delinquent kids have the same idols as other kids. They love their mothers just like other kids. And they draw sharp lines between appropriate and inappropriate targets (or victims) of their criminal activities. In other words, they know what they are doing is wrong. So Sykes and Matza devote their article to the very interesting question: Why do people violate the rules in which they believe? In answer to this question, they note that most of the rules that we learn through socialization are attenuated. That is, early on, one of the first rules that we learn is that there is an exception to every rule. We learn, for example, that it is wrong to kill, but that killing is appropriate in battle, in self-defense, or in legal executions. The problem for the juvenile delinquent, they argue, is that he or she recognizes exceptions to the rules that are not recognized by the authorities. Sykes and Matza describe five categories of exceptions, or techniques that juveniles use to neutralize the wrongfulness of their acts. Importantly, these are not just "lame" excuses that come into play after the deviant act; but the juvenile actually believes in the validity of these exceptions and this belief paves the way for the act.

In the next selection, "A Control Theory of Delinquency," Travis Hirschi starts out with a somewhat different angle than most theories of deviance. Deviance, he argues, is not that hard to explain. If, for example, a person sees something in a store that he or she wants, and they do not have the money or do not feel like spending the money to purchase it, it is not difficult to understand why they might pocket the item and walk out of the store with it. The question is why doesn't everybody do that? The answer, says Hirschi, lies in the strength of the bonds between the individual and society. These bonds act as "controls" and inhibit deviant behavior. Hirschi describes the nature of these controls. In doing so, he sheds light on a perennial question posed by comparative criminologists concerning the high rates of violence and street crime in the United States vis-à-vis other industrialized societies. It is the remarkable emphasis that American society places on the value of individualism that may go a long way in explaining its high crime rates. If it is the bonds between the individual and society that inhibit crime and deviance, then a society that emphasizes individualism will be more prone to crime and deviance.

The next selection, by Jack Gibbs, delineates the differences between the "old" and "new" conceptions of deviance. The old conceptions assumed there to be something *inherent* in the deviant individual and/or inherent in deviant behavior that makes the individual or the behavior "deviant." Sometimes considered the father of criminology, the nineteenth-century Italian researcher Cesare Lombroso argued that criminals were biologically flawed or inherently criminal. Early sociological criminologists—such as the American pioneers in criminology, Shaw, McKay, Sellin, and Sutherland—argued that criminals were not inherently flawed, but that their environments were flawed and predisposed them toward crime. However, in not questioning the meaning of the word "criminal," their works implied that there was something inherent in certain behaviors that made them criminal. Thus, the biologists argued that the criminal was inherently bad and the sociologists, at least by implication, argued the behavior that resulted from criminogenic environments was inherently bad.

Noting that the definitions of crime vary from time to time and place to place, in the 1950s and 1960s sociologists began to question the meanings of the words "crime" and "deviance." Since it is difficult to identify any behaviors that are defined as crime in all cultures throughout history, it follows that there is nothing inherent in crime that makes it a "crime" and, thus, there can be nothing in a person that makes him or her a criminal. With this insight, the labeling theorists and conflict theorists began to examine what kinds of people and what kinds of behaviors were more likely to be labeled deviant. They, thus, began to focus on factors that were *external* to deviance and the deviant. Gibbs sees this shift in perspectives as the emergence of the highly relativistic "new" concept of deviance. This highly relativistic concept of deviance basically argues that "deviance is in the eyes of the beholder," or the eyes of the audience, or the eyes of the culture, or the eyes of the powerful, depending on which variant of theory is employed.

Probably the most often cited name in regards to labeling theory is Howard Becker, who articulated many of its principles in his classic book *Outsiders* in 1963 (Becker, 1963). But as we see in the next reading in this section, Frank Tannenbaum laid a significant part of the groundwork for the development of labeling theory in his book *Crime and Community*, published in 1938. Tannenbaum argues that it is normal for juveniles to engage in rule-breaking behavior and perpetrate general acts of mayhem and that the crucial moment in the delinquent career comes when the normal juvenile is separated from other juveniles for committing those "evil" acts. Once that child's behavior is identified ("labeled") as evil, it is not a far stretch before that child is labeled as evil, and all of his or her subsequent behaviors are seen as a reflection of that evil. Behavior that departs from that label is not recognized by the community, leaving the child with few options other than to conform to the label. Thus, a very important principle that is drawn from Tannenbaum and later theorists is that a deviant label can act as a self-fulfilling prophesy.

Similarly, in 1951, Edwin Lemert elaborated on the self-fulfilling nature of the deviant label, arguing that the reasons for the original deviant acts are myriad—they could be situational, environmental, or even physiological—and, for the most part, they are irrelevant for the sociologist interested in deviance. Lemert's concern was with how societal reaction to the individual and his or her behavior increases the probability "that the integration of existing roles will be disrupted and that reorganization based upon a new role or roles will occur" (Lemert, 1951/1978: 95). Initial acts of deviance (which he calls "primary deviance") are not of concern to the labeling theorist; he or she is instead concerned with the societal reaction to the deviant. This may take the form of labeling and may cause the individual to assume a new role—a deviant role, which increases the likelihood that deviance will be perpetuated. Lemert calls the deviance which is the result of having been labeled "secondary deviance" and once again we see the self-fulfilling nature of the deviant label.

To fully understand why a deviant label may contribute to the initiation and/or perpetuation of deviance, it is important to understand the sociological concept of the "self." Charles Horton Cooley (1902) identified the self as being highly relativistic and as consisting of three components: (a) the imagination of our appearance to others, (b) the imagination of their judgment of that appearance, and (c) pride or shame. In other words, our perception of our self is based on our perceptions of other people's perceptions of us. That is, if you think you are fat, it is because you think other people think you are fat; or if you think you are sexy, it is because you think other people think you are sexy. Cooley called this the "looking-glass self." Thus, according to Cooley, when you look in the mirror what you see is what you think other people see when they look at you.

Labeling theorists more often trace their roots to the work of George Herbert Mead (Mead, 1934/1954) who is considered the father of a branch of sociological thought called "symbolic interactionism." For Mead, human behavior can only be understood in terms of how an individual defines him- or herself and how the individual defines the situation. In between us and reality is our perception or interpretation of reality. That is, we do not respond to reality, but to our perceptions of reality and, importantly, those perceptions are derived from social interaction, that is, our experiences with other people. Since all of us have had hundreds of thousands or millions of such experiences, no two people have had the same sets of experiences and our perceptions of reality are unique and highly relativistic. Thus, according to Cooley and Mead, the ways in which other people react to us has everything to do with how we feel about ourselves; and how we feel about ourselves has everything to do with how we behave. If people react to us differently than they do to others, then we will behave differently than others.

Another way to say that our perceptions of reality are derived from social interaction is to say that reality is "socially constructed." In the next selection, "The Search for Scapegoat Deviants," Jeffery Victor argues that the social construction of deviant categories serves as a sort of release valve for tensions created by social change. In this way, deviants serve as scapegoats, deflecting people's anger and attention away from the true sources of their frustration and onto often power-less victims who come to symbolize what is wrong with society. Along with the construction of deviant categories comes the construction of stereotypes which exaggerate the so-called (so-labeled) deviant's differences and which reinforce the people's anger. The classic example was the medieval witch craze. With the advantage of historical distance, we know that people were not reacting to the reality of witches, but to their perception of witches, which were socially constructed. Anthropologist Marvin Harris (1974) argues that during tremendous economic upheaval, the construction of the witch threat served to divert the peasantry's attention away from the true source of their problems and onto helpless individuals. "The principal result of the witch-hunt system (aside from charred bodies)," he writes, "was that the poor came to believe that they were being victimized by witches and devils instead of princes and popes." Victor's selection is reminiscent of Erikson's functionalist argument made earlier in this text in that they both argue that reactions to deviance serve to unite communities and reinforce their values.

The discussion of deviance and scapegoating also lends itself to the conflict theory of deviance, which focuses on social inequalities and on how the elite use their power to maintain their power. Accordingly, in the case of the medieval witch craze, much as Harris argues, those in power were able to influence the construction of deviant categories to their own advantage by deflecting negative attention away from themselves, by creating the appearance that they were championing the people's values when they prosecuted the deviant, and by uniting the people behind them in a common cause.

Conflict theorists trace their intellectual roots to the works of Karl Marx. Writing at the time of the Industrial Revolution, Marx was concerned with the struggle between the bourgeoisie and the proletariat. The *bourgeoisie* owned the factories and the *proletariat* worked in them. The relationship between the two classes, according to Marx, was one of exploitation. With the state representing the interests of the bourgeoisie, the social structure itself favored the interests of the bourgeoisie; the proletariat were unable to do anything but work for them. All terms of employment favored the employers, and they worked their advantage to the hilt, underpaying their workers and treating them like replaceable parts. Unemployment and the competition for jobs meant the proletariat had to put up with their exploitation or starve. Marx viewed many of the social problems of his day as stemming from these terms of production in capitalist economies. Modern conflict theory, though, is concerned not only with the struggle between employers and employees but also with the struggle between all interest groups: rich and poor, white and black, men and women, Christians and Muslims, etc.

Marx actually had little to say about crime, *per se*. When modern criminologists attribute the causes of crime to the terms of production in a capitalist society, their work is said to fall within the domain of "radical-," "critical-," or "(neo-) Marxist-" criminology. The next article in this section is one of the earliest of such examples, written by Willem Bonger in 1916. Bonger was a Dutch criminologist who was ahead of his time in the belief that crime is the result of social and economic conditions. He reasoned that in an economy that treats men as beasts, men will behave as beasts. Like many of the conflict theorists to follow, he viewed the law as a tool of the elite used to maintain the repressive system of capitalism and, thus, theft committed by the poor will be treated much more severely than theft committed by the rich. While his theoretical formulations are not very apparent in this brief excerpt, Bonger's views on the causes of crime are readily identifiable and easily aligned with the works of Marx.

The last article in this section comes from Jeffrey Reiman's modern classic, *The Rich Get Richer and the Poor Get Prison*. Reiman also makes a causal connection between crime and capitalism when he argues, ". . . most crime is motivated by a desire for property or money and is an understandable way of coping with the pressure of inequality, competition, and insecurity, all of which are essential ingredients of capitalism." He, too, views the law and the criminal justice system as serving the interests of the propertied class in its sanctification of contemporary economic arrangements. We find another common theme from critical criminology in this selection when Reiman notes that our preoccupation with crimes committed by the poor causes "Middle Americans" to fear the poor rather than join forces with them to restrain the elite, who are the real source of their economic insecurity.

The reader will find a more extensive articulation of conflict theory in Article 27 and in the introduction to Part VI on "Corporate, State, and Occcupational Deviance" in this book. Likewise, many of the theories covered in this section are further articulated and illustrated in the selections that follow as well as in the introductions to the sections of articles.

References

Becker, Howard, *Outsiders: Studies in the Sociology of Deviance*. New York: The Free Press, 1963.

Cooley, Charles Horton, *Human Nature and the Social Order*, New York: Scribner's, 1902.

Cohen, Albert K., *Delinquent Boys*, New York: Free Press, 1971. (Original work published 1955)

Durkheim, Emile, *Suicide: A Study in Sociology*, translated by John A. Spaulding and George Simpson, edited with an introduction by George Simpson, New York: The Free Press, 1951. (Original work published 1897)

Harris, Marvin. *Cows, Pigs, Wars and Witches: The Riddles of Culture*, New York: Random House, 1974, p. 237.

Lemert, Edwin M., "Secondary Deviance and Role Conceptions," from *Social Deviance*, edited by Ronald A. Farrell and Victoria Lynn Swigert, New York: J. B. Lippencott, 1978, pp. 94–97. (Original work published 1951)

Mead, George Herbert, *Mind, Self and Society: From the Standpoint of a Social Behaviorist*, edited by Charles W. Morris, Chicago: University of Chicago Press, 1954. (Original work published 1934)

1.

THE NORMAL AND THE PATHOLOGICAL

EMILE DURKHEIM

In one of the most classic statements about crime and deviance in the history of sociology, Durkheim asserts that since crime occurs in all societies throughout history, then it must be seen as normal and not as a sign of an unhealthy society. Because societies allow and encourage a certain diversity of thought, we are all different and that differentness accounts for both deviance and innovation. If it were not for that differentness, there would be no crime and there would be no social change; societies would remain absolutely stagnant—a condition that is not only undesirable but also impossible.

To rephrase Durkheim, crime is the price that we pay for a free society. This is not to say that the more crime the better. Indeed, Durkheim does acknowledge that rising crime rates are cause for concern.

Crime is present not only in the majority of societies of one particular species but in all societies of all types. There is no society that is not confronted with the problem of criminality. Its form changes; the acts thus characterized are not the same everywhere; but, everywhere and always, there have been men who have behaved in such a way as to draw upon themselves penal repression. If, in proportion as societies pass from the lower to the higher types, the rate of criminality, i.e., the relation between the yearly number of crimes and the population, tended to decline, it might be believed that crime, while still normal, is tending to lose this character of normality. But we have no reason to believe that such a regression is substantiated.

Many facts would seem rather to indicate a movement in the opposite direction. From the beginning of the [nineteenth] century, statistics enable us to follow the course of criminality. It has everywhere increased. In France the increase is nearly 300 per cent. There is, then, no phenomenon that presents more indisputably all the symptoms of normality, since it appears closely connected with the conditions of all collective life. To make of crime a form of social morbidity would be to admit that morbidity is not something accidental, but, on the contrary, that in certain cases it grows out of the fundamental constitution of the living organism; it would result in wiping out all distinction between the physiological and the pathological. No doubt it is possible that crime itself will have abnormal forms, as, for example, when its rate is unusually high. This excess is indeed, undoubtedly morbid in nature. What is normal, simply, is the existence of criminality, provided that it attains and does not exceed, for each social type, a certain level, which it is perhaps not impossible to fix in conformity with the preceding rules.[1]

Here we are, then, in the presence of a conclusion in appearance quite paradoxical. Let us make no mistake. To classify crime among the phenomena of normal sociology is not to say merely that it is an inevitable, although regrettable phenomenon, due to the incorrigible wickedness of men; it is to affirm that it is a factor in public health, an integral part of all healthy societies. This result is, at first glance, surprising enough to have puzzled even ourselves for a long time. Once this first surprise has been overcome, however, it is not difficult to find reasons explaining this normality and at the same time confirming it.

In the first place crime is normal because a society exempt from it is utterly impossible. Crime, we have shown elsewhere, consists of an act that offends certain very strong collective sentiments. In a society in which criminal acts are no longer committed, the sentiments they offend would have to be found without exception in all individual consciousnesses, and they must be found to exist with the same degree as sentiments contrary to them. Assuming that this condition could actually be realized, crime would not thereby disappear; it would only change its form, for the very cause which would thus dry up the sources of criminality would immediately open up new ones.

Indeed, for the collective sentiments which are protected by the penal law of a people at a specified moment of its history to take possession of the public conscience or for them to acquire a stronger hold where they have an insufficient grip, they must acquire an intensity greater than that which they had hitherto had. The community as a whole must experience them more vividly, for it can acquire from no other source the greater force necessary to control these individuals who formerly were the most refractory. For murderers to disappear, the horror of bloodshed must become greater in those social strata from which murderers are recruited; but, first it must become greater throughout the entire society. Moreover, the very absence of crime would directly contribute to produce this horror; because any sentiment seems much more respectable when it is always and uniformly respected.

One easily overlooks the consideration that these strong states of the common consciousness cannot be thus reinforced without reinforcing at the same time the more feeble states, whose violation previously gave birth to mere infraction of convention—since the weaker ones are only the prolongation, the attenuated form, of the stronger. Thus robbery and simple bad taste injure the same single altruistic sentiment, the respect for that which is another's. However, this same sentiment is less grievously offended by bad taste than by robbery; and since, in addition, the average consciousness has not sufficient intensity to react keenly to the bad taste, it is treated with greater tolerance. That is why the person guilty of bad taste is merely blamed, whereas the thief is punished. But, if this sentiment grows stronger, to the point of silencing in all consciousnesses the inclination which disposes man to steal, he will become more sensitive to the offenses which, until then, touched him but lightly. He will react against them, then, with more energy; they will be the object of greater opprobrium, which will transform certain of them from the simple moral faults that they were and give them the quality of crimes. For example, improper contracts, or contracts improperly executed, which only incur public blame or civil damages, will become offenses in law.

Imagine a society of saints, a perfect cloister of exemplary individuals. Crimes, properly so called, will there be unknown; but faults which appear venial to the layman will create there the same scandal that the ordinary offense does in ordinary consciousnesses. If, then, this society has the power to judge and punish, it will define these acts as criminal and will treat them as such. For the same reason, the perfect and upright man judges his smallest failings with a severity that the majority reserve for acts more truly in the nature of an offense. Formerly, acts of violence against persons were more frequent than they are today, because respect for individual dignity was less strong. As this has increased, these crimes have become more rare; and also, many acts violating this sentiment have been introduced into the penal law which were not included there in primitive times.[2]

In order to exhaust all the hypotheses logically possible, it will perhaps be asked why this unanimity does not extend to all collective sentiments without exception. Why should not even the most feeble sentiment gather enough energy to prevent all dissent? The moral consciousness of the society would be present in its entirety in all the individuals, with a vitality sufficient to prevent all acts offending it—the purely conventional faults as well as the crimes. But a uniformity so universal and absolute is utterly impossible; for the immediate physical milieu in which each one of us is placed, the hereditary antecedents, and the social influences vary from one individual to the next, and consequently diversify consciousnesses. It is impossible for all to be alike, if only because each one has his own organism and that these organisms occupy different areas in space. That is why, even among the lower peoples, where individual originality is very little developed, it nevertheless does exist.

Thus, since there cannot be a society in which the individuals do not differ more or less from the collective type, it is also inevitable that, among these divergences, there are some with a criminal character. What confers this character upon them is not the intrinsic quality of a given act but that definition which the collective conscience lends them. If the collective conscience is stronger, if it has enough authority practically to suppress these divergences, it will also be more sensitive, more exacting; and, reacting against the slightest deviations with the energy it otherwise displays only against more considerable infractions, it will attribute to them the same gravity as formerly to crimes. In other words, it will designate them as criminal.

Crime is, then, necessary; it is bound up with fundamental conditions of all social life, and by that very fact it is useful, because these conditions of which it is part are themselves indispensable to the normal evolution of morality and law.

Indeed, it is no longer possible today to dispute the fact that law and morality vary from one social type to the next, nor that they change within the same type if the conditions of life are modified. But, in order that these transformations may be possible, the collective sentiments at the basis of morality must not be hostile to change, and consequently must have but moderate energy.

If they were too strong, they would no longer be plastic. Every pattern is an obstacle to new patterns, to the extent that the first pattern is inflexible. The better a structure is articulated, the more it offers a healthy resistance to all modification; and this is equally true of functional, as of anatomical, organization. If there were no crimes, this condition could not have been fulfilled; for such a hypothesis presupposes that collective sentiments have arrived at a degree of intensity unexampled in history. Nothing is good indefinitely and to an unlimited extent. The authority which the moral conscience enjoys must not be excessive; otherwise no one would dare criticize it, and it would too easily congeal into an immutable form. To make progress, individual originality must be able to express itself. In order that the originality of the idealist whose dreams transcend his century may find expression, it is necessary that the originality of the criminal, who is below the level of his time, shall also be possible. One does not occur without the other.

Nor is this all. Aside from this indirect utility, it happens that crime itself plays a useful role in this evolution. Crime implies not only that the way remains open to necessary changes but that in certain cases it directly prepares these changes. Where crime exists, collective sentiments are sufficiently flexible to take on a new form, and crime sometimes helps to determine the form they will take. How many times, indeed, it is only an anticipation of future morality—a step toward what will be! According to Athenian law, Socrates was a criminal, and his condemnation was no more than just. However, his crime, namely, the independence of his thought, rendered a service not only to humanity but to his country. It served to prepare a new morality and faith which the Athenians needed, since the traditions by which they had lived until then were no longer in harmony with the current conditions of life. Nor is the case of Socrates unique; it is reproduced periodically in history. It would never have been possible to establish the freedom of thought we now enjoy if the regulations prohibiting it had not been violated before being solemnly abrogated. At that time, however, the violation was a crime, since it was an offense against sentiments still very keen in the average conscience. And yet this crime was useful as a prelude to reforms which daily became more necessary. Liberal philosophy had as its precursors the heretics of all kinds who were justly punished by secular authorities during the entire course of the Middle Ages and until the eve of modern times.

From this point of view the fundamental facts of criminality present themselves to us in an entirely new light. Contrary to current ideas, the criminal no longer seems a totally unsociable being, a sort of parasitic element, a strange and unassimilable body, introduced into the midst of society.[3] On the contrary, he plays a definite role in social life. Crime, for its part, must no longer be conceived as an evil that cannot be too much suppressed. There is no occasion for self-congratulation when the crime rate drops noticeably below the average level, for we may be certain that this apparent progress is associated with some social disorder. Thus, the number of assault cases never falls so low as in times of want.[4] With the drop in the crime rate, and as a reaction to it, comes a revision, or the need of a revision in the theory of punishment. If, indeed, crime is a disease, its punishment is its remedy and cannot be otherwise conceived; thus, all the discussions it arouses bear on the point of determining what the punishment must be in order to fulfil this role of remedy. If crime is not pathological at all, the object of punishment cannot be to cure it, and its true function must be sought elsewhere.

DISCUSSION QUESTIONS

1. What is the basis for Durkheim's arguing that crime is "normal"?
2. Why, according to Durkheim, is a "society of saints" not only impossible, but also undesirable?

NOTES

1. From the fact that crime is a phenomenon of normal sociology, it does not follow that the criminal is an individual normally constituted from the biological and psychological points

of view. The two questions are independent of each other. This independence will be better understood when we have shown, later on, the difference between psychological and socio-logical facts.

2. Calumny, insults, slander, fraud, etc.

3. We have ourselves committed the error of speaking thus of the criminal, because of a failure to apply our rule (*Division du travail social,* pp. 395–96).

4. Although crime is a fact of normal sociology, it does not follow that we must not abhor it. Pain itself has nothing desirable about it; the individual dislikes it as society does crime, and yet it is a function of normal physiology. Not only is it necessarily derived from the very constitution of every living organism, but it plays a useful role in life, for which reason it cannot be replaced. It would, then, be a singular distortion of our thought to present it as an apology for crime. We would not even think of protesting against such an interpretation, did we not know to what strange accusations and misunderstandings one exposes oneself when one undertakes to study moral facts objectively and to speak of them in a different language from that of the layman.

2.

ON THE SOCIOLOGY OF DEVIANCE

KAI T. ERIKSON

Flowing from Durkheim's assertion that deviance is universal and functional, Erikson speculates about the necessary role performed by deviants in the community. According to Erikson, the deviant helps the community establish its moral boundaries and, therefore, its identity as a community. An understanding of this process helps us to understand why the coverage of crime and deviance constitutes such a large proportion of the daily news in our and other societies. It also helps us to understand one of the great paradoxes in the sociology of social control; that is, do we really believe that we can take society's deviants, force them into extremely deviant environments (e.g., a prison or a mental hospital), and expect them to come out less deviant?

Human actors are sorted into various kinds of collectivity, ranging from relatively small units such as the nuclear family to relatively large ones such as a nation or culture. One of the most stubborn difficulties in the study of deviation is that the problem is defined differently at each one of these levels: behavior that is considered unseemly within the context of a single family may be entirely acceptable to the community in general, while behavior that attracts severe censure from the members of the community may go altogether unnoticed elsewhere in the culture. People in society, then, must learn to deal separately with deviance at each one of these levels and to distinguish among them in his own daily activity. A man may disinherit his son for conduct that violates old family traditions or ostracize a neighbor for conduct that violates some local custom, but he is not expected to employ either of these standards when he serves as a juror in a court of law. In each of the three situations he is required to use a different set of criteria to decide whether or not the behavior in question exceeds tolerable limits.

In the next few pages we shall be talking about deviant behavior in social units called "communities," but the use of this term does not mean that the argument applies only at that level of organization. In theory, at least, the argument being made here should fit all kinds of human collectivity—families as well as whole cultures, small groups as well as nations—and the term "community" is only being used in this context because it seems particularly convenient.[1]

The people of a community spend most of their lives in close contact with one another, sharing a common sphere of experience which makes them feel that they belong to a special "kind" and live in a special "place." In the formal language of sociology, this means that communities are boundary maintaining: each has a specific territory in the world as a whole, not only in the sense that it occupies a defined region of geographical space but also in the sense that it takes over a particular niche in what might be called cultural space and develops its own "ethos" or "way" within that compass. Both of these dimensions of group space, the geographical and the cultural, set the community apart as a special place and provide an important point of reference for its members.

When one describes any system as boundary maintaining, one is saying that it controls the fluctuation of its consistent parts so that the whole retains a limited range of activity, a given pattern of constancy and stability, within the larger environment. A human community can be said to maintain boundaries, then, in the sense that its members tend to confine themselves to a particular radius of activity and to regard any conduct which drifts outside that radius as somehow inappropriate or immoral. Thus the group retains a kind of cultural integrity, a voluntary restriction on its own potential for expansion, beyond that which is strictly required for accommodation to the environment. Human behavior can vary over an enormous range, but each community draws a symbolic set of parentheses around a certain segment of that range and limits its own activities within that narrower zone. These parentheses, so to speak, are the community's boundaries.

People who live together in communities cannot relate to one another in any coherent way or even acquire a sense of their own stature as group members unless they learn something about the boundaries of the territory they occupy in social space, if only because they need to sense what lies beyond the margins of the group before they can appreciate the special quality of the experience which takes place within it. Yet how do people learn about the boundaries of their community? And how do they convey this information to the generations which replace them?

To begin with, the only material found in a society for marking boundaries is the behavior of its members—or rather, the networks of interaction which link these members together in regular social relations. And the interactions which do the most effective job of locating and publicizing the group's outer edges would seem to be those which take place between deviant persons on the one side and official agents of the community on the other. The deviant is a person whose activities have moved outside the margins of the group, and when the community calls him to account for that vagrancy it is making a statement about the nature and placement of its boundaries. It is declaring how much variability and diversity can be tolerated within the group before it begins to lose its distinctive shape, its unique identity. Now there may be other moments in the life of the group which perform a similar service: wars, for instance, can publicize a group's boundaries by drawing attention to the line separating the group from an adversary, and certain kinds of religious ritual, dance ceremony, and other traditional pageantry can dramatize the difference between "we" and "they" by portraying a symbolic encounter between the two. But on the whole, members of a community inform one another about the placement of their boundaries by participating in the confrontations which occur when persons who venture out to the edges of the group are met by policing agents whose special business it is to guard the cultural integrity of the community. Whether these confrontations take the form of criminal trials, excommunication hearings, courts-martial, or even psychiatric case conferences, they act as boundary-maintaining devices in the sense that they demonstrate to whatever audience is concerned where the line is drawn between behavior that belongs in the special universe of the group and behavior that does not. In general, this kind of information is not easily relayed by the straightforward use of language. Most readers of this paragraph, for instance, have a fairly clear idea of the line separating theft from more legitimate forms of commerce, but few of them have ever seen a published statute describing these differences. More likely than not, our information on the subject has been drawn from publicized instances in which the relevant laws were applied—and for that matter, the law itself is largely a collection of past cases and decisions, a synthesis of the various confrontations which have occurred in the life of the legal order.

It may be important to note in this connection that confrontations between deviant offenders and the agents of control have always attracted a good deal of public attention. In our own past, the trial and punishment of offenders were staged in the market place and afforded the crowd a chance to participate in a direct, active way. Today, of course, we no longer parade deviants in the town square or expose them to the carnival atmosphere of Tyburn, but it is interesting that the "reform" which brought about this change in penal practice coincided almost exactly with the development of newspapers as a medium of mass information. Perhaps this is no more than an accident of history, but it is nonetheless true that newspapers (and now radio and television) offer much the same kind of entertainment as public hangings or a Sunday visit to the local gaol. A considerable portion of what we call "news" is devoted to reports about deviant behavior and its consequences, and it is no simple matter to explain why these items should be considered newsworthy or why they should command the extraordinary attention they do. Perhaps they appeal to a number of psychological perversities among the mass audience, as commentators have suggested, but at the same time they constitute one of our main sources of information about the normative outlines of society. In a figurative sense, at least, morality and immorality meet at the public scaffold, and it is during this meeting that the line between them is drawn.

Boundaries are never a fixed property of any community. They are always shifting as the people of the group find new ways to define the outer limits of their universe, new ways to position themselves on the larger cultural map. Sometimes changes occur within the structure of the group which require its members to make a new survey of their territory—a change of leadership, a shift of mood. Sometimes changes occur in the surrounding environment, altering the background against which the people of the group have measured their own uniqueness. And always, new generations are moving in to take their turn guarding old institutions and need to be informed about the contours of the world they are inheriting. Thus single encounters between the deviant and his community are only fragments of an ongoing social process. Like an article of common law, boundaries remain a meaningful point of reference only so long as they are repeatedly tested by persons on the fringes of the group and repeatedly defended by persons chosen to represent the group's inner morality. Each time the community moves to censure some act of deviation, then, and convenes a formal ceremony to deal with the responsible offender, it sharpens the authority of the violated norm and restates where the boundaries of the group are located.

For these reasons, deviant behavior is not a simple kind of leakage which occurs when the machinery of society is in poor working order, but may be, in controlled quantities, an important condition for preserving the stability of social life. Deviant forms of behavior, by marking the outer edges of group life, give the inner structure its special character and thus supply the framework within which the people of the group develop an orderly sense of their own cultural identity. Perhaps this is what Aldous Huxley had in mind when he wrote:

> Now tidiness is undeniably good—but a good of which it is easily possible to have too much and at too high a price. . . . The good life can only be lived in a society in which tidiness is preached and practiced, but not too fanatically, and where efficiency is always haloed, as it were, by a tolerated margin of mess.[2]

This raises a delicate theoretical issue. If we grant that human groups often derive benefit from deviant behavior, can we then assume that they are organized in such a way as to promote this resource? Can we assume, in other words, that forces operate in the social structure to recruit offenders and to commit them to long periods of service in the deviant ranks? This is not a question which can be answered with our present store of empirical data, but one observation can be made which gives the question an interesting perspective—namely, that deviant forms of conduct often seem to derive nourishment from the very agencies devised to inhibit them. Indeed, the agencies built by society for preventing deviance are often so poorly equipped for the task that we might well ask why this is regarded as their "real" function in the first place.

It is by now a thoroughly familiar argument that many of the institutions designed to discourage deviant behavior actually operate in such a way as to perpetuate it. For one thing, prisons, hospitals, and other similar agencies provide aid and shelter to large numbers of deviant persons, sometimes giving them a certain advantage in the competition for social resources. But beyond this, such institutions gather marginal people into tightly segregated groups, give them an opportunity to teach one another the skills and attitudes of a deviant career, and even provoke them into using these skills by reinforcing their sense of alienation from the rest of society.[3] Nor is this observation a modern one:

> The misery suffered in gaols is not half their evil; they are filled with every sort of corruption that poverty and wickedness can generate; with all the shameless and profligate enormities that can be produced by the impudence of ignominy, the range of want, and the malignity of despair. In a prison the check of the public eye is removed; and the power of the law is spent. There are few fears, there are no blushes. The lewd inflame the more modest; the audacious harden the timid. Everyone fortifies himself as he can against his own remaining sensibility; endeavoring to practice on others the arts that are practiced on himself; and to gain the applause of his worst associates by imitating their manners.[4]

These lines, written almost two centuries ago, are a harsh indictment of prisons, but many of the conditions they describe continue to be reported in even the most modern studies of prison life. Looking at the matter from a long-range historical perspective, it is fair to conclude that prisons have done a conspicuously poor job of reforming the convicts placed in their custody; but the very consistency of this failure may have a peculiar logic of its own. Perhaps we find it difficult to change the worst of our penal practices because we *expect* the prison to harden the inmate's commitment to deviant forms of behavior and draw him more deeply into the deviant ranks. On the whole, we are a people who do not really expect deviants to change very much as they are processed through the control agencies we provide for them, and we are often reluctant to devote much of the community's resources to the job of rehabilitation. In this sense, the prison which graduates long rows of accomplished criminals (or, for that matter, the state asylum which stores its most severe cases away in some back ward) may do serious violence to the aims of its founders; but it does very little violence to the expectations of the population it serves.

These expectations, moreover, are found in every corner of society and constitute an important part of the climate in which we deal with deviant forms of behavior.

To begin with, the community's decision to bring deviant sanctions against one of its members is not a simple act of censure. It is an intricate rite of transition, at once moving the individual out of his ordinary place in society and transferring him into a special deviant position.[5] The ceremonies which mark this change of status, generally, have a number of related phases. They supply a formal stage on which the deviant and his community can confront one another (as in the criminal trial); they make an announcement about the nature of his deviancy (a verdict or diagnosis, for example); and they place him in a particular role which is thought to neutralize the harmful effects of his misconduct (like the role of prisoner or patient). These commitment ceremonies tend to be occasions of wide public interest and ordinarily take place in a highly dramatic setting.[6] Perhaps the most obvious example of a commitment ceremony is the criminal trial, with its elaborate formality and exaggerated ritual, but more modest equivalents can be found wherever procedures are set up to judge whether or not someone is legitimately deviant.

An important feature of these ceremonies in our own culture is that they are almost irreversible. Most provisional roles conferred by society, those of the student or conscripted soldier, for example, include some kind of terminal ceremony to mark the individual's movement back out of the role once its temporary advantages have been exhausted. But the roles allotted the deviant seldom make allowance for this type of passage. He is ushered into the deviant position by a decisive and often dramatic ceremony, yet is retired from it with scarcely a word of public notice. And as a result, the deviant often returns home with no proper license to resume a normal life in the community. Nothing has happened to cancel out the stigmas imposed upon him by earlier commitment ceremonies; nothing has happened to revoke the verdict or diagnosis pronounced upon him at that time. It should not be surprising, then, that the people of the community are apt to greet the returning deviant with a considerable degree of apprehension and distrust, for in a very real sense they are not at all sure who he is.

A circularity is thus set into motion which has all the earmarks of a "self-fulfilling prophesy," to use Merton's fine phrase. On the one hand, it seems quite obvious that the community's apprehensions help reduce whatever chances the deviant might otherwise have had for a successful return home. Yet at the same time, everyday experience seems to show that these suspicions are wholly reasonable, for it is a well-known and highly publicized fact that many if not most ex-convicts return to crime after leaving prison and that large numbers of mental patients require further treatment after an initial hospitalization. The common feeling that deviant persons never really change, then, may derive from a faulty premise; but the feeling is expressed so frequently and with such conviction that it eventually creates the facts which later "prove" it to be correct. If the returning deviant encounters this circularity often enough, it is quite understandable that he, too, may begin to wonder whether he has fully graduated from the deviant role, and he may respond to the uncertainty by resuming some kind of deviant activity. In many respects, this may be the only way for the individual and his community to agree what kind of person he is.

Moreover this prophesy is found in the official policies of even the most responsible agencies of control. Police departments could not operate with any real effectiveness if they did not regard ex-convicts as a ready pool of suspects to be tapped in the event of trouble, and psychiatric clinics could not do a successful job in the community if they were not always alert to the possibility of former patients suffering relapses. Thus the prophesy gains currency at many levels within the social order, not only in the poorly informed attitudes of the community at large, but in the best informed theories of most control agencies as well.

In one form or another this problem has been recognized in the West for many hundreds of years, and this simple fact has a curious implication. For if our culture has supported a steady flow of deviation throughout long periods of historical change, the rules which apply to any kind of evolutionary thinking would suggest that strong forces must be at work to keep the flow intact— and this because it contributes in some important way to the survival of the culture as a whole. This does not furnish us with sufficient warrant to declare that deviance is "functional" (in any of the many senses of that term), but it should certainly make us wary of the assumption so often made in sociological circles that any well-structured society is somehow designed to prevent deviant behavior from occurring.[7]

It might be then argued that we need new metaphors to carry our thinking about deviance onto a different plane. On the whole, American sociologists have devoted most of their attention to those forces in society which seem to assert a centralizing influence on human behavior, gathering people together into tight clusters called "groups" and bringing them under the jurisdiction of governing principles called "norms" or "standards." The questions which sociologists have traditionally asked of their data, then, are addressed to the uniformities rather than the divergencies of social life: how is it that people learn to think in similar ways, to accept the same group moralities, to move by the same rhythms of behavior, to see life with the same eyes? How is it, in short, that cultures accomplish the incredible alchemy of making unity out of diversity, harmony out of conflict, order out of confusion? Somehow we often act as if the differences between people can be taken for granted, being too natural to require comment, but that the symmetry which human groups manage to achieve must be explained by referring to the molding influence of the social structure.

But variety, too, is a product of the social structure. It is certainly remarkable that members of a culture come to look so much alike; but it is also remarkable that out of all this sameness a people can develop a complex division of labor, move off into diverging career lines, scatter across the surface of the territory they share in common, and create so many differences of temper, ideology, fashion, and mood. Perhaps we can conclude, then, that two separate yet often competing currents are found in any society: those forces which promote a high degree of conformity among the people of the community so that they know what to expect from one another, and those forces which encourage a certain degree of diversity so that people can be deployed across the range of group space to survey its potential, measure its capacity, and, in the case of those we call deviants, patrol its boundaries. In such a scheme, the deviant would appear as a natural product of group differentiation. He is not a bit of debris spun out by faulty social machinery, but a relevant figure in the community's overall division of labor.

DISCUSSION QUESTIONS

1. According to Erikson, what similar role is played by today's media and yesterday's public executions?
2. "Rites of passage" are rituals used to mark someone's transition from one status in society to another status. What, according to Erikson, is noteworthy about the rites establishing one's passage from non-deviant status to deviant status and back again? Why?

NOTES

1. In fact, the first statement of the general notion presented here was concerned with the study of small groups. See Robert A. Dentler and Kai T. Erikson, "The Functions of Deviance in Groups," *Social Problems*, VII (Fall 1959), pp. 98–107.
2. Aldous Huxley, *Prisons: The "Carceri" Etchings by Piranesi* (London: The Trianon Press, 1949), p. 13.
3. For a good description of this process in the modern prison, see Gresham Sykes, *The Society of Captives* (Princeton, N.J.: Princeton University Press, 1958). For discussions of similar problems in two different kinds of mental hospital, see Erving Goffman, *Asylums* (New York: Bobbs-Merrill, 1962) and Kai T. Erikson, "Patient Role and Social Uncertainty: A Dilemma of the Mentally Ill," *Psychiatry*, XX (August 1957), pp. 263–274.
4. Written by "a celebrated" but not otherwise identified author (perhaps Henry Fielding) and quoted in John Howard, *The State of the Prisons*, London, 1777 (London: J. M. Dent and Sons, 1929), p. 10.
5. The classic description of this process as it applies to the medical patient is found in Talcott Parsons, *The Social System* (Glencoe, Ill.: The Free Press, 1951).
6. See Harold Garfinkel, "Successful Degradation Ceremonies," *American Journal of Sociology*, LXI (January 1956), pp. 420–424.
7. Albert K. Cohen, for example, speaking for a dominant strain in sociological thinking, takes the question quite for granted: "It would seem that the control of deviant behavior is, by definition, a culture goal." See "The Study of Social Disorganization and Deviant Behavior" in Merton et al., *Sociology Today* (New York: Basic Books, 1959), p. 465.

3.

SOCIAL STRUCTURE AND ANOMIE

ROBERT K. MERTON

In one of the most often cited works in the American sociology of deviance, Merton asserts that much of the crime and deviance in our society stems from the extraordinarily strong emphasis our culture places on the goal of financial success. The strong belief that Americans hold in the existence of equal opportunity for all implies that the goal of success is equally available and that those who do not achieve it have only themselves to blame. Yet the problem is that there is not equal opportunity and that millions of Americans are set up to fail. The result can be frustration, hostility, anomie, and crime.

While other countries may have higher rates of poverty, the correlation between crime and poverty is often not as strong in those societies because the emphasis on financial success and the belief in equal opportunity are not as strong as they are in the United States. The physical challenges presented by poverty in poorer countries may be greater, but it may well be that the psychological frustration engendered by poverty is not as keen in these countries as it is in the United States.

There persists a notable tendency in sociological theory to attribute the malfunctioning of social structure primarily to those of man's imperious biological drives which are not adequately restrained by social control. In this view, the social order is solely a device for "impulse management" and the "social processing" of tensions. These impulses which break through social control, be it noted, are held to be biologically derived. Nonconformity is assumed to be rooted in original nature.[1] Conformity is by implication the result of a utilitarian calculus or unreasoned conditioning. This point of view, whatever its other deficiencies, clearly begs one question. It provides no basis for determining the nonbiological conditions which induce deviations from prescribed patterns of conduct. In this paper, it will be suggested that certain phases of social structure generate the circumstances in which infringement of social codes constitutes a "normal" response.[2]

The conceptual scheme to be outlined is designed to provide a coherent, systematic approach to the study of socio-cultural sources of deviate behavior. Our primary aim lies in discovering how some social structures *exert a definite pressure* upon certain persons in the society to engage in non conformist rather than conformist conduct. The many ramifications of the scheme cannot all be discussed; the problems mentioned outnumber those explicitly treated.

Among the elements of social and cultural structure, two are important for our purposes. These are analytically separable although they merge imperceptibly in concrete situations. The first consists of culturally defined goals, purposes, and interests. It comprises a frame of aspirational reference. These goals are more or less integrated and involve varying degrees of prestige and sentiment. They constitute a basic, but not the exclusive, component of what Linton aptly has called "designs for group living." Some of these cultural aspirations are related to the original drives of man, but they are not determined by them. The second phase of the social structure defines, regulates, and controls the acceptable modes of achieving these goals. Every social group invariably couples its scale of desired ends with moral or institutional regulation of permissible and required procedures for attaining these ends. These regulatory norms and moral imperatives do not necessarily coincide with technical or efficiency norms. Many procedures which from the standpoint of *particular individuals* would be most efficient in securing desired values, e.g., illicit oil-stock schemes, theft, fraud, are ruled out of the institutional area of permitted conduct. The choice of expedients is limited by the institutional norms.

To say that these two elements, culture goals and institutional norms, operate jointly is not to say that the ranges of alternative behaviors and aims bear some constant relation to one another. The emphasis upon certain goals may vary independently of the degree of emphasis upon institutional means. There may develop a disproportionate, at times, a virtually exclusive, stress upon the value of specific goals, involving relatively slight concern with the institutionally appropriate modes of attaining these goals. The limiting case in this direction is reached when the range of alternative procedures is limited only by technical rather than institutional considerations. Any and all devices which promise attainment of the all important goal would be permitted in this hypothetical polar case.[3] This constitutes one type of cultural malintegration. A second polar type is found in groups where activities originally conceived as instrumental are transmuted into ends in themselves. The original purposes are forgotten, and ritualistic adherence to institutionally prescribed conduct becomes virtually obsessive.[4] Stability is largely ensured while change is flouted. The range of alternative behaviors is severely limited. There develops a tradition-bound, sacred society characterized by neophobia. The occupational psychosis of the bureaucrat may be cited as a case in point. Finally, there are the intermediate types of groups where a balance between culture goals and institutional means is maintained. These are the significantly integrated and relatively stable, though changing, groups.

An effective equilibrium between the two phases of the social structure is maintained as long as satisfactions accrue to individuals who conform to both constraints, *viz.*, satisfactions from the achievement of the goals and satisfactions emerging directly from the institutionally canalized modes of striving to attain these ends. Success, in such equilibrated cases, is twofold. Success is reckoned in terms of the product and in terms of the process, in terms of the outcome and in terms of activities. Continuing satisfactions must derive from sheer *participation* in a competitive order as well as from eclipsing one's competitors if the order itself is to be sustained. The occasional sacrifices involved in institutionalized conduct must be compensated by socialized rewards. The distribution of statuses and roles through competition must be so organized that positive incentives for conformity to roles and adherence to status obligations are provided *for every position* within the distributive order. Aberrant conduct, therefore, may be viewed as a symptom of dissociation between culturally defined aspirations and socially structured means.

Of the types of groups which result from the independent variation of the two phases of the social structure, we shall be primarily concerned with the first, namely, that involving a disproportionate accent on goals. This statement must be recast in a proper perspective. In no group is there an absence of regulatory codes governing conduct, yet groups do vary in the degree to which these folkways, mores, and institutional controls are effectively integrated with the more diffuse goals which are part of the culture matrix. Emotional convictions may cluster about the complex of socially acclaimed ends, meanwhile shifting their support from the culturally defined implementation of these ends. As we shall see, certain aspects of the social structure may generate countermores and antisocial behavior precisely because of differential emphases on goals and regulations. In the extreme case, the latter may be so vitiated by the goal-emphasis that the range of behavior is limited only by considerations of technical expediency. The sole significant question then becomes, which available means is most efficient in netting the socially approved value.[5] The technically most feasible procedure, whether legitimate or not, is preferred to the institutionally prescribed conduct. As this process continues, the integration of the society becomes tenuous and anomie ensues.

Thus, in competitive athletics, when the aim of victory is shorn of its institutional trappings and success in contests becomes construed as "winning the game" rather than "winning through circumscribed modes of activity," a premium is implicitly set upon the use of illegitimate but technically efficient means. The star of the opposing football team is surreptitiously slugged; the wrestler furtively incapacitates his opponent through ingenious but illicit techniques; university alumni covertly subsidize "students" whose talents are largely confined to the athletic field. The emphasis on the goal has so attenuated the satisfactions deriving from sheer participation in the competitive activity that these satisfactions are virtually confined to a successful outcome. Through the same process, tension generated by the desire to win in a poker game is relieved by successfully dealing oneself four aces, or, when the cult of success has become completely dominant, by sagaciously shuffling the cards in a game of solitaire. The faint twinge of uneasiness in the last instance and the surreptitious nature of public delicts indicate clearly that the institutional rules of the game are *known* to those who evade them, but that the emotional supports of these rules are largely vitiated by cultural exaggeration of the success-goal.[6] They are microcosmic images of the social macrocosm.

Of course, this process is not restricted to the realm of sport. The process whereby exaltation of the end generates a *literal demoralization*, i.e., a deinstitutionalization, of the means is one which characterizes many[7] groups in which the two phases of the social structure are not highly integrated. The extreme emphasis upon the accumulation of wealth as a symbol of success[8] in our own society militates against the completely effective control of institutionally regulated modes of acquiring of fortune.[9] Fraud, corruption, vice, crime, in short, the entire catalogue of proscribed behavior, becomes increasingly common when the emphasis on the *culturally induced* success-goal becomes divorced from a coordinated institutional emphasis. This observation is of crucial theoretical importance in examining the doctrine that antisocial behavior most frequently derives from biological drives breaking through the restraints imposed by society. The difference is one between a strictly utilitarian interpretation which conceives man's ends as random and an analysis which finds these ends deriving from the basic values of the culture.[10]

Our analysis can scarcely stop at this juncture. We must turn to other aspects of the social structure if we are to deal with the social genesis of the varying rates and types of deviate behavior characteristic of different societies. Thus far, we have sketched three ideal types of social orders constituted by distinctive patterns of relations between culture ends and means. Turning from these types of *culture patterning*, we find five logically possible, alternative modes of adjustment or adaptation by *individuals* within the culture-bearing society or group.[11] These are schematically presented in the following table, where (+) signifies "acceptance," (−) signifies "elimination," and (±) signifies "rejection and substitution of new goals and standards."

Our discussion of the relation between these alternative responses and other phases of the social structure must be prefaced by the observation that persons may shift from one alternative to another as they engage in different social activities. These categories refer to role adjustments in specific situations, not to personality *in toto*. To treat the development of this process in various spheres of conduct would introduce a complexity unmanageable within the confines of this paper. For this reason, we shall be concerned primarily with economic activity in the broad sense, "the production, exchange, distribution, and consumption of goods and services" in our competitive society, wherein wealth has taken on a highly symbolic cast. Our task is to search out some of the factors which exert pressure upon individuals to engage in certain of these logically possible alternative responses. This choice, as we shall see, is far from random.

In every society, Adaptation I (conformity to both culture goals and means) is the most common and widely diffused. Were this not so, the stability and continuity of the society could not be maintained. The mesh of expectancies which constitutes every social order is sustained by the modal behavior of its members falling within the first category. Conventional role behavior oriented toward the basic values of the group is the rule rather than the exception. It is this fact alone which permits us to speak of a human aggregate as comprising a group or society.

Conversely, Adaptation IV (rejection of goals and means) is the least common. Persons who "adjust" (or maladjust) in this fashion are, strictly speaking, *in* the society but not *of* it. Sociologically, these constitute the true "aliens." Not sharing the common frame of orientation, they can be included within the societal population merely in a fictional sense. In this category are *some* of the activities of psychotics, psychoneurotics, chronic autists, pariahs, outcasts, vagrants, vagabonds, tramps, chronic drunkards, and drug addicts.[13] These have relinquished, in certain spheres of activity, the culturally defined goals, involving complete aim-inhibition in the polar case, and their adjustments are not in accord with institutional norms. This is not to say that in some cases the source of their behavioral adjustments is not in part the very social structure which they have in effect repudiated nor that their very existence within a social area does not constitute a problem for the socialized population.

This mode of adjustment occurs, as far as structural sources are concerned, when both the culture goals and institutionalized procedures have been assimilated thoroughly by the individual

TABLE 1.1

Modes of Adaptation	Culture Goals	Institutional Means
I. Conformity	+	+
II. Innovation	+	−
III. Ritualism	−	−
IV. Retreatism	−	−
V. Rebellion[12]	±	±

and imbued with affect and high positive value, but where those institutionalized procedures which promise a measure of successful attainment of the goals are not available to the individual. In such instances, there results a two-fold mental conflict insofar as the moral obligation for adopting institutional means conflicts with the pressure to resort to illegitimate means (which may attain the goal) and inasmuch as the individual is shut off from means which are both legitimate *and* effective. The competitive order is maintained, but the frustrated and handicapped individual who cannot cope with this order drops out. Defeatism, quietism, and resignation are manifested in escape mechanisms which ultimately lead the individual to "escape" from the requirements of the society. It is an expedient which arises from continued failure to attain the goal by legitimate measures and from an inability to adopt the illegitimate route because of internalized prohibitions and institutionalized compulsives, *during which process the supreme value of the success-goal has as yet not been renounced*. The conflict is resolved by eliminating *both* precipitating elements, the goals and means. The escape is complete, the conflict is eliminated, and the individual is associated.

Be it noted that where frustration derives from the inaccessibility of effective institutional means for attaining economic or any other type of highly valued "success," that Adaptations II, III, and V (innovation, ritualism, and rebellion) are also possible. The result will be determined by the particular personality, and thus, the particular cultural background, involved. Inadequate socialization will result in the innovation response whereby the conflict and frustration are eliminated by relinquishing the institutional means and retaining the success-aspiration; an extreme assimilation of institutional demands will lead to ritualism wherein the goal is dropped as beyond one's reach but conformity to the mores persists; and rebellion occurs when emancipation from the reigning standards, due to frustration or to marginalist perspectives, leads to the attempt to introduce a "new social order."

Our major concern is with the illegitimacy adjustment. This involves the use of conventionally proscribed but frequently effective means of attaining at least the simulacrum of culturally defined success—wealth, power, and the like. As we have seen, this adjustment occurs when the individual has assimilated the cultural emphasis on success without equally internalizing the morally prescribed norms governing means for its attainment. The question arises, Which phases of our social structure predispose toward this mode of adjustment? We may examine a concrete instance, effectively analyzed by Lohman,[14] which provides a clue to the answer. Lohman has shown that specialized areas of vice in the near north side of Chicago constitute a "normal" response to a situation where the cultural emphasis upon pecuniary success has been absorbed, but where there is little access to conventional and legitimate means for attaining such success. The conventional occupational opportunities of persons in this area are almost completely limited to manual labor. Given our cultural stigmatization of manual labor, and its correlate, the prestige of white collar work, it is clear that the result is a strain toward innovational practices. The limitation of opportunity to unskilled labor and the resultant low income cannot compete in terms of *conventional standards of achievement* with the high income from organized vice.

For our purposes, this situation involves two important features. First, such antisocial behavior is in a sense "called forth" by certain conventional values of the culture *and* by the class structure involving differential access to the approved opportunities for legitimate, prestige-bearing pursuit of the culture goals. The lack of high integration between the means-and-end elements of the cultural pattern and the particular class structure combine to favor a heightened frequency of antisocial conduct in such groups. The second consideration is of equal significance. Recourse to the first of the alternative responses, legitimate effort, is limited by the fact that actual advance toward desired success-symbols through conventional channels is, despite our persisting open-class ideology,[15] relatively rare and difficult for those handicapped by little formal education and few economic resources. The dominant pressure of group standards of success is, therefore, on the gradual attenuation of legitimate, but by and large ineffective, strivings and the increasing use of illegitimate, but more or less effective, expedients of vice and crime. The cultural demands made on persons in this situation are incompatible. On the one hand, they are asked to orient their conduct toward the prospect of accumulating wealth and on the other, they are largely denied effective opportunities to do so institutionally. The consequences of such structural inconsistency are psychopathological personality, and/or antisocial conduct, and/or revolutionary activities. The equilibrium between culturally designated means and ends becomes highly unstable with the progressive emphasis on attaining the prestige-laden ends by any means whatsoever. Within this context, Capone represents the triumph of amoral intelligence over morally prescribed "failure," when the channels of vertical mobility are closed or narrowed[16] *in a society which places a high premium on economic affluence and social ascent for all its members.*[17]

This last qualification is of primary importance. It suggests that other phases of the social structure besides the extreme emphasis on pecuniary success must be considered if we are to understand the social sources of antisocial behavior. A high frequency of deviate behavior is not generated simply by "lack of opportunity" or by this exaggerated pecuniary emphasis. A comparatively rigidified class structure, a feudalistic or caste order, may limit such opportunities far beyond the point which obtains in our society today. It is only when a system of cultural values extols, virtually above all else, certain *common* symbols of success *for the population at large* while its social structure rigorously restricts or completely eliminates access to approved modes of acquiring these symbols *for a considerable part of the same population* that antisocial behavior ensues on a considerable scale. In other words, our egalitarian ideology denies by implication the existence of noncompeting groups and individuals in the pursuit of pecuniary success. The same body of success-symbols is held to be desirable for all. These goals are held to *transcend class lines*, not to be bounded by them, yet the actual social organization is such that there exist class differentials in the accessibility of these *common* success-symbols. Frustration and thwarted aspiration lead to the search for avenues of escape from a culturally induced intolerable situation; or unrelieved ambition may eventuate in illicit attempts to acquire the dominant values.[18] The American stress on pecuniary success and ambitiousness for all thus invites exaggerated anxieties, hostilities, neuroses, and antisocial behavior.

This theoretical analysis may go far toward explaining the varying correlations between crime and poverty.[19] Poverty is not an isolated variable. It is one in a complex of interdependent social and cultural variables. When viewed in such a context, it represents quite different states of affairs. Poverty as such, and consequent limitation of opportunity, are not sufficient to induce a conspicuously high rate of criminal behavior. Even the often mentioned "poverty in the midst of plenty" will not necessarily lead to this result. Only insofar as poverty and associated disadvantages in competition for the culture values approved for *all* members of the society are linked with the assimilation of a cultural emphasis on monetary accumulation as a symbol of success is antisocial conduct a "normal" outcome. Thus, poverty is less highly correlated with crime in southeastern

Europe than in the United States. The possibilities of vertical mobility in these European areas would seem to be fewer than in this country, so that neither poverty per se nor its association with limited opportunity is sufficient to account for the varying correlations. It is only when the full configuration is considered, poverty, limited opportunity, and a commonly shared system of success-symbols, that we can explain the higher association between poverty and crime in our society than in others where rigidified class structure is coupled with *differential class symbols of achievement.*

In societies such as our own, then, the pressure of prestige-bearing success tends to eliminate the effective social constraint over means employed to this end. "The-end-justifies-the-means" doctrine becomes a guiding tenet for action when the cultural structure unduly exalts the end and the social organization unduly limits possible recourse to approved means. Otherwise put, this notion and associated behavior reflect a lack of cultural coordination. In international relations, the effects of this lack of integration are notoriously apparent. An emphasis upon national power is not readily coordinated with an inept organization of legitimate, i.e., internationally defined and accepted, means for attaining this goal. The result is a tendency toward the abrogation of international law, treaties become scraps of paper, "undeclared warfare" serves as a technical evasion, the bombing of civilian populations is rationalized,[20] just as the same societal situation induces the same sway of illegitimacy among individuals.

The social order we have described necessarily produces this "strain toward dissolution." The pressure of such an order is upon outdoing one's competitors. The choice of means within the ambit of institutional control will persist as long as the sentiments supporting a competitive system, i.e., deriving from the possibility of outranking competitors and hence enjoying the favorable response of others, are distributed throughout the entire system of activities and are not confined merely to the final result. A stable social structure demands a balanced distribution of affect among its various segments. When there occurs a shift of emphasis from the satisfactions deriving from competition itself to almost exclusive concern with successful competition, the resultant stress leads to the breakdown of the regulatory structure.[21] With the resulting attenuation of the institutional imperatives, there occurs an approximation of the situation erroneously held by utilitarians to be typical of society generally wherein calculations of advantage and fear of punishment are the sole regulating agencies. In such situations, as Hobbes observed, force and fraud come to constitute the sole virtues in view of their relative efficiency in attaining goals— which were for him, of course, not culturally derived.

It should be apparent that the foregoing discussion is not pitched on a moralistic plane. Whatever the sentiments of the writer or reader concerning the ethical desirability of coordinating the means-and-goals phases of the social structure, one must agree that lack of such coordination leads to anomie. Insofar as one of the most general functions of social organization is to provide a basis for calculability and regularity of behavior, it is increasingly limited in effectiveness as these elements of the structure become dissociated. At the extreme, predictability virtually disappears and what may be properly termed cultural chaos or anomie intervenes. This statement, being brief, is also incomplete. It has not included an exhaustive treatment of the various structural elements which predispose toward one rather than another of the alternative responses open to individuals; it has neglected, but not denied the relevance of, the factors determining the specific incidence of these responses; it has not enumerated the various concrete responses which are constituted by combinations of specific values of the analytical variables; it has omitted, or included only by implication, any consideration of the social functions performed by illicit responses; it has not tested the full explanatory power of the analytical scheme by examining a large number of group variations in the frequency of deviate and conformist behavior; it has not adequately dealt with rebellious conduct which seeks to refashion the social framework radically; it has not examined the relevance of cultural conflict for an analysis of culture-goal and institutional-means malintegration. It is suggested that these and related problems may be profitably analyzed by this scheme.

DISCUSSION QUESTIONS

1. Applying Merton's theory, why is there so much property crime in the United States?
2. What other kinds of crime does Merton's theory help to explain? How so?

NOTES

1. E.g., Ernest Jones, *Social Aspects of Psychoanalysis*, 28, London, 1924. If the Freudian notion is a variety of the "original sin" dogma, then the interpretation advanced in this paper may be called the doctrine of "socially derived sin."

2. "Normal" in the sense of a culturally oriented, if not approved, response. This statement does not deny the relevance of biological and personality differences which may be significantly involved in the incidence of deviate conduct. Our focus of interest is the social and cultural matrix; hence we abstract from other factors. It is in this sense, I take it, that James S. Plant speaks of the "normal reaction of normal people to abnormal conditions." See his *Personality and the Cultural Pattern*, 248, New York, 1937.

3. Contemporary American culture has been said to tend in this direction. See Andre Siegfried, *America Comes of Age*, 26–37, New York, 1927. The alleged extreme(?) emphasis on the goals of monetary success and material prosperity leads to dominant concern with technological and social instruments designed to produce the desired result, inasmuch as institutional controls become of secondary importance. In such a situation, innovation flourishes as the *range of means* employed is broadened. In a sense, then, there occurs the paradoxical emergence of "materialists" from an "idealistic" orientation. Cf. Durkheim's analysis of the cultural conditions which predispose toward crime and innovation, both of which are aimed toward efficiency, not moral norms. Durkheim was one of the first to see that "contrairement aux idees courantes le criminel n'apparait plus comme un être radicalement insociable, comme une sorte d'element parasitaire, de corps étranger et inassimilable, introduit au sein de la société; c'est un agent regulier de la vie sociale." See *Les Règles de la Méthode Sociologique*, 86–89, Paris, 1927.

4. Such ritualism may be associated with a mythology which rationalizes these actions so that they appear to retain their status as means, but the dominant pressure is in the direction of strict ritualistic conformity, irrespective of such rationalizations. In this sense, ritual has proceeded farthest when such rationalizations are not even called forth.

5. In this connection, one may see the relevance of Elton Mayo's paraphrase of the title of Tawney's well-known book. "Actually the problem *is not that of the sickness of an acquisitive society; it is that of the acquisitiveness of a sick society.*" *Human Problems of an Industrial Civilization*, 153, New York, 1933. Mayo deals with the process through which wealth comes to be a symbol of social achievement. He sees this as arising from a state of anomie. We are considering the unintegrated

monetary-success goal as an element in producing anomie. A complete analysis would involve both phases of this system of interdependent variables.

6. It is unlikely that interiorized norms are completely eliminated. Whatever residuum persists will induce personality tensions and conflict. The process involves a certain degree of ambivalence. A manifest rejection of the institutional norms is coupled with some latent retention of their emotional correlates. "Guilt feelings," "sense of sin," "pangs of conscience" are obvious manifestations of this unrelieved tension; symbolic adherence to the nominally repudiated values or rationalizations constitute a more subtle variety of tensional release.

7. "Many," and not all, unintegrated groups, for the reason already mentioned. In groups where the primary emphasis shifts to institutional means, i.e., when the range of alternatives is very limited, the outcome is a type of ritualism rather than anomie.

8. Money has several peculiarities which render it particularly apt to become a symbol of prestige divorced from institutional controls. As Simmel emphasized, money is highly abstract and impersonal. However acquired, through fraud or institutionally, it can be used to purchase the same goods and services. The anonymity of metropolitan culture, in conjunction with this peculiarity of money, permits wealth, the sources of which may be unknown to the community in which the plutocrat lives, to serve as a symbol of status.

9. The emphasis upon wealth as a success-symbol is possibly reflected in the use of the term "fortune" to refer to a stock of accumulated wealth. This meaning becomes common in the late sixteenth century (Spenser and Shakespeare). A similar usage of the Latin fortuna comes into prominence during the first century B.C. Both these periods were marked by the rise to prestige and power of the "bourgeoisie."

10. See Kingsley Davis, "Mental Hygiene and the Class Structure," *Psychiatry*, 1928, 1: esp. 62–63; Talcott Parsons, *The Structure of Social Action*, 59–60, New York, 1937.

11. This is a level intermediate between the two planes distinguished by Edward Sapir; namely, culture patterns and personal habit systems. See his "Contribution of Psychiatry to an Understanding of Behavior in Society," *Amer. J. Sociol.*, 1937, 42:862–870.

12. This fifth alternative is on a plane clearly different from that of the others. It represents a *transitional* response which seeks to *institutionalize* new procedures oriented toward revamped cultural goals shared by the members of the society. It thus involves efforts to change the existing structure rather than to perform accommodative actions within this structure, and introduces additional problems with which we are not at the moment concerned.

13. Obviously, this is an elliptical statement. These individuals may maintain some orientation to the values of their particular differentiated groupings within the larger society or, in part, of the conventional society itself. Insofar as they do so, their conduct cannot be classified in the "passive rejection" category (IV). Nels Anderson's description of the behavior and attitudes of the bum, for example, can readily be recast in terms of our analytical scheme. See *The Hobo*, 93–98, *et passim*, Chicago, 1923.

14. Joseph D. Lohman, "The Participant Observer in Community Studies," *Amer. Sociol. Rev.*, 1937, 2:890–898.

15. The shifting historical role of this ideology is a profitable subject for exploration. The "office-boy-to-president" stereotype was once in approximate accord with the facts. Such vertical mobility was probably more common then than now, when the class structure is more rigid. (See the following note.) The ideology largely persists, however, possibly because it still performs a useful function for maintaining the status quo. For insofar as it is accepted by the "masses," it constitutes

a useful sop for those who might rebel against the entire structure, were this consoling hope removed. This ideology now serves to lessen the probability of Adaptation V. In short, the role of this notion has changed from that of an approximately valid empirical theorem to that of an ideology, in Mannheim's sense.

16. There is a growing body of evidence, though none of it is clearly conclusive, to the effect that our class structure is becoming rigidified and that vertical mobility is declining. Taussig and Joslyn found that American business leaders are being *increasingly* recruited from the upper ranks of our society. The Lynds have also found a "diminished chance to get ahead" for the working classes in Middletown. Manifestly, these objective changes are not alone significant; the individual's subjective evaluation of the situation is a major determinant of the response. The extent to which this change in opportunity for social mobility has been recognized by the least advantaged classes is still conjectural, although the Lynds present some suggestive materials. The writer suggests that a case in point is the increasing frequency of cartoons which observe in a tragi-comic vein that "my old man says everybody can't be President. He says if ya can get three days a week steady on W.P.A. work ya ain't doin' so bad either." See F. W. Taussig and C. S. Joslyn, *American Business Leaders*, New York, 1932; R. S. and H. M. Lynd, *Middletown in Transition*, 67 ff., chap. 12, New York, 1937.

17. The role of the Negro in this respect is of considerable theoretical interest. Certain elements of the Negro population have assimilated the dominant caste's values of pecuniary success and social advancement, but they also recognize that social ascent is at present restricted to their own caste almost exclusively. The pressures upon the Negro which would otherwise derive from the structural inconsistencies we have noticed are hence not identical with those upon lower class whites. See Kingsley Davis, op. cit., 63; John Dollard, *Caste and Class in a Southern Town*, 66 ff., New Haven, 1936; Donald Young, *American Minority Peoples*, 581, New York, 1932.

18. The psychical coordinates of these processes have been partly established by the experimental evidence concerning *Anspruchsniveaus* and levels of performance. See Kurt Lewin, *Vorsatz, Willie and Bedurfnis*, Berlin, 1926; N. F. Hoppe, "Erfolg und Misserfolg," *Psychol. Forschung*, 1930, 14:1–63; Jerome D. Frank, "Individual Differences in Certain Aspects of the Level of Aspiration," *Amer. J. Psychol.*, 1935, 47:119–128.

19. Standard criminology texts summarize the data in this field. Our scheme of analysis may serve to resolve some of the theoretical contradictions which P. A. Sorokin indicates. For example, "not everywhere nor always do the poor show a greater proportion of crime . . . many poorer countries have had less crime than the richer countries. . . . The [economic] improvement in the second half of the nineteenth century, and the beginning of the twentieth, has not been followed by a decrease of crime." See his *Contemporary Sociological Theories*, 560–561, New York, 1928. The crucial point is, however, that poverty has varying social significance in different social structures, as we shall see. Hence, one would not expect a linear correlation between crime and poverty.

20. See M. W. Royse, *Aerial Bombardment and the International Regulation of War*, New York, 1928.

21. Since our primary concern is with the socio-cultural aspects of this problem, the psychological correlates have been only implicitly considered. See Karen Horney, *The Neurotic Personality of Our Time*, New York, 1937, for a psychological discussion of this process.

4.
TECHNIQUES OF NEUTRALIZATION: A THEORY OF DELINQUENCY

GRESHAM M. SYKES AND DAVID MATZA

Why do people violate the rules in which they believe? Put another way, we all need to feel good about ourselves and good people do good things while bad people do bad things. So why do juvenile delinquents do bad things when such behavior can jeopardize their capacity to feel good about themselves? The answer, according to Sykes and Matza, is because juveniles are able to neutralize the wrongfulness of their acts using the techniques outlined in this article.

Key to understanding the role these techniques of neutralization play in deviant behavior is appreciating that these are not mere "rationalizations" that are used to explain the behavior after it has taken place; these techniques are employed before the behavior takes place and pave the way for deviance.

In attempting to uncover the roots of juvenile delinquency, the social scientist has long since ceased to search for devils in the mind or stigma of the body. It is now largely agreed that delinquent behavior, like most social behavior, is learned and that it is learned in the process of social interaction.

The classic statement of this position is found in Sutherland's theory of differential association, which asserts that criminal or delinquent behavior involves the learning of (a) techniques of committing crimes and (b) motives, drives, rationalizations, and attitudes favorable to the violation of law.[1] Unfortunately, the specific content of what is learned—as opposed to the process by which it is learned—has received relatively little attention in either theory or research. Perhaps the single strongest school of thought on the nature of this content has centered on the idea of a delinquent sub-culture. The basic characteristic of the delinquent subculture, it is argued, is a system of values that represents an inversion of the values held by respectable, law-abiding society. The world of the delinquent is the world of the law-abiding turned upside down and its norms constitute a countervailing force directed against the conforming social order. Cohen[2] sees the process of developing a delinquent sub-culture as a matter of building, maintaining, and reinforcing a code for behavior which exists by opposition, which stands in point by point contradiction to dominant values, particularly those of the middle class. Cohen's portrayal of delinquency is executed with a good deal of sophistication, and he carefully avoids overly simple explanations such as those based on the principle of "follow the leader" or easy generalizations about "emotional disturbances." Furthermore, he does not accept the delinquent sub-culture as something given, but instead systematically examines the function of delinquent values as a viable solution to the lower-class, male child's problems in the area of social status. Yet in spite of its virtues, this image of juvenile delinquency as a form of behavior based on competing or countervailing values and norms appears to suffer from a number of serious defects. It is the nature of these defects and a possible alternative or modified explanation for a large portion of juvenile delinquency with which this paper is concerned.

The difficulties in viewing delinquent behavior as springing from a set of deviant values and norms—as arising, that is to say, from a situation in which the delinquent defines his delinquency as "right"—are both empirical and theoretical. In the first place, if there existed in fact a delinquent subculture such that the delinquent viewed his illegal behavior as morally correct, we could reasonably suppose that he would exhibit no feelings of guilt or shame at detection or confinement. Instead, the major reaction would tend in the direction of indignation or a sense of martyrdom.[3] It is true that some delinquents do react in the latter fashion, although the sense of martyrdom often seems to be based on the fact that others "get away with it" and indignation appears to be directed against the chance events or lack of skill that led to apprehension. More important, however, is the fact that there is a good deal of evidence suggesting that many delinquents *do* experience a sense of guilt or shame, and its outward expression is not to be dismissed as a purely manipulative gesture to appease those in authority. Much of this evidence is, to be sure, of a clinical nature or in the form of impressionistic judgments of those who must deal first hand with the youthful offender. Assigning a weight to such evidence calls for caution, but it cannot be ignored if we are to avoid the gross stereotype of the juvenile delinquent as a hardened gangster in miniature.

In the second place, observers have noted that the juvenile delinquent frequently accords admiration and respect to law-abiding persons. The "really honest" person is often revered, and if the delinquent is sometimes overly keen to detect hypocrisy in those who conform, unquestioned probity is likely to win his approval. A fierce attachment to a humble, pious mother or a forgiving, upright priest (the former, according to many observers, is often encountered in both juvenile delinquents and adult criminals) might be dismissed as rank sentimentality, but at least it is clear that the delinquent does not necessarily regard those who abide by the legal rules as immoral. In a similar vein, it can be noted that the juvenile delinquent may exhibit great resentment if illegal behavior is imputed to "significant others" in his immediate social environment or to heroes in the world of sport and entertainment. In other words, if the delinquent does hold to a set of values and norms that stand in complete opposition to those of respectable society, his norm-holding is of a peculiar sort. While supposedly thoroughly committed to the deviant system of the delinquent sub-culture, he would appear to recognize the moral validity of the dominant normative system in many instances.[4]

In the third place, there is much evidence that juvenile delinquents often draw a sharp line between those who can be victimized and those who cannot. Certain social groups are not to be viewed as "fair game" in the performance of supposedly approved delinquent acts while others warrant a variety of attacks. In general, the potentiality for victimization would seem to be a function of the social distance between the juvenile delinquent and others and thus we find implicit maxims in the world of the delinquent such as "don't steal from friends" or "don't commit vandalism against a church of your own faith."[5] This is all rather obvious, but the implications have not received sufficient attention. The fact that supposedly valued behavior tends to be directed against disvalued social groups hints that the "wrongfulness" of such delinquent behavior is more widely recognized by delinquents than the literature has indicated. When the pool of victims is limited by considerations of kinship, friendship, ethnic group, social class, age, sex, etc., we have reason to suspect that the virtue of delinquency is far from unquestioned.

In the fourth place, it is doubtful if many juvenile delinquents are totally immune from the demands for conformity made by the dominant social order. There is a strong likelihood that the family of the delinquent will agree with respectable society that delinquency is wrong, even though the family may be engaged in a variety of illegal activities. That is, the parental posture conducive to delinquency is not apt to be a positive prodding. Whatever may be the influence of parental example, what might be called the "Fagin" pattern of socialization into delinquency is probably rare. Furthermore, as Redl has indicated, the idea that certain neighborhoods are completely delinquent, offering the child a model for delinquent behavior without reservations, is simply not supported by the data.[6]

The fact that a child is punished by parents, school officials, and agencies of the legal system for his delinquency may, as a number of observers have cynically noted, suggest to the child that he should be more careful not to get caught. There is an equal or greater probability, however, that the child will internalize the demands for conformity. This is not to say that demands for conformity cannot be counteracted. In fact, as we shall see shortly, an understanding of how internal and external demands for conformity are neutralized may be crucial for understanding delinquent behavior. But it is to say that a complete denial of the validity of demands for conformity and the substitution of a new normative system is improbable, in light of the child's or adolescent's dependency on adults and encirclement by adults inherent in his status in the social structure. No matter how deeply enmeshed in patterns of delinquency he may be and no matter how much this involvement may outweigh his associations with the law-abiding, he cannot escape the condemnation of his deviance. Somehow the demands for conformity must be met and answered; they cannot be ignored as part of an alien system of values and norms.

In short, the theoretical viewpoint that sees juvenile delinquency as a form of behavior based on the values and norms of a deviant sub-culture in precisely the same way as law-abiding behavior is based on the values and norms of the larger society is open to serious doubt. The fact that the world of the delinquent is embedded in the larger world of those who conform cannot be overlooked nor can the delinquent be equated with an adult thoroughly socialized into an alternative way of life. Instead, the juvenile delinquent would appear to be at least partially committed to the dominant social order in that he frequently exhibits guilt or shame when he violates its proscriptions, accords approval to certain conforming figures, and distinguishes between appropriate and inappropriate targets for his deviance. It is to an explanation for the apparently paradoxical fact of his delinquency that we now turn.

As Morris Cohen once said, one of the most fascinating problems about human behavior is why men violate the laws in which they believe. This is the problem that confronts us when we attempt to explain why delinquency occurs despite a greater or lesser commitment to the usages of conformity. A basic clue is offered by the fact that social rules or norms calling for valued behavior seldom if ever take the form of categorical imperatives. Rather, values or norms appear as qualified guides for action, limited in their applicability in terms of time, place, persons, and social circumstances. The moral injunction against killing, for example, does not apply to the enemy during combat in time of war, although a captured enemy comes once again under the prohibition. Similarly, the taking and distributing of scarce goods in a time of acute social need is felt by many to be right, although under other circumstances private property is held inviolable. The normative system of a society, then, is marked by what Williams has termed flexibility; it does not consist of a body of rules held to be binding under all conditions.[7]

This flexibility is, in fact, an integral part of the criminal law in that measures for "defenses to crimes" are provided in pleas such as non-age, necessity, insanity, drunkenness, compulsion, self-defense, and so on. The individual can avoid moral culpability for his criminal action—and thus avoid the negative sanctions of society—if he can prove that criminal intent was lacking. It is our argument that much delinquency is based on what is essentially an unrecognized extension of defenses to crimes, in the form of justifications for deviance that are seen as valid by the delinquent but not by the legal system or society at large.

These justifications are commonly described as rationalizations. They are viewed as following deviant behavior and as protecting the individual from self-blame and the blame of others after the act. But there is also reason to believe that they precede deviant behavior and make deviant behavior possible. It is this possibility that Sutherland mentioned only in passing and that other writers have failed to exploit from the viewpoint of sociological theory. Disapproval flowing from internalized norms and conforming others in the social environment is neutralized, turned back, or deflected in advance. Social controls that serve to check or inhibit deviant motivational patterns are rendered inoperative, and the individual is freed to engage in delinquency without serious damage to his self-image. In this sense, the delinquent both has his cake and eats it too, for he remains committed to the dominant normative system and yet so qualifies its imperatives that violations are "acceptable" if not "right." Thus the delinquent represents not a radical opposition to law-abiding society but something more like an apologetic failure, often more sinned against than sinning in his own eyes. We call these justifications of deviant behavior techniques of neutralization; and we believe these techniques make up a crucial component of Sutherland's "definitions favorable to the violation of law." It is by learning these techniques that the juvenile becomes delinquent, rather than by learning moral imperatives, values, or attitudes standing in direct contradiction to those of the dominant society. In analyzing these techniques, we have found it convenient to divide them into five major types.

THE DENIAL OF RESPONSIBILITY

Insofar as the delinquent can define himself as lacking responsibility for his deviant actions, the disapproval of self or others is sharply reduced in effectiveness as a restraining influence. As Justice Holmes has said, even a dog distinguishes between being stumbled over and being kicked, and modern society is no less careful to draw a line between injuries that are unintentional, i.e., where responsibility is lacking, and those that are intentional. As a technique of neutralization, however, the denial of responsibility extends much further than the claim that deviant acts are an "accident" or some similar negation of personal accountability. It may also be asserted that delinquent acts are due to forces outside of the individual and beyond his control such as unloving parents, bad companions, or a slum neighborhood. In effect, the delinquent approaches a "billiard ball" conception of himself in which he sees himself as help-lessly propelled into new situations. From a psychodynamic viewpoint, this orientation toward one's own actions may represent a profound alienation from self, but it is important to stress the fact that interpretations of responsibility are cultural constructs and not merely idiosyncratic beliefs. The similarity between this mode of justifying illegal behavior assumed by the delin-quent and the implications of a "sociological" frame of reference or a "humane" jurisprudence is readily apparent.[8] It is not the validity of this orientation that concerns us here, but its func-tion of deflecting blame attached to violations of social norms and its relative independence of a particular personality structure.[9] By learning to view himself as more acted upon than acting, the delinquent prepares the way for deviance from the dominant normative system without the necessity of a frontal assault on the norms themselves.

THE DENIAL OF INJURY

A second major technique of neutralization centers on the injury or harm involved in the delinquent act. The criminal law has long made a distinction between crimes which are *mala in se* and *mala prohibita*—that is, between acts that are wrong in themselves and acts that are illegal but not immoral—and the delinquent can make the same kind of distinction in evaluating the wrongfulness of his behavior. For the delinquent, however, wrongfulness may turn on the ques-tion of whether or not anyone has clearly been hurt by his deviance, and this matter is open to a variety of interpretations. Vandalism, for example, may be defined by the delinquent simply as "mischief"—after all, it may be claimed, the persons whose property has been destroyed can well afford it. Similarly, auto theft may be viewed as "borrowing," and gang fighting may be seen as a private quarrel, an agreed upon duel between two willing parties, and thus of no concern to the community at large. We are not suggesting that this technique of neutralization, labeled the denial of injury, involves an explicit dialectic. Rather, we are arguing that the delinquent frequently, and in a hazy fashion, feels that his behavior does not really cause any great harm despite the fact that it runs counter to law. Just as the link between the individual and his acts may be broken by the denial of responsibility, so may the link between acts and their conse-quences be broken by the denial of injury. Since society sometimes agrees with the delinquent, e.g., in matters such as truancy, "pranks," and so on, it merely reaffirms the idea that the delin-quent's neutralization of social controls by means of qualifying the norms is an extension of common practice rather than a gesture of complete opposition.

THE DENIAL OF THE VICTIM

Even if the delinquent accepts the responsibility for his deviant actions and is willing to admit that his deviant actions involve an injury or hurt, the moral indignation of self and others may be neutralized by an insistence that the injury is not wrong in light of the circumstances. The injury, it may be claimed, is not really an injury; rather, it is a form of rightful retaliation or punishment.

By a subtle alchemy the delinquent moves himself into the position of an avenger and the victim is transformed into a wrong-doer. Assaults on homosexuals or suspected homosexuals, attacks on members of minority groups who are said to have gotten "out of place," vandalism as revenge on an unfair teacher or school official, thefts from a "crooked" store owner—all may be hurts inflicted on a transgressor, in the eyes of the delinquent. As Orwell has pointed out, the type of criminal admired by the general public has probably changed over the course of years and Raffles no longer serves as a hero;[10] but Robin Hood, and his latter-day derivatives such as the tough detective seeking justice outside the law, still capture the popular imagination, and the delinquent may view his acts as part of a similar role.

To deny the existence of the victim, then, by transforming him into a person deserving injury is an extreme form of a phenomenon we have mentioned before, namely, the delinquent's recognition of appropriate and inappropriate targets for his delinquent acts. In addition, however, the existence of the victim may be denied for the delinquent, in a somewhat different sense, by the circumstances of the delinquent act itself. Insofar as the victim is physically absent, unknown, or a vague abstraction (as is often the case in delinquent acts committed against property), the awareness of the victim's existence is weakened. Internalized norms and anticipations of the reactions of others must somehow be activated if they are to serve as guides for behavior; and it is possible that a diminished awareness of the victim plays an important part of determining whether or not this process is set in motion.

THE CONDEMNATION OF THE CONDEMNERS

A fourth technique of neutralization would appear to involve a condemnation of the condemners or, as McCorkle and Korn have phrased it, a rejection of the rejectors.[11] The delinquent shifts the focus of attention from his own deviant acts to the motives and behavior of those who disapprove of his violations. His condemners, he may claim, are hypocrites, deviants in disguise, or impelled by personal spite. This orientation toward the conforming world may be of particular importance when it hardens into a bitter cynicism directed against those assigned the task of enforcing or expressing the norms of the dominant society. Police, it may be said, are corrupt, stupid, and brutal. Teachers always show favoritism and parents always "take it out" on their children. By a slight extension, the rewards of conformity—such as material success—become a matter of pull or luck, thus decreasing still further the stature of those who stand on the side of the law-abiding. The validity of this jaundiced viewpoint is not so important as its function in turning back or deflecting the negative sanctions attached to violations of the norms. The delinquent, in effect, has changed the subject of the conversation in the dialogue between his own deviant impulses and the reactions of others; and by attacking others, the wrongfulness of his own behavior is more easily repressed or lost to view.

THE APPEAL TO HIGHER LOYALTIES

Fifth, and last, internal and external social controls may be neutralized by sacrificing the demands of the larger society for the demands of the smaller social groups to which the delinquent belongs, such as the sibling pair, the gang, or the friendship clique. It is important to note that the delinquent does not necessarily repudiate the imperatives of the dominant normative system, despite his failure to follow them. Rather, the delinquent may see himself as caught up in a dilemma that must be resolved, unfortunately, at the cost of violating the law. One aspect of this situation has been studied by Stouffer and Toby in their research on the conflict between particularistic and universalistic demands, between the claims of friendship and general social obligations, and their results suggest that "it is possible to classify people according to a predisposition to select one or the other horn of a dilemma in role conflict."[12] For our purposes, however, the most important point is that deviation from certain norms may occur not because the norms are rejected but because others' norms, held to be more pressing or involving a higher loyalty, are accorded precedence. Indeed, it is the fact that both sets of norms are believed in that gives meaning to our concepts of dilemma and role conflict.

The conflict between the claims of friendship and the claims of law, or a similar dilemma, has of course long been recognized by the social scientist (and the novelist) as a common human problem. If the juvenile delinquent frequently resolves his dilemma by insisting that he must "always help a buddy" or "never squeal on a friend," even when it throws him into serious difficulties with the dominant social order, his choice remains familiar to the supposedly law-abiding. The delinquent is unusual, perhaps, in the extent to which he is able to see the fact that he acts in behalf of the smaller social groups to which he belongs as a justification for violations of society's norms, but it is a matter of degree rather than of kind.

"I didn't mean it." "I didn't really hurt anybody." "They had it coming to them." "Everybody's picking on me." "I didn't do it for myself." These slogans or their variants, we hypothesize, prepare the juvenile for delinquent acts. These "definitions of the situation" represent tangential or glancing blows at the dominant normative system rather than the creation of an opposing ideology; and they are extensions of patterns of thought prevalent in society rather than something created de novo.

Techniques of neutralization may not be powerful enough to fully shield the individual from the force of his own internalized values and the reactions of conforming others, for as we have pointed out, juvenile delinquents often appear to suffer from feelings of guilt and shame when called into account for their deviant behavior. And some delinquents may be so isolated from the world of conformity that techniques of neutralization need not be called into play. Nonetheless, we would argue that techniques of neutralization are critical in lessening the effectiveness of social controls and that they lie behind a large share of delinquent behavior. Empirical research in this area is scattered and fragmentary at the present time, but the work of Redl,[13] Cressey,[14] and others has supplied a body of significant data that has done much to clarify the theoretical issues and enlarge the fund of supporting evidence. Two lines of investigation seem to be critical at this stage. First, there is need for more knowledge concerning the differential distribution of techniques of neutralization, as operative patterns of thought, by age, sex, social class, ethnic group, etc. On a priori grounds it might be assumed that these justifications for deviance will be more readily seized by segments of society for whom a discrepancy between common social ideals and social practice is most apparent. It is also possible, however, that the habit of "bending" the dominant normative system—if not "breaking" it—cuts across our cruder social categories and is to be traced primarily to patterns of social interaction within the familial circle. Second, there is need for a greater understanding of the internal structure of techniques of neutralization, as a system of beliefs and attitudes, and its relationship to various types of delinquent behavior. Certain techniques of neutralization would appear to be better adapted to particular deviant acts than to others, as we have suggested, for example, in the case of offenses against property and the denial of the victim. But the issue remains far from clear and stands in need of more information.

In any case, techniques of neutralization appear to offer a promising line of research in enlarging and systematizing the theoretical grasp of juvenile delinquency. As more information is uncovered concerning techniques of neutralization, their origins, and their consequences, both juvenile delinquency in particular and deviation from normative systems in general may be illuminated.

DISCUSSION QUESTIONS

1. Why would it be misleading for the student of deviance to think of these techniques of neutralization to be "lame" excuses?
2. Sykes and Matza are referring namely to techniques of neutralization used by juveniles to explain their delinquency. How might these or similar techniques be used by someone committing other acts of deviancy, insider trading for example?

NOTES

1. E. H. Sutherland, *Principles of Criminology*, revised by D. R. Cressey, Chicago: Lippincott, 1955, pp. 77–80.
2. Albert K. Cohen, *Delinquent Boys*, Glencoe, Ill.: The Free Press, 1955.
3. This form of reaction among the adherents of a deviant subculture who fully believe in the "rightfulness" of their behavior and who are captured and punished by the agencies of the dominant social order can be illustrated, perhaps, by groups such as Jehovah's Witnesses, early Christian sects, nationalist movements in colonial areas, and conscientious objectors during World Wars I and II.
4. As Weber has pointed out, a thief may recognize the legitimacy of legal rules without accepting their moral validity. Cf. Max Weber, *The Theory of Social and Economic Organization* (translated by A. M. Henderson and Talcott Parsons), New York: Oxford University Press, 1947, p. 125. We are arguing here, however, that the juvenile delinquent frequently recognizes *both* the legitimacy of the dominant social order and its moral "rightness."
5. Thrasher's account of the "Itschkies"—a juvenile gang composed of Jewish boys—and the immunity from "rolling" enjoyed by Jewish drunkards is a good illustration. Cf. F. Thrasher, *The Gang*, Chicago: The University of Chicago Press, 1947, p. 315.
6. Cf. Solomon Kobrin, "The Conflict of Values in Delinquency Areas," *American Sociological Review*, 16 (October, 1951), pp. 653–661.
7. Cf. Robin Williams, Jr., *American Society*, New York: Knopf, 1951, p. 28.
8. A number of observers have wryly noted that many delinquents seem to show a surprising awareness of sociological and psychological explanations for their behavior and are quick to point out the causal role of their poor environment.
9. It is possible, of course, that certain personality structures can accept some techniques of neutralization more readily than others, but this question remains largely unexplored.

10. George Orwell, *Dickens, Dali, and Others*, New York: Reynal, 1946.
11. Lloyd W. McCorkle and Richard Korn, "Resocialization Within Walls," *The Annals of the American Academy of Political and Social Science*, 293 (May, 1954), pp. 88–98.
12. See Samuel A. Stouffer and Jackson Toby, "Role Conflict and Personality," in *Toward a General Theory of Action*, edited by Talcott Parsons and Edward A. Shils, Cambridge, Mass.: Harvard University Press, 1951, p. 494.
13. See Fritz Redl and David Wineman, *Children Who Hate*, Glencoe, Ill.: The Free Press, 1956.
14. See D. R. Cressey, *Other People's Money*, Glencoe, Ill.: The Free Press, 1953.

5.
A CONTROL THEORY OF DELINQUENCY

TRAVIS HIRSCHI

A great number of theories of deviance look at conditions or traits that are present in the deviant's personality or environment to account for his or her deviance. Control theory is different in that it looks for things that are absent, specifically "controls." In psychoanalytic theory, the superego and the ego act as controls; when they are improperly developed, deviance can be the result. In the sociological version of control theory outlined in this excerpt by Hirschi, controls take the form of bonds between the individual and society. When these bonds are weak or absent, deviance can be the result.

American culture is renowned for the value it places on individualism. The very concept of "individualism" connotes a condition where the bonds between the individual and society are relatively weak. Thus, American culture may be more conducive to deviance than those cultures that place more emphasis on the centrality of the group.

Control theories assume that delinquent acts result when an individual's bond to society is weak or broken. Since these theories embrace two highly complex concepts, the *bond* of the individual to *society*, it is not surprising that they have at one time or another formed the basis of explanations of most forms of aberrant or unusual behavior. It is also not surprising that control theories have described the elements of the bond to society in many ways, and that they have focused on a variety of units as the point of control. . . .

ELEMENTS OF THE BOND

ATTACHMENT

In explaining conforming behavior, sociologists justly emphasize sensitivity to the opinion of others.[1] Unfortunately, . . . they tend to suggest that man is sensitive to the opinion of others and thus exclude sensitivity from their explanations of deviant behavior. In explaining deviant behavior, psychologists, in contrast, emphasize insensitivity to the opinion of others.[2] Unfortunately, they too tend to ignore variation, and, in addition, they tend to tie sensitivity inextricably to other variables, to make it part of a syndrome or "type," and thus seriously to reduce its value as an explanatory concept. The psychopath is characterized only in part by "deficient attachment to or affection for others, a failure to respond to the ordinary motivations founded in respect or regard for one's fellow";[3] he is also characterized by such things as "excessive aggressiveness," "lack of superego control," and "an infantile level of response."[4] Unfortunately, too, the behavior that psychopathy is used to explain often becomes part of the definition of psychopathy. As a result, in Barbara Wootton's words: "[The psychopath] is . . . par excellence, and without shame or qualification, the model of the circular process by which mental abnormality is inferred from anti-social behavior while anti-social behavior is explained by mental abnormality."[5]

The problems of diagnosis, tautology, and name-calling are avoided if the dimensions of psychopathy are treated as causally and therefore problematically interrelated, rather than as logically and therefore necessarily bound to each other. In fact, it can be argued that all of the characteristics attributed to the psychopath follow from, are effects of, his lack of attachment to others. To say that to lack attachment to others is to be free from moral restraints is to use lack of attachment to explain the guiltlessness of the psychopath, the fact that he apparently has no conscience or superego. In this view, lack of attachment to others is not merely a symptom of psychopathy, it *is* psychopathy; lack of conscience is just another way of saying the same thing; and the violation of norms is (or may be) a consequence.

For that matter, given that man is an animal, "impulsivity" and "aggressiveness" can also be seen as natural consequences of freedom from moral restraints. However, since the view of man as endowed with natural propensities and capacities like other animals is peculiarly unpalatable to sociologists, we need not fall back on such a view to explain the amoral man's aggressiveness.[6] The process of becoming alienated from others often involves or is based on active interpersonal conflict. Such conflict could easily supply a reservoir of *socially derived* hostility sufficient to account for the aggressiveness of those whose attachments to others have been weakened.

Durkheim said it many years ago: "We are moral beings to the extent that we are social beings."[7] This may be interpreted to mean that we are moral beings to the extent that we have "internalized the norms" of society. But what does it mean to say that a person has internalized the norms of society? The norms of society are by definition shared by the members of society. To violate a norm is, therefore, to act contrary to the wishes and expectations of other people. If a person does not care about the wishes and expectations of other people—that is, if he is insensitive to the opinion of others—then he is to that extent not bound by the norms. He is free to deviate.

The essence of internalization of norms, conscience, or superego thus lies in the attachment of the individual to others.[8] This view has several advantages over the concept of internalization. For one, explanations of deviant behavior based on attachment do not beg the question, since the extent to which a person is attached to others can be measured independently of his deviant behavior. Furthermore, change or variation in behavior is explainable in a way that it is not when notions of internalization or superego are used. For example, the divorced man is more likely after divorce to commit a number of deviant acts, such as suicide or forgery. If we explain these acts by reference to the superego (or internal control), we are forced to say that the man "lost his conscience" when he got a divorce; and, of course, if he remarries, we have to conclude that he gets his conscience back.

This dimension of the bond to conventional society is encountered in most social control-oriented research and theory. F. Ivan Nye's "internal control" and "indirect control" refer to the same element, although we avoid the problem of explaining changes over time by locating the "conscience" in the bond to others rather than making it part of the personality.[9] Attachment to others is just one aspect of Albert J. Reiss's "personal controls"; we avoid his problems of tautological empirical *observations* by making the relationship between attachment and delinquency problematic rather than definitional.[10] Finally, Scott Briar and Irving Piliavin's "commitment" or "stake in conformity" subsumes attachment, as their discussion illustrates, although the terms they use are more closely associated with the next element to be discussed.[11]

COMMITMENT

"Of all passions, that which inclineth men least to break the laws, is fear. Nay, excepting some generous natures, it is the only thing, when there is the appearance of profit or pleasure by breaking the laws, that makes men keep them."[12] Few would deny that men on occasion obey the rules simply from fear of the consequences. This rational component in conformity we label commitment. What does it mean to say that a person is committed to conformity? In Howard S. Becker's formulation it means the following:

> First, the individual is in a position in which his decision with regard to some particular line of action has consequences for other interests and activities not necessarily [directly] related to it. Second, he has placed himself in that position by his own prior actions. A third element is present though so obvious as not to be apparent; the committed person must be aware [of these other interests] and must recognize that his decision in this case will have ramifications beyond it.[13]

The idea, then, is that the person invests time, energy, himself, in a certain line of activity—say, getting an education, building up a business, acquiring a reputation for virtue. When or whenever he considers deviant behavior, he must consider the costs of this deviant behavior, the risk he runs of losing the investment he has made in conventional behavior.

If attachment to others is the sociological counterpart of the superego or conscience, commitment is the counterpart of the ego or common sense. To the person committed to conventional lines of action, risking one to ten years in prison for a ten-dollar holdup is stupidity, because to the committed person the costs and risks obviously exceed ten dollars in value. (To the psychoanalyst, such an act exhibits failure to be governed by the "reality principle.") In the sociological control theory, it can be and is generally assumed that the decision to commit a criminal act may well be rationally determined—that the actor's decision was not irrational given the risks and costs he faces. Of course, as Becker points out, if the actor is capable of in some sense calculating the costs of a line of action, he is also capable of calculational errors: ignorance and error return, in the control theory, as possible explanations of deviant behavior.

The concept of commitment assumes that the organization of society is such that the interest of most persons would be endangered if they were to engage in criminal acts. Most people, simply by the process of living in an organized society, acquire goods, reputations, prospects that they do not want to risk losing. These accumulations are society's insurance that they will abide by the rules. Many hypotheses about the antecedents of delinquent behavior are based on this premise. For example, Arthur L. Stinchcombe's hypothesis that "high school rebellion . . . occurs when future status is not clearly related to present performance"[14] suggests that one is committed to conformity not only by what one has but also by what one hopes to obtain. Thus "ambition" and/or "aspiration" play an important role in producing conformity. The person becomes committed to a conventional line of action, and he is therefore committed to conformity.

Most lines of action in a society are of course conventional. The clearest examples are educational and occupational careers. Actions thought to jeopardize one's chances in these areas are presumably avoided. Interestingly enough, even nonconventional commitments may operate to produce conventional conformity. We are told, at least, that boys aspiring to careers in the rackets or professional thievery are judged by their "honesty" and "reliability"—traits traditionally in demand among seekers of office boys.[15]

INVOLVEMENT

Many persons undoubtedly owe a life of virtue to a lack of opportunity to do otherwise. Time and energy are inherently limited: "Not that I would not, if I could, be both handsome and fat and well dressed, and a great athlete, and make a million a year, be a wit, a bon vivant, and a lady killer, as well as a philosopher, a philanthropist, a statesman, warrior, and African explorer, as well as a 'tone-poet' and saint. But the thing is simply impossible."[16] The things that William James here says he would like to be or do are all, I suppose, within the realm of conventionality, but if he were to include illicit actions he would still have to eliminate some of them as simply impossible.

Involvement or engrossment in conventional activities is thus often part of a control theory. The assumption, widely shared, is that a person may be simply too busy doing conventional things to find time to engage in deviant behavior. The person involved in conventional activities is tied to appointments, deadlines, working hours, plans, and the like, so the opportunity to commit deviant acts rarely arises. To the extent that he is engrossed in conventional activities, he cannot even think about deviant acts, let alone act out his inclinations.[17]

This line of reasoning is responsible for the stress placed on recreational facilities in many programs to reduce delinquency, for much of the concern with the high school dropout, and for the idea that boys should be drafted into the army to keep them out of trouble. So obvious and persuasive is the idea that involvement in conventional activities is a major deterrent to delinquency that it was accepted even by Sutherland: "In the general area of juvenile delinquency it is probable that the most significant difference between juveniles who engage in delinquency and those who do not is that the latter are provided abundant opportunities of a conventional type for satisfying their recreational interests, while the former lack those opportunities or facilities."[18]

The view that "idle hands are the devil's workshop" has received more sophisticated treatment in recent sociological writings on delinquency. David Matza and Gresham M. Sykes, for example, suggest that delinquents have the values of a leisure class, the same values ascribed by Veblen to *the* leisure class: a search for kicks, disdain of work, a desire for the big score, and acceptance of aggressive toughness as proof of masculinity.[19] Matza and Sykes explain delinquency by reference to this system of values, but they note that adolescents at all class levels are "to some extent" members of a leisure class, that they "move in a limbo between earlier parental domination and future integration with the social structure through the bonds of work and marriage."[20] In the end, then, the leisure of the adolescent produces a set of values, which, in turn, leads to delinquency.

BELIEF

Unlike the cultural deviance theory, the control theory assumes the existence of a common value system within the society or group whose norms are being violated. If the deviant is committed to a value system different from that of conventional society, there is, within the context of the theory, nothing to explain. The question is, "Why does a man violate the rules in which he believes?" It is not, "Why do men differ in their beliefs about what constitutes good and desirable conduct?" The person is assumed to have been socialized (perhaps imperfectly) into the group whose rules he is violating; deviance is not a question of one group imposing its rules on the members of another group. In other words, we not only assume the deviant *has* believed the rules, we assume he believes the rules even as he violates them.

How can a person believe it is wrong to steal at the same time he is stealing? In the strain theory, this is not a difficult problem. (In fact . . . the strain theory was devised specifically to deal with this question.) The motivation to deviance adduced by the strain theorist is so strong that we can well understand the deviant act even assuming the deviator believes strongly that it is wrong.[21] However, given the control theory's assumptions about motivation, if both the deviant and the nondeviant believe the deviant act is wrong, how do we account for the fact that one commits it and the other does not?

Control theories have taken two approaches to this problem. In one approach, beliefs are treated as mere words that mean little or nothing if the other forms of control are missing. "Semantic dementia," the dissociation between rational faculties and emotional control which is said to be characteristic of the psychopath, illustrates this way of handling the problem.[22] In short, beliefs, at least insofar as they are expressed in words, drop out of the picture; since they do not differentiate between deviants and nondeviants, they are in the same class as "language" or any other characteristic common to all members of the group. Since they represent no real obstacle to the commission of delinquent acts, nothing need be said about how they are handled by those committing such acts. The control theories that do not mention beliefs (or values), and many do not, may be assumed to take this approach to the problem.

The second approach argues that the deviant rationalizes his behavior so that he can at once violate the rule and maintain his belief in it. Donald R. Cressey had advanced this argument with respect to embezzlement,[23] and Sykes and Matza have advanced it with respect to delinquency.[24] In both Cressey's and Sykes and Matza's treatments, these rationalizations (Cressey calls them "verbalizations," Sykes and Matza term them "techniques of neutralization") occur prior to the commission of the deviant act. If the neutralization is successful, the person is free to commit the act(s) in question. Both in Cressey and in Sykes and Matza, the strain that prompts the effort at neutralization also provides the motive force that results in the subsequent deviant act. Their theories are thus, in this sense, strain theories. Neutralization is difficult to handle within the context of a theory that adheres closely to control theory assumptions, because in the control theory there is no special motivational force to account for the neutralization. This difficulty is especially noticeable in Matza's later treatment of this topic, where the motivational component, the "will to delinquency," appears *after* the moral vacuum has been created by the techniques of neutralization.[25] The question thus becomes: Why neutralize?

In attempting to solve a strain-theory problem with control-theory tools, the control theorist is thus led into a trap. He cannot answer the crucial question. The concept of neutralization assumes the existence of moral obstacles to the commission of deviant acts. In order plausibly to account for a deviant act, it is necessary to generate motivation to deviance that is at least equivalent in force to the resistance provided by these moral obstacles. However, if the moral obstacles are removed, neutralization and special motivation are no longer required. We therefore follow the implicit logic of control theory and remove these moral obstacles by hypothesis. Many persons do not have an attitude of respect toward the rules of society; many persons feel no moral obligation to conform regardless of personal advantage. Insofar as the values and beliefs of these persons are consistent with their feelings, and there should be a tendency toward consistency, neutralization is unnecessary; it has already occurred.

Does this merely push the question back a step and at the same time produce conflict with the assumption of a common value system? I think not. In the first place, we do not assume, as does Cressey, that neutralization occurs in order to make a specific criminal act possible.[26] We do not assume, as do Sykes and Matza, that neutralization occurs to make many delinquent acts possible. We do not assume, in other words, that the person constructs a system of rationalizations in order to justify commission of acts he *wants* to commit. We assume, in contrast, that the beliefs that free a man to commit deviant acts are *unmotivated* in the sense that he does not construct or adopt them in order to facilitate the attainment of illicit ends. In the second place, we do not assume, as does Matza, that "delinquents concur in the conventional assessment of delinquency."[27] We assume, in contrast, that there is *variation* in the extent to which people believe they should obey the rules of society, and, furthermore, that the less a person believes he should obey the rules, the more likely he is to violate them.[28]

In chronological order, then, a person's beliefs in the moral validity of norms are, for no teleological reason, weakened. The probability that he will commit delinquent acts is therefore increased. When and if he commits a delinquent act, we may justifiably use the weakness of his beliefs in explaining it, but no special motivation is required to explain either the weakness of his beliefs or, perhaps, his delinquent act.

The keystone of this argument is of course the assumption that there is variation in belief in the moral validity of social rules. This assumption is amenable to direct empirical test and can thus survive at least until its first confrontation with data. For the present, we must return to the idea of a common value system with which this section was begun.

The idea of a common (or perhaps better, a single) value system is consistent with the fact, or presumption, of variation in the strength of moral beliefs. We have not suggested that delinquency is based on beliefs counter to conventional morality; we have not suggested that delinquents do not believe delinquent acts are wrong. They may well believe these acts are wrong, but the meaning and efficacy of such beliefs are contingent on other beliefs and, indeed, on the strength of other ties to the conventional order.[29]

DISCUSSION QUESTION

1. According to Hirschi, the strength of the bonds between the individual and society serve to inhibit deviance. Therefore, as mentioned in the introduction to this passage, the emphasis

Americans place on the value of individualism may act to contribute to deviance in the United States. What are some specific indicators of this emphasis and how might they contribute to the incidence of deviance? Conversely, what do you know about more collectivist societies such as Japan or China and how their cultures might inhibit deviance?

NOTES

1. Books have been written on the increasing importance of interpersonal sensitivity in modern life. According to this view, controls from within have become less important than controls from without in *producing* conformity. Whether or not this observation is true as a description of historical trends, it is true that interpersonal sensitivity has become more important in *explaining* conformity. Although logically it should also have become more important in explaining nonconformity, the opposite has been the case, once again showing that Cohen's observation that an explanation of conformity should be an explanation of deviance cannot be translated as "as explanation of conformity has to be an explanation of deviance." For the view that interpersonal sensitivity currently plays a greater role than formerly in producing conformity, see William J. Goode, "Norm Commitment and Conformity to Role-Status Obligations," *American Journal of Sociology*, LXVI (1960), 246–258. And, of course, also see David Riesman, Nathan Glazer, and Rouel Denney, *The Lonely Crowd* (Garden City, New York: Doubleday, 1950), especially Part I.
2. The literature on psychopathy is voluminous. See William McCord and Joan McCord, *The Psychopath* (Princeton: D. Van Nostrand, 1964).
3. John M. Martin and Joseph P. Fitzpatrick, *Delinquent Behavior* (New York: Random House, 1964), p. 130.
4. Ibid. For additional properties of the psychopath, see McCord and McCord, *The Psychopath*, pp. 1–2.
5. Barbara Wootton, *Social Science and Social Pathology* (New York: Macmillan, 1959), p. 250.
6. "The logical untenability [of the position that there are forces in man 'resistant to socialization'] was ably demonstrated by Parsons over 30 years ago, and it is widely recognized that the position is empirically unsound because it assumes [!] some universal biological drive system distinctly separate from socialization and social context–a basic and intransigent human nature" (Judith Blake and Kingsley Davis, "Norms, Values, and Sanctions," *Handbook of Modern Sociology*, ed. Robert E. L. Faris [Chicago: Rand McNally, 1964], p. 471).
7. Emile Durkheim, *Moral Education*, trans. Everett K. Wilson and Herman Schnurer (New York: The Free Press, 1961), p. 64.
8. Although attachment alone does not exhaust the meaning of internalization, attachments and beliefs combined would appear to leave only a small residue of "internal control" not susceptible in principle to direct measurement.
9. R. Ivan Nye, *Family Relationships and Delinquent Behavior* (New York: Wiley, 1958), pp. 5–7.
10. Albert J. Reiss, Jr., "Delinquency as the Failure of Personal and Social Controls," *American Sociological Review*, XVI (1951), 196–207. For example, "Our observations show . . . that delinquent recidivists are less often persons with mature ego ideals or non-delinquent social roles" (p. 204).
11. Scott Briar and Irving Piliavin, "Delinquency, Situational Inducements, and Commitment to Conformity," *Social Problems*, XIII (1965), 41–42. The concept "stake in conformity" was introduced by Jackson Toby in his "Social Disorganization and Stake in Conformity: Complementary Factors in the Predatory Behavior of Hoodlums," *Journal of Criminal Law, Criminology and Police Science*, XLVIII (1957), 12–17. See also his "Hoodlum or Business Man: An American Dilemma,"

The Jews, ed. Marshall Sklare (New York: The Free Press, 1958), pp. 542–550. Throughout the text, I occasionally use "stake in conformity" in speaking in general of the strength of the bond to conventional society. So used, the concept is somewhat broader than is true for either Toby or Briar and Piliavin, where the concept is roughly equivalent to what is here called "commitment."

12. Thomas Hobbes, *Leviathan* (Oxford: Basil Blackwell, 1957), p. 195.

13. Howard S. Becker, "Notes on the Concept of Commitment," *American Journal of Sociology*, LXVI (1960), 35–36.

14. Arthur L. Stinchcombe, *Rebellion in a High School* (Chicago: Quadrangle, 1964), p. 5.

15. Richard A. Cloward and Lloyd E. Ohlin, *Delinquency and Opportunity* (New York: The Free Press, 1960), p. 147, quoting Edwin H. Sutherland, ed., *The Professional Thief* (Chicago: University of Chicago Press, 1937), pp. 211–213.

16. William James, *Psychology* (Cleveland: World Publishing Co., 1948), p. 186.

17. Few activities appear to be so engrossing that they rule out contemplation of alternative lines of behavior, at least if estimates of the amount of time men spend plotting sexual deviations have any validity.

18. *The Sutherland Papers*, ed. Albert K. Cohen et al. (Bloomington: Indiana University Press, 1956), p. 37.

19. David Matza and Gresham M. Sykes, "Juvenile Delinquency and Subterranean Values," *American Sociological Review*, XXVI (1961), 712–719.

20. Ibid., p. 718.

21. The starving man stealing the loaf of bread is the image evoked by most strain theories. In this image, the starving man's belief in the wrongness of his act is clearly not something that must be explained away. It can be assumed to be present without causing embarrassment to the explanation.

22. McCord and McCord, *The Psychopath*, pp. 12–15.

23. Donald R. Cressey, *Other People's Money* (New York: The Free Press, 1953).

24. Gresham M. Sykes and David Matza, "Techniques of Neutralization: A Theory of Delinquency," *American Sociological Review*, XXII (1957), 664–670.

25. David Matza, *Delinquency and Drift* (New York: Wiley, 1964), pp. 181–191.

26. In asserting that Cressey's assumption is invalid with respect to delinquency, I do not wish to suggest that it is invalid for the question of embezzlement, where the problem faced by the deviator is fairly specific and he can reasonably be assumed to be an upstanding citizen. (Although even here the fact that the embezzler's nonsharable financial problem often results from some sort of hanky-panky suggests that "verbalizations" may be less necessary than might otherwise be assumed.)

27. *Delinquency and Drift*, p. 43.

28. This assumption is not, I think, contradicted by the evidence presented by Matza against the existence of a delinquent subculture. In comparing the attitudes and actions of delinquents with the picture painted by delinquent subculture theorists, Matza emphasizes—and perhaps exaggerates—the extent to which delinquents are tied to the conventional order. In implicitly comparing delinquents with a supermoral man, I emphasize—and perhaps exaggerate—the extent to which they are not tied to the conventional order.

29. The position taken here is therefore somewhere between the "semantic dementia" and the "neutralization" positions. Assuming variation, the delinquent is, at the extremes, freer than the neutralization argument assumes. Although the possibility of wide discrepancy between what the delinquent professes and what he practices still exists, it is presumably much rarer than is suggested by studies of articulate "psychopaths."

6.
CONCEPTIONS OF DEVIANT BEHAVIOR: THE OLD AND THE NEW

JACK P. GIBBS

A cross-cultural examination of deviance quickly reveals that deviance is a culturally relative phenomenon. This insight suggests the futility in identifying deviance as the result of inherent or biological qualities of deviant individuals, as was the case in the early days of criminology. It also suggests that there is nothing inherent in deviant behavior that makes it deviant. Instead, deviance is defined by features **external** to the deviant and the deviant act, namely, in the audience that identifies the deviance. As we will see in many of the articles in this text, there are political, economic, and cultural factors that help us understand audience reactions.

The ultimate end of substantive theory in any science is the formulation of empirical relations among classes of phenomena, e.g., X varies directly with Y, X is present if and only if Y is present. However, unless such propositions are arrived at by crude induction or sheer intuition, there is a crucial step before the formulation of a relational statement. This step can be described as the way the investigator comes to perceive or "think about" the phenomena under consideration. Another way to put it is the development of a "conception."

. . . In a field without consensus as to operational definitions and little in the way of systematic substantive theory, conceptions necessarily occupy a central position. This condition prevails in most of the social sciences. There, what purport to be definitions of classes of phenomena are typically general and inconsistent to the point of lacking empirical applicability (certainly in the operational sense of the word). Moreover, what passes for a substantive theory in the social sciences is more often than not actually a loosely formulated conception. These observations are not intended to deride the social sciences for lack of progress. All fields probably go through a "conceptions" stage; it is only more apparent in some than in others.

Of the social sciences, there is perhaps no better clear-cut illustration of the importance of conceptions than in the field identified as criminology and the study of deviant behavior. As we shall see, the history of the field can be described best in terms of changing conceptions of crime, criminals, deviants, and deviation. But the purpose of this paper is not an historical account of major trends in the field. If it is true that conceptions give rise to formal definitions and substantive theory, then a critical appraisal of conceptions is important in its own right. This is all the more true in the case of criminology and the study of deviant behavior, where conceptions are frequently confused with substantive theories, and the latter so clearly reflect the former.

OLDER CONCEPTIONS

In recent years there has been a significant change in the prevailing conception of deviant behavior and deviants. Prior to what is designated here as the "new perspective," it commonly was assumed that there is something inherent in deviants which distinguishes them from non-deviants.[1] Thus, from Lombroso to Sheldon, criminals were viewed as biologically distinctive in one way or another.[2] The inadequacies of this conception are now obvious. After decades of research, no biological characteristic which distinguishes criminals has been discovered, and this generalization applies even to particular types of criminals (e.g., murderers, bigamists, etc.). Consequently, few theorists now even toy with the notion that all criminals are atavistic, mentally defective, constitutionally inferior. But the rejection of the biological conception of crime stems from more than research findings. Even casual observation and mild logic cast doubt on the idea. Since legislators are not geneticists, it is difficult to see how they can pass laws in such a way as to create "born criminals." Equally important, since most if not all "normal" persons have violated a law at one time or another,[3] the assertion that criminals are so by heredity now appears most questionable.

Although the biological conception generally has been rejected, what is here designated as the analytic conception of criminal acts largely has escaped criticism. Rather than view criminal acts as nothing more or less than behavior contrary to legal norms, the acts are construed as somehow injurious to society. The shift from the biological to the analytical conception is thus from the actors to the characteristics of their acts, with the idea being that some acts are inherently "criminal" or at least that criminal acts share intrinsic characteristics in common.

The analytical conception is certainly more defensible than the biological view, but it is by no means free of criticism. Above all, the "injurious" quality of some deviant acts is by no means conspicuous, as witness Durkheim's observation:

> . . . there are many acts which have been and still are regarded as criminal without in themselves being harmful to society. What social danger is there in touching a tabooed object, an impure animal or man, in letting the sacred fire die down, in eating certain meats, in failure to make the traditional sacrifice over the grave of parents, in not exactly pronouncing the ritual formula, in not celebrating holidays, etc.[4]

Only a radical functionalism would interpret the acts noted by Durkheim as literally injuring society in any reasonable sense of the word. The crucial point is that, far from actually injuring society or sharing some intrinsic feature in common, acts may be criminal or deviant because and only because they are proscribed legally and/or socially. The proscription may be irrational in that members of the society cannot explain it, but it is real nonetheless. Similarly, a law may be "arbitrary" in that it is imposed by a powerful minority and, as a consequence, lacks popular support and is actively opposed. But if the law is consistently enforced (i.e., sanctions are imposed regularly on violators), it is difficult to see how it is not "real."

The fact that laws may appear to be irrational and arbitrary has prompted attempts to define crime independently of legal criteria, i.e., analytically. The first step in this direction was Garofalo's concept of natural crime—acts which violate prevailing sentiments of pity and probity.[5] Garofalo's endeavor accomplished very little. Just as there is probably no act which is contrary to law universally, it is equally true that no act violates sentiments of pity and probity in all societies. In other words, cultural relativity defeats any attempt to compile a list of acts which are crimes universally. Also, it is hard to see why the violation of a rigorously enforced traffic regulation is not a crime even though unrelated to sentiments of pity and probity. If it is not a crime, what is it?

The search for an analytic identification of crime continued in Sellin's proposal to abandon legal criteria altogether in preference for "conduct norms."[6] The rationale for the proposal is simple. Because laws vary and may be "arbitrary" in any one society, a purely legal definition of crime is not suited for scientific study. But Sellin's observations on the arbitrariness of laws apply in much the same way to conduct norms. Just as the content of criminal law varies from one society to the next and from time to time, so does the content of extra-legal norms. Further, the latter may be just as arbitrary as criminal laws. Even in a highly urbanized society such as the United States, there is evidently no rationale or utilitarian reason for all of the norms pertaining to mode of dress. True, there may be much greater conformity to conduct norms than to some laws, but the degree of conformity is hardly an adequate criterion of the "reality" of norms, legal or extra-legal. If any credence whatever can be placed in the Kinsey report, sexual taboos may be violated frequently and yet remain as taboos. As a case in point, even if adultery is now common in the United States, it is significant that the participants typically attempt to conceal their acts. In brief, just as laws may be violated frequently and are "unreal" in that sense, the same applies to some conduct norms; but in neither case do they cease to be norms. They would cease to be norms if and only if one defines deviation in terms of statistical regularities in behavior, but not even Sellin would subscribe to the notion that normative phenomena can or should be defined in statistical terms.

In summary, however capricious and irrational legal and extra-legal norms may appear to be, the inescapable conclusion is that some acts are criminal or deviant for the very simple reason that they are proscribed.

THE NEW CONCEPTION

Whereas both the pathological and the analytical conceptions of deviation assume that some intrinsic feature characterizes deviants and/or deviant acts, an emerging perspective in sociology flatly rejects any such assumption. Indeed, as witness the following statements by Kitsuse, Becker, and Erikson, exactly the opposite position is taken.

> Kitsuse: Forms of behavior *per se* do not differentiate deviants from nondeviants; it is the responses of the conventional and conforming members of the society who identify and interpret behavior as deviant which sociologically transform persons into deviants.[7]

> Erikson: From a sociological standpoint, deviance can be defined as conduct which is generally thought to require the attention of social control agencies—that is, conduct about which "something should be done." Deviance is not a property inherent in certain forms of behavior; it is a property conferred upon these forms by the audiences which directly or indirectly witness them. Sociologically,

then, the critical variable in the study of deviance is the social audience rather than individual person, since it is the audience which eventually decides whether or not any given action or actions will become a visible case of deviation.[8]

Becker: From this point of view, deviance is not a quality of the act a person commits, but rather a consequence of the application by others of rules and sanctions to an "offender." The deviant is one to whom that label has successfully been applied; deviant behavior is behavior that people so label.[9]

The common assertion in the above statements is that acts can be identified as deviant or criminal only by reference to the character of reaction to them by the public or by the official agents of a politically organized society. Put simply, if the reaction is of a certain kind, then and only then is the act deviant. The crucial point is that the essential feature of a deviant or deviant act is *external* to the actor and the act. Further, even if the act or actors share some feature in common other than social reactions to them, the feature neither defines nor completely explains deviation. To take the extreme case, even if Lombroso had been correct in his assertion that criminals are biologically distinctive, the biological factor neither identifies the criminal nor explains criminality. Purely biological variables may explain why some persons commit certain acts, but they do not explain why the acts are crimes. Consequently, since criminal law is spatially and temporally relative, it is impossible to distinguish criminals from noncriminals (assuming that the latter do exist, which is questionable) in terms of biological characteristics. To illustrate, if act X is a crime in society A but not a crime in society B, it follows that, even assuming Lombroso to have been correct, the anatomical features which distinguish the criminal in society A may characterize the noncriminal in society B. In both societies some persons may be genetically predisposed to commit act X, but the act is a crime in one society and not in the other. Accordingly, the generalization that all persons with certain anatomical features are criminals would be, in this instance, false. True, one may assert that the "born criminal" is predisposed to violate the laws of his own society, but this assumes either that "the genes" know what the law is or that the members of the legislature are geneticists (i.e., they deliberately enact laws in such a way that the "born criminal" will violate them). Either assumption taxes credulity.

The new perspective of deviant behavior contradicts not only the biological but also the analytical conception. Whereas the latter seeks to find something intrinsic in deviant or, more specifically, criminal acts, the new conception denies any such characterization. True, the acts share a common denominator—they are identified by the character of reaction to them—but this does not mean that the acts are "injurious" to society or that they are in any way inherently abnormal. The new conception eschews the notion that some acts are deviant or criminal in all societies. For that matter, the reaction which identifies a deviant act may not be the same from one society or social group to the next. In general, then, the new conception of deviant behavior is relativistic in the extreme. . . .

DISCUSSION QUESTIONS

1. Contrast the pathological and the analytical conceptions of deviance.
2. What does Gibbs mean when he states that "the new conception of deviant behavior is relativistic in the extreme"? What objections might some people have to such a relativistic conception of deviance?

NOTES

1. Throughout this paper crime is treated as a sub-class of deviant behavior. Particular issues may be discussed with reference to crime, but on the whole the observations apply to deviant behavior generally.
2. Although not essential to the argument, it is perhaps significant that the alleged biological differentiae of criminals have been consistently viewed as "pathological" in one sense or another.
3. See Edwin H. Sutherland and Donald R. Cressey, *Principles of Criminology*, 6th ed., Chicago: J. B. Lippincott, 1960, p. 39.
4. Emile Durkheim, *The Division of Labor in Society*, trans. George Simpson, Glencoe, Illinois: The Free Press, 1949, p. 72.
5. Raffaele Garofalo, *Criminology*, Boston: Little, Brown & Co., 1914, Chapter 1.
6. Thorsten Sellin, *Culture Conflict and Crime*, New York: Social Science Research Council, Bulletin 14, 1938.
7. John I. Kitsuse, "Societal Reaction to Deviant Behavior: Problems of Theory and Method," *Social Problems*, 9 (Winter, 1962), p. 253.
8. Kai T. Erikson, "Notes on the Sociology of Deviance," *Social Problems*, 9 (Spring, 1962), p. 308.
9. Howard S. Becker, *Outsiders*, New York: The Free Press of Glencoe, 1963, p. 9.

7.

DEFINITION AND THE DRAMATIZATION OF EVIL

FRANK TANNENBAUM

At some point in their adolescence, most kids engage in destructive and mischievous behaviors that they define as harmless fun; but only some of them are apprehended by the police and processed through the juvenile justice system. These kids are separated and defined as different from the other kids and the rituals involved in this process of separation, according to Tannenbaum, can be self-defeating if the goal of the juvenile justice system is to minimize the number of kids entering criminal careers. Tannenbaum's exposition from the 1930s is a precursor to labeling theory which would become popular in the 1960s and 1970s.

In the conflict between the young delinquent and the community there develop two opposing definitions of the situation. In the beginning the definition of the situation by the young delinquent may be in the form of play, adventure, excitement, interest, mischief, fun. Breaking windows, annoying people, running around porches, climbing over roofs, stealing from pushcarts, playing truant—all are items of play, adventure, excitement. To the community, however, these activities may and often do take on the form of a nuisance, evil, delinquency, with the demand for control, admonition, chastisement, punishment, police court, truant school. This conflict over the situation is one that arises out of a divergence of values. As the problem develops, the situation gradually becomes redefined. The attitude of the community hardens definitely into a demand for suppression. There is a gradual shift from the definition of the specific acts as evil to a definition of the individual as evil, so that all his acts come to be looked upon with suspicion. In the process of identification his companions, hang-outs, play, speech, income, all his conduct, the personality itself, become subject to scrutiny and question. From the community's point of view, the individual who used to do bad and mischievous things has now become a bad and unredeemable human being. From the individual's point of view there has taken place a similar change. He has gone slowly from a sense of grievance and injustice, of being unduly mistreated and punished, to a recognition that the definition of him as a human being is different from that of other boys in his neighborhood, his school, street, community. This recognition on his part becomes a process of self-identification and integration with the group which shares his activities.

It becomes, in part, a process of rationalization in part, a simple response to a specialized type of stimulus. The young delinquent becomes bad because he is defined as bad and because he is not believed if he is good. There is a persistent demand for consistency in character. The community cannot deal with people whom it cannot define. Reputation is this sort of public definition. Once it is established, then unconsciously all agencies combine to maintain this definition even when they apparently and consciously attempt to deny their own implicit judgment.

Early in his career, then, the incipient professional criminal develops an attitude of antagonism to the regulated orderly life that he is required to lead. This attitude is hardened and crystallized by opposition. The conflict becomes a clash of wills. And experience too often has proved that threats, punishments, beatings, commitments to institutions, abuse and defamation of one sort or another, are of no avail. Punishment breaks down against the child's stubbornness. What has happened is that the child has been defined as an "incorrigible" both by his contacts and by himself, and an attempt at a direct breaking down of will generally fails.

The child meets the situation in the only way he can, by defiance and escape—physical escape if possible, or emotional escape by derision, anger, contempt, hatred, disgust, tantrums, destructiveness, and physical violence. The response of the child is just as intelligent and intelligible as that of the schools, of the authorities. They have taken a simple problem, the lack of fitness of an institution to a particular child's needs, and have made a moral issue out of it with values outside the child's ken. It takes on the form of war between two wills, and the longer the war lasts, the more certainly does the child become incorrigible. The child will not yield because he cannot yield—his nature requires other channels for pleasant growth; the school system or society will not yield because it does not see the issues involved as between the incompatibility of an institution and a child's needs, sometimes physical needs, and will instead attempt to twist the child's nature to the institution with that consequent distortion of the child which makes an unsocial career inevitable. The verbalization of the conflict in terms of evil, delinquency, incorrigibility, badness, arrest, force, punishment, stupidity, lack of intelligence, truancy, criminality, gives the innocent divergence of the child from the straight road a meaning that it did not have in the beginning and makes its continuance in these same terms by so much the more inevitable.

The only important fact, when the issue arises of the boy's inability to acquire the specific habits which organized institutions attempt to impose upon him, is that this conflict becomes the occasion for him to acquire another series of habits, interests, and attitudes as a substitute. These habits become as effective in motivating and guiding conduct as would have been those which the orderly routine social institutions attempted to impose had they been acquired.

This conflict gives the gang its hold, because the gang provides escape, security, pleasure, and peace. The gang also gives room for the motor activity which plays a large role in a child's life. The attempt to break up the gang by force merely strengthens it. The arrest of the children has consequences undreamed-of, for several reasons.

First, only some of the children are caught though all may be equally guilty. There is a great deal more delinquency practiced and committed by the young groups than comes to the attention of the police. The boy arrested, therefore, is singled out in specialized treatment. This boy, no more guilty than the other members of his group, discovers a world of which he knew little. His arrest suddenly precipitates a series of institutions, attitudes, and experiences which the other children do not share. For this boy there suddenly appear the police, the patrol wagon, the police station, the other delinquents and criminals found in the police lock-ups, the court with all its agencies such as bailiffs, clerks, bondsmen, lawyers, probation officers. There are bars, cells, handcuffs, criminals. He is questioned, examined, tested, investigated. His history is gone into, his family is brought into court. Witnesses make their appearance. The boy, no different from the rest of his gang, suddenly becomes the center of a major drama in which all sorts of unexpected characters play important roles. And what is it all about ? about the accustomed things his gang has done and has been doing for a long time. In this entirely new world he is made conscious of himself as a different human being than he was before his arrest. He becomes classified as a thief, perhaps, and the entire world about him has suddenly become a different place for him and will remain different for the rest of his life.

THE DRAMATIZATION OF EVIL

The first dramatization of the "evil" which separates the child out of his group for specialized treatment plays a greater role in making the criminal than perhaps any other experience. It cannot be too often emphasized that for the child the whole situation has become different. He now lives in a different world. He has been tagged. A new and hitherto non-existent environment has been precipitated out for him.

The process of making the criminal, therefore, is a process of tagging, defining, identifying, segregating, describing, emphasizing, making conscious and self-conscious; it becomes a way of stimulating, suggesting, emphasizing, and evoking the very traits that are complained of. If the theory of relation of response to stimulus has any meaning, the entire process of dealing with the young delinquent is mischievous in so far as it identifies him to himself or to the environment as a delinquent person.

The person becomes the thing he is described as being. Nor does it seem to matter whether the valuation is made by those who would punish or by those who would reform. In either case the emphasis is upon the conduct that is disapproved of. The parents or the policeman, the older brother or the court, the probation officer or the juvenile institution, in so far as they rest upon the thing complained of, rest upon a false ground. Their very enthusiasm defeats their aim. The harder they work to reform the evil, the greater the evil grows under their hands. The persistent suggestion, with whatever good intentions, works mischief, because it leads to bringing out the bad behavior that it would suppress. The way out is through a refusal to dramatize the evil. The less said about it the better. The more said about something else, still better.

> The hard-drinker who keeps thinking of not drinking is doing what he can to initiate the acts which lead to drinking. He is starting with the stimulus to his habit. To succeed he must find some positive interest or line of action which will inhibit the drinking series and which by instituting another course of action will bring him to his desired end. (Dewey, 1922: 35)

The dramatization of the evil therefore tends to precipitate the conflict situation which was first created through some innocent maladjustment. The child's isolation forces him into companionship with other children similarly defined, and the gang becomes his means of escape, his security. The life of the gang gives it special mores, and the attack by the community upon these mores merely overemphasizes the conflict already in existence, and makes it the source of a new series of experiences that lead directly to a criminal career.

In dealing with the delinquent, the criminal, therefore, the important thing to remember is that we are dealing with a human being who is responding normally to the demands, stimuli, approval, expectancy, of the group with whom he is associated. We are dealing not with an individual but with a group.

> In a study of 6,000 instances of stealing, with reference to the number of boys involved, it was found that in 90.4 per cent of the cases two or more boys were known to have been involved in the act and were consequently brought to court. Only 9.6 per cent of all the cases were acts of single individuals. Since this study was based upon the number of boys brought to court, and since in many cases not all of the boys involved were caught and brought to court, it is certain that the percentage of group stealing is therefore even greater than 90.4 per cent. It cannot be doubted that delinquency, particularly stealing, almost invariably involves two or more persons. (Shaw and Myers, 1929: 662–63)

That group may be a small gang, a gang of children just growing up, a gang of young "toughs" of nineteen or twenty, or a gang of older criminals of thirty. If we are not dealing with a gang we may be dealing with a family. And if we are not dealing with either of these especially we may be dealing with a community. In practice all these factors—the family, the gang, and the community—may be important in the development and the maintenance of that attitude towards the world which makes a criminal career a normal, an accepted and approved way of life.

Direct attack upon the individual in these circumstances is a dubious undertaking. By the time the individual has become a criminal his habits have been so shaped that we have a fairly integrated character whose whole career is in tune with the peculiar bit of the environment for which he has developed the behavior and habits that cause him to be apprehended. In theory isolation from that group ought to provide occasion for change in the individual's habit structure. It might, if the individual were transplanted to a group whose values and activities had the approval of the wider community, and in which the newcomer might hope to gain full acceptance eventually. But until now isolation has meant the grouping in close confinement of persons whose strongest common bond has been their socially disapproved delinquent conduct. Thus the attack cannot be made without reference to group life.

The attack must be on the whole group for only by changing its attitudes and ideals, interests and habits, can the stimuli which it exerts upon the individual be changed. Punishment as retribution has failed to reform, that is, to change character. If the individual can be made aware of a different set of values for which he may receive approval, then we may be on the road to a change in his character. But such a change of values involves a change in stimuli, which means that the criminal's social world must be changed before he can be changed.

The point of view here developed rejects all assumptions that would impute crime to the individual in the sense that a personal shortcoming of the offender is the cause of the unsocial behavior. The assumption that crime is caused by any sort of inferiority, physiological or psychological, is here completely and unequivocally repudiated.

This of course does not mean that morphological or psychological techniques do not have value in dealing with the individual. It merely means that they have no greater value in the study of criminology than they would have in the study of any profession. If a poor IQ is a bad beginning for a career in medicine, it is also a poor beginning for a career in crime. If the psychiatrist can testify that a psychopath will make an irritable doctor he can prove the same for the criminal. But he can prove no more. The criminal differs from the rest of his fellows only in the sense that he has learned to respond to the stimuli of a very small and specialized group; but that group must exist or the criminal could not exist. In that he is like the mass of men, living a certain kind of life with the kind of companions that make that life possible.

This explanation of criminal behavior is meant to apply to those who more or less consistently pursue the criminal career. It does not necessarily presume to describe the accidental criminal or the man who commits a crime of passion. Here perhaps the theories that would seek the cause of crime in the individual may have greater application than in attempting to deal with those who follow a life of crime. But even in the accidental criminal there is a strong presumption that the accident is the outcome of a habit situation. Any habit tends to have a background of social conditioning.

> A man with the habit of giving way to anger may show his habit by a murderous attack upon some one who has offended. His act is nonetheless due to habit because it occurs only once in his life. The essence of habit is an acquired predisposition to *ways* or modes of response, not to particular acts except as, under special conditions, these express a way of behaving. Habit means special sensitiveness or accessibility to certain classes of stimuli, standing predilections and aversions, rather than bare recurrence of specific acts. It means will. (Dewey, 1922: 42)

In other words, perhaps the accidental criminal also is to be explained in terms such as we used in discussing the professional criminal.

DISCUSSION QUESTION

1. What actions on the part of the criminal justice system and the community contribute to the hardening of a career in delinquency? How so? What alternatives might be employed in responding to a juvenile's commission of a crime?

REFERENCES

Dewey, John. *Human Nature and Conduct.* Henry Holt and Company, New York, 1922.
Shaw, Clifford R. and Earl D. Myers, "The Juvenile Delinquent," *The Illinois Crime Survey,* pp. 662–663. Chicago, 1929.

8.

THE SEARCH FOR SCAPEGOAT DEVIANTS

JEFFERY S. VICTOR

History shows that society is especially inclined to create deviant categories and to hunt for deviants during periods of rapid social change. Change is often unsettling and frequently induces anxiety in people. Scapegoating can provide people with an explanation for their tensions, even if it is false, and sanctioning the deviant can serve to relieve some of these tensions.

There is nothing that makes us feel so good as the idea that someone else is an evildoer.

ROBERT LYND[1]

THE SOCIAL CONSTRUCTION OF IMAGINARY DEVIANTS

Sometimes societies invent new forms of deviance in order to have scapegoats for deep social tensions.[2] New social deviants are sometimes invented when rapid social change in a society results in widespread dislocation in people's lives, and the resulting frustration, fear, and anger, in turn, causes a great many people to seek scapegoats to blame. These scapegoats are "invented" by moral crusaders who target categories of social deviants to bear the blame for threats to a society's past way of life and its basic moral values.

The labels that a society uses to identify a new category of deviance embody socially constructed stereotypes, which are attributed to a category of people regarded as being deviant.[3] For example, the labels "murderer," "rapist," and "child molester" convey deviant stereotypes. In reality, the actual personality patterns and behavior of people involved in these forms of deviance are quite different from the imaginary stereotypes. In some situations, socially constructed labels for newly defined forms of deviance may precede the actual existence of any behavior or persons which fit the stereotypes embodied in the labels. Such was the case of the label "heretic" in the Middle Ages and "subversive" in the 1950s.

Eventually, moral crusades and witch hunts for social deviants, such as "subversives," "heretics," "witches," or "satanists," set society on a path, whereby individuals are found who seem to confirm the stereotype embodied in the deviant label.[4] In other words, moral crusades may be aimed at deviance which does not exist, and may even create a social type of deviant which did not previously exist, by seeking out, apprehending, and punishing some people. Paradoxically, widespread witch hunts, inquisitions, purges, and persecutions function to confirm the existence of new forms of social deviance.[5]

The labels "Satanism" and "Satanic cult" are socially constructed stereotypes. In actual social usage, the label "Satanism" has vague and elastic meanings. In small town newspaper articles, the label "Satanist" is applied loosely to a wide assortment of social deviants, including: teenage vandals, animal mutilators, and gang murderers, and adult psychopathic murderers, child molesters, and vicious rapists. Similarly, the label "Satanic cult" is used to refer to such widely different groups as juvenile delinquent gangs, unconventional religious groups, and Mafia-style criminal syndicates, all of which are supposedly motivated by worship of the Devil. The point is that claims, rumors, and allegations about criminal Satanism and Satanic cults ultimately arise from people's socially constructed predisposition to find Satanism in many unrelated incidents and activities.

As a form of collective behavior, the Satanic cult scare is a moral crusade similar to the "Red Scare" of the 1950s, albeit on a much lesser scale. It is a witch hunt for moral "subversives" and criminals. There isn't any agreed upon term to describe this pattern of collective behavior. It has been called a moral crusade, a witch hunt, or mass hysteria. However, none of these terms convey the complexity and variation of the social processes involved.

The classic case is that of the European witch-hunting craze, which lasted from the fifteenth through the seventeenth century. The frequent waves of anti-Semitic persecutions, beginning in the twelfth century and continuing through the twentieth century, are another familiar set of examples. In the United States, the anti-Catholic movement of the 1840s through the 1850s and the anti-Communist witch hunts of the 1950s are other examples.

SOCIAL CONFLICTS AND THE CREATION OF SCAPEGOAT DEVIANTS

When individuals build up tension from frustration, anger, and fear, they very commonly release their tension in angry attacks upon other people whom they blame for their feelings. For example, when a young husband is suddenly fired from his job, he may come home and verbally attack his wife or kick the family dog. The psychological mechanism is well known. It's called displacement or displaced aggression. We may all use it unintentionally from time to time because it temporarily reduces our feelings of tension. Similarly, when groups of people accumulate a lot of welled-up tension, the collective social process is the same. Groups seek scapegoats to blame, in part, because scapegoating temporarily reduces tension within groups.

However, the creation of scapegoat targets in a society is not only a collective extension of psychological processes. The creation of scapegoat targets tells us a lot about internal social dynamics in a society, because it is also a product of social conflict within a society.

THE SEARCH FOR EXTERNAL ENEMIES

Societies experiencing a lot of internal conflict and tension often seek common external enemies as a way to unify the conflicting elements within the society. The threat of an external enemy functions to pull together conflicting parties within a society and deflects attention and activity away from their grievances against each other. It pushes them to cooperate with each other and to put less emphasis upon defining their differences. Hostility directed at a common external enemy usually causes conflicting groups to set aside, at least temporarily, their hostilities towards each other.

When a society perceives an external enemy, whether or not there exists any genuine threat to that society's security, it collectively manufactures an evil enemy image.[6] The evil enemy image is a stereotype of the enemy group, which portrays the enemy as having those qualities which are considered most immoral in that society. It is a reverse mirror image of one's own society. Onto it, we project all those qualities we most detest and condemn, the ones that violate our culture's highest values. The evil enemy is seen as having no moral scruples whatsoever.

This contrast stereotype of the evil enemy allows people to exaggerate their own virtues. In contrast to the evil enemy, they grow angel's wings. It also discourages any penetrating criticism of the society by internal dissenters, who would immediately be viewed as traitors. The stereotype of Communist "fanatics" and of the "evil empire" of Communism served this social function in American society starting in the late 1940s.[7] Other evil enemy stereotypes held by Americans have been those embodied in the labels "Japs," "Huns," and Indian "savages."

THE SEARCH FOR INTERNAL ENEMIES

A search for internal enemies can serve the same function of providing a target for displaced aggression and a unifying force for conflicting elements in a society. This is done by defining some social category of people as being traitors to, or deviants from, the over-arching moral values of a society. When moral values are in dispute in a society, a witch hunt for moral subversives serves the purpose of clarifying and redefining the limits of moral conduct. The internal enemy can be a useful proxy target, a stand-in, for attacks between powerful conflicting elements in a society. Conflicting groups can direct their attacks safely against the proxy target, without having to engage each other directly. Normally, a society dares not choose genuinely powerful internal enemies to function as scapegoat targets.

Research on American racism illustrates this social dynamic. American scapegoating of Black people becomes more common when there is heightened internal conflict between groups of white people in society. One research study, for example, found a high correlation between the frequency of lynchings of Blacks in the South and periods of economic stress and social conflict arising from sharp drops in the price paid to farmers for cotton.[8] Another study found greater racist behavior in areas of the country in which there was greater income inequality between white people than in areas where the income differences between whites was much less.[9] In Europe, Jews have traditionally served this unifying social function of being a proxy scapegoat target for conflicting groups of Christians.

These same conflict-unifying social functions of scapegoating are also found in small groups.[10] Research on family relationships, for example, has found that conflict-ridden marriages sometimes keep a "united front" by scapegoating a child in the family.[11] Marriage partners can displace their hostilities towards each other by blaming a child for their marital discord. The scapegoated child may actually be responsible for some disturbing behavior, but it gets exaggerated and distorted in the eyes of its parents. In some cases, the behavior may even be entirely a product of the parents' invention. Moreover, the two parents fight each other through their attacks upon the child. Thereby, on the surface at least, they may seem to be cooperating effectively. One of the consequences for the child can be emotional harm.

The fact that the internal enemy, or deviant category, need not actually exist in the society (but is instead socially constructed through the scapegoating process) is recognized by the eminent sociological theorist, Lewis Coser.

> The inner enemy who is looked for, like the outer enemy who is evoked, may actually exist: he may be a dissenter who is opposed to certain aspects of group life or group action and who is considered a potential renegade or heretic. But the inner enemy also may be "found," he may simply be invented, in order to bring about through a common hostility toward him the social solidarity which the group so badly needs. . . . If men define a threat as real, although there may be little or nothing in reality to justify this belief, the threat is real in its consequences—and among these consequences is the increase in group cohesion.[12]

DISCUSSION QUESTION

1. What do you think happened to President George W. Bush's popularity in the aftermath of 9/11? What stereotypes of "terrorist" emerged? Relate your answers to this article.

NOTES

1. Robert Lynd (cited in Rudolf Flesch), *The Book of Unusual Quotations* (New York: Harper Bros., 1957), p. 80.
2. Nachman Ben-Yehuda, *The Politics and Morality of Deviance* (Albany, NY: State University of New York Press, 1990).
3. Erich Goode, *Deviant Behavior*, 3rd ed. (Englewood Cliffs, NJ: Prentice-Hall, 1990).
4. Nachman Ben-Yehuda, "The European Witch Craze of the 14th to 16th Centuries: A Sociologist's Perspective," *American Journal of Sociology* 86, no. 1 (1981): 1–31; Elliott P. Currie, "Crimes Without Criminals: Witchcraft and Its Control in Renaissance Europe," *Law and Society Review* 3, no. 1 (August 1986): 7–32.
5. Albert J. Bergesen, "Political Witch Hunts: The Sacred and the Subversive in Cross-National Perspective," *American Sociological Review* 42, (April 1977): 220–33; Jerry D. Rose, *Outbreaks: The Sociology of Collective Behavior* (New York: The Free Press, 1982).
6. Brett Silverstein, "Enemy Images," *American Psychologist* 44 (June 1989): 903–13; Jerome D. Frank, "The Face of the Enemy," *Psychology Today*, Nov. 1968, 24–29.
7. Howard F. Stein, "The Indispensable Enemy and American-Soviet Relations," *Ethos* 17 (Dec. 1989): 480–503.
8. Joseph T. Hepworth and Stephen G. West, "Lynchings and the Economy: A Time-Series Reanalysis of Hovland and Sears," *Journal of Personality and Social Psychology* 55, no. 2 (1988): 239–47.
9. Michael Reich, "The Economics of Racism," *Problems in Political Economy: An Urban Perspective*, ed. David M. Gordon (Lexington, MA: D. D. Heath, 1971): pp. 107–13.
10. Lynn S. Kahn, "The Dynamics of Scapegoating: The Expulsion of Evil," *Psychotherapy: Theory, Research and Practice* 17 (Spring 1980): 79–84; Jeffrey Eagle and Peter M. Newton, "Scapegoating in Small Groups: An Organizational Approach," *Human Relations* 34, no. 4 (1981): 283–301; Fred

Wright, et al. "Perspectives on Scapegoating in Primary Groups," *Group* 12 (Spring 1988): 33–44; Gary Gemmill, "The Dynamics of Scapegoating in Small Groups," *Small Group Behavior* 20 (Nov. 1989): 406–18.

11. Ezra F. Vogel and Normal W. Bell, "The Emotionally Disturbed Child as the Family Scapegoat," *The Family*, rev. ed. (New York: Free Press, 1960, 1968), pp. 412–25.

12. Lewis Coser, *The Function of Social Conflict* (New York: Free Press, 1956), p. 107.

9.
CRIMINALITY AND ECONOMIC CONDITIONS

WILLEM BONGER

The following piece is an early expression of Marxist criminology published in 1905. Bonger locates the causes of crime in the inequality engendered by the modes of production in a capitalist society. Much crime, he argues, represents a form of reaction by the proletariat against the brutal conditions of employment established by capitalist employers. More specifically, most crime stems from the desperation of impoverishment and is often an expression of vengeance on the part of the oppressed classes. If control over the means of production were shared with the proletariat, there would be greater equality and less crime.

However important crime may be as a social phenomenon, however terrible may be the injuries and the evil that it brings upon humanity, the development of society will not depend upon the question as to what are the conditions which could restrain crime or make it disappear if possible; the evolution of society will proceed independently of this question.

What is the direction that society will take under these continual modifications? This is not the place to treat fully of this subject. In my opinion the facts indicate quite clearly what the direction will be. The productivity of labor has increased to an unheard of degree and will assuredly increase in the future. The concentration of the means of production into the hands of a few progresses continually; in many branches it has reached such a degree that the fundamental principle of the present economic system, competition, is excluded, and has been replaced by monopoly. On the other hand the working class is becoming more and more organized, and the opinion is very generally held among working-men that the causes of material and intellectual poverty can be eliminated only by having the means of production held in common.

Supposing that this were actually realized, what would be the consequences as regards criminality? Let us take up this question for a moment. Although we can give only personal opinions as to the details of such a society, the general outlines can be traced with certainty.

The chief difference between a society based upon the community of the means of production and our own is that material poverty would be no longer known. Thus one great part of economic criminality . . . would be rendered impossible, and one of the greatest demoralizing forces of our present society would be eliminated. And then, in this way those social phenomena so productive of crime, prostitution and alcoholism, would lose one of their principal factors. Child labor and overdriving would no longer take place, and bad housing, the source of much physical and moral evil, would no longer exist.

With material poverty there would disappear also that intellectual poverty which weighs so heavily upon the proletariat; culture would no longer be the privilege of some, but a possession common to all. The consequences of this upon criminality would be very important. For we have seen that even in our present society with its numerous conflicts, the members of the propertied classes, who have often but a veneer of civilization, are almost never guilty of crimes of vengeance. There is the more reason to admit that in a society where interests were not opposed, and where civilization was universal, these crimes would be no longer present, especially since alcoholism also proceeds in large part from the intellectual poverty of the poorer classes. And what is true of crimes of vengeance, is equally true of sexual crimes in so far as they have the same etiology.

A large part of the economic criminality (and also prostitution to a certain extent) has its origin in the cupidity excited by the present economic environment. In a society based upon the community of the means of production, great contrasts of fortune would, like commercial capital, be lacking, and thus cupidity would find no food. These crimes will not totally disappear so long as there has not been a redistribution of property according to the maxim "to each according to his needs," something that will probably be realized, but not in the immediate future.

The changes in the position of woman which are taking place in our present society, will lead, under this future mode of production, to her economic independence, and consequently to her social independence as well. It is accordingly probable that the criminality of woman will increase in comparison with that of man during the transition period. But the final result will be the disappearance of the harmful effects of the economic and social preponderance of man.

As to the education of children under these new conditions it is difficult to be definite. However, it is certain that the community will concern itself seriously with their welfare. It will see to it that the children whose parents cannot or will not be responsible for them, are well cared for. By acting in this way it will remove one of the most important causes of crime. There is no doubt that the community will exercise also a strict control over the education of children; it cannot be affirmed, however, that the time will come when the children of a number of parents will be brought up together by capable persons; this will depend principally upon the intensity that the social sentiments may attain.

As soon as the interests of all are no longer opposed to each other, as they are in our present society, there will no longer be a question either of politics ("a fortiori" of political *crimes*) or of militarism.

Such a society will not only remove the causes which now make men egoistic, but will awaken, on the contrary, a strong feeling of altruism. We have seen that this was already the case with the primitive peoples, where their economic interests were not in opposition. In a larger measure this will be realized under a mode of production in common, the interests of all being the same.

In such a society there can be no question of crime properly so called. The eminent criminologist, Manouvrier, in treating of the prevention of crime expresses himself thus: "The maxim to apply is, act so that every man shall always have more interest in being useful to his fellows than in harming them." It is precisely in a society where the community of the means of production *has* been realized that this maxim will obtain its complete application. There will be crimes committed by pathological individuals, but this will come rather within the sphere of the physician than that of the judge. . . .

"It is society that prepares the crime," says the true adage of Quetelet. For all those who have reached this conclusion, and are not insensible to the sufferings of humanity, this statement is sad, but contains a ground of hope. It is sad, because society punishes severely those who commit the crime which she has herself prepared. It contains a ground of hope, since it promises to humanity the possibility of some day delivering itself from one of its most terrible scourges.

DISCUSSION QUESTIONS

1. When Bonger suggests that improvements made in the status of women could lead to increased rates in female criminality, he was foreshadowing the works of feminist criminologists who came along much later. Indeed he was correct: As women's status improved, female crime rates did increase. Why might that be the case?
2. This piece was first published in 1905. How do you think Bonger would feel about what "progress" has been made in more than a hundred years since its publication?

10.
THE IMPLICIT IDEOLOGY OF CRIMINAL JUSTICE

JEFFREY REIMAN

Two principal concerns of the conflict theorist are inequality and the abuse of power. Namely, the elite use their power to maintain their power and, thus, perpetuate inequality. The elite have many tools at their disposal. Most fundamentally, according to Karl Marx (and Willem Bonger in the previous article), the elite control access to employment and the terms under which people are allowed to earn their livelihood, their survival. But the elite also write the laws and ensure that they rest in their favor.

How can such an unfair arrangement survive? Partly it survives through the use of force, exercised through the criminal justice system. But, more importantly, according to many conflict theorists, it survives on the basis of ideology. An ideology is a system of beliefs that justify a given social system. In this case, the institutions that perpetuate inequality in our society thrive because vast numbers of people subscribe to an ideology which holds that inequality is just. Reiman describes how this works.

Any criminal justice system like ours conveys a subtle yet powerful message in support of established institutions. It does this for two interconnected reasons. First, it concentrates on *individual* wrongdoers. This means that *it diverts our attention away from our institutions, away from consideration of whether our institutions themselves are wrong or unjust or indeed "criminal."*

Second, the criminal law is put forth as the *minimum neutral ground rules* for any social living. We are taught that no society can exist without rules against theft and violence, and thus the criminal law seems to be politically neutral: the minimum requirements for *any* society, the minimum obligations that any individual owes his or her fellows to make social life of any decent sort possible. Thus, the criminal law not only diverts our attention away from the possible injustice of our social institutions, but also bestows upon those institutions the mantle of its own neutrality.

Because the criminal law protects the established institutions (the prevailing economic arrangements are protected by laws against theft, and so on), attacks on those established institutions become equivalent to violations of the minimum requirements for any social life at all. In effect, the criminal law enshrines the established institutions as equivalent to the minimum requirements for *any* decent social existence—and it brands the individual who attacks those institutions as one who has declared war on *all* organized society and who must therefore be met with the weapons of war.

This is the powerful magic of criminal justice. By virtue of its focus on *individual* criminals, it diverts us from the evils of the social order. By virtue of its presumed neutrality, it transforms the established social (and economic) order from being merely *one* form of society open to critical comparison with others into *the* conditions of *any* social order and thus immune from criticism. Let us look more closely at this process.

What is the effect of focusing on individual guilt? Not only does this divert our attention from the possible evils in our institutions, but it also puts forth half the problem of justice as if it were the *whole* problem. To focus on individual guilt is to ask whether the individual citizen has fulfilled his or her obligations to his or her fellow citizens. *It is to look away from the issue of whether the fellow citizens have fulfilled their obligations to him or her.* To look only at individual responsibility is to look away from social responsibility. Writing about her stint as a "story analyst" for a prime-time TV "real crime" show based on videotapes of actual police busts, Debra Seagal describes the way focus on individual criminals deflects attention away from the social context of crime and how television reproduces this effect in millions of homes daily:

> By the time our 9 million viewers flip on their tubes, we've reduced fifty or sixty hours of mundane and compromising video into short, action-packed segments of tantalizing, crack-filled, dope-dealing, junkie-busting cop culture. How easily we downplay the pathos of the suspect; how cleverly we breeze past the complexities that cast doubt on the very system that has produced the criminal activity in the first place.[1]

Seagal's description illustrates as well how a television program that shows nothing but videos of actual events, that uses no reenactments whatsoever, can distort reality by selecting and recombining pieces of real events.

A study of 69 TV law and crime dramas finds that fictional presentations of homicide focus on individual motivations and ignore social conditions:

> Television crime dramas portray these events as specific psychological episodes in the characters' lives and little, if any, effort is made to connect them to basic social institutions or the nature of society within which they occur.[2]

To look only at individual criminality is to close one's eyes to social injustice and to close one's ears to the question of whether our social institutions have exploited or violated the individual. *Justice is a two-way street—but criminal justice is a one-way street.* Individuals owe obligations to their fellow citizens because their fellow citizens owe obligations to them. Criminal justice focuses on the first and looks away from the second. *Thus, by focusing on individual responsibility for crime, the criminal justice system effectively acquits the existing social order of any charge of injustice!*

This is an extremely important bit of ideological alchemy. It stems from the fact that the same act can be criminal or not, unjust or just, depending on the circumstances in which it takes place. Killing someone is ordinarily a crime, but if it is in self-defense or to stop a deadly crime, it is not. Taking property by force is usually a crime, but if the taking is retrieving what has been stolen, then no crime has been committed. Acts of violence are ordinarily crimes, but if the violence is provoked by the threat of violence or by oppressive conditions, then, like the Boston Tea Party, what might ordinarily be called criminal is celebrated as just. This means that when we call an act a crime, *we are also making an implicit judgment about the conditions in response to which it takes place.* When we call an act a crime, we are saying that the conditions in which it occurs are not themselves criminal or deadly or oppressive or so unjust as to make an extreme response reasonable or justified or non-criminal. This means that when the system holds an individual responsible for a crime, *it implicitly conveys the message that the social conditions in which the crime occurred are not responsible for the crime,* that they are not so unjust as to make a violent response to them excusable.

Judges are prone to hold that an individual's responsibility for a violent crime is diminished if it was provoked by something that might lead a "reasonable man" to respond violently and that criminal responsibility is eliminated if the act was in response to conditions so intolerable that any "reasonable man" would have been likely to respond in the same way. In this vein, the law acquits those who kill or injure in self-defense and treats leniently those who commit a crime when confronted with extreme provocation. The law treats understandingly the man who kills his wife's lover, and the woman who kills her brutal husband even when she has not acted directly in self-defense. By this logic, when we hold an individual completely responsible for a crime, we are saying that the conditions in which it occurred are such that a "reasonable man" should find them tolerable. In other words, by focusing on individual responsibility for crimes, *the criminal justice system broadcasts the message that the social order itself is reasonable and not intolerably unjust.*

Thus, the criminal justice system focuses moral condemnation on individuals and deflects it away from the social order that may have either violated the individual's rights or dignity or pushed him or her to the brink of the crime. This not only serves to carry the message that our social institutions are not in need of fundamental questioning, but further suggests that the justice of our institutions is obvious, not to be doubted. Indeed, because it is deviations from these institutions that are crimes, the established institutions become the implicit standard of justice from which criminal deviations are measured.

This leads to the second way in which a criminal justice system always conveys an implicit ideology. It arises from the presumption that the criminal law is nothing but the politically neutral minimum requirements of any decent social life. What is the consequence of this? As already suggested, this presumption transforms the prevailing social order into justice incarnate and all violations of the prevailing order into injustice incarnate. This process is so obvious that it may be easily missed.

Consider, for example, the law against theft. It does seem to be one of the minimum requirements of social living. As long as there is scarcity, any society—capitalist or socialist—will need rules to deter individuals from taking what does not belong to them. The law against theft, however, is more: It is a law against stealing what individuals *presently own.* Such a law has the effect of making the present distribution of property a part of the criminal law.

Because stealing is a violation of the law, this means that the present distribution of property becomes the implicit standard of justice against which criminal deviations are measured. Because criminal law is thought of as the minimum requirements of any social life, this means that the present distribution of property is treated as the equivalent of the minimum requirements of *any* social life. The criminal who would alter the present distribution of property becomes someone who is declaring war on all organized society. The question of whether this "war" is provoked by the injustice or brutality of the society is swept aside. Indeed, this suggests yet another way in which the criminal justice system conveys an ideological message in support of the established society.

Not only does the criminal justice system acquit the social order of any charge of injustice; it also specifically cloaks the society's own crime-producing tendencies. I have already observed that by blaming the individual for a crime, the society is acquitted of the charge of injustice. I would like to go further now and argue that by blaming the individual for a crime, the society is acquitted of the charge of *complicity* in that crime. This is a point worth developing, because many observers have maintained that modern competitive societies such as our own have structural features that tend to generate crime. Thus, holding the individual responsible for his or her crime serves the function of taking the rest of society off the hook for their role in sustaining and benefiting from social arrangements that produce crime. Let us take a brief detour to look more closely at this process.

Cloward and Ohlin argued in their book, *Delinquency and Opportunity*,[3] that much crime is the result of the discrepancy between social goals and the legitimate opportunities available for achieving them. The same point is basic to "strain theory" including recent variations like Messner and Rosenfeld's *Crime and the American Dream*.[4] Simply put, in our society everyone is encouraged to be a success, but the avenues to success are open only to some. The conventional wisdom of our free-enterprise democracy is that anyone can be a success if he or she has the talent and the ambition. Thus, if one is not a success, it is because of one's own shortcomings: laziness, lack of ability, or both. On the other hand, opportunities to achieve success are not equally open to all. Access to the best schools and the best jobs is effectively closed to all but a few of the poor and becomes more available only as one goes up the economic ladder. The result is that many are called but few are chosen. Many who have taken the bait and accepted the belief in the importance of success and the belief that achieving success is a result of individual ability must cope with feelings of frustration and failure that result when they find the avenues to success closed. Cloward and Ohlin argue that one method of coping with these stresses is to develop alternative avenues to success. Crime is such an alternative avenue.

Crime is a means by which people who believe in the American dream pursue it when they find the traditional routes barred. Indeed, it is plain to see that the goals pursued by most criminals are as American as apple pie. One of the reasons that American moviegoers enjoy gangster films— movies in which gangsters such as Al Capone, Bonnie and Clyde, or Butch Cassidy and the Sundance Kid are the heroes, as distinct from police and detective films, whose heroes are defenders of the law—is that even when we deplore the hero's methods, we identify with his or her notion of success, because it is ours as well, and we admire the courage and cunning displayed in achieving that success.

It is important to note that the discrepancy between success goals and legitimate opportunities in America is not an aberration. It is a structural feature of modern competitive industrialized society, a feature from which many benefits flow. Cloward and Ohlin write that

> a crucial problem in the industrial world is to locate and train the most talented persons in every generation, irrespective of the vicissitudes of birth, to occupy technical work roles. Since we cannot know in advance who can best fulfill the requirements of the various occupational roles, the matter is presumably settled through the process of competition. But how can men throughout the social order be motivated to participate in this competition?
>
> One of the ways in which the industrial society attempts to solve this problem is by defining success-goals as potentially accessible to all, regardless of race, creed, or socioeconomic position.[5]

Because these universal goals are urged to encourage a competition to select the best, there are necessarily fewer openings than seekers. Also, because those who achieve success are in a particularly good position to exploit their success to make access for their own children easier, the competition is rigged to work in favor of the middle and upper classes. As a result, "many lower-class persons are the victims of a contradiction between the goals toward which they have been led to orient themselves and socially structured means of striving for these goals."[6]

> [The poor] experience desperation born of the certainty that their position in the economic structure is relatively fixed and immutable—a desperation made all the more poignant by their exposure to a cultural ideology in which failure to orient oneself upward is regarded as a moral defect and failure to become mobile as a proof of it.[7]

The outcome is predictable. "Under these conditions, there is an acute pressure to depart from institutional norms and to adopt illegitimate alternatives."[8]

This means that the very way in which our society is structured to draw out the talents and energies that go into producing our high standard of living has a costly side effect: It produces crime. By holding individuals responsible for this crime, those who enjoy that high standard of living can have their cake and eat it too. They can reap the benefits of the competition for success and escape the responsibility of paying for the costs of the competition. By holding the poor crook legally and morally guilty, the rest of society not only passes the costs of competition on to the poor, but also effectively denies that it (meaning primarily the affluent part of society) is the beneficiary of an economic system that exacts such a high toll in frustration and suffering.

Willem Bonger, the Dutch Marxist criminologist, maintained that competitive capitalism produces egotistic motives and undermines compassion for the misfortunes of others, and thus makes human beings literally *more capable of crime*—more capable of preying on their fellows without moral inhibition or remorse—than earlier cultures that emphasized cooperation rather than competition.[9] Here again, the criminal justice system relieves those who benefit from the American economic system of the costs of that system. By holding criminals morally and individually responsible for their crimes, we can forget that the motives that lead to crime—the drive for success, linked with the beliefs that success means outdoing others and that violence is an acceptable way of achieving one's goals—are the *same motives* that powered the drive across the American continent and that continue to fuel the engine of America's prosperity.

David Gordon, a contemporary political economist, maintains "that nearly all crimes in capitalist societies represent perfectly *rational* responses to the structure of institutions upon which capitalist societies are based."[10] Like Bonger, Gordon believes that capitalism tends to provoke crime in all economic strata. This is so because most crime is motivated by a desire for property or money and is an understandable way of coping with the pressures of inequality, competition, and insecurity, all of which are essential ingredients of capitalism. Capitalism depends, Gordon writes,

> [upon] competitive forms of social and economic interaction and upon substantial inequalities in the allocation of social resources. Without inequalities, it would be much more difficult to induce workers to work in alienating environments. Without competition and a competitive ideology, workers might not be inclined to struggle to improve their relative income and status in society by working harder. Finally, although rights of property are protected, capitalist societies do not guarantee economic security to most of their individual members. Individuals must fend for themselves, finding the best

available opportunities to provide for themselves and their families. Driven by the fear of economic insecurity and by a competitive desire to gain some of the goods unequally distributed throughout the society, many individuals will eventually become "criminals."[11]

To the extent that a society makes crime a reasonable alternative for a large number of its members from all classes, that society is itself not very reasonably or humanely organized and bears some degree of responsibility for the crime it encourages. Because the criminal law is put forth as the minimum requirements that can be expected of any "reasonable man," its enforcement amounts to a denial of the real nature of the social order to which Gordon and the others point. Here again, by blaming the individual criminal, the criminal justice system serves implicitly but dramatically to acquit the society of its criminality.

THE BONUS OF BIAS

We now consider the additional ideological bonus derived from the criminal justice system's bias against the poor. This bonus is a product of the association of crime and poverty in the popular mind. This association, the merging of the "criminal classes" and the "lower classes" into the "dangerous classes," was not invented in America. The word *villain* is derived from the Latin *villanus*, which means a farm servant. The term *villein* was used in feudal England to refer to a serf who farmed the land of a great lord and who was wholly subject to that lord.[12] In this respect, our present criminal justice system is heir to a long tradition.

The value of this association was already seen when we explored the average citizen's concept of the Typical Criminal and the Typical Crime. It is quite obvious that throughout the great mass of Middle America, far more fear and hostility are directed toward the predatory acts of the poor than toward the acts of the rich. Compare the fate of politicians in recent history who call for tax reform, income redistribution, prosecution of corporate crime, and any sort of regulation of business that would make it better serve American social goals with that of politicians who erect their platform on a call for "law and order," more police, fewer limits on police power, and stiffer prison sentences for criminals—and consider this in light of what we have already seen about the real dangers posed by corporate crime and "business as usual."

It seems clear that Americans have been effectively deceived as to what are the greatest dangers to their lives, limbs, and possessions. The very persistence with which the system functions to apprehend and punish poor crooks and ignore or slap on the wrist equally or more dangerous individuals is testimony to the sticking power of this deception. That Americans continue to tolerate the comparatively gentle treatment meted out to white-collar criminals, corporate price fixers, industrial polluters, and political-influence peddlers while voting in droves to lock up more poor people faster and for longer sentences indicates the degree to which they harbor illusions as to who most threatens them. It is perhaps also part of the explanation for the continued dismal failure of class-based politics in America. American workers rarely seem able to forget their differences and unite to defend their shared interests against the rich whose wealth they produce. Ethnic divisions serve this divisive function well, but undoubtedly the vivid portrayal of the poor—and, of course, blacks—as hovering birds of prey waiting for the opportunity to snatch away the workers' meager gains serves also to deflect opposition away from the upper classes.

A politician who promises to keep working-class communities free of blacks and the prisons full of them can get votes even if the major portion of his or her policies amount to continuation of the favored treatment of the rich at their expense. The sensationalistic use, in the 1988 presidential election, of photos of Willie Horton (a convicted black criminal who committed a brutal rape while out of prison on a furlough) suggests that such tactics are effective politics. Recent studies suggest that the identification of race and violent crime continues, albeit in subtler form.[13]

The most important "bonus" derived from the identification of crime and poverty is that it paints the picture that the threat to decent Middle Americans comes from those below them on the economic ladder, not from those above. For this to happen, the system must not only identify crime and poverty, *but also fail enough in the fight to reduce crime that crime remains a real threat.* By doing this, it deflects the fear and discontent of Middle Americans, and their possible opposition, away from the wealthy.

There are other bonuses as well. For instance, if the criminal justice system sends out a message that bestows legitimacy on the present distribution of property, the dramatic impact is greatly enhanced if the violator of the present arrangements is without property. In other words, the crimes of the well-to-do "redistribute" property among the haves. In that sense, they do not pose a symbolic challenge to the larger system in which some have much and many have little or nothing. If the criminal threat can be portrayed as coming from the poor, then the punishment of the poor criminal becomes a morality play in which the sanctity and legitimacy of the system in which some have plenty and others have little or nothing are dramatically affirmed. It matters little whom the poor criminals really victimize. What counts is that Middle Americans come to fear that those poor criminals are out to steal what they own.

There is yet another bonus for the powerful in America, produced by the identification of crime and poverty. It might be thought that the identification of crime and poverty would produce sympathy for the criminals. My suspicion is that it produces or at least reinforces the reverse: *hostility toward the poor.*

There is little evidence that Americans are very sympathetic to poor criminals. Very few Americans believe poverty to be a cause of crime (6 percent of those questioned in a 1981 survey, although 21 percent thought unemployment was a cause—in keeping with our general blindness to class, these questions are not even to be found in recent surveys). Other surveys find that most Americans believe that courts do not deal harshly enough with criminals (67 percent of those questioned in 2002), and that the death penalty should be used for convicted murderers (66 percent of those questioned in 2002).[14]

Indeed, the experience with white-collar crime discussed in Chapter 3 [of Reiman's book] suggests that sympathy for criminals begins to flower only when we approach the higher reaches of the ladder of wealth and power. For some poor ghetto youth who robs a liquor store, five years in a penitentiary is our idea of tempering justice with mercy. When corporate crooks rob millions, incarceration is rare. A fine is usually thought sufficient punishment.

My view is that, because the criminal justice system, in fact and fiction, deals with *individual legal and moral guilt,* the association of crime with poverty does not mitigate the image of individual moral responsibility for crime, the image that crime is the result of an individual's poor character. It does the reverse: It generates the association of poverty and individual moral failing and thus *the belief that poverty itself is a sign of poor or weak character*. The clearest evidence that Americans hold this belief is to be found in the fact that attempts to aid the poor are regarded as acts of charity rather than as acts of justice. Our welfare system has all the demeaning attributes of an institution designed to give handouts to the undeserving and none of the dignity of an institution designed to make good on our responsibilities to our fellow human beings. If we acknowledged the degree to which our economic and social institutions themselves breed poverty, we would have to recognize our own responsibilities toward the poor. If we can convince our selves that the poor are poor because of their own shortcomings, particularly moral shortcomings such as incontinence and indolence, then we need acknowledge no such responsibility to the poor. Indeed, we can go further and pat ourselves on the back for our generosity in handing out the little that we do, and, of course, we can make our recipients go through all the indignities that mark them as the undeserving objects of our benevolence. By and large, this has been the way in which Americans have dealt with their poor.[15] It is a way that enables us to avoid asking the question of why the richest nation in the world continues to produce massive poverty. It is my view that this conception of the poor is subtly conveyed by how our criminal justice system functions.

Obviously, no ideological message could be more supportive of the present social and economic order than this. It suggests that poverty is a sign of individual failing, not a symptom of social or economic injustice. It tells us loud and clear that massive poverty in the midst of abundance is not a sign pointing toward the need for fundamental changes in our social and economic institutions. It suggests that the poor are poor because they deserve to be poor or at least because they lack the strength of character to overcome poverty. When the poor are seen to be poor in character, then economic poverty coincides with moral poverty and the economic order coincides with the moral order. As if a divine hand guided its workings, capitalism leads to everyone getting what he or she morally deserves!

If this association takes root, then when the poor individual is found guilty of a crime, the criminal justice system acquits the society of its responsibility not only for crime *but for poverty as well*.

With this, the ideological message of criminal justice is complete. The poor rather than the rich are seen as the enemies of the majority of decent Americans. Our social and economic institutions are held to be responsible for neither crime nor poverty, and thus are in need of no fundamental questioning or reform. The poor are poor because they are poor of character. The economic order and the moral order are one. To the extent that this message sinks in, the wealthy can rest easily—even if they cannot sleep the sleep of the just.

We can understand why the criminal justice system is allowed to create the image of crime as the work of the poor and fails to reduce it so that the threat of crime remains real and credible. The result is ideological alchemy of the highest order. The poor are seen as the real threat to decent society. The ultimate sanctions of criminal justice dramatically sanctify the present social and economic order, and *the poverty of criminals makes poverty itself an individual moral crime!*

Such are the ideological fruits of a losing war against crime whose distorted image is reflected in the criminal justice carnival mirror and widely broadcast to reach the minds and imaginations of America.

DISCUSSION QUESTIONS

1. What, according to this article, is the connection between crime and capitalism? What role does the criminal justice system play in maintaining capitalism in our society?
2. What does Reiman mean when he states, "Justice is a two-way street—but criminal justice is a one-way street"?
3. How, according to Reiman, does the identification of crime with poverty serve the interests of the elite?

NOTES

1. Debra Seagal, "Tales from the Cutting-Room Floor: The Reality of 'Reality-Based' Television," *Harper's Magazine*, November 1993, p. 52.
2. David Fabianic, "Television Dramas and Homicide Causation," *Journal of Criminal Justice* 25, no. 3: p. 201.
3. Richard A. Cloward and Lloyd E. Ohlin, *Delinquency and Opportunity: A Theory of Delinquent Gangs* (New York: Free Press, 1960), esp. pp. 77–107.
4. Steven Messner and Richard Rosenfeld, *Crime and the American Dream*, 3rd ed. (Belmont, Calif.: Wadsworth), 2000.
5. Ibid., p. 81.
6. Ibid., p. 10.
7. Ibid., p. 107.
8. Ibid., p. 10.
9. Willem Bonger, *Criminality and Economic Conditions*, abridged and with an intro. by Austin T. Turk (Bloomington: Indiana University Press, 1969), pp. 7-1,2, 40-47. Willem Adriaan Bonger was born in Holland in 1876 and died by his own hand in 1940 rather than submit to the Nazis. His *Criminalité et conditions économiques* first appeared in 1905. It was translated into English and published in the United States in Ibid., pp. 3–4.
10. David M. Gordon, "Capitalism, Class and Crime in America," *Crime and Delinquency* (April 1973): p. 174.
11. Ibid.
12. William and Mary Morris, *Dictionary of Word and Phrase Origins*, vol. 2 (New York: Harper & Row, 1967), p. 282.
13. See, for example, Jon Hurwitz and Mark Peffley, "Playing the Race Card in the Post-Willie Horton Era: The Impact of Racialized Code Words on Support for Punitive Crime Policy," *Public Opinion Quarterly* 69, no. 1 (2005): pp. 99–113.
14. *Sourcebook – 1981*, pp. 192, 205, 210–11; and *Sourcebook –2003*, p. 126, Table 2.27; p. 141, Table 2.47; and p. 145, Table 2.50.
15. Historical documentation of this can be found in David J. Rothman, *The Discovery of the Asylum: Social Order and Disorder in the New Republic* (Boston: Little, Brown, 1971); and in Frances Fox Piven and Richard A. Cloward, *Regulating the Poor: The Functions of Public Welfare* (New York: Pantheon, 1971), which brings the analysis up to recent times.

STUDYING DEVIANCE

Introduction

Those of us involved in the sociological study of deviance and deviants are fortunate because our subject matter is so fascinating. There is the temptation to contrast the study of normal behavior to that of deviant behavior and dismiss the former as bland and uninteresting (after all, it is *normal* behavior); but in fact, the two foci are indistinguishable from each other. The norms define deviance and, as we have seen, deviance defines the norm (see Erikson, Article 2).

Both normal and deviant behavior, however, are very difficult to study. Normal behavior is difficult to study because we all grow up surrounded by thousands of norms and learn to take them for granted. We often do not recognize norms until they are violated by deviant behavior. Anthropologist Ralph Linton noted much the same thing about culture when in 1936 he observed,

> It has been said that the last thing that a dweller in the deep sea would discover would be water. He would be conscious of its existence only if some accident brought him to the surface and introduced him to air. . . . The ability to see the culture of one's own society as a whole . . . calls for a degree of objectivity which is rarely if ever achieved. (quoted in Robertson, 1987, p. 72)

Working from Linton's metaphor, the norms are analogous to "water" and deviance is the "air" that brings the norms into sharp relief. So it is the job of the sociologist to expose deviance in order to understand the norms. Exposing deviance, however, is a very difficult task. Since deviance is so often accompanied by censure and a whole host of negative sanctions, those engaged in deviant behavior very often want to keep it a secret.

Sociologists have developed a number of ways for studying people's attitudes, beliefs, and behavior—all with their strengths and weaknesses. The science of survey research was pioneered by sociologists and there are a number of methods by which surveys may be administered. Survey questions can either be "open-ended" or "close-ended." Open-ended questions allow the respondent to freely answer the questions as he or she chooses. Close-ended questions force the respondent to choose among answers provided on the questionnaire (such as "never," "sometimes," or "often"). Open-ended questions allow for more elaborate answers and have the potential to reveal more depth of insight. But it is more difficult to categorize responses and, therefore, more difficult to compare respondents and develop generalizations about the normative qualities of the population. Conversely, close-ended questions tend to reveal less depth of insight, but they produce answers that are more easily coded for entry into a computer database and tabulated for comparison. They are, thus, better adapted for dealing with very large samples and they can produce more breadth of information that is potentially more generalizable to large swaths of the population. As such, they can reveal a good deal of insight about normative behavior.

In studying a deviant group the researcher may also engage in field observation. He or she may do this either as a "participant observer" or as a "non-participant observer." In the former, the researcher engages with the group as a participant. For example, if the researcher is studying a chapter of Alcoholics Anonymous, he or she may actually be an alcoholic or may pretend to be an alcoholic. In either case, they engage in the same activities while present in the group as the other members. If engaging in non-participant observation, the researcher would make it known to the group that he or she is a sociologist and is there to observe. Most likely, he or she would ask for permission to conduct the observations. The advantage of participant observation, of course, is that the subjects are less likely to alter their behavior in the presence of the researcher. One disadvantage of participant observation is that the researcher's objectivity may be compromised as the researcher may become overly sympathetic with his or her subjects. Perhaps a more serious disadvantage is that this method is often criticized for being unethical because the researcher has based a relationship of trust with his or her subjects based on deception or a failure to disclose the full purpose of his or her presence.

Another method that has often yielded important insights into the nature of deviance is the interview. In this method, the researcher develops a relationship of trust with an individual or a number of individuals belonging to a stigmatized group and asks them questions. Like the open-ended questions in a survey, the answers to the interviewer's questions may reveal more depth of insight than a close-ended survey; but unlike a survey, the researcher/interviewer may pursue lines of inquiry off-the-cuff, depending on the respondent's answers to previous questions. This ability to follow up on previous answers until the researcher's curiosity is satisfied has the potential to reveal far more depth of insight than a survey. Interviews are well adapted to understanding why people engage in deviant behavior, how it feels to be a member of a stigmatized group, and what methods they use to deal with their stigma.

Engaging in the sociology of deviance through field observations and/or interviews is inevitably challenging and frequently fascinating. As Susan Palmer recounts in the first article in this section, the sociologist is somewhat caught in the netherworld between the world of the normal and the world of deviance. Lay people often think that the sociologist is suspiciously sympathetic to the deviant and the sociologist's subjects are apt to think that he or she is suspiciously lacking in sympathy. Palmer describes how she negotiates the line between the normal world and the deviant world as well as other trials and tribulations she encounters as she engages in her research on New Religious Movements.

The next selection, "Sex in Boxes," was written by Elizabeth Pisani, an epidemiologist who has worked in various parts of the world trying to reduce the spread of HIV/AIDS. She, too, describes the challenges posed by sociological research. Though she seems somewhat ambivalent about the "sociologist's toolkit," her methods fall squarely within the domain of sociological research. Pisani employs methods ranging from the more qualitative interviews to the more quantitative surveys. There is an ongoing debate within sociology as to which yields the most useful information. The work she describes in this part of her book, *The Wisdom of Whores*, is qualitative, quite informal, and not very systematic. But, she argues, it is necessary in order to lay the groundwork for the more quantitative and systematic aspect of her research.

Understanding the social forces that give rise to and affect deviance requires that we not only understand deviance in our own society in the present, we need also to understand deviance in other societies and in the past. Comparative and historical research, more often than not, involves the use of secondary data analysis. Secondary data is information that has been generated by someone other than the sociologist. Historical documents are used in the case of historical analysis and, in the case of cross-cultural analysis, data collected by various government agencies are often employed. In the next article, I describe the value as well as the limitations of cross-cultural and historical analysis in the study of deviance. I argue that certain sets of assumptions are being made when we employ official data as a measure of crime and deviance in a society and other assumptions are made when we employ such data as a measure of the behavior of the social control agencies that generate the data. In spite of these limitations and assumptions, I argue that cross-cultural and historical analysis has yielded a wealth of insights in the study of deviance and will continue to do so in the foreseeable future.

Reference

Robertson, Ian, *Sociology*, 3rd edition, New York: Worth Publishers, 1987.

11.
CAUGHT UP IN THE CULT WARS: CONFESSIONS OF A CANADIAN RESEARCHER

SUSAN J. PALMER

They are typically called "cults" by the media and the lay public. But sociologists call them New Religious Movements (or NRMs). "Cult" has taken on such negative connotations; the word conjures up images of mass suicide, mass murder, and brainwashed young adults following the mesmerizing commands of a religious fanatic drunk on power.

"New Religious Movement," on the other hand, is far more accurate and less subjective. It puts these religious organizations in their historical context. All of the major religions in the world today were once new, and their adherents were frequently seen as deviants—deluded zealots, mindlessly following the bidding of their fanatical leaders.

The following article describes some of the joys and tribulations of a sociologist who has dedicated her career to the study of deviant subcultures.

> "It would seem, Dr. Palmer, that you have acquired a bit of a reputation for being 'soft on the cults.' Are you indeed . . . a cult-lover?"
>
> —HIGH SOLICITOR

I was standing nervously in the carved oak witness box in the High Court, Lincoln's Inn in London, when the High Solicitor asked this question. It was in 1994, when I became embroiled in what the Children of God's lawyer described as "the longest and second most expensive custody battle in the history of the British Empire." I protested that I strove to be an objective, value-free social scientist when I studied new religions—but then admitted I also felt a sneaking aesthetic appreciation for "the cults." This made the judge smile, but it made me wonder are the two approaches really incompatible?

As a mature researcher, somewhat scarred from my forays into that embattled terrain known as the cult wars, I am now ready to make a confession. I do see myself as a *connoisseur*. For me, NRMs are beautiful life forms, mysterious and pulsating with charisma. Each "cult" is a mini-culture, a protocivilization. Prophets and heretics generate fantasy worlds that rival those of

Philip K. Dick or L. Frank Baum. When I venture into the thickets of wild home-grown spiritual-ity, and explore the rich undergrowth of what society rejects as its "weed" religions, I sometimes think of Dorothy's adventures in The Emerald City of Oz. Dorothy follows the yellow brick road that leads her through Utensia, a city whose inhabitants are kitchen utensils. Managing to escape King Kleaver (who threatens to chop her), she wanders into Bunbury where houses are made of crackers with bread-stick porches and wafer shingles and are inhabited by living buns with cur-rant eyes. She ventures on to meet the evil headless Scoodles, then continues on down the yellow brick road.

New religions are no less phantasmagorical. Immersed in the Oz books as a malingering schoolgirl, I wanted to "have adventures" when I grew up. My wish came true. Today I find myself in the not-quite-respectable, morally problematic, and impecunious field of "cult" studies. Travel-ling the "yellow brick road" of social scientific research, I encounter oddly coherent worldviews constructed higgledy-piggledy out of the most incongruous elements: songs of Solomon, UFO lore, electric bulbs, biofeedback machines, gnostic creation myths—all welded into one seamless syncretism. I drop in on dreams of Utopia and discover quaint communes like Puritan villages, the brothers and sisters marching to a tasteful percussion of Bible-thumping. I have felt trapped in nightmares—racist compounds, parodies of Paradise, Nietzchean dystopias.

Each new religion I encounter evokes in me a sense of awe not unlike what my art historian mother feels when she beholds Greek ruins, German cathedrals, or Renaissance paintings. I see heretical religions as "totems" or testaments—not necessarily of Ultimate Truth, but rather of the creative power of the collective human imagination. Their prophets I approach cautiously, and with respect, as artists of the most radically experimental sort: unpredictable conceptual artists at best, semi-opaque con artists at worst.

This approach seems to aggravate almost everybody; they find it frivolous, irresponsible. One Sufi lady at the Abode of the Messenger stopped me mid-interview and said accusingly, "You're not *really* interested in the spiritual path. I get the impression you have more of a *literary* interest in what we're doing!"

Another time I was effervescing on the sheer *fun* of researching NRMs when a psychologist at a lunchtime lecture for the psychologists at the Montreal General Hospital interrupted: "So I sup-pose you think it's fun and OK for groups like the Solar Temple to go around killing each other!" I was irritated, since I had just spent ten minutes explaining that each "cult" is different, and sta-tistics showed that only a tiny handful engaged in criminal acts, so I responded: "You must excuse me, I prepared this talk for the doctors; I didn't realize that the psychiatric patients would be invited here as well." I don't expect to be invited back.

When asked to define a cult, I explain that it is a baby religion. Personally, I find cults (and babies) attractive. Babies can be heartbreakingly adorable or intensely annoying, depending on the beholder's perspective—but also on the baby's mood and stage of development. So infant religions are not quite toilet-trained, like MOVE, a cult that annoyed neighbors by throwing gar-bage on the street; toddler NRMs, like the Rajneesh, run around naked in the park and knock over tea trays; and teenage missionary movements, like The Family, mooch off their parent society, refuse to get a job, and flaunt their pimply sexuality.

I have heard mothers excuse their obstreperous infants by saying, "It's only a *phase* he's going through!" (teething, bed-wetting, screaming). NRMs also go through phases, shutting out the surrounding culture to form their own identity. NRM scholars may sound like overindulgent mommies making excuses for their spoiled brats when they protest that communal experiments, sexual innovations, and apocalyptic expectations are merely developmental phases, and that society should grit its teeth and give these budding religions a chance to grow up.

Having confessed to singular tastes, perhaps I should explain how I got into "cult studies." My formal debut as a researcher of new religious movements commenced in the 1970s, when meditations—like 100 per cent cotton wear or silk—were Oriental imports, and most of my cool friends had already left for India to seek the right guru. At that time we were, of course, wary of false gurus who sold useless *sadhanas* (spiritual guidelines), or leched after American blondes, but the notion of the charismatic cult leader as obligatory pederast, oppressor of women, and designer of mass suicide had not yet been forged in the media.

Professor Fred Bird was my MA adviser at Concordia University when the department received a grant to study new religious movements in Montreal. I was one of four students hired as research assistants, and was actually paid $60 a week to choose a cult, spy on it, and write up field reports. When I look back on this period the word "halcyon" comes to mind; we researchers were light-hearted and naive, fancying ourselves spiritual PIs. We swapped bizarre anecdotes about our chosen groups and boasted of mild vicarious spiritual highs. As young, counter-cultural types we could easily pass as typical spiritual seekers and, indeed, that's what we were in our own wishy-washy ways.

Like many of my fellow scholars, I have been called a closet cultist. Perhaps there is a grain of truth to this allegation, for although I have never joined a group I've researched, I did start out hanging around meditation centers as a spiritual seeker, and only ended up in the microsociology of NRMs by default—as a failed meditator. I tried many systems, but never got the hang of it. I realize, of course, that the whole point is not to try to be "good" at meditating . . . but I kept trying.

So I began *doing* sociology of religion inadvertently, simply because I was bored with trying to concentrate on my mantra or third eye. Sitting in lotus posture at 4:00 A.M. on a scratchy grey woolen blanket in Swami Vishnu Devananda's quonset hut in Morin Heights, Quebec, I would peek around at my fellow meditators chanting "AUMMMMMM" and observe their subtle social interactions. Making beds and washing sheets, understood as karma yoga, I would question my fellow *chelas* regarding their conversions. At the visiting swamis' evening lectures, I paid more at-tention to the jocular rivalry between these shrewd old disciples of Swami Sivanada than I did to Hindu philosophy. Had I been able to make honest progress in my meditation practice, I would perhaps be living happily in the Himalayas—probably in Swami Shyam's Canadian enclave in Kulu—celibate, sattvic (pure), probably childless, my consciousness percolating up towards my seventh chakra.

Researching NRMs has its pleasures. I meet delightful people. I hear the intimate spiritual confessions of peaceful meditators, unselfish communalists, and disciplined ascetics. But there are disadvantages to taking on the public role of "cult scholar." Courted by the media as an off-beat academic who represents the "other view," TV stations have offered me free travel and luxuri-ous sojourns in Canadian Pacific Railway hotels; but then they edit my interview so I come across as a caricature of a misguided civil libertarian. In anticult circles I am dismissed as a naive dupe, or a closet cultist. In France my name has been listed with the other "revisionists" who deny atrocities *dans les sectes.* As for my Mormon relatives, they urge me to return to the fold lest I end up in the "telestial sphere."

Many cults also look askance at me. Grossed out by the social-scientific method and sick of a sociologist's depressingly secular scrutiny, leaders have denounced me to their disciples as a hireling of a corrupt society. A Rajneesh therapist warned the other "supermoms" not to give me interviews because "she's coming from her head, not from her heart." E. J. Gold (the gnostic guru whose declared mission is "the education of the universe, one idiot at a time"), upon reading my MA thesis (about him), reportedly said, "This lady has the consciousness of a rubber duck!" When I asked a barefoot missionary from the Free Daist Communion for an interview, she explained she must first collect all my writings and send them to Fiji to be vetted. "Do you mean *Da Free John* is going to read my articles?" I asked, thrilled. "Not exactly," she replied. "He *handles* them, and whatever wisdom they contain he absorbs through his fingertips." Da Free John never got back to me.

Excluded from Black Hebrew assemblies as a "leprous pale-eyed Amorite," shunned by the Asatru (racialist Druids) for looking "slightly Jewish," and dismissed by *les sectes Quebecois* as a *carré tête* (square-head or anglophone), I continue the struggle to present myself in such a way that my research attentions will be welcome. But what can be even more disconcerting is when I am besieged by groups *overly eager* to be studied, and subjected to that special kind of "love bombing" that is a product of what sociologist Roland Robertson dubbed philomandarinism: "Susan, we just *love* you! You're so *beautiful*—and so *objective*!" Aside from that sticky feeling of entering a fly-trap, I can foresee the day when they will all turn on me. In fifty years or so, after achieving the status of minority churches with the assistance of the dull ethnographics of academics like myself who function as alkaline neutralizers of the more acid anticult/media reports, these once controversial cults will loose their church historians on me and my peers, and they will condemn our careful writings—all because we tried to include reasonable but unflinching explanations for their bad news, and neglected to indulge in what my Mormon relatives call "faith-promoting incidents."

COVERT RESEARCHER—OR CLOSET CONVERT?

. . . [In some] ways my role as "cult scholar" impedes my research. The wide range of strange groups I have investigated appear in my books, and some straitlaced groups assume I must be immoral to hang out with the Rajneeshees, the Raelians, and The Family, whom they perceive as sinners and sex maniacs. Others feel a little queasy about my overly tolerant attitude towards atheistic or "heretical" groups who claim Jesus was a space alien, and wonder how I can bear to sit down and sup with a mystical pope or a vampire. I received a letter from a Krishna devotee complaining she felt "quite nauseous" that her interview appeared in the same book as a Moonie. Several core-group leaders have expressed jealousy and feelings of abandonment—that since I stopped researching their community I have flitted off to some silly UFO group that even I must realize does not possess the Truth.

When I meet young graduate students researching NRMs today, I envy them their freedom, their naive enthusiasm, their straightforward, unpoliticized curiosity. I recall how effortless it used to be to blend into a following. Even after declaring oneself a researcher, the response was often, "Oh well, you'll soon get over that!" I miss the intensity of real participant observation, the altered states, the grueling ordeals I was subjected to!

I recall how, in the late 70s, I was among a group of neo-gnostics who jumped out of a van at 8:15 A.M. in front of a suburban supermarket. We all wore skin-tight grey leotards, transparent plastic gloves, grey bathing caps, bare feet (painted grey)—and shaved-off eyebrows! We formed a huddle around our core group leader, who instructed us that we were all "hungry ghosts" and our mission was to enter the supermarket by following a customer through the revolving door— "Make sure you touch nothing. If any part of your body makes contact with anything or anybody, go back outside immediately and start over." Having fasted for three days we were hungry, but our exercise was to wander the aisles staring longingly at our favorite food, but to take nothing. After one hour we were meant to leave by shadowing a customer. We didn't last the hour, for one of the cashiers called the police. ("Who are all those weirdos?" we overheard the staff muttering. "They look like a biker gang . . . planning a robbery.") We leaped into the van and squealed off before the police arrived. We lay on the rusty floor, doubled up, holding onto each other as we lurched around corners, hysterical with laughter. The same group, a month before, had me crawling around a giant playpen wearing diapers, undershirt, and bonnet for an entire day, gurgling incoherently, sucking huge bottles of warm milk and playing with building blocks with my fellow "babies." Anticultists might be onto something when they claim an important stage of mind control is to "humiliate the victim" by "reinforcing childish behavior."

Today I am never invited to humiliate myself. I wear suits and shoulder pads and am taken on decorous tours, like visiting royalty. My eyebrows have grown in again, though they've never been quite the same!

Kai Erikson (1967: 373) has argued that "it is unethical for a sociologist to deliberately misrepresent his identity for the purpose of entering a private domain to which he is not eligible; and second, that it is unethical for a sociologist to deliberately misrepresent the character of the research in which he is engaged." I find it difficult not to misrepresent my identity, since most of my informants ignore my staunch protests that I am merely a dreary academic, a boring social scientist doing my job. They insist that, deep down, I am a lost soul desperately struggling towards the light. It is often counterproductive to protest too vigorously, so I just let them think I am on the brink of a conversion—and, indeed, part of me secretly hopes I am still capable of what C. S. Lewis called being "surprised by joy." . . .

WHY I DON'T CONSIDER MYSELF A "KEPT SCHOLAR"

In 1992 I received two grants to study children in new religions. I approached two different sects in Quebec and was refused permission to interview their members (they suspected I was a spy sent by the Catholic school board to undermine their home schooling). Then two international NRMs heard about me and called me up, offering plane tickets to "come on out and study our kids!" I turned them down. The situation made me nervous, for several reasons. First, I was concerned about preserving my "scholarly virginity." Second, I feared that if in the future I did not cooperate with their agenda, they might resort to blackmail (no doubt this is pure paranoia). Finally, I like to feel I am unhampered as a writer, free to poke fun at the group delicately if I feel like it, or mention stuff that is embarrassing. In short, I don't like being censored. I was aware that by choosing to study controversial child-rearing methods in NRMs, I would be vulnerable to criticism, but I didn't realize that I was stepping into the front line of a new battleground in the Cult Wars.

April 1994, I was standing in the witness box at the High Court, Family Division, in Lincoln's Inn to testify during the *Turle vs. Turle* custody battle over the grandson of a millionairess whose mother joined The Family. The same official solicitor who wanted to know if I were "soft on the cults" asked: "Who paid for your trip to San Diego to study The Family's home-school?" Fortunately I was able to respond: "I paid for it out of my SSSR grant"—and could have produced the receipts if necessary.

I have never accepted money from an NRM to study them, but I have had to make deals with leaders who have curtailed the areas I was allowed to go into, I have managed to preserve my scholarly virginity, but have engaged in mutual flattery and love-bombing, if not heavy petting (figuratively speaking), with charismatic leaders and their top aides. Personally, I don't know of any kept scholars in real life, but I am unsuited for the job since I prefer my NRMs wild and virgin. I seek out groups that are almost inaccessible and unselfconscious, groups that know they are not a cult, but I naively swallow what the newspapers say about other cults—groups that have never heard of the term NRM, groups that are suspicious of researchers and assume a sociologist is just a pretentious variety of journalist. Once they start sending out PR reps to conferences wearing suits, groomed hair, and name tags, they're no fun anymore. Well, that's not true. They can still be interesting, but suddenly they seem tame, almost domesticated. Other scholars horn in and conduct schmaltzy interviews in the hotel breakfast nook and arrange visits.

If NRMs are baby religions, scholarly conferences provide the venues to set up *petting zoos.*

A CONDOMINIUM ON THE OUTSKIRTS OF HEAVEN

I have been offered bribes, so I keep all my receipts and correspondence to make it more convenient to sue anyone who suggests my research efforts or opinions can be bought. But I never turn down otherworldly rewards. Three different apocalyptic sects have awarded me a sort of last-minute squeezed-in salvation when the cosmic countdown comes. "We want you to know you will be blessed when Our Saviour returns," a bearded elder told me. Technically I deserve to be consigned to eternal oblivion or fall into the pit amidst other soulless beer-swilling sinners, but I have been promised a condominium on the outskirts of Heaven, according to "The Chosen People." I have been assured by another "biblically based" group that I will be beamed up before Armageddon gets too nasty. I was informed that Da Free John (currently known as Adidam) "meditated me" long before I appeared on their scene. An infamous "cult leader" prophesied I was "one of the three wise women sent by God to assist the Prophet in opening the seventh seal at the end of time." One Raelian guide suggested I might be eligible for cloning when the extraterrestrials arrive. And if linear time is indeed an illusion, I can look forward to a better rebirth, according to a member of Hare Krishna who suggested that I am a devotee of Swami Prahupada "in my heart."

Oddly enough, these assurances make me feel more secure on airplanes when I travel to conferences. . . .

THE SOCIOLOGIST AS UNDERCOVER AGENT

Three months after the Solar Temple perpetrated their shocking mass suicide/homicide ritual "transit" to Sirius, I found myself in an office being grilled by two policemen from the Securité Quebec concerning my belated and rather tentative research efforts into this controversial and criminal order. They wanted me to hand over a list of the Templars or ex-Templars I had met or interviewed. (It was impossible to tell the difference since none of them would admit to a current affiliation.) I refused, saying that to reveal the names of one's informants contravened ethics in the social sciences. "Excuse me, Madame," said one official, "What is that?" It was difficult to explain. Finally the "good cop" in the tweed suit joked, "Be very careful, Madame. But, if you find yourself on Sirius, send us a postcard."

THE SOCIOLOGIST AS SOFT DEPROGRAMMER

I have noticed that the visit of a researcher is sometimes welcomed by NRM adherents as an opportunity for hedonism, a chance to gain access to luxuries and indulgences not normally available within the strict regimen of a commune or the work space of even the more secularized religious institutions. This particular ethical problem has never been identified or discussed in anticult circles, because they view cultists as obedient robots incapable of rebelling. In my experience, the brainwashed are quite capable of sneakiness, of pursuing their own individualistic whims or vices.

The kind of situation I am talking about has occurred quite often, where the people assigned to host me and facilitate my research *very* often suggest we go outside to a local bar or restaurant and order a drink or a meal. Somehow, many NRMs seemed to have gained the impression that most sociologists are borderline alcoholics. After one round of beers (paid for by the cult budget) they have suggested we order another round. The first time this happened I unthinkingly and selfishly said "No thanks," and then saw the anxious, disappointed looks on their faces. I realized this was perhaps their *only* opportunity to indulge in alcoholic beverages for the next few years, so I said, "OK, maybe I will," and paid for the second round. When I left half a glass, I noticed one of them swilled it down quickly as we got up to leave.

Since I privately feel many of the new religions I study are too strict and overly Spartan, I am inclined to collude with my interviewees and encourage their secret rebellions—which places me in a morally dubious position, since I genuinely respect their religious principles and realize the rules are based on sound economics or communal ideals of humility and equality—or necessary measures to avoid assimilation. It puts sociologists like me rather in the position of being a "soft deprogrammer"—by encouraging members to disobey leaders, break out of their conditioning, and place their own selfish desires before the group goals—perhaps the first tentative steps towards eventually leaving?

On one occasion I had arranged to spend a few days living with a rather puritanical, biblically based commune in order to interview members and study communal patterns. Two members in their forties, who had recently been given the exciting task of dealing with the public, picked me up in a car to drive me to the commune four hours away in the countryside. On the way they suggested we stop off at a beautiful hotel by a lake to get some refreshment and so that I could admire the prospect of the mountains. I agreed, still feeling jet-lagged. Upon our arrival at the hotel front desk it became clear they had booked rooms—one for the two women, and the other for the man. Then they turned to me and said, "Susan, you must be really tired with all your teaching and travelling, we thought it would be great for you if we all stayed here for three days. You could interview us, and catch up with your writing projects. We'll double up and give you the private room so you can work in peace." It became clear that their real agenda was to indulge a secret passion they had been harboring for years. It turned out their love affair had started years ago, but had been squelched by the leaders, and they had been encouraged to marry more suitable partners. I was not unsympathetic to their romance, and I could appreciate their need for a little holiday away from the crowded commune.

In this situation we find the sociologist-as-chaperone. The two would no doubt later report to their leaders: "Dr. Palmer *insisted* on stopping at a hotel for three days en route," and they probably had been instructed to indulge a decadent sociologist. I had no problem personally with facilitating their affair, except that I really *did* want to conduct as many interviews as possible and realized if the situation became public this would not be good for my rep: I would very much look like a jet-setting, kept scholar using research trips to enjoy luxurious holidays. So I had to play the priggish spoilsport and say no, although I sat by the lake and reviewed my notes while they went to the room to "rest from the drive." Thus sociologists can have a corrupting effect upon the morals of members.

THE REAL ETHICAL QUESTION: WHO GETS HURT BY WHOM?

. . . Scholars and researchers play an important role as educators in the global process of the pro-liferating new religious pluralism. Often they are the only go-betweens, the ones who have traversed that no man's land between the "cult" and "normal society." In this situation it is tempting to fancy oneself as a "freedom fighter" or a *deus ex machina* who advises cult leaders on how to get out of trouble.

I find myself torn between the need to educate and the desire to entertain. By highlighting spiritual weirdnesses I grab my students' attention and please journalists, but I undermine the groups' struggle for respect. It is only too easy to forget that cult members are human beings too, and that many have found happiness, learned social graces, received spiritual gifts participating in less than respectable religions.

Recently I invited a Knight of the Golden Lotus to speak to my class, after giving the students a rather unfeeling satirical sketch of the late leader's eccentricities. Our speaker appeared in the knights' orange and yellow garments, with mirrors fastened on his headband. His companion wore amulets of swans, rainbows, and mandalas pinned to her ample bosom. I stifled a smirk, and was feeling particularly frazzled—the VCR wasn't working and the audiovisual man refused to help, and he launched into a tirade on the college cutbacks that robbed him of his assistant. My daughter had refused to brush her hair before leaving for school, and my students were now behaving badly, lurching in late and babbling at the back. My Knight of the Golden Lotus stepped forward: "Please be quiet! We have come to present to you our religion and would appreciate respect." The students immediately calmed down and he launched into a fascinating lecture.

Afterwards, walking down the hall beside him, I reflected that, in spite of his leader's execrable taste in architecture, here was an admirable human being. His swift social responses had shown considerable insight and intelligence. I suspected that on this particular day his mental health was superior to my own. In fact, he'd put me in a good mood—perhaps an altered state?

LEARNING HOW TO NAVIGATE THE CULT WARS

All the evidence at hand points to a future filled with a dizzying abundance of ever-proliferating new religions. This phenomenon begs to be studied and offers stimulating hands-on research opportunities for young scholars. And yet, inexperienced and ambitious aspiring academics are likely to be deterred by a kind of miasma hovering around the field, a miasma arising from rumors and stereotypes as well as occasional errors and poor judgment on the part of NRM researchers. Will the young field researcher who wishes to write about the vampire subculture and its rituals hesitate to embark on this project lest she later find herself branded as a morbid blood-drinker once she becomes a famous sociologist? Young scholars may feel reluctant to embark on the study of NRMs like the Church Universal and Triumphant, the Unification Church and The Family, groups that in the past have been known to exhibit "philomandarin" tendencies—to eagerly court, and even pay, scholars to study them. These groups continue to mature, mutate, and institutionalize charisma in fascinating ways . . . but by associating with these groups, are young researchers compromising their most precious commodity: objectivity? Or, even more important, are they compromising their reputations as objective social scientists?

Paradoxically, there is pressure in the academy to steer clear of cults, but the news media exerts considerable pressure on scholars to comment on, and hence to study, the more controversial, outrageous, or dangerous groups—and these are precisely the areas of unpredictable pitfalls. What NRM scholar does not feel trepidation upon hearing the following cautionary, but true tales? (1) A Japanese professor who wrote an encyclopedia entry on Aum Shinrikyo, and whose graduate student was recruited into the movement, was fired by the university—the rationale being, if he knew his stuff he should have been able to recognize danger signals and warn the proper authorities; and (2) an Oregon high-school teacher was fired after inviting two sannyasis from Rajneeshpuram to talk to his class.[1]

Like Dorothy on the yellow brick road, young researchers will occasionally lose their barking "Totos" of objectivity. They will rely on their Cowardly Lions (academic caution) and rusty Tin Woodsmen (quantitative methods) as they wander off into the yet undreamt-of spiritual landscapes of the future. Perhaps in a few years it will be considered quite as respectable to receive research funding from NRMs as it is from the Vatican. Perhaps "religious minority" will have the same earnest ring to it as "sexual minority" or "women of color." The best advice I can offer to my students who aspire to spiritual espionage is this: Be open about what you're doing, don't apologize for mistakes, grow a rhinoceros-hide, but cultivate an empathetic ear for spiritual confessions.

DISCUSSION QUESTIONS

1. Palmer writes, ". . . New religions are no less phantasmagorical. Immersed in the Oz books as a malingering schoolgirl, I wanted to 'have adventures' when I grew up. My wish came true. Today I find myself in the not-quite-respectable, morally problematic, and impecunious field of 'cult' studies." Can you relate? Is there a deviant subgroup that would appeal to your research interests the way "cults" do for Palmer? (You might peruse this book for examples you find most fascinating, or choose a group altogether different from those discussed herein.)

2. Sociology has been referred to as a sort of "slow journalism." In the context of Palmer's research, describe what this means. List at least three different types of "audiences" that might be interested in the kind of work that she does and explain why they might be interested.

3. What are some of the ethical dilemmas described by Palmer? Are these dilemmas likely to compromise the value of her research? Do you think Palmer's prior personal interest in spiritual seeking and meditation is likely to compromise her research or enhance it?

NOTE

1. From *The Oregonian*, a special issue on Rajneeshpuram, August 1985.

REFERENCES

Barker, Eileen. 1996. "The Scientific Study of Religion? You Must Be Joking!" In *Cults in Context*, edited by Lorne L. Dawson, 5–27. Toronto: Canadian Scholars Press.

Baum, L. Frank. 1910. *The Emerald City of Oz*. Chicago: Reilly & Lee.

Erikson, Kai T. 1967. "A Comment on Disguised Observation in Sociology." *Social Problems* 14 (14): 367–73.

Palmer, Susan J. 1994. *Moon Sisters, Krishna Mothers, Rajneesh Lovers: Women's Roles in New Religions*. Syracuse, N.Y.: Syracuse University Press, 105–36.

Palmer, Susan J. 1995. "Women in the Raelian Movement." In *The Gods Have Landed: New Religions from Other Worlds*, edited by James R. Lewis. New York: SUNY.

Singer, Margaret Thaler, with Janja Lalich. 1995. *Cults in Our Midst: The Hidden Menace in Our Everyday Lives*. San Francisco: Jossey-Bass.

12.
SEX IN BOXES

ELIZABETH PISANI

An epidemiologist is a researcher who studies how diseases are transmitted in a society, who is likely to get them, and what conditions—environmental and social—facilitate their transmission. Elizabeth Pisani is an epidemiologist working on strategies to reduce the spread of HIV/AIDS among vulnerable (some would say "deviant") populations in Indonesia. She addresses the distinction between quantitative and qualitative research and notes how the two can complement each other in important ways. Quantitative research in the social sciences often involves surveys of large samples of people; but to know the right questions to ask on such a survey, deviance researchers often find it useful to first conduct qualitative research, asking one-on-one, often more intimate questions of a smaller sample of respondents.

In both the natural and the social sciences, scientific research usually requires the scientist to engage in some process of classifying her or his subjects or their behavior. Pisani discusses the classification difficulties she encountered in her research, especially in dealing with "waria," Indonesia's transgendered sex workers.

I sat in my little office in the grounds of the Ministry of Health; watching rotund civil servants fail to touch their toes in an enthusiastic Friday-morning exercise ritual. Inspired by the fluency of two of the three other foreigners in the Family Health International (FHI) office, I dredged up my Indonesian and went around meeting my new colleagues. There was the venerable Arwati Soepanto, a diminutive retired civil servant with a stern grey bun and a surprising giggle, who had an almost preternatural ability to coax action out of the sclerotic government system. She doled out quiet wisdom to the likes of Made Setiawan, a gangly Balinese research student with hair to his waist. Made set up one of Indonesia's first programs to help drug injectors, and his low opinion of the government was not improved when local officials persecuted the NGO's [nongovernmental organization's] staff. There was Ciptasari Prabawanti, who dressed with Muslim severity and hung out with prostitutes whose condom use she aimed to increase. Even the office janitor Jumiran was surprising—a middle-school dropout, he cheerfully emptied bins and made tea, then stayed late in the evenings, surreptitiously teaching himself software skills and chatting with me in English that he kept hidden from the rest of the staff for fear they would tease him for getting above himself.

Yes, there was plenty that was surprising. Most epidemiologists would rather avoid surprises—we prefer things to be logical. In Geneva, we had spent a lot of time trying to fit the HIV epidemic into an organizational chart of boxes and arrows. People are either in the sex worker box, for example, or the client box or the wife box. But Indonesia was never a country to fit into neat boxes of any sort. I had a hunch that the sex boxes would not be an exception.

Every surveillance cookbook I'd worked on started off with a health warning: don't launch into surveillance without doing "qualitative research" first. None of them actually had much to say about what qualitative research was, why you should do it, or how. But essentially, qualitative research is the step between "hunch" and "epidemiological study." It comes all wrapped up in jargon: key informant interviews, focus group discussions, semi-structured questionnaires. But it boils down to picking the brains of a handful of people who know more about a subject than you do. You try to find out how to reach the people you want to reach in your study, what sort of questions you should be asking them, what sort of language you should be using. If you do your qualitative research right, you'd know not to ask Indonesian rent boys about "sexual orientation" because most of them don't understand sociology-speak. You'd know that you shouldn't do research in brothels on Saturday nights because the owner is likely to be there and he doesn't want his girls disturbed. You'd know all sorts of things that would save you time and energy later on, when you draw up your questionnaires, take them out to tens of thousands of people, collect your surveillance data and try to understand what it means.

A lot of epidemiologists are snobby about qualitative research: it's for sociologists and other "soft" scientists. If you do it by the book it is time-consuming and expensive, and it produces information that can be dismissed with a wave of the hand: interesting, perhaps, but not statistically significant. Epidemiologists would much rather get stuck straight into the serious work of counting things.

I had at least one foot in the "qualitative research is for pussies" camp when I arrived in Indonesia. I could see that Indonesia's sexual landscapes are about as varied as its islands, its cultures, its languages. But in HIV surveillance we already had our cookbooks to hand, with our model questionnaires. We knew what questions we needed to answer—questions that would allow us to spit out indicators prefabricated in Geneva and Washington. And we'd been doing surveillance among sex workers and client groups in Indonesia for five years already. Couldn't we get on with counting things?

Not among waria, certainly. There wasn't even a model questionnaire for waria in the international surveillance cookbooks, and we knew almost nothing about their apparently heterosexual clients. Some "qualitative research" was going to be inescapable. We spent months setting up a study with the University of Indonesia, and we did it by the book, focus group discussions and all. It took forever, but it was worth it. One of the first people we spoke to was Fuad, a twenty-one-year-old lad who occasionally worked as a truck driver's assistant and who bought sex from waria. Fuad's girlfriend lived in Bandung, a university town in the cool hills east of Jakarta. Because his truck work was intermittent, he occasionally supplemented his income by giving blow-jobs or selling anal sex to men who cruised in one of Jakarta's few parks, outside the Finance Ministry beneath the bulging thighs of the monumental, bare-chested Papuan who was symbolically breaking free of the shackles of Dutch colonization. Sex with men was just a cash thing; Fuad was straight. To remind himself of that, he might occasionally want someone to give him a blow-job. But that's not something you can ask of a "nice girl"; Fuad shared a common perception that oral sex is insulting to women, including to female sex workers. So he went to a waria, also known less politely as *banci* (pronounced banchee).

"If I go to a banci, well, it's that I'm thinking of my girlfriend," Fuad told our research team. "I'm 100 per cent into women. Don't think that because I go to a banci I'm a fag. I'm not into that at all."

Fuad's girlfriend was doubtless a nice girl. She also worked the streets of Bandung at night. So here we have a self-proclaimed heterosexual guy who has unpaid sex with a woman who sells sex to other men, while himself also selling sex to other men and buying it from transgendered sex workers. He pushed a lot of the "high risk" buttons for HIV infection, yet he wasn't a female sex worker, a client, a drug injector, a gay man or a student. He didn't fit into a single one of our questionnaire boxes.

The truth is, real people don't have sex in boxes.

Fuad made me realize that counting numbers of partners and tracking condom use was not enough. If I was to make any sense of the "hard science," I was going to have to do a lot more to understand the landscapes of sex and drugs—who buys from whom, who else they have sex with, where they cruise, how they get high. It was to be a long journey, zigzagging back and forth between "hard" and "soft" research. But I also realized that you could get a lot of the information you needed without plodding through the sociologist's toolkit. With the exception of Fuad, most of my best guides were not respondents to surveys. They were the men, women and waria I chatted to in bars or brothels, on street corners or in cinemas, in offices and salons, in police stations, rehab centers and conference halls.

Tika, for example, a waria who sells sex along the train tracks in East Jakarta. Tika is not as complicated as Fuad, thank God. Like most waria, she only has sex with straight men.

"Sex with a homo? No thanks!" said Tika. "Homos" want to have sex with men, she explained, while waria want to be women. In fact, they *are* women, in their heads and in society. This answered one of the questions that worried at me in my first interactions with waria. In Indonesian, people commonly address one another using family terms: Bapak (father) and Ibu (mother) if the person you are talking to is older than you, Mas (brother) and Mbak (sister) if they're your age. Should I call Tika Mas or Mbak? I fudged, using the neutral term "anda" (you), but it felt really clumsy. As Tika told us about her "husband" of fifteen years, it became clear to me that she was a she, regardless of what lurked beneath her skirt. Tika cooks for her husband, washes his clothes, cleans the house. Feminists hold your breath; for Tika that life is the apogee of all that it means to be a Real Woman. Having said that, she still swans off to sell sex on the street whenever she feels like it. "It's where we see our friends, it's how we catch up on the gossip." Who's got a sale on stockings, where to get cheap silicone injections, is that cute new policeman any good at volleyball? (They'll find out at the weekly police vs. waria volleyball match behind the Grand Melia hotel.) Waiting for clients on a street corner is to a waria what going to a mall is to the average Jakarta teenager.

Is being a waria synonymous with selling sex on the streets? If yes, then all waria were probably at high risk for HIV. If no, then we needed to figure out who was selling sex and who wasn't, so that we could focus our HIV prevention efforts on those who needed the services most. To learn more, I went to have a quiet chat with Lenny Sugiharto, a doyenne of Jakarta's waria world, at her hair salon in a neat, working-class district of Jakarta. I got lost in the maze of alleys around her place, and was taken there by a man in a string vest and flip-flops who was bouncing a baby on his shoulder. The local community seemed quite happily to have absorbed a group of men living as women in their midst.

At Lenny's salon, behind careful lace curtains, I met Nancy, head of Jakarta's well-organized waria network. In its structure, the network mirrors the municipal government—a head and vice-head for each of the city's five major districts, and then an overall honcho. Compared with the Jakarta administration, however, the waria network operates at a stratospherically higher level of efficiency. That came in handy when we eventually set up the surveillance system for waria—the district health officers could contact their "counterparts" in the waria structure, who would set everything up for them.

Lenny was busy, so I put my question to Nancy. Do all waria sell sex? "It's not like we *have* to sell sex," she replied. "It's just that cruising is an important social activity for us. And, of course, we have super-charged libidos." In her polyester lilac trouser-suit, amethyst necklace and matching *jilbab* (the Islamic headscarf that was rapidly becoming de rigueur among Indonesian ladies of a certain age), Jakarta's Head Waria would fit right into a Women's Institute meeting. For the last eighteen years, she's been employed by Jakarta's Department of Social Affairs to teach hairdressing and catering skills to fellow waria as a way of enticing them out of sex work. I half expected her to start discussing her favorite recipe for jam tart. But here she was, talking dirty. "It's less about the money than about the orgasms," she said. "Let's face it, we're all human, we've got to get laid." She told me she made it her business to get laid at least once a week. She'll still take money for it if she can (which gave her catering classes the sheen of "do as I say, not as I do") but unpaid is fine too. "What fun is life without orgasms?" she laughed. At the time, Nancy was teetering on the edge of 60.

Nancy was furiously opposed to the new fashion for sex change operations among waria, which she put down, quite simply, to showing off. Not breasts of course—all waria have those these days. But the full-on "op." Indonesia's surgeons are not up to scratch in terms of the removal of the penis and testicles and the fashioning of a false vagina, so the destination of choice for sex change operations is Thailand, just a three-hour flight north. Thailand has been trying to rid itself of a reputation for sex tourism; its in-flight magazines now overflow with ads for medical services for visitors instead. Walk past the Starbucks in the towering atrium of Bangkok's Bumrungrad Hospital and take a gleaming escalator to the third floor, and you'll find the International Medical Centre, a United Nations of smiling nurses and interpreters eager to help you figure out how much money you could save by stocking up on treatment here, rather than at your home-town hospital. Lead competitor Bangkok Hospital boasts a website which declares, "Feel the new sensation of life at Sex Change Clinic Bangkok Hospital" in ten languages. If you don't get the message, the hospital can provide interpreters in a further sixteen.

Both of these hospitals rise out of alleyways crowded with tawdry girlie bars that speak of the earlier tourist industry specialization. Indonesian waria can pile aboard a budget flight to Bangkok and turn a few tricks while waiting for their operation. At around US$6,000, a sex change operation is not exactly a snip. Nancy believes it is a way of signaling to clients that a waria has been a success in a high-paying market like Singapore or in the shadows of the Bois de Boulogne, on the outskirts of Paris. "They come home and stand on the side of the road, not even wearing any underwear, and flash their new pussies at passing cars. It is just showing off. Money and ego is what it is," she growls. For all the Women's Institute niceties, I'm suddenly aware that it would be no fun being on the wrong side of Nancy in a roadside negotiation.

Emerge after midnight from Jakarta's stylish Four Seasons Hotel and you'll see what Nancy means. As you step into the miasma rising off the nearby reservoir you'll be assaulted first by the smell, sour, fetid, heavy with the slough of the millions who scratch out lives alongside the city's waterways. Then come the rats, scuttling purposefully over the moonlit skeletons of daytime food stalls. Finally, as you reach the waste land where miasma meets highway, you'll come across Lydia or Regina, Olive or Baby—perhaps all of them. Most waria go for the classic "Russian hooker" look—the black PVC skirts stretched tight over the fishnet stockings, plunging into the red patent-leather boots. They'll thrust their butt out to the left, dangle their cute imitation Chanel purse to the right—the pose will show off the new breast implants as well as helping them balance on those vertiginous heels.

There's always a lot of flicking of hairdos and endless public display of lip gloss. There are two types of interaction with the slowly cruising cars that hold the lusty, the unfulfilled or the just plain curious. One is a nonchalant disregard; the "girls" chat with one another and feign mild annoyance at being interrupted by guys wanting to negotiate for their services. "I don't need you that badly, so you'd better make it worth my while" is the sales message projected by this crew. The other approach is more brazen—glittering gowns are thrown open as a car crawls up; the full panoply of wares put on display. This sales pitch is favored by those who have invested their savings in "the snip." "Soooooo over the top," sulked Nancy. She herself would never trade orgasms for an operation, she says, but I can't help feeling she's a tiny bit jealous.

Lenny, who was putting on her make-up while Nancy pontificated, laughed. Lenny is not thrilled that the Department of Social Affairs has tossed her, along with all waria, into a box marked "mentally disabled." But she had to agree with "over the top." Lenny had organized a group that was lobbying for equal rights for waria. She interrupted her face-paint ritual to tell of a recent meeting with a parliamentary subcommittee. "We're in the national parliament asking to be taken seriously as a community, and I see that two of the girls are missing. I send someone off to look for them and guess what? They're screwing the security guards in the bathroom." She shook her head in disbelief and went back to her mascara.

Nancy perked up again at the tale. She had reported the miscreants to their *mami,* the long-established cell mothers who oversee the younger waria. "They beat the shit out of them," she said, with visible satisfaction. "No respect, that's the trouble with youngsters these days, no respect."

I had first met Lenny sitting quietly in her *jilbab* and red lipstick during the first planning meeting for the qualitative research among waria and their clients in 2001. Or at least I thought that was when I first met her. But as we spent more time together and started to gossip about our lives, I learned that we had actually known one another since the late 1980s. We were both in different incarnations then; I was a tearabout journalist and Lenny was Mr. Eko, the manager of one of my favorite Jakarta restaurants. In fact, he had helped me organize my farewell dinner when I left Jakarta the first time around. Lenny had a diploma in hotel studies, and had worked in the Mandarin Oriental and other posh hotels in Jakarta and Bali before becoming a restaurant manager. It was a solid career path, but it didn't suit Lenny. She'd turn up to work in her white jacket, assert her authority as Mr. Eko all day, then get picked up after work by her "husband," perching in a ladylike side-saddle on the back of his motorbike. "There I was, Mr. Eko, taking injections," she waved vaguely at her breasts, "being picked up from work by my husband like all the ladies. It just didn't add up." She quit her job and floated into life as a waria, opening a salon, organizing fellow waria, and eventually becoming a stalwart of our research team.

We followed up the qualitative research with a solid survey of syphilis and HIV among waria in 2002. The outcome set Lenny on yet another course. When the lab technician first handed me the test results from that survey, with the positives highlighted in red, I was stunned. For the first and so far only time in my career as a researcher, I felt hot, salty water brimming from my eyes. These tests came from the waria that we'd been teasing, discussing film stars with, playing agony aunt to. One in four of them was infected with a fatal virus, one in four would be dead within a decade, at best, unless we could get them treatment. We'd expected to find some HIV, of course, but nothing like this. When you calculate the number of people you need to include in a study, you have to make assumptions about how much disease you'll find. I'd assumed a worst case scenario of 10 per cent prevalence. Here I was looking at more than twice that. I think I cried as much from the shock of it as anything.

Lenny had been planning to set up an NGO to provide "IEC" to waria. That's AIDS industry jargon for "information, education and communication"—essentially telling people how AIDS is spread and how to avoid it. She had applied to FHI for funding. But as soon as we saw the study results she rewrote the application. It was too late for prevention alone. Waria were going to need doctors, drugs, carers. They also clearly needed treatment for other STIs—close to half of the waria in the study had syphilis. It would be tricky because the current health system forced waria into men's wards. That didn't go down well with people who thought of themselves as women.

On a visit to Jakarta several years later, I dropped by for a gossip with Lenny. She counted off the latest test results—of eleven waria who had drifted into town from the outer islands of Sumatra and faraway Maluku in the previous few weeks, eight had tested positive for HIV. "And three of my girls have died since last Sunday. Not a great week." Lenny doesn't even bother to say what they died of. These days, waria don't seem to die of anything but AIDS.

These very high infection rates have important implications for clients, obviously. Not least because some of the men who buy sex from waria say they do it because they want to reduce their exposure to female sex workers, who they think have AIDS. In fact, a waria is between ten and twenty times more likely to be infected with HIV than a female sex worker in Jakarta, and the discrepancy is even greater in other cities.

One of the reasons that so many waria are infected with HIV is that they are often the receptive partner in anal sex, the "bottom." Of all sexual practices, receptive anal sex is the one most likely to lead to a new HIV infection, assuming that the insertive partner, the "top," is himself infected. Waria get HIV from their clients—the men we were completely ignoring in the national HIV estimates. We had assumed that these men were always the "tops." But it turned out that nearly a third of waria had been paid to be top while the clients took the bottom role. In Nancy's view, this role swapping is another strike against sex change operations. Bad enough that they deprive you of orgasms. But they also deprive you of business, because without your equipment, you'll lose out on any client who wants to be bottom for a change. I didn't say this to Nancy, but I was pretty happy about that. One of the reasons that HIV spreads more quickly in anal sex between men than in any other type of sex is because men can switch roles. People who act as a bottom are highly likely to get infected in anal sex, regardless of their gender. If they have the equipment and the desire to act as top as well, they are highly likely to pass on that infection. Nancy may think sex change operations are bad for business, but they are actually good for slowing the HIV epidemic.

There was so much to try and understand just within the world of waria and their clients. But that was only one feature of the sexual landscape of Indonesia. It was just as important to try to understand how that little corner fed into the broader panorama. We learned from Fuad, the straight rent boy with the female sex worker girlfriend, that guys who buy sex from waria can be eclectic in their taste for partners. When we got around to counting, we found that over 60 per cent of men who said they bought sex from waria were married, and roughly the same proportion said they had casual girlfriends. Fully 80 per cent of clients of waria said they also bought sex from women, real women with two X chromosomes. . . .

Bit by bit, I began to understand that we'd have to work towards a surveillance system that took people out of the neat boxes we had wanted to squish people into in Geneva: "male prostitute," "drug injector," "client of female sex worker." A system that at the very least redrew the boxes as overlapping circles, a great Venn diagram of sex and drugs, desires and needs, hormones and money.

DISCUSSION QUESTIONS

1. Explain the title of this section and discuss the methodological issues involved in Pisani's research.
2. What do you think of the kind of work Pisani does? Can you imagine yourself doing it? What would be the biggest risks and rewards for you?

13.
CROSS-CULTURAL AND HISTORICAL METHODOLOGY

ROBERT HEINER

This book, *Deviance Across Cultures*, is based on the assumption that people can learn something about deviance in their own country by studying deviance in other countries. It assumes that there are certain universals in the sociology of deviance. There are also marked differences between countries when it comes to definitions and reactions to deviance. A fuller understanding of deviance requires an appreciation for both the universals and the differences and that can come only from a comparativist, or cross-cultural approach, such as the one taken in this book.

However, the comparative study of deviance is fraught with ideological assumptions along with formidable methodological complications. These are briefly delineated in this selection. I also discuss the value of such an approach and conclude with some notes about the future of comparative inquiry in the study of deviance.

Crime is present not only in the majority of societies of one particular species but in all societies of all types. There is no society that is not confronted with the problem of criminality. Its form changes; the acts thus characterized are not the same everywhere; but, everywhere and always, there have been men who have behaved in such a way as to draw upon themselves penal repression.

(DURKHEIM, 1938: 65)

The above passage could well be the most definitive, most often reprinted, comparative statement in the sociology of deviance. Writing in his classic *The Rules of the Sociological Method* (originally published in 1895), Durkheim provides the basis for the functionalist approach to the understanding of deviance, arguing that since crime occurs in all societies and always has occurred in all societies, it should be regarded as a normal phenomenon and not as an indicator of social pathology. The basis of his assertion is both cross-cultural ("all societies") and historical ("always"). Interestingly, this statement is not based on systematically acquired empirical data, yet few have challenged its validity.

A couple of years after the publication of *The Rules of the Sociological Method*, Durkheim published *Suicide* (1897). This book, like so many of Durkheim's works, became a classic in sociology, serving as a model of data-driven comparative research. Using secondary data collected in many countries, Durkheim concludes that suicide rates are directly affected by the degree to which a society fosters the integration of its individual members. Namely, suicide rates are high in societies that do not effectively integrate individuals into group affiliations *and* in societies that are overly effective in integrating individuals into groups. In the former, individuals are isolated and lack social support. In the latter, individuals are overcommitted to the group and may sacrifice themselves for the sake of the group (Durkheim, 1951).

THE COMPARATIVE METHOD

A discussion of the comparative method begins with the recognition that virtually all scientific methods employ comparisons: the comparison of fossils formed in one geo-historical period to those formed in another; the comparison of different chemical combinations mixed in differing amounts; the comparison of the ability of a mouse who has received repeated rewards to go through a maze to the ability of one who has not been rewarded; and so on.

In the social sciences, the comparative method usually refers to the comparison of data pertaining to different cultures or to different historical periods. (Historical and cross-cultural research are similar in that comparing different historical periods is essentially the same as comparing different cultures, given that cultures change over time.) Comparative methods are useful, some would argue necessary, in testing the validity of a social theory or the limits of its application. More specifically, "The goal of comparative [research]," write Clinard and Abbott (1973: 2), "should be to develop concepts and generalizations at a level that distinguishes between universals applicable to all societies and unique characteristics representative of one or a small set of societies."

There are, however, two important caveats relevant to our discussion of deviance. First, while there is a great deal of literature on deviance in the past and in cultures around the world, and while there are volumes upon volumes written on sociological methods, a literature on cross-cultural and historical methods specific to the sociology of deviance is relatively spare. Second, one of the most often repeated caveats in the literature on both historical and cross-cultural methods in the social sciences concerns the difficulty (or impossibility) of obtaining reliable, comparable data from the past and from other cultures. Depending on how one looks at it, this latter caveat either applies especially to the study of deviance or it applies not at all—because the data on deviance have always been notoriously flawed in all cultures in all time periods, if only because those who engage in deviant behavior actively try to keep it secret.

Criminologists have long recognized that official crime statistics *within* a given country are problematic; *cross-cultural* comparisons of criminological data are even more problematic. Marvin Wolfgang (1967: 65) summed up the problems as involving "cultural variations in the definition of crime, sentiments of severity, degrees of reportability, probabilities of discovery, types of penalties, and the methods of collecting criminal statistics." When it comes to "deviance," a broader category which includes both criminal and non-criminal behaviors, cross-cultural comparisons become all the more problematic.

Just as researchers in the United States have tried to circumvent the pitfalls of official statistics by using self-report surveys, the same has been done in cross-cultural research. For example,

Vazsonyi and his colleagues (2001) measured the "lifetime deviance" of several thousand adolescents in Hungary, the Netherlands, Switzerland, and the United States using the Normative Deviance Scale. The NDS was designed to measure deviant behaviors that are "independent of penal code and legal definitions" (p. 104) and includes behaviors related to vandalism, alcohol use, drug use, school misconduct, general deviance, theft, and assault. But, while measures included in the NDS are certainly better separated from legal definitions and the biases of social control agents than official statistics, they are still dependent on culturally specific norms and values. For example, several of the items included in the scale deal with drinking alcohol under the age of twenty-one. No matter what the drinking age is in the countries surveyed, such behavior is likely to be more deviant in one country than in another and perhaps not at all deviant in another.

CROSS-CULTURAL METHODS

It is perhaps more so with cross-cultural research than other methodologies that one can see how theory informs method as much as method informs theory. Quantitative cross-cultural studies almost always begin with the obligatory warning that one cannot assume that definitions and measurements are consistent across cultures and then they proceed to use and compare official data from a variety of societies. Most often, they work from a consensus model arguing that there is near-universal condemnation, at least, for certain criminal offenses. These offenses have been called "moral minima" (Scott and Zatz, 1981) and those working from the consensus model argue that while there may be some variation in how these offenses are defined and how the law is applied to such cases, there is not enough variation to invalidate the use of cross-cultural data. Homicide is often taken to be such an offense. In his book *Comparative Deviance: Perceptions and Law in Six Cultures* (1976), Graeme Newman, for example, found strong consensus (disapproval) among survey respondents in India, Indonesia, Iran, Italy, the United States, and Yugoslavia for the acts of robbery and the misappropriation of public funds. Disapproval rates were well above 90 percent in all of these countries. These offenses, then, might also be considered moral minima. Contrary, perhaps, to popular expectations, incest did not reach this threshold because in the New York sample "the proportion disapproving it was down to 75 percent" (Newman, 1976: 113). The exceptionality of New York leaves it an unexplained outlier or calls into question the survey results.

Conflict theorists often take strong exception to the use of official data in the conduct of cross-cultural research, arguing that one cannot assume a consensus with regard to deviance and crime—not even in one's own society, let alone in other societies. They hold that definitions of crime and the application of the law reflect elite interests and how power is distributed in a society. "[W]hen particular kinds of strife become issues of elite or general concern," write Gurr and his colleagues, "a typical response is the passage of laws that criminalize some of the behaviors in question" (Gurr *et al.*, 1977: 753). For example, while Newman (1976) identified near-universal disapproval of the misappropriation of funds in his survey research, since this could be seen as a political crime, it could be that his results may have depended on the timing of the survey and the shifting political winds in one or more countries. (After all, a significant drop in disapproval in only one country would negate the consensus.) That is, the misappropriation of public funds is likely to become the object of public scorn when one regime is losing its grip on power and another is angling to take its place. Thus, the supposed consensus regarding the act would be a temporal reflection of the struggle for power between two or more groups.

The consensus theorist believes that official statistics are generated by the deviant acts of individuals and, therefore, are reflective of the incidence of such behavior in a society; conflict theorists believe them to be a reflection of economic and political conflict in a society. When conflict theorists do use official data, they use them as indicators of the activities of the police, the courts and the prisons. For the conflict theorist, the data do not reflect the kinds of deviance that are being committed in a population; instead, they reflect the activities of social control agents and/or the types of people who are being processed by the criminal justice system. Seeing, for example, that more than half of the prisoners in the United States are racial and ethnic minorities (Bureau of Justice Statistics, 2003) and that immigrants make up more than half the prison population in the Netherlands (Heiner, 2005), the conflict theorist might conclude that prisons are a tool of oppression in these two societies, while the consensus theorist might conclude that minorities commit most of the serious crime in these societies.

Discussions of consensus and conflict perspectives take place within the realm of sociology. Then, of course, there is the work of anthropologists who have contributed enormously to the body of literature on cross-cultural deviance. It is largely their work over the past century or more that has sparked the public imagination with the cultural variability of human behavior. The works of Ruth Benedict and Margaret Mead drew attention to the variability of sexual practices in different parts of the world and encouraged tolerance of practices considered deviant in our own culture. In 1951, *Patterns of Sexual Behavior,* a classic work by Clellan Ford and Frank Beach (1972), catalogued the sexual practices of 190 preindustrial societies (plus those of the United States) using the Human Relations Area Files. Such works effectively challenge prevailing notions about supposed natural sexual behaviors and deviant sexual behaviors. Perceptions of the difference between "natural" and "deviant" behavior, accordingly, are almost always the product of culture. Ford and Beach (1972: 250) conclude,

> One essential way of looking at the evidence involves the achievement of a cross-cultural perspective. Only in this manner can the behavior of men and women in any given society be compared and contrasted with the peoples belonging to quite different societies. The results of our cross-cultural analysis emphasize the important fact that the members of no one society can safely be regarded as "representative" of the human race as a whole.

HISTORICAL METHODS

Historical research is quite similar to cross-cultural research in that it involves the examination of a culture different from the investigator's own—that is, the culture of the past. Historical research may or may not be comparative, depending on whether data are compared over a number of periods of time; if not, they are more appropriately considered case studies (Jones, 1985). Historical investigators often encounter similar problems to those of the cross-cultural researcher as regards the reliability and comparability of data.

Historical research in deviance often yields considerable insight into the nature of social control. One of the best-known examples of such research is Kai Erikson's *Wayward Puritans* (1966). Using mostly older published histories, journals, and documentary evidence, including court records, Erikson reconstructed patterns of social control among the Puritans of Massachusetts in the 17th century to develop his theory of the societal functions of deviance, a theory inspired by Durkheim's assertion some seventy years earlier that "crime is an integral part of all healthy societies" (*The Rules of the Sociological Method*, quoted by Erikson, 1966: 3). Accordingly, a healthy community is one that proudly identifies itself as a community that is morally distinct from other communities. Deviance enables the community to establish and publicize the moral boundaries that distinguish it from other communities. "Deviant persons," Ericson writes, "often supply an important service by patrolling the outer edges of group space and by providing a contrast which gives the rest of the community some sense of their own territorial identity" (p. 196).

Another fine example of historical research in social control is David Musto's *The American Disease: Origins of Narcotic Control* (1987). Using an extensive array of historical documents, legislative records, court records, and the personal papers of people connected to various drug control efforts, Musto reveals a number of important insights into the evolution of drug control in American society. He deftly demonstrates a good deal of disingenuousness behind many historical efforts to control drug use, with those behind such efforts motivated less by concerns about public health or even public morality than by concerns about furthering more personal or political agendas. Most notably, a common thread behind most of the more significant drug control efforts in the United States has been racism and/or xenophobia. Musto (1987: 244) writes,

> The most passionate support for legal prohibition of narcotics has been associated with fear of a given drug's effect on a specific minority. Certain drugs were dreaded because they seemed to undermine essential social restrictions which kept these groups under control: cocaine was supposed to enable blacks to withstand bullets which would kill normal persons and to stimulate sexual assault. Fear that smoking opium facilitated sexual contact between Chinese and white Americans was also a factor in its total prohibition. Chicanos in the Southwest were believed to be incited to violence by smoking marijuana. Heroin was linked in the 1920s with a turbulent age group: adolescents in reckless and promiscuous urban gangs. Alcohol was associated with immigrants crowding into large and corrupt cities. In each instance, use of a particular drug was attributed to an identifiable and threatening minority group.

As regards alcohol control and urban immigrants, Musto confirms the earlier historical analysis by Joseph Gusfield (1963); and analogous conclusions regarding the control of marijuana and Chicanos were derived in the historical work of Richard Bonnie and Charles Whitebread (1974). These and similar historical analyses of drug control reflect a conflict perspective and challenge the popularly held consensus view that certain drugs are illegal because they are inherently wrong or injurious to the user or society.

Those interested in the application of historical methods to the study of deviance might also be interested in a number of treatises on the history of modes of perceiving deviance—both inside and outside the ivory tower. Anne Hendershott's *The Politics of Deviance* (2002), for example, examines fluctuations in definitions of deviance and reactions to deviance since the 1960s, and the cultural and political forces that explain these fluctuations. In *Deviance: Career of a Concept* (2004), Joel Best traces the career of the study of deviance, beginning with the "predecessors" in the study of deviance proper (Durkheim and Merton), proceeding to a discussion of the powerful emphasis on labeling theory in the 1960s and early 1970s, and then to the vigorous attacks on labeling theory in subsequent years. Best also describes the convergence and conflict between the studies of deviance and of crime. Both Hendershott and Best contest the claim that the study of deviance is "dead." Best concludes that, though it is not dead, the field lacks agreement on definitions of deviance and domains of study and is, therefore, too fragmented and in need of revitalization. He writes (Best, 2004: 85),

> The initial focus on crime, mental illness, drug abuse, and sexual misbehavior was soon extended to include disabilities, obesity, nudism, cult membership, red hair and all manner of other phenomena that had relatively little in common with one another except, as the labeling theorists suggested, some degree of social disapproval. . . . No wonder, then, that the field of deviance became fragmented.

FUTURE DIRECTIONS IN COMPARATIVE RESEARCH

Despite the sometimes fragmented research in the study of deviance, globalization perhaps offers the opportunity for the revitalization of the field that is called for by Best. These are interesting times for comparativists and it is likely that there will be more work emerging in cross-cultural research in the coming decades. Research in transnational crime is increasing and will certainly continue to do so. Globalization has made national borders less relevant and, for some crimes, it has become increasingly difficult to establish the country in which they originated (Beirne and Messerschmitt, 2006). The internet has provided pathways for a host of crimes and deviant indulgences that know no national boundaries, including money laundering, fraud, pornography, and sabotage. Crimes are frequently committed that fall within the jurisdictions of several countries. (In the case of child pornography, for example, law enforcement authorities occasionally conduct coordinated international sting operations.) Thorsten Sellin (1938) identified the problem of culture conflict which was especially relevant in the wake of massive immigration to the United States in the early twentieth century and has become relevant again with recent waves of immigration and the influx of refugees in countries throughout the world. And the drug trade, in particular, is notorious for its lack of respect for national boundaries. The market for illegal drugs in the United States, for example, has led to widespread violence in Mexico, some of which spills back into the United States. As with commerce, international boundaries are becoming less relevant when it comes to crime and deviance.

Another effect of globalization has been the homogenization of cultures. Cultures are becoming less distinct. Smaller pre-industrial cultures are being assimilated or overrun by larger, more "modern" cultures in the latter's efforts to expropriate their land and natural resources. Another homogenizing influence has been the proliferation of Western culture and values largely through the media and the export of popular culture. These processes have implications for the construction of deviant categories throughout the world. For example, what Westerners would consider "lesbian" relations have been common, perhaps even normative, among women in Lesotho; but because no penis was involved, local women did not consider these relations "sexual" and, therefore, not as lesbian or deviant. Limakatso Kendall, however, reports the non-deviant status of this behavior is changing as the people of Lesotho become increasingly exposed to Western culture. "I believe that one pressure leading to the demise of batsoalle [the "special friends" relationship] is the increasing Westernization of Lesotho and the arrival, at least in the urban and semi-urban areas and the middle class, of the social construction of 'homophobia' with and without its name" (Kendall, 2008: 104). It is quite possible, even likely, that globalization is similarly affecting deviant categories in cultures throughout the world. The changes—in terms of the types of behavior considered deviant, the frequency of deviance, and the application of sanctions—could be profound and the subject is ripe for investigation by students of deviance.

CONCLUSIONS

Cross-cultural and historical research in deviance is fraught with methodological peril, but considerable knowledge and insight have been derived from these methods. Separately and together, cross-cultural and historical methods have added invaluable breadth to the body of knowledge on deviance. They allow us to understand and appreciate the diversity of human behavior as well as its cultural and historical relativity. They have provided us with tools for better understanding the human condition and allow us to challenge conventional wisdom. They both provide an invaluable aid in understanding the social forces that influence the construction of deviant categories. And popularly held beliefs about deviant behavior being inherently wrong, harmful or offensive have been and will continue to be put to the test by cross-cultural and historical research.

DISCUSSION QUESTIONS

1. According to this article, how do the consensus model and the conflict model differ in their interpretation of official crime statistics?
2. What problems do sociologists face when interpreting cross-cultural data pertaining to crime and deviance?

REFERENCES

Beirne, Piers and James W. Messerschmitt, *Criminology* (4th ed). Los Angeles: Roxbury, 2006.

Best, Joel, *Deviance: Career of a Concept.* Belmont, CA: Wadsworth, 2004.

Bonnie, Richard J. and Charles H. Whitebread, *The Marihuana Conviction: A History of Marihuana Prohibition in the United States.* Charlottesville: University of Virginia Press, 1974.

Bureau of Justice Statistics, "Table 6.34: Prisoners in Federal, State, and Private Adult Correctional Facilities," in *Sourcebook of Criminal Justice Statistics.* Washington, DC: US Department of Justice, 2003. Available at: www.albany.edu/sourcebook/pdf/t634.pdf.

Clinard, Marshall B. and Daniel J. Abbott, *Crime in Developing Countries: A Comparative Perspective.* New York: John Wiley, 1973.

Durkheim, Emile, *The Rules of the Sociological Method,* translated by S. Soloway and J. H. Mueller, edited by G. Catlin. Chicago: University of Chicago Press, 1938 [originally published 1895].

Durkheim, Emile, *Suicide: A Study in Sociology,* translated by J. Spaulding and G. Simpson. New York: Free Press, 1951 [originally published 1897].

Erikson, Kai T., *Wayward Puritans: A Study in the Sociology of Deviance.* New York: John Wiley, 1966.

Ford, Clellan S. and Frank A. Beach, *Patterns of Sexual Behavior.* New York: Harper and Row, 1972 [originally published 1951].

Gurr, Ted Robert, Peter N. Graboski and Richard C. Hula, *The Politics of Crime and Conflict: A Comparative History of Four Cities.* Beverly Hills: Sage, 1977.

Gusfield, Joseph, *Symbolic Crusade: Status Politics and the American Temperance Movement.* Urbana: University of Illinois Press, 1963.

Heiner, Robert, "The Growth of Incarceration in the Netherlands," *Federal Sentencing Reporter,* vol. 17, no. 3, February 2005, pp. 227–230.

Hendershott, Anne, *The Politics of Deviance.* San Francisco: Encounter Books, 2002.

Jones, T. Anthony, "The Evolution of Crime in Pre-industrial Society," in *Comparative Social Research: Deviance,* R. F. Tomasson, ed. Greenwich, CT: JAI Press, 1985.

Kendall, K. Limokatso, "Women in Lesotho and the (Western) Construction of Homophobia," in *Deviance across Cultures,* R. Heiner, ed. New York: Oxford University Press, 2008.

Musto, David F., *The American Disease: Origins of Narcotic Control* (expanded ed.). New York: Oxford University Press, 1987 [originally published 1973].

Newman, Graeme, *Comparative Deviance: Perception and Law in Six Cultures.* New York: Elsevier, 1976.

Scott, Carolyn and Marjorie S. Zatz, "Comparative Deviance and Criminology," *International Journal of Comparative Sociology,* vol. 12, nos. 3–4, 1981, pp. 237–256.

Sellin, Thorsten, *Culture Conflict and Crime.* Bulletin No. 41. New York: Social Science Research Council, 1938.

Vazsonyi, Alexander, Lloyd Pickering, Marianne Junger and Dick Hessing, "An Empirical Test of a General Theory of Crime: Comparative Study of Self-Control and the Prediction of Deviance," *Journal of Research in Crime and Delinquency,* vol. 38, no. 2, May 2001, pp. 91–131.

Wolfgang, Marvin E., "International Criminal Statistics: A Proposal," *Journal of Criminal Law, Criminology and Police Science,* vol. 58, no. 1, 1967, pp. 65–69.

MORAL PANICS

Introduction

Before the fifteenth century, judicial executions of "witches" were relatively rare; but in the following two centuries, hundreds of thousands of people were executed in continental Europe, having been accused of being witches. In 1930, only sixteen of the states in the United States legally banned marijuana; but by 1937, all of the states had implemented such a ban (Goode and Ben-Yehuda, 1994). Before the 1980s, the media paid little attention to serial murderers and few among the public were concerned about the threat that they posed; but in the 1980s and early 1990s, serial murderers were all over the news; they pervaded popular literature and the movies; children were taught to fear strangers; many of the parents who used to let their kids play outside unsupervised stopped doing so; and some had their kids fingerprinted just in case they would ever need to identify their remains. These and events like these often follow in the wake of what are identified in the literature as "moral panics."

The term "moral panic" describes a phenomenon of great interest to many of those interested in the sociology of deviance. Moral panics are usually relatively short-lived (though the European witch hunts went on for centuries) and are described by Eric Goode and Nachman Ben-Yehuda (1994: 149) as "over-heated periods of intense concern." The intensity of that concern is disproportionate to the evidence of any objective threat being posed by the transgressors that are the object of concern (i.e., the deviants). The disproportionality of concern is obvious in the case of the European witch hunts and easily argued in the case of the marijuana user in the 1930s and of the serial killer in the 1980s (the FBI estimated thousands of victims of serial killers annually, whereas the actual number was likely less than a hundred—Jenkins, 1994).

However, the term "moral panic" lacks a good deal of precision because it is unclear how "intense" the concern needs to be to constitute a moral panic. Who and how many people have to be concerned? And how disproportionate does the concern have to be relative to the evidence of threat? With its imprecision, it is vulnerable to criticism. Namely, critics of the term charge that it is employed to dismiss the claims of those who have identified the threat as a social problem— often called in the sociology of deviance literature "moral crusaders" —and that this dismissal is based on the values of those who use the term. Critics charge that the person who calls the intense concern over marijuana in the 1930s a "moral panic" is expressing his or her belief that marijuana is/was not *that* bad, and that someone who calls the serial murder phenomenon of the 1980s a "moral panic" is devaluing the lives of those who actually did die at the hands of a serial killer.

A related problem with the moral panic concept is that it is difficult to identify one in the midst of one. Since moral panics are often short-lived and since a defining characteristic of one is the disproportionality of concern relative to the objective data, often sufficient data has not been generated until after the panic has subsided. Further, to identify a moral panic during the panic is itself a form of deviance. For example, to have identified the concern over the sexual abuse of children in day care centers in the 1980s as a moral panic would put one at risk of being labeled as someone who defends pedophiles and child molesters, the modern-day equivalent of consorting with the devil.

Despite these problems with the moral panic concept, it describes a phenomenon that has very serious implications for countless individuals as well as for society. Hundreds of thousands of people were killed during the witch craze. Hundreds of thousands over the decades have been sent to prison for marijuana possession. Not only was prison likely a devastating experience for them and their families, but it was also costly for the taxpayer. Thanks in part to the serial murder scare, millions of children—most now adults—have grown up fearing strangers and successive generations of children have less freedom to play outside in the sunlight. These are real-life consequences affecting the quality of life of millions of people. Just as importantly, the time, effort, and resources that were spent addressing the threats implicated by various moral panics in history could have instead been spent to address other social problems and could have had untold consequences affecting many, most, or all people.

The term "moral panic" seems to have first been coined in 1971 by Jock Young and then popularized by Stanley Cohen in his book *Folk Devils and Moral Panics* published in 1972. Cohen analyzed a series of incidents involving British youth who were thought to have been "terrorizing" English coastal communities in the 1960s. The first article in this section, by Kenneth Thompson, is a summary and overview of Cohen's classic analysis. Early in that selection, Thompson mentions several concepts that are central to Cohen's work and the subsequent discourse on moral panics. He mentions "folk devils," a phrase contained in the title of Cohen's work; these are the alleged evildoers, the object of the public's wrath; and he identifies the "signification spiral by which the interaction of claims-makers, moral entrepreneurs and the mass media results in the establishment of a discourse in which certain groups are demonized as the source of moral decline." The claims-makers are those who demand something be done about an alleged condition in society; the moral entrepreneurs are those who devote a good deal of time and resources to promoting their moral worldview, who often have a vested interest in doing so; and, in the modern world, the media play a critical role in perpetuating perceptions of folk devils, sensitizing the public to their alleged activities, amplifying their deviance, and, thus promoting and validating people's outrage. Cohen identified another theme common to much of the literature on moral panics (and to the literature on urban legends) and that is that moral panics (and urban legends) take place when there are already pre-existing widespread anxieties in a society that were brought about by social change. That is, people already perceive a vague sense of threat and the folk devil comes to symbolize that threat. Without that raw nerve exposed, people would be more circumspect and more inclined to examine the evidence; consequently, the original claims would not resonate with so large of an audience.

The next article, "The Devil Goes to Day Care" by Mary deYoung, describes a moral panic taking place in the 1980s in which the public was led to believe that children were being used in satanic rituals and being sexually molested in day care centers around the country. It all started with the McMartin case described by deYoung and transformed into scores of cases throughout the country. DeYoung describes the social change that exposed the raw nerve in society and triggered the moral panic. She also describes the societal consequences of the panic.

The next selection, by Heiner, describes a series of moral panics, or "crime scares," also taking place in the 1980s. Undoubtedly there were sweeping social changes that exposed the nerves that made these categories of deviance resonate with the general public, but a major focus of this selection is on the discrepancies between the objective evidence of these social problems and the intensity of concern over them. In addition to identifying the reasons for society's vulnerability to a particular moral panic, an understanding of moral panics also requires an understanding of the interests of the media, and some combination of politicians, moral crusaders, and law enforcement in the creation and perpetuation of a panic. Together, these pieces of information make the seemingly irrational moral panic seem more rational. Thus, another focus of this piece is on how various constituencies benefitted from these panics.

References

Cohen, Stanley, *Folk devils and moral panics*, London: MacGibbon and Kee, 1972.

Goode, Erich and Nachman Ben-Yehuda, "Moral panics: Culture, politics, and social construction," *Annual Review of Sociology*, 1994, vol. 20, pp. 149–171.

Jenkins, Philip, *Using murder: The social construction of serial homicide*, Hawthorne, NY: Aldine de Gruyter, 1994.

14.
THE CLASSIC MORAL PANIC: MODS AND ROCKERS

KENNETH THOMPSON

In this reading, Thompson summarizes one of the first systematic accounts of a moral panic, the case of the Mods and Rockers in 1960s England. Some processes from previous theoretical articles come into play in the creation of a moral panic. For one thing, the creation of a moral panic is likely to occur in the midst of social change and serves to clarify the moral boundaries of a society. For another, it was not so much the behavior of the Mods and Rockers that triggered the panic as it was the needs of various interest groups (i.e., the "audience"), including the media. Note the important role played by the media in "amplifying" deviance and creating "folk devils."

A panic about what was happening to British youth in the 1960s was the occasion for the first sociological analysis of a moral panic (S. Cohen, 1972) and this is significant for [at least two] reasons: first, because concerns about the moral condition of youth have been the object of periodic episodes of moral panic and so they may enable us to pinpoint a major and recurrent source of social anxiety about risk; [and] second, because the moral panic about Mods and Rockers in 1960s Britain provides a good example of the signification spiral by which the interaction of claims-makers, moral entrepreneurs and the mass media results in the establishment of a discourse in which certain groups are demonized as the source of moral decline. . . .

The initial episode of deviant behavior that gave rise to a moral panic and the elevation of a section of British youth to the status of folk devils began in the small seaside town of Clacton in 1964. The rather mundane nature of the event is captured in Cohen's description:

Easter 1964 was worse than usual. It was cold and wet, and in fact Easter Sunday was the coldest for eighty years. The shopkeepers and stall owners were irritated by the lack of business and the young people had their own boredom and irritation fanned by rumors of cafe owners and barmen refusing to serve some of them. A few groups started scuffling on the pavements and throwing stones at each other. The Mods and Rockers factions—a division initially based on clothing and lifestyles, later rigidified, but at that time not fully established—started separating out. Those on bikes and scooters

117

roared up and down, windows were broken, some beach huts were wrecked and one boy fired a starting pistol in the air. The vast number of people crowding into the streets, the noise, everyone's general irritation and the actions of an unprepared and undermanned police force had the effect of making the two days unpleasant, oppressive and sometimes frightening. (S. Cohen, 1972/80: 29)

THE ROLE OF THE MEDIA

Adapting a model of stages of development of certain forms of collective behavior derived from studies of disaster behavior, S. Cohen called this the *initial deviation* or *impact* phase. This was followed by the *inventory* stage, in which observers take stock of what they believe has happened. The most important factor was the way in which the situation was initially interpreted and presented by the mass media, "because it is in this form that most people received their pictures of both deviance and disasters. Reactions take place on the basis of these processed or coded images" (S. Cohen, 1972/80: 30). Cohen shows that the media presentation or inventory of the Mods and Rockers events was crucial in determining the later stages of reaction:

> On the Monday morning following the initial incidents at Clacton, every national newspaper, with the exception of *The Times* (fifth lead on the main news page), carried a leading report on the subject. The headlines are self-descriptive: "Day of Terror by Scooter Groups" (*Daily Telegraph*), "Youngsters Beat Up Town—97 Leather Jacket Arrests" *(Daily Express)*, "Wild Ones Invade Seaside—97 Arrests" (*Daily Mirror*). The next lot of incidents received similar coverage on the Tuesday and editorials began to appear, together with reports that the Home Secretary was "being urged" (it was not usually specified by whom) to hold an inquiry or to take firm action. Feature articles then appeared highlighting interviews with Mods and Rockers. Straight reporting gave way to theories especially about motivation: the mob was described as "exhilarated," "drunk with notoriety," "hell-bent on destruction," etc. (S. Cohen, 1972/80: 30)

The media inventory of the initial incident was analyzed by Cohen under three headings:

- exaggeration and distortion;
- prediction;
- symbolization.

The type of distortion in the inventory lay in exaggerating the seriousness of events in terms of criteria such as the number taking part, the number involved in violence and the amount and effects of any damage or violence. Further distortion took place in the mode and style of presentation characteristic of most crime reporting: the sensational headlines, the melodramatic vocabulary and the deliberate heightening of those elements in the story considered as news. There was frequent use of words and phrases such as "riot," "orgy of destruction," "battle," "attack," "siege," "beat up the town" and "screaming mob." Of the total number of arrests (ninety-seven) at Clacton, only one-tenth were charged with offenses involving violence, and twenty-four were charged with "non-hooligan" sorts of offenses: stealing a half a pint of petrol, attempting to steal drinks from a vending machine and "obtaining credit to the amount of 7d by means of fraud other than false pretenses" (an ice cream) (S. Cohen, 1972/80: 37). The total estimated cost of damage at Clacton was £513. One newspaper reported that "all the dance halls near the seafront were smashed" (ibid: 37); but, in fact, the town had only one dance hall and it had some of its windows broken. Similarly, there was use of the generic plural (if a boat was overturned, reports read "boats were overturned" (ibid: 39)) and the technique, familiar to war correspondents, of reporting the same incident twice to make it look like two different incidents.

Another element in the inventory was that of constant prediction that the event would be followed by more such events involving even worse consequences, and the assertion this was all part of a pattern due to underlying causes that were gathering pace. Subsequently, similar events to those at Clacton were reported during the following holiday period of Whitsun 1964 at Bournemouth, Brighton and Margate, but all of them were in fact of smaller magnitude than those at Clacton. However, the media coverage suggested that they were getting worse, and it is true that the media publicity had led to heightened expectations of dramatic events, which then attracted spectators eager to witness the drama.

The publicity given to the events entailed a form of symbolization in which key symbols (differences in fashion, lifestyle and entertainment) were stripped of their favorable or neutral connotations until they came to evoke unambiguously unfavorable responses:

> There appear to be three processes in such symbolization: a word (Mod) becomes symbolic of a certain status (delinquent or deviant); objects (hairstyle, clothing) symbolize the word; the objects themselves become symbolic of the status (and the emotions attached to the status). (S. Cohen, 1972/80: 40)

Studies of moral panics associated with the Mods and Rockers and other forms of deviance, as well as research on the mass communication process itself (Halloran et al., 1970), suggest that two interrelated factors determine the presentation of deviance inventories: the first is the institutionalized need to create news and the second is the selective and inferential structure of the news-making process. The mass media operate with certain definitions of what is newsworthy:

> It is not that instruction manuals exist telling newsmen that certain subjects (drugs, sex, violence) will appeal to the public or that certain groups (youth, immigrants) should be continually exposed to scrutiny. Rather, there are built-in factors, ranging from the individual newsman's intuitive hunch about what constitutes a "good story," through precepts such as "give the public what it wants" to structured ideological biases, which predispose the media to make a certain event into news. (S. Cohen, 1972/80: 45)

For example, disturbances of various sorts, variously called "hooliganism," "rowdyism" or "gang fights," had been a regular occurrence during the late 1950s and early 1960s in English coastal towns, but it was only with the labeling of the Clacton event as an example of a widespread deviant phenomenon that it became news. "The Mods and Rockers didn't become news because they were new; they were presented as new to justify their creation as news" (S. Cohen, 1972/80: 46). The process of news manufacture is described by Halloran et al. by reference to the development of an inferential structure: this is not intentional bias or simple selection by expectation but rather "a process of simplification and interpretation which structures the meaning given to the story around its original news value" (Halloran et al., 1970: 215–16). The conceptual framework used to locate this process, and one which was taken over by Cohen, is that of Boorstin's notion of the event as news. That is to say, the question of "is it news" becomes as important as "is it real?" The argument is that:

> events will be selected for news reporting in terms of their fit or consonance with pre-existing images—the news of the event will confirm earlier ideas. The more unclear the news item and the

more uncertain or doubtful the newsman is in how to report it, the more likely it is to be reported in a general framework that has already been established. (Halloran et al., 1970: 215–16)

In the light of this, Cohen concludes:

It is only when the outlines of such general frameworks have been discerned, that one can understand processes such as symbolization, prediction, the reporting of non-events and the whole style of presentation. The predictability of the inventory is crucial. So constant were the images, so stylized was the mode of reporting, so limited was the range of emotions and values played on, that it would have been perfectly simple for anyone who had studied the Mods and Rockers coverage to predict with some accuracy the reports of all later variations on the theme of depraved youth: skinheads, football hooligans, hippies, drug-takers, pop-festivals, the Oz trial. (S. Cohen, 1972/80: 47)

However, although the media coverage may have created an interpretative framework for the events, the media did not operate in a vacuum; there were other actors involved—social control agents such as the police and judges, and moral entrepreneurs, particularly politicians.

SOCIAL CONTROL AGENTS AND MORAL ENTREPRENEURS

One of the effects of the symbolization contained in the media reports of deviance is that it sensitizes people to signs of a threat. Incidents and events that might otherwise not be regarded as connected come to be seen as symptoms of the same threatening form of deviance. After the reports of the first disturbances, all kinds of youth misbehavior were interpreted in terms of the same symbolic framework. As a result of sensitization, incidents that might have been written off as "horseplay" or a "dance hall brawl" were interpreted as being part of the Mods and Rockers phenomenon. Public nervousness increased and there was pressure for more police vigilance and stronger action from the forces of law and order. The police then reacted by stepping up patrols and increasing their interventions in potential trouble spots—seaside towns, dance halls, fairs and other public events. Court proceedings reflected the sensitization. In the northern town of Blackburn, many miles from the seaside resorts where the Mods and Rockers disturbances had taken place, a police officer prosecuting two youths for using threatening behavior (they had been in a crowd of twenty flicking rubber bands at passersby) said in court:

This case is an example of the type of behavior that has been experienced in many parts of the country during the last few weeks and it has been slowly affecting Blackburn. We shall not tolerate this behavior. The police will do everything within their power to stamp it out. (*Lancashire Evening Telegraph*, 29 May 1964; quoted in S. Cohen, 1972/80: 80)

According to Cohen, the reaction of the control culture was distinguished by three common elements: diffusion, escalation and innovation. Diffusion could be seen in the way in which control agents distant from the original incidents were drawn in, either by regional and national police collaboration, or by defining their own local activities as coping with the same deviant phenomenon. Escalation of measures to deal with the problem was reflected in calls to "tighten up," "take strong measures," "don't let it get out of hand," which were legitimized by invoking the images of those who had to be protected as "innocent holiday-makers," "old people," "mums and dads," "little children building sand castles" and "honest tradesmen." The final aspect of the control culture was that it extended not only in degree but also in kind through the actual or suggested introduction of new methods of control, e.g. new powers for the police and new penalties. Confiscation of bikes was one suggested punishment, and one magistrate went further in suggesting that offenders should be given hammers to smash up their own bikes: "a childish action should be met with a similar punishment" (quoted in S. Cohen, 1972/80: 91).

Perhaps the most important interface in the control culture is that where state control in the form of legislation and legislators meets pressures of public opinion as channeled by claims-makers and moral entrepreneurs. This is particularly important where the moral entrepreneurs are themselves politicians. The initial reaction in the case of Clacton and the other seaside resorts was shaped by local spokespersons, who defined the hooliganism as a threat to local commercial interests. However, they knew that nothing would be done if the problem was defined in purely local terms—the event had to be magnified to national proportions and the responsibility for it shifted upwards. Calls were made for a government inquiry, for the laws to be "tightened up," for the courts and the police to be given more powers. At some point, in order to have a wider impact, such sporadic general appeals from individuals and local organizations as were reported in the press needed to become formalized into fully fledged action groups. Cohen analyzed the process in terms of Neil Smelser's (1963) theory of collective behavior and the development of social movements. The action groups corresponded to what Smelser calls "norm-oriented movements," and they developed through a sequence of cumulative stages: strain (deviance); anxiety; an identification of the agents responsible; a generalized belief that control was inadequate; a belief that the trouble could be cured by reorganizing the normative structure itself ("there ought to be a law"); and, finally, the formulation of specific proposals to punish, control or destroy the agent. Cohen also provided a detailed profile of one of the typical moral entrepreneurs, a Mr. Blake, who formed an action group, gained publicity for his cause and drew in local politicians and other representatives of authority. This culminated in a resolution in the House of Commons:

> That this House in the light of the deplorable and continual increase in juvenile delinquency and in particular the recent regrettable events in Clacton urges the Secretary of State for Home Department to give urgent and serious consideration to the need for young hooligans to be given such financial and physical punishment as will provide an effective deterrent. (15 April 1964, House of Commons; quoted in S. Cohen, 1972/80: 134)

Legislation was rushed through to deal with "Malicious Damage," justified by explicit reference to the dangers from Mods and Rockers, although the Minister responsible had admitted in the first debate that "Some of the reports of what happened at Clacton over the Easter weekend were greatly exaggerated." Nevertheless, the process had been completed by which a mythology had been created and stereotypes about folk devils had taken hold.

In addition to the control culture, which amplified the deviance, there was also the phenomenon of what Lemert (1952) calls "deviance exploitation." Lemert referred to the "socioeconomic symbiosis between criminal and non-criminal groups" (1952: 310), pointing to the direct or indirect profit derived from crime by persons such as bankers, criminal lawyers, policemen and court officials. There was also *commercial exploitation* of folk devils such as Mods and Rockers by those engaged in marketing teenage consumer goods, who advertised using the groups' style images. The symbiotic relationship between the condemners and the condemned, the "normal" and the "deviant" was shown in the media treatment of the Mod-Rocker differences, as in the

Daily Mail quiz "Are you a Mod or Rocker?," published immediately after Clacton. There was also *ideological exploitation*, which involves a similar ambivalence in the sense that the exploiter "gains" from the denunciation of deviance and would "lose" if the deviance proved to be less real or serious. Such ideological exploitation is not confined to politicians and moral crusaders, but includes a wide variety of groups who could use the symbolic connotations to justify their positions, e.g., "The men in the BBC who feed violence, lust, aimlessness and cynicism into millions of homes nightly must squarely consider their responsibility" (Resolution passed at the Moral Rearmament Easter Conference, 30 March 1964; quoted in S. Cohen, 1972/80: 141).

SOCIAL CONTEXT

The moral panic about Mods and Rockers did not arise in a social vacuum. The media, control agents and moral entrepreneurs required social circumstances conducive to the amplification and willing reception of their message about moral danger. As Cohen explains:

> The Mods and Rockers symbolized something far more important than what they actually did. They touched the delicate and ambivalent nerves through which post-war social change in Britain was experienced. No one wanted depressions or austerity, but messages about "never having it so good" were ambivalent in that some people were having it too good and too quickly: "We've thrown back the curtain for them too soon." Resentment and jealousy were easily directed at the young, if only because of their increased spending power and sexual freedom. When this was combined with a too-open flouting of the work and leisure ethic, with violence and vandalism, and the (as yet) uncertain threats associated with drug-taking, something more than the image of a peaceful Bank Holiday at the sea was being shattered. (S. Cohen, 1972/80: 192)

Cohen suggests that ambiguity and strain was greatest at the beginning of the 1960s. The lines had not yet been clearly drawn and the reaction was part of this drawing of the line. He sees the period as constituting what Erikson (1966), in his study of witchhunts in puritan Massachusetts, had termed a "boundary crisis"—a period in which a group's uncertainty about itself was resolved in ritualistic confrontations between the deviant and the community's official agents. Cohen maintains that it is not necessary to make conspiratorial assumptions about deviants being deliberately "picked out" to clarify normative contours at times of cultural strain and ambiguity to detect in the response to the Mods and Rockers declarations about moral boundaries, about how much diversity can be tolerated. With respect to moral panics, as with the so-called "crime waves," they dramatize the issues at stake when boundaries are blurred and provide a forum to articulate the issues more explicitly. The social and physical mobility of the Mods and Rockers—relatively affluent teenagers who could dress in new styles and travel on their bikes outside working-class areas—provoked unease and hostility:

> Traditionally the deviant role had been assigned to the lower class urban male, but the Mods and Rockers appeared to be less class tied; here were a group of impostors, reading the lines which everyone knew belonged to some other groups. Even their clothes were out of place; without leather jackets they could hardly be distinguished from bank clerks. The uneasiness felt about actors who are not quite in their places can lead to greater hostility. Something done by an out-group is simply condemned and fitted into the scheme of things, but in-group deviance is embarrassing, it threatens the norms of the group and tends to blur its boundaries with the out-group. (S. Cohen, 1972/80: 195)

This analysis of boundary confusion is particularly relevant in the case of the Mods, whose style and social status did not easily fit established norms. The Mod's appearance was different from the stereotypical hooligan personified by the earlier fashion of the Teddy Boy or the leather-jacketed Rockers, who were thought to be imitating the American motor-bike gangs. The Mods seemed to offer some kind of snub to traditional values through their air of distance and ingratitude for what society had given them. Although there can be no doubt that the Mods' and Rockers' behavior did seem to pose a threat to the material interests of local traders and property owners in the resorts where disturbances occurred, the sense of moral outrage they evoked cannot be explained in those terms alone. The statements of the moral crusaders who demonized these youth cultures portrayed them as prematurely affluent, aggressive, permissive and challenging the ethics of sobriety and hard work. Psychologists have attempted to explain such responses in terms of the envy and resentment felt by the lower middle classes, supposedly the most frustrated and repressed of groups, who condemn behavior which they secretly crave. There may be some truth in this, but the fuller sociological explanation that we have suggested needs developing is multifactoral, stressing the interaction of structural conditions, cultural signs and symbols, the actions of key actors and movements, and processes by which typical forms of collective behavior develop.

DISCUSSION QUESTIONS

1. Identify the interest groups involved and describe how they perpetuated and benefitted from the moral panic.
2. How is the theme of social change implicated in the moral panic described by Cohen and Thompson?

REFERENCES

Cohen, S. (1972/80) *Folk Devils and Moral Panics: The Creation of the Mods and Rockers*, London: MacGibbon & Kee; new edition with Oxford: M. Robertson, 1980.

Erikson, K. (1966) *Wayward Puritans: A Study in the Sociology of Deviance*, New York: Wiley.

Halloran, J. D. *et al.* (1970) *Demonstrations and Communications: A Case Study*, Hammondsworth: Penguin.

Lemert, E. M. (1952) *Social Pathology*, New York: McGraw Hill.

Smelser, N. J. (1963) *Theory of Collective Behaviour*, London: Routledge and Kegan Paul.

15.

THE DEVIL GOES TO DAY CARE: MCMARTIN AND THE MAKING OF A MORAL PANIC

MARY DEYOUNG

While many may think that we have come a long way since the Salem witch trials, that we are far too sophisticated to let such a thing happen today, much more recent events suggest otherwise. As in previous articles, we see in the following account how deviance is constructed in the public imagination to encompass folk deviltry on a remarkable scale. Again, we see the role of the media in creating a moral panic. And again we see how the public is "primed" for such a panic by acute, but amorphous, anxieties brought about by social change. Students of the sociology of deviance should try to remain circumspect and examine the evidence when the next potential moral panic emerges. If the allegations seem preposterous, then there is a good chance that they are either unfounded or exaggerated.

A new type of sex crime was discovered during the 1980s—the abuse of very young children in rituals performed by robed and hooded satanists who also happened to be their day care providers. Satanic ritual abuse, as this new sex crime quickly came to be termed, appeared to be epidemic during the 1980s, and the McMartin Preschool was its first *locus delicti*.

The cultural response to the McMartin case had all of the characteristics of what sociologists call a moral panic:[1] it was widespread, volatile, hostile, and overreactive (Goode and Ben-Yehuda, 156–59). From Texas to Tennessee, New Jersey to North Carolina, Maine to Michigan, hundreds of local day care centers were investigated for satanic ritual abuse and scores of day care providers, as many males as females, were arrested and put on trial. From the witness stand, their accusers, the three- and four-year-old children once entrusted to their care, accused them of sexual abuse during satanic ceremonies that included such ghastly practices as blood-drinking, cannibalism, and human sacrifices. Despite the absence of evidence corroborating the children's accounts, many of the day care providers were convicted, and to the cheers and jeers of their deeply divided communities, were sentenced to what often were draconian prison terms.

In the accusatorial post-McMartin climate, day care providers, surrogate parents to this country's youngest children, took measures to protect themselves from their false allegations (Bordin,

80–81). They installed video cameras to record all of their activities, opened up private spaces to public view by taking down doors to bathrooms and closets and, fearing the act now could be misinterpreted, stopped hugging and holding their young charges. State legislatures also took measures. They hurriedly passed laws that mandated the fingerprinting and criminal records check of all current and prospective day care providers; state licensing agencies tightened regulations and by legislative fiat were given more teeth to enforce them. Yet insurance liability premiums soared, forcing many small day care centers out of business and many more, unlicensed and uninsured, to go underground.

Heralded at the start of the decade as playgrounds for children, day care centers were feared at its end as playthings of the devil. The aim of this present article is to analyze the moral panic about satanic day care centers that spread across this country during the 1980s. First, it examines the cultural context of the moral panic by focusing on the social forces and strains peculiar to that decade that not only gave rise to it, but that made what at first blush must appear to be the most innocuous of social institutions, the local day care center, the scene of the most horrific of sex crimes. Second, it interprets the McMartin Preschool case as the trigger that set off the moral panic, and then analyzes the roles that interest, grassroots, and professional groups played in spreading it across the country. Third, the article explains why, after nine long and bitter years, the moral panic finally ended and what "moral," if any, can be derived from it.

CULTURAL CONTEXT OF THE MORAL PANIC

An insightful examination of the social change most critical to the rise of the satanic day care center moral panic during the 1980s is provided by David Bromley and Bruce Busching who examine the changing relation between what they call the covenantal sphere and the contractual sphere of social life at the beginning of that decade. The covenantal sphere is that of the family. Within it, relations are built upon mutual commitment, bonding, and emotional expressiveness, and are articulated through the logic of moral involvement and unity. The contractual sphere, in contrast, is that of the market economy where relations are based upon mutual agreement, negotiation, and exchange, and are articulated through the logic of vested interest and shrewd involvement. By historic necessity, the covenantal and contractual spheres have been always, and uneasily, interdependent. As the locus of socialization, the family always has prepared children for successful participation in the market economy which, in turn, always has provided the legitimate opportunities for gaining the resources needed to sustain the family. In the early 1980s, however, the tension between these two spheres of social life intensified and that most innocent of social institutions, the local day care center, ended up being situated right on the faultline. This heightened tension between family and market economy was largely the result of cultural forces and strains peculiar to that decade. Significant among them were the ideological force of the women's movement that made participation in the market economy an attractive and increasingly accessible alternative to unpaid housework, and the economic strains that made it a necessity.[2] In 1980, in fact, 45% of women with young children had entered the labor market, and because the forces and strains that compelled their doing so had the same impact on their extended families, they had to turn away from relatives as a source of child care, and to public and private day care centers (Hofferth and Phillips, 560–63).

And they did so with more than a little ambivalence. Although day care centers packaged themselves as attractive alternatives to family care, with their use of educational toys to stimulate the mind, playground equipment to develop the body, excursions to cultivate aesthetic taste and, only when needed, just the right kind of discipline administered by trained professionals to shape socially correct behavior, most working parents considered this alternative a change for the worse from their parents' generation (Hutchison, 73–74).

Economic strains of a different type only reinforced that view. For one thing, as the baby-boomer generation went out to look for day care for its own children, it was confronted with a harsh reality: there simply were not enough reputable, licensed, affordable day care centers to meet its needs. Deep cuts in federal funding that over half of the public day centers had received just a few years before now resulted in high costs to working parents, overcrowded facilities, low wages for child care providers, and high staff turnover (Hofferth and Phillips 563–67). Dramatizing this dilemma was a blitz of day care horror stories in popular parents' magazines. Their images of toddlers in soiled diapers forlornly waiting for attention from overworked day care providers in overcrowded centers did little to assuage the anxiety or the guilt of working parents.

Trapped as they were between necessity and risk, working parents reluctantly began transforming the covenantal duty of caring for their young children into contractual arrangements with day care providers. And many feared that in doing so they were relinquishing some control over the socialization of their children. When Kenneth Kenniston wrote of this dilemma a decade before, he was presenting a musical metaphor; now, in the early 1980s, he was describing a discordant reality:

> The parent today is usually a coordinator without voice or authority, a maestro trying to conduct an orchestra of players who have never met and who play from a multitude of different scores, each in notations that the conductor cannot read. If parents are frustrated, it is no wonder: for although they have the responsibility for their children's lives, they hardly ever have the voice, the authority, or the power to make others listen to them. (18)

So, here is the essence of the dilemma experienced by working parents in the early 1980s: on the one hand, the time and energy they were investing in the covenantal sphere of the family was jeopardizing their economic success in the contractual sphere of the market economy; on the other hand, the time and energy they were investing in the contractual sphere of the market economy was diminishing their control over the socialization of their children in the covenantal sphere of the family. And situated on the faultline of this dilemma, where these two once separate spheres of social life were now uncomfortably overlapping, was the local day care center.

The tension produced by this imbrication of covenantal and contractual spheres made the local day care center a target of conflict. But a trigger was needed to set off a moral panic, some kind of spark that in the words of Jeffrey Adler "would link ethereal sentiment to focused activity" (262). That spark was ignited in 1983 at the McMartin Preschool.

TRIGGER OF THE MORAL PANIC

Hardly the dark satanic mill of cultural imagination, the McMartin Preschool was a rambling building on the main boulevard of the southern California town of Manhattan Beach where, if the Chamber of Commerce brochure were to be believed, residents enjoy "small town living, friendly neighbors, and community spirit." Established in the mid-1960s by Virginia McMartin, the family-owned and run day care center had a certain cachet among young, upwardly mobile parents and it filled early each year. So when Judy Johnson[3] went to enroll her two-year-old son in the spring of 1983, there were no openings. She dropped him off anyway. The day care providers arrived early one morning to find him in the yard of the center, and taking pity on the woebegone little boy and his recently separated mother, took him in.

Over the next several months, and without incident, the boy occasionally attended the center. But one day in August of that year, he came home with a reddened anus. His mother, stressed, emotionally unstable, and drinking heavily, immediately suspected that he had been sexually abused (Hubler, A1). She questioned him relentlessly, but to no avail, before she decided on a different tact. Having noticed how her son often pretended to be a doctor like the one who was tending his terminally ill older brother who was living at home, she asked if Raymond Buckey, the only male staff member and grandson of the day care center's founder, had ever given him an injection. The boy said no, but when the question was asked again and again, he finally told his mother that what Buckey really had done was take his temperature. Judy Johnson concluded that the "thermometer" her son described was actually Buckey's penis, and that he had been sexually abused after all (Nathan and Snedeker, 67–70).

The medical exam performed the following day, however, was inconclusive for sexual abuse and the boy disclosed nothing at all to the detective his mother had contacted. But the matter was far from over. Several days later, Judy Johnson called the detective again and informed him that in the privacy of their own home her son was talking about sexual acts of the most perverse kind perpetrated not only on himself, but on other children enrolled at the day care center as well. So convincing was she that the detective demanded she get a second medical opinion. This physician, inexperienced in performing sexual exams and finding nothing of significance anyway in the one she did perform, nonetheless erred on the side of caution and gave the diagnosis that finally confirmed what Judy Johnson was insisting had happened: her son had been sexually abused. Detectives now took a new interest in what the boy allegedly was telling his mother. They telephoned parents with children enrolled in McMartin and asked them to question their young sons and daughters about whether they, too, had been sexually abused. None answered in the affirmative. But in the wake of those telephone contacts that same "small town living, friendly neighbors, and community spirit" that made Manhattan Beach a desirable place to live also assured that rumors would gather and roll. So when the detectives pressed on and later sent the following letter to two hundred families whose children were current or recent enrollees at McMartin, the rumors were reified:

> Please question your child to see if he or she has been a witness to any crime or if he or she had been a victim. Our investigation indicates that possible criminal acts include: oral sex, fondling of genitals, buttocks or chest area, and sodomy, possibly under the pretense of "taking the child's temperature."
> (Cited in Nathan and Snedeker, 72)

The letter also named Buckey as the prime suspect. Over the next several weeks as terrified and outraged parents questioned their children, met with each other to exchange facts and rumors, and questioned their children again, more and more of them answered in the affirmative. The assistant prosecutor appointed to oversee what too many already believed would turn out to be the case of the century, called a community meeting and encouraged parents to take their sons and daughters to the Children's International Institute (CII), a non-profit diagnostic and treatment facility, for evaluation. Over the next year, the CII social workers, already caught up in the fad and folly about satanic sex cults that was still rolling over southern California in the wake of the Bakersfield case,[4] interviewed over 400 McMartin children and determined that 369 of them had been victims of a new and ghastly sex crime—satanic ritual abuse.

In February 1984, the same month that the prosecuting attorney quietly asked the grand jury to issue indictments against Raymond Buckey, as well as his grandmother, mother, sister, and three other McMartin staff members, a KABC reporter broke the story, plunging the local and the national news into what media critic David Shaw describes as "a feeding frenzy" (A1). Bent on proving satanic ritual abuse, the CII social workers kept relentlessly grilling the children who, despite their tender years, soon figured out that "round, unvarnish'd tales" were not what their inquisitors wanted to hear. And so they told other tales—tales about the ritualistic ingestion of feces, urine, blood, semen, and human flesh; the disinterment and mutilation of corpses; the sacrifices of infants; and the orgies with their day care providers, costumed as devils and witches, in the classrooms, in tunnels under the center, and in car washes, airplanes, mansions, cemeteries, hotels, ranches, gourmet food stores, local gyms, churches, and hot air balloons. And they named not only the seven McMartin day care providers as their satanic abusers, but their soccer coaches, babysitters, next-door neighbors, and even their own parents, as well as local businesspeople, the mayor's wife, who was said to drive around town with the corpses of sacrificed infants in the back of her stationwagon, news reporters covering the story, television and film stars, and members of the Anaheim Angels baseball team (Nathan and Snedeker, 78–91).

In 1986, the same year that *Los Angeles Times* reporter Lois Timnick revealed that 80% of the surveyed residents of Los Angeles County were convinced that all seven of the McMartin day care providers were guilty of satanic ritual abuse, the criminal charges against five of them were dismissed for lack of evidence. Now only Raymond Buckey and his mother, Peggy McMartin Buckey, were left to stand trial.

That trial began the following year and lasted twenty-eight months, the longest and, at a cost of $13 million, the most expensive criminal trial in the history of the country (Shaw, A1). The jury listened to 124 witnesses, fourteen of them children, examined 974 major exhibits, and reviewed 64,000 pages of transcripts before returning its verdict after nine weeks of deliberation (DeBenedictis, 29). It acquitted Peggy McMartin Buckey of all of the fifty-two charges against her, and acquitted Raymond Buckey of thirty-nine of the charges, but deadlocked on the remaining thirteen. His second trial on eight of those dead-locked charges ended with a hung jury after two weeks of deliberation. A month later, despite the vehement protests of the parents and many others across the country, the prosecutor dismissed all of the charges against him.

And what of Judy Johnson? The mother of the little boy who never shared his dark secrets with anyone, and who never could even pick out Raymond Buckey's picture from a photo lineup, was institutionalized for a while with the diagnosis of paranoid schizophrenia after she told detectives that her ex-husband also had sodomized her son, and that an intruder had broken into her house and sodomized the family dog. By the time of her death in 1986 from massive liver failure brought on by alcoholism, there had been at least fifty "little McMartin's" across the country; by the fifth anniversary of her death, there were fifty more (Sauer, D1).

SPREAD OF THE MORAL PANIC

The "moral" of the moral panic is now accounted for: the disturbing overlap between the covenantal and contractual spheres of social life had made local day care centers a site of conflict; the McMartin case set the moral boundaries of that conflict by casting day care providers into the role of evil satanists, their young charges into innocent victims, and the parents, social workers, prosecutors, and police into heroes. The "panic" that ensued, however, must be accounted for by yet another set of factors.

First, a clarification of the word "panic." While it tends to conjure up images of frenzied folks frantically fighting more devils than hell can hold, its sociological meaning is different. Panic refers to what Jeffrey Victor describes as a "collective stress reaction in response to a belief in a story about immediately threatening circumstances" (59). For the McMartin Preschool case to set off that collective reaction, that panic, it first had to be narrated, and here the role of interest, grassroots, and professional groups in telling, re-telling, and spreading the McMartin satanic day care story is important to consider.

The major interest group was the news media. After the KABC reporter broke the McMartin story early in 1984 during the local "sweeps week," other press, radio, and television reporters scrambled to surpass his exclusive. "The story had a life of its own," recalled one of them. "We didn't even think at the time about what we were doing. It was, 'We gotta get something new on McMartin; look how big this thing is getting'" (Shaw, A1).

Splattered with words like "grotesque," "bizarre," "chilling," "horrific," and "nightmarish," the early local news stories set the hysterical tone that would be mimicked by the national media and that would resound for nearly a decade throughout the country. And that tone hyperbolized the moral dimensions of the case through the process of what sociologists refer to as role amplification: in each re-telling of the story, the day care providers became more evil; the young children more innocent; the parents, social workers, police, and prosecutors more heroic.

The mass media certainly did nothing to temper that hysterical tone. *People* magazine titled its first feature on the case, "California's Nightmare Nursery"; *Time* magazine's headline was a single, sinister word: "Brutalized!" And on the primetime news magazine, *20/20*, the McMartin Preschool was dubbed "the sexual house of horrors" and the reporter, appearing deeply affected by his own reportage, somberly predicted that the children would never psychologically recover from what they were saying they had experienced.

McMartin had become a household word, synonymous with evil, by the end of 1984. But a household word does not a moral panic make. What yet was needed was that sense of imminent threat that Jeffrey Victor described, that shuddering fear that the mischief the devil had found in a day care center in southern California also was going on in centers in Oregon, Florida, Massachusetts, Iowa, and all places in between. What dissolved the boundaries on the map of imagination was the 1984 Congressional testimony of the CII social worker who had diagnosed satanic ritual abuse for the largest number of the McMartin children. In a widely quoted statement, she told Congress that the McMartin Preschool actually was an "organized operation of child predators" that "serves as a ruse for a larger, unthinkable network of crimes against children" that has "greater financial, legal, and community resources than any of the agencies trying to uncover it" (Brozan, A21). A touch of conspiracy was added to the story.

The plot thickened with its introduction. Not only did the conspiracy theory neatly explain why local and federal investigators were never able to find any evidence of satanic ritual abuse in the McMartin case, but it primed the larger culture's compact and conspiratorial imagination. Now the threat of satanic day care centers was real and exigent, and no community could consider itself immune from it.

That became the message of the grassroots group that also played a significant role in the telling, retelling, and spreading of the McMartin story. "Believe the Children" was formed in 1984 by a coterie of McMartin parents whose activism grew in sophistication from wearing buttons and carrying hand-painted signs to establishing a clearinghouse on satanic ritual abuse, replete with a speakers' bureau, a support network for parents, police, and prosecutors involved in other satanic day care cases, and a referral list of sympathetic professionals ("Believe the Children" n.d.).

Those sympathetic professionals also played a notable role in spreading the moral panic about satanic day care centers across the country. During the bitter years of McMartin, they not only received a great deal of local, national, and international news attention, but also appeared on television talk shows and primetime news magazines. They took to the lecture circuit, gave testimony in government-sponsored hearings, addressed conferences of child abuse professionals, consulted with other professionals as other satanic day care cases began cropping up across the country, and testified as experts in the criminal trials of day care providers. And in each interview, each presentation, each consultation, the story of McMartin was told and re-told in communities that were being primed for the moral panic by the telling.[5]

Originating in cultural anxieties about the socialization and protection of young children, triggered by the McMartin Preschool case, and spread across the country by interest, grassroots, and professional groups, the satanic day care center moral panic swept across the country. It lasted just a year short of a decade. Its longevity, actually quite remarkable by historical standards, is explained not by any corroborative evidence of satanic ritual abuse in day care, there never was any of that, but by its continuing resonance with the prevailing cultural conflict.

MAKE A MORAL OF THE DEVIL

The moral panic ended in 1992 when the last of the alleged satanic day care providers, a wife and her husband, were led off in handcuffs to begin a nearly half-century-long prison sentence.[6] Any temptation to celebrate its end as proof that the forces of good finally and forever triumphed over the forces of evil is best resisted. Instead, its dissolution is better explained in sociological terms: the cultural conflict that spawned and sustained it finally was somewhat ameliorated by it.

But only somewhat. The cultural conflict in question, of course, is that disconcerting overlap between the covenantal and contractual spheres of social life, and that conflict was not at all altered by the satanic day care center moral panic, if any measure of alteration can be found in the rate of public and private day care usage during the years of its duration. The number of working mothers increased both steadily and rapidly between 1983 when the McMartin case started and 1992 when the moral panic finally subsided, and so did the number of young children who were enrolled in public and private day care centers (Hofferth and Phillips, 561). Even with its dramatization, even demonization, of the tension between these two spheres, the moral panic could not thwart the steady encroachment of the contractual sphere into the covenental. But it could, and did, reduce the irritation of its intrusion.

It did so by provoking fear-based changes that had the interesting effect of smoothing the sharp edges of the contractual sphere's penetration into the covenantal sphere by replicating in the former some of the ever so familiar and much valued characteristics of the latter. More to the point, these changes made day care centers more like families, and thus more subject to parental control. Several examples are particularly noteworthy. In reaction to the moral panic, many states hurriedly passed legislation that required the screening of all prospective day care providers not only for criminal and psychiatric histories, but for "good moral character." The intent behind the legislation was almost transparent: it assured that day care providers would have the kind of right-mindedness and trustworthiness of the very best of the working parents who were contracting with them for the care of their children. The care of their children still may be a matter of contract, but it also was being carried out by people with character.

On a more local level, many day care centers reacted to the moral panic by adopting open-door policies. Parents were invited to drop in any time to chat with the staff and admin-istration, observe their children, or even spend time with them. This policy had the effect of replicating within the local day care center the kind of easy informality of interaction that char-acterized the families from which their young charges had come. Accustomed to that style, and practiced in it, parents could monitor, even supervise to some extent, the care of their children by the agents whom they paid to provide it. And they could control that care as well. Day care centers invited parents to play more active roles in the centers, by sitting on their boards of directors, volunteering their time as classroom aides, chaperoning outings, and recruiting other parents to enroll their young children into the happy family that local day care centers fast were becoming.

One less obvious, but certainly sociologically significant, change that occurred in day care during the satanic day care center moral panic was its refeminization. In 1983, the year Judy Johnson's paranoid delusion transmogrified Raymond Buckey into an evil satanist, only 5% of day care providers were male (Weinback, 32). During the nine years of the moral panic, an alarming number of those male providers were accused of that new and horrific sex crime, sa-tanic ritual abuse.[7] As a result of these allegations, males left the profession in droves, seeking the comparative safety of male sex-role stereotyped employment. Day care was refeminized. Once again, and in the time-honored and very familiar tradition of the family, the primary responsibil-ity for the care and socialization of young children was placed on the shoulders of low-paid women.

The satanic day care center moral panic is a fascinating slice of cultural history. Yet in so many ways, this moral panic is really no different from all of the others that have preceded it, and all of the others that inevitably will follow. It originated in an unsettling cultural conflict peculiar to its era and was sustained by that same conflict over time. It set the moral boundaries of that conflict by casting antagonists into the role of evil satanists, and then spread the fear that casting generated. And it ended when it ameliorated that cultural conflict. If there is a moral to this or any other moral panic, it is perhaps nothing more than this: for a little sense of familiarity, a touch of order, a bit of control, the culture always seems willing to pay a most exacting price.

DISCUSSION QUESTIONS

1. Identify the social processes common to this article and the previous article concerning the Mods and Rockers.

2. A sociological principle we see at work in this article states that people do not respond to reality, they instead respond to their perceptions of reality and these perceptions are learned from social interaction. A corollary of this principle is known as the Thomas Theorem, named after sociologist W. I. Thomas; it states that things perceived as real are real in their consequences. How does this theorem apply to the preceding article? How do you think it might apply to the alleged victims of child molestation in this case?

NOTES

1. There is a rich sociological literature on moral panics. Ben-Yehuda (1980), for example, treats the European witchhunts as a moral panic; Cohen (1972) uses the concept to analyze the British reaction to juvenile gangs in the early 1960s; Sindall (1987) uses it to explain the London garroting panics of the 1800s, and Adler (1996) the Boston garroting panics just few years later; and Victor (1993) treats the anti-satanism movement of the 1980s as a moral panic.

2. For an extended discussion on the changing relationship between family and economy, see Negrey (1993), Rubin (1994), and Stacey (1990).

3. Judy Johnson is her real name. Both her name, and the name of her young son, have been widely reported in the media from the very beginning of the McMartin case.

4. Eight child sex rings were uncovered in the greater Bakersfied area in the early 1980s. The largest would come to be known as the Satanic Church case, and would implicate more than sixty adults and seventy-seven children. Virtually every conviction in all eight of the cases has since been overturned. See Nathan and Snedeker (53–66) for an analysis of the Bakersfield cases.

5. Communities really were primed by conferences and workshops conducted by professionals. That priming effect is particularly evident in the Little Rascals Day Care Center case in Edenton, North Carolina, where seven adults, five of them day care providers and the other two unaffiliated with the center, were charged with sexually abusing nearly a hundred children in satanic rituals. Just a few months before the case began, the detective who would go on to investigate the Little Rascals case, the prosecutor who tried it, and the social workers who repeatedly interviewed the children, had attended a three-day conference on satanic ritual abuse in day care centers.

6. That case was Fran's Day Care in Austin, Texas. Day care owner Fran Keller and her husband Dan were each convicted of one count of aggravated sexual assault on a child and were sentenced to 48 years in prison, where they remain today. For a thorough examination of this controversial case, see Gary Cartwright's investigative report, "The Innocent and the Damned."

7. In a sample of 35 major satanic day care center cases, 30 (49%) of the 61 criminally charged day care providers were male.

WORKS CITED

Adler, Jeffrey S. "The Making of a Moral Panic in 19th Century America: The Boston Garroting Hysteria of 1865." *Deviant Behavior* 17 (1996): 259–78.

"Believe the Children." (Brochure). Cary, IL: Author, n.d.

Ben-Yehuda, Nachman. "The European Witch Craze of the 14th and 17th Centuries: A Sociological Perspective." *American Journal of Sociology* 86 (1980): 1–31.

Bordin, Judith A. "The Aftermath of Nonsubstantiated Child Abuse Allegations in Child Care Centers." *Child and Youth Care Forum* 25 (1996): 73–87.

Bromley, David, and Bruce C. Busching. "Understanding the Structure of Contractual and Covenantal Social Relations." *Sociological Analysis* 49 (1989): 15–32.

Brozan, N. "Witness Says She Fears 'Child Predator' Network." *New York Times* 18 Sept. 1984: A21.

Cartwright, Gary. "The Innocent and the Damned." *Texas Monthly* April 1994: 100–05+.

Cohen, Stanley. *Folk Devils and Moral Panics.* London: MacGibbon and Kee, 1972.

DeBenedictis, Don J. "McMartin Preschool's Lessons." *ABA Journal* 55 (1990): 28–9.

Goode, Erich, and Nachman Ben-Yehuda. "Moral Panics: Culture, Politics, and Social Construction." *Annual Review of Sociology* 20 (1994): 149–71.

Hofferth, Sandra L., and Deborah A. Phillips. "Child Care in the United States: 1970–1995." *Journal of Marriage and the Family* 49 (1987): 559–71.

Hubler, Shawn. "Driven to Her Death." *Los Angeles Herald Examiner* 8 Mar. 1987: A1.

Hutchison, Elizabeth D. "Child Welfare as a Woman's Issue." *Families in Society* 73 (1992): 67–77.

Kenniston, Kenneth. *Youth and Dissent: The Rise of a New Opposition.* New York: Harcourt, 1971.

Nathan, Debbie, and Michael Snedeker. *Satan's Silence: Ritual Abuse and the Making of a Modern American Witchhunt.* New York: Basic, 1995.

Negrey, Cynthia. *Gender, Time, and Reduced Work.* Albany, New York: State University of New York Press, 1993.

Rubin, Lillian. *Families on the Fault Line.* New York: Harper, 1994.

Sauer, Mark. "Decade of Accusations: The McMartin Preschool Child Abuse Case Launched 100 Others." *San Diego Union Tribune* 29 Aug. 1993: D1.

Shaw, David. "Reporter's Early Exclusives Triggered a Media Frenzy." *Los Angeles Times* 20 Jan. 1990: A1.

Sindall, Rob. "The London Garrotting Panics of 1856 and 1862." *Social History* 12 (1987): 351–58.

Stacey, Judith. *Brave New Families.* New York: Basic, 1990.

Timnick, Lois. "McMartin Attorneys to Seek Relocation of Trial." *Los Angeles Times* 23 Feb. 1987: A1.

Victor, Jeffrey. *Satanic Panic.* Chicago, IL: Open Court, 1993.

Weinbach, Robert W. "Refeminization of Child Care: Causation, Costs and Cures." *Journal of Sociology and Social Welfare* 14 (1987): 31–40.

16.
CRIME SCARES

ROBERT HEINER

The correlation between the actual incidence of crime and public perceptions of crime is always less than perfect; and there are times when there appears to be no correlation at all. At certain times, crime in general, or certain types of crime receive a great surge of attention from the media, politicians, and the public, though this surge of attention is unwarranted given the objective evidence. That is, suddenly crime becomes a heated social problem, even though the evidence suggests that there has been no sudden surge in criminal activity. The media and the public are whipped into a frenzy; many come to think that social life is very dangerous and/or that society is on the verge of a moral breakdown. We might call this phenomenon a "crime scare." Following are some examples of crime scares that occurred in the late twentieth century.

THE MISSING CHILDREN SCARE

Beginning in the early 1980s, Americans were besieged by reports of missing children. Although the phrase "missing children" actually includes runaways, children taken by a parent who lost legal custody, and abduction by strangers, the public was given the impression that stranger abductions represented the preponderance of the problem. This followed a couple of well-publicized stranger abductions that resulted in the child's death. Most notable was the case of Adam Walsh, who was abducted and whose dismembered body was later found on a riverbank in Hollywood, Florida. His father, John Walsh, subsequently became a leading activist for the cause of missing children and is renowned as the television host of *America's Most Wanted*.

Activists and politicians began describing a social problem of immense proportions. Joel Best describes the situation:

> The crusaders described a stranger-abduction problem of astonishing dimensions. Then U.S. Representative Paul Simon offered "the most conservative estimate you will get anywhere"—50,000 children abducted by strangers annually. Child Find, a leading child-search organization, estimated that parents recovered only 10 percent of these children, that another 10 percent were found dead, and that the remainder—40,000 cases per year—remained missing. In short, the crusaders described a large number of stranger abductions with very serious consequences.[1]

The social problems perspective defines a social problem as a phenomenon recognized as such by a significant part of the population. By the mid-1980s, stranger abduction easily met this definition. The National Center for Missing and Exploited Children had been established, pictures of missing children were showing up on the sides of milk cartons, talk shows devoted considerable air-time to the issue, the estimate of 50,000 stranger abductions per year became popular wisdom, and the press played its role in perpetuating the scare. Best reports that ABC's first news story about the problem stated, "By conservative estimate, 50,000 children are abducted each year, not counting parental kidnappings and custody fights. Most are never found. Four to eight thousand a year are murdered."[2] Meanwhile, surveys showed a growing concern, some might say "paranoia," among parents and children.[3] Parents became ever more watchful of their children, sometimes going so far as to keep identification files with photographs and dental records (in case they should be needed to identify their children's dead bodies). And children were encouraged to be fearful of strangers.

In 1985, however, the 50,000 figure began to be questioned. The *Denver Post*, which later won a Pulitzer Prize for its coverage of the issue, drew attention to the fact that the FBI investigated only 67 cases of stranger abductions in 1984. A *Post* editorial suggested that there are more "preschoolers who choke to death on food each year" than are abducted by strangers.[4]

In actuality, the FBI figure is probably way too low (because they do not investigate all stranger abductions), and the 50,000 figure claimed by the crusaders is certainly way too high. According to Best and extrapolations made by other researchers, the figure is probably in the neighborhood of 500 to 1,000 children abducted by strangers every year.[5] When confronted with the outrageousness of the 50,000 estimate, crusaders would often respond that "one missing child is too many."

As sociologists interested in social problems, we need to look more carefully at this statement. Yes, it is true, one missing child is a tragedy. However, there are millions of tragedies that take place in the world each and every day; few of them are successfully constructed into "social problems." People have a limited amount of time and emotion to attach to social problems, and they cannot do this for the millions of tragedies that take place every day. Potential social problems compete for the public's attention. The public needs accurate information in order to set rational priorities with regard to social problems. Suppose there were "only one" missing-then-murdered child per year, but 5,000 workplace fatalities, many of them resulting from worker safety violations every year. More people might rationally assess worker safety to be a greater threat to themselves and their families. Then, worker safety would become a heated social problem, and public policy might be implemented that would improve the safety conditions of millions of workers. This rational prioritization of social problems is preempted by much of the heated rhetoric and inflated statistics that are often used by activists, capitalized on by politicians, and propagated by the media.

THE SERIAL MURDER SCARE

In the 1980s and 1990s, serial murder came to occupy the public imagination in a big way. This was thanks largely to some highly publicized cases (e.g., Ted Bundy, Henry Lee Lucas, John Wayne Gacy, and later, Jeffrey Dahmer), as well as some very popular fictional books and movies (most notably, *Silence of the Lambs*). The FBI's Behavioral Sciences Unit was also highly instrumental in spreading fear of serial homicide. In the early 1980s, it estimated that approximately one-fifth of all American homicides were cases of serial murders; their estimates went as high as 4,000 or

5,000 cases per year. These estimates were based on the assumption that when the police reported an *unknown* circumstance in a homicide case, that case must have been the work of a serial killer. Phillip Jenkins writes,

> . . . this interpretation of the data is quite unwarranted. In effect, it suggests that an *unknown* circumstance equates to *no apparent motive*, which in turn means that the murder is *motiveless*, or "with no apparent rhyme, reason, or motivation." This is unpardonable. All that can be legitimately understood from an *unknown* circumstance is that, at the time of completing the form, the police agency in question either did not know the exact context of the crime, or did not trouble to fill in the forms correctly.[6]

Nevertheless, in 1983, the U.S. Justice Department held a news conference about the alarming increase in the serial murder phenomenon. At the conference, Justice Department officials reiterated that there were likely several thousand cases of serial murder each year and "that there might be thirty-five such killers active in the United States at any given time."[7] The juxtaposition of these two figures—4,000 victims and 35 serial killers—meant that the average serial killer must have been responsible for over 100 killings per year. Interestingly, there is no confirmed case on record in which a serial killer was responsible for so many murders. At least one of the two statistics was in need of serious readjustment.

According to Jenkins and, indeed, more recent FBI estimates, there may indeed be more than 35 serial killers operating in the United States at any given time, but the annual number of victims, rather than being in the neighborhood of 4,000, is more likely to be in the range of 50– 70.[8] This latter estimate amounts to considerably less than 1 percent of all U.S. homicides. Writes Jenkins,

> In reality, serial homicide accounts for a very small proportion of American murders, and the claims frequently made in the 1980s exaggerated the scale of victimization by a factor of at least twenty. Moreover, such offenses are far from new, and the volume of activity in recent years is little different from conditions in the early part of the present century, while the phenomenon is by no means distinctively American.[9]

Much as in the case of stranger abductions of children, discussed above, misleading statistics and images concerning serial murders captured the public's attention and fostered a deeply ingrained fear of strangers among millions of Americans, even though statistically their chances of being murdered by an acquaintance or loved one were enormously greater than their chances of being murdered by a serial killer. In fact, 70 serial killings per year in a country of over 300 million people means that any person's chances of being murdered by a serial killer were infinitesimally small.

Thus, in the case of serial homicide, the perceived, or subjective, reality of the problem bore little resemblance to the objective reality. We can say, then, that serial homicide was a socially constructed problem. This leads us to the question, Why was this social problem so successfully constructed? Why were such misleading statistics accepted and internalized by so many? The answer, according to Jenkins's constructionist analysis, lies in the fact that a diverse number of interest groups found it to their advantage to perpetuate exaggerated statistics.

The FBI had an interest in perpetuating the myth that there were thousands of victims of crazed killers who roamed the country. They claimed part of the problem lay in the lack of communication between law enforcement agencies, as well as their inability to make the connections between similar crimes happening in very different locations. By exaggerating the extent of these crimes and the extent to which serial killers actually "roam" and by establishing themselves as the experts who could link these disparate killings, the FBI was able to enhance both its jurisdiction and its prestige. Prior to the serial homicide scare, the FBI's jurisdiction was quite limited, restricted to federal crimes and/or crimes that involved the crossing of state lines. However, thanks to the serial homicide scare, the Behavioral Sciences Unit managed to portray themselves as supersleuths, and the public and other law enforcement agencies came to welcome their help rather than resent the intrusion of federal powers, as they might have prior to the scare.

Jenkins argues that the serial killer scare also fit neatly into the ideological framework of the conservative Reagan administration. Conservative ideology places blame for society's problems on weak, immoral, or depraved individuals rather than on the social structure. The serial homicide scare diverted attention away from other crimes—the vast majority of crimes—that can be more readily associated with the social structure. The vast majority of homicides, for example, occur within the lower class and can, therefore, arguably be linked with poverty and similar structural determinants. Serial homicides, on the other hand, are less readily linked to the social structure; they appear to occur randomly, and they seem to be committed by crazed, pathological, immoral individuals who are, quite simply, "evil." Consequently, by shifting society's focus on crime to serial killings, conservatives were able to perpetuate their view that crime has more to do with the moral breakdown of our society than with poverty, inequality, and the dismantling of social welfare programs.

Paradoxically, liberal groups also found an interest in perpetuating the inflated statistics. When the victims were black, as were many of Jeffrey Dahmer's and John Wayne Gacy's victims, black leaders could blame the problem on a lack of concern on the part of law enforcement agencies and their neglect of cases involving missing African Americans. When the victims were gay, similar complaints could be lodged by gay activists. When the victims were female, feminists could blame the patriarchal criminal justice system for its lack of concern for female victims, in which case serial homicide could be "contextualized together with offenses such as rape, child molestation, and sexual harassment."[10]

(Ironically, the serial murder scare also served the interests of those serial murderers who were convicted or were in jail awaiting trial. They received extraordinary amounts of media attention and their exploits, some would say, were "glorified" by the media. Their murderous activities and their perverse "skills" were recounted in numerous books and movies, both fiction and nonfiction. At least one of these convicted murderers, Henry Lee Lucas, even got to escape the drudgery of imprisonment and fly around the country confessing—probably falsely—to unsolved murders.)

In other words, the myths surrounding serial homicide were successfully constructed because many parties had an interest in perpetuating these myths and few had an interest in uncovering the truth. Once again, we can see a connection between crime—in this case, perceptions of crime—and politics. Once again, different groups entered the political arena fighting for their interests and allowing certain misperceptions to reign because it suited them to do so.

THE DRUG SCARE

Beginning in 1986 and continuing for several years, the American public was hit with a barrage of news stories about the problem of drugs, especially crack cocaine. Arnold Trebach refers to

"The Scared Summer of '86," while Craig Reinarman and Harry G. Levine refer to the phenomenon as "The Crack Attack." Reinarman and Levine note that while there have been numerous drug scares in the United States, probably none has paralleled in intensity this most recent "crack attack."[11] Erich Goode and Nachman Ben-Yehuda write, "It is possible that in no other decade has the issue of drugs occupied such a huge and troubling space in the public consciousness."[12]

Powder cocaine is a stimulant that is usually inhaled through the nose (i.e., "snorted"); it is quite expensive, and the "high" that it induces is generally a subtle one. Crack cocaine, however, is crystalline; it is smoked; it is considerably less expensive; and the high it induces is quite intense, though relatively brief. Crack's effects are considerably harsher than those of powder cocaine, and its appeal seems, more or less, limited to residents of impoverished inner-city neighborhoods, the same people, note Reinarman and Levine, who have traditionally gravitated toward heroin.[13]

While a smokable and more intense form of cocaine (namely, "freebase") had been around since the 1970s, crack did not appear on the scene until the mid-1980s. When it did appear, it was referred to by the media, politicians, and many in the drug treatment community as being one of the worst scourges ever to hit America. Numerous stories in the press referred to crack as "instantly addicting."[14] Terms such as "epidemic" and "plague" were popularly used to describe the phenomenon. Crack's popularity in the inner-city ghettos was usually noted, but then news stories went on to explain how the "epidemic" was spreading into middle-class high schools and suburbs. A full-page editorial in *Newsweek*, written by the editor-in-chief and entitled "The Plague Among Us," reported that "An epidemic is abroad in America, as pervasive and dangerous in its way as the plagues of medieval times. [The epidemic] has taken lives, wrecked careers, broken homes, invaded schools, incited crimes, tainted businesses, toppled heroes, corrupted policemen and politicians."[15] The CBS television weekly newsmagazine *48 Hours* aired an episode entitled "48 Hours on Crack Street," which attracted the largest audience in years for a television news documentary. Write Reinarman and Levine,

> In July 1986 alone, the three major TV networks offered 74 evening news segments on drugs, half of these about crack. In the month leading up to the November elections, a handful of national newspapers and magazines produced roughly 1,000 stories discussing crack. Like the TV networks, leading newsmagazines like *Time* and *Newsweek* seemed determined not to be outdone; each devoted five cover stories to crack and the "drug crisis" in 1986 alone.[16]

In 1987, a nonelection year, drug coverage began to subside; then in 1988, it began to pick up again. On September 5, 1989, President George H. W. Bush went on the air with a speech from the Oval Office about the drug crisis in the United States. During the speech, he held up a plastic bag labeled "EVIDENCE" that contained crack, and he announced that it was "seized a few days ago in a park across the street from the White House." It was revealed a couple of weeks later by the *Washington Post* and by National Public Radio that the bag of crack President Bush had held up was little more than a theatrical prop:

> A White House aide told the *Post* that the President "liked the prop. . . . It drove the point home." Bush and his advisors also decided that crack should be seized in Lafayette Park across from the White House or nearby so that the president could say that crack had become so pervasive that men were "selling drugs in front of the White House."[17]

White House and Justice Department operatives, however, found it quite difficult to find any drugs being sold in the vicinity of the White House. As a last resort, they had to entice an 18-year-old to come to the park and sell them the crack. Rather than "seizing" the crack, they bought it from him and sent him on his way. ("Seizure" implies that an arrest was made; and if an arrest had been made, the White House might have had to answer some sticky questions about entrapment and the whole setup would have been brought more readily to the public's attention.)

The "bag of crack speech" provides a good example of how the public was being manipulated throughout the drug scare years. While reporting about the drug "epidemic" was skyrocketing, actual drug use was not. Reports of the "epidemic" rarely, if ever, referred to objective data. Surveys showed that drug use was actually going down at the time of the scare. These surveys did not distinguish between different types of cocaine use, but they did show that cocaine use, in general, was dropping.[18] While the networks were reporting that crack was "flooding America" and that it had become "America's drug of choice," in 1986, report Reinarman and Levine, "*there were no prevalence statistics at all on crack.*"[19]

> The first official measures of the prevalence of crack began with [the] National Institute on Drug Abuse's 1986 high school survey. It found that 4.1 percent of high school seniors reported having tried crack (at least once) in the previous year. This figure dropped to 3.9 percent in 1987, and to 3.1 percent in 1988, a 25 percent decline. This means that at the peak of crack use, 96 percent of America's high school seniors had never tried crack, much less gone on to more regular use, abuse, or addiction.[20]

The objective data hardly indicated a plague or crack epidemic; and if those who touted the problem were so concerned about drug use's threat to our health, they might have mentioned that alcohol and tobacco are, by far, the most popular drugs among Americans, including teenagers, and that they account for far more deaths than do powder or crack cocaine.

While drug use was dropping, surveys indicated that the number of Americans who thought drugs to be the most serious problem facing the country went up dramatically. "The percentage reporting that drug abuse was the nation's most important problem," notes Katherine Beckett, "jumped from 3 percent in 1986 to 64 percent in 1987."[21] Since this dramatic change in the popular perception of drugs was not due to actual increases in drug use, it must have been related to the rhetoric of politicians and/or the intensified media coverage. According to Beckett as well as Reinarman and Levine, the drug scare was largely the result of a political initiative.[22]

As with the serial homicide scare, the drug problem resonated with the conservative ideology that was very popular at the time. Liberal ideology had fallen from grace, and social welfare programs were being defunded. Society's problems were seen, not in terms of inequality and social structural arrangements, but as indicative of a moral breakdown. The solution, according to First Lady Nancy Reagan's anti-drug crusade, was learning to "just say no." To the extent that it was recognized that crack was used disproportionately by poor, inner-city minorities, poverty was considered the effect, not the cause, of drug abuse. Reinarman and Levine write,

> Drug problems fit neatly onto this ideological agenda and allowed conservatives to engage in what might be called sociological denial—to scapegoat drugs for many social and economic problems. For Reagan-style conservatives, people did not so much abuse drugs because they were jobless, homeless, poor, depressed, or alienated; they were jobless, homeless, poor, depressed, or alienated because they were weak, immoral, or foolish enough to use illicit drugs.[23]

Meanwhile, in Congress, this conservative ideology had become so popular that both Republicans and Democrats were jostling to demonstrate who could be tougher on crime. A "feeding frenzy" ensued, resulting in more and more media coverage of the issue and tougher and tougher legislation aimed at drug abuse. Lengthier and mandatory sentences were imposed, and rather than just focusing on sellers, the casual user became the target of stronger law enforcement measures. In the 1980s, the U.S. incarceration rate more than doubled, becoming one of the highest, if not the highest, in the world. This expansion was due in large part to the "War on Drugs" and the legacy of this war is still seen today in the vast numbers of men, women and resources going into our prisons.

From the perspective of critical constructionism, all of these crime scares diverted the public's attention away from other problems whose remedies might threaten elite interests.

DISCUSSION QUESTIONS

1. As we have seen in all of the articles in this section, moral panics (or crime scares) are at least partly explained by a certain conservativism among the public and among those who "promote" the panic. "Conservative" literally means being predisposed to hold onto things the way they are or to return to the way things used to be. Using examples from the readings in this section, explain how this predisposition plays a role in moral panics.

2. As explained in the introduction to this section, it is difficult to identify a moral panic in the midst of one. Why is this the case? What do you think might be some indicators to the layperson or to the sociologist that a moral panic is underway?

NOTES

1. Joel Best, "Missing Children, Misleading Statistics," in W. Feigelman (Ed.), *Readings on Social Problems: Probing the Extent, Causes, and Remedies of America's Social Problems.* Fort Worth, TX: Holt, Rinehart and Winston, 1990, 11–16, at 11.
2. Ibid., 12.
3. Ibid.
4. Ibid.
5. Ibid.
6. Phillip Jenkins, *Using Murder: The Social Construction of Serial Homicide.* New York: Aldine de Gruyter, 1994, 61.
7. Ibid., 64.
8. Ibid.
9. Ibid., 22.
10. Ibid., 17.
11. Arnold S. Trebach, *The Great Drug War: And Radical Proposals That Could Make America Safe Again.* New York: Macmillan, 1987. Craig Reinarman and Harry Levine, "The Crack Attack: America's Latest Drug Scare, 1986–1992," in J. Best (Ed.), *Images of Issues: Typifying Contemporary Social Problems.* New York: Aldine de Gruyter, 1995, 147–186.
12. Erich Goode and Nachman Ben-Yehuda, *Moral Panics: The Social Construction of Deviance.* Cambridge, MA: Blackwell, 1994, 205.
13. Reinarman and Levine, "Crack Attack."
14. Trebach, *The Great Drug War*; Reinarman and Levine, "Crack Attack."

15. Richard Smith, "The Plague Among Us," *Newsweek*, June 16, 1986, 15.

16. Reinarman and Levine, "Crack Attack," 152.

17. Ibid., 155.

18. Ibid.

19. Ibid., 164 (emphasis in original).

20. Ibid.

21. Katherine Beckett, "Setting the Public Agenda: 'Street Crime' and Drug Use in American Politics," *Social Problems*, vol. 41, no. 3, 1994, 425–447.

22. Beckett, "Setting the Public Agenda"; Reinarman and Levine, "Crack Attack."

23. Reinarman and Levine, "Crack Attack," 170.

SEX AND SEXUALITY

Introduction

People are often amused to find out that a course on the sociology of deviance is a standard offering in most sociology departments. When I tell them I teach that course, family, friends, and colleagues often make an off-hand remark along with a knowing, slightly twisted smile and I realize that most lay people equate "deviance" with "perversion." They think I teach a course on sexual perverts. This lay perception is not entirely false because people commonly think that any sexual behavior that departs from the alleged norm in their society is unnatural and, therefore, perverted. Many of the articles included in this section were selected to challenge lay beliefs about what constitutes "natural" sexual behavior. If people were designed by genetics or evolution to have one sexual orientation, then people would possess only one sexual orientation. But, given the amazing diversity of orientations and behaviors within societies and across cultures, this is obviously not the case. While people in probably all societies make assumptions about which sexual behaviors are natural and which are unnatural, a cross-cultural analysis reveals this to be a false dichotomy. Accordingly, many normative sexual behaviors practiced in the United States would appear quite unnatural to peoples in other parts of the world. Ian Robertson writes,

> The conclusion from the cross-cultural data may be disconcerting to some, but it is inescapable. If you were an Alorese mother in Indonesia, you would habitually masturbate your infants to pacify them. . . . If you were a Chewa parent in central Africa, you would encourage your preadolescent daughter to have intercourse in the belief that she would otherwise be infertile when she grew up. If you were a Kwoma male in New Guinea, you would have learned to regard sex as so forbidding that you would never touch your own genitals, even when urinating. If you were an adolescent girl in traditional Mohave society, you would expect your first heterosexual intercourse to involve anal penetration. You would do these things with the full knowledge and approval of your community, and if your personal tastes ran counter to the prevailing norms, you might be considered distinctly odd—even wicked. Being no less ethnocentric than peoples in other societies, you would also regard American sexual attitudes and practices as most peculiar, to say the least. (Robertson, 1981: 211)

While the deviant status of homosexuality has lessened considerably over the past few decades, for many people it is still accompanied by a great deal of stigma and other negative social consequences. Constructions of sexuality in the United States lead to the popular belief that people fall into one of two dichotomous, mutually exclusive categories of homosexual and heterosexual. While some allowances are made for bisexuality, it is considered rare, if it is considered at all. Most people perceive others and perceive themselves as being either gay or straight. If you are gay, they believe, you are not straight; and if you are straight, you are not gay. Gay people should not consider straight sex pleasurable; and straight people should not consider gay sex pleasurable. But this is not the case in many societies and subcultures throughout the world and throughout history. It is well known that men in ancient Greece could engage in homosexual activities with boys without considering themselves homosexual. Albert Reiss (1961), in a classic article from the sociology of deviance, describes a subculture of teenage boys in the United States who prostitute themselves to gay men and who don't define themselves as gay as long as they follow the rules of the subculture (e.g., do it only for money and play only the inserter role in oral sex). Prison inmates, both male and female, often engage in homosexual relationships, not defining themselves as homosexual, and engaging in strictly heterosexual relationships upon their release.

The first three articles in this section describe the circumstances in other cultures and historical periods in which people engage(d) in what most North Americans would consider homosexual relationships without altering their image to others or to themselves as heterosexual. Roger Lancaster describes the case in Nicaragua, a culture that places a high value on the display of machismo among men, but that also allows them to engage in gay relationships without compromising their machismo. Kathyrn Kendall describes the situation in Lesotho in which women, frequently suffering abuse from their husbands and often left alone by their men for extended periods, often develop erotic same-sex friendships; but because there is no penis involved, they do not consider these relationships sexual or homosexual. And Serena Nanda portrays Native American Indian sex/gender systems of the past which were wholly misunderstood and condemned by the Europeans. She describes a variety of such systems among various American Indian peoples and reveals how irrelevant the European heterosexual/homosexual dichotomy is to an understanding of these systems.

All three of these articles implicate the importance of language in categorizing—or not categorizing—people's sexuality. A deviant label is a word, and without the word in one's vocabulary one cannot affix the label. John Lofland (1969) calls the words we use to differentiate between people "pivotal categories," or categories around which our perceptions pivot. These words act as figurative sockets in our brains into which we plug our perceptions. If we do not have the words for categorizing people's differences, then we do not perceive their difference, and then for all social purposes, they are not different. According to Roger Lancaster, while in Nicaragua they have words to describe men who play the passive role in anal intercourse with other men, they have no words that distinguish the male who plays the active role from any other male. The former is considered deviant while the latter is not. The cultures described by Nanda were overrun by people of white European origin who imposed their own language and categories of sexuality upon the natives. Kathryn Kendall expresses her fear that as Western ideas, words, and categories pervade African societies that the "special friendships" that she describes will become stigmatized and avoided. With globalization some old categories of normal are diminishing and some new categories of deviance are being introduced in various parts of the world. The diminishing diversity brought about by globalization is of considerable importance to the sociologist interested in deviance across cultures.

The next two selections address the issue of prostitution. The way people feel about prostitution and its deviant status vary from society to society. In the first of these articles, I describe the stigma attached to prostitution in South Korea. With tens or even hundreds of thousands of women engaged in sex work in this relatively small country, all women are potentially suspect and scrutinized for any signs of participation in the industry. In this patriarchal society, suspect signs of participation happen to be behaviors that might upset the social system in which men exercise control over women and therefore, I argue, prostitution serves a vital role in perpetuating the Korean patriarchy. In the next article, da Silva and Blanchette challenge the presumptively humane characterization of the relationship between the prostitute and the client as being one between victim and victimizer. Paradoxically, they argue that this characterization has led to the criminalization of the prostitute and to counterproductive social policy. They dispel several myths about Brazilian prostitution that may also apply to prostitution in other countries.

Many classic articles in the sociology of deviance reveal the myriad ways in which people manage the stigma that goes along with their deviant status. This section concludes with such a classic, "The Nudist Management of Respectability," which the author, Martin S. Weinberg, has revised and updated for this volume. Weinberg reveals that people who attend nudist resorts are highly sensitive to the perception that non-nudists have of nudists, seeing them as sexual deviants. This sensitivity translates itself into a set of rules for the resort meant to neutralize society's perceptions of nudists. The result is that, while nudists exhort that they are free from society's stilted notions about nudity and sexuality, they have created a very stilted society in which they are in effect less free than their would-be stigmatizers, bound by the extensive rules of the camp governing nudity and sexuality. This article is a classic because of its adept demonstration of the power of conventional norms even among those who band together to resist those norms.

We might distinguish between "anti-conformity" and "true independence." The true independent is someone who does what he or she wishes without regard to the conventional norms. The anti-conformist's behavior, on the other hand, is a *reaction* to conventional norms and, thus, the anti-conformist is very aware of the conventional norms while he or she is violating them. These nudists, then, are anti-conformists, governed by conventional norms as much as the rest of us, but to a different effect. Sociologically speaking, while many of us may fancy ourselves to be true independents or know others who do so, it is difficult to imagine such a person living among us for an extended period. She or he would be so unable or unwilling to negotiate the rules of the social world that their behavior would constantly offend those around them and they would likely end up in prison, a mental hospital, or dead. Such is the power of conventional norms.

References

Lofland John, *Deviance and identity,* Englewood Cliffs, NJ: Prentice-Hall, 1969.

Reiss, Albert J., Jr. "The social integration of queers and peers." *Social Problems,* 1961, vol. 9, pp. 102–120.

Robertson, Ian, *Sociology,* 2nd edition, New York: Worth, 1981.

17.
THE COCHÓN AND THE HOMBRE-HOMBRE IN NICARAGUA

ROGER N. LANCASTER

In the United States, conceptions of sexual orientation are dichotomized. That is, Americans tend to view sexuality in an either-or mode: either you're heterosexual or you're homosexual. If you are homosexual, then you are not heterosexual, and vice versa. If you enjoy sexual relations with the same sex, then you are homosexual and not heterosexual. Many other cultures (and some subcultures within the United States) do not force their members to fit into such mutually exclusive categories. That is, they permit a person to engage in homoerotic behavior without compromising his or her heterosexual status. However, there are rules that such a person must follow in order to maintain their status as "normal." The following article describes the situation in Nicaragua.

THE SOCIAL CONSTRUCTION OF SEXUAL PRACTICES

The *cochón*, at first glance, might be interpreted as a Nicaraguan "folk category." The noun itself appears in both masculine (*el cochón*) and feminine (*la cochón, la cochona*) genders; either case typically refers to a male. The term is loosely translated as "queer" or "faggot" by English-speaking visitors; educated Nicaraguans, if they are fluent in international terminologies, are apt to translate the term in a similar (but more polite) fashion, giving "gay" or "homosexual" as its English equivalents. It becomes clear on closer inspection, however, that the term differs markedly from its Anglo-American counterparts of whatever shade. (And therein lies the danger of treating it as a folk category, which suggests that it is simply the rural version of some larger cosmopolitan concept.) In the first place, the term is not always as derogatory as the slanderous English versions are. Of course, it can be derogatory, and it almost always is. However, it can also be neutral and descriptive. I have even heard it employed in a particular sort of praising manner by ordinary Nicaraguan men: for instance, "We must go to Carnaval this year and see the cochones. The cochones there are very, very beautiful."[1]

Second, and more important, the term marks and delimits a set of sexual practices that partially overlaps but is clearly not identical to our own notion of the homosexual. The term specifies only certain practices in certain contexts. Some acts that we would describe as homosexual bear neither stigma nor an accompanying identity of any special sort whatsoever; others clearly mark their practitioner as a cochón.

If homosexuality in the United States is most characteristically regarded as an oral phenomenon, Nicaraguan homosexual practice is understood in terms of an anal emphasis. The lexicon of male insult clearly reflects this anal emphasis in Nicaraguan culture, even as the North American lexicon generally reflects an oral orientation. Cocksucker is the most common sexually explicit pejorative in the United States. Although equivalents to this term are sometimes used in Nicaragua, men there are more likely to be insulted in reference to anal intercourse. The dominant assumptions of everyday discourse, too, reflect the assumption of privileged, primary, and defining routes of intercourse in each case. That is, in Anglo-American culture, orality defines the homosexual; whatever else he might or might not do, a gay man is understood as someone who engages in oral intercourse with other men. In Nicaragua, anal intercourse defines the cochón; whatever else he might or might not do, a cochón is tacitly understood as someone who engages in anal intercourse with other men. But more is involved here than a mere shifting of the dominant sites of erotic practice or a casting of stigma with reference to different body parts. With the exception of a few well-defined contexts (e.g., prisons) where the rule may be suspended, homosexual activity of any sort defines the Anglo-American homosexual. In Nicaragua, by contrast, it is the passive role in anal intercourse that defines the cochón. Oral or manual practices receive scant social attention; everyday speech does not treat them in great detail, and non-anal practices appear far less significant in the repertoire of actually practiced homosexual activities.

The term *cochón* itself appears to indicate the nature of that status and role. None of my informants was certain about the origin of the term; it is *Nica*, a word peculiar to the Nicaraguan dialect of Spanish. Moreover, one encounters different pronunciations in various neighborhoods, classes, and regions, so there can really be no agreed spelling of the word: I have heard it rendered *cuchón*, *culchón*, and even *colchón*.[2] The last suggests a possible origin of the word: *colchón* means "mattress." As one of my informants suggested when prompted to speculate on the origin of the word, "You get on top of him like a mattress."

In neighboring Honduras, the point is made with even greater linguistic precision. There, "passive" partners in anal intercourse are known as *culeros*, from the term *culo*, meaning "ass," with the standard ending *-ero*. A *zapatero* is a man who works with shoes (*zapatos*); a culero is a man whose sexual activity and identity are defined as anal. As in Nicaragua, the act of insertion carries with it no special identity, much less stigma.

"You get on top of him like a mattress" summarizes the nature of the cochón's status as well as any phrase could, but it also points to the question, *Who* gets on top of him like a mattress? The answer is, Not only other cochones. Indeed, relationships between cochones seem relatively rare and, when they occur, are generally short-term. It is typically a noncochón male who plays the active role in sexual intercourse: a machista or an *hombre-hombre*, a "manly man." Both terms designate a "masculine man" in the popular lexicon; cochones frequently use either term to designate potential sexual partners. Relationships of this type, between cochones and hombres-hombres, may be of any number of varieties: one-time-only affairs; purchased sex, with the purchase running in either direction (although most typically it is the cochón who pays); protracted relationships running weeks or months; or full-scale emotional commitments lasting years.

The last sort is preferred but carries its own type of difficulties, its own particular sadness. As one of my informants related, "I once had a lover for five continuous years. He was a sergeant in the military, an hombre-hombre. During this period of time he had at least fifteen girlfriends, but I was his only male lover. He visited me and we made love almost every day. You have asked me if there is love and romance in these relations; yes, there is. He was very romantic, very tender, and very jealous. But he is married now and I rarely see him."

. . . In spite of my research strategy, and in settings as diverse as the marketplace and the school, I did meet and interview a number of men classified as cochones.[3] In our discussions, many of them told me that they were really comfortable only in the anal-passive position. Others alternate between active and passive roles, depending on whether they are having relations with an hombre-hombre (almost always passive) or with another cochón (passive or active). Some reported practicing oral sex, though not as frequently as anal intercourse. Several of my noncochón informants denied having any knowledge of oral techniques. Nicaraguans in general express revulsion at the idea of oral intercourse, whether heterosexual or homosexual. "Oral sexual relations? What's that?" was a common response to my queries about varied sexual positions in heterosexual intercourse. "*Me disgusta*" (That's disgusting) was the typical response to my descriptions of cunnilingus and fellatio. A series of (not necessarily sexual) aversions and prohibitions concerning the mouth seems to be involved here. The mouth is seen as the primary route of contamination, the major path whereby illness enters the body, and sex is quintessentially *sucio* (dirty). This conception is socialized into children from infancy onward. Parents are always scolding their small children for putting things in their mouths. This oral prohibition curbs the possibilities of oral intercourse.

The resultant anal emphasis suggests a significant constraint on the nature of homoerotic practices. Unlike oral intercourse, which may lend itself to reciprocal sexual practices, anal intercourse invariably produces an active partner and a passive partner. It already speaks the language of "activity" and "passivity," as it were.[4] If oral intercourse suggests the possibility of an equal sign between partners, anal intercourse in rigidly defined contexts most likely produces an unequal relationship: a "masculine" and a "feminine" partner, as seen in the context of a highly gendered ordering of the world. But this anal emphasis is not merely a negative restraint on the independent variable (homosexuality); positively, it produces a whole field of practices and relations.

THE SPECIFIC ROUTES OF STIGMA

There is clearly stigma in Nicaraguan homosexual practice, but it is not a stigma of the sort that clings equally to both partners. Only the anal-passive cochón is stigmatized. His partner, the active hombre-hombre, is not stigmatized at all; moreover, no clear category exists in the popular language to classify him. For all purposes, he is just a normal Nicaraguan male. The term *heterosexual* is inappropriate here. First, neither it nor any equivalent of it appears in the popular language. Second, it is not really the issue. One is either a cochón or one is not. If one is not, it scarcely matters that one sleeps with cochones, regularly or irregularly. Indeed, a man can gain status among his peers as a vigorous machista by sleeping with cochones in much the same manner that one gains prestige by sleeping with many women. I once heard a Nicaraguan youth of nineteen boast to his younger friends: "I am very sexually experienced. I have had a lot of women, especially when I was in the army, over on the Atlantic coast. I have done everything.

I have even done it with cochones." No one in the group thought this a damning confession, and all present were impressed with their friend's sexual experience and prowess. This sort of sexual boasting is not unusual in male drinking talk.

For that matter, desire is not at issue here, and it is irrelevant to what degree one is attracted sexually to members of one's own sex, as long as that attraction does not compromise one's masculinity, defined as activity. What matters is the manner in which one is attracted to other males. It is expected that one would naturally be aroused by the idea of anally penetrating another male. (In neighboring Honduras, it is sometimes said that to become a man, one must sleep with a culero and two women.)

This is not to say that active homosexual pursuits are encouraged or even approved in all social contexts. Like adultery and heterosexual promiscuity, the active role in homosexual intercourse is seen as an infraction. That is, from the point of view of civil-religious authority, and from the point of view of women, it is indeed a "sin" (*pecado* or *mal*). But like its equivalent forms of adultery and promiscuity, the sodomizing act is a relatively minor sin. And in male-male social relations, any number of peccadillos (heavy drinking, promiscuity, the active role in same-sex intercourse) become status markers of male honor.

Nicaraguans exhibit no true horror of homosexuality in the North American style; their responses to the cochón tend rather toward amusement or contempt. The laughter of women often follows him down the street—discreet derision, perhaps, and behind his back, but the amusement of the community is ever present for the cochón. For men, the cochón is simultaneously an object of desire and reproach—but that opprobrium knows tacit limits, community bounds. A reasonably discreet cochón—one who dresses conservatively and keeps his affairs relatively discreet—will rarely be harassed or ridiculed in public, although he may be the target of private jokes. If he is very discreet, his status may never even be publicly acknowledged in his presence, and his practices will occupy the ambiguous category of a public secret. . . .

[T]he hombre-hombre's exemption from stigma is never entirely secure. He might find his honor tainted under certain circumstances. If an hombre-hombre's sexual engagement with a cochón comes to light, for example, and if the nature of that relationship is seen as compromising the former's strength and power—in other words, if he is seen as being emotionally vulnerable to another man—his own masculinity would be undermined, regardless of his physical role in intercourse, and he might well be enveloped within the cochón's stigma. Or if the *activo's* attraction to men is perceived as being so great as to define a clear preference for men, and if this preference is understood to mitigate his social and sexual dominion over women, he would be seen as forgoing his masculine privileges and would undoubtedly be stigmatized. However, the Nicaraguan hombre-hombre retains the tools and strategies to ward off such stigma, both within and even *through* his sexual relationships with other men, and his arsenal is not much less than that which is available to other men who are not sleeping with cochones.

This is a crucial point. These kinds of circumstances are perhaps not exceptions at all but simply applications of the rules in their most general sense. Such rules apply not only to those men who engage in sexual intercourse with other men but also to men who have sex only with women. The sound of stigma is the clatter of a malicious gossip that targets others' vulnerabilities. Thus, if a man fails to maintain the upper hand in his relations with women, his demeanor might well be judged passive, and he may be stigmatized, by degrees, as a *cabrón* (cuckold), *maricón* (effeminate man), and cochón. Whoever fails to maintain an aggressively masculine front will be teased, ridiculed, and, ultimately, stigmatized. In this regard, accusations that one is a cochón are bandied about in an almost random manner: as a jest between friends, as an incitement between rivals, as a violent insult between enemies. Cats that fail to catch mice, dogs that fail to bark, boys who fail to fight, and men who fail in their pursuit of a woman: all are reproached with the term. And sometimes, against all this background noise, the charge is leveled as an earnest accusation.

That is the peculiar and extravagant power of the stigmatizing category: like Nietzsche's "prison-house of language" (Jameson, 1972), it indeed confines those to whom it is most strictly applied; but ambiguously used, it conjures a terror that rules all men, all actions, all relationships.

DISCUSSION QUESTION

1. Much of this article is devoted to language and the words Nicaraguans use to describe particular behaviors and people. What is the significance of language to the sociology of deviance?

NOTES

1. Called "the festival of disguises," Carnaval is a religious celebration held annually in the large agricultural market town of Masaya. It marks the climax of a series of religious festivals in that town, and not the approach of Lent. An important presence among the elaborate masks and disguises of Carnaval is that of the cochones, who don female attire and parade alongside other participants in the day's procession.
2. My spelling throughout conforms to the only spelling I have ever seen in print, in a *Nuevo diario* editorial (6 Dec. 1985).
3. I was not "out"—openly gay—in Erasmus Jimenez. At first, this strategy was to ensure that I could establish good relations with my informants, who, I imagined, would not approve. Later, it became problematic to me just how I would articulate my own understanding of my own sexuality to my informants—as this chapter demonstrates. Covertly, and through various circumlocutions, a few men from the neighborhood attempted to establish sexual liaisons with me; more generally, I encountered cochones in "neutral" and relatively "anonymous" settings such as the marketplace. In either case, for the most part these men assumed that I was an hombre-hombre. If I described myself to them as homosexual or gay, their sexual interest was generally diminished greatly.
4. As Boswell observes (1989, 33–34), fellatio can be considered an "active" behavior; if anything, it is the fellated who is "passive."

REFERENCES

Boswell, John. 1989. "Revolutions, Universals, and Sexual Categories." In Duberman et al., *Hidden from History*, 17–36. New York: NAL Books.

Jameson, Frederic, 1972. *The Prison-House of Language: A Critical Account of Structuralism and Russian Formalism.* Princeton: Princeton University Press.

18.

WOMEN IN LESOTHO AND THE (WESTERN) CONSTRUCTION OF HOMOPHOBIA

KATHRYN KENDALL

Kendall describes the tender, loving, and physical relationships that are often shared by women in Lesotho, an impoverished and harshly patriarchal society. Basotho women see these relationships as nothing more than special friendships while people in the West are inclined to view them as lesbian relationships. The "lesbian" category is foreign to Basotho women; but with globalization, Kendall reasonably fears, these relationships will become increasingly stigmatized.

Globalization could indeed cause radical shifts in the construction of deviant categories in countries throughout the world.

My search for lesbians in Lesotho began in 1992, when I arrived in that small, impoverished southern African country and went looking for my own kind. That was before the president of nearby Zimbabwe, Robert Mugabe, himself mission-educated, declared moral war on homosexuality and insisted that homosexuality was a "Western" phenomenon imported into Africa by the colonists.[1] When I left Lesotho two and a half years later, I had not found a single Mosotho[2] who identified herself as a lesbian. However, I had found widespread, apparently normative erotic relationships among the Basotho women I knew, in conjunction with the absence of a concept of this behavior as "sexual" or as something that might have a name. I learned not to look for unconventionality or visible performance of sex role rejection as indicators of "queerness." Most Basotho women grow up in environments where it is impossible for them to learn about, purchase, or display symbols of gay visibility, where passionate relationships between women are as conventional as (heterosexual) marriage, and where women who love women usually perform also the roles of conventional wives and mothers. I have had to look again at how female sexualities express themselves, how privilege and lesbianism intersect (or do not), and whether what women have together—in Lesotho or anywhere else—should be called "sex" at all. I have concluded that love between women is as native to southern Africa as the soil itself, but that homophobia, like Mugabe's Christianity, is a Western import.

BACKGROUND: LESOTHO AND ITS HISTORY

Surrounded on all sides by South Africa, Lesotho, with no natural resources except population, squirms in an ever-tightening vise. Only 10 percent of the land in Lesotho is arable, but 82 percent of its population of over two million is engaged in subsistence agriculture (Internet World Factbook 1995). Most Basotho have no source of cash income at all, while a few are wealthy even by U.S. standards. Under these circumstances "mean national income per household member" means little, but in 1994 it was [about $13 per month] (Gay and Hall 1994:20). The conclusion of international experts is that Lesotho is experiencing a "permanent crisis" (Gay and Hall 1994:9) exacerbated by unemployment, population growth, decline in arable land, reduction in soil fertility, desertification, and hopelessness. . . .

All women are legally "minors" in Lesotho under customary law. Under common law women are minors until the age of twenty-one, but they revert to minor status if they marry, attaining majority status only if single or widowed (Gill 1992:5). Women cannot hold property; they have no custody rights in the case of divorce; they cannot inherit property if they have sons; they cannot borrow money, own or manage property or businesses, sign contracts, buy and sell livestock, land, or "unnecessary" goods. Nor can a woman obtain a passport without a husband's or father's consent (Gill 1992:5). Although women do now vote, the franchise is one of the few areas in which women have gained legal rights since independence in 1966. A few well-educated middle-class women are fighting for greater equity. The Federation of Women Lawyers has "mounted an awareness campaign on the rights of women" and is trying to secure legal rights for women, but with three legal codes operative in Lesotho (customary law based on tradition and the chieftaincy, common law based on the Roman-Dutch system of South Africa, and constitutional law) the going is difficult, to say the least, for Basotho feminists (Thai 1996:17). . . .

[An] important aspect of the background of this study is that women in Lesotho endure physical abuse almost universally. Marriage is compulsory by custom, and divorce is very expensive; the divorce rate is only 1 percent for this reason (Gill 1992:5). However, women manage up to 60 percent of the households on their own, in small part because of male migrant labor, but in larger part because of de facto separation and divorce occasioned by couples never having been married and then separating, by male abandonment, or by women leaving abusive mates (Gill 1992:21).

In the two years I lived in Lesotho, I met only one woman who said she had never been beaten by a husband or boyfriend, and she said she was the only woman she knew who had been so fortunate. According to precolonial tradition, a man claimed a woman as a wife by raping her, and this custom is still common in the mountain areas. One scholar notes the "apparent tolerance of a man's unbridled right to exploit women sexually" (Epprecht 1995:48). Men are conditioned to abuse women; women are conditioned to accept abuse. In this context, women often seek comfort, understanding, and support from other women. In addition, the homosocial nature of Basotho society, both before and after colonization, separates boys and girls from early childhood and conditions members of one gender group to regard members of the other gender group as a distinct "other." Thus, whatever her sexual desires and impulses may be, a Mosotho woman is likely to establish significant emotional bonds only with other women and with children and to become accustomed to expressing affection toward members of her own sex. Indeed, it is common all over Lesotho to see people of the same sex walking hand-in-hand or arm-in-arm, but it is so rare as to be remarkable to see public displays of affection between males and females. In this context, it is not surprising that some women who experience sexual desire for other women find it easy to express that desire, and it is also not surprising that the lines between what is affection and what is sex or desire blur.

PROBLEMATIZING THE AUTHOR

I cannot claim to have conducted an objective scientific study of Basotho women and sexuality, nor would I want to make such a claim. In every respect, what I see or understand of Basotho women's experience is filtered through my own range of perceptions and beliefs and is colored by my own experience of what is sexual, what is affectional, and what is possible between women. My experience as a lesbian shapes my interpretation of behavior I perceive as being "erotic" or "lesbianlike."[3] My experience as a white working-class woman, who has made it into academe and thereby lost her class connections and identity, shapes my understanding of privilege and its relationship to "lesbianism" as a lifestyle. I have now been "out" for thirty-one years, but I prefer not to share a household with my partner and resent definitions of lesbianism that reify the tidy domestic arrangement that features two middle-class women under one roof, so popular in lesbian communities in the U.S. My personal experience strongly influences my perception of the intersections of class privilege (or the lack of it) and sexual choices in Lesotho. My informants were all black women, Basotho friends, neighbors, and acquaintances, mostly residents of the Roma Valley, an area of Lesotho steeped in and named for the Roman Catholic religion. Although many of the women with whom I discussed women's sexuality had migrated to the Roma Valley from the mountains and can tell about rural women's lives firsthand, nonetheless there is a distance and separation of their experiences from those of the mountain women who have not migrated. The very fact that they were talking to a white woman about bodily functions set them apart from women in the mountains who have never done so. Their lenses, like mine, are unique, and not ideally representative, if indeed such a thing as ideal representativity exists. I speak Sesotho, but not fluently, and I am not an anthropologist. Much of what I have learned about women, class, and sexuality in Lesotho has come to me through lucky coincidences. . . .

WOMEN IN LESOTHO

Probably the most important accident in my quest for lesbians in Lesotho was that on my arrival at the university I was housed at the guest house, where I befriended 'M'e Mpho Nthunya, the cleaning woman.[4] I learned before long that 'M'e Mpho had actually, in a sense, married another woman (more about that later). When I asked her if she knew of any women-loving women in Lesotho, she was puzzled. "Many of us love each other," she said, laughing. Thinking she had misunderstood me, I said I meant not just affectionate loving, but, well, I stammered, "Women who share the blankets with each other," that being the euphemism in Lesotho for having sex.

'M'e Mpho found that uproariously funny. "It's impossible for two women to share the blankets," she said. "You can't have sex unless somebody has a *koai* (penis)." This concise, simple observation led me to two different but related trains of thought.

First, 'M'e Mpho's "impossible" brought to mind one of Greenberg's remarks in *The Construction of Homosexuality*, to wit, "the kinds of sexual acts *it is thought possible to perform*, and the social identities that come to be attached to those who perform them, vary from one society to another" (1988:3, italics mine). Greenberg continues:

> Homosexuality is not a conceptual category everywhere. To us, it connotes a symmetry between male-male and female-female relationships. . . . When used to characterize individuals, it implies that erotic attraction originates in a relatively stable, more or less exclusive attribute of the individual. Usually it connotes an exclusive orientation: the homosexual is not also heterosexual; the heterosexual is not also homosexual.
>
> Most non-Western societies make few of these assumptions. Distinctions of age, gender, and social status loom larger. The sexes are not necessarily conceived symmetrically. (1988:484)

Lesotho is one such non-Western society, and Basotho society has not constructed a social category "lesbian." Obviously in Lesotho the sexes are not conceived symmetrically. Nor is "exclusive orientation" economically feasible for most Basotho women. There is no tradition in Lesotho that permits or condones women or men remaining single; single persons are regarded as anomalous and tragic. Thus women have no identity apart from that of the men to whom they are related; only comparatively wealthy divorced or widowed women could set up housekeeping alone or with each other. As in many other African societies, including that of Swahili-speaking people in Mombasa, Kenya, "a respectable adult is a married adult" (Shepherd 1987:243). However, there is much less wealth in Lesotho than in Mombasa. The lesbian unions Shepherd describes as common and "open" among married and formerly married Swahili-speaking women are based, as she notes, on the constructions of rank and gender in that society, as well as upon the existence of a considerable number of women with sufficient economic power to support other women (1987:262–265). Even more important, Swahili-speaking women, according to Shepherd, do have a concept of the possibility of sexual activity between women. In Swahili the word for lesbian is *msagaji*, which means "a grinder" and has obvious descriptive meanings for at least one variety of lesbian sexual activity. Although I found no evidence of any comparable use of words in the Sesotho language, what is more significant is that Basotho women define sexual activity in a way that makes lesbianism linguistically inconceivable; it is not that "grinding" does not take place, but it is not considered "sexual."

The second train of thought 'M'e Mpho Nthunya's "impossible" led me to is the great mass of scientific sex studies. From Kraft-Ebbing through Kinsey and Hite and on up to the present, these studies repeatedly show that lesbians "have sex" less frequently than heterosexuals or gay men. Marilyn Frye (1992) cites one study by Blumstein and Schwartz that shows that "47% of lesbians in long-term relationships 'had sex' once a month or less, while among heterosexual married couples only 15% had sex once a month or less" (110). Frye is amused by how the sexperts count how many times people have sex. She notes that the question "how many times" they "had sex" is a source of merriment for lesbians. For what constitutes "a time"? Frye continues, "what 85% of long-term heterosexual married couples do more than once a month takes on the average eight minutes to do" (1992:110). In contrast, what lesbians do so much less frequently takes anything from half an hour to half a day to do and can take even longer if circumstances allow. Frye concludes: "My own view is that lesbian couples . . . don't 'have sex' at all. By the criteria that I'm betting most of the heterosexual people used in reporting the frequency with which they have sex, lesbians don't have sex. There is no male partner whose orgasm and ejaculation can be the criterion for counting 'times'" (1992:113).

Or as 'M'e Mpho Nthunya put it: no *koai*, no sex. Diane Richardson writes on a similar tack,

> How do you know you've had sex with a woman? Is it sex only if you have an orgasm? What if she comes and you don't? . . . What if what you did wasn't genital, say you stroked each other and kissed and caressed, would you later say you'd had sex with that woman? And would she say the same? The answer, of course, is that it depends; it would depend on how you and she interpreted what happened. (1992:188)

Since among liberated Western lesbians it is difficult to determine when one has had "sex" with a woman, it is not at all surprising that in Roman Catholic circles in Lesotho, "sex" is impossible without a *koai*. Among Basotho people, as among those surveyed in numerous studies in the U.S. and the U.K., sex is what men have—with women or with each other. The notion of "sex" or the "sex act" is so clearly defined by male sexual function that 'M'e Mpho Nthunya's view of it should not surprise any of us. However, women in Lesotho do, as 'M'e Mpho said, love each other. And in expressing that love, they have *something*.

Judith Gay (1985) documents the custom among boarding school girls in Lesotho of forming same-sex couples composed of a slightly more "dominant" partner, called a "mummy," and a slightly more "passive" partner called a "baby." The girls do not describe these relationships as sexual, although they include kissing, body rubbing, possessiveness and monogamy, the exchange of gifts and promises, and sometimes, genital contact (112). Gay also describes the custom among Basotho girls of lengthening the labia minora, which is done "alone or in small groups" and "appears to provide opportunities for auto-eroticism and mutual stimulation among girls" (1985:101). Certainly there are ample opportunities for Basotho women of various ages to touch each other, fondle each other, and enjoy each other physically. The fact that these activities are not considered to be "sexual" grants Basotho women the freedom to enjoy them without restraint, embarrassment, or the "identity crises" experienced by women in homophobic cultures like those of the U.S. and Europe. Margaret Jackson writes convincingly that the valorization of heterosexuality and the "increasing sexualization of western women [by sexologists] which has taken place since the nineteenth century should not be seen as 'liberating' but rather as an attempt to eroticize women's oppression" (1987:58).

I have observed Basotho women—domestic workers, university students, and secretaries (but not university lecturers)—kissing each other on the mouth with great tenderness, exploring each other's mouths with tongues and this for periods of time of more than sixty seconds—as a "normal," even daily expression of affection. The longest kisses usually take place out of view of men and children, so I presume that Basotho women are aware of the eroticism of these kisses and are protective of their intimacy, yet never have I heard any Mosotho woman describe these encounters as "sexual." When I called attention to this activity by naming it in speaking with a Mosotho professional researcher who was educated abroad, she told me, "Yes, in Lesotho, women like to kiss each other. And it's nothing except—." She seemed at a loss for words and did not finish the sentence but skipped, with some obvious nervousness, to "Sometimes-I-I-I-don't like it myself, but sometimes I just do it."

It is difficult to discuss women's sexuality in Lesotho because of the social taboos (both pre-colonial and postcolonial) against talking about it. Even now, it is socially taboo in Lesotho for a woman who has borne children to discuss sex with girls or women who have not. (Fortunately for my research, I have borne children; a childless American colleague also doing research in

Lesotho found it difficult to have discussions about sexuality with adult Basotho women.) My Basotho women friends would not dream of explaining menstruation to their daughters; rather, they expect girls to learn the mysteries of their developing bodies and of sexual practices from other girls, perhaps a year or two older than themselves. Like everything else in Lesotho, this is changing—very slowly in more remote rural areas and rather quickly in the towns. Sex education two or three generations ago took place in "initiation schools" for boys and girls, but these traditional schools were a major target of missionary disapproval and have now just about disappeared in all but the most remote areas. The taboo on talking about sex certainly hampered the efforts of family planning advocates to institute sex education during the 1970s. The Roman Catholic Church did little to change that, but as a result of concerted efforts of a number of non-governmental agencies and of the Lesotho government itself, birth control information, drugs, and other pregnancy-prevention techniques are now widely available in health clinics. For the most part, the Church now seems to look the other way when women line up at the clinics for pills, IUDs, and injections to prevent pregnancy.

More recently, government-sponsored AIDS education workers have been at pains to dispel dangerous myths kept alive by groups of prepubescent teenagers, to popularize the use of condoms, and to encourage young people to learn about and talk about "safe sex." Over time this may have profound and lasting effects on sexual behavior in Lesotho.

A number of difficulties remain. The Sesotho language was first written down by missionaries, who compiled the first Sesotho-English and Sesotho-French dictionaries; not surprisingly, these dictionaries include few words to describe sexuality or sex acts. If there ever were words for "cunnilingus," "g-spot," or "Do you prefer clitoral or vaginal orgasm?" in Sesotho, they certainly did not make it into the written records of the language nor do translations of these terms appear in phrase books or dictionaries.

My attempts to "come out" to rural women and domestic workers were laughable; they could not understand what I was talking about, and if I persisted, they only shook their heads in puzzlement. Despite this, I had some long conversations with Basotho women, especially older university students and domestic workers, who formed my social cohort in Lesotho and who trusted me enough to describe their encounters in as much detail as I requested. From these I learned of fairly common instances of tribadism or rubbing, fondling, and cunnilingus between Basotho women, with and without digital penetration. This they initially described as "loving each other," "staying together nicely," "holding each other," or "having a nice time together." But not as having sex. No *koai*, no sex.

Lillian Faderman's observation that "A narrower interpretation of what constitutes eroticism permitted a broader expression of erotic behavior [in the eighteenth century], since it was not considered inconsistent with virtue" (1981:191) makes sense here. If these long, sweet Basotho women's kisses or incidences of genital contact were defined as "sexual" in Lesotho, they could be subject to censure both by outside observers who seem to disapprove of sex generally (nuns, visiting teachers, traveling social workers) or by the very women who so enjoy them but seek to be morally upright and to do the right thing. If the mummy/baby relationships between boarding-school girls were defined as "sexual," they would no doubt be subject to the kind of repression "particular friendships" have suffered among nuns.

Since "sex" outside of marriage in Roman Catholic terms is a sin, then it is fortunate for women in this mostly Catholic country that what women do in Lesotho cannot possibly be sexual. No *koai*, no sex means that women's ways of expressing love, lust, passion, or joy in each other are neither immoral nor suspect. This may have been the point of view of the nineteenth-century missionaries who so energetically penetrated Lesotho and who must have found women-loving women there when they arrived. Judith Lorber writes, "Nineteenth-century women were supposed to be passionless but arousable by love of a man; therefore, two women together could not possibly be sexual" (1994:61).

'M'e Mpho Nthunya dictated her entire autobiography to me over the two years I lived in Lesotho, a book called *Singing Away the Hunger: The Autobiography of an African Woman* (1997). In it she describes, in addition to a loving and affectionate (though compulsory) heterosexual marriage, a kind of marriage to a woman that included an erotic dimension. According to Judith Gay (1985), these female marriages were common among women of Nthunya's generation. Gay writes, "elderly informants told me that special affective and gift exchange partnerships among girls and women existed 'in the old days' of their youth" (1985:101).

Nthunya describes how the woman she calls 'M'alineo chose her as her *motsoalle* (special friend) with a kiss. Nthunya writes: "It's like when a man chooses you for a wife, except when a man chooses, it's because he wants to share the blankets with you. The woman chooses you the same way, but she wants love only. When a woman loves another woman, you see, she can love with her whole heart" (1997:69).

Nthunya describes the process of their relationship, the desire that characterized it, the kisses they shared, their hand-holding in church, their meetings at the local cafe. And she describes the two ritual feasts observed by themselves and their husbands, recognizing their relationship. These feasts, held one year apart, involved ritual presentation and slaughter of sheep as well as eating, drinking, dancing, singing, exchanges of gifts, and general merriment and validation of the commitment they made to each other by all the people they knew. "It was like a wedding," Nthunya writes (1997:70). This ritual, which she describes as taking place around 1958, was widespread and well-known in the mountains where she lived. She describes the aftermath of her feast this way:

> So in the morning there were still some people drinking outside and inside, jiving and dancing and having a good time.
> Alexis [my husband] says to them, "Oh, you must go to your houses now. The joala [home-made beer] is finished."
> They said, "We want meat."
> He gave them the empty pot to show them the meat is all gone. But the ladies who were drinking didn't care. They said, "We are not here to see you; we are coming to see [your wife]."
> They sleep, they sing, they dance. Some of them are motsoalle of each other. (1997:71)

It would appear from Nthunya's story that long-term loving, intimate, and erotic relationships between women were normative in rural Lesotho at that time and were publicly acknowledged and honored. Gay (1985) describes an occasion when she was discussing women's relationships with three older women when a twenty-four-year-old daughter-in-law interrupted the discussion by clapping her hands. "Why are you clapping so?" asked the straightforward ninety-seven-year-old woman. "Haven't you ever fallen in love with another girl?" (1985:102). Both Nthunya's and

Gay's accounts emphasize the fact that while such relationships were common and culturally respected up to the 1950s, they no longer seem to exist, or at least young women of the 1980s and 1990s are unaware of this cultural activity so central to their grandmothers' lives. What remains are the affectionate relationships among girls and women, the public kissing and hand-holding, and the normativity of homosocial and homoerotic relationships among working-class or poor women. . . .

HOMOPHOBIA

After an earlier version of this article was published in Lesotho, I received a letter from a young professional woman with whom I had worked closely in writing workshops. She had read my article, came out to me in the letter, observed that she had not deduced that I was a lesbian either, and confirmed, "Life goes on in this place and like you said, we conform, smile and flirt with the male *homo sapiens* that we desperately wish to do without" (Anonymous 1997). She concluded her letter, "You cannot imagine the confusion and loneliness that drove me deeper into myself just wishing all the time I was raised in a different, freer society" (ibid.). This young Mosotho woman found the information about motsoalle relationships an interesting bit of history, and yet clearly, homophobia has now intervened in the lives of professional women to such an extent that she feels she has no permission to express her own sexuality.

In examining the question of options or choices it may be useful to clarify to what extent women in Lesotho have social or sexual options. Five years before Judith Gay wrote her article "Mummies and Babies," she wrote a Ph.D. dissertation at Cambridge called "Basotho Women's Options: A Study of Marital Careers in Rural Lesotho" (1980). In that paper she examined the lives of married women whose husbands are migrant workers and those whose husbands remain at home, of widows, and of separated or divorced women. Gay does not even mention the possibility of single, independent women living alone, or of lesbianism as an option for Basotho women. Instead she states, "marriage is the principal means whereby these women attain adult status and gain access to the productive resources and cash flows which are essential to them and their dependents" (1980:299). She predicts with accuracy the likelihood of growing unemployment among men in Lesotho and conjectures, "It is possible also that the resulting marital conflict and economic difficulties will lead to increasing numbers of independent women who become both heads of matrifocal families and links in matrilateral chains of women and children" (1980:312). That is certainly happening, and perhaps in another decade the lesbian option, as it is experienced in the northern hemisphere (or the "West"), will have come to Lesotho. But its shadow, homophobia, has already preceded it.

'M'e Mpho Nthunya concludes the story of her "marriage" to 'M'e Malineo as follows: "In the old days [note that here she refers to a period up to the late 1950s] celebrations of friendship were very beautiful—men friends and women friends. Now this custom is gone. People now don't love like they did long ago" (1995:7). As Nthunya and I were preparing her autobiography for publication, I asked her if she could add something to the conclusion of that chapter, to perhaps explain why people do not love like they did long ago. She added the following: "Today the young girls only want men friends; they don't know how to choose women friends. Maybe these girls just want money. Women never have money, so young girls, who want money more than love, get AIDS from these men at the same time they get the money" (1996:72). Perhaps that is all there is to it, though I would have thought that women in the "old days" needed money too. And the young professional woman who came out to me via the mail, who does not need money as desperately as the girls in Nthunya's experience, experiences homophobia in what she describes as a "soul-destroying" way (Anonymous 1997).

I believe that one pressure leading toward the demise of the celebration of batsoalle[5] is the increasing westernization of Lesotho and the arrival, at least in urban or semi-urban areas and in the middle class, of the social construction "homophobia" with and without its name. Gay noted in her study of lesbianlike relationships in Lesotho that women who live "near the main road and the South African border" were "no longer involved in intimate female friendships" (1985:102). Living near a "main road" or a South African border would expose a woman to imported ("Western") ideas and values, as would formal education. Women in rural areas would be less likely to suffer the pollution of homophobia.

By scrutinizing homophobia as the "queer" thing it is, given examples of healthy lesbian activity in indigenous cultures in Lesotho and elsewhere, we might conclude that homophobia is an "unnatural" vice, that homophobia is far more likely to qualify as "un-African" . . . than homosexuality, that homophobia is the product of peculiar (Western or northern-hemisphere) cultures.

As Michel Foucault writes in his groundbreaking *History of Sexuality*, it is useful to view sexuality not as a drive, but "as an especially dense transfer point for relations of power" (1981:103). No *koai*, no sex. In that case the loving and egalitarian erotic friendships of Basotho women would not be "sexual" at all, which is exactly what Basotho women have been saying whenever anyone asked them. The freedom, enjoyment, and mutual respect of Basotho women's ways of loving each other, occurring in a context in which what women do together is not defined as "sexual" suggests a need to look freshly at the way Western constructions of sexuality and of homophobia are used to limit and oppress women. Having a (sexualized) "lesbian option" may not be as liberating as many of us have thought.

DISCUSSION QUESTION

1. Do the women discussed in this article engage in sexual relations? Discuss the sociological considerations that go into answering this question.

NOTES

1. Mugabe was quoted in the South African newspaper *Mail and Guardian* declaring homosexuality "immoral," "repulsive," "an 'abhorrent' Western import" (p. 15, August 4–10, 1995).
2. Lesotho is the country; Sesotho is the language; one person from Lesotho is a Mosotho; two or more are Basotho.
3. If by "lesbian" we mean an identity that emerged in the twentieth century in certain Western cultures, then by definition the word cannot be applied to the Basotho situation. Some scholars are using the term "lesbianlike" to describe erotic and deeply affectional relationships among women who do not have the option of identifying themselves as lesbian. See, among others, Vicinus (1994) and Jenness (1992).
4. '*M'e* is the honorific or Sesotho term of address for a mature woman. It literally means "mother" and is used with the woman's first name. It is an insult to speak of her without the honorific or to speak of her by her surname only. In submission to Western academic custom, I sometimes

refer to 'M'e Mpho as "Nthunya" in this paper, but I would never address her in that form. One Mosotho woman said to me, "to speak of a grown woman without using 'M'e is the same as stripping off all her clothes."

5. Plural of motsoalle, special friend.

REFERENCES

Epprecht, Marc. 1995 "'Women's Conservatism' and the Politics of Gender in Late Colonial Lesotho." *Journal of African History* 36:29–56.

Faderman, Lillian. 1981. *Surpassing the Love of Men: Romantic Friendship and Love between Women from the Renaissance to the Present.* New York: William Morrow.

Foucault, Michel. 1981. *The History of Sexuality.* Harmondsworth: Penguin.

Frye, Marilyn. 1992. *Willful Virgin: Essays in Feminism, 1976–1992.* Freedom, CA: The Crossing Press.

Gay, John and David Hall. 1994. *Poverty in Lesotho, 1994: A Mapping Exercise.* Lesotho: Sechaba Consultants.

Gay, Judith. 1980. "Basotho Women's Options: A Study of Marital Careers in Rural Lesotho." Ph.D. diss., University of Cambridge.

———. 1985. "'Mummies and Babies' and Friends and Lovers in Lesotho." *Journal of Homosexuality* 2 (3–4): 97–116.

Gill, Debby. 1992. *Lesotho, a Gender Analysis: A Report Prepared for the Swedish International Development Authority.* Lesotho: Sechaba Consultants.

Greenberg, David E. 1988. *The Construction of Homosexuality.* Chicago: University of Chicago Press.

Internet World Factbook. 1996.: http\www\world.

Jackson, Margaret. 1987. "'Facts of Life' or the Eroticization of Women's Oppression? Sexology and the Social Construction of Heterosexuality." In Pat Caplan, ed., *The Cultural Construction of Sexuality,* pp. 52–81. London: Tavistock.

Jenness, Valerie. 1992. "Coming Out: Lesbian Identities and the Categorization Problem." In Ken Plummer, ed., *Modern Homosexualities: Fragments of Lesbian and Gay Experience,* pp. 65–74. London: Routledge.

Kendall [Kathryn]. 1986. "From Lesbian Heroine to Devoted Wife: Or, What the Stage Would Allow." *Journal of Homosexuality* 12 (3/4): 9–22.

———.1993. "Ways of Looking at Agnes de Castro." In Ellen Donkin and Susan Clement, eds., *Upstaging Big Daddy: Directing Theatre as if Race and Gender Matter,* pp. 107–120. Ann Arbor: University of Michigan Press.

Lorber, Judith. 1994. *Paradoxes of Gender.* New Haven: Yale University Press.

Nthunya, Mpho 'M'atsepo. 1995. "'M'alineo Chooses Me." In K. Limakatso Kendall, ed., *Basali! Stories by and about Basotho Women,* pp. 4–7. Pietermaritzburg: University of Natal Press.

———. 1997. *Singing Away the Hunger: Stories of a Life in Lesotho.* Ed. K. Limakatso Kendall. Pietermaritzburg: University of Natal Press, 1996. Reprint, Bloomington: Indiana University Press.

Richardson, Diane. 1992. "Constructing Lesbian Sexualities." In Ken Plummer, ed., *Modern Homosexualities,* pp. 187–199. London: Routledge.

Shepherd, Gill. 1987. "Rank, Gender, and Homosexuality: Mombasa as a Key to Understanding Sexual Options." In Pat Caplan, ed., *The Cultural Construction of Sexuality,* pp. 240–270. London: Tavistock.

Thai, Bethuel. 1996. "Laws Tough on Basotho Women." *Sowetan* 17.

Vicinus, Martha. 1994. "Lesbian History: All Theory and No Facts or All Facts and No Theory?" *Radical History Review* 60:57–75.

19.
MULTIPLE GENDERS AMONG NORTH AMERICAN INDIANS

SERENA NANDA

While Western societies have traditionally considered there to be only two genders, male and female, Serena Nanda describes the impressive variety of gender variants among Native American Indians. European observers considered those natives who occupied roles that did not fit into their simple gender categories to be perversions of nature. But, as Nanda describes, the gender variants functioned as integral, rather than marginal, members of their communities.

Note that often the community viewed the gender variant role as destined for a particular individual and, therefore, blame and ridicule were not involved. A similar phenomenon has been taking place in modern Western cultures: prejudice and discrimination against those with a minority sexual orientation have become less acceptable as sexual orientation has come to be understood as being not a matter of choice.

The early encounters between Europeans and Indian societies in the New World, in the fifteenth through the seventeenth centuries, brought together cultures with very different sex/gender systems. The Spanish explorers, coming from a society where sodomy was a heinous crime, were filled with contempt and outrage when they recorded the presence of men in American Indian societies who performed the work of women, dressed like women, and had sexual relations with men (Lang 1996; Roscoe in 1995).

Europeans labeled these men "berdache," a term originally derived from an Arabic word meaning male prostitute. As such, this term is inappropriate and insulting, and I use it here only to indicate the history of European (mis)understanding of American Indian sex/gender diversity. The term berdache focused attention on the sexuality associated with mixed gender roles, which the Europeans identified, incorrectly, with the "unnatural" and sinful practice of sodomy in their own societies. In their ethnocentrism, the early European explorers and colonists were unable to see beyond their own sex/gender systems and thus did not understand the multiple sex/gender systems they encountered in the Americas. They also largely overlooked the specialized and spiritual functions of many of these alternative sex/gender roles and the positive value attached to them in many American Indian societies.

By the late-nineteenth and early-twentieth centuries, some anthropologists included accounts of North American Indian sex/gender diversity in their ethnographies. They attempted to explain the berdache from various functional perspectives, that is, in terms of the contributions these sex/gender roles made to social structure or culture. These accounts, though less contemptuous than earlier, largely retained the emphasis on berdache sexuality. The berdache was defined as a form of "institutionalized homosexuality," which served as a social niche for individuals whose personality and sexual orientation did not match the definition of masculinity in their societies, or as a "way out" of the masculine or warrior role for "cowardly" or "failed" men (see Callender and Kochems 1983).

Anthropological accounts increasingly paid more attention, however, to the association of the berdache with shamanism and spiritual powers and also noted that mixed gender roles were often central and highly valued in American Indian cultures, rather than marginal and deviant. These accounts were, nevertheless, also ethnocentric in misidentifying indigenous gender diversity with European concepts of homosexuality, transvestism, or hermaphroditism, which continued to distort their indigenous meanings.

In American Indian societies, the European homosexual/heterosexual dichotomy was not culturally relevant and the European labeling of the berdache as homosexuals resulted from their own cultural emphasis on sexuality as a central, even defining, aspect of gender and on sodomy as an abnormal practice and/or a sin. While berdache in many American Indian societies did engage in sexual relations and even married persons of the same sex, this was not central to their alternative gender role. Another overemphasis resulting from European ethnocentrism was the identification of berdache as *transvestites*. Although berdache often cross-dressed, transvestism was not consistent within or across societies. European descriptions of berdache as *hermaphrodites* were also inaccurate.

Considering the variation in alternative sex/gender roles in native North America, a working definition may be useful: the berdache in the anthropological literature refers to people who partly or completely take on aspects of the culturally defined role of the other sex and who are classified neither as women nor men, but as genders of their own (see Callender and Kochems 1983:443). It is important to note here that berdache thus refers to variant gender roles, rather than a complete crossing over to an opposite gender role.

In the past twenty-five years there have been important shifts in perspectives on sex/gender diversity among American Indians and anthropologists, both Indian and non-Indian (Jacobs, Thomas, and Lang 1997:Introduction). Most current research rejects institutionalized homosexuality as an adequate explanation of American Indian gender diversity, emphasizing the importance of occupation rather than sexuality as its central feature. Contemporary ethnography views multiple sex/gender roles as a normative part of American Indian sex/gender systems, rather than as a marginal or deviant part (Albers 1989:134; Jacobs et al. 1997; Lang 1998). A new emphasis on the variety of alternative sex/gender roles in North America undercuts the earlier treatment of the berdache as a unitary phenomenon across North (and South) America (Callender and Kochems 1983; Jacobs et al. 1997; Lang 1998; Roscoe 1998). Current research also emphasizes the integrated and often highly valued position of gender variant persons and the association of sex/gender diversity with spiritual power (Roscoe 1996; Williams 1992).

A change in terminology has also taken place. Berdache generally has been rejected, but there is no unanimous agreement on what should replace it. One widely accepted suggestion is the term *two-spirit* (Jacobs et al. 1997; Lang 1998), a term coined in 1990 by urban American Indian gays and lesbians. Two-spirit has the advantage of conveying the spiritual nature of gender variance as viewed by gay, lesbian, and transgendered American Indians and also the spirituality associated with traditional American Indian gender variance, but the cultural continuity suggested by two-spirit is in fact a subject of debate. Another problem is that two-spirit emphasizes the Euro-American gender construction of only two genders. Thus, I use the more culturally neutral term, variant genders (or gender variants) and specific indigenous terms wherever possible.

DISTRIBUTION AND CHARACTERISTICS OF VARIANT SEX/GENDER ROLES

Multiple sex/gender systems were found in many, though not all, American Indian societies. Male gender variant roles (variant gender roles assumed by biological males) are documented for 110 to 150 societies. These roles occurred most frequently in the region extending from California to the Mississippi Valley and upper-Great Lakes, the Plains and the Prairies, the Southwest, and to a lesser extent along the Northwest Coast tribes. With few exceptions, gender variance is not historically documented for eastern North America, though it may have existed prior to European invasion and disappeared before it could be recorded historically (Callender and Kochems 1983; Fulton and Anderson 1992).

There were many variations in North American Indian gender diversity. American Indian cultures included three or four genders: men, women, male variants, and female variants (biological females who by engaging in male activities were reclassified as to gender). Gender variant roles differed in the criteria by which they were defined; the degree of their integration into the society; the norms governing their behavior; the way the role was acknowledged publicly or sanctioned; how others were expected to behave toward gender variant persons; the degree to which a gender changer was expected to adopt the role of the opposite sex or was limited in doing so; the power, sacred or secular, that was attributed to them; and the path to recruitment.

In spite of this variety, however, there were also some common or widespread features: transvestism, cross-gender occupation, same sex (but different gender) sexuality, some culturally normative and acknowledged process for recruitment to the role, special language and ritual roles, and associations with spiritual power.

TRANSVESTISM

The degree to which male and female gender variants were permitted to wear the clothing of the other sex varied. Transvestism was often associated with gender variance but was not equally important in all societies. Male gender variants frequently adopted women's dress and hairstyles partially or completely, and female gender variants partially adopted the clothing of men; sometimes, however, transvestism was prohibited. The choice of clothing was sometimes an individual matter and gender variants might mix their clothing and their accoutrements. For example, a female gender variant might wear a woman's dress but carry (male) weapons. Dress was also sometimes situationally determined: a male gender variant would have to wear men's clothing while engaging in warfare but might wear women's clothes at other times. Similarly, female gender variants might wear women's clothing when gathering (women's work), but male clothing when hunting (men's work) (Callender and Kochems 1983:447). Among the Navajo, a male gender variant, *nádleeh*, would adopt almost all aspects of a woman's dress, work, language and behavior; the Mohave male gender variant, called *alyha*, was at the extreme end of the cross-gender continuum in imitating female physiology as well as transvestism (the transvestite ceremony is discussed later in this chapter). Repression of visible forms of gender diversity, and ultimately the almost total decline of transvestism, were a direct result of American prohibitions against it.

OCCUPATION

Contemporary analysis emphasizes occupational aspects of American Indian gender variance as a central feature. Most frequently a boy's interest in the implements and activities of women and a girl's interest in the tools of male occupations signaled an individual's wish to undertake a gender variant role (Callender and Kochems 1983:447; Whitehead 1981). In hunting societies, for example, female gender variance was signaled by a girl rejecting the domestic activities associated with women and participating in playing and hunting with boys. In the arctic and subarctic, particularly, this was sometimes encouraged by a girl's parents if there were not enough boys to provide the family with food (Lang 1998). Male gender variants were frequently considered especially skilled and industrious in women's crafts and domestic work (though not in agriculture, where this was a man's task) (Roscoe 1991; 1996). Female gender crossers sometimes won reputations as superior hunters and warriors.

Male gender variants' households were often more prosperous than others, sometimes because they were hired by whites. In their own societies the excellence of male gender variants' craftwork was sometimes ascribed to a supernatural sanction for their gender transformation (Callender and Kochems 1983:448). Female gender variants opted out of motherhood, so were not encumbered by caring for children, which may explain their success as hunters or warriors. In some societies, gender variants could engage in both men's and women's work, and this, too, accounted for their increased wealth. Another source of income was payment for the special social activities of gender variants due to their intermediate gender status, such as acting as go-betweens in marriage. Through their diverse occupations, then, gender variants were often central rather than marginal in their societies.

Early anthropological explanations of male gender variant roles as a niche for a "failed" or cowardly man who wished to avoid warfare or other aspects of the masculine role are no longer widely accepted. To begin with, masculinity was not associated with warrior status in all American Indian cultures. In some societies, male gender variants were warriors and in many others, males who rejected the warrior role did not become gender variants. Sometimes male gender variants did not go to war because of cultural prohibitions against their using symbols of maleness, for example, the prohibition against their using the bow among the Illinois. Where male gender variants did not fight, they sometimes had other important roles in warfare, like treating the wounded, carrying supplies for the war party, or directing post-battle ceremonials (Callender and Kochems 1983:449). In a few societies male gender variants became outstanding warriors, such as Finds Them and Kills Them, a Crow Indian who performed daring feats of bravery while fighting with the United States Army against the Crow's traditional enemies, the Lakota Sioux (Roscoe 1998:23).

GENDER VARIANCE AND SEXUALITY

Generally, sexuality was not central in defining gender status among American Indians. But in any case, the assumption by European observers that gender variants were homosexuals meant they did not take much trouble to investigate or record information on this topic. In some American Indian societies same-sex sexual desire/practice did figure significantly in the definition of gender variant roles; in others it did not (Callender and Kochems 1983:449). Some early reports noted specifically that male gender variants lived with and/or had sexual relations with women as well as men; in other societies they were reported as having sexual relations only with men, and in still other societies, of having no sexual relationships at all (Lang 1998:189–95).

The bisexual orientation of some gender variant persons may have been a culturally accepted expression of their gender variance. It may have resulted from an individual's life experiences, such as the age at which he or she entered the gender variant role, and/or it may have been one aspect of the general freedom of sexual expression in many American Indian societies. While male and female gender variants most frequently had sexual relations with, or married, persons of the same biological sex as themselves, these relationships were not considered homosexual in the contemporary Western understanding of that term. In a multiple gender system the partners would be of the same sex but different genders, and homogender, rather than homosexual, practices bore the brunt of negative cultural sanctions. The sexual partners of gender variants were never considered gender variants themselves.

The Navajo are a good example (Thomas 1997). The Navajo have four genders; in addition to man and woman there are two gender variants: masculine female-bodied nádleeh and feminine male-bodied nádleeh. A sexual relationship between a female nádleeh and a woman or a sexual relationship between a male-bodied nádleeh and a man were not stigmatized because these persons were of different genders, although of the same biological sex. However, a sexual relationship between two women, two men, two female-bodied nádleeh or two male-bodied nádleeh, was considered homosexual, and even incestual, and was strongly disapproved of.

The relation of sexuality to variant sex/gender roles across North America suggests that sexual relations between gender variants and persons of the same biological sex were a result rather than a cause of gender variance. Sexual relationships between a man and a male gender variant were accepted in most American Indian societies, though not in all, and appear to have been negatively sanctioned only when it interfered with child-producing heterosexual marriages. Gender variants' sexual relationships varied from casual and wide-ranging (Europeans used the term promiscuous), to stable, and sometimes even involved life-long marriages. In some societies, however, male gender variants were not permitted to engage in long-term relationships with men, either in or out of wedlock. In many cases, gender variants were reported as living alone.

There are some practical reasons why a man might desire sexual relations with a (male) gender variant: in some societies taboos on sexual relations with menstruating or pregnant women restricted opportunities for sexual intercourse; in other societies, sexual relations with a gender variant person were exempt from punishment for extramarital affairs; in still other societies, for example, among the Navajo, some gender variants were considered especially lucky and a man might hope to vicariously partake of this quality by having sexual relations with them (Lang, 1998:349).

BIOLOGICAL SEX AND GENDER TRANSFORMATIONS

European observers often confused gender variants with hermaphrodites. Some American Indian societies explicitly distinguished hermaphrodites from gender variants and treated them differently; others assigned gender variant persons and hermaphrodites to the same alternative gender status. With the exception of the Navajo, in most American Indian societies biological sex (or the intersexedness of the hermaphrodite) was not the criterion for a gender variant role, nor were the individuals who occupied gender variant roles anatomically abnormal. The Navajo distinguished between the intersexed and the alternatively gendered, but treated them similarly, though not exactly the same (Thomas 1997; Hill 1935).

And even as the traditional Navajo sex/gender system had biological sex as its starting point, it was only a starting point, and Navajo nádleeh were distinguished by sex-linked behaviors, such as body language, clothing, ceremonial roles, speech style, and work. Feminine, male-bodied nádleeh might engage in women's activities such as cooking, weaving, household tasks, and making pottery. Masculine, female-bodied nádleeh, unlike other female-bodied persons, avoided childbirth; today they are associated with male occupational roles such as construction or firefighting (although ordinary women also sometimes engage in these occupations). Traditionally, female-bodied nádleeh had specific roles in Navajo ceremonials (Thomas 1997).

Thus, even where hermaphrodites occupied a special gender variant role, American Indian gender variance was defined more by cultural than biological criteria. In one recorded case of an interview with and physical examination of a gender variant male, the previously mentioned Finds Them and Kills Them, his genitals were found to be completely normal (Roscoe 1998).

If American Indian gender variants were not generally hermaphrodites, or conceptualized as such, neither were they conceptualized as transsexuals. Gender transformations among gender variants were recognized as only a partial transformation, and the gender variant was not thought of as having become a person of the opposite sex/gender. Rather, gender variant roles were autonomous gender roles that combined the characteristics of men and women and had some unique features of their own. This was sometimes symbolically recognized: among the Zuni a male gender variant was buried in women's dress but men's trousers on the men's side of the graveyard (Parsons quoted in Callender and Kochems 1983:454; Roscoe 1991:124, 145). Male gender variants were neither men—by virtue of their chosen occupations, dress, demeanor, and possibly sexuality—nor women, because of their anatomy and their inability to bear children. Only among the Mohave do we find the extreme imitation of women's physiological processes related to reproduction and the claims to have female sexual organs—both of which were ridiculed within Mohave society. But even here, where informants reported that female gender variants did not menstruate, this did not make them culturally men. Rather it was the mixed quality of gender variant status that was culturally elaborated in native North America, and this was the source of supernatural powers sometimes attributed to them.

SACRED POWER

The association between the spiritual power and gender variance occurred in most, if not all, Native American societies. Even where, as previously noted, recruitment to the role was occasioned by a child's interest in occupational activities of the opposite sex, supernatural sanction, frequently appearing in visions or dreams, was also involved. Where this occurred, as it did mainly in the Prairie and Plains societies, the visions involved female supernatural figures, often the moon. Among the Omaha, for example, the moon appeared in a dream holding a burden strap—a symbol of female work—in one hand, and a bow—a symbol of male work—in the other. When the male dreamer reached for the bow, the moon forced him to take the burden strap (Whitehead 1981). Among the Mohave, a child's choice of male or female implements heralding gender variant status was sometimes prefigured by a dream that was believed to come to an embryo in the womb (Devereux 1937).

Sometimes, by virtue of the power associated with their gender ambiguity, gender variants were ritual adepts and curers, or had special ritual functions (Callender and Kochems 1983:453, Lang 1998). Gender variants did not always have important sacred roles in native North America, however. Where feminine qualities were associated with these roles, male gender variants might become spiritual leaders or healers, but where these roles were associated with male qualities they were not entered into by male gender variants. Among the Plains Indians, with their emphasis on the vision as a source of supernatural power, male gender variants were regarded as holy persons, but in California Indian societies, this was not the case and in some American Indian societies gender variants were specifically excluded from religious roles (Lang 1998:167). Sometimes it was the individual personality of the gender variant rather than his/her gender variance itself, that resulted in occupying sacred roles (see Commentary following Callender and Kochems 1983). Nevertheless, the importance of sacred power was so widely associated with sex/gender diversity in native North America that it is generally agreed to be an important explanation of the frequency of gender diversity in this region of the world.

In spite of cultural differences, some significant similarities among American Indian societies are particularly consistent with multigender systems and the positive value placed on sex/gender diversity (Lang 1996). One of these similarities is a cosmology (system of religious beliefs and way of seeing the world) in which transformation and ambiguity are recurring themes. Thus a person who contains both masculine and feminine qualities or one who is transformed from the sex/gender assigned at birth into a different gender in later life manifests some of the many kinds of transformations and ambiguities that are possible, not only for humans, but for animals and objects in the natural environment. Indeed, in many American Indian cultures, sex/gender ambiguity, lack of sexual differentiation, and sex/gender transformations play an important part in the story of creation (Lang, 1996:187). American Indian cosmology may not be "the cause" of sex/gender diversity but it certainly (as in India) provides a hospitable context for it.

THE ALYHA: A MALE GENDER VARIANT ROLE AMONG THE MOHAVE

One of the most complete classic anthropological descriptions of a gender variant role is from the Mohave, a society that lives in the southwest desert area of the Nevada/California border. The following description, based on interviews by anthropologist George Devereux (1937) with some old informants who remembered the transvestite ceremony and had heard stories about gender variant individuals from their elders, indicates some of the ways in which gender variance functioned in native North America.

The Mohave had two gender variant roles: a male role called alyha and a female role called *hwame*. In this society, pregnant women had dreams forecasting the anatomic sex of their children. Mothers of a future alyha dreamt of male characteristics, such as arrow feathers, indicating the birth of a boy, but their dreams also included hints of their child's future gender variant status. A boy indicated he might become an alyha by "acting strangely" around the age of 10 or 11, before he had participated in the boys' puberty ceremonies. At this age, young people began to engage seriously in the activities that would characterize their adult lives as men and women; boys, for example, learned to hunt, ride horses, make bows and arrows, and they developed sexual feelings for girls. The future alyha avoided these masculine activities. Instead he played with dolls, imitated the domestic work of women, tried to participate in the women's gambling games, and demanded to wear the female bark skirt rather than the male breechclout.

The alyha's parents and relatives were ambivalent about this behavior. At first his parents would try to dissuade him, but if the behavior persisted his relatives would resign themselves and begin preparations for the transvestite ceremony. The ceremony was meant to take the boy by surprise; it was considered both a test of his inclination and an initiation. Word was sent out to various settlements so that people could watch the ceremony and get accustomed to the boy in female clothing. At the ceremony, the boy was led into a circle of onlookers by two women, and the crowd began singing the transvestite songs. If the boy began to dance as women did, he was confirmed as an alyha. He was then taken to the river to bathe and given a girl's skirt to wear. This initiation ceremony confirmed his changed gender status, which was considered permanent.

After this ceremony the alyha assumed a female name (though he did not take the lineage name that all females assumed) and would resent being called by his former, male name. In the frequent and bawdy sexual joking characteristic of Mohave culture, an alyha resented male nomenclature being applied to his genitals. He insisted that his penis be called a clitoris, his testes, labia majora, and anus a vagina. Alyha were also particularly sensitive to sexual joking, and if they were teased in the same way as women they responded with assaults on those who teased them. Because they were very strong, people usually avoided angering them.

Alyha were considered highly industrious and much better housewives than were young girls. It is partly for this reason that they had no difficulty finding spouses, and alyha generally had husbands. Alyha were not courted like ordinary girls, however (where the prospective husband would sleep chastely beside the girl for several nights and then lead her out of her parents' house), but rather courted like widows, divorcees, or "wanton" women. Intercourse with an alyha was surrounded by special etiquette. Like Mohave heterosexual couples, the alyha and her husband practiced both anal and oral intercourse, with the alyha taking the female role. Alyha were reported to be embarrassed by an erection and would not allow their sexual partners to touch or even comment on their erect penis.

When an alyha found a husband, she would begin to imitate menstruation by scratching herself between the legs with a stick until blood appeared. The alyha then submitted to puberty observations as a girl would, and her husband also observed the requirements of the husband of a girl who menstruated for the first time. Alyha also imitated pregnancy, particularly if their husbands threatened them with divorce on the grounds of barrenness. At this time they would cease faking menstruation and follow the pregnancy taboos, with even more attention than ordinary women, except that they publicly proclaimed their pregnancy, which ordinary Mohave women never did. In imitating pregnancy, an alyha would stuff rags in her skirts, and near the time of the birth, drank a decoction to cause constipation. After a day or two of stomach pains, she would go into the bushes and sit over a hole, defecating in the position of childbirth. The feces would be treated as a stillbirth and buried, and the alyha would weep and wail as a woman does for a stillborn child. The alyha and her husband would then clip their hair as in mourning.

Alyha were said to be generally peaceful persons, except when teased, and were also considered to be cowards. They did not have to participate in the frequent and harsh military raids of Mohave men. Alyha did participate in the welcoming home feast for the warriors, where, like old women, they might make a bark penis and go through the crowd poking the men who had stayed home, saying, "You are not a man, but an alyha."

In general, alyha were not teased or ridiculed for being alyha (though their husbands were teased for marrying them), because it was believed that they could not help it and that a child's inclinations in this direction could not be resisted. It was believed that a future alyha's desire for a gender change was such that he could not resist dancing the women's dance at the initiation ceremony. Once his desires were demonstrated in this manner, people would not thwart him. It was partly the belief that becoming an alyha was a result of a "temperamental compulsion" or predestined (as forecast in his mother's pregnancy dream) that inhibited ordinary Mohave from ridiculing alyha. In addition, alyha were considered powerful healers, especially effective in curing sexually transmitted diseases (also called alyha) like syphilis.

The alyha demonstrates some of the ways in which gender variant roles were constructed as autonomous genders in North America. In many ways the alyha crossed genders, but the role had a distinct, alternative status to that of both man and woman (as did the hwame).

Although the alyha imitated many aspects of a woman's role—dress, sexual behavior, menstruation, pregnancy, childbirth, and domestic occupations—they were also recognized as being different from women. Alyha did not take women's lineage names; they were not courted like ordinary women; they publicly proclaimed their pregnancies; and they were considered more industrious than other women in women's domestic tasks.

In spite of the alyha's sexual relations with men, the alyha was not considered primarily a homosexual (in Western terms). In fact, among ordinary Mohave, if a person dreamed of having homosexual relationships, that person would be expected to die soon, but this was not true of the alyha. Most significantly, the alyha were believed to have special supernatural powers, which they used in curing illness.

FEMALE GENDER VARIANTS

Female gender variants probably occurred more frequently among American Indians than in other cultures, although this has been largely overlooked in the historic and ethnographic record (but see Blackwood 1984; Jacobs et al. 1997; Lang 1998; Medicine 1983).

Although the generally egalitarian social structures of many American Indian societies provided a hospitable context for female gender variance, it occurred in perhaps only one-quarter to one-half of the societies with male variant roles (Callender and Kochems 1983:446; see also Lang 1998:262–65). This may be explained partly by the fact that in many American Indian societies women could—and did—adopt aspects of the male gender role, such as warfare or hunting, and sometimes dressed in male clothing, without being reclassified into a different gender (Blackwood 1984; Lang 1998:261ff; Medicine 1983).

As with males, the primary criteria of changed gender status for females was an affinity for the occupations of the other gender. While this inclination for male occupations was often displayed in childhood, female gender variants entered these roles later in life than did males (Lang 1998:303). Among some Inuit, "men pretenders" would refuse to learn women's tasks and were taught male occupations when they were children, by their fathers. They played with boys and participated in the hunt. Among the Kaska, a family who had only daughters might select one to "be like a man"; by engaging in the male activity of hunting, she would help provide the family with food. Among the Mohave, too, hwame refused to learn women's work, played with boys, and were considered excellent providers, as well as particularly efficient healers (Blackwood 1984:30; Lang 1998:286). Among the Cheyenne, the *hetaneman* (defined as a hermaphrodite having more of the female element) were great female warriors who accompanied the male warrior societies into battle. In all other groups, however, even outstanding women warriors were not recast into a different gender role (Roscoe 1998:75). Female gender variants also sometimes entered specialized occupations, becoming traders, guides for whites, or healers. The female preference for male occupations might be motivated by a female's desire to be independent, or might be initiated or encouraged by a child's parents, and in some societies was sanctioned through supernatural omens or in dreams.

In addition to occupation, female gender variants might assume other characteristics of men. Cocopa *warrhameh* wore a masculine hairstyle and had their noses pierced, like boys (Lang 1998:283). Among the Maidu, the female *suku* also had her nose pierced on the occasion of her initiation into the men's secret society. Mohave hwame were tattooed like men instead of women. Transvestism was commonly though not universally practiced: it occurred, for example, among the Kaska, Paiute, Ute, and Mohave.

Like male gender variants, female gender variants exhibited a wide range of sexual relationships. Some had relationships with other females, who were generally regarded as ordinary women. Only rarely, as among a southern Apache group, was the female gender variant (like her male counterpart) defined in terms of her sexual desire for women. Mohave hwame engaged in sexual and marriage relationships with women, although they courted them in a special way, different from heterosexual courtships. If a hwame married a pregnant woman, she could claim paternity of the child, although the child belonged to the descent group of its biological father (Devereux 1937:514). Like an alyha's husband, a hwame's wife was often teased, and hwame marriages were generally unstable. Masahai Amatkwisai, the most well known hwame, married women three times and was also known to have sexual relationships with many men. Masahai's wives were all aggressively teased by male Mohave who viewed "real" sexual relations only in terms of penetration by a penis. At dances Masahai sat with men, described her wife's genitals, and flirted with girls, all typical male behavior. Masahai's masculine behavior was ridiculed, and the men gravely insulted her (though never to her face), by referring to her by an obscene nickname meaning the female genitals. The harassment of Masahai's wives apparently led to the eventual breakup of her marriages.

Sexual relationships between women in American Indian societies were rarely historically documented, but in any case, were generally downplayed in female gender variant roles, even when this involved marriage. One female gender variant, for example, Woman Chief, a famous Crow warrior and hunter, took four wives, but this appeared to be primarily an economic strategy: processing animal hides among the Crow was women's work, so that Woman Chief's polygyny (multiple spouses) complemented her hunting skills.

While most often American Indian women who crossed genders occupationally, such as Woman Chief, were not reclassified into a gender variant role, several isolated cases of female gender transformations have been documented historically. One of these is Ququnak Patke, a "manlike woman" from the Kutenai (Schaeffer 1965). Ququnak Patke had married a white fur trader and when she returned to her tribe, claimed that her husband had transformed her into a man. She wore men's clothes, lived as a man, married a woman and claimed supernatural sanction for her role change and her supernatural powers. Although whites often mistook her for a man in her various roles as warrior, explorer's guide, and trader, such transformations were not considered a possibility among the Kutenai, and many thought Ququnak Patke was mad. She died attempting to mediate a quarrel between two hostile Indian groups.

It is difficult to know how far we can generalize about the relation of sexuality to female gender variance in precontact American Indian cultures from the lives of the few documented female gender variants. These descriptions (and those for males, as well) are mainly based on ethnographic accounts that relied on twentieth-century informants whose memories were already shaped by white hostility toward gender diversity and same-sex sexuality. Nevertheless, it seems clear that although American Indian female gender variants clearly had sexual relationships with women, sexual object choice was not their defining characteristic. In some cases, female gender variants were described "as women who never marry," which does not say anything definitive about their sexuality; it may well be that the sexuality of female gender variants was more variable than that of men.

Occasionally, as with Masahai and Ququnak Patke, and also for some male gender variants, contact with whites opened up opportunities for gender divergent individuals (see Roscoe 1988; 1991). On the whole, however, as a result of Euro-American repression and the growing assimilation of Euro-American sex/gender ideologies, both female and male gender variant roles among American Indians largely disappeared by the 1930s, as the reservation system was well under way. And yet, its echoes may remain. The current academic interest in American Indian multigender roles, and particularly the testimony of contemporary two-spirits, remind us that alternatives are possible and that understanding American Indian sex/gender diversity in the past and present makes a significant contribution to understandings of sex/gender diversity in the larger society.

DISCUSSION QUESTIONS

1. Describe the evolution in the Western European understanding of Native American sex/gender systems.
2. Gender variation beyond the categories of male and female was commonly accepted among Native American Indian peoples. Such acceptance diminished with the arrival of the European settlers. And now some would argue there are signs of a newly emerged acceptance of gender variation in the United States. What is the evidence favoring this argument?

REFERENCES

Albers, Patricia C. 1989. "From Illusion to Illumination: Anthropological Studies of American Indian Women." *In Gender and Anthropology: Critical Reviews for Research and Teaching,* edited by Sandra Morgen. Washington, DC: American Anthropological Association.

Blackwood, Evelyn. 1984. "Sexuality and Gender in Certain Native American Tribes: The Case of Cross-Gender Females." *Signs: Journal of Women in Culture and Society* 10:1–42.

Callender, Charles, and Lee M. Kochems. 1983. "The North American Berdache." *Current Anthropology* 24 (4): 443–56 (Commentary, pp. 456–70).

Devereux, George. 1937. "Institutionalized Homosexuality of the Mohave Indians." *Human Biology* 9:498–587.

Fulton, Robert, and Steven W. Anderson. 1992. "The Amerindian 'Man-Woman': Gender, Liminality, and Cultural Continuity." *Current Anthropology* 33 (5).

Hill, Willard W. 1935. "The Status of the Hermaphrodite and Transvestite in Navaho Culture." *American Anthropologist* 37:273–79.

Jacobs, Sue-Ellen, Wesley Thomas, and Sabine Lang, eds. 1997. *Two-Spirit People: Native American Gender Identity, Sexuality, and Spirituality.* Urbana: University of Illinois Press.

Lang, Sabine. 1996. "There Is More than Just Men and Women: Gender Variance in North America." In *Gender Reversals and Gender Culture,* edited by Sabrina Petra Ramet, pp. 183–96. London and New York: Routledge.

Lang, Sabine. 1998. *Men as Women, Women as Men: Changing Gender in Native American Cultures.* Trans. from the German by John L. Vantine. Austin: University of Texas Press.

Medicine, Beatrice. 1983. "Warrior Women: Sex Role Alternatives for Plains Indian Women." In *The Hidden Half: Studies of Plains Indian Women,* edited by P. Albers and B. Medicine, pp. 267–80. Lanham Park, MD: University Press of America.

Roscoe, Will. 1991. *The Zuni Man-Woman.* Albuquerque: University of New Mexico Press.

Roscoe, Will. 1995. "Cultural Anesthesia and Lesbian and Gay Studies." *American Anthropologist* 97 (3): 448–52.

Roscoe, Will. 1996. "How to Become a Berdache: Toward a Unified Analysis of Gender Diversity." In *Third Sex, Third Gender: Beyond Sexual Dimorphism in Culture and History,* edited by Gilbert Herdt, pp. 329–72. New York: Zone (MIT).

Roscoe, Will. 1998. *Changing Ones: Third and Fourth Genders in Native North America.* London: Macmillan.

Schaeffer, Claude E. 1965. "The Kutenai Female Berdache: Courier Guide, and Warrior." *Ethnohistory: The Bulletin of the Ohio Valley Historic Indian Conference* 12 (3): 173–236.

Thomas, Wesley. 1997. "Navajo Cultural Constructions of Gender and Sexuality." In *Two-Spirit People: Native American Gender Identity, Sexuality, and Spirituality,* edited by Sue-Ellen Jacobs, Wesley Thomas, and Sabine Lang, pp. 156–73. Urbana and Chicago: University of Illinois.

Whitehead, Harriet. 1981. "The Bow and the Burden Strap: A New Look at Institutionalized Homosexuality in Native North America." In *Sexual Meanings: The Cultural Construction of Gender and Sexuality,* edited by Sherry B. Ortner and Harriet Whitehead, pp. 80–115. Cambridge: Cambridge University Press.

Williams, Walter. 1992. *The Spirit and the Flesh: Sexual Diversity in American Indian Culture.* Boston: Beacon.

20.
PROSTITUTION AND THE STATUS OF WOMEN IN SOUTH KOREA

ROBERT HEINER

One of the reasons why people conform to the norms is their fear of being labeled deviant. That is, the potential stigma of a label serves as a powerful form of social control, of ensuring that people keep in line, of maintaining the status quo. The following article demonstrates how labeling helps to maintain the patriarchal status quo in South Korea. Note how the deviant label has a powerfully negative effect on prostitutes in Korea; but note also how the fear of being labeled has an effect on all Korean women and serves to keep them in their submissive roles.

This article was first published in 1992 and much of the research for it was conducted in the 1980s when South Korea was a "newly industrializing country." It has since emerged as an "Asian Tiger" with one of Asia's most successful economies. Modernization is usually accompanied by improvements in the status of women and many of the processes observed then have likely diminished by now, especially in the more urban areas of Korea. But many of them also apply currently to other impoverished, patriarchal societies.

INTRODUCTION

Functionalists have argued that if an allegedly undesirable phenomenon permeates a culture, and if it has always permeated the culture, and if it permeates other cultures as well, then it must exist for a reason. It must serve some useful function for the society. For Durkheim (1947), consensual moral aversion to crime unites a society; and therefore, crime functions to enhance social solidarity. For Erikson (1966), reactions to deviance serve as a means of publicizing those things that are not tolerated in the community; and therefore, the deviant is necessary for maintaining the community's moral boundaries. For Davis (1937), prostitution provides a sexual outlet for the male that does not interfere with his responsibilities to his family; that is, a man utilizing the services of a prostitute is less likely to have an affair and leave his wife for another woman. In this article, it will be argued that prostitution in South Korea does indeed fulfill a function. It functions to perpetuate an extraordinarily patriarchal social structure. Namely, the fear of being labeled a prostitute keeps women dutiful and submissive. This argument will be developed once the situation regarding prostitution and the status of women in South Korea have been discussed.

This examination is based on my experiences and observations having lived for a year in South Korea, having made it a point to visit a large variety of prostitution districts, having badgered a wide variety of Korean citizens with questions about the trade, and having made contacts with "managers" (pimps) who allowed me to interview their "girls" (in all, nineteen women were interviewed). It should be noted that, due to various cultural, political, and methodological constraints, this research is largely impressionistic in nature. Prostitution is a phenomenon not openly discussed in Korea. Though rampant, it is regarded as shameful; and it is technically illegal. As anyone who has studied Korean culture knows, "Koreans are preoccupied with appearances, especially with foreigners" (Gibbons, 1988:234). While in Western cultures it is acceptable to study and write about the seamier side of society, it is much less acceptable in Korean culture. Just as the individual has face that must be guarded at all times, so does the nation; and it is considered somewhat of a betrayal to reveal to an outsider those things that might bring shame to the country.

THE HISTORY AND EXTENT OF PROSTITUTION

Prostitution is rampant in many Asian countries today. Other than being Asian and rife with prostitution, what these countries have in common is that they can trace many of their customs back to Chinese civilization which has been fiercely patriarchal and has a long tradition of prostitution. In Chinese history, and in the history of many of its "relative" cultures, infanticide, the selling, pawning, and enslavement of women were all common practices for centuries. Women were of little economic value in these cultures. When they married, they left their parents' home; and they usually married before they could contribute much to the family in terms of their labor. It was, therefore, in the interest of the family (poorer families especially) to rid themselves of the burden of raising female children. Attitudes towards women can also be traced to Confucianism which established a very strict hierarchy of authority between government and subjects, parents and children, and men and women. Writes one Koreanist, "Anyone familiar with China reads Korean ethnography with a smothering sense of deja vu" (Kendall, 1985:25). Remarkably, Korea has been more strongly influenced by Confucianism than even China (Iyer, 1988). The same history of infanticide, selling, pawning, enslavement, and prostitution of women belongs to Korea.

Also, Korea and China have in common extensive histories of tremendous economic and political unrest and social dislocation—conditions often associated with the prevalence of prostitution (cf. Cohen, 1958; Gronewold, 1982). There have been very few periods of economic and political stability throughout the thousands of years of Korean history. The 20th century was particularly tumultuous with the brutal Japanese occupation, the Korean War, the bifurcation of north and south, and the American "occupation."

Prostitution pervades virtually every sector of Korean society. Every city has a prostitution district. Some have a street devoted to the trade. Some have a neighborhood. Some have many streets scattered throughout. Some have many neighborhoods scattered throughout. Virtually every bus and train station has a series of brothels nearby. There are even small towns devoted to the trade, especially those that cater to the American military bases—such as "Silver Town" outside of Kunsan in the south, and Sunyo-ri near the DMZ in the north—that are known as "villes."

(However, the impression of those who believe that the presence of the American military is responsible for the majority of prostitution in Korea is simply incorrect. Probably more prostitutes serve Japanese tourists; and most clients are Korean nationals—cf. Kim, 1987.)

There are streets and neighborhoods where the prostitutes wait outside and approach all male passersby. More typically, there are streets and neighborhoods where the women, dressed in traditional formal attire, wait together inside rooms with a big window facing the street so men can look in and choose which one they want. There are prostitutes that work all of the large and not-so-large hotels. There are prostitutes who work on the cleaning staffs of innumerable inns. There are prostitutes who work out of the bars. There are prostitutes who work in the restaurants and coffee shops. There are manicurists who ply another trade in dimly lit barbershops. There are prostitutes who work in the many Korean massage parlors. There are even prostitutes who work in the massage parlors located on the American bases. And, most likely, there are other locales where they work of which I have not been informed.

PATRIARCHY AND THE CULT OF THE MALE

The Korean female lives in a society in which it is most advantageous to be male. Sexism and sex discrimination permeate the entire culture. Males are given the best jobs, the better part of the family's inheritance, and the benefit of the doubt. The birth of a son in Korea is always a joyous event, whereas "the birth of a daughter occasions lament" (Kendall, 1980:12). In fact, "given the pressure placed on couples to produce a male heir and the ability to have legal abortions, the [Korean National] assembly [has considered] legislation forbidding doctors from performing tests capable of determining [the sex] of an unborn child" (McBeth, 1987:38). When a male baby is born, its first formal baby picture will likely be of him sitting spread-eagle, displaying the "family jewels," of which the parents are so proud. As he is growing up, relatives and friends of the family will greet and compliment him by a brisk fondling of the genitals as a way of expressing "my what a man you are!" and of signifying respect for the family for their having a male child. (Koreans planning to travel abroad must spend a day at "passport school" where, among other things, they are strongly advised not to pay their compliments to Western families by fondling their little boys' genitals.)

The female will grow up in this cult of the male—in a society where it is considered bad luck if a shopkeeper's first customer in the morning is a woman. She will quickly learn that her role is to serve men. Eventually, she will probably marry. The routes to marriage are varied: perhaps she will marry out of love; perhaps her marriage will be arranged; perhaps she will marry because her younger sisters cannot marry until she is married off; or she may marry because she is approaching her thirties and will soon be over the hill. When she marries, she will find herself subservient to her husband.

Traditionally, the man's world is a public one, while the wife's is private. Korean folklore venerates the woman who refuses to flee her burning home. Today, a frequently used expression referring to "wife" is *annae*, meaning "the one inside." Her husband will quite possibly go out every weekend and get rip-roaring drunk. He is very likely to make use of a prostitute on occasion. And there is more than a slight possibility that he will beat his wife with some regularity. In a national survey, "61 percent of the men queried readily admitted that they beat their wives" (Kim, 1987).

In light of this backdrop, it is probably superfluous to say that sexism plays a major role in Korean prostitution. This phenomenon simply cannot be explained without reference to the patriarchal social structure. Prostitution provides an alternative, though a painful one, to the subjugation imposed by marriage. It also provides an alternative to the subjugation imposed by the legitimate labor market. Writes Elaine Kim:

> The female entertainment industry is particularly attractive to women workers in South Korea, where employment opportunities are limited even for educated women. . . . Women's jobs are predominantly in low-wage factory and service occupations. . . . Women in South Korea work ten hours a month more than men, averaging 59 hours a week, the longest in the world. (Kim, 1987:135)

In fact, the widespread employment of women in the factories for menial wages is one of the factors associated with Korea's current economic success. Their history of being exploited, their willingness to accept low wages, and "the Confucian expectations of a woman—that she be morally strong, self-sacrificing and submissive to men—[have] played and continue to be significant factor[s] in the economic development of the nation" (Yoo, 1985:840).

It is hardly surprising, then, that many young women are drawn to prostitution. While the average monthly salary for working women in Korea was less than 150,000 won (about $170), the average salary for the prostitutes I interviewed was about 800,000 won (about $900). Kim writes, "It is said that it is hard to find pretty bus girls or housemaids any longer, since the good-looking women are all working in the hospitality trade" (1987:136).

FACE AND FAMILY

The most striking paradox of Korean prostitution is that it is so rampant in a society where the worst of all human existences is one involving shame, where there is so much emphasis on keeping face, and where prostitution is seen as such a cause of shame and loss of face. We might expect that a cultural priority emphasizing honor would keep most people honorable; however, such a strong demand for honor has the opposite effect. It provides a standard that is often unrealistic, and those who do not meet this standard are cast out. As labeling theory holds, once labeled and cast out, an honorable existence becomes all the more problematic.

The concept of face is inextricably connected to the Korean concept of *kibun*, perhaps best translated as "harmony of self and others." Paul Crane describes this concept:

> Perhaps the most important thing to an individual Korean is recognition of "selfhood." The state of his inner feelings, his prestige, his awareness of being recognized as a person—all these factors determine his morale, his face, or self-esteem, essentially his state of mind, which may be expressed in Korean by the word kibun. (Crane, 1978:25)

If everyone in a social interaction can keep their face intact (honor), then there is kibun (harmony). Koreans will go out of their way to preserve harmony.

This emphasis on honor and harmony very often has a destructive influence on family relations. It is truly remarkable to live in Korea and hear the continuous litany on the importance of the family, and yet find that family members almost never confide in one another. Things that people are likely to confide are also things that are likely to threaten the family's honor and disrupt the family harmony. Many of the women who find their way into prostitution are women who have already felt themselves to be shamed, who could not confide in their families or who did so with disastrous consequences. A norm that is only recently beginning to change is the one requiring women to be virgins on their wedding night. (The extent to which this expectation has changed is unclear; it almost certainly depends upon the family and their place of residence.) But many of the women I interviewed, at least half (many chose not to answer my questions on the subject), were women who were sexually involved before they left home. They left because they were ashamed to admit it; or because they were prohibited from seeing their lover again; or because the tension created by their indiscretion had become unbearable. As in American society (but more so), when the child does something shameful, she or he brings shame onto the whole family. Many of these women were disowned before they turned to prostitution; and many have been disowned after they turned to prostitution.

THE SPOILED IDENTITY OF THE PROSTITUTE

To be a prostitute is to lose face; to lose face is to be an "unperson." Because of the loss of face associated with prostitution, to have a background in prostitution is to have a spoiled identity. If those with whom she interacts know of her background, then her identity is discredited; if they are not aware of her background, then her identity is *discreditable* (Goffman, 1974). Worse yet, in Korea to associate with an "unperson" is to compromise one's own face, one's own personhood. It is, therefore, important to the Korean to be always on guard, ready to discredit the discreditable.

It is difficult to overstate how attuned Koreans are to the social background of another. As big as the United States is, having once been a dumping ground for England's criminals, and with as much social mobility that has taken place here, it is difficult for Americans to imagine a country in which one cannot escape one's background. In Korea, it is not so easy. Crane addresses this problem of no-escape in his discussion of social relationships gone sour:

> In a tight little country surrounded by water and a hostile boundary to the north, there is no place to escape from the wrath of the enemy. For most people, this means that they must endure when they are under attack or go and hide until the heat subsides. . . . Rarely does a foreigner get more than a peep into the seething, bubbling cauldron of hates and fears and subtle attacks that pressure the average person in Korea, who lacks the mobility of most Americans. (Crane, 1978:31)

Even in the large and populous country of China a hundred years ago, Gronewold (1982) says that it was almost impossible to escape one's background. Communities were tight-knit; and the newly arrived stranger, whose true background was unknown, was assumed to have the worst of backgrounds.

Koreans are acutely aware of any signs of suspect status. The labeling of deviance is easily facilitated under such conditions. As Lofland points out (1969), when there are a "large number of alternatively sufficient indicators," people can be successfully labeled when they meet one of any number of criteria. Flashy dress, employment on an American base, employment as an actress or in other fields of entertainment, employment in certain neighborhoods, living alone without family coming to visit, unfeminine behavior—these are just a few of the conditions that might eventuate in the label of "prostitute." As labeling theory holds, whether or not one engages in deviant behavior is less important than whether or not one is labeled deviant, because once one is labeled, he or she *is* deviant (Schur, 1971).

Prostitutes in Korea suffer all the conditions associated with stigma described by Goffman (1974). The more salient of these include the following. First, they are regarded as less than human by those who are aware of their spoiled identity. Second, their discreditability drives a wall between them and their family and their past. Separating them from their past, their stigma, in effect, means the reconstitution of their entire identity. Third, they live in fear that one day in the future, after they have left the "business" and thought they had "passed" as normal, someone will denounce them. (Many of the women I interviewed expressed hopes of one day getting married, but explained that they were terrified that one day their past would be discovered by their future husbands.) Finally, when they are interacting with someone who does not know of their discreditability, they are aware of the unsettling fact that this person would shun them if he or she knew the truth about their background.

AND THE PATRIARCHY GOES ON

There are, of course, an intricate variety of means by which patriarchal domination is maintained and enhanced in Korea, as in all other patriarchal societies. One of these means in Korea is through the institution of prostitution. Prostitution involves the exploitation of women in the service of men. This position has been well established. However, prostitution in Korea is also a means of subjugating *all* women, not just those involved in the trade. The fact that so many women are involved makes it all the more feasible that any particular woman is or has been involved. In order to stave off the suspicion of their involvement, it becomes necessary for women to strictly adhere to their assigned (submissive) roles in society. To stray from this role is to invite the label of "prostitute," which means reconstitution of herself for the worst. If she divorces her husband, he will probably get the kids, and she will have to reestablish herself by herself. A woman living alone invites suspicion. If a woman works on an American military base or as an entertainer, she might be exposed to ideas that would challenge male domination; but she will also be inviting the label. If she behaves in an "unladylike" manner, she will, by definition, be challenging the norms governing relations between men and women; but she will also be inviting the label. Aside from prostitution, most of the things a woman could do that might eventuate in the label "prostitute" are things that, in one way or another, pose a challenge to patriarchal relations between men and women.

If prostitution is critical in maintaining the moral/patriarchal boundaries in society as I have argued, then, according to Erikson (1966), reactions to deviance that allegedly discourage it may in actuality encourage it. Indeed, this is the case. Many might suppose that the defamatory nature of the label "prostitute" would act to discourage prostitution. However, the ease with which this label is meted out acts as a propellant rather than a repellant. Korean culture has set a vicious cycle in motion. Insistence on adherence to strict ethical principles has led to the "fall" of multitudes of women. The existence of multitudes of fallen women has given rise to a situation in which all women are possibly suspect. When all women are possibly suspect, people become even more attuned to moral strictures in order to identify the status of another, or to demonstrate their own virtuous status. The result is an insistence on adherence to strict ethical principles, which leads to the fall of multitudes of women. And thus, a steady supply of deviant women is insured. To paraphrase Erikson: the prostitute is not a bit of debris spun out by faulty machinery, but an integral component of patriarchal domination.

DISCUSSION QUESTIONS

1. Explain how it is that prostitution serves in the patriarchal oppression of *all* South Korean women.
2. Several references are made to the "function" of prostitution. Does this article represent a functionalist perspective or a conflict perspective or both? Explain your reasoning.

REFERENCES

Cohen, Yehudi (1958). "The sociology of commercialized prostitution in Okinawa." *Social Forces,* 37(December), 160–168.

Crane, Paul (1978). *Korean Patterns.* Seoul, South Korea: The Royal Asiatic Society and Kwangjin Publishing Co.

Davis, Kingsley (1937). "The sociology of prostitution." *American Sociological Review,* 2, 744–755.

Durkheim, Emile (1947). *The Division of Labor in Society.* trans. by G. Simpson. New York: Free Press.

Erikson, Kai (1966). *Wayward Puritans.* New York: John Wiley.

Gibbons, Boyd (1988). "The South Koreans." *National Geographic,* 174 (August), 232–257.

Goffman, Erving (1974). *Stigma: Notes on the Management of Spoiled Identity.* New York: Prentice Hall.

Gronewold, Sue (1982). *Beautiful Merchandise: Prostitution in China, 1860–1936.* New York: Institute for Research in History and Haworth Press.

Iyer, Pico (1988). "The yin and the yang of paradoxical, prosperous Korea." *Smithsonian,* 19 (August), 45–58.

Kendall, Laurel (1980). "Suspect saviors of Korean hearths and homes." *Asia,* 3 (May/June), 121.

Kendall, Laurel (1985). *Shamans, Housewives, and Other Restless Spirits: Women in Korean Ritual Life.* Honolulu: University of Hawaii Press.

Kim, Elaine (1987). "Sex tourism in Asia: A reflection of political and economic inequality." In E. Yu and E. Phillips. eds. *Korean Women in Transition.* pp. 127–144. Los Angeles: Center for Korean-American and Korean Studies, California State University.

Lofland, John (1969). *Deviance and Identity.* Englewood Cliffs, NJ: Prentice-Hall.

McBeth, John (1987). "A family feud for Confucians and women." *Far Eastern Economic Review,* 135 (26) February, 38–41.

Schur, Edwin (1971). *Labeling Deviant Behavior: Its Sociological Implications.* New York: Harper and Row.

Yoo, Ok-Za (1985). "Korean women in the home and the work place." *Korea and World Affairs,* 9 (Winter), 820–872.

21.
SEXUAL TOURISM AND SOCIAL PANICS: RESEARCH AND INTERVENTION IN RIO DE JANEIRO

ANA PAULA DA SILVA AND THADDEUS GREGORY BLANCHETTE

As it is often said, prostitution is one of the oldest professions in the history of the world and what to do about it has long been the subject of controversy. Many argue that most of the women in the trade are being forced to degrade themselves and are routinely subjected to violence and intimidation. Further, where prostitution is prevalent, whole neighborhoods and communities are degraded and threatened by the violence that often accompanies organized crime. On the other hand, there are those who argue that, for most of the women in the business, their participation is voluntary and they should have the right to earn their living however they choose so long as it hurts no one else—especially in patriarchal societies where women have little other recourse or access to jobs with a fair wage and protection from sexual harassment or rape. Many of these issues come into play in the following article.

When it comes to sex, Brazil is so exotic in Western eyes that anything can be said about it and be believed. Since the early nineteenth century, the country has been synonymous with license—a stereotype that baffles those of us who realize just how conservative Brazilians can be in matters sexual. Reality, it seems, is nowhere near as exciting as the fantasy that there is no sin beneath the equator.

These fantasies, of course, have a racialized component. Brazil has a reputation for being a country that encourages miscegenation. If it is true, as Franz Fanon (1968) points out, that blackness is symbolically linked with carnality in racialist thought, it is also true that miscegenation is strongly associated in the Western mind with sensuality and decadence (Young 2005). The brown body is "proof" of past transgressions of the color line and the presumptive "natural sexual order," where like is supposed to mate with like. As such, "race mixing" is endlessly fascinating, even (and perhaps particularly) to those who claim to find it disturbing or repulsive. It is thus no surprise that Rio de Janeiro, Brazil's most iconic city, has turned out to be the premier sexual-tourism destination of the Americas in the early twentieth-first century.[1]

When we began our research of the sex/tourism nexus in the neighborhood of Copacabana in early 2002, we were very much aware of how the history of Western imaginings of miscegenation has deeply influenced foreign and domestic understandings of Brazil. It became apparent to us that while little was known regarding how sexual commerce and tourism interacted in Copacabana, much was imagined. We quickly found out, in fact, that some of the most florid fantasies were serving to orient public policy on how to deal with sexual tourism in our country.

The most persistent of these fantasies might be usefully labeled the "victim/victimizer stereotype." It neatly separates the people involved in sexual tourism into diametrically opposed sets. On one hand, there are the supposedly wealthy or middle-class white, male, middle-aged exploiters from the United States and Europe, empowered by globalism, who travel about the world in search of ever cheaper and more depraved commercial sex; on the other hand, there are the supposedly poor, black, young, female exploited living in Rio de Janeiro, who have been forced by the structural changes of the global economy to prostitute themselves.

In our first months of research in Copacabana, we learned how inadequate the victim/victimizer stereotype of sexual tourism was and how it was being used to criminalize prostitutes, most particularly lower-class, nonwhite prostitutes, in the name of saving them from evil, foreign exploiters.

To begin with, we discovered that the linkages between sex and tourism in Rio de Janeiro are extremely old and varied and produce a diverse set of prostitutions. Rio, of course, is one of the oldest port cities in the Americas. Founded in 1565, the city was a stopover for Asian- or African-bound shipping out of Europe for the better part of four centuries. As a consequence, Rio was quite international from the moment of its founding, and from colonial days on, men and women of all colors and social stations could be found plying the oldest of professions in the city. Of course, many of these people have historically been poor and black or brown, but to focus on them alone (and, more particularly, to cast them as simple and passive victims of structural or economic phenomena) does not adequately explain their lives as individuals or the functioning of the city's sexual market as a social aggregate.

Today, prostitution remains legal in Brazil, and the sex industry of Rio de Janeiro continues to be one of the most diverse in the Americas, with prostitutes ranging from call girls charging thousands of dollars per appointment to streetwalkers working for $2.50 a pop near the Central do Brazil railroad station. Furthermore, the city boasts a booming homosexual prostitution scene (serving both genders) that is equally diversified in terms of status, costs, and work conditions. Both gay and straight commercial sex scenes are diversified in terms of race and class, though the most commonly encountered biotype is the *carioca* (Rio de Janeiro resident) of indeterminate ethnicity whose skin color ranges from light to medium brown.

There is no hard evidence—or even convincing circumstantial evidence—that the city's prostitute population has increased in relative terms over the last twenty years. In fact, what evidence does exist seems to indicate that, percentage-wise, the late twentieth and early twenty-first centuries saw an overall decrease in Rio's prostitute population from the heydays of the early 1900s. Globalization does not seem to have made much of an impact upon the sex trade in Rio, either, outside of spreading foreign tourists more evenly around the annual calendar.

In the heterosexual tourism scene, contact between foreign tourists and *carioca* prostitutes is largely confined to the neighborhood of Copacabana and its immediate environs, with some

63 percent of all reported sexual acts being contracted in that region. A secondary nexus can be found in the downtown: 64 percent of all heterosexual tourist contact with prostitutes is concentrated in ten venues (one disco, one restaurant/bar, one beach, one street "zona,"[2] and six saunas). Of these, all but two are in Copacabana or its immediate environs. Police estimate (and our observations confirm) that some 1,500 female sex workers can be found in this region, probably one-third of whom are working the heterosexual tourism venues at any one time.[3] Significantly, in our seven years of research, we have yet to find a child[4] working in one of the ten main venues.

The prices of the main sexual tourism spots situate them at the upper end of the middle range of carioca sex establishments. The cost paid per sexual act has been floating between US$75 and $150 for close to a decade now, with the women receiving anywhere from 50 to 100 percent of that. Bearing in mind that, as of September 2008, the Brazilian monthly minimum wage was around US$225, sexual work in Copacabana can generate more than a maid's monthly pay in an afternoon.[5] Many of our prostitute informants report wages that are at par with or higher than ours as university professors.

Working conditions in the six main venues that actually employ prostitutes[6] range from average to good, although, as is the case with all paid work in Brazil (including that of university professors), labor laws are more often than not honored in the breach. In general, health conditions are good, with periodic AIDS testing and protected sex being the rule.[7] Sexual labor is also organized in such a fashion that the women generally feel that they are in control, at least vis-à-vis individual clients. The largest number of complaints that we have encountered so far in our (admittedly incomplete) research revolve around labor/management issues that are frankly common across the *carioca* job market—unpaid or late salaries, illegal docking of pay for absenteeism, deduction of labor and raw materials costs from pay, and the like.

We have found the foreign tourists to be no more or less perverse, attractive, or emotionally healthy than men in general. The majority is white and comes from Europe and the United States. An increasing percentage (ranging from 2 to 12 percent depending on time of year and venue), however, is African American. Most are middle-class, but many are working-class, and a substantial number of the latter work in Brazil's growing petroleum industry. With the American war in Iraq and Afghanistan, we have also seen increasing numbers of American servicemen using Rio as a "safe" R&R destination. These men are thus hardly the unambiguous victors of globalization portrayed by so many anti–sexual tourism activists. Nor is the sex that they pay for appreciably cheaper than it is in most parts of the United States (where paid sex can be had for around US$100). Crucially, there is no hard evidence that these men are any more likely to be pedophiles or sex offenders than other men. In fact, a recent study of more than five years of calls to the sexual-exploitation hotline maintained by the Brazilian federal government indicates that members of the clergy are four to five times more likely to be accused of child molestation than foreign tourists (ABRAPIA 2004).

In short, our initial study of Copacabana (Blanchette and Silva 2005) concluded that, all things considered, it was a reasonably well-organized and safe commercial sexual district, with no appreciably greater incidence of violations of human or workers' rights than other, comparable segments of Brazil's tourism economy (most notably, the growing "ethnic tourism" sector patronized by black Americans in Salvador da Bahia).

In early 2003, however, it became increasingly apparent to us that a growing social panic regarding tourism and sex was brewing in the local political scene. A series of police raids were organized and carried out in the name of repressing the sexual exploitation of children (extremely rare in Copacabana) and stamping out the trafficking of women (also rare, if we understand trafficking as necessarily involving violations of fundamental human rights). The organizers of these raids made ample use of the "victim/victimizer stereotype" of sexual tourism as justification for their activities, but the real purpose of police activity seemed to be to harass prostitutes and their clients, with "sexual tourism" and "exploitation of children" being mobilized as legally enabling fictions.

The most notorious of these raids was the Operation Princess series, which was supposedly motivated by denunciations of the sexual exploitation of minors. Though many arrests were made and the raids were internationally reported as being a major blow against sexual tourism and the sexual exploitation of children in Brazil, very few minors were actually encountered, and the cases have not generated much in the way of legal results owing to lack of evidence. This is not to say, however, that they did not generate any results at all: hundreds of sex workers were harassed and detained, often in handcuffs and at gunpoint, simply for being prostitutes. In almost every case, the raids generated many more violations of human and constitutional rights than they resolved.[8]

As we followed Operation Princess and other like activities, it became clear to us that the government was *not* primarily interested in protecting sex workers or even in preventing the sexual exploitation of children; rather, the police were apparently seeking to repress prostitution itself. Again, prostitution is not illegal in Brazil, so in order to repress it, other illegalities needed to be alleged. The immediate motivation behind the raids seemed to be the "revitalization" of Copacabana as a "family tourism district" (a status that the neighborhood has never had in all of its history).

Our research in Copacabana led us to believe that we had uncovered a series of activities that ran counter to the received wisdom regarding sexual tourism. Far from discovering a clean divide between victimizing first-world actors and passive third-world victims, which could be further classified according to color, age, race, and class, we found much diversity among prostitutes and clients. Certainly, some generalizations could be made: Copa prostitutes were generally darker and certainly poorer than most of their foreign clients. Ethnic alterity in this nexus, however, was not so much couched in terms of (foreign) white versus (native) non-white, but rather in terms of presumed foreign "racial purity" versus Brazilian "miscegenation."

Furthermore, most Copacabana sex workers related to us that they felt far less exploited in their current activities than they had in prior jobs. Most, in fact, had left "straight" jobs—often in the tourism industry—in order to work as prostitutes. In short, Copa prostitutes were not under-age sex slaves, "forced" into prostitution against their will or for lack of other work. Their jobs, while perhaps unpleasant, were no more exploitative than those otherwise available in the tourism sector and generated ten to twenty times as much income. The violence they reported did not usually come from pimps or foreign clients but from other prostitutes, the police, or "good citizens" intent on eliminating prostitution.

In the public-policy realm, we discovered that the social panic regarding sexual tourism and the exploitation of children was being used to construct policies that harassed and ultimately endangered sex workers. These policies were almost always justified by recourse to the victim/ victimizer stereotype of sexual tourism, with state agents claiming that their activities were necessary to protect poor, black, exploited women from the ravages of evil white gringo tourists. However, it was precisely the poorer women working as independent prostitutes on the streets who were the preferential targets for the government's repressive activities, and, although African-American sexual tourists are in the vast minority on Copa, two of the last four heavily publicized raids resulted, almost exclusively, in the arrests of African Americans.[9] Women working the closed sexual venues (that is, those who had, to one degree or another, bosses or pimps) and the mostly foreign white sexual tourists who frequented them were rarely discomfited by the crusade.

By late 2004, we felt that, ethically speaking, we needed to take a political stand on this issue. We no longer felt comfortable quietly listening to academic colleagues repeat received wisdom about sexual tourism when we could clearly see, in our fieldwork, that this sort of unreflective discourse was providing the ideological justification for activities that endangered our sex-worker friends and informants. We thus contacted Brazil's main prostitute advocacy group, the Brazilian Prostitutes' Network (RBN). The RBN is a nongovernmental organization run by and for prostitutes and it is extremely active in the fight against AIDS in Brazil. The group's leader, Gabriela Leite, has been one of the main public figures in the struggle for prostitute's rights since the closing years of the Brazilian dictatorship in the 1980s. Gabriela had some formal training as a sociologist before dropping out of school to pursue sex work full time, and her organizational activities had helped the Brazilian federal government to decide to incorporate sex workers in safe-sex educational activities. It would not be an exaggeration to say that Gabriela and the national network of which she was a part were two of the main reasons the HIV crisis in Brazil is not as bad as it potentially could have been.

It was our hope that by presenting the RBN with the results of our study, we could force policy change by giving the organized prostitute movement the means to enter the debate regarding trafficking of women and its supposed connections to sex work in Brazil. Throughout the trafficking debate in Brazil, many people had spoken *about* prostitutes, but sex workers themselves had been largely ignored as participants in policymaking. In part, this was due to the fact that state feminism in Brazil, as represented by the women's secretariat, is divided on the question of prostitution. Brazil's experience with AIDS education, however, shows that actively engaging with prostitutes as educators and agents instead of regarding them as passive victims can have extremely positive results.

Because the RBN is underfunded and overwhelmed, we felt that the prostitutes' movement was not paying attention to how the social panic surrounding sexual tourism was being used to repress prostitution. We hoped that by alerting the RBN as to how the debate regarding the trafficking of women was being used as a Trojan horse in order to repress prostitution, we could help bring about a more honest and far-reaching discussion as to how prostitution and tourism were interwoven in Brazil.

We presented our findings to the women of the RBN and have been working with them ever since. Together, we have attended national, regional, and local conferences discussing sexual tourism, the trafficking of women, and the sexual exploitation of children, providing the results of our ongoing studies of Copacabana as a rational basis for public policy and attempting to undermine the prejudices and stereotypes that currently orient so much of Brazil's laws and police activities in this field.

Concretely, we have pushed policymakers to define clearly the concept of "sexual exploitation" in such a way that it does not automatically presume that all sex work is necessarily exploitative. We have also suggested that, in the struggle against trafficking of women and the sexual exploitation of minors, Brazil could do well by emulating its award-winning anti-AIDS program and integrating prostitutes into educational campaigns as active agents. In our experience, there is no reason to believe that prostitutes and their clients are any more accepting of the sexual abuse of women and children than the public in general. We believe that if sex workers were assured that their accusations would be taken seriously and their anonymity and citizens' rights respected, they would become valuable allies in the repression of sexual crimes. Police and policymakers need to be educated regarding sex workers' rights, and the stereotype of the "worthless" or "feckless whore"—frequently openly expressed by policymakers in Rio—needs to be combated. Finally, we feel that the time has come for sex work—permitted by the Brazilian constitution and qualified as productive labor by the federal labor ministry—to be regulated. We thus support Federal Deputy Fernando Gabeira's 98/2003 bill (inspired by Germany's 2001 laws regarding prostitution), which would put sex work on firm legal ground. One of the effects of this law would be the repeal of Article 231 of the Brazilian Criminal Code, which literally defines any movement of prostitutes whatsoever as human trafficking, regardless of whether or not human rights were violated during said movement.

Our political work has brought us into increased contact with Brazilian policy makers and has given us a better view of how traditional understandings of race, class, and gender underpin policies regarding sexual tourism and prostitution. Basically, the Brazilian government and much of the country's media seem to have decided that, even though sexual tourism is not illegal in Brazil, it is nevertheless a menace that must be combated. In this struggle, there are two types of Brazilian women: those who are and those who are not supposedly threatened by sexual tourism. Prostitutes epitomize the first category, naturally, and there is a growing consensus within Brazil that this sort of woman should not be allowed in contact with foreigners "for her own good." Of course, who is a prostitute and who is not is something that is very much open to question, and this is precisely where the victim/victimizer model of sexual tourism has become codified as policy.

According to the Brazilian federal government, the victims of sexual tourism can be identified by their "vulnerabilities." These are defined as quasi-essential traits based on class, race, education, and gender and that, as a rule, closely follow those adjectives stipulated by the victim/victimizer stereotype. The vulnerable victims of sexual tourism are thus classified as predominantly young, black or brown, poor women who have contact with foreigners. Police officers, tourism agents, and social workers are being trained to spot these "vulnerable" individuals and report any suspicious activities to local authorities.

It does not take much sociological imagination to see what this policy means in practice: poor, black and brown women, especially if they are young and frequent the same places as foreigners are increasingly being subjected to harassment of every sort. What is sinister about this model is that it redefines class and racial profiling and social exclusion as a progressive, human-rights-oriented policy.

Within this context, our goal as politically engaged researchers has been to help people see that prostitutes and their clients are actually strong potential allies in the struggle against trafficking of women and the sexual exploitation of minors. Working with the RBN, we have tried to make policymakers and civil society aware of how anti-prostitution measures disguised to look like human-rights initiatives in the struggle against sexual tourism—a "crime" that does not exist under Brazilian jurisprudence—actually divert resources from finding and jailing the real criminals. Finally, we have tried to bring our and the RBN's work to international audiences in order to provide a more nuanced and balanced picture of sex work in Rio de Janeiro and its similarities and differences with such work in other parts of the world.

DISCUSSION QUESTIONS

1. According to the authors of this article, policymakers and anti-prostitution activists subscribe to a number of myths regarding prostitution in Brazil. What are some of these myths and how, according to the authors, do they lead to bad policymaking?
2. Ostensibly, law enforcement authorities in Brazil act to protect prostitutes, with the view that they are victims of poverty, of racial discrimination, and of their clients. But what, according to the authors, happens instead?

NOTES

1. This affirmation comes from the analysis of some 30,000 public reports filed by self-described sexual tourists on six English-language sex- and travel-oriented bulletin boards. This research is described in Blanchette and DaSilva (2008). We understand "sexual tourism" following the International Labor Organization, which defines it as the use of the tourism infrastructure to travel to foreign lands to purchase sexual services.
2. This is Vila Mimosa, an area that concentrates several prostitution venues frequented by working-class Brazilians and is occasionally visited by foreign sex tourists.
3. This is based on the 2003 statistics of our research presented in Blanchette and Silva (2008). Police estimates can be found in Gripp and Bottarri (2004). The number of prostitutes working Copa varies radically from month to month, but 1,500 seems to be a good average.
4. "Child" is defined here as someone up to fifteen years of age. Only some 2 percent—and sometimes none—of the prostitutes we observe on any given night in Copa appear to be between sixteen and seventeen years old. These girls are hardly ever seen inside the venues in question and tend to work the sidewalks or beach. Police arrest records that have been made public after recent antiprostitution blitzes (which, it must be remembered, specifically look for minors) confirm these findings. See also Blanchette and Silva (2005).
5. It is worth remarking in this context that 20 percent of economically active female Brazilians work as domestic laborers (CEDAW 2003).
6. The disco, beach, and restaurant/bar venues do not directly employ sex workers, and sex does not occur on their premises. They simply serve as meeting places for prostitutes and clients. Only one of these three venues, the disco, charges an entrance fee. Vila Mimosa is a special case: Sex workers are not employed by the venues that make up the Vila, but they do have from 15 percent to 25 percent of their earnings siphoned off by the house in the form of room rentals.
7. Both prostitutes and clients overwhelmingly report that unprotected anal or vaginal sex is almost unheard of, though unprotected oral sex is relatively common.
8. In one raid on an apartment brothel, for example, the apartment owner and the brothel manager were immediately released on bail, while five of the brothel's employees (two telephone

operators, a taxi driver, a maid, and a prostitute) were imprisoned for months as "material witnesses" until a habeas corpus decision in their favor forced their release (Datadez 2006).

9. It is worth pointing out that these men were not involved in the sexual exploitation of minors or the trafficking of women: They were simply clients of adult, self-employed prostitutes. Under Brazilian law, they had committed no crime and, in all but one case, they were immediately released.

WORKS CITED

ABRAPIA. 2004. *Abuso e Exploração Sexual de Crianças e Adolescentes no Brasil. Período: 01 de janeiro de 2000 a 31 de janeiro de 2003.* Rio de Janeiro: ABRAPIA.

Blanchette, T., & A. P. Silva. 2005. "Nossa Senhora da Help": Sexo, turismo e deslocamento transnacional em Copacabana. *Cadernos Pagu, 25,* 249–280.

Blanchette, T., & A. P. Silva. 2008. Mapeamento do sexo turismo no Rio de Janeiro. Presentation at the National Association of Postgraduate Studies in the Social Sciences (ANPOCS) conference, 2008, Caxambú, Minas Gerais.

CEDAW. 2003. Brazilian Report. Paper presented at the 29th CEDAW Session.

Datadez. TJRJ concede habeas corpus a grupo acusado de prostituição na Barra. Datadez, 26 January 2006, www.datadez.com.br.

Fanon, F. 1968. *Black Skin, White Masks.* New York: Grove Press.

Gripp, A., & E. Bottari. 2004. Copacabana e Leme, os mercados do sexo. *O Globo,* 15 February 2004.

Young, R. J. C. 2005. *Desejo Colonial.* Sao Paolo: Perspective.

22.

THE NUDIST MANAGEMENT
OF RESPECTABILITY REVISITED*

MARTIN S. WEINBERG

There is a substantial body of literature in the sociology of deviance dealing with the methods deviants and deviant subcultures use to neutralize or minimize the stigma that they frequently encounter. This article is a classic among such works that has been updated by the author for this volume. Weinberg describes the somewhat rigid set of rules that nudists impose upon themselves as a means of neutralizing the stereotypes non-nudists have of them. Paradoxically, while nudists claim to be free from outsiders' obsession with clothing the body, the myriad rules imposed upon them at nudist resorts suggests something quite the opposite. The student of deviance should be aware of the constraining power of norms on the general population; but what may come as a surprise is that deviant subcultures, often reacting to those constraints, sometimes subject themselves to norms that are no less constraining.

Most people in our society consider public nudity to be inappropriate. Yet there is an organized group whose practices breach this norm. Commonly, they refer to their practices as "social nudism."

A number of questions may be asked about these people. For example, how do they see their behavior as appropriate? Have they constructed their own morality? If so, what characterizes this belief system and what are its consequences?[1]

This article attempts to answer these questions through a study of social interaction in what could be considered traditional nudist camps (i.e., not resorts that are devoted to swinging—although those I've visited ordinarily maintain similar day time practices as in the traditional ones). The data come from a number of sources and at this time from over a period of forty-nine years: at the beginning of this time period, in the early 1960s, from two full summers of participant observation in nudist camps, off-season get-togethers of nudists (e.g., at a commercial Turkish bath house), 101 face to face interviews with nudists in the Chicago area in their homes during the winter months, and 617 mailed questionnaires completed by nudists in the United States and Canada[2];

*Prepared especially for this book and used with the permission of the author and the publisher.

since that time, I have visited nudist and clothing optional resorts and beaches both within and outside of the United States—most recently, a local nudist resort in August, 2012.

THE CONSTRUCTION OF SITUATED MORAL MEANINGS: THE NUDIST MORALITY

The construction of morality in nudist camps is based on the official interpretations that these resorts provide regarding the moral meanings of public heterosexual nudity. These are (1) that nudity and sexuality are unrelated, (2) that there is nothing shameful about the human body, (3) that nudity promotes a feeling of freedom and natural pleasure, and (4) that nude exposure to the sun promotes physical, mental, and spiritual well-being.

Based on my attendance at nudist resorts over a period of almost fifty years, I can report that this official perspective is sustained in nudist camps to an extraordinary degree, illustrating the extent to which adult socialization can affect traditional moral meanings. (This is especially important with regard to the first point of the nudist perspective, which is my primary concern given that this is its most unconventional aspect.) The assumption in the larger society is that indeed nudity and sexuality are related; thus, the resulting emphasis on covering the sexual organs, make the nudist perspective a specifically situated morality. My field work, interview, and questionnaire research show that nudists routinely use a special system of practices to create, sustain, and enforce this situated morality.

STRATEGIES FOR SUSTAINING A SITUATED MORALITY

One strategy used by nudist camps to anesthetize any relationship between nudity and sexuality[3] involves a system of organizational precautions regarding who can come into the resort. Most camps, for example, regard men unaccompanied by a woman as a threat to the nudist morality. They suspect that such men may indeed relate to the nudity as something sexual. Therefore, most resorts either exclude uncoupled men or allow only a small quota of them. Resorts that do allow such unaccompanied men may charge them more than they charge whole families. (This does not, however, seem to discourage them because the cost is still relatively low compared with other resorts. It seems to do little more than create resentment among them, provide organizational backing to the construction that they are not especially desirable, and seems to contribute to their social segregation in nudist resorts.)

Certification by the camp owner/manager is another requirement for attending these resorts, and, in the past at least, letters of recommendation regarding the applicant's character were said to be required. The claim was that these regulations helped to preclude people who might be a threat to the nudist construction of nudity.

As described by one woman:

> [The resort owner] invited us over to see if we were desirable people. Then after we did this, he invited us to resort on probation; then they voted us into resort. [Q: Could you tell me what you mean by desirable people?] Well, not people who are inclined to drink, or people who go there for a peep show. Then they don't want you there. They feel you out in conversation. They want people [going there] for mental and physical health reasons.

In the words of another woman:

> Whom to admit [is the biggest problem of the resort]. [Q][4] Because the world is so full of people whose attitudes on nudity are hopelessly warped. [Q: Has this always been the biggest problem in resort?] Yes. Every time anybody comes, a decision has to be made. [Q] . . . The lady sitting at the gate decides about admittance. The director decides on membership.

Also a limit is sometimes set on the number of trial visits a non-member is allowed to make to the resort. Too, there is usually a restriction on how long a person can remain clothed. This is intended to avoid creating discomfort on the part of the camp's members and marking guests who might not accept the nudist perspective.

Another strategy beyond these organizational precautions for sustaining the nudist morality involves the camp's norms of interpersonal behavior. These are as follows:

No Staring

This rule controls overt signs of over-involvement. As the publisher of one nudist magazine said, "They all look up to the heavens and never look below." Such studied inattention can seem exaggerated among some women. In my observations, they appeared to show no recognition that the men were unclothed. Women also recounted to me while I was in attendance at a resort, how they had initially expected men to stare at them, only to find, when they finally did get up the courage to undress, that no one seemed to notice. One woman stated to me: "I got so mad because my husband wanted me to undress in front of other men that I just pulled my clothes right off thinking everyone would look at me." She said she was amazed (and appeared somewhat disappointed) when no one did. The following statements from the formal interviews conducted off-season illustrate the feeling of constraint that resulted from this norm.

According to one man:

[Q: Have you ever observed or heard about anyone staring at someone's body while at resort?] I've heard stories, particularly about men that stare. Since I heard these stories, I tried not to, and have even done away with my sunglasses after someone said, half-joking, that I hide behind sunglasses to stare. Toward the end of the summer I stopped wearing sunglasses. And you know what; it was a child who told me this.

Another man had this to say:

[Q: Would you stare . . . ?] Probably not, 'cause you can get in trouble and get thrown out. If I thought I could stare unobserved I might. They might not throw you out, but it wouldn't do you any good. [Q] The girl might tell others and they might not want to talk to me. . . . [Q] They disapprove by not talking to you, ignoring you, etc.

A woman said:

[Someone who stares] wouldn't belong there. [Q] If he does that he is just going to the resort to see the opposite sex. [Q] He is just coming to stare. [Q] You go there to swim and relax.

In the words of another woman:

I try very hard to look at them from the jaw up—even more than you would normally.[5]

No Sex Talk

I rarely heard explicit sex talk, or jokes that could be considered off-color, while in nudist resorts. This was in sharp contrast to the talk common in non-nudist resorts. An owner of a large resort in the Midwest put it this way: "It is usually expected that members of a nudist resort will not talk about sex, politics, or religion." Or as one single (unaccompanied) man explained: "It is taboo to make sexual remarks here." Interviewees who mentioned that they had talked about sex qualified this by explaining that such talk was restricted to close friends, was of a "scientific nature," or, if a joke, was a "cute sort." Again, my experience has been that, indeed, this is the case.

Asked what they would think of someone who breached this norm, participants indicated that such behavior would, in effect, cast doubt on the situated morality of the nudist resort:

A woman had this to say:

One would expect to hear less of that at a nudist resort than at other places. [Q] Because you expect that the members are screened in their attitude for nudism—and this isn't one who prefers sexual jokes.

Another woman:

I've never heard anyone swear or tell a dirty joke out there.

In the words of a man:

No. Not at a nudist resort. You're not supposed to. You bend over backwards not to.

Another man:

They probably don't belong there. They're there to see what they can find to observe. [Q] Well, their mind isn't on being a nudist, but to see so and so nude.

Care with Body Contact

Although my fieldwork indicated that the extent to which this is enforced varies from resort to resort, there is at least some degree of informal enforcement in nearly every nudist camp (with less concern apparent outside of the United States). Especially in the U.S., I observed and participants mentioned that they were particularly careful not to brush against anyone or have certain types of body contact for fear of how it might be interpreted:

One man said:

I stay clear of the opposite sex. They're so sensitive, they imagine things.

In the words of a woman:

People don't get too close to you. Even when they talk. They sit close to you, but they don't get close enough to touch you.

And as stated by another woman:

We have a minimum of contact. There are more restrictions [at a nudist resort]. [Q] Just a feeling I had. I would openly show my affection more readily someplace else.

When asked in the interviews to conceptualize a breach of this norm, the following response from a woman was typical of the responses in general:

They are in the wrong place. [Q] That's not part of nudism. [Q] I think they are there for some sort of sex thrill. They are certainly not there to enjoy the sun.

Also, in photographs taken for nudist magazines, the subjects usually were shown having only limited body contact. One woman explained: "We don't want anyone to think we're immoral." Outsiders' interpretations of the photographs, then, were also seen as potentially posing a threat to the nudist reality.

Concern over Alcoholic Beverages

In the past, nudist resorts in the United States prohibited alcoholic beverages. This rule was meant to guard against a loss of sexual inhibitions, and I never observed any blatant disregard for the rule. Even participants who admitted that they had "snuck a beer" went on to say that they fully favored the rule.

A woman said:

> Yes. We have [drunk at resort]. We keep a can of beer in the refrigerator since we're out of the main area. We're not young people or carousers. . . . I still most generally approve of it as a resort rule and would disapprove of anyone going to extremes. [Q] For commonsense reasons. People who overindulge lose their inhibitions, and there is no denying that the atmosphere of a nudist resort makes one bend over backwards to keep people who are so inclined from going beyond the bounds of propriety.

And, in the words of a man:

> Anyone who drinks in a nudist resort is jeopardizing their membership and they shouldn't. Anyone who drinks in a nudist resort could get reckless. [Q] Well, when guys and girls drink they're a lot bolder—they might get fresh with someone else's girl. That's why it isn't permitted, I guess.

Alcoholic beverages are no longer forbidden, but it is expected that participants monitor their intake so uninhibited behavior is less likely to occur. At my most recent visit to a nudist resort, the owner said that a recent party got out of hand and she had to speak to the intoxicated people and explain to them that drunkenness was not permitted at the resort.

Rules Regarding Photography

Photography in a nudist camp is controlled by the resort management. Unless the photographer works for a nudist magazine, his/her moral perspective is sometimes suspect. One photographer's remark to a woman that led to his being so considered was, "Do you think you could open your legs a little more?"

Aside from a general restriction on the use of cameras, when cameras were allowed, it was expected that no pictures will be taken without the subject's permission. I did not observe anyone breaching this rule. Members blamed the misuse of cameras especially on unaccompanied men. As one married man said: "You always see the singles poppin' around out of nowhere snappin' pictures." In general, though, control was maintained, and any infractions that took place were not blatant or obvious. Overindulgence in picture-taking was interpreted as an over-involvement in the subject's nudity and cast doubt on the assumption that nudity and sexuality were unrelated. Thus, one man commented:

> Photographers dressed only in cameras and light exposure meters. I don't like them. I think they only go out for pictures. Their motives should be questioned.

Professional photographers (for nudist magazines) recognized the signs that strain the situated morality and acted accordingly.

One woman who modeled for nudist magazines showed me a soft-core magazine to point out how a model could make a nude picture "sexy"—through the use of various staging, props, and expressions—and in contrast, how a nudist model avoided these techniques to make her pictures "natural." Although it is questionable that a nudist model completely eliminates a sexual perspective for the non-nudist, the model above described how she attempted to do this.

She said:

It depends on the way you look. Your eyes and your smile can make you look sexy. The way they're looking at you. Here, she's on a bed. It wouldn't be sexy if she were on a beach with kids running around. They always have some clothes on too. See how she's "looking" sexy? Like an "oh dear!" look. A different look can change the whole picture. Now here's a decent pose. . . . Outdoors makes it "nature." Here she's giving you "the eye," or is undressing. It's cheesecake. It depends on the expression on her face. Having nature behind it makes it better. Don't smile like "come on honey!" It's that look and the lace thing she has on. . . . Like when you half-close your eyes, like "oh baby," a Marilyn Monroe look. Art is when you don't look like you're hiding it halfway.

In general, the element of trust[6] seemed to play a particularly strong role in socializing women to the nudist perspective. Consider this in the following statements made by another woman who modeled for nudist magazines. She and her husband had been indoctrinated in the nudist ideology by friends. At the time of the interview, however, the couple had not yet been to a nudist resort, although they had posed indoors for nudist magazines.

In this woman's words:

[Three months ago, before I was married] I never knew a man had any pubic hairs. I was shocked when I was married. . . . [And, when we were first married] I wouldn't think of getting undressed in front of my husband. I wouldn't make love with a light on, or in the daytime.

With regard to being a nudist model, this woman continued:

None of the pictures are sexually seductive. [Q] The pose, the look—you can have a pose that's completely nothing, till you get a look that's not too hard to do. [Q: How do you do that?] I've never tried. By putting on a certain air about a person; a picture that couldn't be submitted to a nudist magazine—using [the nudist photographer's] language. . . . [Q: Will your parents see your pictures in the magazine?] Possibly. I don't really care. . . . My mother might take it all right. But they've been married twenty years and she's never seen my dad undressed.[7]

No Accentuation of the Body

Accentuating the body is regarded as incongruent with the nudist ideology. Thus, in my early attendance at nudist camps, I observed a woman who had shaved her pubic area who was said by several other members to be "disgusting." There was a similar reaction to women who sat with their legs widely spread.

One woman said:

I'd think she was inviting remarks. [Q] I don't know. It seems strange to think of it. It's strange you ask it. Out there, they're not unconscious about their posture. Most women there are very circumspect even though in the nude.

According to another woman:

For a girl, . . . [sitting with your legs wide open] is just not feminine or ladylike. The hair doesn't always cover it. [Q] Men get away with so many things. But, it would look dirty for a girl, like she was waiting for something. When I'm in a secluded area I've spread my legs to sun, but I kept an eye open and if anyone came I'd close my legs and sit up a little. It's just not ladylike.

And in the words of a man:

> You can lay on your back or side, or with your knees under your chin. But not with your legs spread apart. It would look to other people like you're there for other reasons. [Q: What other reasons?] . . . To stare and get an eyeful . . . not to enjoy the sun and people.

Because of the current popularity in the general society of shaving the pubertal area, this no longer seemed to be an issue. Instead, when I attended a nudist resort in around 1990, what was remarked on was people wearing nipple and genital jewelry. Currently, according to the owner of a nudist resort, now it is only genital jewelry that is frowned on. In her words, "Even some of the men are pierced, and 'up there' isn't the same as drawing attention 'down there.' If someone complains, I have to talk to the people wearing the jewelry and tell them why it isn't nice in a nudist camp."

No Unnatural Attempts at Covering the Body

"Unnatural attempts" at covering the body can be ridiculed because they call into question the belief that there is no shame in exposing any area of the body. I observed compassion for first time visitors to the resort. Early on, members were more sympathetic, assuming that the person just has not yet fully assimilated the nudist perspective—but this was not as likely after the initial visit.

It was how particular members constructed the meaning of the concealment, however, rather than the behavior itself that determined whether covering up was disapproved.

A man said:

> If they're cold or sunburned, it's understandable. If it's because they don't agree with the philosophy, they don't belong there.

According to a woman:

> I would feel their motives for becoming nudists were not well founded. That they were not true nudists—they're not idealistic enough.

Another element of camp life that was said to be related to the nudist reality was the use of communal (unisex) toilets. While this might now still seem strange, in the 1960s, a unisex public restroom with a number of toilets next to one another in a single room seemed even more so. The large resort where I did most of my early field work did have one, with a sign, "Little Girls Room and Little Boys Too." Although the stalls had three-quarter-length doors, the combined facility still was said by the owner to provide an element of consistency. In his words, "If you are not ashamed of any part of your body or any of its natural functions, men and women do not need separate toilets." Thus, even the physical ecology of this resort was aligned with the nudist point of view about the body. For some, however, communal toilets were going too far.

In the words of one woman:

> I think they should be separated. For myself, it's all right. But there are varied opinions, and for the satisfaction of all, I think they should separate them. There are niceties of life we often like to maintain, and for some people this is embarrassing. . . . [Q] You know, in a bowel movement it always isn't silent.

And, a man responded:

I am so embarrassed by the thought of a woman hearing me poop, that I actually became able to constipate myself over the whole weekend while at the camp.

THE ROUTINIZATION OF NUDITY

In the nudist resort, nudity becomes routinized—its attention-provoking quality recedes, and nudity becomes a taken-for-granted state of affairs (viz., increasingly becoming "ground" and receding as "figure"). Thus, when asked questions about staring ("While at resort, have you ever stared at anyone's body? Do you think you would stare at anyone's body?"), participants indicated that nudity at the resort generally did not invoke their attention.

In the words of a man:

Nudists don't care what bodies are like. They're out there for themselves. It's a matter-of-fact thing. After a while you feel like you're sitting with a full suit of clothes on.

And, a woman said:

To nudists the body becomes so matter-of-fact, whether clothed or unclothed, when you make it an undue point of interest it becomes an abnormal thing. [Q: What would you think of someone staring?] I would feel bad and let down. [Q] I have it set up on a high standard. I have never seen it happen.... [Q] Because it's not done there. It's above that; you don't stare.... If I saw it happen, I'd be startled. There's no inclination to do that. Why would they?

Another woman put it this way:

There are two types—male and female. I couldn't see why they were staring. I wouldn't understand it.

In fact, these questions about staring usually elicited a frame of possibilities in which what was relevant to staring was not the nudity itself, but rather, something unusual, something the observing person seldom saw and thus was not routinized to.[9]

One woman noted:

There was a red-haired man. He had red pubic hair. I had never seen this before.... He didn't see me. If anyone did, I would turn the other way.

And a man said:

Well, once I was staring at a pregnant woman. It was the first time I ever saw this. I was curious, her stomach stretched, the shape.... I also have stared at extremely obese people, cripples. All this is due to curiosity, just a novel sight. [Q] ... I was discreet. [Q] I didn't look at them when their eyes were fixed in a direction so they could tell I was.

A woman had this to say:

[Q: Do you think you would ever stare at someone's body while at resort?] No. I don't like that. I think it's silly.... What people are is not their fault if they are deformed.

In the words of a man:

I've looked, but not stared. I'm careful about that, because you could get in bad about that. Get thrown out by the owner. I was curious when I once had a perfect view of a girl's sex organs, because her legs were spread when she was sitting on a chair. I sat in the chair across from her in perfect view of her organs. [Q] For about ten or fifteen minutes. [Q] Nobody noticed. [Q] It's not often you get that opportunity.[8]

In a nudist resort, the arousal of attention by nudity can be regarded as *unnatural*. Thus, staring can be so considered, especially after a period of grace in which to adjust to the nudist perspective. In the words of one woman:

If he did it when he was first there, I'd figure he's normal. If he kept it up I'd stay away from him, or suggest to the owner that he be thrown out. [Q] At first it's a new experience, so he might be staring. [Q] He wouldn't know how to react to it. [Q] The first time seeing nudes of the opposite sex. [Q] I'd think if he kept staring, that he's thinking of something, like grabbing someone, running to the bushes and raping them. [Q] Maybe he's mentally unbalanced.

From a man:

He just sat there watching the women. You can forgive it the first time, because of curiosity—but not every weekend. [Q] The owner asked him to leave.

Another woman:

These women made comments on some men's shapes. They said, "He has a hairy body . . . ," or "Boy his wife must like him because he's hung big." That was embarrassing. . . . I thought they were terrible. [Q] Because I realized they were walking around looking. I can't see that.

ORGANIZATIONS AND THE CONSTITUTION OF NORMALITY

The norms of an organization and the reality they sustain are a resource for the interpretation of behaviors as "natural" or "unnatural."[9] Over-involvement in nudity, for example, was usually interpreted as being unnatural (and not simply rude). Similarly, both perceptions of suggestive behavior or having a sexual response were often viewed as unnatural.

My observations were that when behaviors were constituted as *unnatural*, efforts to "understand them" were minimal, and what Alfred Schutz calls a reciprocity of perspectives was questioned. (The "reciprocity of perspectives" is the assumption that if one changed places with the other, one would, for all practical purposes, see the world as the other sees it.[10])

I saw this unfold when there was alleged to be a peeper having climbed over the fence into the camp and when some man was reported to have had an erection.

See this interpretation from a woman when she was interviewed:

[Q: What would you think of a man who had an erection at resort?] May be they can't control themselves. [Q] Better watch out for him. [Q] I would tell the resort director to keep an eye on him. And the children would question that. [Q: What would you tell them?] I'd tell them the man is sick or something.

From a man:

[Q: What would you think of a Peeping Tom—a non-nudist trespasser?] They should be reported and sent out. [Q] I think they shouldn't be there. They're sick. [Q] Mentally. [Q] Because anyone who wants to look at someone else's body, well, is a Peeping Tom, is sick in the first place. He looks at you differently than a normal person would. [Q] With ideas of sex. [A trespasser] . . . is sick. He probably uses this as a source of sexual stimulation.

Such occurrences challenged the taken-for-granted notion that nudity in the resort was not related to sexuality.

INHIBITING BREAKDOWNS IN THE NUDIST MORALITY

As described, nudist camps promulgate a nonsexual perspective toward nudity, and they attempt to limit breakdowns in it by controlling both what could be viewed as erotic actions and erotic reactions. In effect, the camp partitions nudity off from other forms of "sexual immodesty" (e.g., types of sex talk, erotic overtures). In this way, it makes it easier for a participant to acquire the organization's interpretation of nudity.[11] When behaviors occurred that were seen to reflect other forms of sexual immodesty (or sexually uninhibited behavior), however, I saw nudists reacting with concern—a fear a voiding of a nonsexual meaning of nudity.

One woman said:

This woman with a sexy walk would shake her hips and try to arouse the men. . . . [Q] These men went to the resort director to complain that the woman had purposely tried to arouse them. The resort director told this woman to leave.

During my attendance in U.S. camps, I saw nudists as being extremely sensitive to the possibility of a breakdown in the nudist morality. I saw them as often exhibiting a very low threshold for interpreting acts as "sexual."

An example from one woman:

Playing badminton, this teenager was hitting the birdie up and down and she said, "What do you think of that?" I said, "Kind of sexy." [The head of the resort] said I shouldn't talk like that, but I was only kidding.

Also, note the following woman's description of "mauling":

I don't like to see a man and a girl mauling each other in the nude before others. . . . [Q: Did you ever see this at resort?] I saw it once. . . . [Q: What do you mean by mauling?] Just, well, I never saw him put his hands on her breasts, but he was running his hands along her arms.

This low threshold also sensitized participants to the possibility that certain of their own, or their partner's behaviors, although not intended as "sexual," might nonetheless be interpreted that way.

A woman said:

Sometimes you're resting and you spread your legs unknowingly. [Q] My husband just told me not to sit that way. [Q] I put my legs together.

Because such behaviors can be defined as unnatural, they can easily be suspect in their intent. Thus, when an individual is thought to be in physical control of the behavior and to know the behavior's meaning within the nudist perspective, sexual intentions were often assigned. Referring to a quotation that was presented earlier, one man said that a woman who was lying with her legs spread may have been doing so unintentionally, "but I doubt it. It wasn't a normal position. Normally you wouldn't lay like this. It's like standing on your head."

What could be interpreted as sexual reactions, as well as those that could be considered sexual actions, are likewise controlled in traditional nudist resorts. Thus, when erotic stimuli came into play, sexual responses were usually suppressed.

One man said:

When lying on the grass already hiding my penis, I got erotic thoughts. And then one realizes it can happen here. With fear there isn't much erection.

Another man:

> Yes, once I started to have an erection. Once. [Q] A friend told me how he was invited by some young lady to go to bed. [Q] I started to picture the situation and I felt the erection coming on; so, I immediately jumped in the pool. It went away.

And a third man:

> I was once in the woods alone and ran into a woman. I felt myself getting excited. A secluded spot in the bushes which was an ideal place for procreation. [Q] Nothing happened, though.

When breaches of the situated morality did occur, nudists' sense of modesty often inhibited negative sanctioning. At the moment, the breach was often ignored. I saw those who observed a breach (e.g., an erection) feign inattention or withdraw from the scene. At the same time, the occurrence was likely to be reported to others and might bring it to the resort director's attention.

From a woman:

> [If a man had an erection] people would probably pretend they didn't see it.

And, another woman:

> [Q: What do you think of someone this happens to?] They should try to get rid of it fast. It don't look nice. Nudists are prudists. They are more prudish. Because they take their clothes off they are more careful. [Q] They become more prudish than people with clothes. They won't let anything out of the way happen.

One man reported:

> We were shooting a series of pictures and my wife was getting out of her clothes. [the photographer] had an erection but went ahead like nothing was happening. [Q] It was over kind of fast. . . . [Q] Nothing. We tried to avoid the issue. . . . Later we went to see [the resort director] and [the photographer] denied it.

As indicated in the remark above, "nudists are prudists," at times, nudists became aware of the fragility of their situated moral meanings.

A woman described the following to illustrate this awareness:

> At _____ [resort], this family had a small boy no more than ten years old who had an erection. Mrs. _____ [the owner's wife] saw him and told his parents that they should keep him in check, and tell him what had happened to him and to watch himself. This was silly, for such a little kid who didn't know what happened.

DEVIANCE AND MULTIPLE SCHEMAS

There are basic social processes that underlie responses to putative deviance. Collectivities can affect thresholds of response to behaviors, influencing the relevance, meaning, and importance of them. In the nudist resort, as pointed out previously, alleged sexual actions and reactions can be regarded as unnatural, and a reciprocity of perspectives can be called into question.

From one woman:

> We thought this [unaccompanied male] single was all right, until others clued us in that he had brought [different] girls up to the resort. [Then we recalled that] . . . he was kind of weird. The way he'd look at you. He had glassy eyes, like he could see through you.[12]

Such an inference in a nudist resort could be said to result from effective socialization to its system of moral meanings. The so-called deviant behavior, on the other hand, could be seen to reflect an ineffective socialization to their perspective.

From a man:

I think it's impossible [to have an erection in a nudist resort]. [Q] In a nudist resort you must have some physical contact and a desire to have one.

From another man:

Sex isn't supposed to be in your mind, as far as the body. He doesn't belong there. [Q] If you go in thinking about sex, naturally it's going to happen. . . . You're not supposed to think about going to bed with anyone, not even your wife.

From a woman:

He isn't thinking like a nudist. [Q] The body is wholesome, not . . . a sex object. He'd have to do that—think of sex.

As these quotes suggest, the unnaturalness or deviance of a behavior is ordinarily determined by relating it to an institutionalized scheme of interpretation. Occurrences that are "not understandable" in one collectivity's schema may, though, be quite understandable in another's.[13] Thus, what was seen as deviance in nudist resorts are typically regarded by members of clothed society as natural and understandable—not unnatural and difficult to understand. For example, a large number of male students in my classes as well as men in the outside society have expressed the opinion that they don't see how a man could not have an erection being around all those nude women.

Finally, people may subscribe to multiple and conflicting interpretive schemes. In fact, the low threshold of social nudists to perceiving events as "sexual" appears to be a function of such marginality—namely, that not having completely suspended the perspective of the clothed society regarding nudity is what leads them to constitute many events in a nudist resort as "sexual" in purpose.

DISCUSSION QUESTIONS

1. How might the rules at nudist resorts described by Weinberg represent a reaction to outsiders' stereotypes of nudists?
2. With this article in mind, if you were to vacation at a nudist resort, what do you anticipate would be the most challenging and the most rewarding parts of the experience?

NOTES

1. In previous papers, I have dealt with other questions that are commonly asked about nudists. How persons become nudists is discussed in "Becoming a Nudist," *Psychiatry*, 29 (February, 1966), 15–24. A report on the nudist way of life and social structure is in *Human Organization*, 26 (Fall, 1967), 91–99. For more about nudism from other authors, an early book describing social nudism from the view of the American Sunbathing Association (which is no longer the name of the national nudist association) is by Donald Johnson, *The Nudists* (Spokane, Washington: Outdoor American Association, 1959). A later book, where William Hartman and Marilyn Fithian teamed

up with Donald Johnson in an updated description is *Nudist Society* (New York: Crown Publishers, 1970). In my opinion, the most sophisticated work on nudism and nudity, which provides a cultural anatomy of human perceptions of nudity in both the past and the present, is by Ruth Barcan, *Nudity: A Cultural Anatomy* (Oxford, NY: Berg, 2004).

2. Approximately one hundred camps were represented in the personal interviews and mailed questionnaires of the initial 1960s study. As noted in the body of the paper, the interviews were conducted in the homes of nudists during the off season. Arrangements for the interviews were initially made with these nudists during the first summer of participant observation; selection of respondents was limited to those living within a one-hundred-mile radius of Chicago. The mailed questionnaires were sent to all members of the National Nudist Council (no longer in existence). The different techniques of data collection provided triangulation and a test of convergent validly. Since that time, I have visited a myriad of nudist resorts and beaches in Europe, in the Caribbean, and in other parts of the United States, and the few changes in ethos that I have observed have been incorporated in this paper.

3. For a discussion of such paired relationships, see Alfred Schutz, *Collected Papers: The Problem of Social Reality,* Maurice Natanson, ed. (The Hague: Nijhoff, 1962), I, 287 ff.

4. [Q] is used to signify a neutral probe by the interviewer that follows the course of the last reply, such as "Could you tell me some more about that?" or "How is that?" or "What do you mean?" Other questions by the interviewer are given in full.

5. Events like a King and Queen Contest, which took place at nudist conventions and other special weekends, allowed for a patterned evasion of the staring rule. Applicants stood before the crowd in front of a so-called "royal platform," and applause was used for selecting the winners. Photography was allowed during the contest and no one was permitted to enter the contest unless willing to be photographed. The major reason for this was that this is a major event, and contest pictures are used in nudist magazines and other media to publicize the resort. At the same time, the large number of photographs sometimes taken by lay photographers (viz., those not working for the media) made a number of members uncomfortable by calling into question a nonsexual construction of the situation.

6. For a deeper but relevant conception of trust, see Harold Garfinkel, "A Conception of, and Experiments with, 'Trust' as a Condition of Stable Concerted Actions," in 0. J. Harvey, ed., *Motivation and Social Interaction* (New York: Ronald, 1963).

7. I was amazed in the initial study at how many nudist women described a similar pattern of extreme clothing modesty among their parents and in their own married life. Included in this group was another woman who was a nudist model, at the time, one of the most photographed of nudist models. Perhaps there are some fruitful data here for cognitive dissonance psychologists.

8. Cf. Schutz, *op. cit.,* p. 74.

9. For some male participants, the female genitalia never become a routinized part of resort nudity: thus its visible exposure did not lose an attention-provoking quality.

10. See: Schutz, *op. cit.,* I, *11,* for his description of reciprocity of perspectives.

11. This corresponds with the findings of learning-theory psychologists.

12. For an interesting study of the process of doublethink, see James L. Wilkins, "Doublethink: A Study of Erasure of the Social Past," unpublished doctoral dissertation, Northwestern University, 1964.

13. Cf. Schutz, *op. cit.,* p. 229 ff. 13. Also, see the notion of a "charter" and a more developed model of these processes, in Martin S. Weinberg, Colin J. Williams, and Douglas Pryor, "Telling the Facts of Life: A Study of a Sex Information Switchboard," *Journal of Contemporary Ethnography,* 17 (July, 1988), 131–163.

DRUGS

Introduction

In 1953, Howard Becker published "Becoming a Marihuana User" in the *American Journal of Sociology*. This became a classic in the sociology of deviance and in the sociology of drug use and it is frequently cited within the context of symbolic interactionism. Evolving from the works of Charles Horton Cooley, George Herbert Mead, W. I. Thomas, and Herbert Blumer, remember from our discussion in earlier chapters that symbolic interactionism rests on the assertion that people do not respond to reality; they instead respond to their perceptions or interpretations of reality; and these perceptions are learned through our interactions with others. Words, people, things and events do not have inherent meaning, but are given meanings based on our experiences with others. Two of the most important types of meanings (perceptions) that affect our behaviors are our "definition of the self" and our "definition of the situation." Thus, Figure 5.1 illustrates the essence of symbolic interactionism.

Returning now to Becker's thesis, he argues a series of conditions needs to occur before one will become a regular marijuana user. Most likely the initiate is introduced to the drug by his or her friends. Before trying it for the first time, their friends must convince him or her that all of the negative things they have heard about the drug's harmful effects are misleading. That is, the initiate learns through social interaction to define the drug as harmless and define him- or herself as one who will not be duped by the anti-drug propaganda. If they do not acquire these definitions, they are not likely to try the drug. Once they try the drug and do get high, it is not the effects of the drug on the mind and body that motivate repeated use; it is the *perception* of the drug's effects. That is, Becker notes, the effects of marihuana are not inherently pleasant. He writes,

> Marihuana-produced sensations are not automatically or necessarily pleasurable. . . . The user feels dizzy, thirsty, his scalp tingles, he misjudges time and distances. Are these pleasurable? He isn't sure. If he is to continue marihuana use, he must decide they are. Otherwise, getting high, while a real enough experience will be an unpleasant one he would rather avoid. (Becker, 1953: 239)

Consequent to the drug-induced high, the initiate's friends might point out the effects of the drug as being hysterically funny. The dry mouth ("cottonmouth") associated with the drug may become a source of amusement. To satisfy the hunger ("the munchies") caused by the drug, the

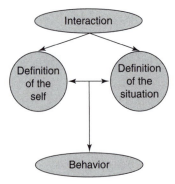

FIGURE 5.1 The Interactionist Model

initiate and his or her friends might make a "raid" on a fast-food joint. There, the time and space distortions produced by the drug could become another source of amusement. The interactions between the initiate and his or her friends, of course, vary; but ultimately, if the initiate learns through social interaction to define the effects of the drug as pleasant and to define him- or herself as cool, fun-loving, and not susceptible to the misinformation propagated by the media, law enforcement, and his or her parents' generation, then he or she is likely to try it again. If they do not acquire such definitions, they are not likely to try it again.

The implications of Becker's thesis are profound. We might think that the mind and body would respond automatically to the physiological changes produced by the chemicals we put in our bodies, much like we respond automatically when we place our hand on a hot burner. But instead, we respond not to the chemicals' effects, but to our perceptions of the chemicals' effects, which we learn through our interactions with others. (The same process explains why some people can tolerate walking on hot coals.)

In the first article in this section, as does Becker, Angus Bancroft takes exception to the popular belief that the drug user responds mainly to the chemical effects of the drug in the user's body. The chemicals' physical actions in the brain and body are certainly not irrelevant, but to emphasize them, as many people in the professional communities of prevention and treatment are inclined to do, ignores the important effects of situational and cultural contexts and reduces our understanding of drugs down to their mechanistic pharmacological properties. If social interactions affect the way we respond to particular drugs, as Becker argues, then it follows that culture will have an influence on the way people respond to drugs. Thus, in some cultures alcohol often makes people more boisterous and perhaps aggressive, while in other cultures, it might make its users more calm and sedate. Bancroft argues that many of the effects of a drug, alcohol in particular, depend not only on its chemical properties, but also on the context in which it is being used and societal expectations of the user's behavior in a given context. Bancroft also describes how the deviant status of alcohol consumption varies from context to context within cultures. More specifically, behaviors that might be considered deviant in ordinary contexts are sometimes accepted if they occur in specific contexts involving alcohol or if they appear to be the result of intoxication during socially sanctioned "time-outs."

Just as people respond to their subjective perceptions of the effects of drugs in their bodies and not to the objective reality of these effects, societies respond to their perceptions of drug "problems" and not to the reality of these phenomena. These perceptions, as Craig Reinarman points out in the second article, are constructed by a variety of social, political, and historical forces. For example, even though opiates were in widespread use throughout the United States in the nineteenth century, the first drug laws were passed in the state of California and they only banned opium *smoking*. These laws received a great deal of popular support. However, the vast majority of opiates, at the time, were consumed in non-smokable forms. It was only Chinese immigrants, who were competing with whites for jobs out West during a severe economic downturn, who smoked opium in significant quantities. Thus, it seems to have been the Chinese immigrants and not opium consumption that were the focus of drug legislation. As Reinarman notes, similar anti-minority sentiments motivated subsequent anti-drug legislation and enforcement and, many would argue, continue to do so today.

Reinarman goes on to identify a variety of elements of a successful drug scare and, while he notes "a kernel of truth" as one such element, none of the other elements have anything to do with the actual harm done to a society by a particular drug. Among these elements, he identifies scapegoating as perhaps the "most crucial" one. Much as we saw in the moral panic literature, during periods of intense "cultural anxiety" brought on by social change, many people are ready and willing to believe that a given folk devil or drug is the source of the worst of society's problems and many politicians and moral entrepreneurs are willing and able to take advantage of their susceptibility. Reinarman notes that the United States stands apart from other countries with the frequency and intensity with which drugs scares occur and he goes on to speculate why Americans are uniquely susceptible them.

Reinarman argues that the social, political, cultural, and historical forces that shape the way Americans perceive illegal drugs interfere with the Unites States' ability to establish sensible and effective drug policy. The next two articles describe what may seem to be sensible and effective drug policies to more people in Europe than they would to people in the United States. Both of these selections describe variations of the "harm reduction" approach to drugs which has gained a good deal of momentum in Western countries other than the United States. This approach holds that, given people are going to use mind-altering drugs whether they are legal or not, policies should be directed toward minimizing the harm done to the user and to those in his or her environment. This emphasis is on public health and not criminalization. The third article in this section is a transcript from the television newsmagazine, *60 Minutes*, describing how this approach is applied in a drug "treatment" program in Liverpool, England. Here, drug users who qualify are prescribed the drug of their choice. The idea would be abhorrent to most Americans, but the case is made that such a policy can be sensible and effective. In the next selection, Bellis, Hughes, and Lowey advocate for a "healthy settings" approach and argue that often the environments in which young people typically use illegal drugs are as or more dangerous than the drugs themselves and that policies should be directed toward making these environments safer.

An honest discussion of drug problems would not just include the use of illegal drugs, but also legal drugs that are being promoted by the pharmaceutical industry. It used to be that people with severe mental disturbances were considered "crazy," stigmatized, marginalized, and perhaps forcefully separated from the rest of us and treated with psychotropic drugs. Today, the word "crazy" is used only colloquially, but millions of people—perhaps most people at some point in their lives—are considered to have varying degrees of various mental illnesses and are prescribed drugs for treatment. Millions more people have physical conditions that were once considered normal, but are now the appropriate target of pharmaceutical intervention. While these conditions and "mental illnesses" do not carry the same stigma as "crazy" once did, pharmaceutical companies have a financial interest in making us feel different from the way we think we are supposed to feel and willing to take drugs to feel better. Thus, pharmaceutical companies engage in what critics often call "disease mongering."

Partly as a result of pharmaceutical marketing, conditions that were never considered medical have recently fallen within the purview of medicine. Acne, once considered a normal part of life, is now a "dermatological condition." Pharmaceutical companies that market acne medications profit when "sufferers" feel their condition lies outside of the norm and seek medical treatment. Today we have drugs to address social anxiety disorder, depression, ADD/ADHD, erectile dysfunction, restless legs, and a host of other conditions. Critics argue, for example, that "social anxiety disorder" is simply a medicalized term for shyness.

There are indeed some people who suffer from extreme forms of these conditions. Some people may be regularly paralyzed by their shyness and may benefit from a prescription for anti-depressants or anti-anxiety drugs. But the drug companies, intent on expanding their markets, have a vested interest in having us believe that that those of us with a modest amount of shyness—that may be part of our personalities—would also benefit from a drug regimen. Some men almost always have difficulty achieving an erection, but critics charge that the drug companies want men who have such problems only on rare occasions to be included among their clientele. Some people cannot stop moving their legs to the point where they cannot relax and the movements can become painful; but some drug manufacturers would profit if the millions more who move their legs while concentrating or as a mild nervous habit were also labeled as suffering from "restless leg syndrome."

As the public comes to accept drugs as a suitable treatment for these milder "afflictions," the boundaries between medical and non-medical, "normal" and "deviant," are shifting and the process of the *medicalization of deviance* is taking place. As the United States is one of the only industrialized countries in the world that allows pharmaceutical companies to advertise directly to the consumer (as opposed to allowing them to market their drugs only to physicians), it is likely that the medicalization of deviance is taking place faster in the United States than elsewhere. But, as Ihara points out in the last article in this section, Western categories of treatable conditions are being disseminated elsewhere. The medicalization of mild to moderate depression that took place in the 1980s and 1990s in the United States reached Japan a decade or so later. Ihara describes the efforts of the pharmaceutical industry to make this happen.

The medicalization of deviance is discussed at more length in Part VIII.

Reference

Becker, Howard, "Becoming a Marijuana User," *American Journal of Sociology*, vol. 59, no. 3, pp. 235–242, 1953.

23.
CUSTOMS, CULTURES AND THE EXPERIENCE OF INTOXICATION

ANGUS BANCROFT

When most scientists, drug educators and treatment specialists tell us what drugs do to us, their explanations are usually reduced to the effects of chemicals on biological processes in the body. We hear about bloodstreams, metabolisms, neurotransmitters, endorphins, synapses, and the like. But social scientists argue that there is much more to explaining the phenomenon of intoxication. People who have used LSD and other hallucinogens know all too well about the importance of set and setting. That is, the mood you were in when you took the drug and the environment in which you took it have a large effect on the quality of intoxication. But set and setting are not only relevant to intoxication induced by hallucinogens. One does not have to be a regular consumer of alcohol to imagine the different qualities of intoxication when you are drinking with your family at a dinner gathering as opposed to drinking with your college buddies on top of a water tower at two o'clock in the morning.

If set and setting are important to explaining intoxication, then it follows that culture is an important variable as well because culture has a pronounced effect on what people expect of a drug and on the occasions in which people are likely to use it. Bancroft argues here that what we think are the automatic effects of alcohol are, in fact, subject to interpretation and our interpretation is learned through our culture.

REMOTE CONTROL FOR THE SOUL

. . . . I was once walking in the broad daylight of a summer afternoon in the full possession of hasheesh delirium. For an hour the tremendous expansion of all visible things had been growing toward its height; it now reached it, and to the fullest extent I realized the infinity of space. Vistas no longer converged, sight met no barrier; the world was horizonless, for earth and sky stretched endlessly onward in parallel planes.

Fitz Hugh Ludlow
"The Apocalypse of Hasheesh," *Putnam's Monthly* (1856, 8: 48)

A few famous attempts have been made to describe the effect of opiates and—less frequently, cannabis—in print, for instance, in Thomas de Quincey's *Confessions of an Opium-Eater*, and Fitz Hugh Ludlow's *Apocalypse of Hasheesh*, quoted above. There is a rather larger body of literature that was created by writers who wrote from their experiences with opium and cocaine in one way or another, such as Samuel Taylor Coleridge's *Kublai Khan* or Sir Walter Scott's *Bride of Lammermoor*. Perhaps reflecting its more mundane status, alcohol has tended to produce reflections on its external effects and changes in behaviour towards others, rather than on internal states, as well as longer, often autobiographical, pieces reflecting on its ills, maudlin sentiment, and the rest of the less flattering end of the range of alcohol-induced emotions. There are two difficulties in constructing some idea of what various intoxications are like, and what makes them like that. One is that so many illicit drug experiences are represented as being exotic, out of this world, as in Ludlow's account, and that alcohol attracts a better class of writer. The other is that alcohol-influenced experiences have the appearance, to a Westerner at least, of being wholly mundane or trivial. Western societies lack a language for drunken intoxication, although they have many words for it, mainly reflecting the supposed disinhibiting nature of alcohol.

A positive language for drug-induced intoxication has been confined to rather outré literary reflections by unreliable interlocutors on opium and cannabis. There is an extensive scientific and policy discourse about problems and damaging side effects of intoxication, which revisits descriptions of states of intoxication, except negatively (in terms of loss of control, inhibition, judgement, coordination and so on). It is mainly in anthropology and symbolic interactionist sociology that we find accounts examining the positive uses of intoxication and the positive steps taken towards achieving states of intoxication. This body of work includes research into how the experience of intoxication is shaped and learnt in local contexts, that looks at, for instance, the cultural shaping of drunkenness, and the learnt effects of cannabis highs. War stories and travellers' tales from the land of opium are beguiling in their outlandishness but detract from our understanding of the more widespread everyday experiences and uses of intoxication. A privileged Victorian gentleman throwing himself towards the extremities of mental experience in opium or cannabis, and returning with tales of the dark side of the moon, will have a very different attitude to his drug of choice than a prostitute using the same drug to numb herself to the cold hours she spends with clients like him. Celebrity dope fiends and abject yet articulate addicts make good copy. They are familiar narratives, endlessly regurgitated in political and media commentary, and in film and literature. Most experiences with psychoactive substances are nothing like that, however. What these images do is to reproduce the idea that illicit drugs, and tobacco and alcohol, are devices that consistently produce the same effects, be they good or bad, in different individuals.

Were you drunk at the weekend? Did you get a bit tipsy, queasy, roaring or catatonic drunk? Or all of them in sequence? If so, how did you get drunk? The answer most people would give, is "By drinking a lot," or "By drinking more than I should have." This is black box pharmacology, in the technological sense of a system whose workings are hidden and in which certain inputs produce predictable outputs. In this case, humans are the black box. The chemicals go in, and the effects come out, like winding up a clockwork toy and setting it to run across the floor, banging into furniture as it goes. The folk knowledge among users about what substances "do" is in practice a lot more sophisticated than this. LSD users, for instance, recognize the subtle effects of environment and mood that can produce radically different hallucinogenic experiences. It is the simpler version that is reproduced in policy and scientific understandings. Their central conceit is that the effects of psychoactive substances are contained within their chemical structure, and that includes not just physical but also behavioral, social and moral effects. This is reflected in academic and policy terminology where, for example, alcohol consumption is said to have "caused" such ills as poverty, murder and robbery (Williams and Brake, 1980: 3), and, more recently, terrorism and sexual violence.

This is the biopharmacological self. Many of the mechanisms through which substances work to induce changes in behavior have been discovered and described. In different instances, smoking tobacco introduces nicotine into the blood, which rapidly crosses the blood–brain barrier and activates the nicotine receptors there and in other parts of the nervous system, raising levels of the neurotransmitter dopamine. It increases heart rate, blood pressure, alertness and memory. The MDMA or similar chemical in an ecstasy pill releases serotonin into the brain's synapses, which has the effect of creating a sense of elation and exhilaration. Heroin, like other opiates, mimics the action of the body's endorphins, and binds to the opioid receptors, tissue to which chemicals bind and thus change brain activity, such chemicals being present in the brain, and also in the gastrointestinal tract and spinal cord. In non-habituated, but not first-time, users it induces a rush of intense euphoria. Cocaine, like nicotine, increases dopamine levels, and hugely stimulates the central nervous system. The user experiences a rush of energy and a sense of self-confidence. Cannabis contains delta^9-tetrahydrocannabinol (THC), the most psychoactive of the sixty or so cannabinoids present in the cannabis plant. Like opiates, it is an agonist for particular receptors, in this case, cannabinoid receptors. The user feels a sense of relaxation and well-being. The biopharmacological view of how drugs and alcohol function and what makes them pleasurable is that the active chemicals they contain alter brain functions, and that these register in the mind as being tipsy, loved-up, aggressive, and so on.

In chapter 2 [of Bancroft's book], I mentioned the historical narrative of an ever more finely tuned understanding of what drugs do. That is it. These findings are illustrated by the very popular presentations of "brain slice" graphics that show sections of the brain lighting up or going dark under the influence of drugs. . . . However, the implications of these processes are much fuzzier than the mechanical representation of them would imply.

It appears at first to be eminently commonsensical, not least to those canny souls who can be seen in off-licences and liquor stores carefully weighing up the comparative price/alcohol ratio of various wines, beers and spirits before making their purchase, as if the other constituents of the drinks were just by-products or pollutants in an alcohol delivery mechanism. Following on from that, drug and alcohol problems are seen to result from overindulgence, or surrendering the self to the substance. Everyone has a limit, which is zero for some people and some substances; everyone should know their limits, and problems begin when that limit is breached. The hangover, the overdose, and the whiteout, are the payback for having had too much of a good thing.

Those same systems that deliver the drug and push our mental buttons also ensure we pay a physical and mental price for our fun. Some of these substances generate dependence and withdrawal symptoms when the user is denied them or chooses to relinquish the chemical crutch. A payback is also demanded following excess use. The moral economy of intoxication is at work, and every pleasure has its price. Some readers will be familiar with the exquisite torture of an alcohol hangover. Ecstasy users often experience a midweek comedown following weekend use of the drug, which leaves them feeling drained and emotionally vulnerable. Cocaine users undergo rapid onset of depression and the slough of despond, which can last for days after heavy ingestion. Heroin withdrawal has its own well-documented horrors, although it takes some time to build up dependence and so generate withdrawal symptoms, contrary to accepted wisdom.

In essence, the drug carries the user on a trip, which they cannot control. They buy their ticket, but after that the drug decides on the ride. This black-box perspective is limiting, not only in the sense of its workings being opaque to human control, but also in the assumption that inputs produce expected outputs, which have little to do with the actions of the people involved. This chapter will examine the evidence that suggests psychoactive drugs are not black boxes of the soul, looking at the social factors shaping intoxication. Two common themes are that most psychoactive substances cause disinhibition and/or sensual and perceptual distortion. Alcohol is the particular stock-in-trade of many of these narratives because a strong folk narrative has built up around it, that of disinhibition.

ALCOHOLIC DISINHIBITION AND STATUS TRANSITION

The culturally loaded definition of alcohol as a substance that disinhibits is reflected in common English language phrases like being "out of one's tree" when drunk, and the ever-repeated stories of drunken antics passed around by friends and dined out on by acquaintances that make up part of a good night out for many. This is more scientifically presented as impairment of the "higher brain functions," the ego, or the reasoning self. It is as if the brain possesses a governor circuit which ethyl alcohol interferes with, reducing the individual to a set of uncontrolled impulses. Alcohol is a substance with the power to cut away the bonds of civilization that hold baser, animal desires in check, rendering individuals myopic towards the consequences of their actions.

Disinhibition may involve disregarding of restraints around sexuality, of norms keeping apart distinct categories of people, situations or objects, or the use of violence. In the case of the biblical story of Lot and his daughters in Genesis, alcohol allows for the violation of the incest taboo. Thinking themselves the only human beings left alive following the divine devastation of Sodom and Gomorrah, Lot's two daughters get their father drunk and have sex with him. The next day, he has forgotten what has happened. They then bear his children. Common regulations on drinking in Western societies reflect these assumptions about what it does. Alcohol in public spaces is monitored and governed. Some United States jurisdictions ban the possession of an open container with alcohol in it in a public place. In many states it is a crime to be or appear to be intoxicated in public. Public drinking is in some circumstances associated with public disorder. Yet the association is oddly inconsistent. Drinking in a beer garden, or a permitted street festival, or a Catholic church service, renders the practice acceptable.

That suggests that there is no such thing as a blanket disinhibition caused by alcohol, which we might expect to happen from this vision of alcohol as gumming up the brain's brake fluid. The form that disinhibitions take is always specific to the situation, if the situation allows for it at all. Anthropological evidence indicates that many taboos—the incest taboo being one, unlike Lot's story—usually remain in place whatever the supposed disinhibiting properties of alcohol may be, as will be seen later on. Those taboos that are broken tend to be broken in a socially acceptable, carefully defined manner. Drinking and collective raucousness commonly go together in the USA, Britain and Finland, but this is not a case of too much fuel in the fire. Alcoholic disinhibition can be used deliberately and creatively to facilitate the fulfillment of a social role, as when young men demonstrate the ability to engage in violent, confrontational masculinity. In other cultures, the associations and uses of drinking and drunkenness run in very different directions.

Despite its limitations, the notion of alcoholized disinhibition is useful because it indicates that being intoxicated often involves a transition between social roles, or a modification of social status. One of the attractions of drinking in Western cultures is its appearance of flattening status hierarchies, for instance, by rendering ugly people attractive, dull people witty and shy people gregarious, even if only in their own eyes. More importantly, drinking situations are supposed to temporarily suspend social hierarchies, such as those of boss and employee. Behavior that is not endorsable when sober will be excused or celebrated when drunk. Like the Shakespearean jester, the drunk may take advantage of his or her temporary role-suspension to make statements that are normally unsayable, and will be forgiven this transgression. Disinhibition therefore implies a surprising clarity—of purpose, desire, and intent—from which the shackles are taken. Distortion is also an effect of intoxication, yet it implies the opposite—a lack of clarity, a sensual and psychic befuddlement.

SENSUAL DISTORTION AND MONSTROUS ENHANCEMENT

> It has also been conjectured that Van Gogh abused digitalis (which was used at this time in the treatment of epilepsy); toxic levels of this drug cause a disturbance of colour vision, which might account for the artist's preference for yellow, beige and ochre.
>
> *J.-C. Sournia*
> A History of Alcoholism (1990: 86)

Jean-Charles Sournia drops the hypothesis into *A History of Alcoholism* that Van Gogh's unique use of colour might have been due to the effect of his heavy use of digitalis. Digitalis was used at the time to treat mania and epilepsy. Van Gogh's doctor may have prescribed it to him in heavy quantities. Its use could have led to the condition of xanthopsia, which gives a yellow tinge to vision, and coronas, which cause the sufferer to perceive halos around light sources (Lee, 1981). Given his use of blue in his work, which should not be common in a painter with xanthopsia, this retrospective diagnosis is far from certain. The list of possible disorders Van Gogh could have suffered from is a long one, including sexually transmitted diseases, temporal lobe epilepsy, Meniere's disease, alcohol poisoning, and various mental illnesses, in which xanthopsia must fight for a place. Some analysts of the painter's work and life ascribe aspects of his work to these other conditions (Blumer, 2002). Eagerness to impute Van Gogh's possible digitalis use to abuse, and his use of colour in some paintings to the consequences of that, reflects another dominant conception of intoxication in Western societies, as consisting of distortion, as well as our contemporary lens for viewing eccentric or abnormal behaviour as symptoms of pathology. Presumably, a healthy Van Gogh would have been a figurative realist painter.

Drinkers in Anglo-Saxon societies in particular are familiar with the notion that the experience of intoxication means encountering various perceptual distortions. "Beer goggles" is a slang term for the common experience in which potential intimates become more attractive the drunker the observer is, often inviting rueful reflections on the morning after by both parties. Beer goggles are now more than a metaphor. A United States company, Drunkbusters, produces "Impairment Goggles" to simulate the effects of alcohol intoxication. The goggles create powerful distortions of visual perception. The wearer experiences double vision, false-depth perception, and blurring of small details such as letters, so that the wearer is required to approach objects and other people slowly to be sure as to their identity and exact location. The goggles are used to demonstrate the effects of alcohol consumption on driving ability, and in sex education. The intention is to demonstrate how badly a primary perceptual faculty is affected by alcohol, and how this impairs one's other abilities. For instance, putting on a condom while drunk becomes very difficult. The drunk person expends time and effort in (over)compensation for their impaired abilities, while insisting that everything is fine.

The beer goggles, in both literal and metaphorical form, encapsulate the understanding that intoxication, especially alcoholic intoxication, equals sensual distortion leading to impairment. It distorts perception, memory, reason and judgement. There is a distinction between distortion and disinhibition. The former relies on an idea of the self as a driver in the body. Alcohol throws oil on the tires and mud on the windscreen. The latter suggests that the self is a balance of forces in the mind which intoxication throws off, allowing some that are normally controlled to come to the fore.

A commonly experienced distortion is alcohol-induced myopia, as it is called, in which alcohol intoxication reduces the effect of factors outside the drinker's immediate environment, past, present and future, whether relationships, anxieties, work worries and other influences. For instance, the future prospect of a hangover in the morning tends to diminish the more one drinks, as does the memory of past hangovers. The moment is made all. There is a double meaning to this, though. "Myopia" meant in this sense can be an enhancement. In other contexts we are expected to strive for this. Focusing the self on the present moment to the exclusion of all else is an ability that is highly valued and desired in athletes and college lecturers with deadlines. One of the effects of cannabis, to encourage a focus on tiny and previously unnoticed details of the environment, could be highly valued by artists. This becomes a problem in terms of the social valuation of the outcome, a night of regretted sexual intercourse not being comparable to a win at tennis. The difference between impairment and enhancement is then a value judgement made outside the experience itself.

The difference between an effect being positively or negatively valued is one of contextual spin. A perceptual distortion may involve finding things funny that aren't. "Aren't" is a localized definition, meaning finding things funny that sober people do not, or that, on sober reflection, do not seem so hilarious. Its brief, pleasant oblivion is paid for by the litany of broken hearts, promises and noses counted the following day, and the slow dripfeed of fragmented returning memories of things said and done that, alas, seemed like a good idea at the time. The issue here is partly that this is not an accurate picture, as we shall see, but also that it is wholly negative. Even the pleasures of intoxication are put down to temporary madness, a madness which in other contexts is highly valued. The conclusion then reached is that the only way to control these negative effects societally is to control the substance itself, either by restricting its availability through taxation and regulation or through banning it altogether, restoring through the state the impairment of judgement presumably lost to the individual.

Illicit drugs also come under the distortion narrative, although here the distortion is not only perceptual, but consists of distortion of the self. In drug mythology, they make you do things you would not otherwise do, and feel what you would not otherwise feel. You can be taken out of your self (heroin), trust people you would not otherwise (ecstasy), or lose the will to resist rape (GHB). They can be monstrous enhancers, such as PCP allegedly gifting the user with superhuman strength. Illicit drugs are thought of as being more specific and precise in their effects than alcohol. They are given various specific classifications that are meant to reflect the effects embodied in them, as stimulants, depressants, psychedelics, deliriants, dissociatives or empathogens. They seem then to be very different from alcohol in the way they act and the effects they have, although the effects of some can be nearly as varied. Their specificity might in fact lie in the culture surrounding their use rather than in their chemical nature. Alcohol has its status as multiple disinhibitor and distorter because it is in such widespread use. We can see every time we go out for a drink how alcohol affects people in wildly different ways; we have some lay understanding of this. As illicit drugs are the habit of a minority, many do not appreciate that the same possibilities apply.

The above disinhibition and distortion explanations of how drugs and alcohol intoxicate tend to treat the individual under the influence of intoxicants as like a car to which the wrong type of fuel has been added. Knowledge of the mechanisms through which intoxicants interact with the body is important, of course, but intoxication cannot be reduced to these mechanisms. In fact, most would recognize that there is a subjective element involved in drug and alcohol experiences, which although subjectively experienced is socially structured. To continue with the same metaphor, the operation of a car depends on its own internal workings, but also on the weather, the layout of the highway, the rules of the road, the behaviour of other drivers, and the experience and skills of whoever is behind the wheel. Intoxication experiences are always individual and specific to the time and place where they happen, but this is not purely a personal reaction to circumstance. It involves a socialized subjectivity that responds to cultural norms and ideological values, along with the sensual elements of its setting.

CROSS-CULTURAL CHEMISTRY

> Specificity of drug action is to a considerable extent a fiction that has served to promote the neglect of the range or multiplicity of drug effects.
>
> *Henry L. Lennard et al.*
> "The Methadone Illusion" (1972: 882)

The effects of alcohol are enumerated with some precision in folk and popular culture. In one episode of *The Simpsons,* the long-running satirical cartoon series, "Selma's Choice," Homer Simpson's sister-in-law Selma takes two of his children, Bart and Lisa, to visit "Duff Gardens." It is a theme park run by the Duff Corporation, who make Duff, Homer's favorite, or only, beer. Duff Gardens is a Disneyland built by the Soviet Commissar for Beer Production. Attractions include the Beerquarium, with the "happiest fish in the world." It also has the "Seven Duffs," characters in beer-bottle costumes who represent various states of drunkenness. Their names are Tipsy, Dizzy, Sleazy, Edgy, Surly, Queasy and Remorseful. They represent some well-recognized stages of drunkenness and effects of drinking in the Anglo-Saxon world. Alcohol has the power to make men by turns angry, violent, lustful and maudlin. This liquid has the notable quality of being gender-specific in some of its effects, not causing women to become loud or boastful, but lowering their sexual inhibitions. This is a clue that there is a lot more at work than pharmacology on its own.

Alcohol is viewed and treated differently between cultures. Across European societies, there is no relationship between the population's propensity for drinking and for getting drunk (ESPAD, 2007). Ireland has a high rate of abstinence and a high level of alcohol problems. Comparative cultural research indicates that the effects of alcohol on behaviour are not related to levels of consumption in the population or to the chemical effect of ethanol, but to social and cultural expectations and beliefs about the effect of alcohol. There is a long-established distinction between the wine-drinking "wet" cultures of Mediterranean Europe—where drinking is part of daily life and mealtimes in particular, and, although heavy and frequent, does not lead to public drunkenness—and the beer- and spirit-drinking "dry" cultures of Northern Europe, where drinking is separate from normal life, and where becoming visibly and publicly drunk is the aim of drinking. Recently, this distinction appears to be losing its force, with drinking behaviour in the Southern wet cultures converging with the Northern dry cultures, in what appears to be a case of cultural diffusion (Allaman et al., 2000).

In some cultural settings inebriation is expected to quickly descend into drunken violence. In others, individuals will be merrily drunk until they pass out. Craig MacAndrew and Robert Edgerton, in their classic *Drunken Comportment* (1969), draw on a wealth of anthropological evidence showing that in different societies people learn not only how to drink—the rules governing who can drink what, when and where—but also how to "do" drunk. In the main, they are concerned with the prevailing assumption in Anglo-Saxon countries that alcohol is a disinhibitor, and that many of its damaging social effects can be put down to its tendency to befuddle the higher brain functions, leaving those circuits of the brain concerned with lust, wrath and gluttony to have their moment.

They collect many examples of continued "inhibition," meaning cultural proprieties being maintained, in states of heavy intoxication, and of disinhibition that takes place within clearly defined limits. There are cultures in which drinking does not lead to clowning around, sexualization, aggression and maudlin remorse. For example, being involved in fighting alongside impeccable maintenance of sexual propriety; or rampant promiscuity alongside the maintenance of complex incest taboos. One people, the Aritama of Colombia, drink themselves into a state of unobtrusive gloom. For them, intoxication is not seen as a state of enjoyment and they seem to seek to challenge themselves through drinking. They work hard, drink hard, but do not play hard. In all, there is no generalized, consistent loss of restraint around alcohol across cultures.

There are forms of drinking that have at best limited analogies with drinking practices in Anglo-Saxon cultures: for instance, ritual drinking "to pull down the clouds" (bring rain); the inducement of drunken visions (holy/religious experiences) and "fiesta" drinking, involving a carnivalesque inversion of social hierarchy. Some of these drinking systems can exist side by side. MacAndrew and Edgerton describe a historical example from Colonial America of the Papago, Native Americans who got drunk on wine in a fiesta fashion, and on white man's whiskey, which was reported as having a violent/chaotic effect on them, absorbing the form of intoxication associated with the drink of the dominant culture. Disinhibition is socially and culturally powerful as much as it is chemically potent. It provides a time out, a script for behaviour that might not be accepted in sobriety. Drunken intoxication is the cultural enactment of alcohol-influenced behaviour. More simply, in any society people quickly learn what drunken behaviour is and how to "do" being drunk. Getting drunk in the wrong way—which might be too often, too much or violating the unspoken rules of drunken comportment—is sanctioned, and the drinker quickly learns to keep himself or less usually herself in check.

For instance, in an Oaxacan village (Dennis, 1975) the drunk has a clearly defined social role, like the savant, seeking out social gatherings and saying what cannot be said by the sober without sanction. This might range from a political critique of official lackadaisical indolence to village gossip. Although formally embarrassing, this is informally welcomed and accepted. The drunk allows information to be transmitted against the strong privacy norms of Oaxacan society. He does not have to conform to the everyday deceptions of polite society, although when sober the same person will be full of apologies for his behaviour.

There are some suggestions as to what aspects of a culture contribute to a particular kind of drunken comportment being the norm. In the society of the Bolivian Camba, the men drink a very high-strength spirit to rapidly attain a drunken state. Dwight Heath notes the fluid and uncertain social bonds of Camba society, suggesting that drinking allows them to engage in "sociable isolation" (Heath, 1962). Ambivalence is common, especially in indigenous Central and South American cultures where there is an ambivalent relationship with the society of the colonizers. In a Brazilian cult, drinking enables a deity to possess the cult member (Leacock, 1964). The *encantados*—the possessing spirits—like to dance and sing, and many also like to smoke and drink, and they enter the body of the cult member to do this. The *encantados* may drink themselves silly, but the cult members claim to never suffer a hangover as a result of the *encantado* drinking. Transgressive behaviour when drunk is explained by the nature of the particular *encantado* possessing them. They are not the ones who are drinking, so they do not experience the ill effects afterwards.

There are limitations in putting cultural variation in drunken comportment down to socialization of drinking norms, without much scope for interactional reflection or agency, or conflict and resistance. This kind of approach can fall into cultural determinism, in which individuals enact society's drunken knowledge. Change comes about only by cultural contamination, such as with Native Americans and the white man's liquor. Yet there is creative, dynamic cultural work being done in intoxication, for instance, reaffirming mythically egalitarian bonds (Paton-Simpson, 2001), or as symbolic resistance (Mitchell, 2004), for instance, the enacting of resistance to class and gender expectations (Friedman and Alicea, 1995), which is especially relevant with the creation and affirmation of group values (Young, 1971) through ritual. . . .

DISCUSSION QUESTIONS

1. What, according to Bancroft, are some of the logical flaws in popular perceptions about the effects of alcohol?
2. Give some examples of when set and setting are likely to affect the quality of a drug's intoxicating effects.

REFERENCES

Allaman, A., Voller, F., Kubicka, L. and Bloomfield, K. (2000), "Drinking Cultures and the Position of Women in Nine European Countries," *Substance Abuse*, 21, 4: 231–47.

Blumer, D. (2002), "The Illness of Vincent Van Gogh," *The American Journal of Psychiatry*, 159:519–26.

Dennis, P. A. (1975), "The Role of the Drunk in a Oaxacan Village," *American Anthropologist*, 77, 4: 856–63.

de Quincey, T. (1886[1822]), *Confessions of an Opium-Eater*, London, George Routledge and Sons.

ESPAD (2007), "The European School Survey Project on Alcohol and Other Drugs," Stockholm, http://www.espad.org.

Friedman, J. and Alicea, M. (1995), "Women and Heroin: The Path of Resistance and Its Consequences," *Gender and Society*, 9, 4: 432–49.

Heath, D. B. (1962), "Drinking Patterns of the Bolivian Camba," in Pittman, D. J. and Snyder, R. (eds), *Society, Culture and Drinking Patterns*, New York, John Wiley and Sons.

Leacock, S. (1964), "Ceremonial Drinking in an Afro-Brazilian Cult," *American Anthropologist*, 66, 2: 344–54.

Lee, T. C. (1981), "Van Gogh's Vision: Digitalis Intoxication," *Journal of the American Medical Association*, 245, 7: 727–29.

Lennard, H. L., Epstein, L. J. and Rosenthal, M. S. (1972), "The Methadone Illusion," *Science*, 176:4037, 881–84.

Ludlow, Fitz Hugh (1856), "The Apocalypse of Hasheesh," *Putnam's Monthly*, 8:48.

MacAndrew, C. and Edgerton, R. B. (1969), *Drunken Comportment*, London: Nelson.

Mitchell, T. (2004), *Intoxicated Identities: Alcohol's Power in Mexican History and Culture*, New York, Routledge.

Paton-Simpson, G. (2001), Socially Obligatory Drinking: A Sociological Analysis of Norms Governing Minimum Drinking Levels," *Contemporary Drug Problems*, 28, 1: 133–77.

Sournia, J. C. (1990), *A History of Alcoholism*, Oxford: Blackwell.

Williams, G. P. and Brake, G. T. (1980), *Drink in Great Britain 1900–1979*, London: Edsall.

Young, J. (1971), *The Drugtakers: The Social Meaning of Drug Use*, London: MacGibbon and Kee.

24.
THE SOCIAL CONSTRUCTION OF DRUG SCARES

CRAIG REINARMAN

Most people would probably contend that certain drugs are illegal because they are harmful to the users and to society. But this contention ignores the fact that cigarettes and alcohol are arguably more dangerous than many illegal drugs and it ignores the historical timing of some of the most prominent drug legislation in U.S. history. Reinarman examines this timing and finds that it coincides with periods of conflict between various interest groups. He argues that periods of intense concern about drugs and the resulting legislation have more to do with who is using them and what the drugs symbolize than with the harmful effects of the drugs. More specifically, drug legislation in the United States has historically targeted certain minorities and groups who pose a symbolic threat, and such legislation has been used as a tool of oppression.

Reinarman describes the essential ingredients of drug scares and speculates as to why American society is particularly susceptible to them.

Drug "wars," anti-drug crusades, and other periods of marked public concern about drugs are never merely reactions to the various troubles people can have with drugs. These drug scares are recurring cultural and political phenomena *in their own right* and must, therefore, be understood sociologically on their own terms. It is important to understand why people ingest drugs and why some of them develop problems that have something to do with having ingested them. But the premise of this chapter is that it is equally important to understand patterns of acute societal concern about drug use and drug problems. This seems especially so for U.S. society, which has had *recurring* anti-drug crusades and a *history* of repressive anti-drug laws.

Many well-intentioned drug policy reform efforts in the U.S. have come face to face with staid and stubborn sentiments against consciousness-altering substances. The repeated failures of such reform efforts cannot be explained solely in terms of ill-informed or manipulative leaders. Something deeper is involved, something woven into the very fabric of American culture, something which explains why claims that some drug is the cause of much of what is wrong with the world are *believed* so often by so many. The origins and nature of the *appeal* of anti-drug claims must be confronted if we are ever to understand how "drug problems" are constructed in the U.S. such that more enlightened and effective drug policies have been so difficult to achieve.

In this chapter I take a step in this direction. First, I summarize briefly some of the major periods of anti-drug sentiment in the U.S. Second, I draw from them the basic ingredients of which drug scares and drug laws are made. Third, I offer a beginning interpretation of these scares and laws based on those broad features of American culture that make *self-control* continuously problematic.

DRUG SCARES AND DRUG LAWS

What I have called drug scares (Reinarman and Levine, 1989a) have been a recurring feature of U.S. society for 200 years. They are relatively autonomous from whatever drug-related problems exist or are said to exist.[1] I call them "scares" because, like Red Scares, they are a form of moral panic ideologically constructed so as to construe one or another chemical bogeyman, a la "communists," as the core cause of a wide array of preexisting public problems.

The first and most significant drug scare was over drink. Temperance movement leaders constructed this scare beginning in the late 18th and early 19th century. It reached its formal end with the passage of Prohibition in 1919.[2] As Gusfield showed in his classic book *Symbolic Crusade* (1963), there was far more to the battle against booze than long-standing drinking problems. Temperance crusaders tended to be native born, middle-class, non-urban Protestants who felt threatened by the working-class, Catholic immigrants who were filling up America's cities during industrialization.[3] The latter were what Gusfield termed "unrepentant deviants" in that they continued their long-standing drinking practices despite middle-class W.A.S.P. norms against them. The battle over booze was the terrain on which was fought a cornucopia of cultural conflicts, particularly over whose morality would be the dominant morality in America.

In the course of this century-long struggle, the often wild claims of Temperance leaders appealed to millions of middle-class people seeking explanations for the pressing social and economic problems of industrializing America. Many corporate supporters of Prohibition threw their financial and ideological weight behind the Anti-Saloon League and other Temperance and Prohibitionist groups because they felt that traditional working-class drinking practices interfered with the new rhythms of the factory, and thus with productivity and profits (Rumbarger, 1989). To the Temperance crusaders' fear of the bar room as a breeding ground of all sorts of tragic immorality, Prohibitionists added the idea of the saloon as an alien, subversive place where unionists organized and where leftists and anarchists found recruits (Levine, 1984).

This convergence of claims and interests rendered alcohol a scapegoat for most of the nation's poverty, crime, moral degeneracy, "broken" families, illegitimacy, unemployment, and personal and business failure—problems whose sources lay in broader economic and political forces. This scare climaxed in the first two decades of this century, a tumultuous period rife with class, racial, cultural, and political conflict brought on by the wrenching changes of industrialization, immigration, and urbanization (Levine, 1984; Levine and Reinarman, 1991).

America's first real drug law was San Francisco's anti-opium den ordinance of 1875. The context of the campaign for this law shared many features with the context of the Temperance movement. Opiates had long been widely and legally available without a prescription in hundreds of medicines (Brecher, 1972; Musto, 1973; Courtwright, 1982; cf. Baumohl, 1992), so neither opiate use nor addiction was really the issue. This campaign focused almost exclusively on what was called the "Mongolian vice" of opium *smoking* by Chinese immigrants (and white "fellow travelers") in dens (Baumohl, 1992). Chinese immigrants came to California as "coolie" labor to build the railroad and dig the gold mines. A small minority of them brought along the practice of smoking opium—a practice originally brought to China by British and American traders in the 19th century. When the railroad was completed and the gold dried up, a decade-long depression ensued. In a tight labor market, Chinese immigrants were a target. The white Workingman's Party fomented racial hatred of the low-wage "coolies" with whom they now had to compete for work. The first law against opium smoking was only one of many laws enacted to harass and control Chinese workers (Morgan, 1978).

By calling attention to this broader political-economic context I do not wish to slight the specifics of the local political-economic context. In addition to the Workingman's Party, downtown businessmen formed merchant associations and urban families formed improvement associations, both of which fought for more than two decades to reduce the impact of San Francisco's vice districts on the order and health of the central business district and on family neighborhoods (Baumohl, 1992).

In this sense, the anti-opium den ordinance was not the clear and direct result of a sudden drug scare alone. The law was passed against a specific form of drug use engaged in by a disreputable group that had come to be seen as threatening in lean economic times. But it passed easily because this new threat was understood against the broader historical backdrop of long-standing local concerns about various vices as threats to public health, public morals, and public order. Moreover, the focus of attention were dens where it was suspected that whites came into intimate contact with "filthy, idolatrous" Chinese (see Baumohl, 1992). Some local law enforcement leaders, for example, complained that Chinese men were using this vice to seduce white women into sexual slavery (Morgan, 1978). Whatever the hazards of opium smoking, its initial criminalization in San Francisco had to do with both a general context of recession, class conflict, and racism, and with specific local interests in the control of vice and the prevention of miscegenation.

A nationwide scare focusing on opiates and cocaine began in the early 20th century. These drugs had been widely used for years, but were first criminalized when the addict population began to shift from predominantly white, middle-class, middle-aged women to young, working-class males, African Americans in particular. This scare led to the Harrison Narcotics Act of 1914, the first federal anti-drug law (see Duster, 1970).

Many different moral entrepreneurs guided its passage over a six-year campaign: State Department diplomats seeking a drug treaty as a means of expanding trade with China, trade which they felt was crucial for pulling the economy out of recession; the medical and pharmaceutical professions whose interests were threatened by self-medication with unregulated proprietary tonics, many of which contained cocaine or opiates; reformers seeking to control what they saw as the deviance of immigrants and Southern Blacks who were migrating off the farms; and a pliant press which routinely linked drug use with prostitutes, criminals, transient workers (e.g., the Wobblies), and African Americans (Musto, 1973). In order to gain the support of Southern Congressmen for a new federal law that might infringe on "states' rights," State Department officials and other crusaders repeatedly spread unsubstantiated suspicions, repeated in the press, that, e.g., cocaine induced African-American men to rape white women (Musto, 1973: 6–10, 67). In short, there was more to this drug scare, too, than mere drug problems.

In the Great Depression, Harry Anslinger of the Federal Narcotics Bureau pushed Congress for a federal law against marijuana. He claimed it was a "killer weed" and he spread stories to the press suggesting that it induced violence—especially among Mexican Americans. Although there was no evidence that marijuana was widely used, much less that it had any untoward effects, his crusade resulted in its criminalization in 1937—and not incidentally a turnaround in his Bureau's fiscal fortunes (Dickson, 1968). In this case, a new drug law was put in place by a militant moral-bureaucratic entrepreneur who played on racial fears and manipulated a press willing to repeat even his most absurd claims in a context of class conflict during the Depression (Becker, 1963). While there was not a marked scare at the time, Anslinger's claims were never contested in Congress because they played upon racial fears and widely held Victorian values against taking drugs solely for pleasure.

In the drug scare of the 1960s, political and moral leaders somehow reconceptualized this same "killer weed" as the "drop out drug" that was leading America's youth to rebellion and ruin (Himmelstein, 1983). Bio-medical scientists also published uncontrolled, retrospective studies of very small numbers of cases suggesting that, in addition to poisoning the minds and morals of youth, LSD produced broken chromosomes and thus genetic damage (Cohen et al., 1967). These studies were soon shown to be seriously misleading if not meaningless (Tijo et al., 1969), but not before the press, politicians, the medical profession, and the National Institute of Mental Health used them to promote a scare (Weil, 1972: 44–46).

I suggest that the reason even supposedly hard-headed scientists were drawn into such propaganda was that dominant groups felt the country was at war—and not merely with Vietnam. In this scare, there was not so much a "dangerous class" or threatening racial group as multi-faceted political and cultural conflict, particularly between generations, which gave rise to the perception that middle-class youth who rejected conventional values were a dangerous threat.[4] This scare resulted in the Comprehensive Drug Abuse Control Act of 1970, which criminalized more forms of drug use and subjected users to harsher penalties.

Most recently we have seen the crack scare, which began in earnest *not* when the prevalence of cocaine use quadrupled in the late 1970s, nor even when thousands of users began to smoke it in the more potent and dangerous form of free-base. Indeed, when this scare was launched, crack was unknown outside of a few neighborhoods in a handful of major cities (Reinarman and Levine, 1989a) and the prevalence of illicit drug use had been dropping for several years (National Institute on Drug Use, 1990). Rather, this most recent scare began in 1986 when free-base cocaine was renamed crack (or "rock") and sold in precooked, inexpensive units on ghetto street corners (Reinarman and Levine, 1989b). Once politicians and the media linked this new form of cocaine use to the inner-city, minority poor, a new drug scare was underway and the solution became more prison cells rather than more treatment slots.

The same sorts of wild claims and Draconian policy proposals of Temperance and Prohibition leaders resurfaced in the crack scare. Politicians have so outdone each other in getting "tough on drugs" that each year since crack came on the scene in 1986 they have passed more repressive laws providing billions more for law enforcement, longer sentences, and more drug offenses punishable by death. One result is that the U.S. now has more people in prison than any industrialized nation in the world—about half of them for drug offenses, the majority of whom are racial minorities.

In each of these periods more repressive drug laws were passed on the grounds that they would reduce drug use and drug problems. I have found no evidence that any scare actually accomplished those ends, but they did greatly expand the quantity and quality of social control, particularly over subordinate groups perceived as dangerous or threatening. Reading across these historical episodes one can abstract a recipe for drug scares and repressive drug laws that contains the following *seven ingredients:*

1. **A Kernel of Truth** Humans have ingested fermented beverages at least since human civilization moved from hunting and gathering to primitive agriculture thousands of years ago. The pharmacopoeia has expanded exponentially since then. So, in virtually all cultures and historical epochs, there has been sufficient ingestion of consciousness-altering chemicals to provide some basis for some people to claim that it is a problem.

2. **Media Magnification** In each of the episodes I have summarized and many others, the mass media has engaged in what I call the *routinization of* caricature—rhetorically recrafting worst cases into typical cases and the episodic into the epidemic. The media dramatize drug problems, as they do other problems, in the course of their routine news-generating and sales-promoting procedures (see Brecher, 1972: 321–34; Reinarman and Duskin, 1992; and Molotch and Lester, 1974).

3. **Politico-Moral Entrepreneurs** I have added the prefix "politico" to Becker's (1963) seminal concept of moral entrepreneur in order to emphasize the fact that the most prominent and powerful moral entrepreneurs in drug scares are often political elites. Otherwise, I employ the term just as he intended: to denote the *enterprise,* the work, of those who create (or enforce) a rule against what they see as a social evil.[5]

   In the history of drug problems in the U.S., these entrepreneurs call attention to drug using behavior and define it as a threat about which "something must be done." They also serve as the media's primary source of sound bites on the dangers of this or that drug. In all the scares I have noted, these entrepreneurs had interests of their own (often financial) which had little to do with drugs. Political elites typically find drugs a functional demon in that (like "outside agitators") drugs allow them to deflect attention from other, more systemic sources of public problems for which they would otherwise have to take some responsibility. Unlike almost every other political issue, however, to be "tough on drugs" in American political culture allows a leader to take a firm stand without risking votes or campaign contributions.

4. **Professional Interest Groups** In each drug scare and during the passage of each drug law, various professional interests contended over what Gusfield (1981: 10–15) calls the "ownership" of drug problems—"the ability to create and influence the public definition of a problem" (1981: 10), and thus to define what should be done about it. These groups have included industrialists, churches, the American Medical Association, the American Pharmaceutical Association, various law enforcement agencies, scientists, and most recently the treatment industry and groups of those former addicts converted to disease ideology.[6] These groups claim for themselves, by virtue of their specialized forms of knowledge, the legitimacy and authority to name what is wrong and to prescribe the solution, usually garnering resources as a result.

5. **Historical Context of Conflict** This trinity of the media, moral entrepreneurs, and professional interests typically interact in such a way as to inflate the extant "kernel of truth" about drug use. But this interaction does not by itself give rise to drug scares or drug laws without underlying conflicts which make drugs into functional villains. Although Temperance crusaders persuaded millions to pledge abstinence, they campaigned for years without achieving alcohol control laws. However, in the tumultuous period leading up to Prohibition, there were revolutions in Russia and Mexico, World War I, massive immigration and impoverishment, and socialist, anarchist, and labor movements, to say nothing of increases in routine problems such as crime. I submit that all this conflict made for a level of cultural anxiety that provided fertile ideological soil for Prohibition. In each of the other scares, similar conflicts— economic, political, cultural, class, racial, or a combination—provided a context in which claims makers could viably construe certain classes of drug users as a threat.

6. **Linking a Form of Drug Use to a "Dangerous Class"** Drug scares are never about drugs *per se*, because drugs are inanimate objects without social consequence until they are ingested by humans. Rather, drug scares are about the use of a drug by particular groups of people who are, typically, *already* perceived by powerful groups as some kind of threat (see Duster, 1970; Himmelstein, 1978). It was not so much alcohol problems *per se* that most animated the drive for Prohibition but the behavior and morality of what dominant groups saw as the "dangerous class" of urban, immigrant, Catholic, working-class drinkers (Gusfield, 1963; Rumbarger, 1989). It was *Chinese* opium smoking dens, not the more widespread use of other opiates, that prompted California's first drug law in the 1870s. It was only when smokable cocaine found its way to the African-American and Latino underclass that it made headlines and prompted calls for a drug war. In each case, politico-moral entrepreneurs were able to construct a "drug problem" by linking a substance to a group of users perceived by the powerful as disreputable, dangerous, or otherwise threatening.

7. **Scapegoating a Drug for a Wide Array of Public Problems** The final ingredient is scapegoating, i.e., blaming a drug or its alleged effects on a group of its users for a variety of preexisting social ills that are typically only indirectly associated with it. Scapegoating may be the most crucial element because it gives great explanatory power and thus broader resonance to claims about the horrors of drugs (particularly in the conflictual historical contexts in which drug scares tend to occur).

Scapegoating was abundant in each of the cases noted previously. To listen to Temperance crusaders, for example, one might have believed that without alcohol use, America would be a land of infinite economic progress with no poverty, crime, mental illness, or even sex outside marriage. To listen to leaders of organized medicine and the government in the 1960s, one might have surmised that without marijuana and LSD there would have been neither conflict between youth and their parents nor opposition to the Vietnam War. And to believe politicians and the media in the past six years is to believe that without the scourge of crack the inner cities and the so-called underclass would, if not disappear, at least be far less scarred by poverty, violence, and crime. There is no historical evidence supporting any of this.

In short, drugs are richly functional scapegoats. They provide elites with fig leaves to place over unsightly social ills that are endemic to the social system over which they preside. And they provide the public with a restricted aperture of attribution in which only a chemical bogeyman or the lone deviants who ingest it are seen as the cause of a cornucopia of complex problems.

TOWARD A CULTURALLY SPECIFIC THEORY OF DRUG SCARES

Various forms of drug use have been and are widespread in almost all societies comparable to ours. A few of them have experienced limited drug scares, usually around alcohol decades ago. However, drug scares have been *far* less common in other societies, and never as virulent as they have been in the U.S. (Brecher, 1972; Levine, 1992; MacAndrew and Edgerton, 1969). There has never been a time or place in human history without drunkenness, for example, but in *most* times and places drunkenness has not been nearly as problematic as it has been in the U.S. since the late 18th century. Moreover, in comparable industrial democracies, drug laws are generally less repressive. Why then do claims about the horrors of this or that consciousness-altering chemical have such unusual power in American culture?

Drug scares and other periods of acute public concern about drug use are not just discrete, unrelated episodes. There is a historical pattern in the U.S. that cannot be understood in terms of the moral values and perceptions of individual anti-drug crusaders alone. I have suggested that these crusaders have benefited in various ways from their crusades. For example, making claims about how a drug is damaging society can help elites increase the social control of groups perceived as threatening (Duster, 1970), establish one class's moral code as dominant (Gusfield, 1963), bolster a bureaucracy's sagging fiscal fortunes (Dickson, 1968), or mobilize voter support (Reinarman and Levine, 1989a, b). However, the recurring character of pharmaco-phobia in U.S. history suggests that there is something about our *culture* which makes citizens more vulnerable to anti-drug crusaders' attempts to demonize drugs. Thus, an answer to the question of America's unusual vulnerability to drug scares must address why the scapegoating of consciousness-altering substances regularly *resonates* with or appeals to substantial portions of the population.

There are three basic parts to my answer. The first is that claims about the evils of drugs are especially viable in American culture in part because they provide a welcome *vocabulary of attribution* (cf. Mills, 1940). Armed with "DRUGS" as a generic scapegoat, citizens gain the cognitive satisfaction of having a folk devil on which to blame a range of bizarre behaviors or other conditions they find troubling but difficult to explain in other terms. This much may be true of a number of other societies, but I hypothesize that this is particularly so in the U.S. because in our political culture individualistic explanations for problems are so much more common than social explanations.

Second, claims about the evils of drugs provide an especially serviceable vocabulary of attribution in the U.S. in part because our society developed from a *temperance culture* (Levine, 1992). American society was forged in the fires of ascetic Protestantism and industrial capitalism, both of which demand *self-control*. U.S. society has long been characterized as the land of the individual "self-made man." In such a land, self-control has had extraordinary importance. For the middle-class Protestants who settled, defined, and still dominate the U.S., self-control was both central to religious worldviews and a characterological necessity for economic survival and success in the capitalist market (Weber, 1930 [1985]). With Levine (1992), I hypothesize that in a culture in which self-control is inordinately important, drug-induced altered states of consciousness are especially likely to be experienced as "loss of control," and thus to be inordinately feared.[7]

Drunkenness and other forms of drug use have, of course, been present everywhere in the industrialized world. But temperance cultures tend to arise only when industrial capitalism unfolds upon a cultural terrain deeply imbued with the Protestant ethic.[8] This means that only the U.S., England, Canada, and parts of Scandinavia have Temperance cultures, the U.S. being the most extreme case.

It may be objected that the influence of such a Temperance culture was strongest in the 19th and early 20th century and that its grip on the American *Zeitgeist* has been loosened by the forces of modernity and now, many say, post-modernity. The third part of my answer, however, is that on the foundation of a Temperance culture, advanced capitalism has built a *postmodern, mass consumption culture* that exacerbates the problem of self-control in new ways.

Early in the 20th century, Henry Ford pioneered the idea that by raising wages he could simultaneously quell worker protests and increase market demand for mass-produced goods. This mass consumption strategy became central to modern American society and one of the reasons for our economic success (Marcuse, 1964; Aronowitz, 1973; Ewen, 1976; Bell, 1978). Our economy is now so fundamentally predicated upon mass consumption that theorists as diverse as Daniel Bell and Herbert Marcuse have observed that we live in a mass consumption culture. Bell (1978), for example, notes that while the Protestant work ethic and deferred gratification may still hold sway in the workplace, Madison Avenue, the media, and malls have inculcated a new indulgence ethic in the leisure sphere in which pleasure seeking and immediate gratification reign.

Thus, our economy and society have come to depend upon the constant cultivation of new "needs," the production of new desires. Not only the hardware of social life such as food, clothing, and shelter but also the software of the self—excitement, entertainment, even eroticism—have become mass consumption commodities. This means that our society offers an increasing number of incentives for indulgence—more ways to lose self-control—and a decreasing number of countervailing reasons for retaining it.

In short, drug scares continue to occur in American society in part because people must constantly manage the contradiction between a Temperance culture that insists on self-control and a mass consumption culture which renders self-control continuously problematic. In addition to helping explain the recurrence of drug scares, I think this contradiction helps account for why in the last dozen years millions of Americans have joined 12-Step groups, more than 100 of which have nothing whatsoever to do with ingesting a drug (Reinarman, 1995). "Addiction," or the generalized loss of self-control, has become the meta-metaphor for a staggering array of human troubles. And, of course, we also seem to have a staggering array of politicians and other moral entrepreneurs who take advantage of such cultural contradictions to blame new chemical bogeymen for our society's ills.

DISCUSSION QUESTIONS

1. Does this article represent the functionalist or the conflict perspective? Explain your answer.
2. Why, according to Reinarman, is American society particularly susceptible to drug scares?

3. Explain the following passage: "[Drugs] provide elites with fig leaves to place over unsightly social ills that are endemic to the social system over which they preside."

NOTES

1. In this regard, for example, Robin Room wisely observes "that we are living at a historic moment when the rate of (alcohol) dependence as a cognitive and existential experience is rising, although the rate of alcohol consumption and of heavy drinking is falling." He draws from this a more general hypothesis about "long waves" of drinking and societal reactions to them: "[I]n periods of increased questioning of drinking and heavy drinking, the trends in the two forms of dependence, psychological and physical, will tend to run in opposite directions. Conversely, in periods of a 'wettening' of sentiments, with the curve of alcohol consumption beginning to rise, we may expect the rate of physical dependence . . . to rise while the rate of dependence as a cognitive experience falls" (1991: 154).

2. I say "formal end" because Temperance ideology is not merely alive and well in the War on Drugs but is being applied to all manner of human troubles in the burgeoning 12-Step Movement (Reinarman, 1995).

3. From Jim Baumohl I have learned that while the Temperance movement attracted most of its supporters from these groups, it also found supporters among many others (e.g., labor, the Irish, Catholics, former drunkards, women), each of which had its own reading of and folded its own agenda into the movement.

4. This historical sketch of drug scares is obviously not exhaustive. Readers interested in other scares should see, e.g., Brecher's encyclopedic work *Licit and Illicit Drugs* (1972), especially the chapter on glue sniffing, which illustrates how the media actually created a new drug problem by writing hysterical stories about it. There was also a PCP scare in the 1970s in which law enforcement officials claimed that the growing use of this horse tranquilizer was a severe threat because it made users so violent and gave them such super-human strength that stun guns were necessary. This, too, turned out to be unfounded and the "angel dust" scare was short-lived (see Feldman et al., 1979). The best analysis of how new drugs themselves can lead to panic reactions among users is Becker (1967).

5. Becker wisely warns against the "one-sided view" that sees such crusaders as merely imposing their morality on others. Moral entrepreneurs, he notes, do operate "with an absolute ethic," are "fervent and righteous," and will use "any means" necessary to "do away with" what they see as "totally evil." However, they also "typically believe that their mission is a holy one," that if people do what they want it "will be good for them." Thus, as in the case of abolitionists, the crusades of moral entrepreneurs often "have strong humanitarian overtones" (1963: 147–48). This is no less true for those whose moral enterprise promotes drug scares. My analysis, however, concerns the character and consequences of their efforts, not their motives.

6. As Gusfield notes, such ownership sometimes shifts over time, e.g., with alcohol problems, from religion to criminal law to medical science. With other drug problems, the shift in ownership has been away from medical science toward criminal law. The most insightful treatment of the medicalization of alcohol/drug problems is Peele (1989).

7. See Baumohl's (1990) important and erudite analysis of how the human will was valorized in the therapeutic temperance thought of 19th-century inebriate homes.

8. The third central feature of Temperance cultures identified by Levine (1992), which I will not dwell on, is predominance of spirits drinking, i.e., more concentrated alcohol than wine or beer and thus greater likelihood of drunkenness.

REFERENCES

Aronowitz, Stanley. 1973. *False Promises: The Shaping of American Working Class Consciousness.* New York: McGraw-Hill.

Baumohl, Jim. 1990. "Inebriate Institutions in North America, 1840–1920." *British Journal of Addiction* 85: 1187–1204.

Baumohl, Jim. 1992. "The 'Dope Fiend's Paradise' Revisited: Notes from Research in Progress on Drug Law Enforcement in San Francisco, 1875–1915." *Drinking and Drug Practices Surveyor* 24: 3–12.

Becker, Howard S. 1963. *Outsiders: Studies in the Sociology of Deviance.* Glencoe, IL: Free Press.

Becker, Howard S. 1967. "History, Culture, and Subjective Experience: An Exploration of the Social Bases of Drug-Induced Experiences." *Journal of Health and Social Behavior* 8: 162–176.

Bell, Daniel. 1978. *The Cultural Contradictions of Capitalism.* New York: Basic Books.

Brecher, Edward M. 1972. *Licit and Illicit Drugs.* Boston: Little Brown.

Cohen, M. M., K. Hirshorn, and W. A. Frosch. 1967. "In Vivo and in Vitro Chromosomal Damage Induced by LSD-25." *New England Journal of Medicine* 227: 1043.

Courtwright, David. 1982. *Dark Paradise: Opiate Addiction in America before 1940.* Cambridge, MA: Harvard University Press.

Dickson, Donald. 1968. "Bureaucracy and Morality." *Social Problems* 16: 143–156.

Duster, Troy. 1970. *The Legislation of Morality: Law, Drugs, and Moral Judgement.* New York: Free Press.

Ewen, Stuart. 1976. *Captains of Consciousness: Advertising and the Social Roots of Consumer Culture.* New York: McGraw-Hill.

Feldman, Harvey W., Michael H. Agar, and George M. Beschner. 1979. *Angel Dust.* Lexington, MA: Lexington Books.

Gusfield, Joseph R. 1963. *Symbolic Crusade: Status Politics and the American Temperance Movement.* Urbana: University of Illinois Press.

Gusfield, Joseph R. 1981. *The Culture of Public Problems: Drinking-Driving and the Symbolic Order.* Chicago: University of Chicago Press.

Himmelstein, Jerome. 1978. "Drug Politics Theory: Analysis and Critique." *Journal of Drug Issues* 8: 37–52.

Himmelstein, Jerome. 1983. *The Strange Career of Marihuana.* Westport, CT: Greenwood Press.

Levine, Harry Gene. 1984. "The Alcohol Problem in America: From Temperance to Alcoholism." *British Journal of Addiction* 84: 109–119.

Levine, Harry Gene. 1992. "Temperance Cultures: Concern about Alcohol Problems in Nordic and English-Speaking Cultures." In G. Edwards et al., eds., *The Nature of Alcohol and Drug Related Problems.* New York: Oxford University Press.

Levine, Harry Gene, and Craig Reinarman. 1991. "From Prohibition to Regulation: Lessons from Alcohol Policy for Drug Policy." *Milbank Quarterly* 69: 461–494.

MacAndrew, Craig, and Robert Edgerton. 1969. *Drunken Comportment.* Chicago: Aldine.

Marcuse, Herbert. 1964. *One-Dimensional Man: Studies in the Ideology of Advanced Industrial Society.* Boston: Beacon Press.

Mills, C. Wright. 1940. "Situated Actions and Vocabularies of Motive." *American Sociological Review* 5: 904–913.

Molotch, Harvey, and Marilyn Lester. 1974. "News as Purposive Behavior: On the Strategic Uses of Routine Events, Accidents, and Scandals." *American Sociological Review* 39: 101–112.

Morgan, Patricia. 1978. "The Legislation of Drug Law: Economic Crisis and Social Control." *Journal of Drug Issues* 8: 53–62.

Musto, David. 1973. *The American Disease: Origins of Narcotic Control.* New Haven, CT: Yale University Press.

National Institute on Drug Abuse. 1990. *National Household Survey on Drug Abuse: Main Findings 1990.* Washington, DC: U.S. Department of Health and Human Services.

Peele, Stanton. 1989. *The Diseasing of America: Addiction Treatment Out of Control.* Lexington, MA: Lexington Books.

Reinarman, Craig. 1995. "The 12-Step Movement and Advanced Capitalist Culture: Notes on the Politics of Self-Control in Postmodernity." In B. Epstein, R. Flacks, and M. Darnovsky, eds., *Contemporary Social Movements and Cultural Politics.* New York: Oxford University Press.

Reinarman, Craig, and Ceres Duskin. 1992. "Dominant Ideology and Drugs in the Media." *International Journal on Drug Policy* 3: 6–15.

Reinarman, Craig, and Harry Gene Levine. 1989a. "Crack in Context: Politics and Media in the Making of a Drug Scare." *Contemporary Drug Problems* 16: 535–577.

Reinarman, Craig, and Harry Gene Levine. 1989b. "The Crack Attack: Politics and Media in America's Latest Drug Scare." In Joel Best, ed., *Images of Issues: Typifying Contemporary Social Problems,* pp. 115–137. New York: Aldine de Gruyter.

Room, Robin G. W. 1991. "Cultural Changes in Drinking and Trends in Alcohol Problems Indicators: Recent U.S. Experience." In Walter B. Clark and Michael E. Hilton, eds., *Alcohol in America: Drinking Practices and Problems,* pp. 149–162. Albany: State University of New York Press.

Rumbarger, John J. 1989. *Profits, Power, and Prohibition: Alcohol Reform and the Industrializing of America, 1800–1930.* Albany: State University of New York Press.

Tijo. J. H., W. N. Pahnke, and A. A. Kurland. 1969. "LSD and Chromosomes: A Controlled Experiment." *Journal of the American Medical Association* 210: 849.

Weber, Max. 1985 (1930). *The Protestant Ethic and the Spirit of Capitalism.* London: Unwin.

Weil, Andrew. 1972. *The Natural Mind.* Boston: Houghton Mifflin.

25.

RX DRUGS

CBS NEWS, *60 MINUTES* (TRANSCRIPT)

There's a certain paradox in our understanding of, and efforts to deal with drug offenders. On the one hand, we often tend to see drug users as having an addiction; that is, they are unable to resist the compulsion to consume the drug of their choice; and addiction is typically regarded as a medical affliction. On the other hand, we often deal with addicts through the criminal justice system, punishing rather than treating them. Neither treatment nor punishment seems to have much success in reforming the addict.

The following is a transcript of a broadcast of the television "newsmagazine" *60 Minutes*. It describes a program in Liverpool, England, in which addicts are prescribed the drug of their choice by a physician. It represents a form of limited legalization: certain addicts may use certain drugs that would otherwise be illegal; but they are kept under medical supervision. What is notable about this program is that addicts can be stabilized, continue their drug consumption, and yet lead otherwise normal lives in terms of both job and family.

This phenomenon certainly goes against the popular belief that the continual use of hard drugs will inevitably produce extremely debilitating effects. A case can be made that it is the very illegality of certain drugs that figures prominently as a cause of their debilitating effects. With drugs illegal and their blackmarket costs being exorbitantly high, addicts constantly have to hustle, rob, and steal to make it to their next fix. As they live this lifestyle, addicts find it increasingly difficult to hold a job and to maintain social and family support systems and their downward spiral is well underway.

ED BRADLEY: Can Britain teach us anything about dealing with drug addicts? That remains to be seen, but one thing seems certain, there's little or nothing we can teach them. They tried our hard-line methods back in the '70s and '80s and all they got for their trouble was more drugs, more crime and more addicts. So they went back to their way, letting doctors prescribe whatever drug a particular addict was hooked on. Does it work? If they're ever going to know, Liverpool, where drugs are out of control, is the place to find out.

This is a gram of 100 percent pure heroin. It's pharmaceutically prepared. On the streets, it would be cut 10 to 15 times and sell for about $2,000. But take it away from the black market, make it legal and heroin's a pretty cheap drug. The British National Health Service pays about $10 for this gram of heroin and for an addict with a prescription, it's free.

(Footage of Dr. John Marks sitting at his desk)

BRADLEY: *(Voiceover)* In Britain, doctors who hold a special license from the government are allowed to prescribe hard drugs to addicts. Dr. John Marks, a psychiatrist who runs an addiction clinic just outside Liverpool, has been prescribing heroin for years.

DR. JOHN MARKS *(Runs Addiction Clinic in Liverpool)*: If they're drug takers determined to continue their drug use, treating them is an expensive waste of time. And really the choice that I'm being offered and society is being offered is drugs from the clinic or drugs from the Mafia.

(Footage of a woman dispensing a drug and a patient talking to Dr. Marks, a nurse and a social worker)

BRADLEY: *(Voiceover)* To get drugs from the clinic rather than from the Mafia, addicts have to take a urine test to prove they're taking the drugs they say they are. And unlike most other addiction clinics, where you have to say you want to kick the habit before they'll take you in, addicts here have to convince Dr. Marks, a nurse, and a social worker that they intend to stay on drugs come what may. But doesn't Dr. Marks try to cure people?

DR. MARKS: Cure people? No. Nobody can. Regardless of whether you stick them in prison, put them in mental hospitals and give them electric shocks—we've done all these things—put them in a nice rehab center away in the country; give them a social worker; pat them on the head. Give them drugs; give them no drugs. Doesn't matter what you do. Five percent per annum, one in 20 per year, get off spontaneously. Compound interested up, that reaches about 50 percent. Fifty-fifty after 10 years are off. They seem to mature out of addiction regardless of any intervention in the interim. But you can keep them alive and healthy and legal during that 10 years if you so wish to.

BRADLEY: By giving them drugs?

DR. MARKS: It doesn't get them off drugs. It doesn't prolong their addiction either. But it stops them offending; it keeps them healthy and it keeps them alive.

(Footage of Julia pushing her daughter on a swing)

BRADLEY: *(Voiceover)* That's exactly what happened to Julia. Although she doesn't look it, Julia is a heroin addict. For the last three years, the heroin she injects every day comes through a prescription. Before she had to feed her habit by working as a prostitute, a vicious circle that led her to use more heroin to cope with that life.

JULIA *(Heroin Addict)*: And once you get in that circle, you can't get out. And I didn't think I was ever going to get out.

BRADLEY: But once you got the prescription . . .

JULIA: I stopped straight away.

BRADLEY: Never went back?

JULIA: No, I've never. I went back once just to see, and I was almost physically sick just to see these girls doing what I used to do.

(Footage of Julia talking to her daughter)

BRADLEY: *(Voiceover)* Julia says she's now able to have normal relationships, to hold down a job as a waitress and to care for her three-year-old daughter.

Without that prescription, where do you think you'd be today?

JULIA: I'd probably be dead by now.

DR. MARKS: OK.

UNIDENTIFIED MAN: OK.

DR. MARKS: One sixty then . . .

MAN: If I can, yes.

DR. MARKS: . . . of heroin.

(Footage of a man sitting in Dr. Marks' office)

BRADLEY: *(Voiceover)* Once they've got their prescriptions, addicts must show up for regular meetings to show they're staying healthy and free from crime. But how can anyone be healthy if they're taking a drug like heroin?

MR. ALLAN PARRY *(former drug information officer)*: Pure heroin is not dangerous. We have people on massive doses of heroin.

(Footage of Parry talking to Bradley)

BRADLEY: *(Voiceover)* Allan Parry is a former drug information officer for the local health authority and now a counselor at the clinic. So how come we see so much damage caused by heroin?

MR. PARRY: The heroin that is causing that damage is not causing damage because of the heroin in it. It's causing the damage because of brick dust in it, coffee, crushed bleach crystals, anything. That causes the harm. And if heroin is 90 percent adulterated, that means only 10 percent is heroin; the rest is rubbish. Now you inject cement into your veins, and you don't have to be a medical expert to work out that's going to cause harm.

OK, George, let's put your leg up. Let's have a look.

(Footage of George having his leg looked at)

BRADLEY: *(Voiceover)* Many at the clinic, like George, still suffer from the damage caused by street drugs. Allan Parry believes you can't prescribe clean drugs and needles to addicts without teaching them how to use them.

(Footage of George in the office)

MR. PARRY: *(Voiceover)* The other major cause of ill health to drug injectors is not even the dirty drugs they take; it's their bad technique, not knowing how to do it.

I've seen drug users in the States with missing legs and arms, and that is through bad technique.

Can I have a look at your arms. Have you been . . .

(Footage of George in the office)

BRADLEY: *(Voiceover)* George's legs have ulcerated and the veins in his arms have collapsed. To inject, he must use a vein in his groin which is dangerously close to an artery.

MR. PARRY: Now when you go in there, you getting any sharp pains?

GEORGE *(Addict)*: No.

MR. PARRY: If you hit the artery, how would you recognize it?

GEORGE: If I hit the artery?

MR. PARRY: Yeah.

GEORGE: By me head hitting the ceiling.

MR. PARRY: So we show people how to—not how to inject safely, but how to inject less dangerously. We have to be clear about that. You know, stoned people sticking needles into themselves is a dangerous activity, but the strategy is called "harm minimization."

(Footage of a billboard with the words: Heroin screws you up; police entering a building and a man under arrest)

BRADLEY: *(Voiceover)* In the '70s, the British weren't content with minimizing the harm of drug abuse. They adopted the American policy of trying to stamp it out altogether. Prescription drugs were no longer widely available, and addicts who couldn't kick the habit had to find illegal sources. The result? By the end of the '80s, drug addiction in Britain had tripled. In Liverpool, there was so much heroin around it was known as smack city. And then came a greater threat.

More than anything else, it's been the threat of AIDS that has persuaded the British to return to their old policy of maintaining addicts on their drug of choice. In New York, it's estimated that more than half of those who inject drugs have contracted the AIDS virus through swapping contaminated needles. Here in Liverpool, the comparable number—the number of known addicts infected—is less than 1 percent.

(Footage of a pharmacist Jeremy Clitherow dispensing cigarettes containing heroin)

BRADLEY: *(Voiceover)* In an effort to get addicts away from injecting, Liverpool pharmacist Jeremy Clitherow has developed what he calls "heroin reefers." They're regular cigarettes with—heroin in them. Whatever you feel about smoking, he says, these cigarettes hold fewer risks than needles for both the addicts and the community.

MR. JEREMY CLITHEROW *(Pharmacist)*: So we then use this to put in a known volume of pharmaceutical heroin into the patient's cigarette. And there we are, one heroin reefer containing exactly 60 milligrams of pharmaceutical heroin.

BRADLEY: So the National Health Service will pay for the heroin, but not for the cigarettes.

MR. CLITHEROW: Oh yes. Yes, of course. It's the patient's own cigarette, but with the National Health prescription put into it.

(Footage of the outside of Clitherow's pharmacy and people waiting in line inside the store)

BRADLEY: *(Voiceover)* Addicts pick up their prescriptions twice a week from his neighborhood pharmacy. And how does this affect his other customers?

MR. CLITHEROW: *(Voiceover)* The patient who comes in to pick up a prescription of heroin in the form of reefers would be indistinguishable from a patient who picks up any other medication.

PAUL *(Heroin Addict)*: Good morning.

MR. CLITHEROW: Hello, Paul. How are you doing?

PAUL: Fine.

MR. CLITHEROW: All right.

PAUL: Cigarettes next week?

MR. CLITHEROW: That's my sheet. Anything else we can do for you?

PAUL: No, that's fine . . .

MR. CLITHEROW: The prescription is ready and waiting, and they pick it up just as they would pick up their Paracetamol, aspirin or bandages.

BRADLEY: But with all of these drugs available to—to—to most people, plus the hard drugs which you have here, what's your security like?

MR. CLITHEROW: Like Fort Knox. But we keep minimal stocks. We buy the stuff in— regularly, frequently. It comes in, goes out.

(Footage of Clitherow filling a prescription)

BRADLEY: *(Voiceover)* And heroin isn't the only stuff to come in and out of here. Clitherow also fills prescriptions for cocaine, and that's 100 percent pure freebase cocaine—in other words, crack. So in fact when you're putting cocaine in here . . .

MR. CLITHEROW: Yes.

BRADLEY: . . . you're actually making crack cigarettes?

MR. CLITHEROW: Yes.

BRADLEY: In America that has a very negative connotation . . .

MR. CLITHEROW: Mm-hmm.

BRADLEY: . . . but not for you?

MR. CLITHEROW: It depends which way you look at it. If they continue to buy on the street, whether it's heroin, methadone, crack or whatever, sooner or later they will suffer from the—the merchandise that they are buying. I want to bring them into contact with the system. And let's give them their drug of choice—if the physician agrees and prescribes it— in a form which won't cause their health such awful deterioration.

BRADLEY: And you don't have any problems giving people injectable cocaine or cocaine cigarettes.

DR. MARKS: No, not in principle. I mean, there are—there are patients to whom I've prescribed cocaine and to whom I've then stopped prescribing the cocaine because their lives do not stabilize. They continue to be thieves or whatever. But there are equally many more to whom we prescribe cocaine who've then settled to regular, sensible lives.

(Footage of Mike)

BRADLEY: *(Voiceover)* Mike is one of those who has settled into a regular, sensible life on cocaine. He has a prescription from Dr. Marks for both the cocaine spray and the cocaine cigarettes. Before he got that prescription, the cocaine he bought on the street cost him $1,000 a week, which at first he managed to take from his own business. But it wasn't long before it cost him much more than that.

So you lost your business.

MIKE *(Cocaine Addict)*: Yeah.

BRADLEY: You lost your—your wife.

MIKE: Yeah.

BRADLEY: You lost the kids.

MIKE: Yeah.

BRADLEY: And the house.

MIKE: Yeah.

BRADLEY: But you kept going after the cocaine.

MIKE: Yeah. That's what addiction is. That's the whole—the very nature of addiction is the fact that one is virtually—chemically and physically—forced to continue that way.

(Footage of Mike sitting in a chair writing)

BRADLEY: *(Voiceover)* Now after two years of controlled use on prescription cocaine, Mike has voluntarily reduced his dose. He's got himself a regular job with a trucking company and is slowly putting his life back together again.

Where do you think you would be now if—if Dr. Marks had not given you a—a prescription for cocaine?

MIKE: I wouldn't be here now talking to you, and you probably wouldn't be interested in talking to me, either. I'd be on the street.

BRADLEY: Dr. Marks, how would you reply to critics who would say that you're nothing more than a legalized dealer, a pusher?

DR. MARKS: I'd agree. That's what the state of England arranges, that there's a legal, controlled supply of drugs. The whole concept behind this is control.

(Footage of Bradley talking to Parry while they're walking outside)

BRADLEY: *(Voiceover)* And there are signs that control is working. Within the area of the clinic, Allan Parry says the police have reported a significant drop in drug-related crime. And since addicts don't have to deal anymore to support their habit, they're not recruiting new customers. So far fewer new people are being turned on to drugs.

What do the dealers around the area of the clinic think about it all?

MR. PARRY: *(Voiceover)* Well, there aren't any around the clinic.

BRADLEY: *(Voiceover)* You—you've taken away their business.

MR. PARRY: Exactly. There's no business there. The scene is disappearing. So if you want to get rid of your drug problem, which presumably all societies do, there are ways of doing it, but you have to counter your own moral and political prejudice.

BRADLEY: What would you say to people who would ask, "Why give addicts what they want? Why give them drugs?"

JULIA: So they can live. So they have a chance to live like everyone else does. No one would hesitate to give other sorts of maintaining drugs to diabetics. Diabetics have insulin. In my mind it's no different. It's the same. I need heroin to live.

(Show motif-)

(Announcements)

DISCUSSION QUESTIONS

1. What popular stereotypes of drugs and drug users are challenged by this article?
2. Would you support the establishment of such programs in your country? Why or why not?

26.

HEALTHY NIGHTCLUBS AND RECREATIONAL SUBSTANCE USE: FROM A HARM MINIMIZATION TO A HEALTHY SETTINGS APPROACH

MARK A. BELLIS, KAREN HUGHES, AND HELEN LOWEY

The drug treatment program described in the previous article provides us with one example of a harm minimization. The following article describes a healthy settings approach. Both approaches recognize that criminalization is either an ineffective or insufficient means of control— *if* the goal of control is to safeguard the health of drug users and/or the public. Both approaches take a realistic perspective, recognizing that some people are going to use drugs come what may; but many of the associated risks of drug-taking can be reasonably reduced. The following article demonstrates how the health of drug users is compromised by many factors—beyond the biochemical effects of a given substance—that can be controlled without criminalization.

INTRODUCTION

In the UK alone, approximately 3.5 million individuals go to nightclubs each week (Mintel International Group, 2000). Most of these are younger people and a large proportion of them consume illegal drugs often in combination with alcohol (Measham, Aldridge, & Parker, 2001). The relationship between recreational drug use and dance music events is now well established (Release, 1997; Winstock, Griffiths, & Stewart, 2001). In the UK, for instance, estimates of ecstasy, amphetamine, and cocaine use in regular clubbers (i.e. attendees at nightclubs) or those travelling abroad to visit international nightclub resorts (e.g. Ibiza) far exceed average levels of consumption by individuals in the general population (Bellis, Hale, Bennett, Chaudry, & Kilfoyle, 2000) (Table 5.1).

The acute and long-term problems relating to recreational (i.e. ecstasy, amphetamine, and cocaine) drug use are the subject of a wide range of studies (Parrott, Milani, Parmar, & Turner, 2001; Reneman et al., 2001) and form the rationale for a variety of health interventions (Niesnk, Nikken, Jansen, & Spruit, 2000; Page, 2000). Thus, ecstasy use has been linked to short-term health effects such as hyperthermia (Henry, Jeffreys, & Dawning, 1992) as well as long-term effects such as memory problems (Reneman et al., 2001). Interventions addressing recreational

TABLE 5.1 LEVELS OF DRUG USE IN THREE UK SURVEYS

	British Crime Survey[a] (%)	Ibiza Uncovered Survey[b] (%)	Dancing on Drugs Survey[c] (%)
Cannabis	22	51	69.5
Ecstasy	5	39	51.4
Amphetamine	5	27	53.5
Cocaine	5	26	27.1

[a]16–29-year-olds in the general population; drugs used in last 12 months (Ramsay, Baker, Goulden, Sharp, & Sondhi, 2001).
[b]16–29-year-olds who visited Ibiza during Summer 2000; drugs used in last 6 months (Bellis et al., 2000).
[c]15–57-year-olds attending dance events; drugs used in last 3 months (Measham et al., 2001).

drug use have often been outreach based (Crew 2000, 2001) and focused on disseminating information on adverse effects of drugs and how to avoid them, problems around combining substances (often drugs and alcohol), and courses of action necessary when acute adverse effects are experienced. However, there is now a growing recognition that the adverse effects of club drugs are strongly related to the environment in which they are used rather than resulting solely from the toxic properties of substances themselves (Calafat et al., 2001). Often, reports of ecstasy-related deaths refer to the temperature of the environment—The most likely cause of death is heatstroke. The temperature inside the club had reached 40° C [104° F](Burke, 2001) or in other instances the lack of basic facilities to redress the effects of dancing and substance use—A number of people complained about lack of water (Bowcott, 2001).

In this paper, we argue that the relationship between the health effects of substance use and the environment in which they are used is much wider than temperature control and access to water and extends across the entire nightlife setting. We explore the wide range of factors that contribute to risk in nighttime environments and describe initiatives that effectively address these issues without curtailing fun. Consequently, we argue that by adopting a broad settings approach (World Health Organization, 1997) to nightclubs, inclusive solutions to reducing harm in clubs (including that caused by drugs) can be better developed and disseminated.

Furthermore, the same approach can also facilitate multidisciplinary involvement in nightlife health, taking health issues solely from health departments and placing the responsibility also in the hands of organizations such as local authorities, police, voluntary organizations, club owners and managers, door staff, and clubbers themselves. Finally, we suggest that with worldwide growth in dance music tourism, this multidisciplinary approach needs to be extended to include travel and tourism organizations and requires collaboration on an international level.

HEALTHY SETTINGS AND NIGHTCLUBS

A healthy settings approach (World Health Organization, 1997) recognizes that the effects of any particular setting on an individual's health are related to the general conditions within that setting, perhaps more than they are to provision of health or other care facilities. The nightclub setting at its most basic is a building that provides loud music, often with a repetitive beat, a dance area that usually has low background light and intermittent bright lighting effects and a licensed bar. Developing this environment as a healthy setting must recognize that large numbers of clubbers regularly consume substances such as alcohol, drugs, and tobacco (often in combination) and consequently experience a variety of psychological and physiological effects. Furthermore, the criminal nature of some drug use and environmental factors such as poor ventilation mean substance consumption can directly affect staff, for example, pressure of door staff to allow drugs into clubs (Morris, 1998) and passive smoking affecting bar staff, respectively (Jones, Love, Thomson, Green, & Howden-Chapman, 2001).

Some settings approaches to club health are well established. Harm minimization messages advising sipping water, avoiding mixing alcohol with ecstasy, and taking periods of rest provide the essential information for individuals to protect their health (London Drug Policy Forum, 1996). However, without cool areas within the club, often referred to as chill out areas (London Drug Policy Forum, 1996) and access to free cold water, such advice cannot be implemented. Equally, when adverse reactions to drugs are experienced, a separate appropriately stocked first-aid room, trained staff, and access [to] emergency services are all required to allow the best chance of recovery. However, other often more deleterious effects on health are also related to nightlife and substance use. In the UK in 1999, 19% of all violent acts (n = 3,246,000) occurred outside a pub or club. Overall, 40% of violent incidents were related to alcohol use and 18% to drugs (Kershaw et al., 2000). The paraphernalia of alcohol use also contributes to harm, with 5,000 people being attacked with pint glasses every year of whom many are scarred for life (Deehan, 1999). Thus, both the promotion of aggression by, for instance, alcohol (Institute of Alcohol Studies, 2001) and the paraphernalia of substance use play parts in the harm caused by violence.

Less frequently addressed issues, which are important to a settings approach to club health, include the risk of smoking and in particular fire. Large amounts of electrical equipment, the use of old converted premises, low lighting, and a high proportion of smokers (Measham et al., 2001) all contribute to making nightclubs high-risk environments. Additionally, substance use can mean that patrons can be disorientated, leading to further implications particularly if an emergency evacuation of the building is required. A healthy setting should promote well-marked fire exits (some have been known to be camouflaged to fit in with club decor), crowd control training (Newcombe, 1994), and strict compliance with fire limits on the building's capacity (Ministry of Health, 1999). The effects of fires in clubs can be horrific, as graphically illustrated by the loss of life associated with recent incidents (*BBC News*, 2000; CNN, 2000; *The Guardian*, 2001). However, the effects of smoking alone may also be significant. Dancing while holding a cigarette can result in damage to eyes of those nearby (Luke, 1999), whilst nonsmoking bar staff are subject to heavy exposure to environmental tobacco smoke while at work (Jarvis, Foulds, & Feyerabend, 1992).

Noise levels in clubs can also pose a substantial risk to health. UK guidance on protection at work suggests earplugs are used when levels regularly exceed 90 dB (Health and Safety Executive, 1999). However, noise levels in many nightclubs reach 120 dB (Royal National Institute for Deaf People, 1999) and at some points noise can approach the pain threshold (140 dB) (Walsh, 2000). However, those utilizing the nighttime environment are unlikely to recognize the effects on their hearing. The clubbing experience, especially in conjunction with substance use, distracts from concerns about health effects and in the case of some drugs (e.g. ketamine or cocaine) may even anaesthetize the user against pain (European Monitoring Center for Drugs and Drug Addiction, 2000).

As increasing numbers of young people are exposed to loud music in dance clubs, it would be expected that more young people would develop hearing problems. In fact, a survey by the Medical Research Council Institute of Hearing Research found that 66% of club goers reported temporary hearing problems after attending a nightclub (Smith & Davis, 1999). Policies about maximum noise levels in clubs can address some of these issues. However, noise is not just a concern within the club but may also affect the surrounding environment, either through loud music contaminating nearby residential areas or through the noise of inebriated clubbers appearing on the street when clubs finally close (BBC Devon, 2001). Such noise may also be associated with violence (often related to alcohol and drug use), lack of appropriate access to public transport (leaving long waits or drink/drug driving as the only alternatives), and difficulties in coordinating an adequate police presence when clubs close (Calafat et al., 2001).

Furthermore, any comprehensive approach to a healthy club setting should recognize the close relationship between substance use and sexual health. A variety of studies identify the relaxation of safe sex measures (particularly condom use) associated with alcohol and drug-taking (e.g. Poulin & Graham, 2001). One study has identified individuals using drugs, particularly GHB, specifically in order to temporarily forget safe sex messages they have previously heard (Clark, Cook, Syed, Ashton, & Bellis, 2001). Addressing such issues means providing safe sex information within the club setting and combining this with easy access to condoms. Fire, noise, sex, and other areas for health promotion and protection in the nighttime environment as well as their relationship with substance use are summarized in Table 5.2.

TABLE 5.2 SOME WIDER CLUB HEALTH ISSUES, THEIR RELATIONSHIP WITH SUBSTANCE USE, AND DEVELOPING A SETTING RESPONSE

Health Risk	Relationship to Substance Use	Setting Response	Groups Involved
Dehydration and hyperthermia	Ecstasy alters thermoregulation (McCann, Slate, & Ricaurte, 1996) Increased energetic dancing Alcohol consumption causes dehydration	Prevent overcrowding Well ventilation and temperature control Cool and quieter *chill out* areas or ability to leave and reenter Access to cool, free water Information on effects of taking drugs Pill testing First-aid room and staff training	Club owners/staff Drug outreach workers Health promotion groups Licensing authority Club goers Local A&E
Fire	High levels of smoking among club goers Intoxication leads to disorientation when exiting clubs Flammable clubbing clothes (e.g. PVC)	Prevent overcrowding High visibility and accessible emergency exits Availability and maintenance of all fire equipment Ensure electrical equipment is safe Encourage use of noncombustible material	Club owners/staff Fire authorities Building inspectors Licensing authority Club goers

Damage to hearing	Alchohol and drugs reduce awareness of potential hearing damage Greater exposure to noise due to prolonged dancing	Set maximum levels on systems Restricted areas around speakers Make earplugs available Information on the effects of excessive noise Information on signs of hearing damage	Club owners/staff Club goers Environmental inspectors Licensing authoirty Health promotion Club goers
STIs and unwanted pregnancies	Alcohol and drugs reduce inhibitions (Calafat et al., 2001) Substances help forget safe sex message (Clark et al., 2001)	Easy availability of condoms Information on safer sex	Health promotion groups Public health department Contraception services Club owners Club goers

Accident
  Glass
  Burns
  Falls
  General
	Disorientation
	Anaesthetising effect of substances (European Monitoring Centre for Drugs and Drug Addiction, 2000)
	Lack of fear and increased confidence
	Increased risk-taking
		Toughened glass or plastic bottles
		No drinking/smoking on dance floor
		Provide places to dispose of cigarettes
		Well-lit and clear stairwells
		Restricted access to potentially dangerous areas
		Secure fixtures and fittings are secure
		On-site first-aid
			Club owners/staff
			Public health departments
			Health promotion groups
			Licensing authority
			Club goers

Violence	Alcohol and drugs increase aggression Drug dealing (Morris, 1998) Steroid and cocaine use by door staff (Lenehan & McVeigh, 1998) Increased risk-taking, lower inhibitions	Stagger closing times Increase public transport availability throughout night Plastic/toughened glass Registration and training of door staff Complaints procedures and Policing	Club owners/staff Police Licensing authority Club goers Transport authority
Drink/drug driving	Increased confidence Lack of coordination Increased risk-taking, lower inhibitions (Crowley & Courney, 2000)	Provide cheap soft drinks Public transport: taxis, buses, and trains available Information of safety issues Special club buses provided by clubs	Club owners/staff Health promotion group Club goers Police Transport authority
Passive smoking	Increased smoking when out Many "occasional" smokers Link between smoking and other substance use (Lewinsohn, Rohde, & Brown, 1999)	Adequate ventilation (especially behind the bar) Adequate "break areas" for staff No smoking areas Information on dangers of smoking	Club owners Outreach workers Smoking prevention groups Health promotion groups Licensing authority Club goers

DISSEMINATING KNOWLEDGE AND DEVELOPING SOLUTIONS

The use of substances often contributes to the dangers presented within the nighttime environment. Previously, harm minimization has tended to focus on direct effects of drug use. However, basic measures to alter the environment can substantially reduce substance-related harm. Measures to reduce violence in and around clubs include training and registration of door staff, good lighting around the main entrance, and public transport integrated into the nighttime environment so that individuals can quickly and easily leave city centers (London Drug Policy Forum, 1996; Calafat et al., 2001). Specific measures to reduce spillage of bottles from bars and clubs onto streets can also reduce the risk of glass-related injuries (The Kirklees Partnership, 1999). Inside, club design should anticipate and acknowledge the exuberant behavior and intoxicated state of patrons by restricting access to any areas where falls are likely and ensuring exits are well lit and distinctive (London Drug Policy Forum, 1996).

Importantly, the process of tackling harm reduction across the entire nightlife setting legitimizes the inclusion of a wide variety of organizations and individuals who may have felt that they could not engage in dialogue solely on a drug use agenda. These groups may include club and bar owners, club goers and club staff, event promoters, local authorities and politicians, environmental health officials, and travel and tour operators as well as youth services, health services, police, and other emergency services. Furthermore, sometimes, this mix of individuals produces novel solutions. For example, to reduce night crime and increase public safety, the owners of a number of neighboring venues have supported the employment of a uniformed police officer dedicated to patrolling outside their premises (Greater Manchester Police, 2001). Also, in North Devon, a police initiative involved handing out free lollipops as clubbers left nightclubs in order to reduce noise in the surrounding areas (BBC Devon, 2001).

INTERNATIONAL CONSIDERATIONS

The recent clubbing phenomenon probably has its roots in Ibiza where the mix of music (known as the Balearic Beat) and concurrent use of ecstasy rose to popularity (Calafat et al., 1998). Today, traveling in the form of dance music tourism (individuals specifically traveling abroad to attend dance events or choosing to holiday in destinations renowned for their nightlife) is more popular than ever. Major international clubbing resorts include Ibiza in Spain, Rimini in Italy, and Ayia Napa in Cyprus. Clubbing has additional elements of risk when undertaken in an unfamiliar country. Thus, geography abroad is often unfamiliar, and combined with a different language, this can mean health services or other forms of help are difficult to locate and access. Furthermore, accessing items such as condoms or emergency contraception may also prove more difficult. Legislation can be different and poorly understood, leading to unexpected confrontations with judicial services. If drugs are purchased, the supplier will often be untested, raising the possibility of counterfeits. Equally, alcohol measures may vary in size and purity from standard measures within individuals' home countries. When alcohol and drugs are consumed, a combination of hotter climates, longer periods of dancing, and possible gastrointestinal infections increase the risk of severe dehydration. Importantly, however, along with environmental change, individuals abroad are often free from the social constraints of work and family that restrict their substance use and sexual behavior (Ryan and Kinder, 1996). Thus, an individual may go clubbing one night per week while at home, whereas during a 2-week trip abroad the same individual may visit a club every night. This in turn can significantly alter an individual's exposure to substances. For instance, around a third of all young people from the UK who visited Ibiza in 1999 used ecstasy while on the island. The vast majority of these also used ecstasy in the UK (Bellis et al., 2000). However, the way in which people used ecstasy while abroad was significantly different. Of ecstasy users, only 3% used the drug 5 or more days a week in the UK while 45% of the same group used the drug 5 or more days a week while in Ibiza. Similar trends in increased frequency of use were also seen for alcohol, amphetamine, and cocaine.

Little is currently known about the health effects of such periods of intense substance use. Clearly, the opportunities for adverse reactions are substantially increased where multiple drugs are being regularly consumed along with alcohol on a nightly basis. Furthermore, intense periods of consumption provide at least the possibility that more frequent drug use could continue when individuals return home, potentially moving individuals' habits further towards problematic use.

In order to address the health needs of the increasingly large numbers of young people who regularly travel to experience international nightlife, new approaches to health promotion and protection are required. New literature and campaigns are needed that provide international information on substance use and nightlife health for those traveling abroad. They should tackle the broad range of risks to health, including environmental considerations, but should also address the changes in substance use that occur while abroad (Bellis et al., 2000). Access to such information can utilize new technologies affiliated with club culture (e.g. the Internet) and popular with the major clubbing age groups (Hughes & Bellis, in press). Good examples of such sites are already available (www.dancesafe.org and www.ravesafe.org).

CONCLUSIONS

Around the world, clubbing is now well established as a major feature of the nighttime environment. It provides a social outlet for millions of individuals every week and developing a popular club scene has reinvigorated many cities, bringing money and employment. Substance use in clubs is strongly affiliated with relaxation, exercise (Gaule, Dugdill, Peiser, & Guppy, 2001), and meeting new sexual partners. Whether these pastimes lead to increased well-being or ill health depends on the environment and the specific behavior of individuals. Developing clubs as a healthy setting requires interventions that protect and promote health while retaining fun as a central feature. Where interventions or regulations substantially reduce fun, young people may look elsewhere for their entertainment (e.g. illegal parties). Consequently, organizations need to recognize the importance of involving young people in the development of nighttime health interventions.

Substance use is one of the major risks to health in the nighttime environment both through its direct effects on individuals' health and through the alterations in behavior and perception that it causes. However, many organizations and individuals do not feel either comfortable or equipped to engage in drug-specific interventions or even discussions. By developing a healthy settings approach to clubs, the emphasis of health interventions can be diverted away from solely drug use to include a wider range of issues.

This means key individuals and organizations (including club owners, staff, promoters, and major industries) can be engaged in a harm minimization agenda that includes drug use along with alcohol, tobacco, transport, security, and other environmental issues. Furthermore, tackling a broad range of issues in the nighttime environment reaches groups that are difficult to reach through education or occupational settings, such as those who play truant or are unemployed.

Some countries have already engaged in this more holistic approach to nighttime health by generating broader guidelines on safer clubs and clubbing (e.g. London Drug Policy Forum, 1996; Ministry of Health, 1999; Newcombe, 1994). However, with cheaper air travel and young people having greater expendable income (Calafat et al., 2001) combined with the international nature of the clubbing phenomenon, a significant proportion of an individual's annual clubbing nights can be spent in nightclubs abroad where risks to health may be even greater. As a result, guidelines are required to provide basic standards for nightclubs on an international basis and different interventions need to be developed to address local and international needs. Efforts to develop international guidelines on club health are already underway (www.clubhealth.org.uk). However, empirical evidence on changes in individuals' behavior when abroad (Bellis et al., 2001) and the resultant effects on health are both rare and urgently needed. Without such intelligence, the appropriate structure of health interventions to minimize harm for millions of dance music tourists remains unclear and the burden of ill health carried especially by younger people may unnecessarily be increasing.

DISCUSSION QUESTIONS

1. The United States expends vast resources for the control of illegal drugs, both in terms of the war on drugs and the costs of incarceration—all in the name of protecting society's safety. Should U.S. policymakers work to balance these efforts with implementing the kind of measures suggested in this article?
2. What would be the challenges with implementing the suggestions put forth in this article?

REFERENCES

BBC Devon News (2001). Lollipops gag late-night revellers. *BBC News* (online).

BBC News (2000). Mexico club blaze kills 19. *BBC News*, Friday, 20 October 2000.

Bellis, M. A., Hale, G., Bennett, A., Chaudry, M., & Kilfoyle, M. (2000). Ibiza uncovered: Changes in substance use and sexual behaviour amongst young people visiting an international night-life resort. *International Journal on Drug Policy*, 11, 235–244.

Bellis, M. A., Hughes, K., Bennett, A., & Chaudry, M. (2001). *Three years of research on risk behaviour in Ibiza* (in preparation).

Bowcott, O. (2001). Ecstasy deaths may have been caused by heat, not a bad batch. *The Guardian*, Saturday, 30 June 2001.

Burke, J. (2001). Ecstasy's death toll "set to go on rising." *The Guardian*, Sunday, 1 July 2001.

Calafat, A., Fernandez, C., Juan, M., Bellis, M. A., Bohrn, K., Hakkarainen, P., Kilfoyle-Carrington, M., Kokkevi, A., Maalste, N., Mendes, F., Siamou, I., Simojn, J., Stocco, P., & Zavatti, P. (2001). *Risk and control in the recreational drug culture: SONAR project.* Spain: IREFREA.

Calafat, A., Stocco, P., Mendes, F., Simon, J., van de Wijngaart, G., Sureda, M., Palmer, A., Maalste, N., & Zapatti, P. (1998). *Characteristics and social representation of ecstasy in Europe.* Valencia: IREFREA and European Commission.

Clark, P., Cook, P. A., Syed, Q., Ashton, J. R., & Bellis, M. A. (2001). *Re-emerging syphilis in the North West: Lessons from the Manchester outbreak.* Liverpool: Public Health Sector, Liverpool John Moores University.

CNN (2000). Christmas fire kills at least 309 at China shopping center. *CNN,* 27 December 2000.

Crew 2000 (2001). Development of strategies for secondary prevention in drug use. Patterns of drug use amongst young people at clubs and pre-club bars in Edinburgh. *Project Report.* Edinburgh: Crew 2000.

Deehan, A. (1999). *Alcohol and crime: Taking stock.* Policing and Reducing Crime Unit, Crime Reduction Research Series Paper 3. London: Home Office.

European Monitoring Center for Drugs and Drug Addiction (2000). *Report on the risk assessment of ketamine in the framework of the joint action on new synthetic drugs.* Portugal: EMCDDA.

Gaule, S., Dugdill, L., Peiser, B., & Guppy, A. (2001). *Moving beyond the drugs and deviance issues: Rave dancing as a health promoting alternative to conventional physical activity.* Proceedings of Club Health 2002. Liverpool John Moores University and Trimbos Institute. Available at: www.clubhealth.org.uk.

The Guardian (2001). Dutch fire toll climbs to 10 with 17 fighting for life. *The Guardian,* Wednesday, 3 January 2001.

Greater Manchester Police (2001). *Manchester City Center venues team up with police to reduce night crime.* Press release.

Health and Safety Executive (1999). *Introducing the noise at work guidelines: A brief guide to the guidelines controlling noise at work.* INDG75 (rev) C150-11/99. Suffolk: HSE Books.

Henry, J. A., Jeffreys, K. J., & Dawling, S. (1992). Toxicity and deaths from 3,4-methylenedioxymethamphetamine ("Ecstasy"). *Lancet,* 340, 384–387.

Hughes, K., & Bellis, M. A. (2002). *Disseminating public health information and the public health evidence base: Assessing the current and future potential for the Internet and e-mail.* Health Development Agency and North West Public Health Observatory (in press).

Institute of Alcohol Studies (2001). Alcohol and crime. *IAS factsheet.* Cambridgeshire: Institute of Alcohol Studies.

Jarvis, M. J., Foulds, J., & Feyerabend, C. (1992). Exposure to passive smoking among bar staff. *British Journal of Addiction,* 87, 111–113.

Jones, S., Love, C., Thomson, G:, Green, R., & Howden-Chapman, P. (2001). Second-hand smoke at work: The exposure, perceptions and attitudes of bar and restaurant workers to environmental tobacco smoke. *Australian and New Zealand Journal of Public Health,* 25, 90–93.

Kershaw, C., Budd, T., Kinshott, G., Mattinson, J., Mayhew, P., & Myhill, A. (2000). *The 2000 British crime survey.* Home Office Statistical Bulletin 18/00. London: Home Office.

The Kirklees Partnership (1999). *Boiling point preventer: A code of practice for dealing with drugs and violence in pubs and clubs.* Yorkshire: The Kirklees Partnership.

London Drug Policy Forum (1996). *Dance till dawn safely: A code of practice on health and safety at dance venues.* London: Drug Policy Forum.

Luke, C. (1999). A little nightclub medicine. In M. Kilfoyle & M. A. Bellis (Eds.), *Club health: The health of the clubbing nation.* Liverpool: Department of Public Health, Liverpool John Moores University.

McCann, U. D., Slate, S. O., & Ricaurte, G. A. (1996). Adverse reactions with 3,4-methylenedioxy-methamphetamine (MDMA: "ecstasy"). *Drug Safety,* 15, 107.

Measham, F., Aldridge, J., & Parker, H. (2000). *Dancing on drugs: Risk, health and hedonism in the British club scene.* London: Free Association Books.

Ministry of Health (1999). *Guidelines for SAFE dance parties: The big book.* New Zealand: Ministry of Health.

Mintel International Group (2000). *Nightclubs and discotechques: Market size and trends.* Report Code 11/2000, London.

Morris, S. (1998). *Clubs, drugs and doormen.* Crime Detection and Prevention Series Paper 86, Police Research Group, London: Home Office.

Newcombe, R. (1994). *Safer dancing: Guidelines for good practice at dance parties and nightclubs.* Liverpool: 3D Pub.

Niesnk, R., Nikken, G., Jansen, F., & Spruit, L. (2000). *The drug information and monitoring service (DIMS) in the Netherlands: A unique tool for monitoring party drugs.* Proceedings of club health 2002. Liverpool John Moores University and Trimbos Institute. Available at: www.club health. org.uk.

Page, S. (2000). *Death on the dancefloor.* Proceedings of Club Health 2002. Liverpool John Moores University and Trimbos Institute. Available at: www.clubhealth.org.uk.

Parrott, A. C., Milani, R. M., Parmar, R., & Turner, J. D. (2001). Recreational ecstasy/MDMA and other drug users from the UK and Italy: Psychiatric problems and psychobiological problems. *Psychopharmacology*, 159, 77–82.

Poulin, C., & Graham, L. (2001). The association between substance use, unplanned sexual intercourse and other sexual behaviours among adolescent students. *Addiction*, 96, 607–621.

Release (1997). *Drugs and dance survey: An insight into the culture.* London: Release.

Reneman, L., Lavalaye, J., Schmand, B., de Wolff, F. A., van den Brink, W., den Heeten, G. J., & Booij, J. (2001). Cortical serotonin transporter density and verbal memory in individuals who stopped using methylenedioxymethamphetamine (MDMA or "ecstasy"): preliminary findings. *Archives of General Psychiatry*, 58, 901–906.

Royal National Institute for Deaf People (1999). *Safer sound: An analysis of musical noise and hearing damage.* London: RNID.

Ryan, C., & Kinder, R. (1996). Sex, tourism and sex tourism: Fulfilling similar needs? *Tourist Management*, 17, 507–518.

Smith, P., & Davis, A. (1999). Social noise and hearing loss. *Lancet*, 353, 1185.

Walsh, E. (2000). *Dangerous decibels: Dancing until deaf.* San Francisco: The Bay Area Reporter, Hearing Education and Awareness for Rockers.

Winstock, A. R., Griffiths, P., & Stewart, D. (2001). Drugs and the dance music scene: A survey of current drug use patterns among a sample of dance music enthusiasts in the UK. *Drug and Alcohol Dependence*, 64, 9–17.

World Health Organization (1997). *The Jakarta declaration on leading health promotion into the 21st century.* Fourth International Conference on Health Promotion, Jakarta, 21–25 July 1997.

27.

A COLD OF THE SOUL: A JAPANESE CASE OF DISEASE MONGERING IN PSYCHIATRY

HIROSHI IHARA

The phrase "drug abuse" has many different connotations. It can refer to the use of any kind of illegal drug; or it can refer to the excessive use of legal drugs, namely alcohol; or it can refer to the illegal or excessive use of prescription drugs. In any of these cases, the deviant perpetrator is the drug user. If we expand our conceptualization of "drug abuse" to include the unnecessary use of drugs or the use of unnecessary drugs, then a new set of perpetrators comes to mind, namely the medical and pharmaceutical industries. Critics charge that the expansive use of psychiatric and "lifestyle" drugs in the United States has been the result of a self-serving promotional campaign on the part of these two industries, especially the pharmaceutical industry. (The role of medical professionals in the "medicalization of deviance" is discussed at greater length in Part VIII of this volume.)

In the United States today, the word "depression" describes a clinical condition that is often treated by prescription drugs. In the past, it was only the most severe cases of depression that were considered to require pharmaceutical intervention. Today hundreds of thousands, perhaps millions, of prescriptions are written every year for people with what once would have been considered mild cases (or normal "bouts") of depression. Pharmaceutical companies and medical professionals may claim that this change came about because of increased understanding of the biochemical causes of depression and the development of more effective drugs that can treat the condition. Critics charge that the pharmaceutical industry and the medical profession have a conflict of interest and are biased in favor of creating more patients and more drug-consuming customers. In either case, conceptions of "normal" states of being are changing as a result.

Ihara describes the process that took place decades ago in the United States and more recently in Japan.

INTRODUCTION

Disease mongering has recently begun to have an adverse influence on both psychiatrists and patients in Japan. Indeed, this problem has been widely discussed internationally. [9, 17, 21]. But, there has been a relative paucity of reports concerning the current state of disease mongering in

Japan, due perhaps to a language barrier. This paper will discuss disease mongering in the Japanese context, with a particular focus on depression.

DISEASE MONGERING

Frequently used in an uncomplimentary sense, disease mongering connotes a widening of the diagnostic boundaries of illness. It is most often employed for activities of pharmaceutical companies, or others with similar interests, who conduct disease awareness campaigns on the pretext of educating the public about the prevention of illness or the promotion of health. Under the cover of early detection and early treatment, they strain the conceptual domain of diagnostic categories to their own advantage. Encouraged by these disease awareness advertisements, the public gradually becomes concerned that they are ill and require medical treatment. As a result, pharmacotherapy is increasingly being applied to ever-milder conditions, leading to potentially unnecessary medication, wasted resources, and adverse side effects [9, 17, 21].

Proponents of these practices justify disease awareness campaigns, arguing that the pharmaceutical industry is simply providing the public with information about its options and that the option of receiving medication is a matter to be discussed between patient and physician. Opponents however refute this argument, claiming that the true intent of disease awareness campaigns is primarily or even exclusively to produce profit for the drug companies. Furthermore, opponents suggest that by inspiring fear of illness, these campaigns drive patients to demand potentially unnecessary prescriptions, which may have unfavorable consequences instead of benefits [18].

Among all fields of clinical medicine, psychiatry is perhaps the most vulnerable to the dangers of disease mongering. The psychiatric conditions most commonly targeted by the pharmaceutical industry include social anxiety disorder, ADHD, bipolar disorder, and depression [15].

DEPRESSION MONGERING IN JAPAN

Depression before SSRI in Japan

Until the late 1990s, Japanese psychiatrists focused almost exclusively on psychosis and endogenous depression, the latter being severe enough to require conventional forms of antidepressants, known as tricyclic antidepressants, and even hospitalization [1, 11].

At this time, the public's attitude toward depression was generally unfavorable. This stigma was in part due to the negative connotations of the Japanese word for clinical depression, "utsubyou." This word, which suggests severe mental illness, contrasts strikingly with the English word "depression," which has a much broader meaning. Even in the psychiatric context, "depression" can be used alongside various subdivisions: organic, endogenous, neurotic, major, minor, reactive, vascular, juvenile, postpartum, premenstrual, senile, etc.

"Utsubyou," on the other hand, means only major depressive disorder or the depressive phase in manic-depressive disorder. It is a highly technical term and is almost unheard of outside clinical medicine. To talk about a feeling of gloominess, the general public uses a variety of everyday expressions such as "ki ga omoi" (heavy spirit), "ki ga harenai" (cloudy mood), "ki ga meiru" (dented mood), and so on. Even when relying on the so-called psychiatric vocabulary, people prefer the term "noiroze," a Japanized adaptation of the German word "Neurose."

In the past and also now, Japan's culture is strongly influenced by a Confucian tradition characterized by family centered and socio-centered attitudes and collectivism [19]. Over time, a worldview that encourages the acceptance of sadness, even the sharing of life's miseries with others, has emerged [22]. In Japan, it was natural that mild depression was rarely seen as a medical condition, and it was never thought that such feelings should be counteracted with chemical substances.

Depression after SSRI in Japan

This situation began to change after the 1999 introduction of Fluvoxamine (Luvox-Fujisawa, Depromel-Meiji Seika), the first selective serotonin re-uptake inhibitor (SSRI) to receive approval in Japan. Direct-to-consumer advertising (DTC advertising) is prohibited in Japan, and so pharmaceutical companies initiated educational campaigns focusing on mild depression. In order to aid the drug's acceptance by the Japanese public, they coined the catchphrase "*kokoro no kaz*," which literally means "a cold of the soul" [14]. Thus armed with this phrase, the pharmaceutical industry embarked on a mission to lessen the stigma of depression [10].

The campaign accelerated when GlaxoSmithKline received approval for another SSRI, Paxil (paroxetine) [24]. Subsequently, sertraline (J-Zoloft-Pfizer), milnacipran (Toledomin-Asahi Kasei-Janssen) and duloxetin (Cymbalta-Eli Lilly) have also entered the market in Japan. According to national data from the Ministry of Health, Labour and Welfare [16], the number of patients with a diagnosis of mood disorder increased from 441,000 in 1999 to 1,041,000 in 2003 (Fig. 5.2).

In an article entitled "Did Antidepressants Depress Japan?" *The New York Times* reports that in Japan, "GlaxoSmithKline alone saw its sales of Paxil increase from $108 million in 2001 to $298 million in 2003." [7]. Thanks to marketing practices that equate depression with a cold, Japan has proven to be fertile ground for selling antidepressants.

"A Cold of the Soul": A Japanese Case of Depression Mongering

The catchphrase "*kokoro no kaze*" or "a cold of the soul" masks a critical difference between the common cold and depression [3]. While medicines for the former are taken for a few days at

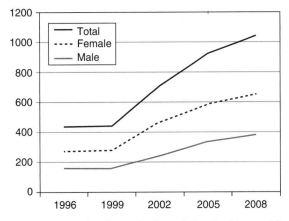

FIGURE 5.2 National trends in patients with a diagnosis of mood disorder (thousands) (Ministry of Health, Labour and Welfare)

most, those for the latter are usually consumed for months, years, or even for life. Thus, as pa-tients began to see antidepressants as medicine for "a cold of the soul," they became more likely to justify pharmacological treatment. However, once psychiatrists began prescribing antidepres-sants, they took for granted that their patients would be under treatment for months or much longer [2, 20, 23]. Indeed, once patients have begun to take antidepressants, many cannot help but continue. In this sense, the pharmaceutical companies' marketing claims falsified the nature of treatment for depression by concealing the documented duration of medication. Thanks to this distortion of information, pharmaceutical companies were assured a steady stream of profits.

These depression awareness campaigns have been based on the syllogism: "Your depression may be a disease. It can be cured by antidepressants. Therefore, your depression should be cured by antidepressants." This psychopharmacological reasoning is, even if valid, applicable only to the biological aspects of depression. It is utterly absurd to claim that antidepressants can cure depression caused by family difficulties, a dissolved relationship, a demanding job, or intractable indebtedness.

The neglect of psychotherapy has also contributed to the spike in antidepressant usage. Patients are frequently given only one option: pharmacotherapy. In fact, much variability exists among sufferers of depression. For some, depression is not linked to a chemical imbalance but rather is associated with inescapable life events such as separation, interpersonal conflicts, and unexpected adversities that are central to being human. Treatment should hence be multifaceted rather than depending solely on antidepressants. Patients, however, face difficulty in finding psy-chiatrists familiar with psychotherapy as well as with antidepressants.

The Pharmacological Model of Depression

Perhaps most importantly, the pharmacological model of depression lacks a robust scientific foundation. Indeed, pharmacological treatment is based on the assumption that depression is caused by an imbalance of mood-regulating chemicals in the brain, although there is actually little evidence that the pharmacological model is really adequate for patients with less severe depression [13].

Recent meta-analyses [5, 12] have also called into question previous research, which postu-lated that antidepressants have a specific pharmacological effect in comparison to placebo in patients with mild to moderate symptoms. According to these meta-analyses, the benefit of med-ication relative to placebo depends on the initial severity of depression symptoms. Excluding patients with very severe depression, the benefit of medication over a placebo may be minimal or even nonexistent.

CONCLUSIONS

Japanese psychiatrists can learn a great deal from their experience with the aggressive marketing of antidepressants. It can be argued that in the case of depression, over-medication did more harm than good. The same risk exists with other conditions, including bipolar disorder, to which the pharmaceutical industry has recently been shifting its focus [4]. Disease mongering may occur whenever the interests of a pharmaceutical company exceed the expected benefits from the proposed pharmacotherapy on those affected by the putative psychiatric disorder. In cases that are not severe enough for aggressive medication, psychiatrists should propose natural alternatives, such as an alteration of lifestyle and psychotherapy [6, 8].

DISCUSSION QUESTIONS

1. What, according to Ihara, is particularly misleading about euphemistically equating depression to "a cold of the soul"?
2. The United States and New Zealand are the only industrialized countries that allow pharmaceutical companies to engage in direct-to-consumer advertising. Why do you think other countries have banned the practice? Do you think it should be allowed?
3. How does this article relate to the sociology of deviance?

REFERENCES

[1] K. Appelbaum, Educating for global mental health: The adoption of SSRIs in Japan, In: Petryna A, Lakoff A, Kleinman A (Eds.). *Global Pharmaceuticals: Ethics, Markets, Practices.* Duke University Press, Durham, NC, 2006, pp. 85–110.

[2] M. Bauer, T. Bachor, A. Pfenning, et al., World Federation of Societies of Biological Psychiatry (WFSBP) guidelines for biological treatment of unipolar depressive disorders in primary care, *The World Journal of Biological Psychiatry* 8(2) (2007), 67–104.

[3] A. Brady, Film explores antidepressant use in Japan. *The Japan Times,* 2007. Available from: http://www.japantimes.co.jp/news/2007/07/12/national/film-explores-antidepressant-use-in-japan/.

[4] Elli Lilly, Advertisement of Olanzapine, *Seishinka Chiryogaku (Psychiatric Practice)* 25(11) (2010), page not specified. (in Japanese).

[5] J. C. Fournier, R. J. DeRubeis, S. D. Hollon, A. Dimidjian, J. D. Amsterdam, R. C. Shelton and J. Fawcett, Anti depressant drug effects and depression severity. A patient-level meta-analysis, *JAMA* 303(1) (2010), 47–53.

[6] E. Frank, H. A. Swartz and D. J. Kupfer, Interpersonal and social rhythm therapy: Managing the chaos of bipolar disorder, *Biol Psychiatry* 48 (2000), 593–604.

[7] Kathryn Schulz, Did Antidepressants Depress Japan? *New York Times,* August 22, 2004. Available at: http://www.nytimes.com/2004/08/22/magazine/did-antidepressants-depress-japan.html?pagewanted=all&src=pm.

[8] F. Goodwin and K. Jamison, *Manic-Depressive Illness,* Second Edition. Oxford University Press, New York, 2007, pp. 869–906.

[9] D. Healy, The latest mania: Selling bipolar disorder, *PLoS Medicine* 3 (2006), e185, 441–444.

[10] E. Ingrams, Long-taboo. "mood disorder" is now being seen as the common and crippling disease it is, *The Japan Times* 10 (2005), http://www.japantimes.co.jp/text/fl20050710x1.html

[11] L. J. Kirmayer, Psychopharmacology in a globalizing world: The use of antidepressants in Japan, *Transcultural Psychiatry* 39 (2002), 295–322.

[12] I. Kirsch, B. J. Deacon, T. B. Huedo-Medina, A. Scoboria, T. J. Moore and B. T. Johnson, Initial severity and antidepressant benefits: A meta-analysis of data submitted to the Food and Drug Administration, *PLoS Medicine* 5 (2008), 250–268.

[13] L. R. Lacasse and J. Leo, Serotonin and depression. A disconnect between the advertisements and the scientific literature, *PLoS Medicine* 2 (2005), e392, 1211–1216.

[14] P. Landers, Drug companies push Japan to change view of depression, *Wall Street Journal Online*, 2002, http://www.chelationtherapyonline.com/technical/p98.htm

[15] C. Lane, *Shyness: How normal behavior became a sickness*. Yale University Press, New Haven, 2007.

[16] Ministry of Health, Labour and Welfare. *Heisei 20 nen Kanja Chosa* (The investigation of patients in 2008) (in Japanese), 2008. Available from: http://www.mhlw.go.jp/toukei/saikin/hw/kanja/10syoubyo/suiihyo18.html

[17] R. Moynihan, E. Doran and D. Henry, Disease mongering is now part of the global health debate, *PLoS Med* 5 (2008), e106.

[18] R. Moynihan, I. Heath and D. Henry, Selling sickness. The pharmaceutical industry and disease mongering, *BMJ* 324 (2002), 886–891.

[19] C. Nakane, *Tate Shakai no Ningen Kankei* (Human relationships in the vertical society). Kodansha, Tokyo, 1967.

[20] National Institute for Health and Clinical Excellence: The treatment and management of depression in adults, 2009. Available at: http://www.nice.org.uk/nicemedia/live/12329/45888/45888.pdf

[21] A. Saddichha, Disease mongering in psychiatry: Is it fact or fiction? *World Medical & Health Policy* 2 (2010), 15.

[22] K. Schulz, Did antidepressants depress Japan? *New York Times*, 2004, http://www.nytimes.com/2004/08/22/magazine/did-antidepressants-depress-japan.html?pagewanted=all&src=pm22DEPRESS.html?ex=1250913600&en=cbf6990f7aecfcc7&ei=5090&partner=rssuserland&pagewanted=all

[23] TMAP (Texas Medications Algorithm Project) Manuals and algorithms: Major depressive disorder nonpsychotic algorithm, 2008. Available at: http://www:dshs.state.tx.us/mhprograms/pdf/TIMA_MDD_MDDAlgoOnly_080608.pdf

[24] E. Watters, How big pharma changed the nature of depression in Japan. *The Scavenger*, 2010, http://www.thescavenger.net/health/how-big-pharma-changed-the-nature-of-depression-in-japan-78235-466.html

CORPORATE, STATE, AND OCCUPATIONAL DEVIANCE

Introduction

This section deals with a type of deviance committed by those with some degree of institutionalized power over others; it is variously known as "white collar crime," "corporate deviance," "bureaucratic deviance," or "elite deviance." Relative to the kinds of deviance already discussed in this text, conflict theorists argue that elite deviance does inordinately more harm to society, yet it receives relatively little attention from the public and the authorities. Kappeler and Potter adeptly note in the first selection that most deviance is often the subject of a great deal of myth-making, involving exaggeration and sensational accounts of the threat and harm done by the deviant; these myths increase the deviant's vulnerability to social stigmatization and a punitive response from the state. However, they argue, elite deviance is the exception in that the myths surrounding it actually downplay the threat and harm caused by the deviant, which lessens the likelihood of social stigmatization and punishment and which, in the case of elite deviance, is often more deserved. Kappeler and Potter go on to detail the stark contrast between society's treatment of lower-class criminals and its treatment of upper-class criminals. These contrasts reveal a great deal about how extensive elite deviance is in society and how much political and economic power the elite wield in American society—enough to shape public perceptions of their crimes as being benign or even necessary, enough to shape legislation so that their crimes are not "crimes," and enough to avoid prosecution and/or receive minimal punishment even when their crimes are "crimes." On a sobering note, the article concludes, "There are two very different justice systems. One is for the poor and defenseless, and the other is for the rich and powerful."

Conflict theorists are likely to include in their definition of elite deviance behaviors that are not illegal, but would be illegal if the elite did not have such influence over the legislative process. Using this definition, elite deviance is part of the normal conduct of business in the United States and occurs thousands of times every day. If we restrict our concern only to those behaviors that are illegal, then certainly there is far less deviance, but still enough that few are surprised when incidents come to light. However, in some parts of the world, even illegal forms of elite deviance—namely, in the forms of bribery and corruption—are institutionalized into the normal conduct of business and government bureaucracies. Ling Li describes the situation in China where bureaucrats throughout the government hierarchy are notorious for their routine exchange of bribes, often with very deleterious effects on Chinese society. Recent railway accidents, bridge collapses, and a host over other man-made disasters have been attributed to the corruption of Chinese bureaucrats, engineers, and contractors. Given the pervasiveness and illegality of corrupt transactions, their preparation and escalation often follow a delicate set of rules that have evolved over generations of corruption. *Guanxi* is not easily translated, but it refers to a traditional management style in China where it is expected that personal relationships will bear on bureaucratic decision-making. As Li describes, guanxi lends itself to widescale corruption as people use gifts and bribes to establish personal relationships with those in power. As China modernizes, it is likely that tolerance for guanxi will diminish fairly rapidly. At the same time, however, as Li notes, guanxi is evolving to resist efforts to ban it.

The next article also deals with deviance in a bureaucratic environment. Namely, Richard Rubenstein employs principles developed by the early twentieth-century sociologist and economist,

Max Weber, to explain the Holocaust. Weber considered bureaucracies to be the culmination of a process that has been taking place throughout the history of civilization that he called "rationalization." As societies become more rationalized, informal methods and procedures in the workplace are replaced by more formal, carefully calculated and systematic methods and procedures. McDonald's restaurants have been identified as the model of rationalization. (In fact, the process has been referred to as "McDonaldization.") At McDonald's, all tasks have been boiled down to very simple, carefully calculated routines. Employees are not meant to exercise creativity or invention; they are just supposed to mindlessly execute the routines developed by those at the top. This makes the employees easily replaceable parts in the machine and consolidates power at the top of the hierarchy. McDonald's is the model, but rationalization is taking place throughout the workplace and, as a result, the workplace is becoming increasingly dehumanized. Rubenstein argues that it was this process of rationalization and the resulting dehumanization that made the Holocaust possible. The selection comes from Rubenstein's book, *The Cunning of History: The Holocaust and the American Future*. The subtitle serves as Rubenstein's bleak warning that the ongoing process of rationalization could make another holocaust possible.

In the last article in this section, Stuart Hills employs a political economic explanation for corporate deviance in a capitalist society, arguing that the profit imperative in the highly competitive cutthroat business world has produced a corporate culture in which ethical considerations take low priority in the conduct of business. For executives focused on improving shareholder value and employees focused on advancement within the organization, discussions about ethics are nothing less than "awkward." Like Rubenstein in the previous article, Hills identifies the depersonalized nature of bureaucracies that contributes to the lack of moral compunction often displayed in the behavior of their corporate executives and their employees. But these are people who are usually highly regarded by the general public, often seen as upholding the cherished American values of hard work, ambition, innovation, and financial success. Not surprisingly, they often see themselves in the same light. So how do they so often engage in unethical, frequently illegal behavior and still maintain their positive self-image? Hills applies the same "techniques of neutralization" to understanding executive malfeasance that Sykes and Matza applied to understanding juvenile delinquency in Article 4 in this volume. These techniques have been used in the literature to explain all kinds of deviance, from deer poaching to entering daughters into beauty pageants to genocide. Hills applies them very adeptly to corporate deviance and simultaneously implicates the capitalist ethos as exacerbating such deviance.

28.
CORPORATE CRIME AND "HIGHER IMMORALITY"

VICTOR E. KAPPELER AND GARY W. POTTER

The United States has the highest known incarceration rate in the world and the vast majority of inmates in U.S. prisons are from the lower and working classes, convicted for street crimes and drug offenses. In spite of its inordinately high incarceration rate, many politicians and large segments of the U.S. population think the problem of crime stems from the leniency of the criminal justice system. Ironically, it is often these same constituencies who think there are far too many regulations on corporate conduct and who want to "get the government off our backs." A strong case can be made, however, that corporate crime and the paucity of corporate regulations pose a far greater threat both to our physical safety and our economic well-being than street crime. For the conflict theorist, the juxtaposition of these facts suggests the enormous power that the corporate elite wield over the public's perceptions of criminal threat and over legislation and law enforcement in the United States.

> The law does not pretend to punish everything that is dishonest. That would seriously interfere with business.
>
> CLARENCE S. DARROW

Myths of crime and criminal justice, for the most part, revolve around two central themes. First, there is a criminal act or behavior. That behavior is seized upon by the media, law enforcement bureaucracies, and politicians as a way to attract public attention and to win support for policy issues related to crime. The behavior is exaggerated through political rhetoric, sensational reporting, and misrepresentations to create a distorted view of the threat to society and to individuals in that society. The burgeoning myths frequently target minority populations or groups with unpopular beliefs. Thus, we have had crime scares about women and witchcraft, homosexuals and molested children, Satanists and ritual murders, people of color and drugs, and immigrants and political subversion.

The second recurring theme in myths of crime and criminal justice is a massive law enforcement response to the behavior in question. New laws are passed outlawing certain aspects of the behavior, prison sentences are increased, new powers are granted to investigating agencies, and a proactive campaign of enforcement is launched in an attempt to control the perceived danger. In taking these steps we frequently overreact and make the problem we are trying to solve much worse than it was originally.

In this chapter, we explore a very different type of myth. This myth *downplays* the importance of criminal behavior and justifies a policy of **lax** enforcement. This myth mitigates responsibility and excuses misconduct. This myth argues for less enforcement, fewer laws, and less stringent punishment; it protects those with political and economic power. The mythology of corporate crime consists of three myths that neutralize and explain away this type of crime.

The first of these myths is that corporate criminality causes less damage, both economic and physical, than traditional "street crimes." Government officials have tried to present the issue of corporate crime in terms of individual misconduct, ignoring the more pervasive and dangerous criminality of corporations. The second myth is that corporate crimes are accidents or oversights— that they are unintended crimes lacking the criminal intent found in crimes of violence and theft. The third myth is that current laws and enforcement efforts are more than sufficient to deal with the problem. This argument is frequently carried a step further to suggest that present laws are too stringent and that they are out of proportion to the danger of the behavior.

"REAL" CORPORATE CRIME

When most people think of crime, they think of acts of interpersonal violence or property crimes. A crime occurs when someone breaks into your house and steals your plasma television; a crime occurs when a mugger steals your wallet; a crime occurs when a sniper shoots someone pumping gas. The FBI and other law enforcement agencies monitor the amount of street crime and gauge the threat of crime to society in that context. We spend billions of dollars a year and employ more than one million police officers, almost 750,000 correctional officers, and nearly 500,000 prosecutors and judges in the battle against street crime (Bauer & Owens, 2004; Maguire & Pastore, 2003).

While murder, rape, robbery, and other violent crimes in society are frightening, our exclusive emphasis on these crimes conceals two fundamental truths about crime in the United States: (1) the criminal justice system can do very little to control street crimes—and next to nothing to prevent them; (2) the total of all violent crime and all property crime combined is less of a threat to society than the crime committed by corporations.

The reality of corporate crime in U.S. society changes little from year to year. Corporate crime is rampant; corporations are criminal recidivists; corporate crime causes exponentially more economic damage than all street crimes put together; corporate crime kills, maims, and injures enormously larger numbers of innocent people than all street crimes combined; and corporate crime is treated with kid gloves by government agencies and the criminal justice system. In the words of C. Wright Mills (1952), corporate crime creates a "higher immorality" in U.S. society. It does more damage to the social fabric, health, and safety of the country than all the murderers, rapists, terrorists, and property criminals combined. As Clinard and Yeager point out, corporate crime reveals a terrible social hypocrisy:

> It is hypocritical to regard theft and fraud among the lower classes with distaste and to punish such acts while countenancing upper-class deception and calling it "shrewd business practice." A review of

corporate violations and how they are prosecuted and punished shows who controls what in law enforcement in American society and the extent to which this control is effective. Even in the broad area of legal proceedings, corporate crime is generally surrounded by an aura of politeness and respectability rarely if ever present in cases of ordinary crime. Corporations are seldom referred to as lawbreakers and rarely as criminals in enforcement proceedings. Even if violations of the criminal law, as well as other laws are involved, enforcement attorneys and corporation counsels often refer to the corporation as "having a problem": one does not speak of the robber or the burglar as having a problem. (Clinard and Yeager, 1980, p. 21)

THE COSTS OF CORPORATE CRIME

Jeffrey Reiman (2004) notes that the crimes tracked by government agencies do not include the majority of crimes that cost the public dearly.

> The general public loses more money *by far* . . . from price fixing and monopolistic practices and from consumer deception and embezzlement than from all the property crimes in the FBI's Index combined. Yet these far more costly acts are either not criminal, or, if technically criminal, not prosecuted, or, if prosecuted, not punished, or if punished, only mildly. In any event, although the individuals responsible for these acts take more money out of the ordinary citizen's pocket than our Typical Criminal, they rarely show up in arrest statistics and almost never in prison populations. (p. 61)

The Uniform Crime Reports estimated losses from street crime at $16.6 billion in 2002 (Federal Bureau of Investigation, 2003); Enron alone cost investors, pensioners, and employees an estimated $60 billion. Lee Drutman (2003) also points out that the UCR data do not list environmental pollution crimes, food safety violations, occupational diseases, product safety violations, workplace safety violations, "and countless other crimes that kill, injure, and sicken millions of Americans each year. . . . Most credible estimates confirm that, in the aggregate, white-collar and corporate crimes cost the U.S. hundreds of billions of dollars annually" (p. B13).

"Crime of the street variety . . . is much less significant in cost and social disruption than are white-collar crimes—those committed by middle-class and upper-middle-class people in their business and social activities" (Eitzen & Zinn, 2004, p. 347). The costs of air pollution, toxic chemical dumping, diseases caused by industrial carcinogens, adverse patient reactions to unsafe drugs, and the like are impossible to calculate with any degree of accuracy. The very conservative estimate of economic costs from corporate crime as $400 to $500 billion a year is roughly 30 times the cost of street crime. The economic loss from corporate crime is about $1,730 per person, far in excess of the average loss of less than $59 from street crimes in the United States.

But economic loss is only a minor part of the corporate crime story. As Steven Barkan (2001) points out, conservative estimates of the victims of corporate crime would include 55,000 annual deaths resulting from injuries or illnesses occurring at work; 30,000 annual deaths from the sale of unsafe consumer products; and 20,000 deaths from various forms of environmental pollution. There is no way to determine how many people die from inadequately tested or inappropriately marketed prescription drugs, or inadequate nursing home care delivered by corporate health giants, or the denial of medical care in order to maximize insurance company profits. A conservative estimate would be that more than 100,000 people die each year as a result of corporate crime compared to an annual homicide total of about 16,000, or a ratio of about 6 to 1. These numbers do not reflect the 4.4 million nonfatal workplace injuries and the almost 300,000 newly reported cases of occupational illnesses in 2002. More than half of these 4.7 million workplace-related injuries or illnesses were sufficiently serious to cause days away from work (Bureau of Labor Statistics, 2003), unlike the typical assault reported to the police.

The numbers are huge, but the specifics are even more shocking. Many of the 230 employees at Roe Imperial Food Products in Hamlet, North Carolina, lived in Larry Hubbard Homes, a housing project less than 10 minutes from the one-floor, windowless brick building with one entry door. The plant produced chicken tenders for fast-food outlets. The interior of the plant consisted of conveyor belts, concrete floors, and vats of grease with temperatures that could reach 500 degrees. There was no automatic sprinkler system, no fire alarms, only one fire extinguisher, and most of the exits were locked or blocked to prevent stealing. Twenty-three out of every 100 workers became seriously ill or injured each year. In 11 years of operation, the plant had never been inspected for safety or health violations. On September 3, 1991, a hydraulic line ruptured and spilled flammable liquid into gas burners under the frying vats. A 30-second fireball sent toxic smoke through the plant. Ninety workers were in the plant at the time. Twenty-five employees were killed, and 56 suffered injuries, including severe burns, respiratory diseases caused by smoke inhalation, post traumatic stress syndrome, neurological and brain damage, and blindness. Nineteen of the 25 workers killed were single mothers (Haygood, 2002). A state official was quoted as saying, "the doors at a chicken processing plant where a fire killed 25 people probably wouldn't have been locked if the workers hadn't been stealing from their employer" (Norton, 2002). North Carolina's Occupational Safety and Health Administration (OSHA) proposed a record $808,150 in civil penalties against Imperial Foods and recommended criminal action against company management. The owner, Emmett Roe, his son Brad (the operations manager), and the plant manager, James Hair, were all indicted on 25 counts each of involuntary manslaughter. Under a plea agreement, Emmett Roe was sentenced to 19 years in prison, and charges were dismissed against Brad Roe and James Hair. Emmett Roe served 54 months in prison and was paroled in 1997.

Numerous civil suits were filed after the fire, including one against the North Carolina Department of Labor and its OSHA division for breaching its public duty to inspect the plant. Although lower courts had ruled in favor of the plaintiffs, the North Carolina Supreme Court ruled on February 6, 1998, that:

> Just as the limited resources of law enforcement were recognized in *Braswell*, the limited resources of the defendants in this case are recognized and a judicially imposed overwhelming burden of liability for failure to prevent every employer's negligence resulting in injuries or deaths to employees is refused. . . . A government ought to be free to enact laws for the *public protection* without thereby exposing its supporting taxpayers to liability for failures of omission in its attempt to enforce them. It is better to have such laws, even haphazardly enforced, than not to have them at all. (*Stone v. N.C. Dept. of Labor*, **1998**)

While locked doors might seem to be a draconian approach that could never happen in the twenty-first century, an investigation by the *New York Times* in 2004 proved otherwise. The *Times* found that for more than 15 years, Wal-Mart had locked the doors in about 10 percent of its Wal-Mart and Sam's Club stores while employees were working the overnight shift. The policy originated to keep robbers out and, according to some managers, to prevent employee theft. Incidents that occurred during the policy included a worker suffering a heart attack in Indiana, employees locked-in when hurricanes hit in Florida, and employees who couldn't leave when their wives went into labor. Michael Rodriguez suffered a smashed ankle at 3 a.m. in Corpus Christi and had to wait until a manager arrived an hour later to let him out before he could go to the hospital. Although there was a fire exit, management had repeatedly warned that workers would be fired if the exit was used for anything but a fire. In January 2004, Wal-Mart changed its policy and required that a manager with a key be present during such shifts (Greenhouse, 2004).

In 1996 Secretary of Labor Robert Reich called DeCoster Egg Farm "an agricultural sweatshop." DeCoster owned farms in Iowa, Maine, Minnesota, and Ohio. At DeCoster's farm in Turner, Maine, Mexican migrant workers labored for ten to fifteen hours a day without even minimum safety precautions. They collected and discarded dead chickens with their bare hands. They handled Salmonella-infected manure with no gloves. Workers injured on the job were routinely left untreated. One worker lost three fingers in a machine used to scrape chicken manure from the barns. There were no safeguards on equipment, and barn roofs were improperly constructed and at risk of collapse. Workers lived in company trailers with faulty plumbing that allowed raw sewage into bathtubs and shower stalls. DeCoster paid $2 million for OSHA violations in 1996 (Blanding, 2002).

DeCoster had a history of violating immigration and labor laws and contesting fines for violations. In 1998 the Mexican government filed suit on behalf of approximately 1,500 workers employed from 1991 through 1997, charging DeCoster with discrimination in housing and slave-like working conditions. This was an unprecedented instance of a foreign government taking legal action on behalf of its citizens against a U.S. employer (Corchado, 2002). An initial settlement of $6 million was reached in 2000; DeCoster later contested the amount, and the parties eventually reached a $3.2 million settlement in 2002, which was finally dispersed to approximately 1,500 workers in 2004 ("Egg farm," 2004).

While DeCoster still owns the livestock and real estate in Maine, other companies took over operations in September 1997. OSHA inspections between November 1998 and June 1999 found 78 violations and fined the successor companies $224,625. In 2002 OSHA proposed another $344,810 in fines for 27 offenses including unguarded equipment, defective eye wash stations, hazardous electrical equipment, exposed asbestos, unsanitary shower facilities, unsupported roof rafters, the use of defective cranes and trucks, and unprotected propane fuel tanks (Blanding, 2002).

In 2002 DeCoster settled a federal discrimination lawsuit filed on behalf of Mexican women who said they were raped or sexually harassed by supervisors at four northern Iowa egg farms. The suit alleged that DeCoster supervisors in the four locations sexually assaulted female employees and threatened to kill those who complained. DeCoster was fined $1.53 million (Seibert, 2002).

Austin J. DeCoster, owner of DeCoster Farms, was sentenced in federal court to five years probation in 2003 for knowingly and repeatedly hiring illegal workers; in 1989 he had been fined for similar charges. Although DeCoster could have been sentenced to up to a year in prison, U.S. District Judge Mark W. Bennett said: "I don't think you deserve prison time. You've done an extraordinary amount of work with the government," referring to what the judge characterized as sincere efforts to comply with complex immigration regulations. DeCoster paid $2 million in fines and assessments for the cost of monitoring his egg farms over the next five years. Bennett stated that while he was concerned that it could look as though DeCoster were buying his way out of prison, people who have worked hard should not be penalized for making money (Associated Press, 2003a). The "three strikes" correctional policy apparently does not apply to the world of corporate crime.

Managers at the Shell Motiva refinery in 2001 ignored employee warnings that a tank filled with spent sulfuric acid was severely corroded and overdue for maintenance and issued orders to a crew to perform some tasks near the tank. A welding torch ignited leaking vapors and the explosion flung one of the workers into the tank. The acid consumed everything except for the steel shanks of his boots. In the last decade Shell and its partners were assessed $4.3 million in fines for 11 deaths (Barstow, 2003b).

Hanford Environmental Health Foundation, funded by the Department of Energy for 38 years, is under allegations of fraud, supervisory misconduct, and falsification of medical records. Hanford Nuclear Reservation is the largest and most expensive nuclear waste cleanup site in the United States. The government spends $2 billion a year on cleanup. The Government Accountability Project, a nonprofit watchdog group, describes the Hanford culture as "dominated by profit-minded contractors and meekly supervised by federal bureaucrats—where there are powerful financial incentives to cover up worker complaints, falsify reports of work-loss injuries and subordinate safety to production bonuses" (Harden, 2004).

Great White, a heavy-metal band, was fined $7,000 and club owners were fined $82,200 after 100 people were killed and more than 180 were injured when the band's pyrotechnics ignited a fire at a nightclub in Rhode Island. Three months before the show, a fire inspector cited the nightclub for having an exit door that opened inward instead of outward. The violation was not corrected, and the door caused a fatal bottleneck the night of the fire (Daly, 2003).

McWane, Inc., one of the world's largest manufacturers of cast-iron sewer and water pipe, has 10 major foundries in the United States and employs 5,000 workers. Five plants (in Alabama, Utah, Texas, and New Jersey) have been designated "high priority" violators by the Environmental Protection Agency; one in New York was convicted of possessing hazardous waste, a felony (Barstow & Bergman, 2003a). McWane foundries are dangerous places to work. Since 1995, the various locations have been cited for more than 400 safety violations and 450 environmental violations. McWane employees suffered at least 4,600 injuries during that time, and 9 workers were killed, 3 because of willful violations of federal safety standards (Barstow & Bergman, 2003c). McWane workers at the various locations have been maimed, burned, sickened, and killed by the same failures to comply with federal safety and health regulations (Barstow & Bergman, 2003b). Current and former managers said McWane viewed regulatory fines as far less costly than complying with safety and environmental rules. For example, after an employee was run over by a forklift that had known safety defects and brakes that were not working properly, McWane paid $10,500 to settle OSHA violations for operating unsafe forklifts and failing to train drivers.

Corporate crime is not limited to workers on the job or to adults. A 1995 study found traces of pesticides, all either neurotoxins or probable human carcinogens, in 53 percent of all baby food from major national manufacturers (Rosoff, Pontell, & Tillman, 2004). In 1997, Andrew and Williamson Sales Company, a major fruit distributor in the United States, pled guilty to criminal charges in connection with an outbreak of hepatitis that made 198 school children and teachers dangerously ill (CCR, 1997b). Odwalla, Inc., a company that bases its advertising on the provision of pure, clean, and nutritious juice drinks, pled guilty to criminal charges of selling contaminated apple juice that killed a 16-month-old girl and made at least 70 others sick (*CCR*, 1998).

Corporate criminals often assault their victims when they are most vulnerable. In 1995 three executives of C. R. Bard, Inc., a manufacturer of balloon tips used in angioplasty, pled guilty to 391 counts of fraud. Bard had concealed from the FDA malfunctions in its products including balloon ruptures, deflations, and breakages that caused serious heart injuries resulting in emergency coronary bypass surgery. Approximately 22,000 people had used the catheters before they were recalled; at least one of them died, and at least 10 patients had to undergo emergency heart surgery (Simon, 2002). Warner-Lambert, a Fortune 500 drug company, pled guilty in 1995 to felony charges related to its production of an anti-epileptic drug named Dilantin. Adulterated shipments of the drug had been distributed, and FDA efforts to determine the potency of the drug shipments had been obstructed (Mokhiber & Wheat, 1995). Copley Pharmaceutical pled guilty to conspiracy charges and agreed to pay a fine of $10.65 million after changing FDA-mandated manufacturing methods for its prescription drugs, falsifying batch records submitted to the FDA, and submitting false annual reports to the FDA (*CCR*, 1997a). For example, Genentech, Inc. pled guilty to charges that it illegally marketed its synthetic human growth hormone, Protropin, to doctors and hospitals for the treatment of medical conditions for which the drug had never been approved by the FDA (*CCR*, 1999).

The incidents continue year after year. Some of the most recent are highlighted below.

- GlaxoSmithKline was indicted for consumer fraud for not disclosing all of its data about the effects of its antidepressant Paxil on adolescents (Meier, 2004).
- Mitsubishi Motors Corporation admitted in June 2004 that it had failed to disclose defects in its vehicles for a decade (Zaun, 2004).
- IBM and National Semiconductor face lawsuits that claim the chip industry ignores the risks of exposure to dangerous chemicals in their pursuit of profits. Some suits allege that exposure to the chemicals caused birth defects in their children; others claim the exposure is responsible for illnesses (Sorid, 2004).
- Mexicans workers are 80 percent more likely to die at work than native-born workers and are twice as likely to die as other immigrant workers. Two Mexican teenagers died in South Carolina in 2003 while building a suburban high school when the walls of a trench collapsed and buried them. OSHA fined the employers $50,475 for the safety violations (Pritchard, 2004).
- Parents are often unaware of the range of carcinogenic exposures that "pervade the landscape of our children's lives, seeping into their bodies through contaminated drinking water, chemically preserved wooden playground sets, pediatric prescription drugs—even the flea collar around Fido's neck" (Epstein & Young, 2003, p. 17).
- From 1982 to 2002, OSHA investigated 1,242 deaths in which workers were buried alive, burned beyond recognition, decapitated, electrocuted, or crushed by machinery because employers willfully violated workplace safety laws; in 93 percent of the cases, OSHA declined to seek criminal prosecution (Barstow, 2003a).
- Two dairy workers at Aguiar-Faria & Sons dairy in Gustine, California, drowned in a sump hole of manure and wastewater. The Circuit Prosecutor Project indicted the general manager

and herdsman for involuntary manslaughter after the California agency known as CalSHA determined the deaths were caused by willful safety violations. From 1990 to 2002, California prosecuted 36 percent of the deaths caused by willful violation, compared to 3.9 percent prosecuted by OSHA and 4.6 percent prosecuted by other state-run OSHA agencies (Barstow, 2003c).

THE NORMALCY OF CORPORATE CRIME

Despite the damage to society from corporate and white-collar crimes, government officials, corporate executives, and even some law enforcement experts argue that these crimes differ from street crimes in several important respects. They attempt to mitigate the impact of corporate crime by pointing to a lack of *mens rea* (criminal intent). They claim that corporate violators do not set out to commit crime, unlike muggers, rapists, and murderers. Violations happen because of oversights, occasionally from negligence, and from the pressures inherent in the business world—not from a conscious decision to do harm or to inflict injury.

The argument that corporate offenders lack criminal intent is one of a series of neutralizing myths employed by white-collar criminals to excuse their conduct. Unfortunately, the facts simply belie the myth. Studies have shown clearly that injuries and deaths caused by corporate violations are not simply a matter of carelessness or neglect; many are the direct result of willful violations of the law. Corporate criminals are also criminal recidivists, committing their predations over and over again.

Consider Edwin Sutherland's findings in his groundbreaking research on white-collar crime conducted more than a half-century ago (Sutherland, 1949). Sutherland searched the records of regulatory agencies/commissions and federal, state, and local courts looking for adverse decisions handed down against the seventy largest corporations in America over a twenty-year period:

> Each of the 70 large corporations has 1 or more decisions against it, with a maximum of 50. The total number of decisions is 980, and the average per corporation is 14.0. Sixty corporations have decisions against them for restraint of trade, 53 for infringement, 44 for unfair labor practices, 43 for miscellaneous offenses, 28 for misrepresentation in advertising, and 26 for rebates. (Sutherland, 1949, p. 15)

Sutherland found that major corporations engaged in widespread criminality; 97.1 percent of the corporations in his study were recidivists. The numbers were even more compelling considering how little effort was put into discovering and prosecuting corporate violations. The adverse decisions found by Sutherland represented only a tiny portion of the actual crime committed.

Marshall Clinard and Peter Yeager's (1980) findings with regard to crimes committed by the 477 largest manufacturing corporations and the 105 largest wholesale, retail, and service corporations in the United States in 1975 and 1976 were equally disturbing. In that two-year period, the 582 companies were the subjects of 1,553 federal cases. Because these numbers included only cases brought against the corporations, they again represented only a tiny portion of the total amount of crime committed by the corporations. Clinard and Yeager stated that they had uncovered only "the tip of the iceberg of total violations" (p. 111). They found that in just two years, 60 percent of the corporations had at least 1 action initiated against them, 42 percent of the corporations had 2 or more actions, and the most frequent violators were averaging 23.5 violations.

An investigation of white-collar crime by *U.S. News & World Report* ("Corporate Crime," 1982) found that during the decade of the 1970s almost 2,700 corporations were convicted of federal criminal charges. Sociologist Amatai Etzioni found that 62 percent of the Fortune 500 companies were involved in at least one act of bribery, price fixing, tax fraud, or environmental crime between 1975 and 1984. A similar study by the *Multinational Monitor* found that the twenty-five largest Fortune 500 corporations had all been convicted of a criminal act or fined and required to make civil restitution between 1977 and 1990 (Donahue, 1992, pp. 14–19).

Congress passed the Occupational Safety and Health Act in 1970. The Act made it a misdemeanor to cause the death of a worker by willfully violating safety laws. The maximum sentence was six months in jail—half the maximum jail time for harassing a wild burro on federal lands (Barstow, 2003b). Despite subsequent efforts to raise the violation to felony status, it remains a misdemeanor. Fines have been increased only once since OSHA was created. In 1990, the maximum sanction for a safety violation was increased to $70,000 from $10,000. In over three decades, OSHA has proposed fines exceeding $1 million against only 15 employers (Barstow & Bergman, 2003b).

OSHA's charter is prevention, not punishment. There are approximately 2,200 inspectors in over 200 offices, with a budget of $450 million; 26 states also conduct workplace inspections. There are more than 115 million workers at 7.1 million sites in the United States. With the exception of miners, transportation workers, and many public employees, OSHA is charged with setting and enforcing standards for the safety and health of U.S. workers. In 2003, it conducted almost 40,000 federal inspections and found 83,600 violations. Of those, 406 were willful, meaning the employer intentionally and knowingly violated safety standards; 59,899 were "serious," meaning death or serious physical harm could result from the hazard and that the employer knew, or should have known, about the danger. There were 2,152 repeat violations, which consist of finding a similar violation upon reinspection. The remaining 21,000 violations were either "failure to abate" a prior violation, "other," or "unclassified." Penalties totaled $82 million. There were approximately 59,000 state inspections that found 196 willful violations, 59,693 serious violations, 2,686 repeat violations, and 77,253 in the last 3 categories (OSHA, 2004).

Before making a determination of willful disregard for worker safety, OSHA subjects the case to intense scrutiny—up to thousands of hours of gathering evidence. The maximum fine for a willful violation can be up to 10 times higher than any other fine. Since 1990, OSHA downgraded 202 fatality cases from "willful" to "unclassified." Defense lawyers seek the designation because it makes any future prosecution much more difficult. McDermott, Will & Emery, a law firm in Washington, DC, makes the following claims on its Web site: "Our group pioneered the approach of amending the citations from 'willful' to 'unclassified' that has become a common tool today for proactively resolving difficult issues while avoiding unnecessary complication presented by harmful labels."

Numbers are the key element in OSHA's culture—numbers of inspections and numbers of violations. If OSHA decides to use its ultimate enforcement tool—the ability to refer cases to federal or state prosecutors—the increased burden of proof means that those cases will detract from hours available to pursue other numbers. The reluctance to pursue such cases is so entrenched that the agency had never done a comprehensive study to track repeat offenders across jurisdictions, leaving multiple-location companies, such as DeCoster egg farms or McWane, free to commit precisely the same violations from one state to another with impunity unless inspectors happened to schedule a visit. Rarely does OSHA pursue criminal charges, whether because of scarce resources, fear of bad publicity, or a persistent belief that the Justice Department does not like such cases. Many OSHA directors believe that the solicitors' office is a "black hole" where cases disappear because the lawyers are too busy, too willing to settle, or too intimidated if the employer is a powerful corporation (Barstow, 2003a)—or uninterested in pursuing cases where the burden of proof is high and the maximum penalty is a misdemeanor. Since OSHA was created, only 151 cases have been referred to the Justice Department; federal prosecutors decided not to act on more than half of those referrals, and 11 people have been sentenced to prison—the longest sentence was the maximum six months (Barstow & Bergman, 2003b). Safety violations that kill workers may also be prosecuted under state manslaughter and reckless homicide statutes, but state agencies are also often reticent about pursuing criminal convictions.

The *New York Times* conducted a comprehensive study of the more than 170,000 workers killed on the job between 1982 and 2002. OSHA investigated less than a quarter of those deaths. The newspaper reporters analyzed 1,798 investigations (1,242 OSHA investigations plus those of 21 states and one territory) using a computer analysis of OSHA inspection data plus thousands of government records and hundreds of interviews. The 2,197 deaths from willful safety violations occurred at companies ranging in size from Shell Oil to local plumbing and painting contractors. In the 1,242 OSHA cases, 70 employers were repeat offenders whose willful safety violations resulted in additional deaths. Fines for the deaths over the span of 20 years totaled $106 million. Fatality cases designated as willful often have fines reduced from the maximum $70,000 to $25,000 if companies agree not to challenge the findings and to correct safety hazards. Cases that are downgraded from willful to less severe violations have even deeper reductions (Barstow, 2003b). Jail sentences for the 2,197 deaths totaled less than 30 years over the two-decade span. Twenty of those thirty years were assessed for a single incident—the state criminal prosecution of the fire at Imperial Foods that killed 25 workers in 1991. In contrast, the Environmental Protection Agency in a single year (2001) obtained prison sentences totaling 256 years (Barstow, 2003a). The willful violations were downgraded or removed completely in 427 cases; 196 cases were referred to state or federal prosecutors; there were 81 convictions and 16 jail sentences.

The litany of numbers belie the myth that corporate criminality is random, isolated, and lacking intent. The neutralizing myth has resulted in a workplace death being a misdemeanor with fines substantially reduced if the company voices its cooperation. The myth is so entrenched that it leads to absurd reasoning. For example, after OSHA warnings in 1984, 1985, and 1986 about trench safety and a $700 fine, a worker for Moeves Plumbing in Cincinnati was buried alive when the walls of a trench collapsed in 1989. Moeves then agreed to inspect each job to make sure it followed safety regulations. In 2002, two weeks after an OSHA inspector shut down another Moeves job site for inadequate trench precautions, another worker died. One day after OSHA reached a determination of a willful violation, it changed the designation to "unclassified." The second death was clear proof that the 1989 agreement was not followed, yet that very negligence became the reasoning for not pursuing steeper fines or criminal liability. In essence, because the owner of the company had violated the duty to make sure each job was inspected, that failure meant that she did not have specific knowledge about the dangers of the trench (Barstow, 2003a).

A POLICY OF NONENFORCEMENT

Just like street criminals, corporate criminals defy the law and break the rules. They maim and kill and cause immense economic hardship and loss, but the neutralizing myth is that current laws are more than adequate to address the problems. Bertram Gross commented years ago that the U.S. criminal justice system has a "dirty little secret":

> We are not letting the public in on our era's dirty little secret: that those who commit the crime which worries citizens most—violent street crime—are, for the most part, products of poverty, unemployment, broken homes, rotten education, drug addiction, alcoholism, and other social and economic ills about which the police can do little if anything. . . . But, all the dirty little secrets fade into insignificance in comparison with one dirty big secret: Law enforcement officials, judges as well as prosecutors and investigators, are soft on corporate crime. . . . The corporation's "mouthpieces" and "fixers" include lawyers, accountants, public relations experts and public officials who negotiate loopholes and special procedures in the laws, prevent most illegal activities from ever being disclosed and undermine or sidetrack "overzealous" law enforcers. In the few cases ever brought to court, they usually negotiate penalties amounting to "gentle taps on the wrist." (Gross, 1980, pp. 113–115)

A corollary to the myth that current laws are sufficient to halt corporate crime is that business is "overregulated."

> Opponents of government regulation and legal intervention also argue that, since most businesses are law-abiding, there is no need for state controls. This position seems no more logical than proposing to raze our prisons, since most citizens are law-abiding. (Rosoff, Pontell, & Tillman, 2004, p. 29)

Not only are corporations underregulated, but they also actively participate in defining their own criminality. When legislatures write laws outlawing rape, burglary, armed robbery, larceny, and theft, they do not consult or negotiate with the criminals who committed the crimes. But when legislatures enact laws regulating corporations, they actively seek input and advice from those they are ostensibly setting out to punish. How effective is a regulatory system enacted only with the consent of the perpetrators? The earliest regulatory laws were the antitrust acts of the late 1800s. These laws were in fact initiated and supported by the very businesses they ostensibly regulated. Legal prohibitions against monopolies and price-fixing were used by the robber barons to stabilize the market and to make the economy more predictable. Smaller competitors could no longer employ the tactics that the large corporations had used to create their dominant economic positions (Pearce, 1976; Weinstein, 1968). The 1906 Meat Inspection Act is one example. Ostensibly, the act was passed to protect consumers from spoiled, contaminated meat products. In fact, the meatpacking laws had the full support of the large meatpacking companies because they kept imported meat off the United States market at government expense, and they hindered smaller meatpacking companies by making it hard for them to survive and to compete with the major corporations (Kolko, 1963). The contemporary situation is no different. For example, the automobile industry has successfully blocked legislation that would criminalize knowing and willful violations of federal auto safety laws.

Another way in which corporate criminals successfully avoid regulation, prosecution, and investigation is through the incestuous relationships between the government and the major corporations. The relatively few regulators employed by the government to enforce laws against corporate misconduct are hardly in an adversarial relationship with the industries they regulate.

Those in charge of many of the regulatory agencies and commissions are people who have come to government service from the same corporations they are supposed to be regulating. Contacts between the regulators and the regulated have been cordial and frequently collaborative. Regulators who have come to the government from private enterprise are often more concerned with the needs of the corporations they are regulating than with the safety or economic health of the public.

The reciprocity works both ways. Many agency employees leave government service to work for the companies they regulated—compelling evidence of a very cozy relationship. This conflict of interest has been apparent in several cases, but the most blatant example can be found in the Environmental Protection Agency during the Reagan administration. Rita Lavelle was appointed by the president to oversee the government's "superfund" program, designed to clean up the most threatening cases of corporate pollution resulting from improper disposal of toxic waste. She had previously been employed at Aerojet-General Corporation in California. During her tenure at the EPA, she participated in decisions relating to her former employer (a clear conflict of interest), entered into "sweetheart deals" with major polluters, and used the superfund allocations for political purposes. In 1983, Lavelle was convicted on four felony counts (Hagan, 2002).

Government actions even facilitate corporate and white-collar crime, as happened with the savings and loan scandal of the 1980s. The Reagan administration deregulated the savings and loan industry in order to stimulate growth in the banking industry. In addition, they increased insurance protection for depositor's accounts at these institutions from $40,000 to $100,000. The administration argued that deregulation would make S & L's more competitive. What it did was make them more criminal. Following deregulation, S & L executives began using institutional funds for their private expenses, thereby robbing their own banks (Calavita, Pontell, & Tillman, 1999). In addition, the new federal regulations allowed the S & L to engage in such practices as accepting deposits contingent upon loans being made to the depositors. The depositors then defaulted on the loans. Not only did those depositors essentially obtain interest-free money to invest in high-risk speculations but the go-betweens also were paid very generous "finder's fees" for arranging the loans. The S & L's profited because the deposits artificially inflated the assets of the bank, which resulted in higher dividends being paid to stockholders and extravagant bonuses being paid to S & L executives (Calavita, Pontell, & Tillman, 1999). Charles Keating, Jr., the former CEO of Lincoln Savings & Loan in Irvine, California, was the central figure in the scandal. When Lincoln Savings & Loan went bankrupt, it cost taxpayers $3.4 billion. Keating was convicted of defrauding investors of $200 million. He served more than four years in prison before succeeding in having the charges thrown out. In April 1999, he pled guilty to four felony counts in a deal to keep him out of prison (Hamilton, 2002). Eventually hundreds of savings and loans failed, costing U.S. taxpayers over $500 billion to cover federally insured losses—and much more to investigate the bank failures (Brewton, 1992).

To make a successful case against an offender, cooperation is almost always necessary, as we noted in the discussion of OSHA investigations. Unmotivated, understaffed, underfunded enforcement agencies are not able to litigate even those few cases of corporate crime that actually come to their attention. As a result, the consent decree is the common remedy. Under the terms of a consent decree, a defendant corporation negotiates with the government over the violations the corporation has committed. It agrees to alter its pattern of conduct. In return, the government agrees that the company will not have to admit guilt. The company does not have to admit its culpability, but it does have to promise to stop committing the crime. The irony of this "sanction" is made clear by Peter Wickman and Phillip Whitten:

> Corporations that have been involved in polluting the environment sign consent decrees with the EPA and announce that they are working on the problem. Imagine the public reaction if a common street criminal were to be dealt with in this fashion. Here's the scene: Joe Thug is apprehended by an alert patrolman after mugging an eighty-five-year-old woman in broad daylight on the streets of Paterson, New Jersey. Brought down to police headquarters, he holds a press conference with the assistant police chief. While not admitting his guilt, he promises not to commit any future muggings and announces that he is working on the problem of crime in the streets. (Wickman & Whitten, 1980, p. 367)

No matter how serious the crime or how flagrant the violation, the fact is that severe sanctions are rarely applied in the case of corporate criminals. In their study, Clinard and Yeager found that the sanctions applied to corporate criminals were weak at best (Clinard & Yeager, 1980). The most common sanction was a warning (44 percent of the cases). Corporate criminals were assessed fines 23 percent of the time, although those fines were negligible. In 80 percent of the cases, they were for five thousand dollars or less—hardly a significant sanction to corporations earning billions of dollars a year. The Senate Governmental Affairs Subcommittee noted an even more disturbing fact. Over a thirty-month period, 32,000 fines levied against white-collar crime offenders had gone uncollected by the government. In only 1.5 percent of the cases was a corporate officer convicted of a crime, and in only 4 percent of those convictions did the offender go to jail. Even so, their terms of incarceration were very light—averaging thirty-seven days (Clinard & Yeager, 1980; Senate Permanent Subcommittee on Investigations, Committee on Governmental Affairs, 1983). This pattern appears to be consistent throughout United States history. Albert McCormick, Jr., studied antitrust cases brought by the Department of Justice from 1890–1969 and found that only 2 percent of the violators served any prison time at all (McCormick, 1977). . . .

A CRIMINAL MONOPOLY

Corporations in the United States have made the most of their ability to define the standards by which they are regulated. One hundred corporations, out of the approximately 200,000 operating in the United States, control 55 percent of all industrial assets in the United States. The largest 500 industrial corporations control 75 percent of all manufacturing assets. In the transportation and utilities industries 50 of the 67,000 corporations control two-thirds of the assets in the airline, railroad, communications, electricity, and gas industries. Only 50 of the approximately 15,000 banks in the United States control 64 percent of all banking assets. And in the insurance industry fifty of the roughly 2,000 companies control 80 percent of all insurance assets (Simon, 2002). Shared monopolies can now be found in the tire industry, aluminum industry, soap industry, tobacco industry, cereals, bread and flour, milk and dairy products, processed meats, canned goods, sugar, soups, and light bulbs.

Not only do a few corporations control most of the manufacturing capacity and wealth in the United States, but they have also entered into mutually cooperative exchanges. Chief executive officers of 233 of the 250 largest U.S. corporations sit on the board of directors of at least one of the other 250 largest corporations. In many cases, they participate in deciding policy for ostensibly competing corporations, which could be interpreted as a violation of the Clayton Antitrust Act of 1914 (Simon, 2002).

Corporate criminals engage in profiteering and theft, they endanger consumers and workers, and they defraud the state with relative immunity. And they do so with virtually no interference from those who are charged with the responsibility of exposing corruption in U.S. society. The predations of corporate criminals are given little attention by the news media, politicians, and even academics. Agencies funding research into crime are far more concerned about dubious data derived from urine tests on arrestees and unproven models attempting to predict career criminality among the poor than they are about the insidious nature of corporate crime.

The many of cases of wanton criminality discussed above represent only the tiniest tip of the corporate crime iceberg. For every successful prosecution of a corporate offender, there are literally thousands of others never caught or even investigated. For every corporate offender convicted of a crime, fined, or even jailed, there are hundreds of others who face only mild reprimands by the criminal justice system. Even more debilitating to the moral fabric of U.S. society is that for every corporate offender prosecuted and convicted of a criminal act there are thousands of others whose criminality is overlooked and whose profitability is celebrated as an example of the American dream of success. Millions of dollars in political contributions and millions of dollars spent on legislative lobbying have perverted the law-making process. Congress and legislatures focus on street crime and ignore or pass toothless regulations for corporations. For every corporate criminal tried and convicted, thousands of others escape prosecution because of the immense resources they can bring to bear in their defense, often overwhelming prosecutors and investigators.

CONCLUSION

Stanley Eitzen and Maxine Zinn (2004) argue that profit is so central to capitalism that many corporate decisions look only at the bottom line, without consideration for the consequences to customers and employees. Punishments for white-collar crime do not match the harm. The myths that corporate crime is unintentional and less costly results in differential treatment for certain offenders. There is a double standard of justice operating in the United States. Many states have "three strikes and you're out" laws for individuals, but corporate recidivists do not confront such intransigence. Eitzen and Zinn cite the example of General Electric Corporation. From 1990 to 2001, the company was fined 42 times and ordered to make restitution for crimes involving environmental violations, defense contracting fraud, consumer fraud, workplace safety, and employment discrimination.

If street criminals were guilty of so many repeat offenses, there would be calls for preventive detention (lock them up before they commit more crimes), automatic add-on sentences for being career criminals (keep them in jail so they can't commit more crime), as well as for stepped-up enforcement efforts (increased surveillance, sting operations, profiling). But does this happen when the criminal justice system confronts corporate crime? Are there calls for a massive crackdown on corporate violence? Do the police break down the front doors of Ford, General Motors, and General Electric in midnight raids? The answer is no. We make little effort to enforce the law against these criminals, and often subscribe to the myth that current laws are too severe and businesses are overregulated. In the few instances when we do bring charges, the punishment is essentially a slap on the wrist, especially if they agree to make changes—even if the pledges are never executed or enforced.

The available evidence on corporate crime leads to several clear conclusions. Criminality in the corporate sector is widespread and pervasive, and few corporate criminals are ever caught or prosecuted. Corporate criminals are recidivists; they commit crimes over and over again with great frequency. The label "career criminal" applies. When apprehended, these criminals are treated with kid gloves, warned, given small fines, or allowed to bargain out of prosecution altogether. In those very rare cases where they are convicted of a crime and sentenced to prison, they are treated with far more consideration and leniency than traditional offenders.

This evidence leads us inexorably to one more myth about the criminal justice system in the United States. Contrary to popular notions and official pronouncements, in opposition to slogans chiseled in marble on courthouses across the country, we do not have an equal system of justice. There are two very different justice systems. One is for the poor and defenseless, and the other is for the rich and powerful. The evidence speaks clearly. Our political institutions and our criminal justice system, in helping to perpetuate these myths about corporate crime, have institutionalized C. Wright Mills's "higher immorality."

DISCUSSION QUESTIONS

1. What do the authors mean by the phrase "neutralizing myths" as it applies to corporate crime? What are these myths?
2. A key argument made in this article is that corporate crime does far more harm to individuals and to society than does street crime. Do you think that most Americans believe this? Do you think the authors made their argument convincingly? Why or why not?

REFERENCES

Associated Press. (2003a, November 26). DeCoster given probation. *Globe Gazette*, p. 1.

Associated Press. (2003b, December 4). Police: Parents beat daughter to death with umbrella [Online]. Available: http://www.edition.cnn.com/2003/US/South/12/03/child.beatingdeath.ap/.

Barkan, S. (2001). *Criminology: A sociological understanding* (2nd ed.). Upper Saddle River, NJ: Prentice-Hall.

Barstow, D. (2003a, December 21). A trench caves in: A young worker is dead. Is it a crime? *New York Times*, p. 1.

Barstow, D. (2003b, December 22). When workers die. U.S. rarely seeks charges for deaths in workplace. *New York Times*.

Barstow, D. (2003c, December 23). California leads prosecution of employers in job deaths. *New York Times*, Sec. A, p. 1.

Barstow, D., & Bergman, L. (2003a, January 9). Dangerous business: A family's fortune, a legacy of blood and tears. *New York Times*, p. Al.

Barstow, D., & Bergman, L. (2003b, January 10). Deaths on the job, slaps on the wrist. *New York Times*, p. 1.

Barstow, D., & Bergman, L. (2003c, March 11). OSHA to address persistent violators of job safety rules. *New York Times*, p. A6.

Bauer, L., & Owens, S. (2004, May). *Justice expenditure and employment in the United States, 2001* (NCJ 202792). Washington, DC: Bureau of Justice Statistics, Office of Justice Programs.

Blanding, M. (2002, October). The invisible harvest. *Boston* magazine [Online]. Accessed June 18, 2004. Available: http://www.bostonmagazine.com/ArticleDisplay.php?id

Brewton, P. (1992). *Untold story.* New York: SPI Books.

Bureau of Labor Statistics. (2003). *Number and rates of fatal occupational injuries for select occupations, 2002.* Washington, DC: U.S. Government Printing Office.

Calavita, K., Pontell, H., & Tillman, R. (1999). *Big money crime: Fraud and politics in the savings and loan crisis.* Berkeley: University of California Press.

Clinard, M., & Yeager, P. (1980). *Corporate crime.* New York: Macmillan.

Corchado, A. (2002, July 2). Mexico settles lawsuit that alleged laborers worked in slavelike conditions in Maine. Knight Ridder Tribune News Service *(The Dallas Morning News).*

Corporate Crime Reporter. (1997a). June 2, 22(1).

Corporate Crime Reporter. (1997b). November 17, 44(4).

Corporate Crime Reporter. (1998). July 27, 30(1).

Corporate Crime Reporter. (1999). April 19, 16(3).

Corporate crime: The untold story. (1982, September 6). *U.S. News & World Report,* 25.

Daly, S. (2003, September 7). A tearful Great White, playing only with fog. *Washington Post,* p. Dl.

Donahue, J. (1992). The missing rap sheet: Government records on corporate abuses. *Multinational Monitor,* 14, 14–19.

Drutman, L. (2003, November 4). Corporate crime acts like a thief in the night. *Los Angeles Times,* p. B13.

Egg farm pays settlement to migrant workers. (2004, February 16). *Kennebec Journal* [Online]. Available: http://www.centralmaine.com/news/loca1/419172.shtml.

Eitzen, D. S., & Zinn, M. (2004). *Social problems* (9th ed.). Boston: Allyn & Bacon.

Epstein, S. S., & Young, Q D. (2003, June 17). Stark rise in childhood cancer: The sad truth about the stark rise in childhood cancer. *Chicago Tribune,* p. 17.

Federal Bureau of Investigation. (2003). Crime in the United States, 2002, uniform crime reports. Washington, DC: U.S. Department of Justice.

Greenhouse, S. (2004, January 18). Workers assail night lock-ins by Wal-Mart. *New York Times,* p. Al.

Gross, B. (1980). *Friendly fascism: the new face of fascism in America.* New York: M. Evans.

Hagan, E (2002). *Introduction to criminology* (5th ed.). Belmont, CA: Wadsworth.

Hamilton, W. (2002, July 13). Crisis in corporate America: more time for executive crime; already tougher sentencing rules may play big role in latest scandals. *Los Angeles Times,* p. C1.

Harden, B. (2004, February 24). Waste cleanup may have human price. *Washington Post,* p. Al.

Haygood, W. (2002, November 10). Still burning: After a deadly fire, a town's losses were just beginning. *Washington Post,* p. F1.

Kolko, G. (1963). *The triumph of conservatism.* New York: Free Press.

Maguire, K., & Pastore, A. (Eds.). (2003). *Sourcebook of criminal justice statistics 2002* [Online]. Available: http://www.albany.edu/sourcebook.

McCormick, A., Jr. (1977). Rule enforcement and moral indignation: Some observations on the effects of criminal antitrust convictions upon societal reaction process. *Social Problems,* 25, 30–39.

Meier, B. (2004, June 3). Two studies, two results, and a debate over a drug. *New York Times.*

Mills, C. W (1952). A diagnosis of moral uneasiness. In I. Horowitz (Ed.), *Power, politics and people* (pp. 330–339). New York: Ballantine.

Mokhiber, R., & Wheat, A. (1995, December). Shameless: 1995's 10 worst corporations. *Multinational Monitor, 16,* 12.

Norton, K. (2002). The investigation, indictment, incarceration and parole [Online]. Accessed June 19, 2004. Available: http://www.tcnj.edu/~white2/hamlet/essays/govt-legal05.html.

Occupational Safety and Health Administration. (2004). OSHA facts [Online]. Accessed June 21, 2004. Available: http://www.osha.gov/as/opa/oshafacts.html.

Pearce, F. (1976). *Crimes of the powerful: Marxism, crime and deviance.* London: Pluto. *Peek v. Florida,* 488 So. 2d 52, 56 (1986).

Pritchard, J. (2004, March 14). Mexican-born workers more likely to die on job; risky work, compliant attitude and language barrier contribute to the trend, AP study shows. *Los Angeles Times,* p. A1.

Reiman, J. (2004). *The rich get richer and the poor get prison* (7th ed.). Boston: Allyn & Bacon.

Rosoff, S., Pontell, H., & Tillman, R. (2004). *Profit without honor: White-collar crime and the looting of America* (3rd ed.). Upper Saddle River, NJ: Prentice-Hall.

Seibert, M. (2002, October 1). DeCoster to pay for alleged abuse. *Des Moines Register* [Online]. Accessed June 18, 2004. Available: http://www.desmoinesregister.com/news/stories/c4788993/19355746.html.

Senate Permanent Subcommittee on Investigations, Committee on Governmental Affairs. 98th Congress, First Session (August 13, 1983).

Simon, D. (2002). *Elite deviance* (7th ed.). Boston: Allyn and Bacon.

Sorid, D. (2004, March 19). Chip industry to probe cancer rates of workers. Reuters News Service. Available: http://nucnews.net/nucnews/2004nn/0403nn/040319nn.htm#642

Stone v. North Carolina Department of Labor, 347 NC 473 (81PA97), (1998).

Sutherland, E. (1949). *White collar crime.* New York: Holt, Rinehart and Winston.

Weinstein, J. (1968). *The corporate ideal in the liberal state: 1900–1918.* Boston: Beacon Press.

Wickman, P., & Whitten, P. (1980). *Criminology: Perspectives on crime and criminality.* Lexington, MA: DC Heath.

Zaun, T. (2004, June 3). Mitsubishi says it hid defects; recall is set. *New York Times.*

29.
PERFORMING BRIBERY IN CHINA: GUANXI-PRACTICE, CORRUPTION WITH A HUMAN FACE

LING LI

When deviance is institutionalized, but illegal, participants often must engage in ritualized forms of conduct (or "performance") in order to create the opportunity for "plausible deniability." Bribery is a prime example. The rituals involved are often not very challenging or strenuous because those in charge of enforcing the laws against corruption are often taking bribes as well. This article describes guanxi-practice in China. Guanxi-practice refers to a traditional management style in China where it is expected that personal relationships will bear on bureaucratic decision-making. This management style lends itself to widespread corruption as people offer bribes to bureaucrats in order to establish such relationships. Similar corruption runs rampant in many developing countries and often helps to explain the enormous gaps between rich and poor found in these countries.

. . . According to a survey among 100 people [in China], who were prosecuted for bribe-giving, 94.2% stated that they would "warm up the relationship" first before they would bribe with money.[1] The "warm-up" always starts with the offering of gifts or other gratuitous services for the benefit of the bribed and at the expense of the briber. Gifts foster a sense of indebtedness,[2] as experienced guanxi-practitioners often say: "The thing is half done once the gift is accepted."[3] When an official accepts a gift, it normally means that the official is willing to repay the debt to the gift-giver in their future encounters. Gift-giving has, therefore, almost become an expert skill of experienced guanxi-practitioners, such as the protagonist of *Celadon*.[4] [*Celadon* is a "quasi-autobiographical" novel written by a convicted "insider" that provides details about the world of guanxi-practice.] In analyzing this process of gift-giving, it is worthwhile to introduce the following themes.

CHOOSING A "GIFT"

A good gift draws the bribed into a relationship. A poor one repels the bribed and invites rejection. Zhang's first gift to Judge Hou, the case of liquor, is an example of a good gift. First of all, the gift is valuable: "It costs millions just for the trademark and formula;" yet, the fact that the product has not yet been put on the market results in a sense of ambiguity in terms of its value, which can be employed as a defense for any possible future corruption investigation. Zhang's meticulous deliberation impressed the judge, who responded in the book, "You really used your brain in choosing this gift. If people from the procuratorate ask about it, we can simply say I am helping you to conduct a pre-market customer evaluation."[5] Zhang's second gift, the tutorship for Judge Hou's son, was probably the most appreciated. It is not only because the service is of great value to the judge but also because it demonstrates Zhang's "sincere" care for the judge's family. Following that, the trust in the relationship between Zhang and the judge reached a high level. Zhang's third delivery, consequently, that of the cash, is no longer perceived as threatening and disturbing.

Evidently, what constitutes a good gift varies from case to case and from time to time. What was popular as a gift in the 1960s, such as a basket of eggs or a piece of fine cloth, will now be considered contemptible and inappropriate, even in rural villages. Twenty years ago banqueting in VIP chambers of restaurants used to be a popular inducement on its own. Nowadays it only serves as a "get-to-know-each-other" exercise.[6] The contemporary increase in the economic value of gifts seems to be commensurate with the increase in the GDP of the country. In recent years international luxury items have frequently appeared in the evidence lists in corruption prosecutions.[7] At the time of writing, prosecutors in Chongqing City had found more than 100 items of international designer clothes and 200 pairs of expensive shoes in the residence of a local official, who took bribes worth RMB1,600,000.[8] According to some studies, the rapid rise of consumption of luxury-products in China, being the third largest in the world,[9] is closely linked to the spreading of corruption.[10]

Choosing a good gift is not always easy. From a briber's viewpoint, the first issue to be decided is how much should be spent on the gift. It should not be too expensive so as to contain the briber's risk of economic loss in case the bribed official fails to deliver the expected service in the future. It certainly should not be too cheap to invite rejection either. A rule of thumb is that the value of the gift should be proportional to the value of the service that one has in mind to request. Two packs of cigarettes will be unlikely to go down well if one desires to obtain a public procurement contract worth millions. In fields where corruption takes place regularly, bribes are taken as regular kickbacks, the rate of which is more or less commonly understood by the "insiders."[11]

Once its value has been decided, the choice of the gift becomes easier to make. After all, the best gift is the gift most appreciated by its recipient. China is no longer an economy of acute scarcity. Ordinary commodities will hardly please sophisticated officials, who already enjoy various privileges and benefits. Some bribers spend a lot of time investigating and discovering the personal preferences of targeted officials. An interviewee told me in confidence: "One has to have some kind of hobby."[12] Many do. Mai Chongkai, former president of Guangdong High Court, was able to perfect his performance in golf-playing after having played on numerous golf-courses across the country, all as treats from his favor-seekers.[13] Hao Heping, the main character in the notorious national drug-safety scandal in 2007, once accepted three golf-club membership cards with a total value of RMB500,000 from pharmaceutical manufacturers in exchange for favors in license application.[14] During an anti-corruption campaign in 2000 in Guangdong province where 70 golf courses were in operation, 135 golf-club payment-cards were confiscated from officials and five officials were asked to resign from their honorary positions in various golf associations.[15]

Mahjiong, a popular gambling game in China, is also often used as a setting for bribing. For a long time, *mahjiong*-playing became a routine program of guanxi-practice after banquets. It is a service provided by almost all tea-houses, nightclubs or other entertaining establishments. While playing the game, bribers can bribe, for instance, by deliberately losing to the targeted official. Bribers call this game-playing yewupai (game-for-business),[16] since it is not really a gambling contest if one party contrives to lose. The only problem with this approach to bribing is that the bribed could also attribute his winning to his own good luck or good skill rather than to "generous help" from the briber. To avoid this kind of "misunderstanding," experienced bribers would organize a game for the targeted official with others and provide the official with the betting-money, instead of participating and deliberately losing. If the official wins, the briber would insist that the official keep the winnings as *"xinkufei,"* meaning allowance for the labor.[17] *"Yingle shi nide, shule shi wode"* (whatever won is yours, whatever lost is mine), as the briber would say. Bribing-through-gambling has become so popular that this approach to bribing was recently recognized and incorporated in the criminal law against bribery.[18] When some officials are no longer content with the challenge of traditional *mahjiong* games, they visit Macau, the closest place to mainland China where professional casinos legally operate.[19] One of the most notorious gamblers is Ma Xiangdong, former deputy mayor of Shenyang City, Liaoning Province, who visited Macau 17 times in a period of two and half years. When he lost all his bets, he called in "help" from his briber. Once, when a briber complained about the liquidity problem of his company, the deputy mayor, who was in charge of zoning and public construction, waived taxation worth RMB12 million for a construction project undertaken by the briber's company. In exchange, Ma was able to "borrow" from the briber US$500,000, all being spent in casinos.[20] Not surprisingly, these big-spending officials soon became the favorite clients of those casino-owners.[21]

In comparison to these gamblers, some officials are found to be amenable to artistic gratification. A few corporation executives once commissioned the State Orchestra to play a symphony composed by Wang Yi, former vice-chairman of the China Securities Regulatory Commission, who, "by accident," discovered his "talent" in composing in his late 40s during a trip to the Tibet Plateau.[22] Compared with Wang's hobby, art collection is more popular among "artistically minded" officials, which possibly coincides with a significant boost to the antique and art markets in China.[23] A director of a local police bureau in Wenzhou City, Zhejiang Province, had collected several hundred antique items as presents from "friends."[24] In a poorly monitored auction industry, pieces of art constitute a wise choice of bribe favored by some for their money-laundering function. The usual practice is that firstly the would-be bribed puts a piece of antique of little value up for auction and then the briber buys off the piece in the auction at the agreed price with the agreed terms of payment.[25] In another case discovered by prosecutors in Nanjing City, a real-estate developer bought two paintings directly from an official, who was in charge of state confiscation of land. The appraised value of the paintings was RMB3,000, whereas the developer paid RMB1,000,000.[26]

In general, gifts are preferred over pure money at the initial stage of guanxi-practice, when the trust is not yet strong. Meanwhile, a modern invention—the shopping-card (*gouwuka*, basically a voucher in the shape of a plastic card with a magnetic stripe, on which information regarding credit can be stored)—makes the perfect bridge between money and gift.[27] The State Council issued a regulation prohibiting shopping-card issuance in 2001 but the cards are simply too popular to be banned in practice.[28] Usually, such cards are issued by large shopping malls, which offer a wide range of product lines to satisfy the diversified needs of card holders. During one of my interviews, an owner of an intermediating company excused herself in the middle of the conversation and told me she had to rush off to deliver some shopping-cards as presents for the upcoming Spring Festival to her "patrons," who helped her in winning some public procurement biddings that her company represented.[29] According to a local procuratorate, 92% of the officials prosecuted for bribe-taking in its jurisdiction in 2007 had accepted shopping-cards from bribers, among whom one had taken as many as 45 cards, worth RMB110,000. None of these officials had rejected a shopping-card when it was offered to them.[30] Some officials are completely at ease when receiving piles of shopping cards but feel uncomfortable with cash.[31] A RMB5,000-bribe was rejected twice by a county official in Shandong Province but was accepted when the same amount was transferred onto a shopping-card delivered by the same briber.[32] Shopping-cards are accepted as a popular form of bribe because they provide recipients with the discretion to choose or consume the gifts at their own convenience. It is transferable and is accurate in value, which makes it much easier for both bribers and the bribed to register how much has been offered and accepted. In short, it is as good as money but without the latter's projection of venality.

ADDRESSING A "GIFT"

After a bribe has been chosen, the next step is the delivery. It is only at that point that one would realize that how to address the bribe becomes "an issue." As Noonan detected, "there is no specific, unambiguous word for bribe" and "no common terms designating and denigrating the briber and the bribee."[33] Bribers with some common sense would understand that a bribe should not be addressed as a "bribe" or explained as an "inducement" for an illicit service, since those words project dashing instrumentality of the briber and illegality to its recipient, who is the last person a briber wants to offend. As demonstrated in the story between Zhang and Judge Hou in *Celadon*, the choice of language is all important. Some words shall never be used in any circumstances. Some can be used only in relation to certain persons, with whom a trusting relationship has been established. Risk and trust are both subjective perceptions, which respond to the slightest observation of behavior. This is certainly the case in the Chinese culture, where reading between the lines is a regular communicative practice.[34] Therefore, when a term of reference to the bribe is required, a euphemism is indispensable. In all the cases investigated in this research, terms such as "bribe" (*huijin*), "bribery" (*huilu*), "bribe-giving/taking" (*xinghui/shouhui*) were never employed by bribery practitioners for self-references. In this context, the euphemism is probably the most noticeable behavioral pattern in the performance of bribery.

In the course of this research, the following common euphemisms have been found, for example, "*yanjiuqian*" (money for cigarettes and liquor), "*yidian xiaoyisi*" or "*yidian biaoshi*" (a little expression [of gratitude]) and *haochu* (benefits). Coded language is employed in circumstances where a higher degree of discreteness is required. For example, in one scene of delivery, a briber pointed to a shopping bag and said to Tang Jikai, former vice-president of Changsha Intermediate Court, "there is *mi* (refers to cash but literally means rice) in it."[35] Euphemisms are also applied when bribers talk about their own act of bribery to a third party. . . . The most frequently used phrases include *"dadian,"*[36] *"goudui"*[37] and most notable of all, the "guanxi-practice" expressions as listed in the introduction of this paper. These "guanxi-practice" expressions include, for instance, *"zou guanxi"* (go through guanxi), *"tuo guanxi"* (to do something through guanxi), *"guanxi yunzuo"* (operation of guanxi), *"huodong guanxi"* (to activate guanxi), etc.[38] In some public sectors, in which corruption is pervasive and bribery a common practice, euphemisms become less evasive: *"xiaoyisi"* (a little expression) is substituted by comparatively more direct terms, such as, *"haochufei"* (benefit-fee) or *"xinkufei"* (fee for the labor), which suggest what is offered is payment for a service.[39]

In general, we use euphemisms when we are reluctant to utter some semantically transparent terms to denote unsettling topics.[40] In the account of bribery, nothing is more "unsettling" than the concept of corruption and any normative terms related to it. Not to rub something into the face of the bribed is the least a briber can do and the least that would be expected from him by the bribed.[41] There is little doubt that no briber wants to present himself as offensive or threatening when he is at the mercy of the bribed.

ACCEPTANCE OF A "GIFT"

Sometimes when the bribed official has difficulties to settle with a venal image, only employing euphemisms will not be sufficient for the bribe to be accepted. This is especially the case when an official is offered a bribe for the first time.[42] Under such a circumstance, further persuasion becomes necessary. According to a survey among 100 officials who were prosecuted for bribe-taking, the most convincing persuasions are "This is what you deserve. Don't be too humble" and "you are not giving me face if you don't accept it."[43] Another common but somewhat circuitous tactic consists of setting up an imaginary straw man first and then to claim that the bribe is to cover the expense of engaging the straw man rather than the bribed to carry out the necessary corrupt acts. For example, one of my interviewees reported that she had once invited an official to dinner, to whom she had submitted an application for a residence permit. After dinner she handed the official an envelope containing cash. At first, the official declined to accept it. My interviewee insisted, saying, "Please take it. What I requested is not an easy task. This (the money in the envelope) is not for you but for you to *dadian* [44] other officials. This is just to cover your expenses."[45] As she expected, the envelope was then accepted.

The auction house owner Zhang in *Celadon* excelled in this art of performance. In order to avoid possible rejection of the gift or gratuity that he offered, Zhang always thoughtfully provided the judge with alternative reasons for acceptance, thereby neutralizing the venality projected by the gift. For example, during his first visit, Zhang stage-managed the scene by carrying the heavy liquor-case all the way up to the judge's apartment on the seventh floor. When the judge saw Zhang appear at his doorstep, next to the liquor-case, breathing heavily, the judge said, "I shall accept your kind intent . . . If I don't accept your gift and insist that you carry it all the way back downstairs, you would curse me in your mind, wouldn't you?" In this twisted discourse, it looks as though the judge had decided to accept the gift not because it was a gift which he would actually enjoy having but because he did not want to be *"bujin renqing"* (behaving without any consideration for the other party). In fact, the judge appeared to be actually doing Zhang a favor by accepting his gift.

Great resemblance is found in a similar speech by the Empress Dowager over a century ago when she accepted gifts at her extravagant 60th birthday party, which took mandarins two years to prepare. Having announced previously that she did not want anything costly in view of the hardship of foreign wars inflicted upon the country at that moment, nevertheless, the Empress decided to take the treasures sent in from all corners of the country. In her acceptance speech, she said, "The gifts were presented by officials, who want to comply with tradition. Their intent is sincere. If I don't accept them . . . it will be me being unreasonable . . . I will grant them a favor and accept the gifts."[46]

In order to reduce the venality of bribe-taking, many bribers choose to deliver the gifts at traditional holidays or other ritual occasions, including weddings and funerals in the family of the targeted official, when gifts are customarily exchanged. According to the aforementioned survey conducted by Haizhu Procuratorate among 100 bribers, 45.8% of the respondents said they would choose to bribe during the spring festival.[47] Such occasions seem to have provided more legitimacy to cash bribes, addressed as *"lijin"* (gift-money) wrapped in red envelopes (*hongbao*). When the competition for favor is intense, in order to maintain a good relationship with the targeted official, bribers feel compelled to send *hongbao* on any occasion which entails financial costs for the family of the targeted official, such as traveling, illness, moving, and the start of school-terms of the official's children. According to the same survey among 100 bribers mentioned above, 50.2% of the respondents had chosen to bribe during the months of August and September, the time of the commencement of new school terms.[48]

For risk-conscious officials, whether to accept a bribe does not only involve an issue as to what is offered but also as to who offers it. According to the previously mentioned survey among bribe-taking officials, 80% of the respondents stated that they would choose to accept bribes selectively depending on who the bribers were. Some 47% chose to accept from "people who look loyal and trust-worthy;" 40% chose to accept from "people who look rich."[49] The weight of these "extra variables" increases as the value of the public resources that an official is entrusted to allocate increases. This is because these officials are usually "chased after" by many bribers.[50] Hence they can afford to be "picky" and choose to exchange only with bribers, who are not only generous with "gifts" but also have "likable" disposition. It will be overambitious to attempt to generalize the qualities required for "likableness." However, in the context of bribery, a few characteristics are quite identifiable, for example, generosity, loyalty and discreetness, all as indications of whether the briber is likely to act opportunistically. This is exactly why, in situations where guanxi-practice is called for, the participants would emphasize the importance of the quality of the personal relationship between the favor-seeker and the favor-grantor. This is also why "guanxi-practice" phrases are named after the word "guanxi," which indicates the existence of a personal relationship. The quality of this relationship (guanxi) is a variable that affects the decision of the person concerned on whether he would engage in a certain exchange. . . .

CONCLUSION

By investigating the interactions between bribers and the bribed in the process of initiating corrupt transactions, this paper finds that the illegality of corruption compels its practitioners to resort to "alternative operating mechanisms" to break down the legal, moral and cognitive barriers so that the contracting process can proceed. Guanxi-practice functions exactly as this "alternative operating mechanism." It facilitates the contracting process of an illegal transaction not only by minimizing the otherwise prohibitively high transactional costs created by the legal barrier, but also by removing the moral and cognitive constraints of the bribed. Gifts, its main prop, are used as an initial payment from the briber, to demonstrate the briber's commitment, to close his distance to the targeted official and to set up an alternative social context, in which the exchange activities can be rationalized and redefined. Performed with tactics and etiquettes, guanxi-practice seamlessly grafts a corrupt and legally unenforceable agreement upon a social setting, in which venality is neutralized and rationalized. In this re-defined social reality of corruption, an instrumental relationship is perceived or at least presented as a reciprocal relationship based on social commitment.

Therefore, this paper contends that corruption, in particular bribery, is not a "cold," "impersonal" transaction, oriented at immediate short-term gain, but an exchange with a rather "human" interface between its practitioners, which is designed to prepare the bribed to overcome the legal, moral and cognitive barriers that will otherwise obstruct the exchange from taking place. Furthermore, this paper postulates that the causality link between guanxi-practice and corruption is the inverse of the view held by many. It is not that the participants of corruption are compelled to corrupt conduct because of the existence of certain reciprocal relationship, but on the contrary, these participants adopt guanxi-practice as an enabling operating mechanism that facilitates corruption. In this sense, guanxi-practice is not only "fuelling" corruption, but it is a necessary and integral part of corruption in China.

It is rather ironic that contrary to the views advanced by some Western China scholars, who attempt to distinguish gifts from bribes, and guanxi-practice from corruption, guanxi-practitioners are striving to blur these boundaries. The very existence of equivocation, excuses and camouflage, so characteristic of guanxi-practice, demonstrates a shared sense of awareness of the illegality and impropriety of the conduct. Were it not for this awareness, such a heavy-loaded masquerade would be meaningless. In fact, the very term of "guanxi-practice" is a euphemism, used to conceal the confrontation with the "unsettling topic" of corruption.

As some authors pertinently observed, with corruption embedded in the deep-rooted social institution of guanxi-practice, the elimination of the corrupt mechanism through a formal legal system is a "Herculean task."[51] It is difficult to ascertain whether it is corruption that is embedded in the guanxi institution or the converse since both have a long tradition in Chinese history. What can be ascertained, however, is that by being connected to the social institution of guanxi-practice, corruption has become institutionalized as well. This institutionalization stabilizes and facilitates corrupt transactions. The roles of corrupt participants are structurally assigned and assumed and the acts of these participants are governed by their own codes of conduct. Through this endogenous process, corruption develops a life of its own, capable of "mutation" and adjustment to the changing external environments, and of survival in the battles waged against it in China.

DISCUSSION QUESTION

1. Bribery and other forms of corruption are part of business-as-usual in many developing countries around the world. As we have seen in this book, those who break the law are often able to

neutralize their deviance and see nothing wrong with what they are doing. This is probably all the more the case with the type of institutionalized corruption described in this article. List as many reasons as you can think of as to why such corruption can be harmful.

NOTES

1. According to the survey report, 85 of the 100 persons responded. The survey was conducted by Haizhu District Procuratorate in Guangdong Province in collaboration with the Clean Politics and Governance Research Center of Qsinghua University: Gufeng Huang and Rui Li, *Haizhuqu Jianchayuan Dui Xinghui Renyuan De Wenjuan Diaocha Baogao [Survey Report of Bribe-Giving Conducted by Haizhu District Procuratorate]*, (2006).
2. Marcel Mauss, **The Gift**, trans. Ian Cunnison (New York: Norton, 1967).
3. This is a statement that the author heard very often during her fieldwork in China.
4. Popular self-help books can be easily found on how to have your gifts accepted. By searching on the online bookstore, www.dangdang.com, the key word "gift-offering" (*songli*) produces 203 results. If one puts in the words "*lingdao*" (superior) and "*songli*" (gift-giving) in the search column of www.baidu.com, suggested topics include "how to give gifts to [your] superior," "what gifts to give to [your] superior," "what to say when presenting a gift to [your] superior," "skills of gift-giving to [your] superior," etc.
5. Fushi, *Qingci [Celadon]* (Changsha: Hunan Wenyi, 2006), ch. 2, p. 18.
6. Interview T.028.
7. Just to name two examples, see the case of Wang Xuebing, former Chairman of China Construction Bank, and the case of Mu Suixin, former Mayor of Shenyang City, Liaoning Province.
8. See http://news.xinhuanet.com/legal/2008-12/16/content_10510994.htm.
9. It is estimated that China will consume 29% of the world's luxury goods by 2015, making it second only to Japan: http://seekingalpha.com/article/81603-luxury-products-in-china.
10. See http://service.china.org.cn/link/wcm/Show_Text?info_id ¼ 128850&p_qry ¼ SARS.
11. For example, according to an internal analytical report on judicial corruption by Huang Jianliang, a journalist of *The Procuratorate Daily*, some "customary practice" (*hanggui*) has developed among participants of corruption in courts. For instance, the distributing ratio of profit gained from court auctions is known to be 4:3:3, which means that 40% goes to judges involved, 30% goes to the auction house and 30% is spent on expenses of running costs and the cost to "*dadian*," other officials on contingent issues. An excerpt of the report can be seen at http://news .sohu.com/20061202/n246751848.shtml.
12. Interview T.028.
13. See http://www.southcn.com/news/gdnews/gdtodayimportant/200312200081.htm.
14. See http://sports.sohu.com/20070612/n250528660.shtml.
15. See http://news.xinhuanet.com/house/2004-05/25/content_1489203.htm.
16. *Celadon* [see note 5] has an elaborated description of such a scene in Chapter 3.
17. "Former Chief-prosecutor bribe-taking in gambling games and was sentenced for 8.5 years" (29 August 2007), available at: http://news.china.com/zh_cn/domestic/945/20061029/13707123_3 .html. Also see the Defendant's Statement in the public prosecution against Tian Zixiang, the Director of the Appraisal Center of Agricultural Machinery.
18. *Guanyu Banli Shouhui Xingshi Anjian Shiyong Falü Ruogan Wenti De Yijian [Opinions on the Prosecution and Adjudication on Cases of Bribe-Taking]*, jointly issued by the Supreme People's Court and the Supreme Procuratorate in 2007, Art. 5.

19. See report available at: http://news.tom.com/1002/3291/2005121-1785942.html. Also see "Chinese officials 'lost millions'," BBC News (10 January 2009), available at: http://news.bbc.co.uk/1/hi/world/asia-pacific/7821747.stm.

20. Court judgment: Nanjing City Procuratorate vs. Ma Xiangdong, Criminal Division, Nanjing Intermediate Court [2001], no. 110.

21. See report available at: http://www.chinanews.com.cn/zhonghuawenzhai/2001-04-01/new/(12)%201.html.

22. See the link http://www.caijing.com.cn/2008-06-12/100069029.html.

23. For a brief history of the development of the art market in China since the economic reform, see http://www.china.com.cn/culture/txt/2008-11/30/content_16875708.htm.

24. See http://www.zjol.com.cn/05zjc/system/2006/11/04/007969601.shtml.

25. See http://finance.sina.com.cn/money/collection/yspmarket/20050413/11231513614.shtml; also see http://www.cnhubei.com/200502/ca691716.htm.

26. See http://news.xinhuanet.com/legal/2008-02/26/content_7670023.htm.

27. The shopping card is so popular that an online market of swapping and exchanging has been established in some cities. To name just a few, see http://shop.nnsky.com/zhuanti/card/card.asp (for shopping-cards issued in Nanning city); http://bj.fenlei168.com/F_MaiMai/17B457S0Q0S0S0S0S0B0Z1.html (for Beijing); and http://sz.ganji.com/gouwuka/ (for Shenzhen).

28. See *Notification of the Termination of Issuance and Circulation of Shopping Vouchers*, (2001), Issued by the Ministry of Economy and Trade, The People's Bank and the Jiufeng Office of the State Council.

29. Interview M.033.

30. Jinzeng Lu, *Shopping-Card Induces Civil Servant Crimes [Gouwuka Yi Youfa Zhiwu Fanzui]*, available at: http://www.jcrb.com/200707/ca616445.htm.

31. See prosecutors' commentary, available at: http://news.xinhuanet.com/legal/2008-02/19/content_7627862.htm.

32. Interview M.033.

33. John T. Noonan, *Bribes* (University of California Press, 1984).

34. Bob Hodge and Kam Louie, *The Politics of Chinese Language and Culture: The Art of Reading Dragons* (London and New York: Routledge, 1998), ch. 5, pp. 96–119. Ambiguity of the Chinese language as a linguistic feature was discussed in the following literature: Matthew Ricci, *China in the Sixteenth Century: The Journals of Matthew Ricci 1583–1610* (New York: Random House, 1953); Hui-ching Chang, "The 'well-defined' is 'ambiguous'—indeterminacy in Chinese conversation," *Journal of Pragmatics* 31, (1999); Q. S. Tong, "Inventing China—The use of orientalist views on the Chinese language," Interventions 2(1), (2000).

35. Court Judgment: *Ruanling County Procuratorate vs. Tang Jikai*, 2nd instance, Huaihua Intermediate Court [2006], no. 52.

36. Among these expressions, *dadian* is the only one that was inherited from imperial times and is still popularly applied. The term "*dadian guanxi*" produced 2,120,000 results when searched on www.baidu.com (8 December2007). If one expands the search and includes terms such as "*shangxia* (literally means up and down) *dadian*," "*qianhou* (literally means front and back) *dadian*," the number of hits will be even higher.

37. The term was originally used to refer to wine blending. This evolved meaning is more popularly used in the southwest of China.

38. As a linguistic phenomenon, the semantic meaning of "guanxi" in these phrases has evolved beyond "a status of relatedness" and become an independent entity by itself, which the practitioners can "operate," "activate" and "do something through."

39. These terms repetitively appeared in the cases investigated in this research and can be easily located incorruption reports in the media.

40. Matthew S. McGlone and Jennifer A. Batchelor, "Looking out for number one: Euphemism and face," *Journal of Communication* 53(2), (2003), p. 251.

41. Experiments also found that instead of concern for the addressee's feelings, speakers apply euphemisms "out of concern for themselves for self-presentational purposes" (*Ibid*).

42. Gufeng Huang and Rui Li, *Haizhuqu Jianchayuan Dui Xinghui Renyuan De Wenjuan Diaocha Baogao.*

43. *Ibid.*

44. See Court Judgment: *Ruanling County Procuratorate vs. Tang Jikai,* 2nd instance, Huaihua Intermediate Court [2006], no. 52.

45. Interview H.022.

46. Hengjun Ren, *Rules in the Officialdom of Late Qing Dynasty [Wanqing Guanchang Guize Yanjiu]* (Haikou:Hainan, 2003), pp. 125–126.

47. See http://www.csonline.com.cn/news/chsh/200608/t20060806_504840.htm.

48. *Ibid.*

49. Gufeng Huang and Rui Li, *Haizhuqu Jianchayuan Dui Xinghui Renyuan De Wenjuan Diaocha Baogao.*

50. For example, Xu Guoyuan, former mayor of Chifeng City, confessed that people who had bribed him were so many that it was easier for him to recollect the names of those who had not bribed him rather than those who had. See http://china.huanqiu.com/roll/2009-08/534042.html.

51. Matthias Schramm and Markus Taube, "Private ordering of corrupt transactions," in Johann Graf Lambsdorffet al., eds, *The New Institutional Economics of Corruption: Norms, Trust, and Reciprocity* (London: Routledge, 2004), p. 193.

30.

THE CUNNING OF HISTORY: BUREAUCRATIC DOMINATION AND THE HOLOCAUST

RICHARD L. RUBENSTEIN

The age-old question with regard to the Holocaust has been "How could it have happened?" How could loving fathers and sons and law-abiding citizens turn into such "monsters" and engage in the cruelest behavior imaginable? In the following selection Richard Rubenstein draws upon the work of the preeminent sociologist Max Weber to explain the Holocaust. Weber saw bureaucratic organization to be one of the most significant developments in modern civilization. Bureaucracies reduce human labor to very specific and precise mechanical routines. This process consolidates the power of those at the top of the bureaucratic hierarchy who specify the routines workers must follow and enhances the efficiency of the bureaucracy as workers become more specialized in their routines. But in the process, workers lose their capacity to engage creatively with their work and they are transformed into mindless, replaceable parts in the bureaucratic machine. Rubenstein argues that the Nazis refined this process and it is the ensuing depersonalization of the workplace that made the Holocaust possible. Rubenstein portends a future when another holocaust is possible because bureaucratic organizational structures remain an entrenched part of the modern social landscape.

Usually the progress in death-dealing capacity achieved in the twentieth century has been described in terms of technological advances in weaponry. Too little attention has been given to the advances in social organization that allowed for the effective use of the new weapons. In order to understand how the moral barrier was crossed that made massacre in the millions possible, it is necessary to consider the importance of bureaucracy in modern political and social organization. The German sociologist Max Weber was especially cognizant of its significance. Writing in 1916, long before the Nazi party came to prominence in German politics, Weber observed:

> When fully developed, bureaucracy stands . . . under the principle of *sine ira ac studio* (without scorn and bias). *Its specific nature which is welcomed by capitalism develops the more perfectly the more bureaucracy is "dehumanized,"* the more completely it succeeds in eliminating from official business love, hatred,

and all purely personal, irrational and emotional elements which escape calculation. *This is the specific nature of bureaucracy and it is appraised as its special virtue.*"[1] (Italics added.)

Weber also observed:

> The decisive reason for the advance of bureaucratic organization has always been its purely technical superiority over any other kind of organization. *The fully developed bureaucratic mechanism compares with other organizations exactly as does the machine with the nonmechanical modes of organization.*
>
> Precision, speed, unambiguity, knowledge of the files, continuity, discretion, unity, strict subordination, reduction of friction and of material and personal costs—these are raised to the optimum point in the strictly bureaucratic organization."[2] (Italics added.)

Weber stressed "the fully developed bureaucratic mechanism." He was aware of the fact that actual bureaucracies seldom achieve the level of efficiency of the "ideal type" he had constructed.[3] Nevertheless, he saw clearly that bureaucracy was a machine capable of effective action and was as indifferent to "all purely personal . . . elements which escape calculation" as any other machine.

In his time Karl Marx looked forward to the eventual domination of the proletariat over the body politic because of its indispensability to the working process. Max Weber was convinced that political domination would rest with whoever controlled the bureaucratic apparatus because of its indisputable superiority as an instrument for the organization of human action. But, to the best of my knowledge, even Weber never entertained the possibility that the police and civil service bureaucracies could be used as a death machine to eliminate millions who had been rendered superfluous by definition. Even Weber seems to have stopped short of foreseeing state-sponsored massacres as one of the "dehumanized" capacities of bureaucracy.

Almost from the moment they came to power, the Nazis understood the bureaucratic mechanism they controlled. When they first came to power, there were a large number of widely publicized bullying attacks on Jews throughout Germany, especially by the SA, the brown-shirted storm troopers. However, it was soon recognized that improperly organized attacks by individuals or small groups actually hindered the process leading to administrative massacre. The turning from sporadic bullying to systematic anonymous terror paralleled the decline in influence of the SA and the rise of Heinrich Himmler and the SS. Himmler does not seem to have been a sadist. During the war, he did not like to watch killing operations and became upset when he did.[4] But, *Himmler was the perfect bureaucrat.* He did what he believed was his duty *sine ira et studio*, without bias or scorn. He recognized that the task assigned to his men, mass extermination, was humanly speaking exceedingly distasteful. On several occasions, he praised the SS for exercising an obedience so total that they overcame the feelings men would normally have when engaged in mass murder. The honor of the SS, he held, involved the ability to overcome feelings of compassion and achieve what was in fact perfect bureaucratic objectivity.[5]

Himmler objected to private acts of sadism, but his reasons were organizational rather than moral. He understood that individual and small group outbursts diminished the efficiency of the SS. One of his most important "contributions" to the Nazi regime was to encourage the systematization of SS dominance and terror in the concentration camps. At the beginning of Hitler's rule, Himmler, as head of the SS, was subordinate to Ernst Rohm, the head of the SA, the storm troopers. Himmler's position was transformed when Hitler ordered Rohm murdered on June 30, 1934. He ceased to be a subordinate. In the aftermath of the Rohm *Putsch,* there was a general downgrading of the SA. SA guards were removed from the concentration camps. Their places were taken by Himmler's SS.[6] By 1936 Himmler was appointed *Reichsfuhrer SS* and *Chef der Deutschen Polizei.* He then dominated the entire German police apparatus.

One of the examples of Himmler's organizing ability was his involvement in the concentration camp at Dachau which he founded in 1933. Originally, there was little to distinguish Dachau from any of the early "wild" Nazi camps. Under Himmler's guidance, Dachau became a model for the systematically managed camps of World War II. Under his direction, the sporadic terror of the "wild" camps was replaced by impersonal, systematized terror. Much of the systematization was carried out with Himmler's approval by Theodor Eicke who became commandant at Dachau in June 1933.[7] Eicke had spent most of his career in police administration. His organization of the camp was modern and professional. His "discretionary camp regulations," issued on October 1, 1933, provided for a strictly graded series of punishments including solitary confinement and both corporal and capital punishment for offending prisoners. When corporal punishment was inflicted, Eicke's directives provided that the punishment be carried out by several SS guards in the presence of the other guards, the prisoners and the commandant. In a report dated May 8, 1935, Eicke's successor as Dachau commandant wrote to Himmler that individual guards were "forbidden to lay hands on a prisoner or to have private conversations with them."[8] The intent of Eicke's regulations was to eliminate all arbitrary punishment by individual guards and to replace it with impersonal, anonymous punishment. The impersonal nature of the transaction was heightened by the fact that any guard could be called on to inflict punishment. Even if a guard was struck by a prisoner, he could not retaliate personally, at least insofar as the regulations were concerned. Like everything else at the camps, under Himmler punishment was bureaucratized and depersonalized. Bureaucratic mass murder reached its fullest development when gas chambers with a capacity for killing two thousand people at a time were installed at Auschwitz. As Hannah Arendt has observed, the very size of the chambers emphasized the complete depersonalization of the killing process.[9]

Under Himmler, there was no objection to cruelty, provided it was disciplined and systematized. This preference was also shared by the German civil service bureaucracy. According to Hilberg, the measure that gave the civil service bureaucrats least difficulty in exterminating their victims was the imposition of a starvation diet.[10] In a bureaucratically controlled society where every individual's ration can be strictly determined, starvation is the ideal instrument of "clean" violence. A few numbers are manipulated on paper in an office hundreds of miles away from the killing centers and millions can be condemned to a prolonged and painful death. In addition, both the death rate and the desired level of vitality of the inmates can easily be regulated by the same bureaucrats. As starvation proceeds, the victim's appearance is so drastically altered that by the time death finally releases him, he hardly seems like a human being worth saving. The very manner of death confirms the rationalization with which the killing was justified in the first place. The Nazis assigned the paranthropoid identity of *a Tiermensch,* a subhuman, to their victims. By the time of death that identity seemed like a self-fulfilling prophecy. Yet, the bureaucrat need lose no sleep over his victims. He never confronts the results of his distinctive kind of homicidal violence.

A crucial turning point in the transformation of outbursts of hatred into systematized violence occurred in the aftermath of the infamous *Kristallnacht*, the Nazi anti-Jewish riots of November 10, 1938. It is generally agreed that the riots were an unsuccessful attempt on the part of Propaganda Minister Joseph Goebbels and the SA to gain a role in the anti-Jewish process. On November 9, 1938, a young Jew, Herschel Grynzpan assassinated Legationsrat Ernst vom Rath in the German embassy in Paris. At Goebbels's instigation, SA formations set out to burn down every synagogue in Germany.[11] Jewish stores were burned and looted and Jews were attacked throughout the country.

The SS was not informed that the operation was to take place. When Himmler heard that Goebbels had instigated a pogrom, he ordered the detention of twenty thousand Jews in concentration camps under his control and ordered the police and the SS to prevent widespread looting. According to Hilberg, Himmler dictated a file memorandum in which *he* expressed his distaste for the Goebbels pogrom.[12]

In the wake of the *Kristallnacht*, there was widespread negative reaction against the pogrom from such leading Nazis as Goering, Economy Minister Walter Funk and the German Ambassador to the United States, Hans Dieckhoff.[13] Goering was especially vehement in his opposition to *Einzelaktionen*, undisciplined individual actions. He expressed his opposition to pogroms and riots which led to unfavorable foreign repercussions and which permitted the mob to run loose. Goering's feelings were shared by the entire German state bureaucracy. This was simply not the way to "solve" the Jewish problem. According to Hilberg, the effect of the Nazi outrages of the thirties on the state bureaucracy was to convince the Nazi and the non-Nazi bureaucrats alike that measures against the Jews had to be taken in a rational organized way.[14] Every step in the *methodical* elimination of the Jews had to be planned and carried out in a thoroughly *disciplined* manner. Henceforth, there would be neither emotional outbursts nor improvisations. The same meticulous care that goes into the manufacture of a Leica or a Mercedes was to be applied to the problem of eliminating the Jews. *Kristallnacht* was the last occasion when Jews had to fear street violence in Germany. Henceforth no brown-shirted bullies would assail them. Hilberg points out that when a decree was issued in September 1941 requiring Jews to wear the yellow star, Martin Bormann, the Chief of the Party Chancellery, issued strict orders against the molestation of the Jews as beneath the dignity of the Nazi movement.[15] "Law and order" prevailed. There were no further state-sponsored incidents. The hoodlums were banished and the bureaucrats took over. Only then was it possible to contemplate the extermination of millions. A machinery was set up that was devoid of both love and hatred. *It was only possible to overcome the moral barrier that had in the past prevented the systematic riddance of surplus populations when the project was taken out of the hands of bullies and hoodlums and delegated to bureaucrats.*

When Max Weber wrote about bureaucratic domination, he did not have the Nazis in mind, nor was he proposing a prescription for slaughter. Yet, almost everything Weber wrote on the subject of bureaucracy can in retrospect be read as a description of the way the bureaucratic heirarchies of the Third Reich "solved" their Jewish problem. . . .

In the case of the German Jews, the Nazis used a very simple bureaucratic device to strip them of citizenship. On November 25, 1941 the Reich Citizenship Law was amended to provide that a Jew "who takes up residence abroad" was no longer a Reich national.[16] The property of such persons was to be confiscated by the state. Thus, as soon as the SS transported Jews beyond the

German border, no matter how unwilling the Jews were to be "transported," they lost all rights as German nationals. No government anywhere was concerned with what happened to them. The last legal impediment to dealing with them in any fashion the German government elected had been removed.

Men without political rights are superfluous men. They have lost all right to life and human dignity. Political rights are neither God-given, autonomous nor self-validating. The Germans understood that no person has any rights unless they are guaranteed by an organized community with the power to defend such rights. They were perfectly consistent in demanding that the deportees be made stateless before being transported to the camps. They also understood that *by exterminating stateless men and women, they violated no law because such people were covered by no law.* Even those who were committed by religious faith to belief in natural law, such as the hierarchy of the Roman Catholic Church, did not see fit to challenge the Nazi actions publicly at the time.

Once the Germans had collected the stateless, rightless, politically superfluous Jews, they exercised a domination over them more total than was ever before exercised in history by one people over another. In the past, political or social domination was limited by the ruler's or the slaveholder's need to permit at least a minimal level of subsistence for his charges. The dominated almost always had some economic value for their masters. Until the twentieth-century camps, there were few situations in which masses of dominated men and women were as good as dead, cut off from the land of the living, and, at the same time, of no long-term use to their masters. Furthermore, the SS knew that in occupied, overpopulated Europe the supply of superfluous, totally dominated people was almost inexhaustible. All that was required, should the supply of Jews be depleted, was the setting apart of other categories of men and women to be condemned to the camps. There is abundant evidence that such indeed was the intention of the Germans. Hilberg quotes a letter written by Otto Thierack, the German minister of justice, on October 13, 1942:

> With a view to freeing the German people of Poles, Russians, Jews and Gypsies, and with a view to making the eastern territories which have been incorporated into the Reich available for settlement by German nationals, I intend to turn over criminal jurisdiction over Poles, Russians, Jews and Gypsies to the *Reichsfuhrer-SS* (Himmler). In so doing, I stand on the principle that the administration of justice can make only a small contribution to the extermination of these peoples.[17]

The minister of justice regarded the concentration camps as a place in which to execute such policies for which the normal judicial procedures could make "only a small contribution." He also understood that the scope of the extermination policy was not to be restricted to Jews.

For the first time in history, a ruling elite in the heart of Europe, the center of Western civilization, had an almost inexhaustible supply of men and women with whom they could do anything they pleased, irrespective of any antique religious or moral prejudice. The Nazis had created a society of total domination. Among the preconditions for such a society are: (a) a bureaucratic administration capable of governing with utter indifference to the human needs of the inmates; (b) a supply of inmates capable of continuous replenishment; (c) the imposition of the death sentence on every inmate as soon as he or she enters. Unless the supply is more or less inexhaustible, the masters will be tempted to moderate their treatment of the inmates because of their labor value. If the supply is capable of replenishment, the masters can calculate the exact rate at which they wish to work the prisoners before disposing of them. Both use and riddance can be calculated in terms of the masters' requirements, with only minimal concern for the survival requirements of the slaves. Furthermore, there must be no hope that any inmate might eventually return to normal life. Total domination cannot be achieved if camp guards are apprehensive that some of the inmates might be persons to be reckoned with at some future time. Such cautionary calculation could inhibit the extremities of behavior the camp personnel might otherwise indulge in. The Germans were able to create a society of total domination because of the competence of their police and civil service bureaucracies and because they possessed millions of totally super- fluous men whose lives and sufferings were of absolutely no consequence to any power secular or sacred and who were as good as dead the moment they entered the camps.

DISCUSSION QUESTION

1. Rubenstein implicates the development of modern bureaucratic organizational structures as making the Holocaust possible and he predicts these structures make another holocaust pos- sible. Do events taking place since World War II add to or detract from his argument? Explain your answer.

NOTES

1. Weber, "Bureaucracy" in *From Max Weber: Essays in Sociology*, trans. and ed. H. H. Gerth and C. Wright Mills (New York: Oxford University Press, 1946), pp. 215–16.
2. *Ibid.*, p. 214.
3. For Weber's discussion of his use of ideal types, see Weber, "Religious Rejections of the World and Their Directions" in Gerth and Mills, *From Max Weber*, pp. 323–24. For a further discussion of Weber's use of ideal types, see Talcott Parsons, Introduction to Max Weber, *The Sociology of Religion*, trans. Ephraim Fischoff (Boston: Beacon, 1963), pp. lxv f. Reinhard Bendix, *Max Weber: An Intellectual Portrait*, (Garden City, NY: Doubleday, 1960), pp. 278 ff. Julien Freund, *The Sociol- ogy of Max Weber*, trans. Mary Ilford (New York: Pantheon, 1970), pp. 59–71.
4. The root of Himmler's behavior is succinctly characterized by Manvell and Fraenkel, *Himmler*, p. 183: "Himmler was a man of violence, not by nature, but by conviction." For a description of Himmler's reaction to actual killing, see Raul Hilberg, *The Destruction of the European Jews* (Chicago: Quadrangle Books, 1967), pp. 218 f.
5. Perhaps the best known example of this is Himmler's speech to SS officers in Posen, October 4, 1943 (Nuremberg Document PS-1918). The speech is printed in *Nazi Conspiracy and Aggression, 10* vols. (Washington: 194648), 4: 558–78. The theme of overcoming the difficulty involved in the work of extermination is also expressed by Himmler in his May, 1944 speech to the Nazi Gauleit- ers; *see* Manvell and Fraenkel, *The Incomparable Crime* (New York: Putnam, 1967), pp. 43 f.
6. Martin Broszat, "The Concentration Camps" in Helmut Krausnick and Martin Broszat, *Anatomy of the SS State*, trans. Dorothy Long and Marian Jackson (London: Paladin, 1968), pp. 165 ff.
7. Ibid., pp. 165 ff.
8. Ibid., p. 179.
9. Hannah Arendt, *The Origins of Totalitarianism* (New York: Harcourt Brace, 1951), p. 449.
10. Hilberg, *The Destruction*, p. 235; *see* also pp. 101 ff.

11. Helmut Krausnick, "The Persecution of the Jews" in Krausnick and Broszat, *Anatomy*, pp. 57 ff.; Hilberg, *The Destruction*, pp. 23–30. The view that Goebbels was the instigator is not universally held. Nora Levin places the responsibility on Heydrich in *The Holocaust*, pp. 80 ff. Albert Speer, however, insists that Goebbels was responsible: See Albert Speer, *Inside the Third Reich*, trans. Richard and Clara Winston (New York: Macmillan, 1970), p. 112.

12. Hilberg, *The Destruction*, pp. 23–30.

13. *Ibid.*

14. *Ibid.*

15. Nuremberg Document NG-1672, cited by Hilberg, *The Destruction*, p. 29.

16. Hilberg, *The Destruction*, p. 301.

17. Thierack to Bormann, Nuremberg Document, NG-558, cited by Hilberg, *The Destruction*, p. 296.

31.
CORPORATE VIOLENCE AND THE BANALITY OF EVIL

STUART L. HILLS

Ronald Kramer defines corporate violence as

> corporate behavior which produces an unreasonable risk of physical harm to employees, the general public, and consumers, which is the result of deliberate decision-making by persons who occupy positions as corporation managers or executives, which is organizationally based, and which is intended to benefit the corporation itself (Ronald Kramer, "A Prolegomenon to the Study of Corporate Violence," *Humanity and Society*, vol. 7, 1983, p. 166).

Hills gives many examples of such violence and, much like Rubenstein in the previous article, he attributes the inhumane behavior of corporate personnel to the structure and culture of bureaucratic organizations. Hills adds a political-economic element to his explanation in suggesting that such behavior is inherent to the competitive, unregulated environment fostered by a capitalist economic system. He further applies Sykes and Matza's "techniques of neutralization" to show how corporate personnel can engage in destructive behavior without thinking any less of themselves, resulting in what philosopher and Holocaust scholar Hannah Arendt famously referred to as "the banality of evil."

How is it possible that men who are basically moral and decent in their own families—perhaps even generous in civic and charitable contributions—are able to engage in corporate acts that have extraordinarily inhumane consequences? The key to understanding this fundamental human enigma lies not in the pathology of evil individuals but in the culture and structure of large-scale bureaucratic organizations within a particular political economy. Thus, in addition to whatever else may be involved in explaining corporate violence, some insight may be provided by a brief examination of the organizational pressures and dilemmas that confront corporate executives in a capitalistic economy.

GOALS, PRIORITIES, AND PRESSURES

Although large corporations may have other goals—enhanced prestige and power, increased market shares, product diversification into potentially competing industries, growth and stability, or other short-range goals—the long-run profitability of the corporation is ultimately the most basic and over-riding goal. "No matter how strongly managers prefer to pursue other objectives and no matter how difficult it is to find profit-maximizing strategies in a world of uncertainty and high information costs, failure to satisfy this criterion means ultimately that a firm will disappear from the economic scene."[1] In a capitalistic economy, profit-seeking firms must often compete in an uncertain and unpredictable environment. Competitive market pressures, fluctuating sales, increasing costs for safety and health measures, consumer and environmental concerns, government regulations, and other constraints may limit the ability of the business firm to achieve its profit goals through legitimate opportunities. Thus, some corporations may evade and violate the law or engage in practices that many Americans would consider unethical, endangering the well-being of workers, consumers, and citizens.

In response to the request of the Dupont corporation to use safety glass in the Chevrolet cars, Alfred P. Sloan, the former president of General Motors, succinctly stated this corporate priority of profit—sometimes at any cost:

> I am trying to protect the interest of the stockholders of General Motors and the corporation's operating position—it is not my responsibility to sell safety glass. . . . You can say perhaps that I am selfish, but business is selfish. We are not a charitable institution—we are trying to make a profit for our stockholders.[2]

As the case of the Ford Pinto reveals, the automobile industry has not only been indifferent to pleas for greater auto safety, but in some instances has actively lobbied to prevent safety regulations that threatened corporate profits. From the rejection of safety glass and airbags to the refusal to redesign flawed gas tanks, the conviction that "safety doesn't sell" has needlessly destroyed human lives and caused crippling injuries.

For new employees joining a firm, the *internal organizational climate*—the corporate subculture—is not typically an environment suffused with ethical sensibilities and discussions of social responsibility. Instead, quantifiable performance criteria based on production goals, sales quotas, volume, costs, market shares, and quarterly profits pervade the corporate atmosphere. If socialized into a job routine that includes illegal or questionable ethical practices, the new job holder is apt to look for guidance from immediate superiors or peers and experiences pressures to "get on board and up to speed quickly."[3] Frequently, the illegal or unethical practices are so institutionalized that they simply appear to be part of the *normal* routine and are unreflected upon. Indeed, executives who are convicted of violating the law often react with surprise and shock that their actions were considered criminal or unethical by people outside the insulated occupational world of the corporation. One General Electric official, convicted for his part in the heavy electrical equipment conspiracy commented that price-fixing "had become so common and gone on for so many years that we lost sight of the fact that it was illegal."[4] As James Carey describes the attitudes of the pharmaceutical executives involved in the marketing of an anticholesterol drug with dangerous side effects: "No one involved expressed any strong repugnance or even opposition to selling the unsafe drug. Rather, they all seemed to drift into the activity without thinking a great deal about it."[5]

For the newcomer, subtle cues and shared corporate vocabularies ("he's a team player," "she's a producer," "he's on a fast track") clearly indicate the preferred role models and where the rewards lie. "Conversations about moral and ethical issues are almost doomed to be awkward, halting, and time-consuming to the point of painfulness"—and therefore unlikely to occur.[6] And powerful executive supervisors have many ways to keep conscience-troubled subordinates in line: the threat of demotion, transfer to a less desirable position, and subtle innuendo regarding the employee's abilities and future with the company.

Faced with the choice of refusing to follow orders and risking the stigma of organizational disloyalty, or "going along," many employees will reluctantly pursue the latter course. In a survey of 400 corporate managers in eighteen different industries, 50 percent of top-level and 84 percent of lower-level managers agreed to some degree with this statement: "Managers today feel under pressure to compromise personal standards to achieve company goals."[7] Two other surveys, one a random sample of corporate managers and the other a study of Uniroyal executives, found that between 64 and 70 percent of the managers perceived that their peers "would not refuse orders to market off-standard and possibly dangerous items" (although a majority of the managers said they would personally reject such orders).[8] John De Lorean, recalling his experiences as a former senior vice-president at General Motors commented on corporate pressures and the importance of being a "team player":

> There wasn't a man in top GM management who had anything to do with the Corvair who would purposely build a car that he knew would hurt or kill people.
>
>   But, as part of a management team pushing for increased sales or profits, each gave his individual approval in a group to decisions which produced the car in the face of serious doubts that were raised about its safety, and then later sought to squelch information which might prove the car's deficiencies.[9]

Or consider the case of the NASA space shuttle, Challenger. On the frigid morning of January 28, 1986, the shuttle disintegrated minutes after lift-off, killing all seven astronauts. A presidential investigation revealed that despite numerous warnings by engineers for Morton Thiokol, Inc. that the solid rocket booster seals might prove defective at low temperatures, top management overruled their own engineers and gave approval for the ill-fated flight. Under strong pressure from a team of senior-level executives and NASA officials to make the shuttle launch—and procure the renewal of the lucrative $400 million solid booster contract at stake—the vice-president for engineering at Thiokol testified that he changed his position regarding the safety of the flight after being told "to shed his role as an engineer and take the role of a management person."[10] As the probe of the shuttle disaster deepened, evidence of a tangled web of NASA mismanagement, fraud, and corporate misconduct emerged revealing pressures to accommodate NASA launch schedules and enhance corporate profits that jeopardized the safety of the space shuttle program. (Government documents, for example, revealed that as early as 1980, Rockwell International, the prime contractor for the space shuttle, failed to report promptly to NASA defects in components of the space orbiter whose malfunction could threaten the Challenger or its crew. According to 1983 documents in the NASA Inspector General's office, officials at Jet Air, Inc., a subcontractor for Rockwell International, routinely falsified X-ray reports to conceal defective welds on the Challenger "to avoid the costs of rewelding.")[11]

For managers with a heavy stake in their position in the company, the moral trade-offs from corporate pressures to violate the law may sometimes cause severe discomfort. One laboratory supervisor, who was asked to go along with the cover-up of falsified test data on aircraft brakes to meet a deadline for a defense contract, explained:

> I've been an engineer for a long time, and I've always believed that ethics and integrity were every bit as important as theorems and formulas, and never once has anything happened to change my beliefs. Now this . . . Hell, I've got two sons I've got to put through school and I just . . .[12]

Another conspirator in the doctored test data commented on a similar dilemma:

> At forty-two, with seven children, I had decided that the Goodrich Company would probably, be my "home" for the rest of my working life. The job paid well, it was pleasant and challenging, and the future looked reasonably bright. My wife and I had bought a home and we were ready to settle down into a comfortable, middle-age, middle-class rut. If I refused to take part in the . . . fraud, I would have to either resign or be fired.[13]

In the heavy-electrical-industry price-fixing conspiracy, the sentencing judge summarized the predicament of the participants:

> They were torn between conscience and an approved corporate policy, with the rewarding objective of promotion, comfortable security, and large salaries. They were the organization, or company man; the conformist who goes along with his superiors and finds balm for his conscience in additional comforts and security of his place in the corporate set-up.[14]

There is some empirical evidence that corporate managers who are shrewd and ambitious, men with "flexible moralities" and an eye on both the company's bottom line and their own career mobility, are likely to experience considerable success in today's executive suites. Indeed, as Edward Gross argues, high positions in corporate organizations seem to demand persons with such personal characteristics and "non-demanding moral codes": executives who can both sleep at night and make the cold, calculated decisions "for the good of the company." And it seems likely that after long years of service, such top-level executives gradually internalize the ideologies and goals of the company—and make them their own, as they profit personally from such goal attainment and organizational loyalty.[15]

NEUTRALIZING GUILT

In view of the commitment of respectable corporate executives to the conventional social order, it is necessary for corporate officials who violate the law to neutralize the potential feelings of guilt and self-condemnation. There are many justifications and rationalizations that enable corporate functionaries to accomplish this social-psychological task and avoid any definition of themselves as criminal. Indeed, the very availability of these shared "vocabularies of rationalization" already existing within the corporate occupational culture is precisely what permits many managers to violate the law without any great burden of guilt or threat to their self-respect. The following mechanisms are some "techniques of neutralization" to help assuage one's conscience and rationalize criminal acts.[16]

Denial of Responsibility

A distinguishing characteristic of large-scale corporations is the fragmentation of responsibilities. In a hierarchical labyrinth of specialized tasks and segmented organizational units, employees can easily evade any sense of personal responsibility for the ultimate consequences of their actions. In the B.F. Goodrich scandal where the falsification of airplane test data jeopardized the safety of airplane pilots, officials who participated in the cover-up by falsifying data or by verbally approving the fraudulent reports repeatedly denied that their responsibility extended beyond that specific action. One test lab supervisor who "fudged" the data for the flawed aircraft brakes commented: "After all, we're just drawing some curves, and what happens to them after they leave here, well, we're not responsible for that."[17] Another supervisor, when confronted by a lab technician who demanded that the supervisor report the cover-up to the chief engineer of the plant, refused. When asked to justify his refusal, the supervisor replied: "Because it's none of my business, and it's none of yours. I learned a long time ago not to worry about things over which I had no control. I have no control over this." The lab technician persisted, however, appealing to the supervisor's conscience and pointing out that pilots might be killed or injured during flight tests if the brakes failed to hold. Becoming rather exasperated, the supervisor replied, "I just told you I have no control over this thing. Why should my conscience bother me?"[18]

In a bureaucratic organization, most employees see only a small part of the whole corporate enterprise and can conveniently ignore—or choose not to see—the larger implications of their occupational decisions. Bureaucracies *depersonalize,* and corporate officials rarely confront the victims whose faces are melted beyond recognition in fiery automobile crashes when defective gas tanks explode. It is unlikely that the senior executives at the Robins company who made the decision to keep the Dalkon Shield IUD on the market ever met any of the women who suffered from painful pelvic infections, or the mothers whose children were born retarded, or the women who lost their ovaries and can never have any children. One can only wonder what would have been the response of the executives who marketed thalidomide if they could have personally confronted some of the 8,000 children born with horrible deformities that this drug was suspected of producing. Would these officials have continued to "lie, suppress, bribe and distort" to keep this highly profitable, "non-toxic tranquilizer" on the market if they had come face to face with children such as Terry Wiles—"sixteen years old now but only two feet high, born without arms or legs, and with a protruding eye that had to be surgically removed—and . . . mothers ravaged by guilt . . .?"[19]

Decision-making must, to a large degree, be decentralized in mammoth corporations with multidivisional organizational structures (e.g., research and planning divisions, engineering departments, legal offices, production plants, sales and marketing divisions, corporate subsidiaries). Important operational decisions are made in a series of small steps at each organizational level in the corporate hierarchy, thereby diffusing responsibility. In this bureaucratic labyrinth, it is often difficult to find any specific individual at higher executive levels on whom to place the responsibility for short-cuts in product safety or distorted drug test results. Harried managers under pressure to achieve results may filter and edit information (e.g., questionable safety findings) before sending it up the corporate line of command to make their own department look good. Consequently, top company officials may sometimes have only partial information regarding what goes on at middle and lower levels of management.

Yet, to absolve themselves of any legal responsibility, upper-echelon executives may make it quite clear that they do not wish to be informed of all the sordid details used "to meet the competition" or "cope with the regulators," while they, at the same time, hold lower-level managers responsible for failure to meet production deadlines or profit quotas. Under excruciating pressure to meet extremely demanding goals, and aware that he or she can easily be replaced, the desperate manager, searching for a quick fix, can find illegal or unethical means attractive. In the heavy-electrical-equipment price-fixing conspiracy, top executives, after setting profit goals and market shares that virtually required price-fixing, made it quite clear to middle-level managers that they did not wish to learn of any illegal means that might be used to achieve these objectives.[20]

Denial of Injury

Another social-psychological device to avoid moral responsibility and alleviate feelings of guilt is to define what occurs as an unfortunate "accident" or the hazards inherent in dangerous work. None of the officials at the Ford Motor Company, at A. H. Robins, or at the Scotia Coal Company wished anyone to die or suffer from badly burned faces and mangled limbs, or lose their reproductive organs. Managers can suppress medical data and reports of injuries or hazardous conditions and contend that they are acting in the best interest of their company. Speeding up production, taking shortcuts on product safety, falsifying lab tests, refusing to recall defective products or implement costly safety measures in the workplace—all are done, it can be rationalized, to enhance the company's profits. Although the consequences may be viewed as unfortunate, the insistence that there is no *intention* to harm (despite deliberate violations of safety and health regulations) takes the offender off the moral hook. Since the manager does not intend to hurt anyone, workers or consumers or the general public, such semantic sleight-of-hand conveniently insulates the company manager from realizing that his behavior is morally blameworthy, much less "criminal" (a view reinforced by the media stereotype of the criminal as the low-class predatory street offender).

In cases of work-related health problems (e.g., brown lung and asbestosis), company doctors and officials may argue that "more research is needed" to prove any link between the occurrence of cancer or other disabling ailments that may take years to develop, and the conditions existing in the textile and asbestos factories. That only a certain percentage of workers will develop the occupationally induced diseases, and the belief that those who do will be "compensated," helps blunt any sense of moral culpability from the failure to inform the workers at risk or to redesign a safer workplace. A former Johns-Manville medical director who developed the company policy of not informing asbestos workers that their routine physical examination revealed asbestosis explains his actions:

> Eventually, compensation will be paid to each of those men. But, as long as a man is not disabled it is felt he should not be told of his condition so that he can live and work in peace *and the company can benefit by his many years of experience.*[21]

Similarly, the difficulty in securing conclusive scientific evidence that chemical effluents contaminated groundwater used for drinking, and therefore caused an outbreak of cancer years later, helps to deflect any self-conception of company officials as criminally negligent. Between 1969 and 1986, twenty children in Woburn, Massachusetts, developed leukemia; eleven of them died. According to the U.S. Centers for Disease Control, the frequency of childhood leukemia in East Woburn, is seven times higher than expected on a chance basis.[22] Yet, even to win the case in a civil court, the parents of the dead children must prove a causal chain of events: that the companies were negligent in allowing dangerous chemicals to be disposed of in the soil; that these pollutants migrated to underground water supplies; and that the victims were exposed in sufficient quantities to cause cancer or death.

Denial of the Victim

One way to neutralize the moral implications of one's actions is to blame the victim for the harm. Corporate officials may insist that it was not any flaw in the intrauterine contraceptive device that caused the life-threatening pelvic infection, but the improper insertion of the IUD, or the lifestyles of "promiscuous women." Asbestos workers who develop lung cancer smoke too much and are predisposed to die from cancer anyway, "so why blame us?" A favorite argument in the automobile industry is that cars are not unsafe but road conditions and irresponsible drivers are the problem.

> It is an extraordinary experience to hear automotive "safety engineers" talk for hours without ever mentioning cars. They will advocate spending billions educating youngsters, punishing drunks and redesigning street signs. Listening to them, you can momentarily begin to think that it is easier to control 100 million drivers than a handful of manufacturers. They show movies about guardrail design and advocate the clear-cutting of trees 100 feet back from every highway in the nation. If a car is unsafe, they argue, it is because its owner doesn't drive properly. Or, perhaps, maintain it.[23]

Another way corporate officials can neutralize their guilt is to deny the victim full human status. In the Film Recovery Systems factory in Illinois, it was easier to force illegal Hispanic or Polish aliens to handle a deadly cyanide solution without adequate safeguards, and consequently, jeopardize their lives. Anonymous victims, often of another race, from impoverished Third World nations— may help business managers avoid confronting their own qualms for dumping carcinogenic garments, dangerous drugs, highly toxic pesticides, or other products banned or under strict controls in this country. A recent report provides a vivid example of the risks involved in Central American countries where pesticide poisoning is a major problem among farmers and agricultural workers:

> A farm-supply store in Haiti is packed with multi-colored drums of pesticides—many of them banned in the United States. Clerks scoop out the toxic white powders with their bare hands and put them into unlabeled plastic bags for sale to farmers on their crops. When the drums are empty, they are sold, unwashed, to peasants who use them as water containers.[24]

In response to the report, an official for Dow Chemical denied any moral responsibility for improper use of these exported pesticides (some so highly toxic that a teaspoon full of the chemicals can cause the death of an adult). "After a product has been removed to some banana plantation in Guatemala, you find it's difficult if not impossible to police and control its use."[25] Yet, no mention is made of how workers might become aware of the dangers involved when warning labels are printed in English or written in highly technical language, or, as occurs frequently with exports, warnings of the full extent of the dangers are glossed over or omitted entirely. As Robert Jackall points out, "In a world where the actual and symbolic interconnectedness of human action can be denied and where the faces of victims are unseen until it is too late, almost anything becomes permissible."[26] A University of California entomologist, who has studied the effects of toxic pesticides dumped in Central American countries, describes what may happen when agricultural workers are regarded as less than human:

> The people who work in the fields are treated like half humans. . . . When an airplane flies over to spray, they can leave if they want, but they won't be paid their seven cents a day, or whatever. They often live in huts in the middle of the fields. Their homes, their children and their food get contaminated.[27]

Condemn the Condemners

A technique by which corporate officials may neutralize the moral bind of the law is to deny its legitimacy and to condemn not only it, but those government regulatory agencies that enforce such "unfair laws." In the 1980s, the campaign promise of "getting the government off our backs" symbolized the sanctity of the unfettered pursuit of profit in a "free-enterprise" system and the growing resistance to health, safety, and environmental regulations. Conservative business groups stepped up their attacks on the regulatory laws contending that they were oppressive, ambiguous, unnecessary, that they lowered profits and productivity, and in general, made it more difficult for American businesses to compete effectively in the world-wide economy. In 1983, a new senior administrator in the ideologically revamped Environmental Protection Agency, who had worked previously for a corporation under investigation for pollution violations, bitterly accused the EPA's own general counsel of overzealous enforcement and "alienating the primary constituents of this administration, the business community."[28]

In 1985, a chemical leak at the Union Carbide plant in Institute, West Virginia, hospitalized 135 workers. After an exhaustive investigation (partly prompted by international publicity of the gas leak in 1984 that killed 2,000 persons at the Carbide plant in Bhopal, India), the Occupational Safety and Health Administration imposed a $1.4 million fine on the company for over 200 violations of 55 federal safety and health laws. OSHA accused Union Carbide of willful and blatant disregard of the health and safety of its workers at the Institute plant. Among the alleged violations was the customary practice of asking workers to detect the presence of highly toxic phosgene gas by "sniffing the air after alarms indicated a leak." As Labor Secretary Brock sardonically commented: "They used to use canaries for that." (Phosgene, used in chemical warfare during World War I, is one of the most dangerous industrial gases; it causes lung damage and often results in death.) Angry at the magnitude of the proposed civil penalties and the adverse publicity, the president of Union Carbide lashed out at OSHA and condemned the agency as having "grossly distorted the actual safety conditions of the plant. Most of the citations are entirely unjustified."[29]

Appeal to Higher Loyalties

Finally, corporate managers may rationalize their evasions of laws and ethical constraints by appealing to a "morally superior" set of business ethics to justify their actions: the pursuit of profits in a free enterprise market economy unhampered by government interference. The belief in the moral superiority of this system of free enterprise—the provider of the nation's wealth and abundance, and the basis of human freedom and the American way of life—may release the manager from any feeling of moral obligation to comply with the law simply because it is merely a government regulation.[30] The only responsibility is to maximize profits for shareholders. And with a cultural legacy of "caveat emptor" (let the buyer beware) and a compensation insurance system for some work-related injuries, corporate management may refuse to recognize any further ethical responsibility for saving human lives and preventing harm. Conservative social critic and economist Milton Friedman has provided a strong ideological defense of this view of limited corporate social responsibility.

> There is one and only one social responsibility of business—to use its resources and engage in activities designed to increase its profits so long as it stays within the rules of the game . . . [and] engages in open and free competition, without deception or fraud. . . . Few trends could so thoroughly undermine the very foundations of our free society as the acceptance by corporate officials of a social responsibility other than to make as much money for their stockholders as possible.[31]

If the only legitimate consideration is corporate profitability—with scant concern for ethical considerations—the use of cost-benefit analysis provides an impersonal and economically rational tool to help shape corporate decision-making. If voluntarily recalling millions of defective cars or deadly birth control devices, or lowering the level of cotton dust becomes too costly to the company— even if thousands of lives and much human suffering could be prevented—the executive may, with good conscience, reject such demands as not being "cost effective."

The company manager may also justify legal violations by appealing to another kind of higher morality. For instance, a factory manager may knowingly violate state or federal regulations on chemical dumping of pollutants or installation of expensive safety equipment, justifying these actions as necessary to keep corporate headquarters from closing the factory. Compliance with the law, the manager may contend, would make the plant unprofitable and make a ghost town of the community. Thus, "saving jobs" takes a higher ethical priority than obeying the law. One Texas political official commented on a federal investigation into the impact of asbestos on workers' health at the Pittsburgh-Corning plant in Tyler, Texas: "I think we are all willing to have a little bit of crud in our lungs and a full stomach rather than a whole lot of clean air and nothing to eat."[32] Eventually, the Tyler plant did close down, throwing hundreds of people out of work after an OHSA investigation found numerous safety violations. In recent years, many multinational corporations have tried to avoid such problems by relocating factories in foreign countries where labor costs are cheaper and there are no safety laws to erode corporate profits. As Raymond Michalowski points out, "rather than cease violations against worker health and safety, they have sought to locate new and less powerful victims."[33]

CONTROLLING CORPORATE VIOLENCE, WHITHER AMERICA?

Many social critics have pointed out the massive difficulties in controlling corporate crime. Not only is it extremely hard to pinpoint individual responsibility in the complex maze of corporate bureaucracy, but the very evidence that would legally incriminate officials is often concealed within the corporation. The complexity of the task and the ability of corporate officials to thwart investigations often overwhelm enforcement agencies' limited resources. Beleaguered regulatory agencies find their legal powers eroded, their budgets slashed, and their enforcement efforts hampered by the intervention of politically connected, powerful corporate interests. Even when corporations are convicted, the use of administrative or civil courts and pleas of "nolo contendere" (no contest), largely removes the stigma of criminality. And since corporations cannot be imprisoned, the miniscule fines ("overhead business expenses") meted out to multibillion dollar companies hardly constitute a meaningful deterrent.

As the toll of human suffering from grave physical harms continues to rise, legal scholars and sociologists, in recent years, have proposed a variety of legal reforms to contain this wave of corporate violence. For example, a congressional committee in 1980 considered a proposal that would have required corporate managers who discover life-threatening safety and health hazards in the workplace or in a product to notify an appropriate federal agency or risk a $50,000 fine or two years in prison. After vigorous lobbying by manufacturers, the proposal died quietly in committee.

Indeed, there are innovative proposals to control corporate crime: e.g., requiring corporations convicted of crimes to advertise their injurious actions as both a form of punishment and consumer information; appointing public interest representatives on corporate boards to oversee court-mandated organizational and procedural reforms in the corporate decision-making process.

From proposals for a civil "bill of rights" to protect and encourage whistle-blowers, to draconian criminal penalties such as "corporate capital punishment" (revoking the corporate charter or placing the "habitual criminal corporation" in federal receivership), social critics have made numerous proposals to make the criminal justice system more effective in controlling corporate crime.[34]

Yet, in the present political climate, these proposals, whatever their merit, stand little chance of implementation. Moreover, these kinds of legal reforms do nothing to change the basic economic forces in a capitalistic system that continue to generate pressures to use illegal or morally questionable means to achieve corporate goals. Few elected political officials in America seem willing to risk the economic dislocation that a radical attack on corporate criminality might precipitate. Only the most courageous legislators are apt to challenge the massive political power of corporations by writing effective laws. And even when a highly-publicized disaster goads reluctant lawmakers into advocating marginal legal reforms, especially in the crucial area of occupational safety and health, the power of corporations to weaken the laws with legal loopholes, to co-opt or otherwise render impotent the ability of governmental agencies to enforce new laws, all too often makes a mockery of this exercise in symbolic politics. Congressmen can reassure their constituents that they are safeguarding the public interest with this legal charade, but the ability of large corporations to continue to enhance their profits at the expense of human lives is likely to continue.

Despite such obstacles, pressures to control the antisocial acts of irresponsible corporations persist. During the last two decades, the Nader-inspired consumer protection movement, organized labor's demands for greater safety in the workplace, and the grass-roots efforts of angry families to save their communities from poisonous waste disposal have all helped to transform the individual victim's injury into an issue of public policy. Ultimately, however, a broad-based democratic political movement will be necessary to prevent further massive environmental destruction and human suffering caused by the practices of multinational corporations whose marketing and production facilities now span the entire globe. While incremental liberal reforms may save some lives and prevent some injuries, efforts that are valuable and should not be denigrated, such reforms are not easily won or sustained in the deregulatory conservative political climate of the present era. In the 1970s, new health and safety regulations, many of them now under attack, saved thousands of lives in factories, coal mines, and homes. Legal reforms led to a 50 percent reduction in crib deaths; a Consumer Product Safety Commission ruling requiring difficult-to-remove safety caps on pill bottles reduced emergency-room treatments for poisoning by 230,000 between 1973 and 1978 and prevented the deaths of 200 to 300 preschool children.[35]

Perhaps at this juncture in the American criminal justice system, a necessary and crucial step is to educate the public to the horrendous consequences of corporate wrongdoing—the damaged human lives, disease-stricken bodies, and other illnesses and injuries inflicted on workers and consumers. Until there is greater public understanding of the relationship between corporate decision-making and human suffering, indeed, until there is a public sensibility that provokes moral outrage at this corporate indifference, the far-reaching structural reforms that could make a major and lasting difference are unlikely to occur. Until more citizens perceive that assaulting a woman's body with a dangerously designed birth control device is as serious as assaulting her in the streets; that concealing the level of cotton dust particles is as unconscionable a crime as mugging an old man in an alleyway; that manufacturing and keeping on the market a defective car known to explode and burn on rear-end impact is as morally repugnant as any conventional form of criminal manslaughter—only when such acts are defined as "real crime," will further fundamental reform of the criminal justice system be possible.

The writings and research efforts of social scientists to foster this public awareness may lead to charges that such efforts are "biased." If such pejorative labels mean simply that sociologists are not indifferent to the outcome of what happens in their world, then most of us must plead guilty. As observers of social behavior, we cannot avoid being morally involved in what we study. Nor are we any less biased by cloaking ourselves in a pseudo-scientific garb of "value-neutrality," assuming the posture of moral eunuchs. To be as objective as possible about our research data, to be aware of how our moral commitments shape our perceptions and conclusions, to be extremely clear about the criteria used to delineate crimes and make policy recommendations, all are imperative if we are to develop a more critical reflexivity toward our responsibilities as social researchers.[36] To pretend, however, that we are morally indifferent regarding the outcome of our research is to risk making our work sterile and socially irrelevant. And to refuse to make our values explicit, using instead the prevailing legalistic conceptions of crime, merely means that the value judgments provided by dominant political groups will continue to pervade the criminal justice system and distort public conceptions of the locus of harmful behavior in society.

Social scientists should not underestimate the difficulties of publicizing corporate violence in trying to change conceptions of criminality. Powerful political and economic interests strongly resist such reformulations of crime. It is the hope of a more humanistic criminology, however, that once a large part of the public broadens its conception of what constitutes criminal violence and begins to perceive more clearly the connections between callous decision-making in corporate bureaucracies and serious physical harms, more citizens will become actively involved in a political movement to bring about fundamental changes in the political economy and quality of American life.[37]

With such formidable obstacles to achieving major reforms, it is easy for sociologists to sink into a cynical mood of despair or detachment and withdraw into the politically safe study of conventional crimes of the poor and powerless. To retreat from a vigorous effort to expose corporate criminality in the face of these difficulties, however, leaves citizens not only with a myopic view of crime, but also ensures that such injurious corporate behavior will continue to erode the moral texture of the world in which our children shall grow up.

DISCUSSION QUESTIONS

1. One of the implications of Hills's argument is that there are times when corporations or companies that act ethically are at a competitive disadvantage to those that don't. Can you think of real or hypothetical examples? (You might extrapolate examples from this article.)

2. In the case of *Citizen's United v. Federal Elections Commission,* the U.S. Supreme Court ruled in 2010 that corporations could spend unlimited funds on political campaign advertising. How might this decision exacerbate the problems identified in this article?

3. Referring to the criticism that those social scientists who call attention to the deleterious effects of corporate violence have an anti-corporate bias, Hills writes ". . . And to refuse to

make our values explicit, using instead the prevailing legalistic conceptions of crime, merely means that the value judgments provided by dominant political groups will continue to pervade the criminal justice system and distort public conceptions of the locus of harmful behavior in society." Explain what he means and how it relates to conflict theory.

NOTES

1. F. M. Scherer, quoted in Marshall B. Clinard, *Corporate Ethics and Crime* (Beverly Hills, Calif.: Sage, 1983), p. 18.

2. Quoted in James W. Coleman, *The Criminal Elite* (New York: St. Martin's Press, 1985), p. 40.

3. James A. Waters, "Catch 20.5: Corporate Morality as an Organizational Phenomenon." *Organizational Dynamics* (Spring 1978), p. 6.

4. Quoted in Gilbert Geis, "The Heavy Electrical Equipment Antitrust Cases of 1961." In *White Collar Crime*, edited by Gilbert Geis and Robert F. Meir (New York: Free Press, 1977, rev. ed.), p. 123.

5. James T. Carey, *Introduction to Criminology* (Englewood Cliffs, NJ: Prentice-Hall, 1978), p. 384.

6. Waters, p. 10.

7. Archie B. Carroll, "Managerial Ethics: A Post-Watergate View." *Business Horizons* (April 1975), p. 77.

8. Carl Madden, quoted in Marshall B. Clinard and Peter C. Yeager, *Corporate Crime* (New York: Free Press, 1980), p. 67.

9. Quoted in Mark Green and John F. Berry, *The Challenge of Hidden Profits* (New York: Morrow, 1985), pp. 270–71.

10. Philip M. Boffey, "Rocket Engineers Tell of Pressure for a Launching." *New York Times*, 26 February 1986, p. B-7. See also "Pointing Fingers." *Newsweek*, 10 March 1986, p. 40.

11. Stuart Diamond, "NASA Cut or Delayed Safety Spending." *New York Times*, 24 April 1986, p. B-4.

12. Kermit Vandivier, "Why Should My Conscience Bother Me?" In *In the Name of Profit*, by Robert L. Heilbroner et al. (New York: Doubleday, 1972), p. 22.

13. Ibid., p. 24.

14. Geis, in Geis and Meier, p. 125.

15. Edward Gross, "Organizational Crime: A Theoretical Perspective." In *Studies in Symbolic Interaction*, edited by Norman K. Denzin, vol. 1. (Greenwich, CT: Jai Press, 1978), pp. 67–72; Box, pp. 38–43.

16. Gresham M. Sykes and David Matza, "Techniques of Neutralization: A Theory of Delinquency." *American Sociological Review* 22 (December 1957), pp. 667–70; Michael L. Benson, "Denying the Guilty Mind: Accounting for Involvement in a White-Collar Crime." *Criminology* 23 (November 1985), pp. 583–607.

17. Vandivier, p. 22.

18. Ibid., pp. 23–24.

19. Robert Jackall, "Crime in the Suites." *Contemporary Sociology* 9 (May 1980), p. 357.

20. See Geis, "The Heavy Electrical Equipment Antitrust Cases of 1961."

21. M. David Ermann and Richard J. Lundman, *Corporate Deviance* (New York: Holt, Rinehart and Winston, 1982), p. 73.

22. "Water Pollution Trial Against 2 Corporations Opens in Massachusetts." *Syracuse Post-Dispatch*, 11 March 1986, p. 8; "Why Business Is Watching This Pollution Case." *Business Week*, 24 March 1986, p. 39.

23. Mark Dowie, "Pinto Madness." *Mother Jones* (September/October 1977), p. 24.

24. Nancy Frank, *Crimes Against Health and Safety.* (New York: Harrow and Heston, 1985), p. 57.

25. Ibid.

26. Jackall, p. 356.

27. Quoted in David Weir, with Mark Schapiro and Terry Jacobs, "The Boomerang Crime." *Mother Jones* (November 1979), p. 42.

28. "Mrs. Gorsuch Pollutes the E.P.A." *New York Times,* 16 February 1983, p. A-30.

29. All quotes in this paragraph from Kenneth B. Noble, "Union Carbide Faces Fine of $1.4 Million on Safety Violations," *New York Times,* 2 April 1986, pp. A-1, A-15.

30. Box, p. 57.

31. Quoted in Simon and Eitzen, p. 239.

32. Quoted in Raymond J. Michalowski, *Order, Law, and Crime* (New York: Random House, 1985), p. 334.

33. Ibid. See also Barry I. Castleman, "The Double Standard in Industrial Hazards." *Multinational Monitor* (September 1984), pp. 4–8.

34. See John Braithwaite and Gilbert Geis, "On Theory and Action for Corporate Crime Control." *Crime and Delinquency* 27 (April 1982), pp. 292–314; Christopher D. Stone, *Where the Law Ends: The Social Control of Corporate Behavior* (New York: Harper & Row, 1975); Ermann and Lundman, pp. 131–75.

35. Mark Green and Norman Waitzman, *Business War on the Law.* rev. 2d ed. (Washington, DC: The Corporate Accountability Research Group, 1981), p. 157; John Braithwaite, "White Collar Crime," edited by Ralph H. Turner and James F. Short, Jr. *Annual Review of Sociology 11* (Palo Alto, Calif.: Annual Reviews Inc., 1985), pp. 15–16; David Bollier and Joan Claybrook, *Freedom from Harm: The Civilizing Influence of Health, Safety, and Environmental Regulation* (Washington, DC, and New York: The Public Citizen and Democracy Project, 1986).

36. Ronald Kramer, "Studying Crime Where There Is No Law: Corporate Crime in the Multinational Context" (unpublished paper presented at the American Society of Criminology (November 1984, revised February 1985). See also Ronald C. Kramer, "Defining the Concept of Crime: A Humanistic Perspective." *Journal of Sociology and Social Welfare* 12 (September 1985), pp. 469–87.

37. See Simon and Eitzen, pp. 251–271; Martin Carnoy and Derek Shearer, *Economic Democracy: The Challenge of the 1980's* (Armonk, NY: M. E. Sharpe, 1980); Michael Harrington, *Decade of Decision: The Crisis of the American System* (New York: Simon and Schuster, 1980); Samuel Bowles, David M. Gordon and Thomas E. Weisskopf, *Beyond the Wasteland: A Democratic Alternative to Economic Decline* (Garden City, NY: Doubleday/Anchor, 1984).

RELIGIOUS DEVIANCE

Introduction

Most textbooks and readers in the sociology of deviance do not include a separate section on religion. But religion plays such a recognized and powerful influence in the creation of moral and behavioral codes that its role in the construction of deviant categories cannot be ignored. There have been centuries of religious conflict between and within countries in which large numbers of people have been "otherized," ostracized and demonized in the name of religion, often with catastrophic consequences. The medieval witch craze and the Nazi persecution of the Jews are but two examples that come to mind. To the modern observer, the decade or more following the events on 9/11 may seem particularly tumultuous, but it is only one among many such periods of intense religious conflict in the history of the world.

Religion has long played an important role in the social and political life of the United States. While there is a considerable amount of religious freedom in the United States, there is an implicit assumption that a "good American" is a religious American. According to surveys of American religious beliefs, the odds are that there are some in the U.S. House and Senate who doubt the existence of God and, yet, there are few if any known atheists or even agnostics among them. Political candidates who have their religious doubts know that to confess their doubts would amount to political suicide. More than that, they are frequently called upon to express their religious convictions in public and they usually comply. This situation is especially the case in the southern United States. The first article deals with the marginalization of those who are outspoken about their religious doubts in the Deep South. I describe the persecution of non-religious deviants variously called "freethinkers," "apostates," "atheists," and "heathens." My sample was not a representative sample of doubters, but a group of doubters who meet regularly to support one another in dealing with their marginalization. Deviants often form groups to provide one another with moral support in the face of persecution and to develop means of neutralizing their deviant status. These particular freethinkers are part of a national network of such groups. In the face of real and perceived persecution, many members of these groups have developed an antagonism to Christianity and its more fervent followers. This antagonism serves as a method of neutralizing the pain of ostracism, but it also serves to increase their marginalization. I conclude the article on a note reminiscent of Erikson (Article 2), arguing that freethinkers play a role in establishing the moral boundaries of the religious community. Rather than threatening the religious community, as might be their intention, they serve to reinforce it.

The next article about the controversy surrounding the wearing of traditional Muslim attire in many Western European countries essentially deals with the importance of symbolism in the sociology of deviance. Again, we can draw from the theoretical concepts developed in symbolic interactionism. Accordingly, people do not respond to reality, but to their interpretations of reality which are determined by their personal histories of social experience. The *burqa* and the *niqab* have no inherent meaning, but are assigned meanings by Muslim doctrine which varies from place to place and time to time. Further, they have different meanings to the women who wear them, depending on their experience; to some they are simply a symbol of their faith; to others they are a symbol of defiance; to others, they mean quite the opposite as a symbol of repression. To Western observers, they may symbolize the oppression of Muslim women, or they may symbolize

Muslim defiance of Western culture, or they may symbolize the right of women to express themselves freely. These, of course, are very different and contradictory interpretations. Among Western observers, the contradictory nature and ambiguity of these meanings undoubtedly creates anxiety among many and that anxiety has led to a movement in some European countries to legally define those who wear such garments as deviant. For those Muslim women who interpret the wearing of these garments positively, the movement to ban them amounts to nothing less than persecution.

When many of us think of the connection between deviance and religion, religious violence comes to mind. September 11, 2001, brought religiously inspired violence into the public eye and subsequent wars between largely Christian and largely Muslim countries have kept it there. In the third article in this section, Nepstad discusses an inherently contradictory feature of religions: On one hand, they often inspire adherents toward violence, and on the other hand, they often inspire adherents toward peacemaking. If religious violence is to be seen as a form of deviance, then religious peacemaking may also be seen as a form of deviance, perhaps "positive deviance." While we detest and abhor the violent zealot, we often admire and respect the peacemaking zealot. Mahatma Gandhi and Martin Luther King, Jr. are remembered for their doctrines of non-violence, but both inspired political protest which was unwelcome and was regarded as deviance by the elites of their time. Brothers Daniel and Philip Berrigan, both ordained priests and peace activists, protested against the Vietnam War and later broke into military facilities and vandalized nuclear warheads. They were seen by some as heroes and others as traitors. Both had been on the FBI's Ten Most Wanted List and both spent time in prison. Nepstad begins the article by arguing that religiously inspired violent actors and peacemakers have many qualities in common. She then proceeds to identify important differences in their beliefs and worldviews. These differences are critical in determining whether zealotry will lean toward peaceful or violent means.

32.
NONES ON THE RUN: EVANGELICAL HEATHENS IN THE DEEP SOUTH

ROBERT HEINER

Not surprisingly, people who do not conform to the norms often seek the company of others who do not conform, creating what are often called in the literature "deviant subcultures." Often shunned by others, they can find comfort and companionship in the group. In the company of others like themselves, they frequently establish beliefs, practices, and rituals that aid them in neutralizing the stigma attached to them by outsiders. Following is a discussion of atheists and other nonbelievers who have banded together in the Deep South, a region of the United States which is renowned for the intensity of religious expression among its residents.

INTRODUCTION

Despite the important role religion plays in the social life of the United States and the thousands upon thousands of books and articles published on the subject, relatively little has been written about atheism. Although atheism predates Christianity by millennia, in 1971 James Thrower could refer to the history of atheism as "the so far neglected and well-nigh unrecorded history of unbelief."[1] But the student of deviance should be well aware of the fact that historically the deviant is often neglected in the professional literature. Because religious beliefs prevail in virtually every culture, and religion dates back to prehistory, it is possible that atheism has existed as a deviant status in most cultures since nearly the beginning of humankind.

But this study is not just about atheists; it is about atheists and other unbelievers (e.g., agnostics and deists), people sometimes referred to as *nones* because they check the word "none" on surveys that ask their religion. They are also referred to as apostates in the sociology of religion literature, referring to people who have turned away from religion.[2] The nones examined in this article are not ordinary nones; they are rather extraordinary (and deviant) because they are outspoken and *organized*. In the minds of the fervently religious, they are all atheists, but they like to call themselves "freethinkers." This term seems a bit immodest and self-congratulatory, and as a sociologist, I am inclined to doubt the very existence of such a thing as a freethinker. But the word has a history of almost 300 years and for lack of a better term, it will be used in this article to refer to the loosely connected nationwide group of unbelievers who call themselves "freethinkers."

The dearth of writings on the subject of atheism and freethought in the deviance literature is especially notable considering the pervasive and extensive history of the persecution of unbelievers in Western civilization. Until 1610 in England, outspoken unbelievers could be burned as heretics. Legal codes prohibiting blasphemy continued beyond this date, and ecclesiastical courts could imprison heretics for as long as six months. Laws prohibited blasphemers from holding public office, owning land, or bringing suit in courts, and blasphemers who repeated their offenses could be imprisoned for as long as three years.[3] Persecutory measures, in one form or another, have been officially exercised throughout Christendom to the present century. The list of notable figures who have been so persecuted includes Denis Diderot (French philosopher and atheist who was imprisoned for three years for blasphemy), Thomas Paine (British deist, American Revolutionary hero, banished from England, shunned in America for his outspoken deistic ideas), Richard Carlile (American publisher who spent more than nine years in prison for publishing such heretical works as Paine's *The Age of Reason*), and Annie Besant (British social reformer, deemed unfit to maintain custody of her children because of her beliefs).

Today in the United States, some state constitutions still ban unbelievers from holding public office (e.g., South Carolina, Arkansas, and Pennsylvania), and unbelievers continue to experience a good deal of prejudice and discrimination (this will be discussed in further detail later). In fact, while some of the worst atrocities perpetrated against unbelievers occurred in Europe in previous centuries, the twentieth century has probably seen "more de facto discrimination and prejudice [in the United States] than in any other Western country."[4]

Considering that the sociology of deviance has traditionally examined groups that are oppressed, the study of unbelievers is a chapter sorely lacking in the literature. This article is a preliminary effort to fill that void.

In a society such as our own in which religion plays an important role in the lives of so many, the transition from belief to unbelief is likely to be accompanied by a good deal of uncertainty, self-doubt, and anomie. The unbelievers examined in this study are organized at least to the extent that they hold regular meetings (many of them pay dues to a national organization of unbelievers). That they band together on the basis of their deviant status makes them similar to various other deviant subcultures described in the literature.[5] Belonging to such groups fulfills certain basic needs for its members. Writes Simmons:

> In response to society's disapproval and harassment deviants usually band together with others in the same plight. Beyond the ties of similar interests and views which lie at the base of most human associations, deviants find that establishing fairly stable relationships with other deviants does much to ease procurement and coping problems and to provide a stable and reliable source of direct support and interaction.[6]

Among the more important functions of the group is providing its members with the situated morality necessary to neutralize their deviancy. According to Goode, "Deviance neutralization is an effort to render a positive image of oneself while engaging in behavior and accepting an identity one knows is odious and obnoxious to others."[7] In the case of these freethinkers, neutralization consists of a series of arguments that strongly suggest both an intellectual and a moral superiority of freethought over religious conviction. Natural byproducts of such neutralization tactics are hostility and disdain on the part of freethinkers toward those who hold religious beliefs.

Such hostile feelings toward the majority can be problematic. Freethinkers are often estranged not only from the general society, but also from members of their own families and from their own upbringings. These are the issues that will be addressed in this article. It will further be argued that the unbeliever plays an integral role in boundary maintenance for the religious community. But first, we will begin with a description of the group and the environment—the prejudice and discrimination—that gave rise to its formation.

THE STUDY SETTING AND METHOD

Southland (pseudonym) is a city in the Deep South with a population of roughly 200,000. Church attendance is very high, fundamentalism thrives, and religious bookstores and media programming do a booming business. The unbelievers examined in this analysis are not deviant simply because they are unbelievers, but because they are organized unbelievers, often outspoken, in a city where religion has a prominent influence. This group of unbelievers meets once a month as the Southland Freethought Association (SFA). Between 10 and 25 people attend each meeting, with the average attendance being between 12 and 15 people. This is one of many freethought associations around the country that are a part of the Freedom from Religion Foundation (FFRF), headquartered in Madison, Wisconsin. The stated goals of FFRF are to defend the First Amendment guarantee of separation of church and state and to educate the public about nontheistic beliefs. It claims a nationwide membership of 3,800. Membership is between $30 and $35 per year. Each member receives a monthly newspaper, *Freethought Today*.

SFA is one of the two freethought associations in the state. The other one is in Big City (pseudonym), a city with a population of about 300,000 residents about 250 miles from Southland. Both of these groups are aligned with various other liberal interest groups in the state. They are well connected with the National Organization for Women and the American Civil Liberties Union. In addition to separation of church and state, SFA's main political cause, members also tend to take liberal positions regarding abortion rights and the environment. Many SFA members also attend the Unitarian Fellowship, another one of a very few liberal organizations in Southland.

The data in this study come from notes taken during eight of the monthly SFA meetings (where I continually introduced myself as a sociologist and observer). I also interviewed 10 people who regularly attended the meetings. I interviewed people in both Southland and Big City; the interviews lasted between 45 minutes and one and a half hours. Data also include passages from the FFRF publication *Freethought Today*.

Deviant subcultures have their own rituals that serve to reaffirm the situated morality of the group.[8] As part of one such ritual, many members of these two freethought associations apparently take great pleasure in having letters published in the local newspapers. These letters usually involve some kind of attack on religious doctrine or local religious leaders. Members often photocopy their letters for distribution at the monthly meetings. These letters were also used as a source of information.

I can make no claims as to the representativeness of the 10 respondents. Admittedly, I especially sought to interview those who were most outspoken, expressive, eloquent, politically active, and cantankerous. Excerpts from *Freethought Today* are used to give a little breadth, if not representativeness, to the data obtained from the meeting notes, interviews, and letters.

Though the people I chose for my sample, those who write letters, and those who write for *Freethought Today* may or may not be typical members of FFRF, they are the most outspoken, and they appear to dominate the direction and nature of the activities of FFRF and its association meetings.

Of the respondents I interviewed, one identified herself as an agnostic, one identified himself as a deist, and the rest identified themselves as atheists. Three had college degrees, two were college students (nontraditional students, one age 48, the other age 36), one had his GED, the rest were high school graduates. Most came from parents who did not graduate from high school. They ranged in age from 33 to 87. Five were female, five were male. Their occupations were varied, including a journalist, a self-employed insurance salesman, an electrician, a secretary, a retired radar technician, and a retired mechanic. Included in the sample were the director of the Southland chapter and his wife, and the director of the Big City chapter and his wife (the wives in both cases were very active and might best be considered co-directors). One of the respondents was once a rural Southern fundamentalist minister. Another respondent has spent most of his adult life as an atheist activist (he drives a car that is covered in decals spelling out atheistic and antireligious slogans). His name is of some renown among various atheistic circles around the country.

The respondents also come from various religious backgrounds. None reported having two freethinking parents. Interestingly, though, most of the respondents reported that their mothers were very religious (Pentecostal, Assembly of God, Southern Baptist, Methodist, Roman Catholic) and insisted on a good deal of religious adherence, while their fathers were either agnostic, atheist, or completely uninvolved in religion.

> R3: My dad was a closet heretic, I think. But because of his career [an undertaker], he couldn't be open about his beliefs.
>
> R4: My dad was an atheist, but he only started to talk about it when he found out I was interested [in her late twenties]. He never would have brought it up on his own.
>
> R8: I never heard my father mention the word "religion" other than when he was cussing preachers.
>
> R10: My mother was a fanatic. My father made me go to church; but he didn't believe none of it no how.

PREJUDICE AND DISCRIMINATION

Atheism has often been associated with immorality, anarchy, and during the Cold War, communism; some fundamentalists are taught that atheists are in league with the Devil. Furthermore, atheists and unbelievers get very strong signals from some of our nation's leaders when they are trying to appeal to the religious right. A flyer distributed by SFA quotes presidential candidate George H. W. Bush as saying, "I don't know that atheists should be considered as citizens, nor should they be considered patriotic. This is one nation under God." They are often misunderstood, sometimes suspected, occasionally despised. A social distance survey reported by Stark and Bainbridge asked respondents if they "would feel friendly and at ease" with various kinds of people. Only 23% of Protestant respondents and 24% of Catholic respondents said that they would feel friendly and at ease with an atheist.[9] As mentioned earlier, the state constitutions of Arkansas, Pennsylvania, and South Carolina have clauses that prohibit atheists from holding certain public offices; this practice "grew out of the conviction that people who were not believers were not trustworthy."[10] According to Robertson,

There is an implicit cultural assumption that Americans should be religious—not necessarily by attending church or synagogue, but at least by expressing a belief in God and in religious principles. A 1983 Gallup poll found that only 42 percent of Americans would be willing to vote for an atheist for president (compared with 66 percent who would vote for a Jew, 77 percent for a black, 80 percent for a woman, and 92 percent for a Catholic).[11]

Members of FFRF are acutely aware of prejudice and discrimination directed toward them. The passage below is from the *Freethought Today* "Letter Box."

> As freethinkers in this country, we are a despised minority fighting to maintain our Constitutional right to exist. Our program is primarily one of image. People don't hate us for what we are. They hate us for what they're being told we are by their preachers.[12]

A respondent expressed similar feelings of persecution.

> R10: They'd burn me at the stake if they thought they could get away with it. There's no God protecting me; there's only a Constitution protecting me.

Almost all of the respondents had stories of being victims of prejudice and discrimination that they were anxious to tell. Many of these accounts dealt with relations in their own families.

> R1: We have family who are ultra-religious who keep their children away from us.
> R2: My nephew is not allowed to be around me.
> R7: My family is less likely to be cooperative with my ideas now than when they thought I was a Christian.
> R7: My sister will not allow me to discuss freethought. Her children are very special to me, but we don't see them as much since we [the respondent and her husband] came out of the closet.
> R7: Our next-door neighbors don't knock on our door anymore. But one good thing about it is the preachers don't come knocking either.

Relations at the workplace are also strained when employers and co-workers become aware of their unbelief.

> R1: I would have to work on holidays so the good Christians could go home. . . . The Christians could take off for church business, but I couldn't take off for freethought.
> R2: [After an article came out in the local newspaper about his involvement in SFA] I got fired. I became an antichrist. Nobody would even get in a car with me.
> R5: [About being an atheist] I don't wear it on my sleeve; but I don't deny it either. . . . A guy at work harasses me; he enjoys putting me on the spot to make me look bad.
> R10: [Retired and confined to a wheelchair] I get very little pension for one thing. I think I would get a lot more if I weren't an atheist. I can't belong to the VFW or the American Legion, because I won't swear an oath to God. And so they're fighting against me and not for me.

One respondent expressed concern about her child facing prejudice because of her beliefs.

> R5: I worry about how to bring up my girl so she doesn't get beat over the head.

Another source of embitterment and feelings of persecution is the fact that various local businesses offer discounts to customers who present a church bulletin when paying for goods or services.

Several issues that came up frequently at SFA meetings were related to members' concerns about prejudice and public attitudes. First, they were concerned about how to "reach out" to atheists who were afraid to "come out of the closet."

> R10: [Speaking out during a meeting] One out of every four of your neighbors is an atheist. But Christians are such a violent people, nobody don't dare speak their mind.

Likewise, some members were concerned that their involvement with SFA be kept from public knowledge. Also, some members emphasized the importance of the organization's being involved in community and charitable service in order to counteract the public image of the unbeliever as being immoral.

Ever-conscious of the unpopularity of their beliefs, these people seek refuge in FFRF groups. The groups provide a place where they can speak openly, a kind of group therapy.

> R6: It's nice to be around people who think like you. There are so few freethinkers around.
>
> R4: [Answer to the question "What do you get out of the Freethought meetings?"] The opportunity to express feelings you're not free to discuss in outside society . . . to be free of recriminations . . . to be with like-minded people.

Expressing similar sentiments are the following letters typical of those published in *Freethought Today*.

> Thank you for being an oasis of reason in a desert of religious fanaticism.[13]
>
> It is so helpful getting from one day to the next knowing that despite the way it often looks, I am not alone in my dedication to rationality.[14]

ANOMIE AND CONVERSION

Given the degree of prejudice and discrimination against the unbeliever in our society, it is rather remarkable that anyone would become an unbeliever, especially an acknowledged unbeliever. Lofland and Stark describe "conversion" in the following terms:

> All men and all human groups have ultimate values, a world view, or a perspective furnishing them with a more or less orderly and comprehensive picture of the world. . . . When a person gives up one such perspective or ordered view of the world for another we refer to this process as conversion.[15]

The authors are referring, of course, to religious conversions. Formerly religious members of Freethought have been through religious *unconversions*, or perhaps more precisely, unreligious conversions, in that they have merely converted from one orderly and comprehensive picture of the world to an unreligious (they say "rational") picture. Given their religious upbringing, and the often fiercely negative attitudes in the religious community toward unbelievers, an important question is how did their conversion to unbelief come about. Fear of unbelief and the wrath of God is often instilled at very young ages.

> R4: My mother told me the only sin you'll never be forgiven for is questioning whether or not there is a God.

Naturally, many traced the earliest stirrings of doubt to unanswered questions during their childhood.

> R2: I got chewed out for asking the question, where did God come from? I asked another question about whether dinosaurs were on the Ark.

In between religiousness and conversion, there appear to be periods of experimentation with doctrinal ideas, fear, normlessness, self-doubt, and a grasping for meaning. When religion

(1) does not measure up to its claims, (2) does not achieve empirical validity, (3) contradicts other expectations or values of the believer, or (4) threatens the believer or his or her family, the believer can be thrust into a state of anomie; that is, previously held beliefs lose their meeting. This is the beginning of a lengthy process whose result may be unbelief. Following are examples of situations that respondents claimed caused them to doubt the value of religion.

An example of religion not measuring up to its claims:

> R5: [Took the fundamentalist path to hold her family together] I went to church and got saved. People told me that if you stay in church, he's [her alcoholic husband] gonna break. I went for a year, stopped wearing makeup, jewelry, the whole nine yards; but he didn't change.

An example of religion not achieving empirical validity:

> R9: [Talking about his childhood when the children in the neighborhood would blaspheme and raise hell] Mother said I mustn't talk like that or the Devil would come out of a crack in the ground and drag me down to hell alive. But I doubted that, because he never dragged the other little bastards down.

An example of religion contradicting the believer's expectations or values:

> R4: In my twenties, I was a religious nut, and I could get pretty preachy. But my earliest turn-off came when I tried to give testimony in church. I waved my hand in the air, but the preacher would never call on me. Later I asked him why, and he told me that women were not allowed to talk in church.

An example of religion threatening the believer:

> R7: My son and husband would jokingly blaspheme. They would call each other "God" and "Jesus." And that would scare me. But I started thinking: They were good people, they had good values, what kind of God would send them to hell?

While conversion to unbelief is usually preceded by anomie, in a culture where people are sometimes called upon to affirm their religious beliefs, anomie may persist beyond conversion to freethought. Unbelievers are frequently put in the position of deciding whether or not to identify themselves to others as deviant. The following are excerpts from an autobiography by Neysa Dickey entitled "Grace: It's Not So Amazing" published in *Freethought Today*.

> When friends invite my husband and me for dinner, I still bow my head for grace—sometimes. . . . You see it's like this: My life as an atheist is filled with fits and spurts. . . . [I wish I didn't] bow my head for grace. Sometimes I don't! I also don't hold my hand over my heart during the "Star-Spangled Banner." I continue to believe people have a right to burn the flag in protest. . . . I continue not having babies and trying to be more vocal on all points, but it's hard when your personality is such that acceptance feels like lifeblood, and rejection or controversy leads to panic attacks![16]

During the transition from religion to freethought, when they are losing faith in their religious upbringing, along with anomie comes self-doubt. Much like Dank's description of the gay male's coming out of the closet, the self-doubt comes from society's stereotype of the deviant.[17]

> R2: For a long time I was lying to myself because my beliefs were too radical for anybody. I did not believe there were any nonbelievers out there. If you didn't believe in Jesus, you were un-American, and I considered myself a patriot.

And with conversion to freethought often comes resentment of past religious indoctrination.

> R10: I didn't attend church—but my mother brainwashed me. She'd have neighbors over and hold church at home. I was brainwashed . . . believed in Jesus until I was 35 . . . never had a thought of my own until I was 35. . . . I was a parrot.

CLAIMS OF SUPERIORITY

Perhaps one has no control over whether one believes or not, but one does have some control over whether or not other people know that one is an unbeliever. People are not likely to publicly acknowledge their disbelief unless they are able to neutralize this deviant status. Through their organization, it is apparent that freethinkers are quite effective in neutralizing their deviance (at least among themselves). Judging by the way they present themselves, although they may be cynical, freethinkers appear to feel pretty good about themselves. They place a high value on rationality and obviously feel themselves to be superior to the devoutly religious, whom they believe to be irrational. They see themselves as having been duped, but take great pride in the fact that they have overcome their religious indoctrination, unlike many in their families, their neighborhoods, and their places of employment. As with other deviant subcultures,[18] they have their own cultural heroes. They take pride in the intellectual heritage of freethought. Many of them, even the lesser educated, are quite familiar with the works of Voltaire, Thomas Paine, Robert Ingersoll, and Bertrand Russell; Mark Twain seems to be a favorite of almost all of them. Most also see themselves as patriotic and take heart in the fact that many of the founding fathers of the United States were deists.

It is often thought that two of the most important functions of religion are to motivate people to follow the rules and to provide people with a sense of meaning in their lives. Both of these are accomplished in part by providing the promise of an afterlife, which is a reward for doing good and a reason to put up with the often miserable contingencies of earthly existence. Freethinkers strongly assert their moral superiority in that they do not need the promise of heaven or the threat of hell to conduct themselves in a moral fashion. They view Christians, especially fundamentalists, as hypocrites who are more concerned with their own self-aggrandizement or salvation than they are with the welfare of others. Even when their deeds are good, their motives are not.

> R8: I know a lot of good caring people, but they care for the wrong reason— because they're afraid not to.

By the same token, these unbelievers believe that freethinkers are more humanitarian than their Christian counterparts. They say they are concerned about the here and now and not the welfare of themselves and others in the hereafter. Lack of concern about the hereafter is liberating. But, though it liberates, unbelievers say, it also makes one aware of all the suffering in the here and now. Unbelievers do not wait for God to make things better.

> R1: Freethinkers have been the ones to advance humanitarian ideas in this country. Humanitarian people are doers. Religious people are prayers; they sit back and wait for God to do it. We focus on our lives right now, not on an afterlife.
>
> R7: I have to compare it to a visiting preacher who knocks on your door. I don't think he's as concerned about the individual as he is about the soul. . . . A freethinker knocks on the door and sees the human, the humane part of it. . . . A preacher sees a poor pregnant woman and doesn't think about her present needs.

R8: I feel real concerned about protecting the environment, which I think kind of developed through freethought. . . . Once you start freethinking, you stop living in a fantasy world and start becoming aware of the world around you.

Furthermore, they argue that the idea that one can pray for forgiveness is destructive and leads to the rampant commission of misdeeds throughout the Christian world.

R9: Atheists might be inclined to be more humanitarian because they have no God to go to for forgiveness.

R10: The only ones who are like Christians are atheists. They're the only ones with good morals. Christians are all sinners.

They often go a step farther in arguing that unbelievers are humanists, while Christian doctrine is inherently misanthropic, especially the notion that we are all born in sin.

R9: Atheists are humanists; Christians aren't. They hate the human race. All they believe is war. They were born in sin. They think the human race is no good. I say everyone is born an atheist. They could have been taught something good, but instead they were taught evil Christianity.

HOSTILITY

As has already become quite apparent, freethinkers display a good deal of hostility in their communications. It is difficult to vehemently claim superiority without, at least, some disdain for the allegedly inferior group. A believer who showed up at one of these meetings would likely be quite offended. Without a doubt, one of the most pronounced characteristics of most of these unbelievers is their fervent distaste for religion, especially fundamentalism. Their monthly meetings provide members an opportunity to delight in their mutual abhorrence of religion. One favorite pastime is pointing out contradictions in the Bible. One regular section in *Freethought Today*, entitled "The Unreasoning Clergy," is written every month by sociologist Michael Hakeem. Below is an excerpt:

He talked of seeing "spiritual" bodies. Generally by "spiritual" he meant "supernatural." In fact the resurrected Jesus that he claimed he saw was not a physical but a "spiritual body." (This oxymoron should cast suspicion on Paul's authenticity in the eyes of the vast numbers of Christians who insist that Jesus was resurrected in his physical form; but it doesn't because their capacity for embracing mutually exclusive ideas is without limit).[19]

And from the *Freethought Today* "Letter Box":

Easter Message to Christians
Jesus Christ was a fraud. He cannot "save" you! He couldn't even save himself! (Matt. 27:46, Mark 15:34).[20]

Another attraction is taking quotes from the Bible so as to indicate that Christianity is lewd, pornographic, cruel, hypocritical, or ridiculous. Below are some liberally interpreted excerpts from the Bible taken from an article in *Freethought Today* entitled "The X-Rated Book: Sex and Obscenity in the Bible.

Genesis 17:9–14 Circumcision mandated
19:1–8 Righteous man impregnates his daughters while drunk
32:25 God grabs Jacob's testicles
Kings I 1:1–4 Virgin as therapy for sick old man unsuccessful.[21]

Along the same lines, it is popular to recount Biblical stories of God's cruelty. One article in *Freethought Today* is entitled "Does Your God Kill Babies?" and is emblazoned with the passage "God's crimes against humanity make Hitler and Stalin look like flower children."[22]

Another repeated theme in their anti-Christian liturgy has to do with providing accounts of the harm done by Christianity. Such accounts include stories of Christian Scientists allowing their children to die because they refused to seek medical help, stories of faith healers duping their followers with illusions, stories of fundamentalist churches being sued by their parishioners for inflicting psychological trauma, and stories of priests sexually abusing children in their parish. Christianity is also blamed for racism.

> R10: I remember when we didn't think nuthin' of it if they hung a black next door, because we were good Christians.
> R8: When I was a Christian (or thought I was a Christian), I was a racist. And I feel I've grown out of that since I became aware of being an atheist.

One unbeliever who attends meetings on occasion summed up this sentiment, saying, "I think all religions are an abomination. It's the worst thing that ever happened to mankind."

Of course, this contempt for religion and the religious is often expressed as ridicule. Another regular section in *Freethought Today* is entitled "You Won't Believe You're Reading This." Following are a few entries:

Satan Works in Strange Ways
A naked family of three was charged with arson after taking off their demon-infested clothing and burning them in a Holiday Inn bathroom.

One Less Church in the World
Although lava from the Kilauea Volcano ignited and consumed the much-prayed-for church on Kalapana, Hawaii, it spared a nearby store.

Safer to Be a Freethinker
The disgruntled chairman of a church building committee shot two parishioners, held a bleeding church deacon hostage for six hours, then committed suicide at St. Sebastian By-the-Sea Episcopalian church in Melbourne Beach, Florida.[23]

DISCUSSION

In his study of the "nudist management of respectability," Weinberg [Article 22 in this volume] found that, much like these freethinkers, nudists displayed a good deal of disdain for social convention. He found that nudists went out of their way to prove to themselves and others that they were free of society's stilted views regarding sex and nudity.[24] The key phrase here is that "they went out of their way." The very fact that they went out of their way to demonstrate their freedom from social conventions indicates that they were not free of them. They used as their point of reference the very conventions they said were meaningless to them. Likewise, though the term freethought would seem to be a declaration of independent thinking, these freethinkers seem to think in a rather formulaic way. They define themselves not so much in terms of what they are, but in terms of what they are not—Christians. Le Blond writes that atheism represents a reaction against religion and a negation which presupposes an antecedent affirmation. But, it is abundantly clear that current atheism, at least that of the Occident, draws its nourishment from Christianity and can only be fully understood in relation to Christianity.[25]

These unbelievers are ever-conscious of their deviant status, flaunting and defending it. Their group would be of no significance, would not even exist, if it were not for the Christians "all around them." Their beliefs, rather than being independent of religion, are a reaction to religion; and, in that sense, their beliefs are based on religious beliefs.

In their anticonformist activities, they cannot avoid taking on the characteristics of their religious counterparts; they cannot avoid using the same techniques. They spin anti-Christian liturgy with the same zeal Christians spin their liturgy. They exhibit the same degree of intolerance as their religious counterparts, of whom they are intolerant because of their intolerance. They get together and give "testimony" to their antireligious revelations and conversion, just as their fundamentalist counterparts give testimony to their revelations and conversion. Freethinkers may not use the word "sin," but they frequently and vehemently accuse their religious counterparts of the moral equivalent. It is often said among Christians that "there are no atheists in foxholes." Conversely, it is often heard among freethinkers that religious leaders are really closet atheists. Here again, freethinkers are resorting to the same rationale as their opponents. Both are saying of the other, "They can't really believe what they say they believe."

The profane is the antithesis of the sacred, and yet the profane could not exist without the sacred.[26] Likewise, freethought is the antithesis of religion, yet it could not exist without religion. It appears that neither belief system could exist without the other. As Erikson noted, a community cannot exist without boundaries; it is the presence of the other that gives each group its boundaries.[27] Their relationship is symbiotic. Christianity could not exist without sinners (in this case, freethinkers); nor could freethought exist without religion (in this case, Christians). It follows, then, that the hostility between the two groups contributes to the continued survival of each group. The hostility toward freethought exhibited by the religious community takes the form of prejudice and discrimination. This creates a need in the deviant freethinking subculture to neutralize their deviance. In neutralizing their deviance, they become haughty, self-righteous, and smug, much like their oppressors. This further alienates them from the religious community and thus further increases the likelihood of their oppression, contributing to the continued survival of the deviant subculture and, therefore, of the religious community. To paraphrase Erikson, a freethinker does not represent a failure of the religious community to encompass the entire citizenry; he or she, instead, plays a prominent role in the religious indoctrination of the rest of the community.

In summary, this article has examined a group of deviants who represent a subset of a larger group of deviants; that is, a group of organized unbelievers who are part of the much larger group of all unbelievers. Unbelief in our society represents a deviation from the recognized norm (the word "recognized" is used deliberately, because we cannot be sure of actual normative beliefs). Remarkably, very little research has been done in this area. In a society in which so many people profess religious belief (84% of Americans say they believe in God),[28] the sociology of deviance needs to look more closely at those who do not believe. To be sure, the organized unbelievers considered in this study represent the more extreme and deviant group of unbelievers; but to what extent do they represent other unbelievers? To what extent do other unbelievers experience anomie, hostility, or feelings of superiority? To what extent do they feel different? How do they neutralize their deviance, and how does their deviance impinge upon their lifestyles? To what extent are they hesitant to disclose their unbelief, and to whom and under what circumstances are they likely to make such disclosures? Is it important to them that they find other unbelievers with whom to associate? For what types of people and in what environments is unbelief likely to be most problematic? As for the theory of boundary maintenance, can the symbiotic relationship between freethought and religion be empirically demonstrated? Is there a point at which the religiosity of a community might preclude the evolution of unbelievers? Or would the development of such a religious community be impossible without the presence of unbelievers? These are some of the questions that could be advanced in future research. They are significant questions because, as students of deviance learn early in their studies, the best way to understand the norm is to study deviations from the norm. That is, we cannot fully understand belief without first understanding unbelief.

DISCUSSION QUESTIONS

1. To an extent this article is about orthodoxy and the rigid intolerance that people sometimes have of those who believe differently than they do. Can you think of examples of this in your own social circles? Are there things that you believe that you would hesitate to tell your family? Things you would hesitate to tell your friends? How does this phenomenon relate to the sociology of deviance?
2. Are there schisms within your family or among your friends between those with intense religious beliefs and those without?

NOTES

1. Thrower, J. (1971), *A short history of Western atheism*. London: Pemberton.
2. See Hunsberger, B. & Brown, L. B. (1984), Religious socialization, apostasy, and the impact of family background. *Journal for the Scientific Study of Religion*, 23(3), 239–251; and Hadaway, C. K. (1989), Identifying American apostates: A cluster analysis. *Journal for the Scientific Study of Religion*, 28, 201–215.
3. Mossner, E. C. (1972), Deism. In P. Edwards (Ed.), *The Encyclopedia of Philosophy*, Vol. 2. (pp. 326–336). New York: Macmillan.
4. Edwards, F. (1972), Atheism. In *The Encyclopedia of Philosophy*, Vol. 1. New York: Macmillan; p. 175.
5. See Weinberg, M. S. (1981), The nudist management of respectability. In E. Rubington and M. Weinberg, (Eds.), *Deviance: The interactionist perspective*. (pp. 336–345). New York: Macmillan; Simmons, J. L. (1969), *Deviants*. Berkeley: Glendessary Press; Schur, E. (1971), *Labeling deviant behavior: Its sociological implications*. New York: Harper & Row.
6. Simmons, J. L. (1969), *Deviants*; p. 88.
7. Goode, E. (1978), *Deviant behavior: An interactionist approach*. Englewood Cliffs, NJ: Prentice-Hall; p. 71.
8. Cf. Simmons, J. L. (1969), *Deviants*.
9. Stark, R. & Bainbridge, W. S. (1985), *The future of religion: Secularization, revival, and cult formation*. Berkeley: University of California Press.

10. *The Christian Century* (1990), Atheist Candidate. Vol. 107(20), 627.

11. Robertson, I. (1987), *Sociology*. New York: Worth; p. 410.

12. *Freethought Today*, September 1990, p. 15.

13. *Freethought Today*, April 1990, p. 3.

14. *Freethought Today*, March 1990, p. 14.

15. Lofland, J. & Stark, R. (1965), Becoming a world saver: Theory of conversion to a deviant perspective. *American Sociological Review*, 30, p. 862.

16. *Freethought Today*, March 1990, p. 11.

17. Dank, B. (1971), Coming out in the gay world. *Psychiatry*, 34, 180–197.

18. Cf. Simmons, J. L. (1969), *Deviants*.

19. *Freethought Today*, April 1990, p. 5.

20. Ibid., p. 2.

21. Ibid., p. 7.

22. *Freethought Today*, October 1990, p. 12.

23. *Freethought Today*, August 1990, pp. 19–20.

24. Weinberg, M. S. (1981), The nudist management of respectability. In *Deviance: The interactionist perspective*. E. Rubington and M. Weinberg, eds. New York: Macmillan, 336–345.

25. Le Blond, J. (1965), The contemporary status of atheism. *International Philosophical Quarterly*, 5(1), p. 39.

26. Durkheim, E. (1961), *The Elementary Forms of Religious Life*. (J. Swain, Trans.). Glencoe, IL: Free Press.

27. Erikson, K. T. (1966), *Wayward puritans: A study in the sociology of deviance*. New York: Wiley.

28. Stark, R. & Bainbridge, W. S. (1985), *The future of religion*.

33.
LIBERTÉ, EGALITÉ—DE FÉMINISTES! REVEALING THE BURQA AS A PRO-CHOICE ISSUE

AMANDA KNIEF

Deviance and deviants are often created through legislation. For example, once opiates were criminalized in the early part of the twentieth century in the United States, users were stigmatized and relegated to the margins of society. Users not only faced the stigma for being "users," but now they were "criminals" as well. Criminalization almost inevitably results in the production of more deviants. Conflict theory most obviously applies in the sociology of deviance when the normative behaviors of a subcultural minority are criminalized.

The following article describes efforts by some European governments to criminalize certain religious attire often worn by Muslim women. Knief considers such legislation to be misguided and oppressive. Women wearing such garments are already marginzalized by certain segments of the community, but such legislation legitimates their marginalization with the government imprimatur and contributes to further marginalization as these women are criminalized.

"Ban the burqa! Ban the burqa!" Across Western Europe this resounds as the rallying cry of the day among the public and politicians. At least Belgium, France, Austria, Italy, Switzerland, Spain, and the United Kingdom are in various stages of proposing, voting, or enforcing legislation that would prohibit a person from wearing a facial covering in public places that hides the identity of the person. The words "burqa" which describes a Muslim garment that covers the body and includes a mesh covering over the face, and "niqab" referring to a Muslim facial covering that leaves only a slit revealing the eyes, do not appear in any nation's ban. However, the rhetoric accompanying the legislation in these countries leaves no doubt that it is Muslim women who are targeted—not those citizens who are wearing woolen scarves to keep their faces warm in cold weather.

Animosity against the burqa, the niqab, and even Muslim headscarves isn't new. France banned the wearing of conspicuous religious symbols in public schools in September 2004. The law had the effect of preventing Muslim schoolgirls from wearing headscarves. In spring of 2010 a sixteen-year-old Spanish girl was expelled from her school in suburban Madrid for wearing a headscarf, which violated the school's dress code. The student was readmitted after the national education ministry intervened, stating that the Spanish Constitution requires government institutions to respect religious beliefs. Turkey bans the covering of the face and neck; however, since 2008 loose headscarves are allowed. Some areas of Italy have used a national law against hiding one's identity in public, which predates any discussion of a burqa ban, to prevent Muslim women from wearing the burqa and the niqab in public.

It's worth noting that the burqa, the niqab, and other Muslim clothing traditions are not consistent among Muslim cultures. According to the Muslim Women's League, the Koran only states that women should dress modestly. From there, how women should dress is open to interpretation. The differences in how Muslim women dress reflects the diversity of the women themselves, which is often overlooked. The Muslim Women's League states that "stereotypical assumptions about Muslim women are as inaccurate as the assumption that all American women are personified by the bikini-clad cast of Baywatch."

The burqa and the niqab are striking symbols for those who wear them and for those who don't. When Western government officials and the public blindly insist that the burqa and niqab are used to oppress these women, they are in effect denying that women are intelligent individuals capable of making their own choices. There is no denying that the burqa and niqab have been and are still being used as tools to oppress some Muslim women—both individually by family members or peer groups and collectively by governments. But banning head and facial coverings is also a tool used to oppress Muslim women in Muslim and secular countries. Prior to the revolution in 1979 in Iran, women were prohibited from wearing religious head coverings, called chadors, as expressions of their faith. Many women wore the chadors while marching in the streets to protest the repressive regime. Iranian women were then forced to wear them every day by those who seized power after the revolution. In Turkey, the ban on facial coverings stems from the belief imposed by Turkish authorities that the facial coverings and even headscarves are representative of radical Muslim groups who threaten the country's secularism. Therefore, women who wear facial coverings are prevented from holding public offices and jobs. In short, oppression in the form of forced apparel goes both ways.

There is a presumption among many Western non-Muslim men and women, many of them otherwise religious, that wearing the burqa or niqab or even a headscarf can't be an intelligent or rational choice for a woman but rather is always a patriarchal imposition—one that robs women of their identity and equality. Yet after the repressive Muslim Taliban regime was overthrown in 2002 in Afghanistan, women who were thought to have been forced to wear the burqa didn't cast it off—confusing many Westerners who failed to understand that force is different from choice. Amnesty International, the American Civil Liberties Union, the Parliamentary Assembly of the Council of Europe (PACE), Human Rights Watch, and many other Western human rights groups have stated that wearing the burqa or niqab is a religious and individual choice and should be protected—not banned. After adopting a unanimous resolution against any general prohibition on wearing the burqa or niqab on June 23, 2010, PACE, which includes parliamentarians from forty-seven European countries, stated in a press release that the burqa or niqab is often perceived "as a symbol of the subjugation of women to men" but a general ban would deny women "who genuinely and freely desire to do so" the right to cover their faces.

The reactions of the women themselves to a burqa and niqab ban should be considered. In March, after France began debating the issue, a woman wearing a niqab posted a YouTube video demonstrating how to wear a medical mask under the burqa or niqab so that when required to remove either, her face would still be covered. The fully masked and clothed woman, even wearing gloves, boasted that authorities couldn't make her take off the medical mask because it is for her health. In May, according to Italian press reports, when Amel Marmouri was fined 500 euros for wearing a niqab at a Northern Italian post office, she threatened to stay indoors and never leave her home. Rather than freeing Muslim women and assimilating them into European society, these early examples seem to indicate a fierce backlash may erupt within the Muslim community from the very persons the bans are purported to help. Each passed or proposed ban includes monetary fines for appearing in public wearing a facial covering that expresses some Muslim women's religious faith—in effect a burqa and niqab ban criminalizes the behavior of the very victims the legislation is supposed to help.

The French ban would fine women wearing face coverings 150 euros (about $190) and require them to take a citizenship course. The fines are much stiffer, however, for anyone convicted of forcing a woman or girl to wear a face covering—30,000 euros and a year in prison (doubled if the victim is a minor). The ability of the government to convict a person of forcing another to wear a burqa or niqab has not been tested in Western Europe. Yet, its effectiveness must be questioned when the manner of proof against the defendant would likely reside upon the statement of a woman or girl forced to wear the garment, who must also have been under the authority of that same defendant. It's not unlike asking a domestic violence victim to make a statement against her abuser. And will there be shelters and assistance for those victims who turn against their parents, imams, or spouses?

Advocating for women's emancipation means that all the possible choices a woman may make should be respected including how a woman chooses to express her sexuality: from the extreme of exploitation (like pornography) to the extreme of complete camouflage (like the burqa, niqab, or a nun's habit). The responsibility of government and society is only to ensure that women have the freedom and education to make these choices for themselves. These bans target what is actually a very small minority of Muslim women who wear the burqa or niqab. In Belgium, it is estimated that only 300 women wear such garments. In France, where there are more than 5 million Muslim immigrants, less than 2,000 Muslim women wear the burqa or niqab according to French police. Individuals' religious rights or civil liberties must be protected no matter how few people are being persecuted, which here are the small numbers of Muslim women wearing the burqa or niqab.

Every person is indoctrinated into their society but the variables at play and the degree of their influence aren't always the same. A woman learns what is normal for females based on the religion, culture, lifestyle, and family she's born into. But in our global society it's presumptuous to assume that another's beliefs are wrong simply because those beliefs conflict with a society's standards—as is being assumed by Western countries' views of the burqa and niqab. French President Nicolas Sarkozy showed this kind of sexism and presumption earlier this year when he stated that "the full veil is not welcome in France because it is contrary to our values and contrary to the ideals we have of a woman's dignity."

Practically, there must be proof that another's beliefs are harmful. Take, for example, the sects of fundamentalist Latter-Day Saints (Mormons) in the United States and Canada that practice polygamy.

In these sects, girls under the age of legal consent are married off to much older men. This is harmful to the girls by societal standards and is a crime. In one of these fundamentalist Mormon sects in the southwest United States, the women wear their hair in the same elaborate coiffed and braided style and wear matching blue prairie-style ankle-length dresses. The intent is to make sure that everyone knows they're part of the sect. Using the same arguments that Western European governments are applying to the burqa and niqab for judging the rights of women, the women in this sect are certainly being oppressed. Furthermore, based upon the known religious principles of the sect, a majority of these women are likely victims of punishable crimes. Yet, there is no law banning these women's dresses or hairstyles because a hairstyle and dress style aren't outwardly harmful to the women, and such a law wouldn't stop the sect's polygamy nor free the women from the sect's oppression.

Unlike a polygamous sect, Islam is not predicated on a religious doctrine that violates the law in a Western country. There is no evidence that simply by wearing a burqa or niqab, a woman is oppressed or the victim of a crime. Many of these women have even stated that they have chosen the burqa or niqab as a way to express their faith. In order to assist others who may truly be oppressed, all Western governments must be ready to provide assistance to any and all Muslim women if they look to the government for help—and not assume any or all of them will come wearing a burqa or niqab.

It's true a prairie-style dress and coiffed, braided hairstyle don't raise the same security concerns that Western European governments claim the burqa and niqab do. The government of France claims that hiding one's face in public is a security risk. Yet its proposed ban exempts a number of face coverings, including motorcycle helmets and masks worn for health reasons, fencing, skiing, or carnivals. And while the Belgian law would prohibit any clothing that obscures the identity of the wearer in public places, such as parks and sidewalks, any country's ban will likely include similar exceptions.

So while a government may make laws in the interest of the welfare, safety, and health of its citizens, a law banning facial coverings does not relate to any of these interests. In order to have an effective law about facial coverings to ensure an individual's identification on the street, a government would have to pass a law of extremes: no oversized sunglasses, no hats that shade the face, no facial hair (real or fake) that obscures the lines of the face, and no bangs or hairstyles that hide the eyes. Lady Gaga would be banned from every Western European country.

Specific situations do favor facial identification. In fact, at a time when identity theft has become a major crime, identity checks are a safety accommodation for government, business, and the consumer when services are being provided or exchanged. Religious customs don't prevent private businesses from requiring patrons to show their faces for service. In the United States, it is common to show photo identification when using a credit card. The purchaser's face must be visible for comparison. Reasonable security precautions allow for a government to require every person who enters a secured government building to have his or her identity checked—including showing her or his face. Whether the services a person receives from the government are a right or a privilege, it is reasonable to expect a person to confirm his or her identity facially in order to receive such services. Reciprocally, the government should be expected to provide a female official to check the identities of women who are wearing facial coverings in order to respect religious practices. A business will make such an accommodation for its consumers based on the monetary incentive; the government is required upfront to be more equitable to its citizenry.

This was the case in 2002, when a Florida appellate court ruled that the state did not violate a Muslim woman's rights by requiring her to remove her niqab in order to take a driver's license photograph. Florida provided Sultaana Freeman with a private room and a female employee to take the photograph. The court stated that hiding one's face on a photo identification defeats the purpose of having the photo identification.

There is an argument that wearing the burqa or niqab violates the secularism of the society. In France, this is a particularly strong opinion among the public as reported by the French media. One could say the ban is really to help the French retain their cherished principle of liberty–at the expense of the personal liberty of those masked. Others argue that banning the burqa and niqab will only further isolate Muslim women and girls, in turn reinforcing the negative stereotype many Muslims have of Western governments and preventing younger generations of Muslim women from considering a different way of life and making different choices. Religious tolerance and freedom of expression allow all ideas to bubble to the surface and be heard—from the mainstream to the wacky and scary. At the surface, sunshine is the best disinfectant. The laws banning the burqa and niqab are wholesale laws restricting expressions of religion and culture without proof of harm and are the antithesis of a free and open secular society.

If the goal of Western European countries and all Western governments is truly to fight the oppression of women and encourage cultural and societal integration, there are more positive alternatives to explore than banning the burqa and niqab. Instead these governments should create an outreach network, including a hotline, emergency services, and counseling, with education and work programs so that if and when Muslim women who are truly oppressed by their religion, culture, or relatives–whether or not they wear a burqa or niqab–choose to leave their families, their religion, their culture, their entire lives, they will have the resources to move on and start a new life, and, importantly, a society that will welcome them instead of shying away.

Most Muslim women will likely not leave their faith, but that doesn't mean they don't want the same things as Western women, including the right to education, access to healthcare, marriage and divorce rights, and equal pay for equal work. Western governments should form coalitions with Muslim women's groups to assist their efforts. These Western governments will find that such overtures and actions will provide Muslim women with opportunities to improve their lives in their communities and to act as agents of change. Muslim women should be viewed as partners in accommodating cultures and religion. To start such a process, Western governments should learn and understand Islam and Muslim women enough to accept that wearing a headscarf, burqa, or niqab doesn't mean a woman is acquiescing to the male-dominated version of Islam, but until proven otherwise, she is making a valid choice to honor her faith.

DISCUSSION QUESTIONS

1. What does Knief mean when she argues that laws requiring women to wear specific religious garments *and* laws that prohibit these garments can both be used as tools in the oppression of women?
2. Do you think it is reasonable for countries to ban wearing the burqa or the niqab in public places? Why or why not?
3. How does this article relate to the sociology of deviance?

34.
RELIGION, VIOLENCE, AND PEACEMAKING

SHARON ERICKSON NEPSTAD

September 11, 2001, and recent military conflicts in the Middle East have made us so attuned to the connection between religion and violence that many of us often neglect the connection between religion and peace. Some of the most famous peacemakers in modern history have been religious leaders, most notably Mahatma Gandhi and Martin Luther King, Jr. In the name of peace, both stirred a good deal of controversy and both had their enemies. They may be good examples of what has been called "positive deviance" in that they distinguished themselves from the norm by taking values and behaviors that most people admire to new heights, and they put themselves at risk by doing so.

Nepstad discusses how religion can inspire both violence and peacemaking and she discusses the factors that distinguish religious leaders who inspire violence from those who devote their lives to promoting peace.

The recent rise of religiously inspired terrorism has revived interest in religion's darker capacities. Although the events of September 11 occurred only a few years ago, religion and political violence have been intertwined for centuries. Holy wars, forced conversions, witch hunts, and heresy executions led early social theorists to question why and how the religious imagination fosters and is fueled by cultures of violence. Although these are critical questions to revisit in light of contemporary political concerns, it is also important to recognize that religion has historically played a significant role in curbing violence, constraining aggression, and promoting reconciliation and understanding between disputing groups. Church history, for example, demonstrates that Christianity was responsible for the brutal Crusades but has also tried to place limits on fighting through Ambrose and Augustine's Just War criteria. Furthermore, it has inspired nonviolent groups that denounce militarism and have heroically intervened in war.

Since religion can be both bellicose and pacifying, what are the conditions that, on the one hand, make it a force that foments violence or, on the other hand, promotes peace? In his book *Terror in the Mind of God*, Mark Juergensmeyer (2000) offers an answer to the first part of this question by examining the social dynamics that foster religious violence. Comparing terrorist groups in several faith traditions, he concludes that religious terrorists share the following attributes. First, they consider contemporary forms of religion as weakened versions of the true, authentic faith. These terrorists embrace a more demanding, "hard" religion that requires sacrifice. Second, they refuse to compromise with secular institutions, critiquing "soft" religions for readily accommodating to the mainstream culture. Thus Islamic radicals call for a stronger stance against Western influence, Jewish settlers denounce Israeli politicians who are willing to negotiate over the occupied territories, and abortion clinic bombers reject U.S. Christians' complacency vis-à-vis the *Roe v. Wade* Supreme Court decision. These activists feel justified in defying laws since they view their responsibilities as citizens as secondary to their faith and religious obligations. Finally, Juergensmeyer notes that religious terrorists reject the public-private split whereby faith is considered a private matter to be kept outside the realm of politics. Some even hope that their actions will contribute to the demise of the secular state, ultimately leading to the establishment of a theocracy.

Yet these same attributes are also typical of many religious activists who aim to *stop* political violence. For example, the U.S. Catholic Left repudiates "soft Christianity" that acquiesces to expanding American militarism. This group commits radical acts of peacemaking by breaking into weapons production sites and military compounds to disarm weapons of mass destruction through sabotage. Those who participate in these "plowshares actions" face lengthy prison sentences, but this does not deter them since they believe that authentic faith yields the same consequences that Christ and the early apostles faced, namely, prison and death (Nepstad 2004). Similarly, Quakers have a longstanding tradition of rejecting compromises with secular institutions such as the government. They refused conscription and military service (which most religious groups accept) and denounced slavery. Yet Quakers did not confine their convictions to a personal refusal to own slaves or private decisions to boycott goods produced by slave labor. They actively interfered with the institution of slavery by participating in the Underground Railroad and obstructing slave hunters' efforts after the passage of the Fugitive Slave Act. Perhaps the best-known religious peacemaker, Mahatma Gandhi, also rejected a complete public-private split, stating: "I could not be leading a religious life unless I identified myself with the whole of mankind, and that I could not do unless I took part in politics. . . . You cannot divide social, economic, political and purely religious work into watertight compartments" (Gandhi 1958:63).

If these three traits—rejection of soft religion, the public-private split, and compromises with secular society—characterize religious terrorists as well as peacemakers, then why is religion sometimes divisive and destructive and sometimes a powerful force for peace? Aside from ethical differences on the use of force, there are several factors that distinguish peaceful religious movements from violent ones. I offer some reflections on these differences by examining commonalties in the philosophy and practice of several prominent religious peacemakers of various faiths—Gandhi (Hindu), Daniel Berrigan (Catholic), Martin Luther King Jr. (Protestant), and Thich Nhat Hanh (Buddhist). Although this type of comparative analysis could include a variety of other factors, I focus on distinctions in the worldviews and religious imaginations of these groups.

DISTINCTIONS BETWEEN VIOLENT AND NONVIOLENT RELIGIOUS ACTIVISTS
VIEWS ON THE NATURE OF GOOD AND EVIL

One notable point of divergence between radical religious peacemakers and religious activists who use violence is found in their view of good and evil. For religious terrorists, there is no ambiguity: they perceive their enemies as completely wicked and consider themselves the protectors of righteousness. James Aho (1994) argues that this tendency to view conflicting parties in Manichean terms is not unique to religious groups. In fact, he states that both religious and secular groups manufacture enemies because this provides the opportunity to valiantly battle evil, thereby establishing themselves as heroes and granting meaning and purpose to their existence. Furthermore, Aho notes that enemies function as a societal enema, allowing groups to transfer their own negative attributes to others and purifying themselves in the process.

> We represent right, *Recht*, law and morality. We are righteousness; we are rigid; we are, to use a term familiar to clinical psychologies of anality, "rectal." We comprise the social rectum, as it were. The enemy is what is wrong, what is left, not right, what is left behind, that which remains. What remains is waste material, the refuse of the social body, what it refuses, that which is not permitted. . . . Moral campaigns purge the social body of its refuse. They represent public enemas of sorts, collective "escapes from evil." (Aho 1994:109)

When religiosity is mixed into the process of constructing an enemy, it can intensify the conflict. If people believe that they are carrying out a divine mandate, they may be less willing to negotiate, since the devout will not compromise the will of God. Furthermore, earthly struggles may take on cosmic significance, reflecting a transcendent battle between good and evil. This type of worldview often leads people to draw rigid, impermeable divisions between groups. Evil is no longer an individual trait but rather a characteristic of an entire group that is considered incapable of change. "A satanic enemy cannot be transformed," Juergensmeyer states, "it can only be destroyed" (2000:217). The only way to completely eliminate evil, therefore, is to annihilate the wicked and any means used to accomplish this are morally justified.

For religious peacemakers, the line between good and evil lies within each individual, not between groups. By acknowledging that we are all capable of evil, the basis for moral self righteousness is removed and it becomes difficult to condemn others for weaknesses that all people possess. Thich Nhat Hanh, a Vietnamese Buddhist monk, frequently emphasizes this point. He deconstructs rigid dualisms and simplistic moral judgments as he speaks about a letter he received from a Southeast Asian refugee who recounted how he and others fled by boat, only to encounter a pirate who raped one of the refugees—a 12-year-old girl. The girl became so despondent that she threw herself into the ocean and drowned. Hanh writes:

> When you first learn of something like that, you get angry at the pirate. You naturally take the side of the girl. As you look more deeply you will see it differently. If you take the side of the little girl, then it is easy. You only have to take a gun and shoot the pirate. But . . . in my meditation I saw that if I had been born in the same village of the pirate and raised in the same conditions as he was, there is a great likelihood that I would become a pirate. I cannot condemn myself so easily. In my meditation, I saw that many babies are born along the Gulf of Siam, hundreds every day, and if we educators, social

workers, politicians, and others do not do something about the situation, in 25 years a number of them will become sea pirates. . . . If you take a gun and shoot the pirate, you shoot all of us, because all of us are to some extent responsible for this state of affairs. (1987:62)

Recognizing that everyone is capable of committing injustices, religious peacemakers also believe that all individuals are redeemable. Unlike the religious terrorists who argue that the wicked cannot be transformed, advocates of nonviolence assert that anyone can be converted. Rather than shunning their enemies and accentuating divisions, peacemakers intentionally traverse group boundaries to have dialogue and develop relationships with their opponents. Daniel Berrigan, a Jesuit priest who destroyed draft files during the Vietnam War and damaged missiles during the nuclear arms race, underscores this point.

[T]he Christian (if he follows Christ's example) will constantly want to cross over and be with the ex-communicated, or be with the stigmatized, or be with the so-called "enemy." . . . For those who belong to the radical religious community, I don't care whether it is located in the East or West, whether it is Christian or Buddhist, there is a constant insistence that . . . whatever judgments are rendered, they are not retributive so much as redemptive. Mercy is the point. We are trying to say even to those who in the name of law or in the name of power commit most awful actions against others—we are declaring that those people are redeemable too. (Berrigan and Coles 1971:165)

This should not be misunderstood as unrealistic optimism or naïve faith in the essential goodness of humanity. Martin Luther King Jr. called people to be realistic pacifists who would not ignore "the glaring reality of collective evil" (King 1958:99). He emphasized that all humans have the capacity for both good and evil but he argued that the use of violence expands an individual's malevolence whereas nonviolence calls forth virtuosity.

VIEWS ON THE NATURE OF TRUTH

A second fundamental distinction between nonviolent and violent religious activists centers on their views of truth. Religious terrorists maintain that there is only one truth that is timeless and unchanging. Protecting this divine, absolute truth is of paramount importance and thus ideas take precedence over people. In contrast, Thich Nhat Hanh argues that this mindset is dangerous, leading to dogmatism and a readiness to kill in the name of truth. His religious principles encourage the opposite—nonattachment to ideas. He describes the first three precepts of the Tiep Hien Order of Engaged Buddhism.

First: Do not be idolatrous about or bound to any doctrine, theory, or ideology, even Buddhist ones. All systems of thought are guiding means; they are not absolute truth. . . . Human life is more precious than any ideology, any doctrine. . . . [I]f you have an ideology and stick to it, thinking it is the absolute truth, you can kill millions. This precept includes the precept of not killing in its deepest sense. Humankind suffers very much from attachment to views. In the name of truth, we kill each other. . . . Second: Do not think that the knowledge you presently possess is changeless, absolute truth. Avoid being narrow-minded and bound to present views. Learn to practice nonattachment from views in order to be open to receive others' viewpoints. . . . Third: Do not force others, including children, by any means whatsoever, to adopt your views, whether by authority, threat, money, propaganda, or even education. However, through compassionate dialogue, help others renounce fanaticism and narrowness. (Hanh 1987:89–91)

This alternative perspective is perhaps most clearly exemplified in Gandhi's life and work. Gandhi maintained that "Truth is God," in contrast to the more common premise that God is truth. Since humans do not know God completely and fully, then they do not possess absolute truth and hence are not in a position to punish others. Thus, rather than being protectors of the truth, Gandhi argued that we should be pursuers of it, which is tantamount to seeking God. This quest for truth requires individuals to unmask falsehoods, persistently persuading oppressors to stop perpetrating injustices. Yet it also requires truthseekers to remain unceasingly open to other views, including their opponent's. This is the heart of the Gandhian concept of *satyagraha*, translated as "holding on to truth" or "truth force." Joan Bondurant (1958) described it as a "Gandhian dialectic" since the ultimate goal of *satyagraha* is to synthesize the truths of both parties in a conflict, thereby expanding their common ground and bringing each closer to God. In practice this means that religious activists cling to their understanding of truth, aiming to resolve conflicts through persuasion of their opponents in word and action. Yet simultaneously the *satyagrahi* (truthseeker) invites the other side to demonstrate the correctness of its position. Bondurant carefully notes that this is not equivalent to compromise. She states:

> [T]he Gandhian technique proceeds in a manner qualitatively different from compromise. What results from the dialectical process of conflict of opposite positions as acted upon by satyagraha, is a synthesis, not a compromise. The satyagrahi is never prepared to yield any position which he holds to be the truth. He is, however, prepared—and this is essential—to be persuaded by his opponent that the opponent's position is the true, or the more nearly true, position. . . . When persuasion has been effected, what was once the opponent's position is now the position of both antagonist and protagonist. There is no victory in the sense of triumph of one side over the other. . . . There is no "lowering" of demands, but an aiming at a "higher" level of adjustment which creates a new, mutually satisfactory, resolution. (1958:197)

Satyagraha does not mean that religious peacemakers are any less radical than religious activists who use violence. Gandhi's faith and convictions inspired him to fight for comprehensive social change in India's political, economic, and cultural realms. His movement had revolutionary goals—to free India from British colonial rule, to move toward economic self-sufficiency, and eliminate the caste system. This is not the "soft" compromising religion that religious terrorists repudiate. The Gandhian pursuit of Truth/God, the Catholic Left's efforts to abolish weapons of mass destruction, and Engaged Buddhists' efforts to stop the Vietnam War required serious sacrifice. Similar to religious terrorists, these religious peacemakers were willing to die for their faith and their cause. However, they were not willing to kill for it.

VIEWS OF RELIGION

The discussion of Gandhi's view of truth reveals that religious terrorists and religious peacemakers also think of faith in fundamentally different ways. For religious terrorists, *religion is an end in itself*. Often, their struggle is not only to defeat earthly evil but also to usher in an era in which their religion dominates. For some, this may take the form of a theocracy while others believe their actions will inaugurate an apocalypse that will culminate in a spiritual transformation of the world (Juergensmeyer 2000). Because religion is the end goal, people may be sacrificed in order to establish or preserve a religious foothold in society.

For religious peacemakers, *religion is viewed as a means to an end*, namely, enlightenment, truth, or spiritual fulfillment. Thich Nhat Hanh asserts that religious principles and practices are methods designed to guide individuals toward this destination. "Buddha's teaching is only a raft to help you cross the shore, a finger pointing to the moon," he states. "Don't mistake the finger for the moon. The raft is not the shore" (Hanh 1987:89). Moreover, many religious peacemakers hold that the type of vessel one uses to reach the shore is not so important. Gandhi commented:

> Religions are different roads converging to the same point. What does it matter that we take different roads, so long as we reach the same goal? In reality, there are as many religions as there are individuals. If a man reaches the heart of his own religion, he has reached the heart of others too. So long as there are different religions, every one of them may need some distinctive symbol. But when the symbol is made into a fetish and an instrument of proving the superiority of one's religion over others, it is fit only to be discarded. ([1958] 1999:54)

For religious peacemakers, therefore, the goal is spiritual enlightenment and truth—not only for individuals but also for society as a whole. This is not to be confused with religious terrorists' desire to establish a religious government or culture but rather to integrate religiously inspired principles of justice and respect for all people into the fabric of society.

CONCLUSION

A comprehensive discussion of the factors that contribute to religion's capacity to promote respect, dialogue, and nonviolent resolution of conflicts—or, conversely, promote a climate of terror—requires a more systematic, in-depth investigation than I offer in this brief essay. Although I examine key differences in the worldviews of religious peacemakers and terrorists, future research ought to explore the broader structural influences on religious actors' decisions to adopt nonviolent or violent tactics. For instance, recent debates suggest that the spread of democracy may inhibit violent revolutionary movements and foster nonviolent protest as opposition groups can now work for reform within the system. Although the nature of religious terrorism is fundamentally different from political acts of violence, we do not have systematic data that determines whether or how various forms of government affect religious activists' tactical choices. Juergensmeyer (2000) also suggests that key historical developments and economic shifts have contributed to the global rise of religious violence; we need similar comparative information about the type of environmental changes that foster the emergence and vitality of faith-based peacemaking movements. Additionally, the social organization within religious groups is another factor that merits further consideration. Do hierarchical religious institutions encourage moral dualism and dogmatic views of truth more or less often than decentralized groups that determine and implement doctrine at the local level?

I have not presented a definitive theoretical account of why religion sometimes promotes violence and at other times fosters peace. Rather, I drew attention to the fact that religion is not inherently dogmatic, rigid, socially intolerant, and exclusive. It can be—and this is true for both conservative as well as progressive faiths. However, when religious teachers and practitioners reject simplistic moral dualism and define themselves as truthseekers rather than truth protectors, then religion can undercut the polarizing dynamics of conflict. It can be a potent force that encourages disputing parties to see the limitations of their own perspectives, the humanity of the opposing side, and the possibility of transforming even hardened hearts. Religion can operate as a moral compass that values human life over ideas. Those who seek fulfillment through a "hard" faith will find that many nonviolent faith traditions require resolute commitment and sacrifice, including the willingness to offer one's life as Gandhi, King, and other religious peacemakers have done. Radical religious peacemaking demands the type of altruism that accepts suffering but does not inflict it on others.

DISCUSSION QUESTIONS

1. According to Nepstad, what do religiously inspired violent activists have in common with religiously inspired peacemaking activists? What are the essential differences between the two?
2. It was suggested that peacemaking religious activists like Gandhi, King, and Berrigan might best be considered positive deviants because they devoted their lives to acting on values and ideals which most people admire and they were persecuted for doing so.. Why would it be so difficult for most of us to do as they did?

REFERENCES

Aho, J. 1994. *This thing of darkness: A sociology of the enemy.* Seattle, WA: University of Washington Press.

Berrigan, D. and R. Coles. [1971] 2001. *The geography of faith: Underground conversations on religious, political and social change.* Woodstock, VT: SkyLight Paths Publishing.

Bondurant, J. V. 1958. *Conquest of violence: The Gandhian philosophy of conflict.* Princeton, NJ: Princeton University Press.

Gandhi, M. K. [1958] 1999. *All men are brothers: Autobiographical reflections.* New York: Continuum.

Hanh, T. N. 1987. *Being peace.* Berkeley, CA: Parallax Press.

Juergensmeyer, M. 2000. *Terror in the mind of God: The global rise of religious violence.* Berkeley, CA: University of California Press.

King Jr., M. L. 1958. *Stride toward freedom.* San Francisco, CA: Harper Collins.

Nepstad, S. E. 2004. Persistent resistance: Commitment and community in the Plowshares Movement. *Social Problems* 51(1):43–60.

MENTAL ILLNESS

Introduction

There have always been people whose thoughts and behaviors departed so far from the norm that they were unable to function as productive members of society. For most of the past several centuries in the West, with some historical exceptions, these people were routinely subjected to medically sanctioned "treatments" that were often indistinguishable from punishment. The first article in this section describes some of these treatments. It is worth noting that at the time they were theoretically justified and regarded as humane. The article also introduces the concept of the "medicalization of deviance," and questions the scientific basis of modern psychiatric treatments. The medicalization of deviance is very controversial in the mental health treatment community but finds a good deal of support among those interested in the sociology of deviance.

A longstanding interest of sociology has been in the methods societies use to induce compliance to the norms. These methods are referred to as "social controls" and the medicalization of deviance thesis argues that psychiatrists and others in the mental health profession are acting as agents of social control under the pretext of medical science. Given that psychiatric patients often experience relief from severe distress as a result of treatment, critics of modern psychiatric practices are sometimes seen as inhumane and unsympathetic to the plight of those suffering from mental illness. The critics often counter that the sources of suffering for the mentally ill are as much or more social than they are biological and that treating the problem with pharmaceuticals obviates the need to address the environmental sources of the problem. Beyond the original sources of the problem—be they biological or social—greater tolerance for difference would go a long way in alleviating the suffering of those considered mentally ill.

Today there are millions of people in the United States and beyond who are being prescribed psychoactive drugs for the treatment of various emotional and mental disorders. Until three or four decades ago, it used to be that people in need of psychiatric medication were stigmatized and marginalized, that is, treated as deviants. Since then, the medical community has been so effective in getting so many millions of people on these drugs that those people are coming to represent the "new normal." Indeed, it is positive that the people on psychiatric medications are subject to less stigma than in the past, but the fact that there are so many more now than in the past has profound implications for the sociology of deviance.

The presumption is that patients taking these drugs suffer from some sort of brain defect or chemical imbalance and that it is normal to be so afflicted at some point in one's life. Diagnoses of these conditions, however, almost never involve empirical observations of the patients' brains or measurements of their chemical imbalances. Nonetheless, these explanations are popularly accepted and the acceptance of these explanations overshadows sociological explanations which attribute peoples' thinking, feelings, and actions to their environments.

The acceptance of biophysical explanations for troubling psychological and emotional states means that rectifying troubling environments will often be overlooked as a solution for people's difficulties. The result is that the often-damaging status quo remains intact and millions rely on drugs as a solution to their problems. As the implications of the medicalization of deviance have such sociological significance, most of the articles in this section address this issue in one way or another and challenge the orthodoxy that underpins it. And because the orthodoxy that underpins the medicalization of deviance is so well entrenched in Western society, undoubtedly many readers will take offense. The controversy involved is a theoretical one and there is most likely truth to both the biophysical and the sociological models of mental disorders.

The next article is a classic in the sociology of deviance. In it, David Rosenhan deftly accomplishes two tasks: first, he effectively challenges the scientific basis of psychiatric diagnoses and second, he demonstrates how powerfully labels associated with mental illness can affect people's lives. By temporarily, if not momentarily, faking a single symptom of schizophrenia, Rosenhan and his colleagues managed to get themselves diagnosed "schizophrenic" and admitted to psychiatric hospitals. Once admitted, even their most normal behaviors were seen as symptomatic of their schizophrenia and were used by hospital staff to reaffirm their diagnosis. That is, everything they did was seen through the prism of their labels.

Since schizophrenia is regarded in Western society as incurable, patients will carry their label with them for the rest of their lives. For example, years after release from the hospital, the ex-patient could vehemently disagree with a family member and the family member could dismiss their emotion-laden argument as a symptom of schizophrenia. In other words, the costs of diagnosing a healthy patient as sick—that is, the costs of a "false positive"—are enormous to the patient; yet there is almost no cost to the doctor. However, as Rosenhan recounts, in the next "phase" of the study, when the psychiatric staff were told in advance that pseudopatients would be trying to gain admission to their institution, the staff were then aware that their credibility was on the line. This awareness acted as a new variable in the equation: perceived cost to the doctor of a false positive. Rosenhan actually sent no more pseudopatients, but the doctors and their staff identified some of their real patients as faking their symptoms. Presumably, some of these patients who were suspected as being pseudopatients truly met the psychiatric definition of "schizophrenic" and these cases might be considered "false negatives." Thus, when there is no perceived cost to the doctors for making a false positive, they tend to over-label; and when there is a perceived cost for such an error, they tend to under-label. This is a frightening situation if you are on the receiving end of a psychiatric diagnosis and, of course, this situation would not be possible if there were a sound scientific basis for such diagnoses.

The next article, by Schubert, Hansen, and Rapley, concerns how entrenched medical conceptions of ADHD are in Australia. Remarkably, the absence of any empirically verifiable biological markers for ADHD rarely presents a significant impediment to the biomedical model's dominance in public discourse on the subject. (Although, in this article a proponent of the biomedical model is treated with a good deal of skepticism.) The authors examine this public discourse and the linguistic contortions members of the mental health community have to go through in order to justify and maintain the popular belief that the troublesome behavior of some kids belongs within the domain of medicine. A principle theme underlying this book is that of social constructionism, which holds that deviant categories are socially constructed; that is, there are no qualities *inherent* in actions or people that make them deviant; but that social groups determine what behavior and which people are considered deviant. This article starts with that position and examines how the medical community reifies medical constructions of ADHD through public discourse.

As noted earlier, schizophrenia is regarded as incurable in Western psychiatry; but, as Richard Warner describes in the next article, it seems to be a transitory state for many people in the

Third World who frequently fully recover from this condition. How is it that the prognosis for schizophrenia is worse in affluent countries, with their advanced medical science and technology, than it is in poor countries? Warner answers this question in terms of the social and cultural differences between First and Third World countries. One important difference is that in advanced industrialized countries we expect people to be productive within a highly specialized division of labor. In poor countries, the workforce is not so specialized and, therefore, people with limited abilities are still able to contribute in ways that will be appreciated by those around them. Furthermore, in the First World, people who display the behavioral symptoms of mental illness are often shunned. In some Third World countries, they are often embraced by their families and community. Often the folk diagnoses presume that there are supernatural forces at work and the very presence of the mentally ill serves to confirm their religious beliefs. Those who experience delusional states may be seen as experiencing temporary bouts of spiritual sensitivity, acting as conduits to the spiritual world. These differences, among others, help to explain why societal reactions to mental illness are generally much more negative in the First World than in the Third World. Thus a cross-cultural examination reveals that societal reaction to schizophrenia may have more to do with recovery than correcting biological defects or chemical imbalances.

In the next article in this section, Ethan Watters describes how Western psychiatry is being diffused throughout the world. As a result, he says mental illnesses in the Western "repertoire" are spreading across the globe and replacing indigenous expressions of mental illness. The Western psychiatric model assumes that mental illnesses are biological in origin and pays little attention to environmental causes; therefore, when the Western model crosses international borders, cultural differences in the definition and expression of mental illness are implicitly or explicitly discarded as irrelevant. Presumably, the biological model is both more scientific and more humane because it is supposed to relieve the patient of blame for his or her aberrant condition. Watters cites evidence suggesting that the biological model may have the opposite effect, resulting in greater stigmatization of the mentally ill. Watters' arguments have serious implications for the sociology of deviance in an increasingly globalized world. The arrival of the Western psychiatric model in non-Western countries portends that more people will be labeled mentally ill and many of those so labeled will have worse prognoses than they would have before its arrival.

We end this section on what many readers will consider a lighter note. Robert Bartholomew discusses *koro*, a condition in which people think that their genitalia are disappearing into their bodies. Koro is taken seriously by friends and family of its victims and sometimes by medical practitioners. There have been occurrences in which koro strikes a significant number of people in a society within a short period of time, much like an epidemic. It is difficult to classify this phenomenon. In the first edition of this book, this article was included in the "moral panics" section. However, these occurrences are not technically moral panics because they do not necessarily involve folk devils (although sometimes in some parts of the world, folk devils are invoked when the victims claim someone is stealing their penis or putting a spell on them.) Koro is one of many deviant behavioral patterns that are specific to certain cultures, sometimes called "culture-bound syndromes." Non-native observers and many in the psychiatric community view koro's victims as suffering from bouts of mental illness. But this is a controversial point of view because, as we have seen, mental illness is popularly conceived in the West as being biological in origin.

Critics of this perspective argue that such behaviors can only be understood as expressions of deep-seated cultural tensions and that a psychiatric approach leads to misunderstanding.

While Westerners may laugh at those societies in which koro occurs, keep in mind that only a tiny fraction of the residents in these societies experience koro. We should also keep in mind that many things happen in Western countries that seem "crazy" to outsiders. As we have seen in the moral panics literature, people in Western societies are probably no less susceptible to collective delusions; and we seem to be more susceptible when social tensions are at high levels.

35.
THE MEDICALIZATION OF DEVIANCE

ROBERT HEINER

Sociologists are frequently critical of psychiatry, arguing that it has clouded the study of deviance with pseudoscientific nomenclature and biomedical explanations that have not risen to empirical verification. Through "medicalizing" deviance, critics argue, psychiatry has become little more than an institution of social control, much like the police and the courts—but more insidious than the police and the courts because psychiatry is not recognized for its control function.

Psychiatrists would likely argue that we have come a long way in treating mental disorders from the day when those afflicted were isolated and tortured to the modern day when those who are afflicted are treated with the same care and compassion as those afflicted by any other disease. Critics of psychiatry suggest otherwise. According to the critics, the medications used today may offend the modern sensibilities less than treatments of the past; but the scientific understanding of mental disorders and the motives for treatment have not progressed as much as most people think; and the appearance of medications as being more humane than treatments of the past is a socially constructed reality specific to our times.

The seven million people in prison, jail, on probation or on parole are under the control of the criminal justice system. At least that many more, some say, are under the control of the medical profession, psychiatry in particular. All societies have ways of ensuring that their people follow the norms. Sociologists call the means societies have for keeping people in line "social control mechanisms." These include informal mechanisms, such as rumor, gossip or ostracism, and formal mechanisms, such as after-school detention or prison. Agencies of social control include the police and the church. According to Thomas Szasz, as societies have secularized and religion has played a diminishing role in keeping people in line, psychiatry has risen to take up the slack.[1]

The problem, says Szasz, is that unlike other branches of medicine which base their diagnosis on objective observation of structure, psychiatry bases its diagnosis on behavior which can only be subjectively observed. Millions of Americans taking psychiatric medications have been and are being told that their afflictions are biologically based when, in fact, no biological defect has been detected in them. "Thus," he writes, "whereas in modern medicine new diseases were discovered, in modern psychiatry they were invented. Paresis was proved to be a disease, hysteria was declared to be one."[2] Modern psychiatry, he says, has progressed very little from the days when escaped slaves were diagnosed with the disease "drapetomania," which causes an overwhelming desire to run away and in the late 19th century when women with a variety of symptoms, including a tendency to cause trouble, were diagnosed with hysteria or a "wandering womb."

In the 1960s, hundreds of thousands of American children were diagnosed with MBD, "minimal brain damage," and prescribed methylphenidate, brand name Ritalin, which is chemically quite similar to cocaine.[3] The diagnosis was based, not on objective observation of biological defect, but on behavior which deviated from the norm. Unable to identify a biological etiology, the diagnosis eventually became "minimal brain dysfunction," and then "hyperkinesis," or "hyperactivity," and now "attention deficit disorder." While it is nearly fifty years later and the drug regimen has changed slightly, there are still no biological tests involved in the diagnosis of this "medical" disorder. The same can be said for schizophrenia, bipolar disorder, depression, and virtually all other psychiatric "diseases."

The social control implications of the "medicalization of deviance" are profound. In the 1970s, blacks, women, and poor people who went to the doctor complaining of anxiety were more likely to be prescribed anti-anxiety medications than whites, men, and middle class patients who complained of anxiety.[4] What blacks, women, and poor patients had in common, of course, is that they may well have had good reasons for feeling anxious and the source of their anxiety may have had something to do with how their status in society affected their life chances. Treating the individual with chemicals diverts attention away from the societal sources of stress. Change the individual, maintain the status quo. And, if a child has an "attention deficit disorder," maybe what he or she needs is more attention. Instead, with the medicalization of deviance, rather than investing more time and money in that child, he or she is likely to be given amphetamines.

It is said that "necessity is the mother of invention." Perhaps anxiety is the true mother of invention. If the status quo induces stress in someone, perhaps he or she will be motivated to change it. Perhaps society today would be different if hundreds of thousands, perhaps millions, of African Americans, women, and poor people were not having their stress levels chemically reduced in the 1970s.

The more traditional means of social control through the criminal justice system may be described as the "coercive model" of social control, whereas the medicalization of deviance offers an alternative model, the "treatment model." The coercive model says "we are going to *force* you to fit in;" the treatment model says "we're going to *help* you to fit in." The treatment model may be more effective because people like to be helped and they do not like to be forced. They even volunteer themselves for the help offered by the medical profession. The treatment model may also be more cost-effective because people (or their insurance companies) will even pay for the help. But, the critical constructionist warns, the treatment model is also more insidious because people do not recognize it as a form of social control and it is, therefore, more difficult to limit its application. So for the critical constructionist, not only are the constructions of crime and deviance at issue, but so too are the constructions of punishment and treatment.

When we look through history and apply modern sensibilities to the "treatments" applied to those diagnosed mentally ill, they appear to be nothing more than torturous punishments. Robert

Whitaker writes of treatments in the 18th century, "The various depleting remedies—bleeding, purgings, emetics, and nausea-inducing agents—were also said to be therapeutic because they inflicted considerable pain, and thus the madman's mind became more focused on this sensation rather than on his usual raving thoughts."[5] Benjamin Rush, the "father" of American medicine and renowned Quaker humanist, treated some of his mentally disordered patients with blistering agents, leaving the wounds open for months or years to "induce 'permanent discharge' from the overheated brain."[6] Some 19th century psychiatrists dabbled with drowning therapies.[7] In the first half of the 20th century, various methods of inducing violent convulsions in patients were developed as these were believed to be therapeutic; and in the 1940s and 1950s, tens of thousands of lobotomies were performed on psychiatric patients.

All of these treatments were, at one time, believed to be the humane approach to relieving the suffering associated with mental illness. Today, powerful drugs—some with very unpleasant or even dangerous side-effects—are often prescribed to psychiatric patients, who are frequently led to believe that they suffer some sort of chemical imbalance in their brains. Yet the chemicals in their brains have not been measured and no one has specified what the proper balance of chemicals should be in a "healthy" brain. It is quite likely that decades from now people will look back on the chemical treatment of psychiatric patients as part of the long tradition of punishing those who do not fit in. In any case, the millions of people under correctional supervision, plus the millions more under medical supervision, suggest the United States has very little tolerance for nonconformity—in a country whose claim to fame is the value it places on individual freedom.

DISCUSSION QUESTION

1. It is argued that, contrary to popular belief, the medical profession has made very little progress over the centuries in the treatment of mental disorders. What is the basis of this argument? Do you agree or disagree? Why?

NOTES

1. Thomas Szasz (interview), in F. W. Miller et al. (eds.), *The Mental Health Process.* Mineola, NY: The Foundation Press, 1976.
2. Thomas Szasz, *The Myth of Mental Illness.* New York: Harper and Row, 1974, 12.
3. Richard Hughes and Robert Brewin, *The Tranquilizing of America: Pill Popping and the American Way of Life.* New York: Harcourt, Brace, Jovanovich, 1979. Richard DeGrandpre, *The Cult of Pharmacology: How America Became the World's Most Troubled Drug Culture.* Durham, NC: Duke University Press, 2006.
4. Jane Prather, "The Mystique of Minor Tranquilizers," paper presented to the U.S. Senate Subcommittee on Health and Scientific Research, September 1979; Hughes and Brewin, *The Tranquilizing of America*; Richard Tessler, Randall Stokes, and Marianne Pietras, "Consumer Response to Valium," *Drug Therapy*, February 1978.
5. Robert Whitaker, *Mad in America: Bad Science, Bad Medicine, and the Enduring Mistreatment of the Mentally Ill,* Cambridge, MA: Perseus, p. 7.
6. Ibid., p. 15.
7. Ibid., p. 17.

36.
ON BEING SANE IN INSANE PLACES

DAVID L. ROSENHAN

In this classic article, Rosenhan calls into question the scientific validity and reliability of psychiatric diagnoses. Since this article was written in the 1970s, psychiatry has moved to improve the reliability of diagnoses; and, yet, still today, when a criminal defendant enters an insanity plea, so often there is an expert claiming he or she is sane and another claiming that he or she is insane.

The article is also a classic in its demonstration of the power of psychiatric labels in affecting the lives of those so diagnosed.

If sanity and insanity exist, how shall we know them?

The question is neither capricious nor itself insane. However much we may be personally convinced that we can tell the normal from the abnormal, the evidence is simply not compelling. It is commonplace, for example, to read about murder trials wherein eminent psychiatrists for the defense are contradicted by equally eminent psychiatrists for the prosecution on the matter of the defendant's sanity. More generally, there are a great deal of conflicting data on the reliability, utility, and meaning of such terms as "sanity," "insanity," "mental illness," and "schizophrenia." Finally, as early as 1934, [Ruth] Benedict suggested that normality and abnormality are not universal.[1] What is viewed as normal in one culture may be seen as quite aberrant in another. Thus, notions of normality and abnormality may not be quite as accurate as people believe they are.

To raise questions regarding normality and abnormality is in no way to question the fact that some behaviors are deviant or odd. Murder is deviant. So, too, are hallucinations. Nor does raising such questions deny the existence of the personal anguish that is often associated with "mental illness." Anxiety and depression exist. Psychological suffering exists. But normality and abnormality, sanity and insanity, and the diagnoses that flow from them may be less substantive than many believe them to be.

At its heart, the question of whether the sane can be distinguished from the insane (and whether degrees of insanity can be distinguished from each other) is a simple matter: Do the salient characteristics that lead to diagnoses reside in the patients themselves or in the environments and contexts in which observers find them? From Bleuler, through Kretchmer, through the formulators of the recently revised *Diagnostic and Statistical Manual of the American Psychiatric Association*, the belief has been strong that patients present symptoms, that those symptoms can be categorized, and, implicitly, that the sane are distinguishable from the insane. More recently, however, this belief has been questioned. Based in part on theoretical and anthropological considerations, but also on philosophical, legal, and therapeutic ones, the view has grown that psychological categorization of mental illness is useless at best and downright harmful, misleading, and pejorative at worst. Psychiatric diagnoses, in this view, are in the minds of observers and are not valid summaries of characteristics displayed by the observed.

Gains can be made in deciding which of these is more nearly accurate by getting normal people (that is, people who do not have, and have never suffered, symptoms of serious psychiatric disorders) admitted to psychiatric hospitals and then determining whether they were discovered to be sane and, if so, how. If the sanity of such pseudopatients were always detected, there would be prima facie evidence that a sane individual can be distinguished from the insane context in which he is found. Normality (and presumably abnormality) is distinct enough that it can be recognized wherever it occurs, for it is carried within the person. If, on the other hand, the sanity of the pseudopatients were never discovered, serious difficulties would arise for those who support traditional modes of psychiatric diagnosis. Given that the hospital staff was not incompetent, that the pseudopatient had been behaving as sanely as he had been out of the hospital, and that it had never been previously suggested that he belonged in a psychiatric hospital, such an unlikely outcome would support the view that psychiatric diagnosis betrays little about the patient but much about the environment in which an observer finds him.

This article describes such an experiment. Eight sane people gained secret admission to 12 different hospitals. Their diagnostic experiences constitute the data of the first part of this article; the remainder is devoted to a description of their experiences in psychiatric institutions. Too few psychiatrists and psychologists, even those who have worked in such hospitals, know what the experience is like. They rarely talk about it with former patients, perhaps because they distrust information coming from the previously insane. Those who have worked in psychiatric hospitals are likely to have adapted so thoroughly to the settings that they are insensitive to the impact of that experience. And while there have been occasional reports of researchers who submitted themselves to psychiatric hospitalization, these researchers have commonly remained in the hospitals for short periods of time, often with the knowledge of the hospital staff. It is difficult to know the extent to which they were treated like patients or like research colleagues. Nevertheless, their reports about the inside of the psychiatric hospital have been valuable. This article extends those efforts.

PSEUDOPATIENTS AND THEIR SETTINGS

The eight pseudopatients were a varied group. One was a psychology graduate student in his 20's. The remaining seven were older and "established." Among them were three psychologists, a pediatrician, a psychiatrist, a painter, and a housewife. Three pseudopatients were women, five were men. All of them employed pseudonyms, lest their alleged diagnoses embarrass them later.

Those who were in mental health professions alleged another occupation in order to avoid the special attentions that might be accorded by staff, as a matter of courtesy or caution, to ailing colleagues.[2] With the exception of myself (I was the first pseudopatient and my presence was known to the hospital administration and chief psychologist and, so far as I can tell, to them alone), the presence of pseudopatients and the nature of the research program was not known to the hospital staffs.[3]

The settings are similarly varied. In order to generalize the findings, admission into a variety of hospitals was sought. The 12 hospitals in the sample were located in five different states on the East and West coasts. Some were old and shabby, some were quite new. Some had good staff-patient ratios, others were quite understaffed. Only one was a strict private hospital. All of the others were supported by state or federal funds or, in one instance, by university funds.

After calling the hospital for an appointment, the pseudopatient arrived at the admissions office complaining that he had been hearing voices. Asked what the voices said, he replied that they were often unclear, but as far as he could tell they said "empty," "hollow," and "thud." The voices were unfamiliar and were of the same sex as the pseudopatient. The choice of these symptoms was occasioned by their apparent similarity to existential symptoms. Such symptoms are alleged to arise from painful concerns about the perceived meaninglessness of one's life. It is as if the hallucinating person were saying, "My life is empty and hollow." The choice of these symptoms was also determined by the absence of a single report of existential psychoses in the literature.

Beyond alleging the symptoms and falsifying name, vocation, and employment, no further alterations of person, history, or circumstances were made. The significant events of the pseudopatient's life history were presented as they had actually occurred. Relationships with parents and siblings, with spouse and children, with people at work and in school, consistent with the aforementioned exceptions, were described as they were or had been. Frustrations and upsets were described along with joys and satisfactions. These facts are important to remember. If anything, they strongly biased the subsequent results in favor of detecting insanity, since none of their histories or current behaviors were seriously pathological in any way.

Immediately upon admission to the psychiatric ward, the pseudopatient ceased simulating any symptoms of abnormality. In some cases, there was a brief period of mild nervousness and anxiety, since none of the pseudopatients really believed that they would be admitted so easily. Indeed, their shared fear was that they would be immediately exposed as frauds and greatly embarrassed. Moreover, many of them had never visited a psychiatric ward; even those who had, nevertheless had some genuine fears about what might happen to them. Their nervousness, then, was quite appropriate to the novelty of the hospital setting, and it abated rapidly.

Apart from that short-lived nervousness, the pseudopatient behaved on the ward as he "normally" behaved. The pseudopatient spoke to patients and staff as he might ordinarily. Because there is uncommonly little to do on a psychiatric ward, he attempted to engage others in conversation. When asked by staff how he was feeling, he indicated that he was fine, that he no longer experienced symptoms. He responded to instructions from attendants, to calls for medication (which was not swallowed), and to dining-hall instructions. Beyond such activities as were available to him on the admissions ward, he spent his time writing down his observations about the ward, its patients, and the staff. Initially these notes were written "secretly," but as it soon became clear that no one much cared, they were subsequently written on standard tablets of paper in such public places as the dayroom. No secret was made of these activities.

The pseudopatient, very much as a true psychiatric patient, entered a hospital with no fore-knowledge of when he would be discharged. Each was told that he would have to get out by his own devices, essentially by convincing the staff that he was sane. The psychological stresses associated with hospitalization were considerable, and all but one of the pseudopatients desired to be discharged almost immediately after being admitted. They were, therefore, motivated not only to behave sanely, but to be paragons of cooperation. That their behavior was in no way disruptive is confirmed by nursing reports, which have been obtained on most of the patients. These reports uniformly indicate that the patients were "friendly," "cooperative," and "exhibited no abnormal indications."

THE NORMAL ARE NOT DETECTABLY SANE

Despite their public "show" of sanity, the pseudopatients were never detected. Admitted, except in one case, with a diagnosis of schizophrenia,[4] each was discharged with a diagnosis of schizophrenia "in remission." The label "in remission" should in no way be dismissed as a formality, for at no time during any hospitalization had any question been raised about any pseudopatient's simulation. Nor are there any indications in the hospital records that the pseudopatient's status was suspect. Rather, the evidence is strong that, once labeled schizophrenic, the pseudopatient was stuck with that label. If the pseudopatient was to be discharged, he must naturally be "in remission"; but he was not sane, nor, in the institution's view, had he ever been sane.

The uniform failure to recognize sanity cannot be attributed to the quality of the hospitals, for, although there were considerable variations among them, several are considered excellent. Nor can it be alleged that there was simply not enough time to observe the pseudopatients. Length of hospitalization ranged from 7 to 52 days, with an average of 19 days. The pseudopatients were not, in fact, carefully observed, but this failure speaks more to traditions within psychiatric hospitals than to lack of opportunity.

Finally, it cannot be said that the failure to recognize the pseudopatients' sanity was due to the fact that they were not behaving sanely. While there was clearly some tension present in all of them, their daily visitors could detect no serious behavioral consequences—nor, indeed, could other patients. It was quite common for the patients to "detect" the pseudopatient's sanity. During the first three hospitalizations, when accurate counts were kept, 35 of a total of 118 patients on the admissions ward voiced their suspicions, some vigorously. "You're not crazy. You're a journalist, or a professor (referring to the continual note-taking). You're checking up on the hospital." While most of the patients were reassured by the pseudopatient's insistence that he had been sick before he came in but was fine now, some continued to believe that the pseudopatient was sane throughout his hospitalization. The fact that the patients often recognized normality when staff did not raises important questions.

Failure to detect sanity during the course of hospitalization may be due to the fact that physicians operate with a strong bias toward what statisticians call the Type 2 error. This is to say that physicians are more inclined to call a healthy person sick (a false positive, Type 2) than a sick person healthy (a false negative, Type 1). The reasons for this are not hard to find: it is clearly more dangerous to misdiagnose illness than health. Better to err on the side of caution, to suspect illness even among the healthy.

But what holds for medicine does not hold equally well for psychiatry. Medical illnesses, while unfortunate, are not commonly pejorative. Psychiatric diagnoses, on the contrary, carry with them personal, legal, and social stigmas. It was therefore important to see whether the tendency toward diagnosing the sane insane could be reversed. The following experiment was arranged at a research and teaching hospital whose staff had heard these findings but doubted that such an error could occur in their hospital. The staff was informed that at some time during the following three months, one or more pseudopatients would attempt to be admitted into the psychiatric hospital. Each staff member was asked to rate each patient who presented himself at admissions or on the ward according to the likelihood that the patient was a pseudopatient. A 10-point scale was used, with a 1 and 2 reflecting high confidence that the patient was a pseudopatient.

Judgments were obtained on 193 patients who were admitted for psychiatric treatment. All staff who had had sustained contact with or primary responsibility for the patient—attendants, nurses, psychiatrists, physicians, and psychologists—were asked to make judgments. Forty-one patients were alleged, with high confidence, to be pseudopatients by at least one member of the staff. Twenty-three were considered suspect by at least one psychiatrist. Nineteen were suspected by one psychiatrist and one other staff member. Actually, no genuine pseudopatient (at least from my group) presented himself during this period.

The experiment is instructive. It indicates that the tendency to designate sane people as insane can be reversed when the stakes (in this case, prestige and diagnostic acumen) are high. But what can be said of the 19 people who were suspected of being "sane" by one psychiatrist and another staff member? Were these people truly "sane" or was it rather the case that in the course of avoiding the Type 2 error the staff tended to make more errors of the first sort—calling the crazy "sane"? There is no way of knowing. But one thing is certain: any diagnostic process that lends itself too readily to massive errors of this sort cannot be a very reliable one.

THE STICKINESS OF PSYCHODIAGNOSTIC LABELS

Beyond the tendency to call the healthy sick—a tendency that accounts better for diagnostic behavior on admission than it does for such behavior after a lengthy period of exposure—the data speak to the massive role of labeling in psychiatric assessment. Having once been labeled schizophrenic, there is nothing the pseudopatient can do to overcome the tag. The tag profoundly colors others' perceptions of him and his behavior.

From one viewpoint, these data are hardly surprising, for it has long been known that elements are given meaning by the context in which they occur. Gestalt psychology made the point vigorously, and Asch[5] demonstrated that there are "central" personality traits (such as "warm" versus "cold") which are so powerful that they markedly color the meaning of other information in forming an impression of a given personality. "Insane," "schizophrenic," "manic-depressive," and "crazy" are probably among the most powerful of such central traits. Once a person is designated abnormal, all of his other behaviors and characteristics are colored by that label. Indeed, that label is so powerful that many of the pseudopatients' normal behaviors were overlooked entirely or profoundly misinterpreted. Some examples may clarify this issue.

Earlier, I indicated that there were no changes in the pseudopatient's personal history and current status beyond those of name, employment, and, where necessary, vocation. Otherwise, a veridical description of personal history and circumstances was offered. Those circumstances were not psychotic. How were they made consonant with the diagnosis modified in such a way as to bring them into accord with the circumstances of the pseudopatient's life, as described by him?

As far as I can determine, diagnoses were in no way affected by the relative health of the circumstances of a pseudopatient's life. Rather, the reverse occurred: the perception of his circumstances was shaped entirely by the diagnosis. A clear example of such translation is found in the case of a pseudopatient who had had a close relationship with his mother but was rather remote from his father during his early childhood. During adolescence and beyond, however, his father became a close friend, while his relationship with his mother cooled. His present relationship with his wife was characteristically close and warm. Apart from occasional angry exchanges, friction was minimal. The children had rarely been spanked. Surely there is nothing especially pathological about such a history. Indeed, many readers may see a similar pattern in their own experiences, with no markedly deleterious consequences. Observe, however, how such a history was translated in the psychopathological context, this from the case summary prepared after the patient was discharged.

> This white 39-year-old male . . . manifests a long history of considerable ambivalence in close relationships, which begins in early childhood. A warm relationship with his mother cools during his adolescence. A distant relationship with his father is described as becoming very intense. Affective stability is absent. His attempts to control emotionality with his wife and children are punctuated by angry outbursts and, in the case of the children, spankings. And while he says that he has several good friends, one senses considerable ambivalence embedded in those relationships also . . .

The facts of the case were unintentionally distorted by the staff to achieve consistency with a popular theory of the dynamics of a schizophrenic reaction. Nothing of an ambivalent nature had been described in relations with parents, spouse, or friends. To the extent that ambivalence could be inferred, it was probably not greater than is found in all human's relationships. It is true the pseudopatient's relationships with his parents changed over time, but in the ordinary context that would hardly be remarkable—indeed, it might very well be expected. Clearly, the meaning ascribed to his verbalizations (that is, ambivalence, affective instability) was determined by the diagnosis: schizophrenia. An entirely different meaning would have been ascribed if it were known that the man was "normal."

All pseudopatients took extensive notes publicly. Under ordinary circumstances, such behavior would have raised questions in the minds of observers, as, in fact, it did among patients. Indeed, it seemed so certain that the notes would elicit suspicion that elaborate precautions were taken to remove them from the ward each day. But the precautions proved needless. The closest any staff member came to questioning those notes occurred when one pseudopatient asked his physician what kind of medication he was receiving and began to write down the response. "You needn't write it," he was told gently. "If you have trouble remembering, just ask me again."

If no questions were asked of the pseudopatients, how was their writing interpreted? Nursing records for three patients indicate that the writing was seen as an aspect of their pathological behavior. "Patient engaged in writing behavior" was the daily nursing comment on one of the pseudopatients who was never questioned about his writing. Given that the patient is in the hospital, he must be psychologically disturbed. And given that he is disturbed, continuous writing must be a behavioral manifestation of that disturbance, perhaps a subset of the compulsive behaviors that are sometimes correlated with schizophrenia.

One tacit characteristic of psychiatric diagnosis is that it locates the sources of aberration within the individual and only rarely within the complex of stimuli that surrounds him. Consequently, behaviors that are stimulated by the environment are commonly misattributed to the patient's disorder. For example, one kindly nurse found a pseudopatient pacing the long hospital corridors. "Nervous, Mr. X?" she asked. "No, bored," he said.

The notes kept by pseudopatients are full of patient behaviors that were misinterpreted by well-intentioned staff. Often enough, a patient would go "berserk" because he had, wittingly or unwittingly, been mistreated by, say, an attendant. A nurse coming upon the scene would rarely inquire even cursorily into the environmental stimuli of the patient's behavior. Rather, she assumed that his upset derived from his pathology, not from his present interactions with other staff members. Occasionally, the staff might assume that the patient's family (especially when they had recently visited) or other patients had stimulated the outburst. But never were the staff found to assume that one of themselves or the structure of the hospital had anything to do with a patient's behavior. One psychiatrist pointed to a group of patients who were sitting outside the cafeteria entrance half an hour before lunchtime. To a group of young residents he indicated that such behavior was characteristic of the oral-acquisitive nature of the syndrome. It seemed not to occur to him that there were very few things to anticipate in a psychiatric hospital besides eating.

A psychiatric label has a life and an influence of its own. Once the impression has been formed that the patient is schizophrenic, the expectation is that he will continue to be schizophrenic. When a sufficient amount of time has passed, during which the patient has done nothing bizarre, he is considered to be in remission and available for discharge. But the label endures beyond discharge, with the unconfirmed expectation that he will behave as a schizophrenic again. Such labels, conferred by mental health professionals, are as influential on the patient as they are on his relatives and friends, and it should not surprise anyone that the diagnosis acts on all of them as a self-fulfilling prophecy. Eventually, the patient himself accepts the diagnosis, with all of its surplus meanings and expectations, and behaves accordingly.

The inferences to be made from these matters are quite simple. Much as Zigler and Phillips have demonstrated that there is enormous overlap in the symptoms presented by patients who have been variously diagnosed,[6] so there is enormous overlap in the behaviors of the sane and the insane. The sane are not "sane" all of the time. We lose our tempers "for no good reason." We are occasionally depressed or anxious, again for no good reason. And we may find it difficult to get along with one or another person—again for no reason that we can specify. Similarly, the insane are not always insane. Indeed, it was the impression of the pseudopatients while living with them that they were sane for long periods of time—that the bizarre behaviors upon which their diagnoses were allegedly predicated constituted only a small fraction of their total behavior. If it makes no sense to label ourselves permanently depressed on the basis of an occasional depression, then it takes better evidence than is presently available to label all patients insane or schizophrenic on the basis of bizarre behaviors or cognitions. It seems more useful, as Mischel[7] has pointed out, to limit our discussions to *behaviors*, the stimuli that provoke them, and their correlates.

It is not known why powerful impressions of personality traits, such as "crazy" or "insane," arise. Conceivably, when the origins of and stimuli that give rise to a behavior are remote or unknown, or when the behavior strikes us as immutable, trait labels regarding the behavior arise. When, on the other hand, the origins and stimuli are known and available, discourse is limited to the behavior itself. Thus, I may hallucinate because I am sleeping, or I may hallucinate because I have ingested a peculiar drug. These are termed sleep-induced hallucinations, or dreams, and drug-induced hallucinations, respectively. But when the stimuli to my hallucinations are unknown, that is called craziness, or schizophrenia—as if that inference were somehow as illuminating as the others. . . .

THE CONSEQUENCES OF LABELING AND DEPERSONALIZATION

Whenever the ratio of what is known to what needs to be known approaches zero, we tend to invent "knowledge" and assume that we understand more than we actually do. We seem unable to acknowledge that we simply don't know. The needs for diagnosis and remediation of behavioral and emotional problems are enormous. But rather than acknowledge that we are just embarking on understanding, we continue to label patients "schizophrenic," "manic-depressive," and "insane," as if in those words we captured the essence of understanding. The facts of the matter are that we have known for a long time that diagnoses are often not useful or reliable, but we have nevertheless continued to use them. We now know that we cannot distinguish sanity from insanity. It is depressing to consider how that information will be used.

Not merely depressing, but frightening. How many people, one wonders, are sane but not recognized as such in our psychiatric institutions? How many have been needlessly stripped of their privileges of citizenship, from the right to vote and drive to that of handling their own accounts? How many have feigned insanity in order to avoid the criminal consequences of their behavior, and, conversely, how many would rather stand trial than live interminably in a psychiatric hospital—but are wrongly thought to be mentally ill? How many have been stigmatized by well-intentioned, but nevertheless erroneous, diagnoses? On the last point, recall again that a "Type 2 error" in psychiatric diagnosis does not have the same consequences it does in medical diagnosis. A diagnosis of cancer that has been found to be in error is cause for celebration. But psychiatric diagnoses are rarely found to be in error. The label sticks, a mark of inadequacy forever.

DISCUSSION QUESTIONS

1. How did the environment affect the way the pseudopatients were perceived by others?
2. What variable did Rosenhan introduce to the equation which caused a reversal from the doctors' tendency to make Type 2 errors toward a tendency to make Type 1 errors? (You will find a discussion of this also in the introduction to this section of readings.)

NOTES

1. R. Benedict, *J. Gen. Psychol.*, 10 (1934), 59.
2. Beyond the personal difficulties that the pseudopatient is likely to experience in the hospital, there are legal and social ones that, combined, require considerable attention before entry. For example, once admitted to a psychiatric institution, it is difficult, if not impossible, to be

discharged on short notice, state law to the contrary notwithstanding. I was not sensitive to these difficulties at the outset of the project, nor to the personal and situational emergencies that can arise, but later a writ of habeas corpus was prepared for each of the entering pseudopatients and an attorney was kept "on call" during every hospitalization. I am grateful to John Kaplan and Robert Bartels for legal advice and assistance in these matters.

3. However distasteful such concealment is, it was a necessary first step to examining these questions. Without concealment, there would have been no way to know how valid these experiences were; nor was there any way of knowing whether whatever detections occurred were a tribute to the diagnostic acumen of the hospital's rumor network. Obviously, since my concerns are general ones that cut across individual hospitals and staffs, I have respected their anonymity and have eliminated clues that might lead to their identification.

4. Interestingly, of the 12 admissions, 11 were diagnosed as schizophrenic and one, with the identical symptomatology, as manic-depressive psychosis. This diagnosis has more favorable prognosis, and it was given by the private hospital in our sample. On the relations between social class and psychiatric diagnosis, see A. deB. Hollingshead and F. C. Redlich, *Social Class and Mental Illness: A Community Study* (New York: John Wiley, 1958).

5. S. E. Asch, *J. Abnorm. Soc. Psychol.,* 41 (1946), *Social Psychology* (Englewood Cliffs, NJ: Prentice_ Hall, 1952).

6. E. Zigler and L. Phillips, *J. Abnorm. Soc. Psychol.* 63 (1961), 69. See also R. K. Freudenberg and J. P. Robertson, *A.M.A. Arch. Neurol. Psychiatr.,* 76 (1956), 14.

7. W. Mischel, *Personality and Assessment* (New York; John Wiley, 1968).

37.

"THERE *IS* NO PATHOLOGICAL TEST": MORE ON ADHD AS RHETORIC

SARAH SCHUBERT, SUSAN HANSEN, AND MARK RAPLEY

Like so many other mental and emotional disorders, there are no biological markers that set those who are diagnosed ADHD apart from those who are not. This exposes the psychiatric and mental health communities to substantial criticism given that these conditions are allegedly biological in origin and given that the professionals who utilize these diagnostic categories claim a scientific expertise. When people believe strongly in something, but lack the objective evidence of its existence, then their belief is based on faith. Thomas Szasz (see Article 35 in this section) argued, psychiatry and religion are similar to each other in that they both act as agencies of social control; and, arguably, the authority of both religion and psychiatry is based on faith.

In the following article, the authors deconstruct a pediatrician's testimony before the Western Australian parliament to show how the medical model of deviance rests on the authority of the medical profession rather than on scientific evidence.

A DHD is the most commonly diagnosed and researched psychiatric label given to children today (Radcliffe and Timimi, 2004). At the same time, while ADHD remains a questionable diagnosis, it is the justification for putting tens of thousands of Australian children on psychostimulant drugs every year (Jacobs, 2003). ADHD has been defined and conceptualized in a variety of ways over the past several decades. In contemporary Western societies the dominant discourse surrounding both illness and behavior that is not "normal" is the discourse of scientific medicine. The prevailing cultural belief about ADHD is that it is a medical disorder, and like other mythical entities such as "schizophrenia," this belief is underpinned by widespread social acceptance of the concept's scientific status and legitimacy (Boyle, 2002; Brown, 2004; Sarbin, 1990).

ADHD exists, then, in contemporary western Anglophone societies primarily because it has been positioned by its proponents within the empiricist tradition of medical research (Radcliffe and Timimi, 2004).[1] Once thousands of scientific papers, not to mention advice columns in popular media, have been published about some-thing, the some-thing becomes reified—becomes a *something*: an objective entity that exists "out there" (Hansen, McHoul and Rapley, 2003; Jacobs, 2003).

The successful reification of ADHD makes it extremely difficult for alternative voices to propose that, unlike say tertiary syphilis, Von Economo's encephalitis or tuberculosis, which *are* caused by an objectively discoverable pathogen and which have a demonstrable pathology, ADHD is a purely *hypothetical* construct. And this is despite the fact that even the medical and psy-professions acknowledge that after decades of research there are no cognitive, physiological, metabolic, or neurological markers for ADHD: that there is absolutely no *medical* basis *at all* for the diagnosis (APA, 1994; Jacobs, 2003; NHMRC, 1997). However, while acknowledging that—even by their own lights—ADHD cannot remotely be considered a *bona fide* medical problem, the psy-professions do not, by and large, endorse the alternative view of ADHD which proposes that ADHD is a social construct (Radcliffe and Timini, 2004; Singh, 2002), an invented notion, whose meaning has evolved over time and which is but a reflection of the *social* rather than the *physical* world in which we live (Berger and Luckman, 1987). ADHD is not then a scientifically discovered disorder, but rather a concept created via the discourse of psy to police behaviors that are socially unaccept-able (Foucault, 1963; Jacobs, 2003; Radcliffe and Timimi, 2004). This unwanted conduct, once reified, medicalized, and solidified into dis-ease, of course requires medical professionals to "treat" those who "suffer" from "it."

The primary treatment for children diagnosed with ADHD is psychostimulant medication—usually Ritalin™ (methylphenidate) and dexamphetamine—whose pharmacological properties are similar to the street drugs speed and cocaine (Jacobs, 2003; Radcliffe and Timimi, 2004; Vance and Luk, 2000). Children in Western Australia, some as young as four, are the highest users of licit psychostimulants in the world after their peers in the USA and Canada (Berbatis, Sutherland and Bulsara, 2002). Prescriptions in WA [the state of Western Australia] are four times higher than the Australian average (Mackey and Kopras, 2001). One in twenty-two children in WA take "medica-tion" for ADHD, representing the consumption of nearly 12.9 *million* tablets of dexamphetamine and 2.2 *million* tablets of Ritalin™ in WA every year (Berbatis, et al, 2002).

Concern within the Western Australian community led to a government inquiry into ADHD in 2003-4 (Education and Health Committee, 2004). The inquiry's main aim was to establish why WA has such high incidence rates for ADHD, with concomitant massive levels of psychostimulant (mis)use. A subsidiary aim was to investigate why and how public perceptions in WA appear to have shifted from endorsing the "War on Drugs" slogan that "all drugs are harmful" to "not medicating your child is unethical." The evidence to the inquiry of one of the key players shaping this social debate, a high school principal, was considered by Hewlett, Hansen and Rapley (2005). Here we examine evidence to the inquiry from another professional in a crucial position to influ-ence public beliefs about ADHD: one of the gatekeepers of caseness, a pediatrician.

APPROACH AND ANALYSIS

We draw upon work in discursive psychology, which: "adopts the social constructionist notion that reality is a product of history and culture and is formed through the ways in which language is put together in particular ways, with particular effects" (Tuffin and Howard, 2001, p.199). That is, we view contemporary understandings of (problematic) conduct in children as "knowledge" still in the process of manufacture, a product of the ways in which we talk about or describe the world, rather than assuming that reality is evident, stable and waiting to be discovered (Pilgrim and Rogers, 1993).

We employ Membership Categorization Analysis (Sacks, 1995; see also Silverman, 1998) to examine the categories associated with ADHD, how they are created and maintained through talk, and the consequences of choosing one category rather than another. That is, although there are potentially infinite alternative ways to categorize (unruly) conduct, the categorization of such conduct *as* "ADHD" influences how it is understood by members, and has implications for the interventions considered most appropriate to "treat" those "diagnosed" with it. The descriptions in the evidence here are not, then, just *about* ADHD, they are active in *producing* ADHD *as such*. They are not mere representations of the pediatrician's expert knowledge of ADHD, but are designed to influence committee members' beliefs about ADHD, and in turn to flavor the committee's recommendations to government on the management of ADHD in the community. The evidence considered here had the potential to influence how ADHD was understood in the wider community at many levels, from individuals, families and schools, to health practitioners, the health care system, and State health policy.

ADHD AS A "REAL" DISEASE: PROBLEMS OF STAKE AND INTEREST

"P," the pediatrician, categorizes himself in his opening statement as a medical professional, a practitioner in behavioral and developmental pediatrics.[2] Categorizing himself as a member with medical expertise entitles him to certain rights, and one of these rights is that, as he possesses legitimate knowledge about medicine and medical conditions, his reports and descriptions should be given special credence (Potter, 1996). His category membership is not only crucial to his entitlement to speak on topic but *provides for* his credibility and the "truth" of his descriptions. However, although P's category-bound knowledge entitlement might be expected to warrant the facticity of his statements, it is also the case that bald membership claims may reveal the interest of the speaker in the position they advance (Potter, 1996). As such it is necessary for P to buttress his case and, as we see in Extract 1, he clearly orients to precisely this need.

That is, this privileged access to truth granted by category incumbency is oriented to by P early on in his evidence. Implicitly positioning himself as of both higher social status than, and as occupying an epistemologically privileged position relative to, the committee members he addresses, in Extract 1 P constructs his role in the inquiry as being to enlighten the uninformed and "out-of-date" committee members (1. 6) on the contemporary realities of ADHD.[3]

Extract 1
P
1. ADHD is a real disorder; it is recognized by all major
2. government health organizations throughout the
3. world and medical associations and is the most common
4. psychiatric disorder affecting children. I will not go
5. through my submission today because you have read it.
6. I want to try to bring you up to date with the things that
7. have happened

It is apparent, however, that P is all too well aware of the precariousness of the facticity of ADHD and the truth-value to be accorded to medical practitioners. This is made explicit in Extract 1 via the fact that P not only relies on his *own* category membership to imbue his evidence with credibility but also, through appealing to other prestigious bodies ("all major government health organizations throughout the world and medical associations"), constructs extreme case formulated corroboration and consensus warrants to justify his construction of ADHD as "truth" (cf. LeCouteur, Rapley and Augoustinos, 2000; Rapley, 1998).

ADHD is characterized as both a "real" (1.1) and a "psychiatric" disorder (1.4).[4] By using the term "disorder" and, via extreme case formulations (Pomerantz, 1986), citing the ratification of ADHD as such by *"all* major government health organizations and "medical associations *throughout the world"* ADHD is produced as belonging, unequivocally, to scientific medical discourse. Categorizing ADHD as such suggests that it is an illness, a medical condition, which in turn requires treatment. The unproblematized categorization of ADHD as "the *most common* psychiatric disorder" (1.3–4) also works neatly to recuperate the potentially disreputable practice of psychiatry into medicine proper. Categorizing ADHD within medical discourse allows it to be spoken of as an objective entity discovered through science, an entity that exists like other medical illnesses such as chickenpox or the flu and, moreover, one that is certified as such by governments (Boyle, 2002; Brown, 2004).

However, as Potter (1996) has noted, although a number of categories may provide for potentially correct categorizations, the "correct" category—that is, the one we actually select and use, on any occasion—tends to be the category that best supports our interests, on that occasion. Because this is a piece of well-appreciated cultural common sense, anything P says has the potential to be discounted as a product of his stake or interest in a *particular* version of reality. His stake and interest in the matter thus present P with an immediate problem in establishing the factual status of his particular account. As Mandy Rice-Davies famously put it, "he would say that wouldn't he?" To establish as "fact" the notion that ADHD is a medical disorder P provides a lengthy, elaborate, and detailed account of the "proper medical" process involved in diagnosing ADHD that is too long to reproduce here (see Education & Health Committee, 2004). Via specific, intricate, and technical details P attempts to shore up the credibility of his account. However a problem with providing richly detailed accounts is that speakers leave themselves open to being undermined in various ways (Potter, 1996). Within P's evidence the irresolvable paradox of a pathology-free "real" disease, and the questionable scientificity of psychiatric classification (precisely the issues that P's opening in Extract 1 attempted to bury) were identified as problematic by the committee.

THERE IS NO PATHOLOGICAL TEST

In Extract 2 a committee member attempts to clarify the paradox central to P's detailed description of diagnostic practice.

Extract 2

CM

1. To be absolutely clear: do you regard ADHD as a
2. neurological disorder for which there is no clinical test
3. and for which diagnosis is based on observation of
4. behavior?

P

5. Yes; there is no pathological test. The clinical test is the
6. symptoms and the exclusion of other disorders. . . . One

7. thing about medicine and behavior is that it is very
8. difficult to be black and white.

In Extract 2 P acknowledges that it is "absolutely clear" (2.1) that ADHD is a neurological disorder that, miraculously, not only has no clinical test, but also no apparent pathology. ADHD is, then, a biological disease without physical means of support (cf. Newnes, 2002). Unlike other run-of-the-mill neurological disorders where neuropathology is evident—motor neurone disease for instance—in the case of ADHD, biological abnormality is not required. Instead, the test for caseness is simply to appear symptomatic. To all intents and purposes P's evidence here amounts to saying "trust me, I'm a doctor—I know it when I see it." It is difficult to imagine any other branch of medicine where such a cavalier approach to disease identification would be countenanced: the equivalent in general practice might be to refer any and all presentations of fever randomly around specialties not on the basis of blood tests, but rather of a gut feeling that *this* fever is malarial, *that* one is septicemic and *the one over there in the corner is a* case of rubella.[5] Should this sound alarmingly subjective, P proceeds to imply a process of differential diagnosis via his citing of the practice of "exclusion" of other disorders.[6] Further (as P makes clear in lines 6–8 one needs to be a special kind of expert in order to identify such cases—given that whereas medicine is straightforward and precise, "medicine and behavior" combined create a specialty in which it is "difficult to be black and white."

In Extract 3, in an attempt to repudiate committee members' skepticism about his account of the scientificity of the diagnosis of ADHD, P appeals to expertise, both his own extensive experience in diagnosing children with ADHD and the reliability and "sophistication" (3.5) of the authors of the DSM-IV.[7]

Extract 3

P

1. It is reliable because the people who created the
2. diagnostic manuals such as the DSM-IV do not just
3. write down a list of symptoms and say that is how you
4. do it. They create ways they think are appropriate from
5. a sophisticated committee. They then run a field trial
6. to see how well this particular symptom differentiates
7. children who are normal from children who are
8. impaired.

Rather than strengthening his position with this statement, here P unwittingly undermines the credibility of the disorder—and indeed, arguably, the wider psy complex. P's account is presumably designed to accentuate the objectivity, reliability, scientificity, and above all, *medical* basis of ADHD through invoking the magisterial authority of the DSM. However, his account serves also to expose the very process through which ADHD was arbitrarily *invented by committee* and exists as a social construct, rather than being the object, like penicillin perhaps, of accidental but physical medical discovery (see Jacobs, 2003 especially pp. 10–11). P's evidence in Extract 3 also clearly demonstrates the taken-for-grantedness of the power of such "sophisticated" professions knowledge by its custodians. It appears that P takes it as given that when powerful interests (psy, for example) define phenomena as "real," by committee or by *fiat*, the phenomena in question are expected to be uncritically accepted as such by the public at large.[8]

However, in the face of this description of the rigors of the construction of reliable diagnostic criteria—by *scientific* committee—the *parliamentary* committee appeared unconvinced. Pursuing the issue of differential diagnosis and medication, P was asked about the incidence of ADHD. While even the American Psychiatric Association (1994) concedes that there is no proven biological etiology for ADHD, the primary treatment of choice for P, as we see in Extract 4, is individual intervention in the form of a biological treatment—psychostimulant medication.

Extract 4
CM
1. I am trying to get a handle on the number of people
2. who may present and who seek alternatives or who
3. end up on prescription drugs. Does the vast majority
4. end up on a prescription or is that only a small percentage?
5. How many?

P
6. I do not have exact figures. It is my impression that
7. the percentage has been changing over the years. Fifteen
8. or 20 years ago when they were first presenting and had not
9. been diagnosed, many of the children who came to see
10. me were put onto medication because legitimate
11. diagnoses of ADHD were made. My impression is that
12. there are far fewer now. As an estimate, at least a
13. quarter of my patients who present do not end up on
14. medication.

Of importance here is not so much what is being said, but what is *not* being said, and that is that *seventy-five per cent* of children who present end up on medication (cf. Zito, et al., 1999). This is apparently something to do with the changing "legitimacy" of diagnoses "over the years," but what constitutes a "legitimate" diagnosis is not explained.[9] Here, strangely, P offers neither detailed, precise and accurate statistics, nor even bald "fact" statements of the "ADHD is a real disorder" variety. There are no "exact figures," but rather "impressions," and "estimates." In the face of such imprecision, given that one of the committee's main terms of reference was to investigate the consequences of WA's massive prescription rates, committee members sought reassurance about the scientific evidence base of psychostimulant treatment. In Extract 5 P describes studies examining the long-term effects of psychostimulant consumption.

Extract 5
P
1. There are no studies looking at medication that go
2. beyond two years in any country in the world. The
3. statement from the expert panel brought out by
4. Professor George Lipton, which included Lawrence
5. Greenhill and psychiatrists from all over Australia,
6. stated clearly that these medications have been in use
7. for 50 or 60 years and no long-term side effects have
8. been identified. It is highly unlikely that we will see
9. long-term effects.

CM

10. This is what worries me. We have children of four-and-a-
11. half years of age on psychostimulants; yet, we have
12. acknowledged there are side effects but there are no
13. long-term studies to show whether they are safe.

P

14. It is not an unusual position in medicine. The side effects of
15. the original disorder may be far worse than the potential
16. side effects of the medication. We know what the side
17. effects of the original disorder may be over time because
18. that has been studied carefully.

Quite apart from the fact that it is simply ungrammatical to talk of the "side effects of the original disorder" (5.14–15, 17–18), P's evidence here again reveals the fragility of the psy-account of ADHD simply by virtue of the work that has to be done to buttress it. Once more relying on extreme case formulations (5.2 "in *any* country in the world"; 5.5 "psychiatrists from *all over* Australia") P constructs wide consensus on the harmlessness of psychostimulants and corroboration of this position and by associating his views with those of "Professors" and nameless "expert panels" who have access to "careful studies" (5.18)[10] This works to draw attention away from the nonsensical nature of his claims (cf. Wittgenstein, 1958) while at the same time seeking to strengthen them as fact. Of course to say "no long-term side effects have been identified" (5.7–8) immediately after suggesting that two years is the upper limit of extant studies (5.1–2) obscures the fact that if long-term side effects have not been *looked for,* then of course they will not have been *found.*

It is noteworthy that, when challenged (5.10–13), P again relies upon the morally coercive power of "medical" discourse to dismiss the concerns of his interlocutor. He simply and confidently states that an absence of long-term studies of drug safety is "not unusual"; that is presumably it is normal and acceptable, as a prelude to a frankly incoherent, but at face value "scientific," set of claims about what is known in "medicine."

In concluding his evidence, the pediatrician makes a series of recommendations to the committee about the proper management of ADHD. Having proposed to the committee that it would be desirable (presumably in the interest of social justice) to "make long-acting medications available to everybody—equity of access," P once more deploys scientistic jargon to reiterate the empiricism of psychiatric pediatrics.

Extract 6

P

1. My third recommendation is that we must use the
2. scientific method when we are dealing with this
3. disorder. We need to use the kinds of algorithms and
4. diagnostic methodologies I talked about earlier on to
5. teach our pediatricians and our trainees how this
6. disorder is diagnosed and best treated in the future.

ADHD is, then, to the last a medical disorder that needs to be diagnosed and treated via the use of "scientific method," "algorithms" and "diagnostic methodologies." Of course such a construction absolutely precludes the possibility of alternative ways of knowing and "dealing with" the unruly or uninterested conduct of small persons.

SOME CONCLUDING OBSERVATIONS

There are always different ways in which a story can be told, a concept described, or phenomena categorized. What we hope to have highlighted here is that the ways in which ADHD is talked about by currently influential members of society, the manner in which unruly or irritating conduct—forgetting one's pencils for instance—is categorized, has direct implications for how that conduct is comprehended and addressed. Practitioners in genuine sciences seem to feel little need to reassure us of the status of their endeavors as "scientific." However, in much the same way that clinical psychologists relentlessly claim to be "scientist-practitioners" engaged in "evidence-based practice," here we have seen the paradox of a neurological disease with "symptoms" but no "pathology."

Less paradoxical perhaps, and more encouraging, is the critical reception by *parliamentary* committee, of the science-by-committee methods of the DSM, and accordingly of the quality of any associated expert evidence. It seems that while appeals to *soi-disant* "scientific knowledge" are *often* convincing, they are not *necessarily* so—especially in the face of the growing self-evidence of the need for concern over the "alarming" rates of ADHD diagnosis in our young people—or, alternatively stated, the clear imposition of a particularly violent regime of *moral* truth.

DISCUSSION QUESTIONS

1. What do you think of the pediatrician's testimony? What is the point of the article?
2. What do you think of the technique the authors use to analyze their data? Is it subject to bias?

NOTES

1. As McHoul and Rapley note , speaking a language other than English seems, strangely, to confer near immunity from the dis-ease.
2. Hewlett, Hansen and Rapley (2005) note how the high school principal whose evidence they examined was also careful to claim special expertise by virtue of his co-membership in the categories of "education professional" and "father of an ADHD child."
3. In Extracts P is the pediatrician, CM denotes a committee member.
4. That this claim needs to be made at all points to the very real doubt that there must be about the notion of ADHD as a "real," as opposed to a mythical, anything. Can we sensibly imagine a gastroenterologist *needing* to say "bowel cancer is a *real* disorder," a marine biologist assuring a parliamentary inquiry that "a kipper is a *real* fish," or a chemist having to defend the idea that "sulphur is a *real* chemical"?
5. That P is not an anomaly in this respect may be confirmed by an inspection of the diagnostic session conducted by another Perth pediatrician discussed in McHoul and Rapley (2005).
6. This roughly translates as "if I can't think of anything else that might cause Johnny to have symptoms like forgetting his pencils, avoiding his homework and squirming in his seat (APA, 1994) he must have ADHD." It is now of course, impossible to imagine a child ever being bored to distraction. . . .
7. Of course, the argument here is akin to an Inquisitor claiming that witch burning was the correct procedure for the salvation of souls because of the scrupulousness with which the identificatory strategies outlined by the theologically sophisticated authors of the *Malleus Maleficarum* (Kramer and Sprenger, 1468) were adhered to.

8. We are reminded that, as Michael Moore points out in *Fahrenheit 9/11*, all sorts of things—like imaginary Nigerian yellowcake, Iraqi links to al-Qaeda and WMDs—can be made to be "real" simply by the relentless repetition of their "reality" by those in positions of power.

9. *En passant,* we note that diagnoses of masturbatory insanity, feeble-mindedness, drapetomania, moral defectiveness, dementia praecox—and even of minimal brain dysfunction—also appear to have declined "over the years."

10. Presumably P is unaware that the DSM-IV lists Amphetamine Dependence Disorder and Amphetamine Psychosis as potential effects of psychostimulant consumption. He also seems not to have noticed that the label on pharmacy-dispensed bottles of dexamphetamine in WA reads: "Controlled Drug. Possession without authority illegal. Keep out of reach of children."

REFERENCES

American Psychiatric Association (1994) *Diagnostic and Statistical Manual of Mental Disorders* (4th ed). Washington DC: APA.

Berbatis, C., Sunderland, V. and Bulsara, M. (2002) Licit Psychostimulant Consumption in Australia, 1984–2000: International and jurisdictional comparison. *Medical Journal of Australia, 177,* 539–52.

Berger, P. and Luckman, T. (1987) *The Social Construction of Reality. A treatise in the sociology of knowledge.* Reading: Penguin.

Boyle, M. (2002) *Schizophrenia: A scientific delusion?* (2nd ed). London: Routledge.

Brown, F. (2004) Scientific narratives and ADHD. *Clinical Psychology, 40,* 17–20.

Education and Health Committee (2004) *Attention Deficit Disorder and Attention Deficit Disorder in Western Australia.* Transcript of evidence taken at Perth, June 30, 2004, from Dr Kenneth Rowland Whiting. Retrieved August 29, 2004, from http://www.parliament.wa.gov.au/parliament/commitnsf/ 0/ AC486CC98EB18ADD48/web/newwebparlnsf/framewebpages/committees+-+past>

Foucault, M. (1963/73). *The Birth of the Clinic. An archeology of medical perception.* Trans. by S. Smith. London: Tavistock.

Hansen, S., McHoul, A. and Rapley, M. (2003) *Beyond Help: A consumer's guide to psychology.* Ross-on-Wye: PCCS Books.

Hewlett, T., Hansen, S. and Rapley, M. (2005) "Like bees to a honey pot": ADHD as rhetoric. *Journal of Critical Psychology, Counselling and Psychotherapy, 5*(2), 94–103.

Jacobs, B. (2003) *Western Australian Parliamentary Inquiry into ADD and ADHD.* Retrieved September 15, 2004, from http://www.yarig.org.au/index.pl?page=getdoc&lnk_id=180&doc_id=113.

Kramer, H. and Sprenger, J. (1468/1971) *The Malleus Maleficarum of Heinrich Kramer and James Sprenger.* Translated with an Introduction, Bibliography & Notes by the Reverend Montague Summers. New York: Dover Publications.

LeCouteur, Rapley, M. and Augoustinos (2000) "This is a very difficult debate about Wi." Stake, voice and the management of membership categories in race politics. *British Journal of Social Psychology, 40,* 35–57.

Mackey, P. and Kopras, A. (2001) *Medication for Attention Deficit/Hyperactivity Disorder (ADHD): An analysis by federal electorate.* Retrieved March 31, 2004, from http://www.aphgov.au/library/pubs/cib/2000-01cib11.htm.

McHoul, A. and Rapley, M. (2005) A Case of ADHD Diagnosis: Sir Karl and Francis B slug it out on the consulting room floor. *Discourse and Society, 16*(3), 419–49.

Newnes, C. (2002) Brainwashed. *The Guardian,* 10 January.

NHMRC (1997) *Attention Deficit Hyperactivity Disorder.* Retrieved March 15, 2005, from http://www .nhmrc.gov.au/ publications/ adhd/ contents.htm.

Pilgrim, D. and Rogers, A (1993) A *Sociology of Mental Health and Illness.* Buckingham: Open University Press.

Pomerantz, A. M. (1986) Extreme case formulations: A way of legitimizing claims. *Human Studies, 9,* 219–30.

Potter, J. (1996) *Representing Reality: Discourse, rhetoric and social construction.* London: Sage.

Radcliffe, N. and Timimi, S. (2004). The rise and rise of ADHD. *Clinical Psychology, 40,* 8–16.

Rapley, M. (1998). "Just an ordinary Australian": Self-categorisation and the discursive construction of facticity in "new racist" political rhetoric. *British Journal of Social Psychology, 37,* 325–44.

Sacks, H. (1995) *Lectures on Conversation.* Oxford: Blackwell.

Sarbin, T. R. (1990) Toward the obsolescence of the schizophrenia hypothesis, *Journal of Mind and Behaviour, 11*(3 and 4), 131–38/259–84.

Silverman, D. (1998) *Harvey Sacks: Social science and conversation analysis.* New York: Oxford University Press.

Singh, I. (2002) Biology in Context: Social and Cultural Perspectives on ADHD. *Children & Society, 16,* 360–67.

Tuffin, K., and Howard, C. (2001) Demystifying discourse analysis: Theory, method and practice. In A. McHoul and M. Rapley (eds.) (2001) *How to Analyse Talk in Institutional Settings: A casebook of methods.* London: Continuum.

Vance, A. L. A. and Luk, E. S. L. (2000) Attention deficit hyperactivity disorder: Current progress and controversies. *Australian and New Zealand Journal of Psychiatry, 34,* 719–30.

Wittgenstein, L. (1958) *Philosophical Investigations.* Oxford: Blackwell.

Zito, J. M., Safer, D. J., dosReis, S., Magder, L. S., Gardner, J. F. and Zarin, D. (1999) Psychotherapeutic Medication Patterns for Youths with Attention-Deficit/Hyperactivity Disorder. *Archives of Pediatrics and Adolescent Medicine, 153,* 1257–63.

38.
SCHIZOPHRENIA IN THE THIRD WORLD

RICHARD WARNER

Paradoxically, while the United States is presumed to have among the most advanced medical treatments in the world, schizophrenia patients in many Third-World countries often have better prognoses than those in the United States. That is, schizophrenia is generally considered incurable in the United States, whereas frequently patients in the Third World who exhibit the symptoms of the "disease" frequently get over it. As you will see in the following article, many of the factors that are strongly correlated with recovery from schizophrenia are social and environmental factors, thus calling into question the role of biological and medical factors alleged by Western psychiatrists.

Sixteen billion dollars was spent on the treatment of schizophrenia in the United States in 1990[1]—about 0.3 per cent of the gross domestic product. This figure excludes social security benefits paid to people with schizophrenia and other indirect costs. Such a substantial investment should surely have yielded Americans significantly better rates of recovery than in less affluent parts of the world. By contrast, psychiatric care is very low on the list of priorities in developing countries. Despite this fact, the evidence points overwhelmingly to much better outcome from schizophrenia in the Third World. It is worth looking at this evidence in some detail.

BRIEF PSYCHOSIS IN THE THIRD WORLD

There are numerous reports that psychoses have a briefer duration in the Third World, and virtually none to indicate that such illnesses have a worse outcome anywhere outside the Western world. Transitory delusional states (*bouffées délirantes*) in Senegal, for example, with such schizophrenia-like features as "derealization, hallucinations, and ideas of reference dominated by themes of persecution and megalomania"[2] occasionally develop the classic, chronic course of schizophrenia, but generally recover spontaneously within a short period of time. Acute paranoid reactions with a favorable course and outcome are common in the Grande Kabylie of northern Algeria[3] and throughout East Africa.[4] Acute psychotic episodes with high rates of spontaneous remission are frequent in Nigeria,[5] and brief schizophrenia-like psychoses have been reported to account for four-fifths of the admissions to one psychiatric hospital in Uganda.[6] Indistinguishable from schizophrenia, acute "fear and guilt psychoses" in Ghana manifest hallucinations, inappropriate emotional reactions, grotesque delusions and bizarre behavior. Under treatment at local healing shrines, such illnesses are generally cured within a week or so, although they may occasionally progress to chronic schizophrenia.[7] Doris Mayer, a psychiatrist, also found typical schizophrenic states to be more readily reversible in the Tallensi of northern Ghana.[8] Many more examples could be given of the prevalence of such brief psychoses in Singapore, Papua and other developing countries.[9] "Acute, short lasting psychoses," according to Dr H. B. M. Murphy, a Canadian psychiatrist with much research experience in cross-cultural psychiatry, "form a major part of all recognized mental disorders . . ." in the Third World.[10]

NOT REALLY SCHIZOPHRENIA

But are they schizophrenia? Some psychiatrists would argue that these acute psychoses are indeed schizophrenia in view of the typical schizophrenic features such as hallucinations, delusions, bizarre behavior and emotional disturbances. They would also point to the minority of cases, initially indistinguishable, which develop the chronic schizophrenic picture. Others would deny that any brief psychosis can be schizophrenia precisely because schizophrenia, by definition, is a long-lasting illness. According to the American Psychiatric Association's *Diagnostic and Statistical Manual* (DSM-IV),[11] a psychosis must last six months to be labeled schizophrenia. This is a terminological issue that must not be allowed to obscure the point of logic. If schizophrenia has a more benign course in the developing world (and there is considerable evidence to show that this is the case), then we might well find many schizophrenia-like episodes in these societies that are of a shorter duration than six months. To argue that these are not schizophrenia is to prejudge the issue.

Could these be cases of organic psychosis? Certainly, some could be. There is a high prevalence in Third World countries of trypanosomiasis, pellagra and related parasitic, nutritional and infectious disorders that may develop into psychotic states. Malaria, in particular, is often associated with acute psychotic episodes.[12] It is unlikely, however, that all brief episodes in the Third World are organic in origin. In conducting their social psychiatric survey of four aboriginal tribes in Taiwan, two psychiatrists, Hsien Rin and Tsung-Yi Lin, were particularly concerned about the diagnosis of organic and functional psychoses. They carefully separated schizophrenia from malarial psychosis, drug-induced psychosis and unclassifiable cases. Although skeptical at the outset of the study, after cross-checking their information and cross-validating their diagnoses they were forced to conclude that psychoses in general, and schizophrenia in particular, had a particularly benign course among these Formosan farmers and hunters. Of ten confirmed cases of schizophrenia only two had been active for more than two years and five had been ill for less than a year.[13]

. . . Schizophrenia in the Third World has a course and prognosis quite unlike the condition as we recognize it in the West. The progressive deterioration that Kraepelin considered central to his definition of the disease is a rare event in non-industrial societies, except perhaps under the dehumanizing restrictions of a traditional asylum. The majority of people with schizophrenia in the Third World achieve a favorable outcome. The more urbanized and industrialized the setting, the more malignant becomes the illness. Why should this be so?

WORK

It [has been argued] that the dwindling cure rates for insanity during the growth of industrialism in Britain and America, and the low recovery rates in schizophrenia during the Great Depression, were possibly related to labor-force dynamics. . . . The picture that has now been drawn of schizophrenia in the Third World gives more support to the notion that the work role may be an important factor shaping the course of schizophrenia.

In non-industrial societies that are not based upon a wage economy, the term "unemployment" is meaningless. Even where colonial wage systems have been developed, they frequently preserve the subsistence base of tribal or peasant communities, drawing workers for temporary labor only.[14] In these circumstances, underemployment and landlessness may become common but unemployment is rare. Unemployment, however, may reach high levels in the urbanized and industrial areas of the Third World.

The return of a person suffering from psychosis to a productive role in a non-industrial setting is not contingent upon his or her actively seeking a job, impressing an employer with his or her worth or functioning at a consistently adequate level. In a non-wage, subsistence economy, people with mental illness may perform any of those available tasks that match their level of functioning at a given time. Whatever constructive contributions they can make are likely to be valued by the community and their level of disability will not be considered absolute. Dr. Adios Lambs, a psychiatrist well known for developing a village-based treatment and rehabilitation program in Nigeria, reports that social attitudes in Nigerian rural communities permit the majority of those with mental disorders to find an appropriate level of functioning and thus to avoid disability and deterioration.[15] In India, research workers for the World Health Organization's [WHO] follow-up study of schizophrenia encountered difficulty in interviewing their cases as the ex-patients were so busy—the men in the fields and the women in domestic work.[16] In rural Sichuan, China, more than three-quarters of people with schizophrenia who had never been treated were working; even people with significant psychotic symptoms were doing housework or farm work.[17] The more complete use of labor in pre-industrial societies may encourage high rates of recovery from psychosis.

But what of the nature of the work itself? John Wing, a British social psychiatrist who undertook a great deal of research on schizophrenia, identified two critical environmental factors that lead to optimal outcome from the illness. The first of these, which we will return to later, is freedom from emotional over-involvement—smothering or criticism—from others in the household. His second criterion, which is relevant here, is that there should be stable expectations precisely geared to the level of performance that the individual can actually achieve.[18] Industrial society gives relatively little leeway for adapting a job to the abilities of the worker. High productivity requirements and competitive performance ratings may be particularly unsuitable for a person recovering from schizophrenia. In a peasant culture he or she is more likely to find an appropriate role among such tasks of subsistence farming as livestock management, food- and fuel-gathering or child-minding. . . .

In each setting there is wide individual variation. In pre-revolutionary Russia, for example, peasant farmers in Volokolamsk worked between 79 days a year in the least industrious households and 216 in the most industrious.[19] This compares with an expectation of around

230 to 240 working days a year for employees in modern industrial society. Work demands in many cultures are particularly low for young, unmarried adults[20] (who may be at higher risk for developing schizophrenia), but whatever the usual pattern, workload expectations are more readily adjusted to meet the capacities of the marginally functional individual in a village setting than in the industrial labor market. There can be little doubt that it is simpler for a person with schizophrenia to return to a productive role in a non-industrial community than in the industrial world. The merits of tribal and peasant labor systems are apparent. As in the West during a period of labor shortage, it is easier for family and community members to reintegrate the sick person into the society, and the sufferer is better able to retain his or her self-esteem. The result may well be not only better social functioning of the sick person but also more complete remission of the symptoms of the illness.

OCCUPATION AND OUTCOME

[The] WHO Pilot Study data more clearly document an association between occupation and outcome. Farmers were more likely than patients of any other occupation to experience the most benign pattern of illness—full remission with no relapses—and the unemployed were least likely to experience such a mild course to the psychosis. In urbanized Cali and Taipei patients from high-status professional and managerial occupations were found to achieve good overall outcome, while this was not the case in the largely rural catchment area around Agra, India.[21] This pattern confirms the impression that schizophrenia may be more benign in the successful upper classes in the industrialized setting, but more malignant among the better educated in India who are known to suffer rates of unemployment several times greater than the poorly educated and illiterate.[22] The data from Nigeria do not fit as neatly. Even though many patients in the sample appear to have come from rural districts, Nigerians with schizophrenia in managerial jobs experienced good overall outcome.[23] This could be explained by a strong local demand for educated labor at that time or, again, the high mobility of the migrant labor force may confuse the picture; patients who were unable to continue in managerial positions could return to a less demanding role in their farming community.

Migrant-labor practices allow people with schizophrenia in the Third World to change occupation and residence after developing psychotic symptoms. Level of education, however, is less easily changed. It is therefore interesting to note that a *high* level of education is one of the few strong and consistent indicators of *poor* outcome in the Third World,[24] thus standing in contrast to Western patterns of recovery. This point, then, may be one of the most useful pieces of evidence in the WHO study, pointing to a link between good outcome for schizophrenia in the Third World and the maintenance of traditional occupational roles. . . .

A PSYCHOTIC EPISODE IN GUATEMALA

Maria, a young Indian woman living in a village on Lake Atitlan in Guatemala, alienates her close relatives and the people of the community by her irresponsible behavior before finally suffering a full-blown psychotic episode. She hallucinates, believing that spirits are surrounding her to take her to the realm of the dead, and she walks about the house arguing with ghosts. A local shaman perceives that she is *loca* (crazy) and diagnoses her as suffering the effect of supernatural forces unleashed by the improper behavior of certain relatives. He prescribes a healing ritual that calls for the active participation of most of her extended family. Her condition requires her to move back to her father's house, where she recovers within a week. Benjamin Paul, the anthropologist who describes Maria's case, points out several features of interest. Maria is never blamed for her psychotic behavior or stigmatized by her illness, because her hallucinations of ghosts are credible supernatural events and she is innocently suffering the magical consequences of the wrongdoing of others. The communal healing activities lead to a dramatic reversal of Maria's course of alienation from family and community. In the West, a psychotic episode is likely to lead to increased alienation. In the case of Maria, conflict resolution and social reintegration are central to her recovery and result from the folk diagnosis and treatment of her symptoms.[25]

THE FOLK DIAGNOSIS OF PSYCHOSIS

Throughout the non-industrial world, the features of psychosis are likely to be given a supernatural explanation. The Shona of Southern Rhodesia, for example, believe visual and auditory hallucinations to be real and sent by spirits.[26] In Dakar, Senegal:

> one can have hallucinations without being thought to be sick. A magical explanation is usually resorted to and native specialists are consulted. There is no rejection or alienation by society. The patient remains integrated within his group. As a result, the level of anxiety is low.[27]

The psychiatrist who gives this report claims that 90 per cent of the acute psychoses in Dakar are cured because the patient's delusions and hallucinations have an obvious culturally relevant content, and he or she is not rejected by the group.

Similarly, in the slums of San Juan, Puerto Rico:

> If an individual reports hallucinations, it clearly indicates to the believer in spiritualism that he is being visited by spirits who manifest themselves visually and audibly. If he has delusions . . . his thoughts are being distorted by interfering bad spirits, or through development of his psychic faculties spirits have informed him of the true enemies in his environment. Incoherent ramblings, and cryptic verbalizations indicate that he is undergoing a test, an experiment engineered by the spirits. If he wanders aimlessly through the neighborhood, he is being pursued by ambulatory spirits who are tormenting him unmercifully.[28]

In many cases where a supernatural explanation for psychotic features is used, the label "crazy" or "insane" may never be applied. I once remarked to a Sioux mental health worker from the Pine Ridge Reservation in South Dakota that most Americans who heard voices would be diagnosed as suffering from psychosis. Her response was simple. "That's terrible."

STIGMA

Psychiatrists working in the Third World have repeatedly noted the low level of stigma that attaches to mental disorder. Among the Formosan tribesmen studied by Rio and Lin, mental illness is free of stigma.[29] Sinhalese families freely refer to their psychotic family members as *pissu* (crazy) and show no shame about it. Tuberculosis in Sri Lanka is more stigmatizing than mental illness.[30] The authors of the WHO follow-up study suggest that one of the factors contributing to the good outcome for people with schizophrenia in Cali, Colombia, is the "high level of tolerance of relatives and friends for symptoms of mental disorder"—a factor that can help the "readjustment to family life and work after discharge."[31]

The possibility that the stigma attached to an illness may influence its course is illustrated by research on Navajos who suffer from epilepsy conducted by anthropologist Jerrold Levy in cooperation with the Indian Health Service. Sibling incest is regarded as the cause of generalized seizures, or Moth Sickness, in Navajo society, and those who suffer from the condition are highly stigmatized for supposed transgressions of a major taboo. It is interesting to learn that these individuals are often found to lead chaotic lives characterized by alcoholism, promiscuity, incest, rape, violence and early death. Levy and his co-workers attribute the career of the Navajo epileptic to the disdain and lack of social support that he or she is offered by the community.[32] To what extent, we may wonder, can features of schizophrenia in the West be attributed to similar treatment?

HIGH STATUS IN PSYCHOSIS

It seems strange in retrospect that tuberculosis should have been such a romantic and genteel illness to eighteenth- and nineteenth-century society that people of fashion chose to copy the consumptive appearance.[33] Equally curious, the features of psychosis in the Third World can, at times, lead to considerable elevation in social status. In non-industrial cultures throughout the world, the hallucinations and altered states of consciousness produced by psychosis, fasting, sleep deprivation, social isolation and contemplation, and hallucinogenic drug use are often a prerequisite for gaining shamanic power.[34] The psychotic features are interpreted as an initiatory experience. For example, whereas poor Puerto Ricans who go to a psychiatric clinic or insane asylum are likely to be highly stigmatized as *locos* (madmen), people who suffer from schizophrenia who consult a spiritualist may rise in status. Sociologists Lloyd Rogler and August Hollingshead report: "The spiritualist may announce to the sick person, his family, and friends that the afflicted person is endowed with *facultades* (psychic faculties), a matter of prestige at this level of the social structure. . . ."[35]

The study indicates that Puerto Ricans with schizophrenia who consult spiritualists may not only lose their symptoms, they may also achieve the status of mediums themselves. So successful is the social reintegration of the male Puerto Ricans with schizophrenia that, after some readjustment of family roles, their wives found them *more* acceptable as husbands than did the wives of normal men. . . .

GROUP PARTICIPATION

The process of curing in pre-industrial societies, it is clear, is very much a communal phenomenon tending not only to reintegrate the deviant individual into the group but also to reaffirm the solidarity of the community. Thus, the N'jayei secret society of the Mende tribe in Sierra Leone, which aims to treat mental illness by applying sanctions to those who are presumed to have committed a breach of social rules, provides members with a mechanism for social reintegration and, simultaneously, reinforces the integrity and standards of the culture.[36] Such a dual process of unification of the group and integration of the individual is seen to result from the great public healing ceremonies of the Zuni medicine societies[37] or from the intense communal involvement and dramatic grandeur of a Navajo healing ceremony. The Navajo patient, relatives and other participants alike take medicine and submit to ritual procedures in a symbolic recognition that illness is a problem for the community as a whole.[38]

Nancy Waxler, in her research on people suffering from psychosis in Sri Lanka, was impressed with the way in which the intense community involvement in treating mental illness prevents the patient from developing secondary symptoms from alienation and stigma and results in the sick person being reintegrated into society. She writes:

> Mental illness is basically a problem of and for the family, not the sick person. Thus we find among the Sinhalese that almost all treatment of mental illness involves groups meeting with groups. When a mad person is believed to have been possessed by a demon the whole family, their relatives and neighbors, sometimes the whole village, join together to plan, carry out and pay for the appropriate exorcism ceremony. The sick person is usually the central focus, but often only as the vehicle for the demon, and during some parts of these ceremonies the patient is largely ignored.[39]

The importance of this process of social reintegration is confirmed by data from the two WHO outcome studies. In both the developed and developing worlds, social isolation was found to be one of the strongest predictors of poor outcome in schizophrenia.[40] Several other researchers have found this factor to be important in the genesis and outcome of schizophrenia.[41]

THE FAMILY

One of John Wing's criteria for good outcome in schizophrenia mentioned earlier in the chapter was freedom for the patient from excessive emotional demands or criticism within the family. His recommendation is backed up by a good deal of social psychiatric research from the Medical Research Council in London. . . . The family environment for people with schizophrenia in the Third World is different from the West. In India, spouses, parents or siblings are willing to provide for a relative, however disabled.[42] The multiple caregivers in an Indian extended family will handle most of the problems presented by a family member with schizophrenia without seeking outside assistance—self-neglect and dirtiness seem to be of the greatest concern.[43] At the end of the twentieth century, however, with urbanization, increased female employment and the break-up of the extended family, the level of tolerance was declining.[44] Increased acceptance, nevertheless, can bring better outcomes. In Qatar, on the Persian Gulf, people with schizophrenia in extended families have been reported to show better outcome at follow-up than those who return to nuclear family households.[45] The extended family structure, which is more common in the Third World, allows a diffusion of emotional over-involvement and interdependence among family members.

The emphasis on community involvement in the treatment of mental illness in non-industrial societies similarly tends to reduce family tensions. Responsibility is shared broadly and the patient often escapes blame and criticism, allowing the family to be more supportive. According to one study, for example, relatives of people with schizophrenia in Chandigarh, north India, are much less likely to be demanding or critical of their psychotic family member than are the relatives of people with schizophrenia in the industrial world. In London, nearly a half of patients with schizophrenia have such emotionally stressful relatives; in Rochester, New York, the proportion is similar; but in north India, fewer than a fifth of subjects with schizophrenia were found to have critical and demanding relatives. . . .[46] [T]his difference might be a consequence of the higher achievement expectations placed on Westerners suffering from psychosis or of the emotional isolation so common for families of people with schizophrenia in the West but so much rarer in the developing world.

In the Third World, it appears, the person with a psychotic disorder is more likely to retain his or her self-esteem, a feeling of value to the community and a sense of belonging. These are things that . . . sixteen billion dollars does not buy the person with schizophrenia in the United States or elsewhere in the Western world.

DISCUSSION QUESTION

1. What sociological conditions may contribute to the better rates of recovery from schizophrenia in some developing countries than in the West? Can an understanding of these conditions contribute to better recovery rates in the West? If so, how? If not, why not?

NOTES

1. Norquist, G. S., Regier, D. A. and Rupp, A., "Estimates of the cost of treating people with schizophrenia: Contributions of data from epidemiological survey," in M. Moscarelli, A. Rupp and N. Sartorius (eds), *Handbook of Mental Health Economics and Health Policy: Volume I: Schizophrenia*, Chichester: John Wiley and Sons, 1996, pp. 96–101.
2. Collomb, H., "Bouffées délirantes en psychiatrie Africaine," *Transcultural Psychiatric Research*, 3: 29–34, 1966, p. 29.
3. Schwartz, R., "Beschreibung einer ambulanten psychiatrischen Patienten-population in der Grossen-Kabylie (Nordalgerien): Epidemiologische und Klinische Aspekte," *Social Psychiatry* (West Germany), 12: 207–18, 1977.
4. Smartt, C. G. F., "Mental maladjustment in the East African," *Journal of Mental Science*, 102: 441–66, 1956.
5. Opler, M. K., "The social and cultural nature of mental illness and its treatment," in S. Lesse, (ed.), *An Evaluation of the Results of the Psychotherapies*, Springfield, Illinois: C. C. Thomas, 1968, pp. 280–91.
6. Tewfik, G. I., "Psychoses in Africa," in *Mental Disorders and Mental Health in Africa South of the Sahara*, CCTA/CSA-WFMH-WHO meeting of specialists on mental health, Bukavu, London: 1958.
7. Field, M. J., *Search for Security, An Ethno-Psychiatric Study of Rural Ghana*, Chicago: Northwestern University Press, 1962.
8. Fortes, M. and Mayer, D. Y., "Psychosis and social change among the Tallensi of northern Ghana," in S. H. Foulkes and G. S. Prince (eds.), *Psychiatry in a Changing Society*, London: Tavistock, 1969, pp. 33–73.
9. Berne, E., "Some oriental mental hospitals," *American Journal of Psychiatry*, 106:376–83, 1949; Seligman, C. G., "Temperament, conflict and psychosis in a stone-age population," *British Journal of Medical Psychology*, 9:187–202, 1929; Jilek, W. G. and Jilek-Aall, L., "Transient psychoses in Africans," *Psychiatrics Clinica* (Basel), 3: 337–64, 1970.
10. Murphy, H. B. M., "Cultural factors in the genesis of schizophrenia," in D. Rosenthal and S. S. Kety (eds.), *The Transmission of Schizophrenia*, Oxford: Pergamon, 1968, p. 138.
11. American Psychiatric Association, *Diagnostic and Statistical Manual of Mental Disorders (DSM–III)*, Washington, DC: Author, 1968.

12. Wintrob, R. M., "Malaria and the acute psychotic episode," *Journal of Nervous and Mental Disease*, 156: 306–17, 1973.
13. Rin, H. and Lin, T., "Mental illness among Formosan aborigines as compared with the Chinese in Taiwan," *Journal of Mental Science*, 108: 134–46, 1962.
14. Harris, M., *Culture, Man and Nature. An Introduction to General Anthropology*, New York: Thomas Y. Crowell, 1971, p. 480.
15. Lambo, T., "The importance of cultural factors in psychiatric treatment," in I. Al-Issa and W. Dennis (eds.), *Cross-Cultural Studies of Behavior*, New York: Holt, Rinehart & Winston, 1970, pp. 548–52.
16. World Health Organization, *Schizophrenia: An International Follow-Up Study*, Chichester, England: Wiley, 1979, p. 104.
17. Ran, M., Xiang, M., Huang, M. and Shan, Y. "Natural course of schizophrenia," *British Journal of Psychiatry*, 178, 2001.
18. Wing, J. K., "The social context of schizophrenia," *American Journal of Psychiatry*, 135: 1333–9, 1978.
19. Chayanov, A. V., *The Theory of Peasant Economy*, Homewood, Illinois: Richard D. Irwin, 1966, p. 77, cited in M. Sahlins, *Stone Age Economics*, Chicago: Aldine-Atherton, 1972, p. 89.
20. Richards, A. I., *Land, Labor and Diet in Northern Rhodesia*, London: Oxford University Press, 1939, p. 402; Douglas, M., "Lele economy as compared with the Bushong," in G. Dalton and P. Bohannen, *Markets in Africa*, Evanston, Illinois: Northwestern University Press, 1962, p. 231, cited in Sahlins, *Stone Age Economics*, pp. 52–4.
21. World Health Organization, *Schizophrenia: An International Follow Study*, Chichester, England: Wiley, 1979, pp. 271, 283.
22. Squire, L. *Employment Policy in Developing Countries*, New York: Oxford University Press, 1981, p. 71.
23. World Health Organization, *Schizophrenia*, p. 283.
24. Ibid., pp. 287–8.
25. Paul, B. D., "Mental disorder and self-regulating processes in culture: A Guatemalan illustration," in R. Hunt (ed.), *Personalities and Cultures: Readings in Psychological Anthropology*, Garden City, New York: Natural History Press, 1967.
26. Gelfand, M., "Psychiatric disorders as recognized by the Shona," in A. Kiev (ed.), *Magic, Faith and Healing*, New York: Free Press, 1964, pp. 156–73.
27. Collomb, "Bouffées délirantes en psychiatrie Africaine," p. 30.
28. Rogler, L. H. and Hollingshead, A. B., *Trapped: Families and Schizophrenia*, New York: Wiley, 1965, p. 254.
29. Rin and Lin, "Mental illness among Formosan aborigines."
30. Waxler, N. E., "Is mental illness cured in traditional societies? A theoretical analysis," *Culture, Medicine and Psychiatry*, 1: 233–53, 1977, p. 242.
31. World Health Organization, *Schizophrenia*, p. 105.
32. Levy, J. E., Neutra, R. and Parker, D., "Life careers of Navajo epileptics and convulsive hysterics," *Social Science and Medicine*, 13: 53–66, 1979.
33. Sontag, S., *Illness as Metaphor*, New York: Vintage Books, 1979.
34. Eliade, M., *Shamanism: Archaic Techniques of Ecstasy*, Princeton: Princeton University Press/ Bollingen Paperback, 1972; Black Elk, *The Sacred Pipe*, Baltimore: Penguin, 1971.
35. Rogler and Hollingshead, *Trapped. Families and Schizophrenia*, New York: Wiley, 1965, p. 254.
36. Dawson, J., "Urbanization and mental health in a West African community," in Kiev, *Magic, Faith and Healing*, pp. 305–42.

37. Benedict, R., *Patterns of Culture*, Boston: Houghton-Mifflin, 1934, p. 72.

38. Kaplan, B. and Johnson, D., "The social meaning of Navajo psychopathology and psychotherapy," in Kiev, *Magic, Faith and Healing*, pp. 203–29; Leighton, A. H. and Leighton, D. C., "Elements of psychotherapy in Navaho religion," *Psychiatry*, 4: 515–23, 1941.

39. Waxler, "Is mental illness cured in traditional societies?," p. 241.

40. World Health Organization, *Schizophrenia*, p. 288; Jablensky et al., "Schizophrenia: Manifestations, incidence and course in different cultures. A World Health Organization ten-country study," *Psychological Medicine*, monograph supplement 20, 1991. Table 4.17.

41. Hare, E. H., "Mental illness and social conditions in Bristol," *Journal of Mental Science*, 102:349–57, 1956; Stein, L., "Social class' gradient in schizophrenia," *British Journal of Preventive and Social Medicine*, 11:181–95, 1957; Cooper, B., "Social class and prognosis in schizophrenia: Part I," *British Journal of Preventive and Social Medicine*, 15:17–30, 1961; Jaco, E. G., "The social isolation hypothesis and schizophrenia," *American Sociological Review*, 19: 567–77, 1954.

42. Thara, R. and Rajkumar, S. "Gender differences in schizophrenia: Results of a follow-up study in India," *Schizophrenia Research*, 7: 65–70, 1992.

43. Srinivasan, T. N., Rajkumar, S., and Padmavathi, R. "Initiating care for untreated schizophrenic patients and results of a one year follow-up," *International Journal of Social Psychiatry*, 47: 73–80, 2001.

44. Thara, "Gender differences in schizophrenia."

45. El-Islam, M. F., "A better outlook for schizophrenics living in extended families," *British Journal of Psychiatry*, 135: 343–7, 1979.

46. Wig, N. N., Menon, D. K. and Bedi, H., "Coping with schizophrenic patients in developing countries: A study of expressed emotions in the relatives" presented at the Seventh World Congress of Psychiatry, Vienna, July 11–16, 1983; J. Leff, *Psychiatry Around the Globe*, New York: Dekker, 1981, p. 157.

39.
THE AMERICANIZATION OF MENTAL ILLNESS

ETHAN WATTERS

As Watters describes, anorexia was quite uncommon in Hong Kong and the expression of the disease was quite different before Western notions of the condition arrived in the 1990s and incidents of anorexia climbed sharply. That is, the apparent causes of the condition, the way people understood the condition, and the way patients expressed the condition—all changed as Western constructions came to replace native constructions. The same can be said for a number of psychiatric conditions throughout the world.

Western medical professionals might argue that the only thing that is being exported is the scientific understanding of psychiatric ailments. That does not explain why the sets of conditions that cause these ailments often change; nor does it explain why the symptoms often vary from culture to culture. Presumably, with the diffusion of a scientific understanding would come better treatments, resulting in fewer and less severe cases. Watters argues that the opposite is often the result of the spread of Western psychiatric categories.

It is frequently presumed that the medical model is more humane because it takes the blame off of the individuals who are afflicted and they, therefore, suffer less stigma. Watters cites evidence to the contrary and he suggests some of the ways that Westerners respond to mental illness that may actually exacerbate the condition. And while, as Warner described in the previous article, recovery rates are frequently better in the developing world than in the developed world, poor countries may lose that significant advantage as Western psychiatric categories come to pervade the world.

For more than a generation now, we in the West have aggressively spread our modern knowledge of mental illness around the world. We have done this in the name of science, believing that our approaches reveal the biological basis of psychic suffering and dispel prescientific myths and harmful stigma. There is now good evidence to suggest that in the process of teaching the rest of the world to think like us, we've been exporting our Western "symptom repertoire" as well. That is, we've been changing not only the treatments but also the expression of mental illness in other cultures. Indeed, a handful of mental-health disorders—depression, post-traumatic stress disorder and anorexia among them—now appear to be spreading across cultures with the speed of contagious diseases. These symptom clusters are becoming the lingua franca of human suffering, replacing indigenous forms of mental illness.

Dr. Sing Lee, a psychiatrist and researcher at the Chinese University of Hong Kong, watched the Westernization of a mental illness firsthand. In the late 1980s and early 1990s, he was busy documenting a rare and culturally specific form of anorexia nervosa in Hong Kong. Unlike American anorexics, most of his patients did not intentionally diet nor did they express a fear of becoming fat. The complaints of Lee's patients were typically somatic—they complained most frequently of having bloated stomachs. Lee was trying to understand this indigenous form of anorexia and, at the same time, figure out why the disease remained so rare.

As he was in the midst of publishing his finding that food refusal had a particular expression and meaning in Hong Kong, the public's understanding of anorexia suddenly shifted. On Nov. 24, 1994, a teenage anorexic girl named Charlene Hsu Chi-Ying collapsed and died on a busy downtown street in Hong Kong. The death caught the attention of the media and was featured prominently in local papers. "Anorexia Made Her All Skin and Bones: Schoolgirl Falls on Ground Dead," read one headline in a Chinese-language newspaper. "Thinner Than a Yellow Flower, Weight-Loss Book Found in School Bag, Schoolgirl Falls Dead on Street," reported another Chinese-language paper.

In trying to explain what happened to Charlene, local reporters often simply copied out of American diagnostic manuals. The mental-health experts quoted in the Hong Kong papers and magazines confidently reported that anorexia in Hong Kong was the same disorder that appeared in the United States and Europe. In the wake of Charlene's death, the transfer of knowledge about the nature of anorexia (including how and why it was manifested and who was at risk) went only one way: from West to East.

Western ideas did not simply obscure the understanding of anorexia in Hong Kong; they also may have changed the expression of the illness itself. As the general public and the region's mental-health professionals came to understand the American diagnosis of anorexia, the presentation of the illness in Lee's patient population appeared to transform into the more virulent American standard. Lee once saw two or three anorexic patients a year; by the end of the 1990s he was seeing that many new cases each month. That increase sparked another series of media reports. "Children as Young as 10 Starving Themselves as Eating Ailments Rise," announced a headline in one daily newspaper. By the late 1990s, Lee's studies reported that between 3 and 10 percent of young women in Hong Kong showed disordered eating behavior. In contrast to Lee's earlier patients, these women most often cited fat phobia as the single most important reason for their self-starvation. By 2007 about 90 percent of the anorexics Lee treated reported fat phobia. New patients appeared to be increasingly conforming their experience of anorexia to the Western version of the disease.

What is being missed, Lee and others have suggested, is a deep understanding of how the expectations and beliefs of the sufferer shape their suffering. "Culture shapes the way general psychopathology is going to be translated partially or completely into specific psychopathology," Lee says. "When there is a cultural atmosphere in which professionals, the media, schools, doctors, psychologists all recognize and endorse and talk about and publicize eating disorders, then people can be triggered to consciously or unconsciously pick eating-disorder pathology as a way to express that conflict."

The problem becomes especially worrisome in a time of globalization, when symptom reper-toires can cross borders with ease. Having been trained in England and the United States, Lee knows better than most the locomotive force behind Western ideas about mental health and ill-ness. Mental-health professionals in the West, and in the United States in particular, create official categories of mental diseases and promote them in a diagnostic manual that has become the worldwide standard. American researchers and institutions run most of the premier scholarly journals and host top conferences in the fields of psychology and psychiatry. Western drug com-panies dole out large sums for research and spend billions marketing medications for mental illnesses. In addition, Western-trained traumatologists often rush in where war or natural disas-ters strike to deliver "psychological first aid," bringing with them their assumptions about how the mind becomes broken by horrible events and how it is best healed. Taken together this is a juggernaut that Lee sees little chance of stopping.

"As Western categories for diseases have gained dominance, micro-cultures that shape the illness experiences of individual patients are being discarded," Lee says. "The current has become too strong." . . .

Even when the underlying science is sound and the intentions altruistic, the export of Western biomedical ideas can have frustrating and unexpected consequences. For the last 50-odd years, Western mental-health professionals have been pushing what they call "mental-health literacy" on the rest of the world. Cultures became more "literate" as they adopted Western biomedical conceptions of diseases like depression and schizophrenia. One study published in *The Interna-tional Journal of Mental Health*, for instance, portrayed those who endorsed the statement that "mental illness is an illness like any other" as having a "knowledgeable, benevolent, supportive orientation toward the mentally ill."

Mental illnesses, it was suggested, should be treated like "brain diseases" over which the pa-tient has little choice or responsibility. This was promoted both as a scientific fact and as a social narrative that would reap great benefits. The logic seemed unassailable: Once people believed that the onset of mental illnesses did not spring from supernatural forces, character flaws, semen loss or some other prescientific notion, the sufferer would be protected from blame and stigma. This idea has been promoted by mental-health providers, drug companies and patient-advocacy groups like the National Alliance on Mental Illness in the United States and SANE in Britain. In a sometimes fractious field, everyone seemed to agree that this modern way of thinking about mental illness would reduce the social isolation and stigma often experienced by those with mental illness. Trampling on indigenous prescientific superstitions about the cause of mental illness seemed a small price to pay to relieve some of the social suffering of the mentally ill.

But does the "brain disease" belief actually reduce stigma?

In 1997, Prof. Sheila Mehta from Auburn University Montgomery in Alabama decided to find out if the "brain disease" narrative had the intended effect. She suspected that the biomedical explanation for mental illness might be influencing our attitudes toward the mentally ill in ways we weren't conscious of, so she thought up a clever experiment.

In her study, test subjects were led to believe that they were participating in a simple learning task with a partner who was, unbeknownst to them, a confederate in the study. Before the experi-ment started, the partners exchanged some biographical data, and the confederate informed the test subject that he suffered from a mental illness.

The confederate then stated either that the illness occurred because of "the kind of things that happened to me when I was a kid" or that he had "a disease just like any other, which affected my biochemistry." (These were termed the "psychosocial" explanation and the "disease" explanation respectively.) The experiment then called for the test subject to teach the confederate a pattern of button presses. When the confederate pushed the wrong button, the only feedback the test subject could give was a "barely discernible" to "somewhat painful" electrical shock.

Analyzing the data, Mehta found a difference between the group of subjects given the psycho-social explanation for their partner's mental-illness history and those given the brain-disease explanation. Those who believed that their partner suffered a biochemical "disease like any other" increased the severity of the shocks at a faster rate than those who believed they were paired with someone who had a mental disorder caused by an event in the past.

"The results of the current study suggest that we may actually treat people more harshly when their problem is described in disease terms," Mehta wrote. "We say we are being kind, but our actions suggest otherwise." The problem, it appears, is that the biomedical narrative about an illness like schizophrenia carries with it the subtle assumption that a brain made ill through bio-medical or genetic abnormalities is more thoroughly broken and permanently abnormal than one made ill though life events. "Viewing those with mental disorders as diseased sets them apart and may lead to our perceiving them as physically distinct. Biochemical aberrations make them almost a different species."

In other words, the belief that was assumed to decrease stigma actually increased it. Was the same true outside the lab in the real world?

The question is important because the Western push for "mental-health literacy" has gained ground. Studies show that much of the world has steadily adopted this medical model of mental illness. Although these changes are most extensive in the United States and Europe, similar shifts have been documented elsewhere. When asked to name the sources of mental illness, people from a variety of cultures are increasingly likely to mention "chemical imbalance" or "brain disease" or "genetic/inherited" factors.

Unfortunately, at the same time that Western mental-health professionals have been convincing the world to think and talk about mental illnesses in biomedical terms, we have been simultane-ously losing the war against stigma at home and abroad. Studies of attitudes in the United States from 1950 to 1996 have shown that the perception of dangerousness surrounding people with schizophrenia has steadily increased over this time. Similarly, a study in Germany found that the public's desire to maintain distance from those with a diagnosis of schizophrenia increased from 1990 to 2001.

Researchers hoping to learn what was causing this rise in stigma found the same surprising connection that Mehta discovered in her lab. It turns out that those who adopted biomedical/genetic beliefs about mental disorders were the same people who wanted less contact with the mentally ill and thought of them as more dangerous and unpredictable. This unfortunate rela-tionship has popped up in numerous studies around the world. In a study conducted in Turkey, for example, those who labeled schizophrenic behavior as *akil hastaligi* (illness of the brain or reasoning abilities) were more inclined to assert that schizophrenics were aggressive and should not live freely in the community than those who saw the disorder as *ruhsal hastagi* (a disorder of the spiritual or inner self). Another study, which looked at populations in Germany, Russia and

Mongolia, found that "irrespective of place . . . endorsing biological factors as the cause of schizophrenia was associated with a greater desire for social distance."

Even as we have congratulated ourselves for becoming more "benevolent and supportive" of the mentally ill, we have steadily backed away from the sufferers themselves. It appears, in short, that the impact of our worldwide antistigma campaign may have been the exact opposite of what we intended.

Nowhere are the limitations of Western ideas and treatments more evident than in the case of schizophrenia. Researchers have long sought to understand what may be the most perplexing finding in the cross-cultural study of mental illness: people with schizophrenia in developing countries appear to fare better over time than those living in industrialized nations.

This was the startling result of three large international studies carried out by the World Health Organization over the course of 30 years, starting in the early 1970s. The research showed that patients outside the United States and Europe had significantly lower relapse rates—as much as two-thirds lower in one follow-up study. These findings have been widely discussed and debated in part because of their obvious incongruity: the regions of the world with the most resources to devote to the illness—the best technology, the cutting-edge medicines and the best-financed academic and private-research institutions—had the most troubled and socially marginalized patients.

Trying to unravel this mystery, the anthropologist Juli McGruder from the University of Puget Sound spent years in Zanzibar studying families of schizophrenics. Though the population is predominantly Muslim, Swahili spirit-possession beliefs are still prevalent in the archipelago and commonly evoked to explain the actions of anyone violating social norms—from a sister lashing out at her brother to someone beset by psychotic delusions.

McGruder found that far from being stigmatizing, these beliefs served certain useful functions. The beliefs prescribed a variety of socially accepted interventions and ministrations that kept the ill person bound to the family and kinship group. "Muslim and Swahili spirits are not exorcised in the Christian sense of casting out demons," McGruder determined. "Rather they are coaxed with food and goods, feted with song and dance. They are placated, settled, reduced in malfeasance." McGruder saw this approach in many small acts of kindness. She watched family members use saffron paste to write phrases from the Koran on the rims of drinking bowls so the ill person could literally imbibe the holy words. The spirit-possession beliefs had other unexpected benefits. Critically, the story allowed the person with schizophrenia a cleaner bill of health when the illness went into remission. An ill individual enjoying a time of relative mental health could, at least temporarily, retake his or her responsibilities in the kinship group. Since the illness was seen as the work of outside forces, it was understood as an affliction for the sufferer but not as an identity.

For McGruder, the point was not that these practices or beliefs were effective in curing schizophrenia. Rather, she said she believed that they indirectly helped control the course of the illness. Besides keeping the sick individual in the social group, the religious beliefs in Zanzibar also allowed for a type of calmness and acquiescence in the face of the illness that she had rarely witnessed in the West.

The course of a metastasizing cancer is unlikely to be changed by how we talk about it. With schizophrenia, however, symptoms are inevitably entangled in a person's complex interactions with those around him or her. In fact, researchers have long documented how certain emotional reactions from family members correlate with higher relapse rates for people who have a diagnosis of schizophrenia. Collectively referred to as "high expressed emotion," these reactions include criticism, hostility and emotional overinvolvement (like overprotectiveness or constant intrusiveness in the patient's life). In one study, 67 percent of white American families with a schizophrenic family member were rated as "high EE." (Among British families, 48 percent were high EE; among Mexican families the figure was 41 percent and for Indian families 23 percent.)

Does this high level of "expressed emotion" in the United States mean that we lack sympathy or the desire to care for our mentally ill? Quite the opposite. Relatives who were "high EE" were simply expressing a particularly American view of the self. They tended to believe that individuals are the captains of their own destiny and should be able to overcome their problems by force of personal will. Their critical comments to the mentally ill person didn't mean that these family members were cruel or uncaring; they were simply applying the same assumptions about human nature that they applied to themselves. They were reflecting an "approach to the world that is active, resourceful and that emphasizes personal accountability," Prof. Jill M. Hooley of Harvard University concluded. "Far from high criticism reflecting something negative about the family members of patients with schizophrenia, high criticism (and hence high EE) was associated with a characteristic that is widely regarded as positive."

Widely regarded as positive, that is, in the United States. Many traditional cultures regard the self in different terms—as inseparable from your role in your kinship group, intertwined with the story of your ancestry and permeable to the spirit world. What McGruder found in Zanzibar was that families often drew strength from this more connected and less isolating idea of human nature. Their ability to maintain a low level of expressed emotion relied on these beliefs. And that level of expressed emotion in turn may be key to improving the fortunes of the schizophrenia sufferer.

Of course, to the extent that our modern psychopharmacological drugs can relieve suffering, they should not be denied to the rest of the world. The problem is that our biomedical advances are hard to separate from our particular cultural beliefs. It is difficult to distinguish, for example, the biomedical conception of schizophrenia—the idea that the disease exists within the biochemistry of the brain—from the more inchoate Western assumption that the self resides there as well. "Mental illness is feared and has such a stigma because it represents a reversal of what Western humans . . . have come to value as the essence of human nature," McGruder concludes. "Because our culture so highly values . . . an illusion of self-control and control of circumstance, we become abject when contemplating mentation that seems more changeable, less restrained and less controllable, more open to outside influence, than we imagine our own to be."

Cross-cultural psychiatrists have pointed out that the mental-health ideas we export to the world are rarely unadulterated scientific facts and never culturally neutral. "Western mental-health discourse introduces core components of Western culture, including a theory of human nature, a definition of personhood, a sense of time and memory and a source of moral authority. None of this is universal," Derek Summerfield of the Institute of Psychiatry in London observes. He has also written: "The problem is the overall thrust that comes from being at the heart of the one globalizing culture. It is as if one version of human nature is being presented as definitive, and one set of ideas about pain and suffering. . . . There is no one definitive psychology."

Behind the promotion of Western ideas of mental health and healing lie a variety of cultural assumptions about human nature. Westerners share, for instance, evolving beliefs about what type of life event is likely to make one psychologically traumatized, and we agree that venting emotions by talking is more healthy than stoic silence. We've come to agree that the human mind is rather fragile and that it is best to consider many emotional experiences and mental states as illnesses that require professional intervention. (The National Institute of Mental Health reports that a quarter of Americans have diagnosable mental illnesses each year.) The ideas we export often have at their heart a particularly American brand of hyperintrospection—a penchant for "psychologizing" daily existence. These ideas remain deeply influenced by the Cartesian split between the mind and the body, the Freudian duality between the conscious and unconscious, as well as the many self-help philosophies and schools of therapy that have encouraged Americans to separate the health of the individual from the health of the group. These Western ideas of the mind are proving as seductive to the rest of the world as fast food and rap music, and we are spreading them with speed and vigor.

No one would suggest that we withhold our medical advances from other countries, but it's perhaps past time to admit that even our most remarkable scientific leaps in understanding the brain haven't yet created the sorts of cultural stories from which humans take comfort and mean-ing. When these scientific advances are translated into popular belief and cultural stories, they are often stripped of the complexity of the science and become comically insubstantial narratives. Take for instance this Web site text advertising the antidepressant Paxil: "Just as a cake recipe re-quires you to use flour, sugar and baking powder in the right amounts, your brain needs a fine chemical balance in order to perform at its best." The Western mind, endlessly analyzed by generations of theorists and researchers, has now been reduced to a batter of chemicals we carry around in the mixing bowl of our skulls.

All cultures struggle with intractable mental illnesses with varying degrees of compassion and cruelty, equanimity and fear. Looking at ourselves through the eyes of those living in places where madness and psychological trauma are still embedded in complex religious and cultural narratives, however, we get a glimpse of ourselves as an increasingly insecure and fearful people. Some philosophers and psychiatrists have suggested that we are investing our great wealth in researching and treating mental illness—medicalizing ever larger swaths of human experience—because we have rather suddenly lost older belief systems that once gave meaning and context to mental suffering.

If our rising need for mental-health services does indeed spring from a breakdown of meaning, our insistence that the rest of the world think like us may be all the more problematic. Offering the latest Western mental-health theories, treatments and categories in an attempt to ameliorate the psychological stress sparked by modernization and globalization is not a solution; it may be part of the problem. When we undermine local conceptions of the self and modes of healing, we may be speeding along the disorienting changes that are at the very heart of much of the world's mental distress.

DISCUSSION QUESTIONS

1. Following from Watters's argument, is the incidence of mental illness in the world likely to increase or decrease in the coming decades? Why?
2. Why, according to Watters, are Americans more likely to react to a family member's mental illness with "high expressed emotion" than are people in many other countries? What is the correlation between expressed emotion and recovery rates?

40.

PENIS PANICS

ROBERT BARTHOLOMEW

The following is one of those articles that is difficult to categorize. In the first edition of this book, this article was placed in the "Moral Panics" section of readings. While not technically a moral panic, the following article describes a well-documented phenomenon with similar mechanics of a moral panic—in terms of the dispersion of poorly premised alarm in a population—without the "moral" character of a moral panic. As with moral panics, incidents of koro are often precipitated by some sort of generalized anxiety in the population.

Many Westerners reading this article will be amused and will consider the people who share the collective fears described herein to be "crazy." Indeed, incidents of koro have been described, explained, and treated by psychiatrists. Koro is one of many "culture-bound syndromes" for which most agree the medical model provides little understanding and which can best be understood in the context of the cultures in which they occur. An understanding of their cultural context makes their occurrence something far less than outrageous.

It sounds like something from a poor B movie. It might even make the 1978 cult film *Attack of the Killer Tomatoes* seem plausible. I'm referring to scares where communities are swept up in the fear that their sex organs are rapidly shrinking. In parts of Asia entire regions are occasionally overwhelmed by terror-stricken men who believe that their penises are shriveling up or retracting into their bodies. Those affected often take extreme measures and place clamps or string onto the precious organ or have family members hold the penis in relays until an appropriate treatment is obtained, often from native healers. Occasionally women are affected, believing their breasts or vaginas are being sucked into their bodies. Episodes can endure for weeks or months and affect thousands. Psychiatrists are divided as to the cause of these imaginary scares. Some believe that it is a form of group psychosis triggered by stress, while others view it as mass hysteria. How can groups of people come to believe that their sex organs are shrinking? We will try to unravel this mystery by briefly describing several genital-shrinking scares, their similarities, and the factors involved in triggering them.

While genitalia-shrinking is known by a variety of names in different cultures, psychiatrists refer to it with the generic term "koro." A Malay word of uncertain derivation, koro may have arisen from the Malay word "keruk," meaning to shrink (Gwee, 1968, 3), although it is more likely a reflection of the Malaysian-Indonesian words for "tortoise" (kura, kura-kura, and kuro). In these countries, the penis, especially the glans or tip, is commonly referred to as a tortoise head. This led Dutch scientist P.M. Van Wulfften-Palthe to conclude that this is how the modern term "koro" most likely got its name: "The fact that a tortoise can withdraw its head with its wrinkled neck under its shell literally into its body, suggested . . . the mechanism . . . in 'koro' ('kura') and gave it its name" (1936, 536).

THE ANATOMY OF MASS HYSTERIA

The first well-documented outbreak in modern times occurred in October and November, 1967, when hospitals on the tiny Southeast Asian island nation of Singapore were inundated by frantic citizens who were convinced that their penises were shrinking and would eventually disappear, at which time, many believed, death would result. "Victims" used everything from rubber bands to clothes pins in desperate efforts to prevent further perceived retraction. These methods occasionally resulted in severe organ damage and some pretty sore penises. At the height of the scare the Singapore Hospital treated about 75 cases in a single day. The episode occurred amid rumors that eating pork vaccinated for swine fever prior to slaughter could trigger genitalia shrinkage. One erroneous report even claimed that a pig dropped dead immediately after inoculation when its penis suddenly retracted!

The panic abruptly ended when the Singapore Medical Association and Health Ministry held public news conferences to dispel fears. Writing in the prestigious *British Journal of Psychiatry*, Singaporean doctor C.T. Mun described two typical cases. In one, a pale 16 year-old boy rushed into the clinic accompanied by his parents and clutching his penis. After providing reassurance and a sedative, there was no recurrence. The frightened boy said that he had heard the rumors of contaminated pork at school, had eaten pork that morning, and upon urinating, his penis appeared to have shrunk. At that point he hung on for all he was worth and shouted for help. In a second case, a mother dashed into the clinic clutching the penis of her 4-month-old baby frantically seeking help. Dr. Mun said that:

> The child had not been well for two days with cold and a little diarrhea. The mother was changing his napkin . . . when the child had colic and screamed. The mother saw the penis getting smaller and the child screamed and [she] thought he had koro. She had previously heard the rumors. The mother was first reassured, and the baby's cold and diarrhea treated. The child was all right after that.

Most Singaporeans are of Chinese origin where there is a common belief in the reality of shrinking genitalia. Chinese medical texts from the 19th century even describe such cases as caused by an actual disease. Pao Sian-Ow's book, *New Collection of Remedies of Value* published in 1834, states that episodes occur when "the penis retracts into the abdomen. If treatment is not instituted at once and effective, the case [patient] will die. The disease is due to the invasion of cold vapors and the treatment is to employ the 'heaty' drugs."

At least 5,000 inhabitants in a remote area of southern Guangdong province, China, were affected by a genital-shrinking panic between August 1984 and the summer of 1985 (Jilek, 1986, 273). Male residents of the region are reared to practice restraint in matters of sexual desire and activity, as excessive semen discharge is believed to cause poor physical and mental health, even death. If that wasn't enough to worry about, many residents believe that certain spirits of the dead, especially female fox maidens, wander in search of penises that will give them powers. Each of the 232 "victims" surveyed by University of Hawaii psychiatrist Wen-Shing Tseng and his colleagues, was convinced that an evil female fox spirit was the culprit, while 76 percent of those affected had witnessed others being "rescued." Most of these cases occurred at night following a chilly sensation which would appear before a feeling of penile shrinkage. Tseng and his researchers reported: "Thinking this [chill] to be a fatal sign and believing that they were affected by an evil ghost, they [koro 'victims'] became panic stricken and tried to pull at their penises, while, at the same time, shouting for help" (Tseng et al., 1988, 1540). Interestingly, several children reported shrinkage of their tongue, nose and ears, reflecting the prevalent ancient Chinese belief that any male (yang) organs can shrink or retract. Tseng investigated a separate episode in 1987, affecting at least 300 residents on the Leizhou Peninsula of Guangdong province. Genital-shrinking panic is well-known in southern China, with episodes recorded in 1865, 1948, 1955, 1966, and 1974, all involving at least several hundred residents (Bartholomew, 1998).

Dr. Tseng has sought to determine why episodes repeatedly occur in the vicinity of Leizhou Peninsula and Hainan Island, but never spread to the principal section of Guangdong province or other parts of China, and why it is that only certain residents in a region report koro, while others do not. It was found that those affected held the more intense koro-related folk beliefs relative to a control group from the adjacent nonaffected area (Tseng et al. 1992, 122), helping to explain "why each time the koro epidemic spread from the Peninsula, it would cease when it reached the urban area of Guangzhou, where the people are more educated and hold less belief in koro." While recognizing the importance of rumors and traditional beliefs in precipitating episodes, Tseng considers koro outbreaks in southern China to be a psychiatric disorder ("genital retraction panic disorder") which primarily affects susceptible individuals, such as the poorly educated and those possessing below normal intellectual endowment who are experiencing social crisis or tension (1988, 1542; 1992, 117).

Another koro episode happened in northeast Thailand between November and December, 1976, affecting about 2,000 people, primarily rural Thai residents in the border provinces of Maha Sarakham, Nakhon Phanom, Nong Khai, and Udon Thani. Symptoms included the perception of genitalia shrinkage and impotence among males, while females typically reported sexual frigidity, with breast and vulva shrinkage. Other symptoms were panic, anxiety, dizziness, diarrhea, discomfort during urination, nausea, headaches, facial numbness, and abdominal pain. Some patients temporarily lost consciousness, and many were fearful of imminent death. Of 350 subjects studied in detail, irrespective of whether they sought treatment from native healers or physicians, "most patients had recovered within one day and all within one week" (Suwanlert and Coates, 1979, 65).

The episode began at a technical college in Udon Thani province, with rumors that Vietnamese immigrants had deliberately contaminated food and cigarettes with a koro-inducing powder. During this period, there was a strong anti-Vietnamese sentiment throughout Thailand following communist victories in Southeast Asia in 1975, the growing influence of the Communist Party of Thailand, and the perceived control of Cambodia and Laos by the Vietnamese. Anti-Vietnamese sentiments in the region were especially strong in the month before the episode (Andelman, 1976a, 1976b), with allegations by Thailand's Interior Minister that there was "solid evidence" of a plot whereby "Vietnamese refugees would incite rioting in northeast Thailand, providing Vietnam with an excuse to invade" on February 15 (Andelman, 1976c). As the episode continued, the poisoning rumors became self-fulfilling as numerous Thai citizens recalled that previously consumed food and cigarettes recently purchased from Vietnamese establishments had an unusual smell and taste. However, an analysis of suspected sources by the Government Medical Science Department "detected no foreign substance that could possibly cause sexual impotence or contraction of the male sex organ" (Jilek and Jilek-Aall, 1977, 58).

Koro rumors, combined with pre-existing awareness of the "disease," served to foster and legitimate its plausible existence. Suwanlert and Coates (1979, 65) found that 94 percent of "victims" studied "were convinced that they had been poisoned." Negative government analysis of alleged tainted substances was undermined by contradictory statements issued by authority figures in the press. Security officials attributed the tainting substances believed responsible for causing the koro in food to a mixture of vegetable sources undetectable by medical devices (1977a, 58).

Another outbreak occurred in northeastern India from July to September, 1982. Cases numbered in the thousands, as many males believed their penises and testicles were retracting while women felt their breasts "going in." Indian psychiatrist Ajita Chakraborty said the panic reached such proportions that medical personnel toured the region, reassuring those affected with loud speakers (Chakraborty, Das, and Mukherji et al., 1983). Some parents tied string to their sons' penises to reduce or stop retraction, a practice that occasionally produced penile ulcers. Authorities even went to the extent of measuring penises at intervals to allay fears. A popular local remedy was to have the "victim" tightly grasp the affected body part, drink lime juice and be dowsed with buckets of cold water (Sachdev and Shukla, 1982, 1161). While there was evidence of pre-existing koro-related beliefs among some residents, the episode spread across various religious and ethnic groups, social castes, and geographical areas by way of rumors. Based on interviews with 30 "victims," investigating physicians were unable to identify obvious signs of psychological disturbance (Sachdev and Shukla, 1982). . . .

UNRAVELING THE MYSTERY

"Victims" of genitalia-shrinking panics recover within hours or days after being convinced that the "illness" is over or never existed, and most clearly lack any psycho-sexual problems. Episodes also share similar symptoms: anxiety, sweating, nausea, headache, transient pain, pale skin, palpitations, blurred vision, faintness, insomnia, and a false belief that body parts are shrinking. These symptoms are normal body responses to extreme fear. The penis, scrotum, breasts, and nipples are the most physiologically plastic external body parts, regularly changing size and shape in response to various stimuli from sexual arousal to temperature changes. Studies also reveal that stress, depression, illness, and urination can cause small but discernible penis shrinkage (Oyebode, Jamieson, and Davison, 1986; Thase, Reynolds, and Jennings, 1988). Another key factor is the nature of human perception, which is notoriously unreliable (Ross, Reade, and Toglia, 1994). Perception is also preconditioned by a person's mental outlook and social and cultural reference system. In each of the countries reporting epidemic koro, there were preexisting beliefs that genitalia could shrivel up under certain circumstances.

Far from exemplifying group psychosis, disorder or irrationality, penis-shrinking panics are a timely reminder that no one is immune from mass delusions, and that the influence of culture and society on individual behavior is far greater than most of us would like to admit. This is a valuable lesson to remember at the dawn of a new millennium. It is all too easy to think of past or non-Western delusions with a wry smile as if we are somehow now immune or those involved were naive and gullible. Yet, the main reason for the absence of penis-shrinking epidemics in Western societies is their incredible nature. It is simply too fantastic to believe. But any delusion is possible if the false belief underlying it is plausible. So while we may laugh at the poor "misguided" Indian or Chinese for believing in penis and breast-shrinking panics, we are haunted by our own unique delusions of crashed saucers, alien abductors, and CIA cover-ups of just about everything.

DISCUSSION QUESTION

1. What is the cultural context of koro outbreaks that contributes to their occurrence? What types of people are more likely to experience a bout of koro? Why?

BIBLIOGRAPHY

Andelman, D. 1976a. "Thai Junta Re-Examines Relations with Neighbor Nations and U.S." *New York Times*, October 18, 1976.

———. 1976b. "Vietnam Accuses Thai Regime and Demands That It Free 800." *New York Times*, October 28, p. 30.

———. 1976c. "Campaign Grows Against Vietnamese in Thailand Region." *New York Times*, December 12, p. 3.

Bartholomew, R. E. 1998. "The Medicalization of Exotic Deviance: A Sociological Perspective on Epidemic Koro." *Transcultural Psychiatry* 35 (1):5–38.

———. 1994. "The Social Psychology of 'Epidemic' Koro." *The International Journal of Social Psychiatry* 40 (1):46–60.

Berrois, G. E., and Morley, S. J. 1984. "Koro-like Symptoms in a Non-Chinese Subject." *British Journal of Psychiatry* 145:331–334.

Chakraborty, A., Das, S., and Mukherji, A. 1983. "Koro Epidemic in India." *Transcultural Psychiatric Research Review* 20:150–151.

Devan, G. S., and Hung, O. S. 1987. "Koro and Schizophrenia in Singapore." *British Journal of Psychiatry* 150:106–107.

Cremona, A. 1981. "Another Case of Koro in a Briton." Letter. *British Journal of Psychiatry* 138:180.

Edwards, J. G. 1970. "The Koro Pattern of Depersonalization in an American Schizophrenic Patient." *American Journal of Psychiatry* 126 (8):1171–1173.

Emsley, R. A. 1985. "Koro in Non-Chinese Subject." Letter. *British Journal of Psychiatry* 146:102.

Gittelson, N. L. and S. Levine. 1966. "Subjective Ideas of Sexual Change in Male Schizophrenics." *British Journal of Psychiatry* 112:1171–1173.

Gwee, A.-L. 1968. "Koro—Its Origin and Nature as a Disease Entity." *Singapore Medical Journal* 9(1):3–6.

Ilechukwu, S. T. C. 1992. "Magical Penis Loss in Nigeria: Report of a Recent Epidemic of a Koro-Like Syndrome." *Transcultural Psychiatric Research Review* 29:91–108.

————. 1988. "Letter from S.T.C. Ilechukwu, M.D." (Lagos, Nigeria) which describes interesting koro-like syndromes in Nigeria. *Transcultural Psychiatric Research Review* 25:310–314.

Jilek, W. G. 1986. "Epidemics of 'Genital Shrinking' (Koro): Historical Review and Report of a Recent Outbreak in Southern China." *Curare* 9:269–282.

————and Jilek-Aall, L. 1977. "A Koro Epidemic in Thailand." *Transcultural Psychiatric Research Review* 14:56–59.

Kendall, E. M., and Jenkins, P. L. 1987. "Koro in an American Man." *American Journal of Psychiatry* 144 (12):1621.

Mun, C. I. 1968. "Epidemic Koro in Singapore." Letter. *British Medical Journal* i: 640–641, March 9.

Oyebode, F., Jamieson, M. J., and Davison, K. 1986. "Koro: A Psychophysiological Dysfunction." *British Journal of Psychiatry* 148:212–214.

Ross, D. F., Read, J. D., and Toglia, M. P. 1994. *Adult Eyewitness Testimony: Current Trends and Developments.* Cambridge: Cambridge University Press.

Sachdev, P. S., and Shukla, A. 1982. "Epidemic Koro Syndrome in India." *The Lancet*: 161.

Suwanlert, S., and Coates, D. 1979. "Epidemic Koro in Thailand—Clinical and Social Aspects." Abstract of the report by F. R. Fenton appearing in *Transcultural Psychiatric Research Review* 16:64–66.

Thase, M. E., Reynolds, C. F., and Jennings, J. R. 1988. "Nocturnal Penile Tumescence is Diminished in Depressed Men." *Biological Psychiatry* 24:33–46.

Tseng, W. S., Mo, K. M., Hsu, J., Li, L. S., Ou, L. W., Chen, G. Q., and Jiang, D. W. 1988. "A Sociocultural Study of Koro Epidemics in Guangdong, China" *American Journal of Psychiatry* 145 (12):1538–1543.

Tseng, W. S., Mo, K. M., Li, L. S., Chen, G. Q., Ou, L. W., and Zheng, H. B. 1992. "Koro Epidemics in Guangdong, China: A Questionnaire Survey." *The Journal of Nervous and Mental Disease* 180 (2):117–123.

Van Wulfften-Palthe, P. M. 1936. "Psychiatry and Neurology in the Tropics" p. 525–547. In C. de Langen and A. Lichtenstein (eds.), *Clinical Textbook of Tropical Medicine*. Batavia: G. Kolff and Company.

A FREEDOM/DEVIANCE TRADE-OFF?

41.
LESSONS IN ORDER

DAVID H. BAYLEY

To end this volume full circle, we can return to the very first article in which Emile Durkheim asserts that crime and deviance are the price we pay for a free society. It is the freedom to think and act differently from others that account for both crime and progress. Many societies have lower crime rates than the United States, and a myriad of factors account for the differences. The following article concerns the extraordinarily low rates of street crime in Japan relative to the United States. For example, the United Nations Office on Drugs and Crime reports that in 2009 the homicide rate in the United States was more than 10 times greater than that of Japan's; the U.S. robbery rate was more than 35 times greater than Japan's rate.* (These figures are rates and are, therefore, adjusted for the population size of the respective countries.) Bayley attributes the difference to the relatively strong—Americans might say, "extreme"—emphasis the Japanese place on conformity to the group.

To say that freedom and individualism account for high rates of deviance in the United States, however, is an oversimplication. In some respects, the Japanese culture described by Bayley resembles Durkheim's "society of saints" relative to the United States. According to Durkheim, in such a society, while there may be fewer instances of what **we** consider deviance; with such high standards of behavior, there will be more instances of what **they** consider deviance.

. . . Looking generally then at the circumstances within which Japanese and Americans live, there are some differences that would explain the lower crime rates in Japan. On the one hand, income distribution is more equitable in Japan, unemployment is less, and poverty is less concentrated in particular localities, especially neighborhoods defined by race or ethnicity. Japan also regulates gun ownership much more stringently than does the United States. On the other hand, its popular culture is as violent as that of the United States, and its criminal justice system, while more efficient, is less rigorous in its punishments. Criminal prosecution is hampered by civil rights, very much as in the United States except for the extended pre-charge detention period.

*United Nations Office on Drugs and Crime, "Crime and Criminal Justice Statistics," http://www.unodc.org/unodc/en/data-and-analysis/statistics/crime.html. Retrieved November 29, 2012.

It is impossible to determine scientifically, given limitations on data in both countries, whether these differences in social circumstances can account entirely for Japan's enviable crime record. At the same time, it is clear that there are other processes at work in Japan that help to produce its remarkable orderliness. These are processes of social interaction, part of general culture, that bear directly on the behavior of the Japanese. Crime, more generally the impulse to deviance, is inhibited by mechanisms that are peculiar to Japan in their strength and extensiveness. Although these mechanisms can be found in American society too, they are much weaker and more attenuated. Control of deviant behavior in Japan, I shall argue, is obtained through a unique combination of propriety, presumption, and pride.

FIRST: PROPRIETY

Japanese are bound by an infinite number of rules about what is proper. To an American, Japan is supremely upright. There is nothing casual or relaxed about it. In order to avoid giving offense, modes of speech shift as one addresses a man or a woman, a child or an adult, an older or a younger sibling, an elderly person, one's peer, a first-time acquaintance or a long-time friend, a workmate or an outsider, and so forth. Informal dress codes are strict, and people dress exactly so as to conform to what is expected on particular occasions as well as in particular roles. All schoolchildren wear the uniform distinctive of the school they attend, identical down to purses, backpacks, width of trousers, and length of skirts. Businessmen and government bureaucrats invariably wear dark suits, dark ties, white shirts, and black shoes. Construction workers can be recognized by knickers, soft two-toed boots, and woolen belly-warmers. Female street sweepers wear long scarves; truck and taxi drivers often wear white gloves. Revealingly, a customer in a Western-style dress shop will be asked, "What size are you?"; in a kimono store, "How old are you?"[1] People in Japan are what they look like, which means they must conform in order to be what they want to be.

Decorum is all-encompassing: not sitting on desks and surfaces people use for work; not putting shod feet on chairs, so that mothers carefully take off the tiny tennis shoes of their children when they pull them onto subway seats; encasing wet umbrellas in disposable plastic sacks when entering department stores; tying a *ukata* (bathrobe) one way for a man, another for a woman; and not looking directly into the eyes of another person in public. Japanese calculate the depth as well as the number of bows so that proper deference is shown. Department stores have mechanical calibrators that help personnel learn the appropriate bowing angle for different sorts of people.[2] Late one morning in a popular Tokyo restaurant I heard chanting from the kitchen. Peering surreptitiously through an open door, I saw the manager rehearsing the staff in saying, "What can I do for you?" "How can I help you?" and "Thank you, come back," in the proper bright and cheery way.

Japanese are surrounded by rules in all they do, from the serious to the trivial. In relation to Americans, they are compulsively watchful about decorum. Etiquette, civility, morality, and law blend together. Japanese learn early that someone is paying attention to everything they do, and that departures from propriety will be met with visible expressions of disapproval. A sense of constraining order is always present in Japanese life. A person is never offstage.

The pervading sense of propriety produces startling demonstrations of orderliness. An English businessman was so astonished at the absence of litter that he personally inspected 1,200 yards of subway corridors in the Yurakicho-Ginza subway station during an evening rush hour to count discarded trash. Although this complex is ten times larger than London's Piccadilly Circus Underground station, he found only nineteen cigarette ends, twenty-eight matchsticks, eleven candy wrappers, and four pieces of paper.[3] Japanese pedestrians rarely jaywalk, dutifully waiting for the crossing-lights to turn green even if there is no car in sight and it is late at night.

The instinctive obedience to shared rules of order is wonderfully captured in a story about a burglar who was caught fleeing an apartment in the daytime. It is important to understand that Japanese remove their shoes on entering a private home, especially if its floor is the traditional raised floor made of thick woven-straw (tatami). The burglar had crossed such a room to ransack a bureau, but was apprehended by the police because, when he heard them, he had stopped to put his shoes back on.[4]

Japanese orderliness in large matters, such as crime, seems to be related to orderliness in small things. If this is true, then the lack of regimentation that Americans value in personal life may affect the amount of criminal disorder in public life. Would Americans, one wonders, be willing to obtain a greater measure of safety if they were required to tie their bathrobes in a prescribed way?[5]

SECOND: PRESUMPTION

Japanese are enmeshed in closely knit groups that inhibit behavior through informal social controls. Japanese are not raised to stand alone, develop their individual potential, or "do their own thing." They are taught to fit into groups and to subordinate themselves to the purposes of those groups. The most important and enduring groups are family, school, and workplace. Becoming an organic part of them—belonging—is the source of the deepest emotional satisfaction Japanese feel. Thus, fitting in becomes the ultimate discipline in Japan. Japanese are encapsulated in small groups of well-known people who have the presumptive right to tell them how to behave.

Accepting the obligations of belonging is not like being directed to conform, though that is the result. Japanese tolerate the presumptions of membership because in exchange they are nurtured, supported, and cared for. This may take the form of lifetime employment, or the covering up of errors, or assistance in carrying out tasks, or simply an understanding of personal problems. Americans are more calculating about the costs and benefits of membership. Groups are instruments of individual purpose, rather than being ends in themselves. Americans are therefore less bound by the obligations of membership in any particular group, whether it be family, marriage, job, sports team, or social club. Because Japanese depend so entirely on a much smaller number of affiliations, they lose the ability to discriminate between the claims of the individual and those of the group, the obligations of the personal as opposed to those of the public.

The difference between Japanese and Americans is not in valuing the favorable regard of others or in the need to conform; it lies in the range of significant external references. Americans are "outer directed," to use David Reisman's famous phrase, in a generalized way; Japanese are "outer directed" in a focused way.[6] Studies have in fact shown that among strangers Americans conform more quickly than Japanese.[7] Japanese do not accept the presumptions of any group, but only of a small number of groups. The universal desire for fellowship and community provides enormous leverage in Japan because it is not counterbalanced by the obligations of other affiliations.

The presumptive control that immediate social groups can exercise can be seen in the importance placed on unspoken communication in Japan. People who properly belong do not have to be told; they understand instinctively what the wishes of the group are. For example, a husband in a properly attuned marriage does not need to apologize to his wife if he spills hot tea-water on her hand, because she understands without being told that he did not intend to hurt her and also that he is sorry. The most cutting remark a man can make about his wife is that she has to be told what he needs.[8] Businessmen complain that they do not like to be sent abroad for long periods because they lose instinctive knowledge of their group. When they return they feel like strangers, having to be told what everyone else understands. As the Japanese say, the expectation in most of life is that when you talk "others can finish the sentence." It is not an acceptable excuse in Japan to say "I wasn't told."[9]

Japanese learn the value of belonging early in life. In schools children advance automatically, as a group, helping one another as they go. Individual achievements are de-emphasized in favor of group accomplishments. Children learn not to embarrass schoolmates by showing them to be wrong. Instead, they correct others by saying "I want to help Yakuda-kun" or "I agree with Kato-san but I also think this way."[10] Individual test scores are not known among classmates. Separation according to ability occurs impersonally, usually as the result of formal examinations allowing students to move from one level of schooling to another. Young children compete athletically by classes, not as individuals. Students also perform together many of the custodial chores at schools, like sweeping floors, washing dishes after lunch, picking up trash, putting away equipment, and rearranging chairs. Teachers and students explain constantly to laggards what is expected, reiterating that unless something or other is done the class will be disappointed, the student will be letting down the side, or everyone will be ashamed if the student does not try. Emotional blackmail, Americans would call this, and would resent it.

Even before schooling, Japanese children learn that fitting in brings warmth and love. Observers of early child-raising practices have noted that Japanese mothers carry their children with them everywhere, both inside and outside the house. Children sleep with their parents until the age of four or five. American mothers put down happy children, encouraging them to play by themselves. American children are left with baby-sitters, a practice still uncommon in Japan. They learn early to attract attention by crying and demanding; Japanese mothers anticipate the needs of their children so they do not have to cry or demand.[11]

When Japanese preschool children misbehave, parents threaten them with being locked out of the home. They tearfully bang on the front doors, pleading to be allowed back in. In the United States parents threaten badly behaving children with exactly the reverse–being kept in. The children are "grounded." The effect is that American children are taught that it is punishment to be locked up with one's family; Japanese children are taught that punishment is being excluded from one's family.[12] Small wonder, then, that Japanese schools and work groups have leverage over individual behavior later in life—and that adult affiliations in the United States have less.

The power of informal social control is what the Japanese criminal justice system relies on when it accepts apologies for minor infractions, does not insist on arresting suspects, allows people to be free without bail pending trial, and suspends prosecution or the execution of sentences. The vitality of group supervision is what allows police, prosecutors, and judges to act on the philosophy that they "hate the crime but not the criminal." The Japanese criminal justice system is founded not on deterrence but rather on "reintegrative shaming."[13] The purpose of the system is to shame individuals into accepting the obligations of their social setting and to shame groups into accepting responsibility for the errant member. Individuation makes sense in Japan, as it often does in the United States as well, when people are situated in specific, binding social networks.

Learning to accept the presumptions of groups does not mean that groups are without conflict and disagreement. Japanese often feel frustrated and inhibited. Unlike Americans, however, they are more willing to manage the conflict, deflecting or repressing it.[14] They make an explicit distinction linguistically between what is apparent and what is real in social situations. *Tatemae* refers to the appearance that must be maintained; *honne* is the inside story, what is truly felt. Americans too understand the tension between gut-feeling and propriety, but are more likely to be led by the former. Conversely, they value sincerity, being uncomfortable with hollow conformity. Japanese stifle nonconformity for the sake of maintaining the *tatemae* of group harmony, even though they know it is a pretense.

Social order in an individualistic society like the United States requires the discipline of conscience; social order in a communitarian society like Japan requires the discipline of presumption. Both societies learn to accommodate some of the other perspective. Japanese society does not wholly trample individual identity; American society does not forfeit entirely the capacity for cooperative endeavor. But the balance is different. As two observers of both countries have said, "One may even venture to suggest that while Americans learn to live with an illusion of complete self-reliance, self-sufficiency and autonomy, many Japanese tend to live with an illusion of total harmony, mutual understanding and consensus among them."[15]

THIRD: PRIDE

Discipline is maintained in Japan because people take enormous pride in performing well the roles demanded of them. Distinctive occupational dress is one indication of the prideful identification people have with their work. Japanese society is hierarchical in terms of authority, but it is egalitarian in its evaluation of the worth of work. What is important is the dedication brought to the job, not its status. Interestingly, anyone who teaches in Japan, from university professors to instructors in cutting up raw fish, are called *sensei*. One reason Japanese women have accepted differentiated sex roles more readily than American women may be that the emotional rewards are greater. Being a wife and mother is regarded as a demanding and responsible job in Japan. It is not denigrated as being "just housework."[16]

The essential ingredient in achieving success at anything is *seishin*, literally "spirit." But the word has strong overtones of effort, discipline, self-control, and even suffering. Inner fulfillment comes from developing the *seishin* necessary to accept demanding obligations willingly, whether artistic and craft skills, work routines, athletic feats, or social responsibilities. Japanese respect the *seishin* shown by the daughter-in-law who uncomplainingly performs her duties in the house of an overbearing mother-in-law for the sake of the family, or the student who practices tea-ceremony for years in order to achieve a higher ranking, or the baseball player who trains despite personal injury without asking for time off.[17] In arts, crafts, and social relations, Japanese learn by rote, by endlessly copying approved behavior. High achievement is obtained by fanatical application, not by gifted innovation. Great effort earns great respect. Indeed, Japanese tend to excuse marginal performance as long as exemplary *seishin* was shown. By being perfectionist in effort, Japanese protect themselves against censure. Americans, on the other hand, are more ends-oriented, excusing slipshod preparation if the results are good.

Pride given to work helps Japanese accept conformity. As Edwin O. Reischauer, former ambassador to Japan, has said, "social conformity to the Japanese is no sign of weakness but rather the proud, tempered product of inner strength."[18] A symbol of this is the bonsai tree, a unique expression of aesthetic taste with which Japanese identify. Bonsai is a dwarf tree that has been restricted by binding and pruning so that it grows into strange, artificial shapes. A bonsai tree achieves beauty by being constricted, some might say deformed. Japanese orderliness is achieved in the same way.

In conclusion, propriety, presumption, and pride can be analytically and anecdotally separated, but they are part of a single dynamic. The enwrapping web of propriety is held in place by the myriad presumptive corrections of primary social groups. Careful attention to the forms of human interaction allows tightly knit groups to hold together despite the vagaries of circumstance and personality. Pride allows for the internalization of the discipline necessary for subordination to small groups. Presumption becomes bearable when society rewards those who accept it.

Americans can understand, perhaps even empathize with, this dynamic. But they reverse the values. Propriety in the United States is limited, individuals being free to live their lives bound only by the commodious limits of the law. Behavior is bound more exclusively by law, or a very general morality, because the texture of American society is too loosely knit to rely on the presumptive enforcement of small groups. Norms of decorum and civility are not shared across the spectrum of American life. American pride is rooted in individual accomplishment, not in the acceptance of the disciplines of primary social groups. Americans kick against the restrictions of propriety, having been taught to question conventions of dress, language, taste, and morality.

If crime is caused to an important extent by customary patterns of social interaction, then Japan and the United States may both be getting what they have contrived.

DISCUSSION QUESTIONS

1. Bayley asks the question, "Would Americans, one wonders, be willing to obtain a greater measure of safety if they were required to tie their bathrobes in a prescribed way?" What does he mean by the question and what would be your answer?

2. In this article, Bayley explains why Japanese society has less deviance than American society. But the introduction to this article suggests that Japanese society, as Bayley describes it, may actually have *more* deviance than American society. What is the basis of that argument?

NOTES

1. W. Caudill and H. Weinstein, "Maternal Care and Infant Behavior in Japan and America," in *Japanese Culture and Behavior*, T. S. and W Lebra, eds. (Honolulu: University of Hawaii Press, 1974), pp. 225–76.
2. Peter Hazelhurst, formerly Tokyo correspondent for the *Sunday Times* and the *Straits Times*.
3. Peter Hazelhurst.
4. Robert Trumbull, formerly Tokyo correspondent for the *New York Times*. I once saw a squad of plainclothes detectives break into a yakuza apartment on a drug-bust and stop inside the front door to remove their shoes before undertaking their search.
5. James Q. Wilson and George L. Kelling have argued that police should concentrate on maintaining decorum on the streets in order to discourage more serious criminal behavior. "Broken

Windows," *Atlantic Monthly* (March 1982), pp. 29–38. Experimental evidence for a connection between visible signs of disorder and criminal actions was found by Professor Philip Zimbardo, Stanford University, in 1969.

6. David Reisman, *The Lonely Crowd* (Garden City, NY: Doubleday, 1953).

7. H. Wagatsuma and Arthur Rosett, "Cultural Attitudes toward Contract Law: Japan and the U.S. Compared" (Draft article, 1982), p. 22.

8. Robert J. Smith, *Japanese Society: Tradition, Self, and the Social Order* (Cambridge: Cambridge University Press, 1983), pp. 57–58.

9. In *Hidden Differences: Doing Business with the Japanese* (New York: Anchor Press/Doubleday, 1987), Part I, Edward T. and Mildred R. Hall describe Japan as a "high context" society, meaning that people need a great deal of information about the people they work with in order to work together successfully. Americans, on the other hand, need much less, preferring to limit the dimensions of interaction with the people they work with. The same distinction is made by Howard Gardner, *Frames of Mind* (New York: Basic Books, 1985), in distinguishing "particle" societies, where autonomous individuals interact, from "field" societies, where individuals are subordinated to groups.

10. Takie S. Lebra, *Japanese Women: Constraint and Fulfillment* (Honolulu: University of Hawaii Press, 1984), chap. 5.

11. See Caudill and Weinstein (n. 1 above).

12. *Mura hachibu* is the term for being excluded. It was a very serious punishment in villages. This is similar to the practice in the British labor movement of sending colleagues "to Coventry," not talking to them, when they defied group norms.

13. John Braithwaite, *Crime, Shame, and Reintegration* (Cambridge: Cambridge University Press, 1989).

14. Takie S. Lebra, "Nonconfrontational Strategies for Management of Interpersonal Conflicts," in Ellis S. Krauss et al., *Conflict in Japan* (Honolulu: University of Hawaii Press, 1984), chap. 3.

15. Wagatsuma and Rosett, "Cultural Attitudes."

16. Suzanne H. Vogel, "Professional Housewife: The Career of Urban Middle Class Japanese Women," *Japan Interpreter* 12, no. 1 (Winter 1978): 16–43.

17. Robert Whiting, *You Gotta Have Wa* (New York: Macmillan, 1989), p. 317.

18. *The Japanese Today* (Cambridge: Harvard University Press, 1988), p. 166.